Frommer's
Costa Rica 2005

POSTCARDS FROM

W9-DFK-059

Mischievous squirrel monkeys live in and around Manuel Antonio National Park (see chapter 7) and the Osa Peninsula (see chapter 8). © Norman Owen Tomalin/Bruce Coleman, Inc.

With thermal pools, lush gardens, waterfalls, a swim-up bar, and spa services, Tabacón Hot Springs Resort, at the base of Arenal Volcano, is a playground for adults. See chapter 6.
© Robert Winslow/Viesti Collection, Inc.

Coffee and sugar cane thrive in the rich, verdant, volcanic soil of the Central Valley. You can visit a coffee farm as a side trip from San José. See chapter 4. © Nicholas DeVore III/Bruce Coleman, Inc.

Costa Rica boasts an astounding diversity of tropical plant life. Here, the brilliant blooms of the heliconia marginata *appear to unfold like origami birds.*
© Margarette Mead/Getty Images.

Coffee is one of Costa Rica's most important crops, and coffee farms dot the fertile Central Valley. See chapter 4.
© J-C Carton/Bruce Coleman, Inc.

The Monteverde Biological Cloud Forest Reserve is lush and largely untouched, with thousands of exotic ferns, orchids, and bromeliads, plus 400 varieties of birds and 100 species of mammals. Its well-organized infrastructure helps guarantee a rewarding experience for first-time eco-adventurers. See chapter 6. © Drew Thate/Bruce Coleman, Inc.

White-faced capuchin monkeys abound in Manuel Antonio National Park. See chapter 7.
© Wolfgang Kaehler Photography.

Throughout the country, sunbathing iguanas are a common sight.
© Russell Mittermeier/Bruce Coleman, Inc.

Green turtles nest and hatch in Tortuguero National Park. This just-hatched youngster is ready to plunge into the surf. See chapter 9. © Kevin Schafer/Getty Images.

A tiny red-eyed tree frog. © *James Carmichael/Getty Images.*

A tropical land crab. © *Margarette Mead/Getty Images.*

Although the cone is often socked in by fog, Arenal Volcano experiences nearly constant rumblings and eruptions. See chapter 6. © *Macduff Everton/Getty Images.*

Costa Rica's Pacific coast is lined with glorious beaches, including this uncrowded stretch of sand in Corcovado National Park. See chapter 8. © *Houserstock, Inc.*

Frommer's

Costa Rica

2005

by Eliot Greenspan

WILEY

Wiley Publishing, Inc.

About the Author

Eliot Greenspan is a poet, journalist, and travel writer who took his backpack and typewriter the length of Mesoamerica before settling in Costa Rica in 1992. Since then, he has worked steadily as a travel writer, freelance journalist, and translator, and continued his travels in the region. He is the author of *The Tico Times Restaurant Guide to Costa Rica* and *Frommer's Belize,* as well as the chapter on Venezuela in *Frommer's South America,* and is co-author of *Frommer's Cuba.*

Published by:

Wiley Publishing, Inc.

111 River St.
Hoboken, NJ 07030-5774

ISBN 0-7645-6768-3

Editor: Myka Carroll Del Barrio
Production Editor: Suzanna R. Thompson
Cartographer: Roberta Stockwell
Photo Editor: Richard Fox
Production by Wiley Indianapolis Composition Services

Front cover photo: Tabacón Hot Springs, near Arenal Volcano
Back cover photo: A devastatingly handsome red-eyed tree frog

For information on our other products and services or to obtain technical support, please contact our Customer Care Department within the U.S. at 800/762-2974, outside the U.S. at 317/572-3993 or fax 317/572-4002.

Wiley also publishes its books in a variety of electronic formats. Some content that appears in print may not be available in electronic formats.

Manufactured in the United States of America

5   4   3   2   1

Contents

List of Maps   vi

What's New in Costa Rica   1

1 The Best of Costa Rica   3

1 The Best of Natural Costa Rica . . .3

2 The Best Beaches 6

3 The Best Adventures 8

4 The Best Day Hikes &
Nature Walks 9

5 The Best Bird-Watching 11

6 The Best Destinations
for Families 12

7 The Best Luxury Hotels &
Resorts 13

8 The Best Moderately Priced
Hotels 14

9 The Best Ecolodges & Wilderness
Resorts 15

10 The Best Bed-and-Breakfasts &
Small Inns 16

11 The Best Restaurants 17

12 The Best Views 18

13 The Best After-Dark Fun 19

14 The Best Websites About
Costa Rica 20

2 Planning Your Trip to Costa Rica   21

1 The Regions in Brief 21

2 Visitor Information 24

3 Entry Requirements &
Customs 24

4 Money 26

*The Colón, the U.S. Dollar &
the Euro* 27

5 When to Go 29

Costa Rica Calendar of Events . . .31

6 Health & Insurance 32

7 Specialized Travel Resources . . .36

Getting Married in Costa Rica . . .38

8 Planning Your Trip Online 40

*Frommers.com: The Complete
Travel Resource* 41

9 The 21st-Century Traveler 41

Online Traveler's Toolbox 42

10 Getting There 43

*What Travel Agents
Don't Tell You* 45

11 Package Deals for the
Independent Traveler 47

12 Getting Around 48

Car-Rental Tips 50

13 Spanish-Language Programs . . .53

14 Tips on Accommodations 54

15 Tips on Dining 56

16 Tips on Shopping 57

17 Suggested Itineraries 58

18 Recommended Reading 58

Fast Facts: Costa Rica 60

3 The Active Vacation Planner   64

1 Organized Adventure Trips 64

2 Activities A to Z 66

*Where to See the
Resplendent Quetzal* 69

In Search of Turtles 76

3 Costa Rica's Top National
Parks & Bioreserves 77

Monkey Business 81

4 Tips on Health, Safety &
Etiquette in the Wilderness 82

5 Ecologically Oriented
Volunteer & Study Programs ...82

4   San José   84

1 Orientation 85

*"I Know There's Got to Be a
Number Here Somewhere . . .":
The Arcane Art of Finding an
Address in San José* 89

The Neighborhoods in Brief 90

2 Getting Around 91

Fast Facts: San José 93

3 Where to Stay 96

4 Where to Dine 109

*Only in the Central Valley:
Dining Under the Stars on a
Mountain's Edge* 113

5 What to See & Do 117

Suggested Itineraries 117

6 Outdoor Activities &
Spectator Sports 122

7 Shopping 124

Joe to Go 125

8 San José After Dark 129

9 Side Trips from San José 134

*Holy Smoke!: Choosing
the Volcano Trip That's
Right for You* 138

5   Guanacaste & the Nicoya Peninsula:
The Gold Coast   144

1 Liberia 146

2 La Cruz 152

3 Playa Hermosa, Playa
Panamá & Papagayo 154

4 Playa del Coco &
Playa Ocotal 160

5 Playas Flamingo, Potrero,
Brasilito & Conchal 164

6 Playa Tamarindo &
Playa Grande 170

7 Playa Junquillal 181

8 Playa Nosara 183

9 Playa Sámara 188

10 Playa Tambor 193

11 Playa Montezuma 195

12 Malpais/Santa Teresa 202

6   The Northern Zone: Mountain Lakes,
Cloud Forests & a Volcano   206

1 Puerto Viejo de Sarapiquí 206

2 Arenal Volcano &
La Fortuna 213

Boats, Horses & Taxis 215

*Taking a Soothing Soak in
Hot Springs* 217

3 Along the Shores of
Lake Arenal 226

4 Monteverde 230

7 The Central Pacific Coast: Where the Mountains Meet the Sea   245

1 Puntarenas 245
  Diving Trips to Isla del Coco (Cocos Island) 249
2 Playa de Jacó 251
3 Manuel Antonio National Park 262
4 Dominical 279
5 San Isidro de El General: A Base for Exploring Chirripó National Park 285

8 The Southern Zone   291

1 Drake Bay 291
  Those Mysterious Stone Spheres 296
2 Puerto Jiménez: Gateway to Corcovado National Park 299
3 Golfito: Gateway to the Golfo Dulce 307
4 Playa Zancudo 312
5 Playa Pavones: A Surfer's Mecca 315

9 The Caribbean Coast   317

1 Barra del Colorado 318
2 Tortuguero National Park 321
3 Limón: Gateway to Tortuguero National Park & Southern Coastal Beaches 328
4 Cahuita 332
5 Puerto Viejo 338

Appendix A: Costa Rica in Depth   350

1 The Natural Environment 350
2 Costa Rica Today 352
3 History 101 353
  Dateline 353
4 *Gallo Pinto,* Ceviche & *Frescos:* Costa Rican Food & Drink 356

Appendix B: Glossary of Spanish Terms & Phrases   359

1 Basic Words & Phrases 359
2 Some Typical Tico Words & Phrases 360
3 Menu Terms 361

Index   363

General Index 363
Accommodations Index 368

List of Maps

The Best of Costa Rica   4

The Regions in Brief   23

San José   86

The Central Valley   135

Guanacaste & the Nicoya Peninsula   145

Tamarindo   171

The Northern Zone   207

Monteverde   231

The Central Pacific Coast   247

Manuel Antonio   263

The Southern Zone   293

Corcovado National Park   301

The Caribbean Coast   319

Acknowledgments

I'm eternally grateful to Anne Becher and Joe Richey, who were instrumental in getting me this gig—*muchas gracias*. I'd also like to thank my parents, Marilyn and Warren Greenspan, who showed unwavering love, support, and encouragement (well, one out of three ain't bad) as I pursued words and world-wandering over a more stable and lucrative career. Jody and Ted Ejnes (my sister and brother-in-law) deserve a mention; they risked life and limb (literally) leading to two important tips that may help you save yours. And a tip of the hat to Myka Del Barrio for her editorial diligence.

An Invitation to the Reader

In researching this book, we discovered many wonderful places—hotels, restaurants, shops, and more. We're sure you'll find others. Please tell us about them, so we can share the information with your fellow travelers in upcoming editions. If you were disappointed with a recommendation, we'd love to know that, too. Please write to:

Frommer's Costa Rica 2005
Wiley Publishing, Inc. • 111 River St. • Hoboken, NJ 07030-5774

An Additional Note

Please be advised that travel information is subject to change at any time—and this is especially true of prices. We therefore suggest that you write or call ahead for confirmation when making your travel plans. The authors, editors, and publisher cannot be held responsible for the experiences of readers while traveling. Your safety is important to us, however, so we encourage you to stay alert and be aware of your surroundings. Keep a close eye on cameras, purses, and wallets, all favorite targets of thieves and pickpockets.

Other Great Guides for Your Trip:

Frommer's Belize
Frommer's Cancún, Cozumel & the Yucatán
Frommer's Cuba
Frommer's Mexico
Frommer's South America

Frommer's Star Ratings, Icons & Abbreviations

Every hotel, restaurant, and attraction listing in this guide has been ranked for quality, value, service, amenities, and special features using a **star-rating system.** In country, state, and regional guides, we also rate towns and regions to help you narrow down your choices and budget your time accordingly. Hotels and restaurants are rated on a scale of zero (recommended) to three stars (exceptional). Attractions, shopping, nightlife, towns, and regions are rated according to the following scale: zero stars (recommended), one star (highly recommended), two stars (very highly recommended), and three stars (must-see).

In addition to the star-rating system, we also use **seven feature icons** that point you to the great deals, in-the-know advice, and unique experiences that separate travelers from tourists. Throughout the book, look for:

Finds	Special finds—those places only insiders know about
Fun Fact	Fun facts—details that make travelers more informed and their trips more fun
Kids	Best bets for kids and advice for the whole family
Moments	Special moments—those experiences that memories are made of
Overrated	Places or experiences not worth your time or money
Tips	Insider tips—great ways to save time and money
Value	Great values—where to get the best deals

The following **abbreviations** are used for credit cards:

AE	American Express	DISC	Discover	V	Visa
DC	Diners Club	MC	MasterCard		

Frommers.com

Now that you have the guidebook to a great trip, visit our website at **www.frommers.com** for travel information on more than 3,000 destinations. With features updated regularly, we give you instant access to the most current trip-planning information available. At Frommers.com, you'll also find the best prices on airfares, accommodations, and car rentals—and you can even book travel online through our travel booking partners. At Frommers.com, you'll also find the following:

- Online updates to our most popular guidebooks
- Vacation sweepstakes and contest giveaways
- Newsletter highlighting the hottest travel trends
- Online travel message boards with featured travel discussions

What's New in Costa Rica

Costa Rica is a vibrant and growing tourist destination, and changes are nearly constant. Here are some of the highlights of the new air routes, hotels, restaurants, and attractions you'll find.

PLANNING YOUR TRIP

Two new direct routes were added to the Juan Santamaría International Airport in San José. **United Airlines** (© 800/538-2929; www.united.com) has a daily direct flight originating in Washington, D.C., while **America West** (© 800/363-2957; www.americawest.com) has a daily direct flight from Phoenix.

The **Daniel Oduber Airport** (© 668-1117) in Liberia now receives a steady stream of scheduled commercial and charter flights throughout the year. **Delta** (© 800/241-4141; www.delta.com) has five weekly direct flights between its Atlanta hub and Liberia; **American Airlines** (© 800/433-7300; www.aa.com) offers three weekly direct flights between Miami and Liberia; and **Continental** (© 800/525-0280; www.continental.com) has three weekly direct flights between Houston and Liberia.

SAN JOSE

Up at the La Paz Waterfall Gardens, the **Peace Lodge** (© 482-2720 or 225-0643; www.waterfallgardens.com) has opened, with some of the most impressive rooms you'll find anywhere in the country.

The dining scene has gotten a welcome wake-up call from **Bakea** (© 248-0303), which is serving up very creative fare in a wonderful setting in the heart of downtown.

A little farther east, chef Tony D'Alaimo has returned with his latest local venture **Il Ritorno** (© 225-0543), serving excellent Italian cuisine and thin-crust wood-fired pizzas.

The local nightlife scene is getting a boost from the opening of **Meridiano al Este** (© 256-2705), a well-designed club and restaurant featuring live music and other performances nightly.

Atmósfera, one of the better downtown gift shops and art galleries, suffered a fire and has apparently closed for good.

See chapter 4 for complete coverage of San José.

GUANACASTE & THE NICOYA PENINSULA

Pardon the pun, but the growing action sport of kiteboarding is taking off in the Bahía Salinas area of Guanacaste. If you're interested in lessons or a test flight, check in with the **Kitesurfing Center** (© 826-5221; www.suntoursandfun.com).

The **Four Seasons Resort Costa Rica** (© 800/819-5053 in the U.S., or 696-0098; www.fourseasons.com/costarica) has opened for business on a stunning section of the Papagayo Peninsula. Within its first month of operation, reliable rumors placed both Michael Jordan and Madonna as guests.

Also on the Papagayo peninsula, the **Fiesta Premier Resort & Spa** (© 296-6263 or 672-0000; www.fiestapremier.com), located on a newly rehabilitated property, is an excellent option in the all-inclusive market.

In Montezuma, the popular **Luz de Mono** restaurant and hotel has been closed, with no indication of whether it's temporary or permanent.

See chapter 5 for all the latest on this rapidly developing region.

THE NORTHERN ZONE

The **Tabacón Hot Springs Resort & Spa** (© 256-1500; www.tabacon. com) has added 24 new rooms, a gym, and a business center, and has also remodeled the reception area.

In the La Fortuna area, **Pure Trek Canyoning** (© 479-9940; www.pure trek.com) offers the opportunity to test out this new adventure craze: You hike alongside and through a jungle river, with periodic breaks to rappel down the face of a rushing waterfall.

Eco Termales (© 479-8484) is a new and beautiful hot springs option in the La Fortuna/Arenal area. Reservations are essential here.

Up on Lake Arenal, kiteboarders are now flying alongside windsurfers on a regular basis. Check in with the **Tilawa Windsurfing Center** (© 695-5050; www.windsurfcostarica.com) for more information.

Located in downtown Santa Elena, the **World of Insects** (© 645-6859) is the newest nature-based educational attraction in the Monteverde area.

Full details on the northern zone can be found in chapter 6.

CENTRAL PACIFIC COAST

The folks at the Rain Forest Aerial Tram have opened a sister project, **Aerial Tram Pacific** (© 257-5961; www.rainforestram.com), just outside of Jacó.

In a similar vein, the new **Turu BaRi Tropical Park** (© 428-6070; www. turubari.com), located outside the town of Orotina, has a gondola-style tram ride through the canopy, along with a more traditional zip-line canopy tour, a butterfly garden, and several other attractions.

See chapter 7 for complete coverage of this region.

THE CARIBBEAN COAST

The new **Azania Bungalows** (© 750-0540; www.azania-costarica.com) is yet another excellent midrange option located just south of Puerto Viejo.

See chapter 9 for complete coverage of this area.

The Best of Costa Rica

For years, Costa Rica was the well-kept secret of a few biologists, backpackers, and beachcombers, but that's all changed. The secret is out. Today the country is a major international vacation and adventure-travel destination, and tourism has become the nation's number-one source of income. Despite the boom in vacationers, Costa Rica remains a place rich in natural wonders and biodiversity, far from the madding crowds. Here you can still find unsullied beaches that stretch for miles, small lodgings that haven't attracted hordes of tourists, jungle rivers for rafting and kayaking, and spectacular cloud and rainforests with ample opportunities for bird-watching and hiking. In addition to the country's trademark eco- and adventure tourism offerings, recent years have seen the opening of a handful of large luxury resorts and golf courses, with more on the way.

This is my ninth year putting this book together, and the "best of" experiences keep on coming. In this chapter, I've selected the very best of what this unique country has to offer. Most of these places and experiences are covered in greater detail elsewhere in the book; this chapter is merely meant to give you an overview of the highlights so you can start planning your own adventure.

1 The Best of Natural Costa Rica

- **Rincón de la Vieja National Park** (northeast of Liberia, in Guanacaste): This is an area of rugged beauty and high volcanic activity. The Rincón de la Vieja Volcano rises to 1,848m (6,061 ft.), but the thermal activity is spread out along its flanks, where numerous geysers, vents, and fumaroles let off its heat and steam. This is a great place to hire a guide and a horse for a day of rugged exploration. There are waterfalls and mud baths, hot springs, and cool jungle swimming holes. You'll pass through pastureland, scrub savanna, and moist secondary forest; the bird-watching is excellent. See p. 148.

- **The Río Sarapiquí Region** (north of San José between Guanacaste in the west and the Caribbean coast in the east): This is a prime place for an ecolodge experience. Protected tropical forests climb from the Caribbean coastal lowlands up into the central mountain, affording you a glimpse of a plethora of life zones and ecosystems. **Braulio Carrillo National Park** borders several other private reserves here, and there's a variety of ecolodges to suit any budget. See "Puerto Viejo de Sarapiquí" in chapter 6.

- **Arenal Volcano/Tabacón Hot Springs** (near La Fortuna, northwest of San José): When the skies are clear and the lava is flowing, Arenal Volcano provides a thrilling light show accompanied by an earthshaking rumble that defies description. You can even see the show while soaking in a natural hot spring and having a drink at

The Best of Costa Rica

0   25 mi
0   25 km

Airport ✈
Ferry − − −
Mountain ▲

Lake Nicaragua

Golfo de Santa Elena

GUANACASTE RANGE

1

SANTA ROSA NATIONAL PARK

Murciélagos Islands

Rincón de la Vieja ▲

RINCON DE LA VIEJA NATIONAL PARK

3

35

Golfo de Papagayo

Río Tempisque

Interamerican Hwy.

Liberia

Lake Coter

Río Frío

Lake Arenal

TILARAN RANGE

142

Arenal Volcano

Monteverde

8

9

Tamarindo

PALO VERDE NATIONAL PARK

21

18

160

NICOYA PENINSULA

160

Puntarenas

1

160

Golfo de Nicoya

10

PACIFIC OCEAN

12   13

Cabo Blanco Absolute Nature Reserve

160

14

34

Isla del Coco (Coco Island)

THE BEST OF NATURAL COSTA RICA

Arenal Volcano/Tabacón Hot Springs 5
Braulio Carrillo National Park 19
Manuel Antonio National Park 26
Monteverde Cloud Forest Reserve 6
Osa Peninsula & Corcovado National Park 27
Rincón de la Vieja National Park 2
The Río Sarapiquí Region 15
Tortuguero Village & Jungle Canals 16

THE BEST BEACHES

The Beaches Around Playa Sámara 10
Malpais 12
Manuel Antonio 26
Playa Montezuma 13
Playa Tamarindo 9
Punta Uva & Manzanillo 22
Santa Rosa National Park 1

THE BEST ADVENTURES

Battling a Billfish off the Pacific Coast 25
Diving off Isla del Coco 11
Hiking Mount Chirripó 23
Kayaking Around Golfo Dulce 28
Rafting the Upper Reventazón River 17
Surfing & Four-Wheeling Guanacaste 8
Surfing Pavones 29
Windsurfing Lake Arenal 4

THE BEST BIRD-WATCHING

Aviarios del Caribe 21
Caño Negro Wildlife Refuge 3
Carara Biological Reserve 14
Cerro de la Muerte 24
La Selva Biological Station 18
Parque del Este 20
Río Tempisque Basin 7
Wilson Botanical Gardens 30

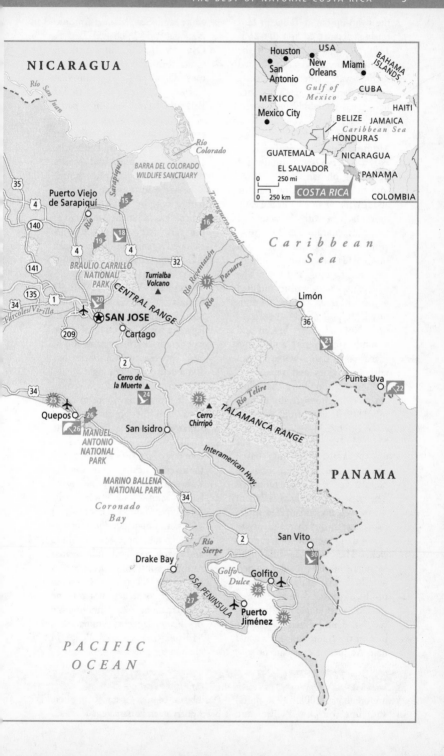

NICARAGUA

Río San Juan

BARRA DEL COLORADO
WILDLIFE SANCTUARY

35
4
140

Puerto Viejo
de Sarapiquí

Río Sarapiquí

Río Colorado

15

16

Tortuguero Canal

Caribbean
Sea

141
135
34
1
209

4
19
18
4

BRAULIO CARRILLO
NATIONAL
PARK

32
Turrialba
Volcano

CENTRAL RANGE

Río Reventazón
Río Pacuare

17

Río Parismina

20
SAN JOSE

Cartago

Limón

36

21

2
Cerro de
la Muerte
24

Río Telire

23
Cerro
Chirripó

TALAMANCA RANGE

Punta Uva

22

34
25
Quepos
26
26

MANUEL
ANTONIO
NATIONAL
PARK

San Isidro

Interamerican Hwy.

PANAMA

MARINO BALLENA
NATIONAL PARK

34

Coronado
Bay

Río Sierpe

2
San Vito

30

Drake Bay

Golfo
Dulce

Golfito

28

OSA PENINSULA

27

Puerto
Jiménez

29

PACIFIC
OCEAN

USA
Houston
New
Orleans
Miami
San
Antonio

Gulf of
Mexico

BAHAMA
ISLANDS

CUBA

HAITI

MEXICO

Mexico City

BELIZE
JAMAICA
Caribbean Sea
HONDURAS

GUATEMALA
NICARAGUA
EL SALVADOR
PANAMA
COSTA RICA
COLOMBIA

0   250 mi
0   250 km

the swim-up bar at **Tabacón Hot Springs Resort & Spa** (© 256-1500; www.tabacon.com). If the rushing torrent of volcano-heated spring water isn't therapeutic enough, you can get a massage here at an incredibly inexpensive price. See "Arenal Volcano & La Fortuna" in chapter 6.

- **Monteverde Biological Cloud Forest Reserve** (in the mountains northwest of San José): There's something both eerie and majestic about walking around in the early morning mist with the sound of bird calls all around and the towering trees hung heavy in broad bromeliads, flowering orchids, and hanging moss and vines. The reserve itself has a well-maintained network of trails, and the community is truly involved in conservation. Not only that, but in and around Monteverde and Santa Elena, you'll find a whole slew of related activities and attractions, including canopy tours that allow you to swing from treetop to treetop while hanging from a skinny cable. See p. 234.

- **Manuel Antonio** (near Quepos on the central Pacific coast): There's a reason this place is so popular and renowned: monkeys! The national park here is full of them, even the endangered squirrel monkeys. But there's plenty to see and do outside the park as well. The road leading into Manuel Antonio provides numerous lookouts that consistently produce postcard-perfect snapshots of steep jungle hills meeting the sea. Uninhabited islands lie just off the coast, and the beaches here are perfect crescents of soft,

white sand. See "Manuel Antonio National Park" in chapter 7.

- **Osa Peninsula** (in southern Costa Rica): This is Costa Rica's most remote and biologically rich region. **Corcovado National Park,** the largest remaining patch of virgin lowland tropical rainforest in Central America, takes up much of the Osa Peninsula. Jaguars, crocodiles, and scarlet macaws all call this place home. Whether you stay in a luxury nature lodge in Drake Bay or outside of Puerto Jiménez, or camp in the park itself, you will be surrounded by some of the most lush and most intense jungle this country has to offer. See chapter 8.

- **Tortuguero Village & Jungle Canals** (on the Caribbean coast, north of Limón): Tortuguero Village is a small collection of rustic wooden shacks on a narrow spit of land between the Caribbean Sea and a dense maze of jungle canals. It's been called Costa Rica's Venice, but it actually has more in common with the South American Amazon. You can fly into the small airstrip, but it's better to take one of the slow boats that ply the river and canal route. On the way you'll see a wide variety of herons and other water birds, three types of monkeys, three-toed sloths, and huge American crocodiles. If you come between June and October, you might be treated to the awe-inspiring spectacle of a green turtle nesting—the small stretch of Tortuguero beach is the last remaining major nesting site of this endangered animal. See "Tortuguero National Park" in chapter 9.

2 The Best Beaches

With more than 1,200km (750 miles) of shoreline on its Pacific and Caribbean coasts, Costa Rica offers beachgoers an embarrassment of riches.

- **Santa Rosa National Park:** If you really want to get away from it all, the beaches here in the northwest corner of Costa Rica are a good bet. You'll have to four-wheel-drive or hike 13km (8 miles) from the central ranger station to reach the beach. And once you get there, you'll find only the most basic of camping facilities: outhouse latrines and cold-water showers. But you will probably have the place almost to yourself. In fact, the only time it gets crowded is in October, when thousands of olive Ridley sea turtles nest in one of their yearly *arribadas* (arrivals). See p. 152.

- **Playa Tamarindo:** Although it's on the verge of becoming a little too overdeveloped, crowded, and chaotic, Tamarindo is still hanging on to its place on this list. Tamarindo has ample lodgings to suit every budget, as well as excellent restaurants at almost every turn. The beach here is long and broad, with sections calm enough for swimmers and others just right for surfers. Located about midway along the beaches of Guanacaste province, Tamarindo makes a good base for exploring other nearby stretches of sand. There are plenty of surfers here, as well as one of the liveliest nightlife scenes on this coast. See "Playa Tamarindo & Playa Grande" in chapter 5.

- **The Beaches Around Playa Sámara:** Playa Sámara itself is nice enough, but if you venture just slightly farther afield, you'll find some of the nicest and least developed beaches along the entire Guanacaste coast. **Playa Carillo** is a long, almost always deserted crescent of palm-backed white sand located just south of Sámara, while **Playa Barrigona** and **Playa Buena Vista** are two hidden gems tucked down a couple of dirt roads to the north. See "Playa Sámara" in chapter 5.

- **Playa Montezuma:** This tiny beach town at the southern tip of the Nicoya Peninsula has weathered fame and infamy, and yet retains a funky sense of individuality. European backpackers, vegetarian yoga enthusiasts, and UFO seekers choose Montezuma's beach over any other in Costa Rica. The waterfalls are what set it apart from the competition, but the beach stretches for miles, with plenty of isolated spots to plop down your towel or mat. Nearby are the Cabo Blanco and Curu wildlife preserves. See "Playa Montezuma" in chapter 5.

- **Malpais:** If you're looking to visit Costa Rica's newest hot spot before the throngs discover it, head out to Malpais. Here you'll find miles of nearly deserted beaches, great surf, and just a smattering of lodges, surf camps, and simple *cabinas.* If Malpais is too crowded for you, head farther on down the road to Santa Teresa, Playa Hermosa, and Manzanillo. See "Malpais/Santa Teresa" in chapter 5.

- **Manuel Antonio:** The first beach destination to become popular in Costa Rica, it retains its charms despite burgeoning crowds and mushrooming hotels. The beaches inside the park are idyllic, and the views from the hills approaching the park are enchanting. This is one of the few remaining habitats for the endangered squirrel monkey. Rooms with views tend to be a bit expensive, but many a satisfied guest will tell you they're worth it. See "Manuel Antonio National Park" in chapter 7.

- **Punta Uva & Manzanillo:** Below Puerto Viejo, the beaches of Costa Rica's eastern coast take on true Caribbean splendor, with turquoise waters, coral reefs, and palm-lined stretches of nearly deserted white-sand beach. Punta Uva and Manzanillo are the two most sparkling gems of this coastline. Tall coconut palms line the shore, providing shady respite for those who like to spend a full day on the sand, and the water is usually quite calm and good for swimming. See "Puerto Viejo" in chapter 9.

3 The Best Adventures

- **Mountain-Biking the Back Roads of Costa Rica:** The lack of infrastructure and paved roads that most folks bemoan is a huge boon for mountain bikers. There are endless back roads and cattle paths to explore. Tours of differing lengths and all difficulty levels are available. Contact **Coast to Coast Adventures** (© **280-8054;** www. ctocadventures.com). See p. 67.

- **Swinging Through the Treetops on a Canopy Tour:** This unique adventure is becoming quite the rage. In most cases, after a strenuous climb using ascenders, you strap on a harness and zip from treetop to treetop while dangling from a cable. There are canopy tours all around Costa Rica. **The Original Canopy Tours** (©/fax **257-5149;** www.canopytour.com) runs operations in locations around the country. See p. 70.

- **Rafting the Upper Reventazón River** (near Turrialba): The Class V Guayabo section of this popular river is serious white water. Only experienced and gutsy river runners need apply. If you're not quite up to that, try a 2-day Pacuare River trip, which passes through primary and secondary forests and a beautiful steep gorge that, sadly, might be dammed soon. Get there quick! **Ríos Tropicales** (© **233-6455;** www.riostropicales.com) can arrange either of these tours. See p. 76.

- **Surfing & Four-Wheeling Guanacaste Province:** This northwestern province has dozens of respectable beach and reef breaks, from Witch's Rock at Playa Naranjo near the Nicaraguan border to Playa Nosara more than 100km (62 miles) away. In addition to these two prime spots, try a turn at Playa Grande, Punta Langosta, and playas Negra, Avellanas, and Junquillal. Or, find your own secret spot. Rent a four-by-four with a roof rack, pile on the boards, and explore. See chapter 5.

- **Battling a Billfish off the Pacific Coast:** Billfish are plentiful all along Costa Rica's Pacific coast, and boats operate from Playa del Coco to Playa Zancudo. Costa Rican anglers hold world records for both blue marlin and Pacific sailfish. Go to Quepos (just outside Manuel Antonio) for the best après-fish scene, or head down to Drake Bay, the Osa Peninsula, or Golfo Dulce, if you want some isolation. **Costa Rica Outdoors** (© **800/308-3394** in the U.S., or 282-6743 in Costa Rica; www. costaricaoutdoors.com) can help you find a good charter skipper or specialized fishing lodge. See chapter 5; "Manuel Antonio National Park" in chapter 7; and chapter 8.

- **Windsurfing Lake Arenal:** With steady gale-force winds and stunning scenery, the northern end of Lake Arenal has become a major international windsurfing hot spot. If you're an avid boardsailor, be sure to check in with Norm at **Rock River Lodge** (©/fax **692-1180;** www.rockriverlodge.com).

See "Along the Shores of Lake Arenal" in chapter 6.

- **Diving off the Shores of Isla del Coco** (off the Pacific coast): Legendary among treasure seekers, pirate buffs, and scuba divers, this small island is consistently rated one of the 10 best dive sites in the world. A protected national park, Isla del Coco is surrounded by clear Pacific waters, and its reefs are teeming with life (divers regularly encounter large schools of hammerhead sharks, curious manta rays, and docile whale sharks). Because the island is so remote and has no overnight facilities for visitors, the most popular way to visit is on 10-day excursions on a live-aboard boat, where guests live, eat, and sleep onboard—with nights spent anchored in the harbor. See p. 249.

- **Hiking Mount Chirripó** (near San Isidro de El General on the central Pacific coast): The highest mountain in Costa Rica, Mount Chirripó is one of the few places in the world where (on a clear day) you can see both the Caribbean Sea and the Pacific Ocean at the same time. Hiking to Chirripó's 3,724m (12,215-ft.) summit will take you through a number of distinct bioregions, ranging from lowland pastures and a cloud forest to a high-altitude *páramo,* a tundralike landscape with stunted trees and morning frosts. See "San Isidro de El General: A Base for Exploring Chirripó National Park" in chapter 7.

- **Kayaking Around the Golfo Dulce:** Slipping through the waters of the Golfo Dulce by kayak gets you intimately in touch with the raw beauty of this underdeveloped region. Spend several days poking around in mangrove swamps, fishing in estuaries, and watching dolphins frolic in the bay. **Escondido Trex** (© 735-5210; www.escondidotrex.com) provides multiday custom kayaking trips out of Puerto Jiménez on the Osa Peninsula. See "Puerto Jiménez: Gateway to Corcovado National Park" in chapter 8.

- **Surfing Pavones** (on the southern Pacific coast): Just 13km (8 miles) from the Panamanian border at the southern reaches of Costa Rica's Pacific coast, Pavones is reputed to have one of the longest rideable waves in the world. When this left-point break is working, surfers enjoy rides of almost a mile in length. Much more can be said about this experience, but if you're a surfer, you've heard it all before. Contact **Casa Siempre Domingo** (© 820-4709; www.casa-domingo.com), the most comfortable hotel in town, for current wave reports and other local information. See "Playa Pavones: A Surfer's Mecca" in chapter 8.

4 The Best Day Hikes & Nature Walks

- **Lankester Gardens:** If you want a really pleasant but not overly challenging day hike, consider a walk among the hundreds of distinct species of flora on display here. Lankester Gardens (© 552-3247) is just 27km (17 miles) from San José and makes a wonderful day's expedition. The trails meander from areas of well-tended open garden to shady natural forest. See p. 122.

- **Rincón de la Vieja National Park:** This park has a number of wonderful trails through a variety of ecosystems and natural wonders. My favorite hike is down to the Blue Lake and Cangrejo Falls. It's 5.1km (3¼ miles) each way, and you'll want to spend some time at the base of this amazing lake; plan on spending at least 5 hours on the outing, and bring along lunch and plenty of water. You can also hike up to two craters and a crater lake here, and there's the Las Pailas loop for those seeking a less strenuous hike. This remote volcanic national park is located about an hour north of Liberia (it's only 25km/16 miles, but the road is quite rough), or about 5 hours from San José. See p. 148.

• **La Selva Biological Station:** This combination research facility and rustic nature lodge has an extensive and well-marked network of trails. You'll have to reserve in advance (© **766-6565**) and take the guided tour if you aren't a guest at the lodge. But the hikes are led by very informed naturalists, so you might not mind the company. The Biological Station is located north-northeast on the Caribbean slope of Costa Rica's central mountain range. It'll take you about 1½ hours to drive from San José via the Guápiles Highway. See p. 211.

• **Arenal National Park & Environs:** There's great hiking all around this area. The national park itself has several excellent trails that visit a variety of different ecosystems, including rainforest, secondary forest, savanna, and, my favorite, old lava flows. Most of them are on the relatively flat flanks of the volcano, so there's not too much climbing involved. There's also great hiking on the trails at the Arenal Observatory Lodge, and the trail down to the base of the La Fortuna Waterfall is a fun scramble. It's about a 3½-hour drive from San José to La Fortuna and Arenal National Park. See "Arenal Volcano & La Fortuna" in chapter 6.

• **Monteverde Biological Cloud Forest Reserve:** In morning rush of high season, when groups and tours line up to enter the reserve, you'd think the sign said CROWD FOREST. Still, the guides here are some of the most professional and knowledgeable in the country. Take a tour in the morning to familiarize yourself with the forest, and then spend the late morning or afternoon (your entrance ticket is good for the whole day) exploring the reserve. Once you get off the main thoroughfares, Monteverde reveals its rich mysteries with stunning regularity. Walk through the gray mist and look up at the dense tangle of epiphytes and vines. The only noises you'll hear are the rustlings of birds or monkeys and the occasional distant rumble of Arenal Volcano. The trails are well marked and regularly tended. It's about 3½ hours by bus or car to Monteverde from San José. See p. 234.

• **Corcovado National Park:** This large swath of dense lowland rainforest is home to Costa Rica's second-largest population of scarlet macaws. The park has a well-designed network of trails, ranger stations, and camping facilities. Most of the lodges in Drake Bay and Puerto Jiménez offer day hikes through the park, but if you really want to experience it, you should hike in and stay at one or more of the campgrounds. This is strenuous hiking, and you will have to pack in some gear and food, but the reward is some of Costa Rica's most spectacular and unspoiled scenery. Because strict limits are placed on the number of visitors allowed into the park, you'll always be far from the madding crowd. See "Puerto Jiménez: Gateway to Corcovado National Park" in chapter 8.

- **Cahuita National Park:** The trails here are flat, well-maintained paths through thick lowland forest. Most of the way, they parallel the beach, which is usually no more than 90m (295 ft.) away, so you can hike out on the trail and back along the beach, or vice versa. White-faced and howler monkeys are quite common here, as are brightly colored land crabs. See p. 333.

5 The Best Bird-Watching

- **Observing Oropendula & Blue-Crowned Motmot at Parque del Este:** A boon for city bird-watchers, this San José park rambles through a collection of lawns, planted gardens, and harvested forest, but it also includes second-growth scrub and dense woodland. Oropendula and blue-crowned motmot are common species here. Take the San Ramón/Parque del Este bus from Calle 9 between Avenida Central and Avenida 2. See p. 123.

- **Spotting Hundreds of Marsh & Stream Birds along the Río Tempisque Basin:** Hike around the Palo Verde Biological Station, or take a boat trip down the Bebedero River with **TAM Tours** (© 668-1037; www.tamtravel.com) or **Safaris Corobici** (© 669-6191; www.nicoya.com). This area is an important breeding ground for gallinules, jacanas, and limpkins, as well as a common habitat for numerous heron and kingfisher species. Palo Verde is about a 3½-hour drive from San José. See p. 149.

- **Looking for More Than 300 Species of Birds in La Selva Biological Station:** With an excellent trail system through a variety of habitats, from dense primary rainforest to open pasturelands and cacao plantations, this is one of the finest places for bird-watching in Costa Rica. With such a variety of habitats, the number of species spotted runs to well over 300. Contact the **Organization for Tropical Studies** (© 240-6696; www.ots.ac.cr) or see p. 211.

- **Sizing Up a Jabiru Stork at Caño Negro National Wildlife Refuge:** Caño Negro Lake and the Río Frío that feeds it are incredibly rich in wildlife and a major nesting and gathering site for aquatic bird species. These massive birds are getting less common in Costa Rica, but this is still one of the best places to see one. **Caño Negro Lodge** (© 471-1426; www.canonegrolodge.com) sits right on the edge of the refuge and makes a great base for exploring this region. See p. 219.

- **Catching a Scarlet Macaw in Flight over Carara Biological Reserve:** Home to Costa Rica's largest population of scarlet macaws, Carara Biological Reserve is a special place for devoted bird-watchers and recent converts. Macaws are noisy and colorful birds that spend their days in the park but choose to roost in the evenings near the coast. They arrive like clockwork every morning and then head for the coastal mangroves around dusk. These daily migrations give birders a great chance to see these magnificent birds in flight. The reserve is located about 2 hours from San José along the central Pacific coast. See p. 255.

- **Looking for a Resplendent Quetzal in the Cerro de la Muerte:** Don't let the name (Hill of Death) scare you away from the opportunity to see this spectacular bird, revered by the ancient Aztecs and Mayas. Serious bird-watchers won't want to leave Costa Rica without crossing this bird off their life lists, and neophytes might be hooked for life after seeing one of these iridescent green wonders fly overhead, flashing its brilliant red breast and trailing 2-foot-long tail feathers. **Trogon Lodge** (© 293-8181; www.grupomawamba.com) can almost guarantee a sighting. The Cerro de la Muerte is a high mountain pass located along the way to San Isidro de El General about 1½ hours from San José. See "En Route to San Jose: Three Places to See Quetzals in the Wild" in chapter 7.

• **Spotting Hundreds of Species at Wilson Botanical Gardens:** With more than 7,000 species of tropical plants and flowers, the well-tended trails and grounds of this beautiful research facility are fabulous for bird-watching. Hummingbirds and tanagers are particularly plentiful, but the bounty doesn't end there—more than 330 different species of birds have been recorded here. Wilson Gardens is located about an hour outside the town of Golfito. See "Golfito: Gateway to the Golfo Dulce" in chapter 8.

• **Taking Advantage of the Caribbean's Best Birding at Aviarios del Caribe:** In just a few short years, Aviarios del Caribe (© 750-0775) has established itself as the prime bird-watching resort on the Caribbean. If it flies along this coast, chances are good that you'll spot it here; more than 310 species of birds have been spotted so far. Located on the Caribbean coast, Aviarios del Caribe is about a 3-hour drive from San José. See p. 331.

6 The Best Destinations for Families

• **San José:** If you're spending any time in San José, you'll probably want to be outside the rough-and-tumble downtown area. The best place for all of you to experience Costa Rica's capital city (and still get a decent night's sleep) is the **Meliá Cariari** (© 888/956-3542 in the U.S. and Canada, or 239-0022; www.solmelia.com). With facilities that include several large pools, an 18-hole golf course, 11 tennis courts, and a game room (not to mention a babysitting service), there's something here for everyone. If you're traveling with teens, they'll feel right at home at the new Mall Cariari, which has a multiplex theater, an indoor skating rink, and, of course, a food court. Located just 15 minutes from downtown, it's well situated for exploring all of the city's sights and attractions. See p. 106.

• **Playa Hermosa:** The protected waters of this Pacific beach make it a family favorite. However, just because the waters are calm doesn't mean it's boring here. Check in at **Aqua Sport** (© 672-0050), where you can rent sea kayaks, sailboards, paddleboats, beach umbrellas, and bicycles. See "Playa Hermosa, Playa Panamá & Papagayo" in chapter 5.

• **Allegro Papagayo Resort** (© 248-2323; www.allegropapagayo.com) This large all-inclusive resort probably has the most extensive facilities, widest array of tours and activities, and best-run children's program set up in the country so far. The hotel is located on a very calm section of Bahía Culebra, and it even has a separate "Fun

Club" on a beautiful nearby white-sand beach. See p. 157.

- **Playa Tamarindo:** This lively surf town has a bit of something for everything. This is a great spot for teens to learn how to surf or boogie-board, and there are a host of tours and activities to please the entire family. **Hotel Capitán Suizo** (© 653-0353; www.hotel capitansuizo.com; p. 177) has an excellent location on a calm section of beach, spacious rooms, and a great pool for kids and adults alike. See "Playa Tamarindo & Playa Grande" in chapter 5.

- **Monteverde:** Located about 160km (99 miles) northwest of San José, this area not only boasts the country's most famous cloud forest, but it also sports a wide variety of related attractions and activities. After hiking through the reserve, you should be able to keep most kids happy and occupied riding horses, squirming at the local serpentarium, or visiting the butterfly farm and humming-bird gallery. More adventurous families can take a horseback ride or one of the local zip-line canopy tours. See "Monteverde" in chapter 6.

- **Playa de Jacó:** On the central Pacific coast, this is Costa Rica's liveliest and most developed beach town. The streets are lined with souvenir shops, ice-cream stands, and inexpensive eateries; there's even a miniature-golf course. Older kids can rent a surf- or boogie board, although everyone should be careful with the rough surf here. The **Club del Mar Condominiums & Resort** (©/fax 643-3194; www.clubdelmarcosta rica.com; p. 256) is situated at the calm southern end of the beach. The hotel has a large, free-form pool and some shady grounds, and is accommodating to families traveling with small children. See "Playa de Jacó" in chapter 7.

- **Manuel Antonio:** Manuel Antonio has a little bit of everything: miles of gorgeous beaches, tons of wildlife (with almost guaranteed monkey sightings), and plenty of active tour options. There's a load of lodging options, but **Hotel Sí Como No** (© 777-0777; www. sicomono.com), with its large suites, two pools, water slide, and nightly movies, is probably your best bet. See "Manuel Antonio National Park" in chapter 7.

7 The Best Luxury Hotels & Resorts

"Luxury" is a relative term in Costa Rica. Several major resorts and a couple of fabulous boutique hotels have done their darndest to meet the needs of upscale travelers. With the recent opening of a Four Seasons resort in the northern province of Guanacaste, the bar has been raised even further.

- **Marriott Costa Rica Hotel** (San Antonio de Belén, San José area; © 800/228-9290 in the U.S. and Canada, or 298-0844; www.marriott.com): Of all the contenders in the upscale urban market, the Marriott seems to be

doing the best job. Maybe that's just because it's the newest, but everything is in great shape, the service is bend-over-backward, the restaurants are excellent, and there are all the facilities and amenities you could want. See p. 106.

- **Four Seasons Resort Costa Rica** (Papagayo Peninsula; © 800/819-5053 in the U.S., or 696-0098; www.fourseasons.com/costarica): This is the first major resort to really address the luxury market in Costa Rica. Within its first month of operation, both Madonna and

Michael Jordan were notable guests. A beautiful setting, wonderful installations, and stellar service make this the current king of the hill in the upscale market. See p. 156.

- **Paradisus Playa Conchal** (on the northern Pacific coast; ℭ **888/ 336-3542** in the U.S., or 654-4123; www.solmelia.com): If you're looking for a large and luxurious all-inclusive resort with all the trappings, including an 18-hole Robert Trent Jones golf course, this place fits the bill. As a bonus, it's located on one of the nicest beaches in Costa Rica, the seashell-strewn wonder of Playa Conchal. See p. 167.
- **Hotel Punta Islita** (on the Pacific coast in central Guanacaste; ℭ **231-6122;** www.hotelpunta islita.com): This is a great getaway. Perched on a high, flat bluff overlooking the Pacific Ocean, Punta Islita is popular with honeymooners, and rightly so. The rooms are large and comfortable, the food is excellent, and the setting is stunning. If you venture beyond your room and the hotel's inviting hillside pool, there's a long, almost always deserted beach for you to explore, as well as a wealth of activities for the more adventurous. See p. 192.
- **Flor Blanca Resort** (Playa Santa Teresita; ℭ **640-0232;** www.flor blanca.com): The individual villas at this intimate resort are some of the largest and most luxurious in the country. The service and food are outstanding, and the location

is breathtaking, spread over a lushly planted hillside just steps off of Playa Santa Teresita. See p. 203.

- **Marriott Los Sueños Ocean & Golf Resort** (Playa Herradura; ℭ **800/228-9290** in the U.S., 298-0844 or 630-9000; www. marriott.com): With large, luxurious rooms, an 18-hole golf course, tons of facilities and amenities, and a large maze of a pool built to resemble the canals of Venice, this is one of the finest luxury resorts in Costa Rica. The only real downside here is the decidedly mediocre beach. See p. 258.
- **Villa Caletas** (north of Jacó; ℭ **637-0606;** www.hotelvilla caletas.com): Spread out over a steep hillside, high above the Pacific Ocean, these individual villas have a Mediterranean feel. The Greek Doric amphitheater follows the same motif. Carved into the steep hillside, the theater frequently features evening concerts of jazz or classical music. The "infinity pool" here was one of the first in Costa Rica and is still the most interesting. Sitting in a lounge chair at the pool's edge, you'll swear that it joins the sea beyond. See p. 259.
- **Hotel Sí Como No** (Manuel Antonio; ℭ **777-0777;** www.si comono.com): Although there are fancier and more posh places in Costa Rica, the large modern suites and villas, spectacular views, attentive service, and first-rate facilities here earn this small resort a spot on this list. See p. 272.

8 The Best Moderately Priced Hotels

- **Hotel Grano de Oro** (San José; ℭ **255-3322;** www.hotelgranode oro.com): San José boasts dozens of old homes that have been converted into hotels, but few offer

the luxurious accommodations or professional service that can be found at the Grano de Oro. Throughout all the guest rooms, you'll find attractive hardwood furniture, including old-fashioned wardrobes in some rooms. When it comes time to relax, you can soak in a hot tub or have a drink in the rooftop lounge while taking in the commanding view of San José. See p. 101.

- **Hotel Le Bergerac** (San José; © 234-7850; www.bergerachotel. com): This classy little hotel has been pleasing diplomats, dignitaries, and other discerning travelers for years. Ask for one of the garden rooms, or get the old master bedroom with its small private balcony. See p. 103.

- **Villa del Sueño Hotel** (Playa Hermosa; ©/fax 672-0026; www. villadelsueno.com): It's not right on the beach (you'll have to walk about 90m/295 ft.), but everything else about this place is right on the money, including clean, comfortable rooms; a nice refreshing pool; and an excellent restaurant. You can't do better in Playa Hermosa. See p. 159.

- **El Sano Banano Beach Resort** (Playa Montezuma; © 642-0638; www.elbanano.com): Isolated, private cabins with outdoor showers set amid lush grounds a stone's throw from the Pacific Ocean add up to my idea of a tropical paradise. See p. 199.

- **Hotel El Sapo Dorado** (Monteverde; © 645-5010; www.sapo dorado.com): Spacious wooden cabins with fireplaces and private porches are spread across an open hillside planted with fruit trees and tropical flowers. The hotel has an excellent restaurant and is a great place to enjoy some of the best sunsets in town. See p. 240.

- **Cariblue Bungalows** (Playa Cocles; © 750-0035; www.cari blue.com): Try to get one of the private wooden bungalows here. If you do, you might be so happy and comfortable that you won't want to leave. Just 90m (295 ft.) or so away, however, are the warm waves of the Caribbean Sea. See p. 345.

9 The Best Ecolodges & Wilderness Resorts

The term "ecotourism" is fast becoming ubiquitous within the travel industry, particularly in Costa Rica. Ecolodge options in Costa Rica range from tent camps with no electricity, cold-water showers, and communal buffet-style meals to some of the most luxurious accommodations in the country. Generally, outstanding ecolodges and wilderness resorts are set apart by an ongoing commitment (financial or otherwise) to minimizing their effect on surrounding ecosystems and to supporting both conservation efforts and the residents of local communities. They should also be able to provide naturalist guides and plentiful information. All of the following do.

- **La Selva Biological Station** (south of Puerto Viejo; © 240-6696; www.ots.ac.cr): Sure, this place is geared more toward researchers than tourists, but that (along with the surrounding rainforest and extensive trail system) is what makes this one of the best ecotourism spots in the country. See p. 211.

- **Arenal Observatory Lodge** (near La Fortuna; © 290-7011; www. arenal-observatory.co.cr): Originally a research facility, this lodge has upgraded quite a bit over the years and now features comfortable rooms with impressive views of the Arenal Volcano. There are also excellent trails to nearby lava flows and a nice waterfall. Toucans frequent the trees near the lodge, and howler monkeys provide the wake-up calls. See p. 222.

- **La Paloma Lodge** (Drake Bay; ✆ 239-2801; www.lapaloma lodge.com): If your idea of the perfect nature lodge is one where your front porch provides some prime-time viewing of flora and fauna, this place is for you. If you decide to leave the comfort of your porch, the Osa Peninsula's lowland rainforests are just outside your door. See p. 297.
- **Bosque del Cabo Rainforest Lodge** (Osa Peninsula; ✆/fax 735-5206; www.bosquedelcabo.com): Large and comfortable private cabins perched on the edge of a cliff overlooking the Pacific Ocean and surrounded by lush rainforest make this one of my favorite spots in the country. There's plenty to do, and there are always great guides here. See p. 305.
- **Corcovado Lodge Tent Camp** (Playa Carate; ✆ 257-0766; www.costaricaexpeditions.com): Located right on the border of Corcovado National Park, these accommodations are in spacious individual tents set within walking distance of the crashing surf. The whole operation is run by the very dependable and experienced Costa Rica Expeditions. See p. 306.
- **Tortuga Lodge** (Tortuguero; ✆ 257-0766; www.costarica expeditions.com): The canals of Tortuguero snake through a maze of lowland primary rainforest. The beaches here are major sea-turtle nesting sites. This is not only the most comfortable option in the area, but it's also another of the excellent ecolodges run by Costa Rica Expeditions. See p. 326.
- **Selva Bananito Lodge** (in the Talamanca Mountains south of Limón; ✆/fax 253-8118; www.selvabananito.com): This is one of the few lodges providing direct access to the southern Caribbean lowland rainforests. There's no electricity here, but that doesn't mean it's not plush. Hike along a riverbed, ride horses through the rainforest, climb 30m (100 ft.) up a ceiba tree, or rappel down a jungle waterfall. There's fabulous bird-watching here, and the Caribbean beaches are nearby. See p. 331.

10 The Best Bed-and-Breakfasts & Small Inns

- **Finca Rosa Blanca Country Inn** (Santa Bárbara de Heredia; ✆ 269-9392; www.fincarosa blanca.com): If the cookie-cutter rooms of international resorts leave you cold, then perhaps the unique rooms of this unusual inn will be more your style. Square corners seem to have been prohibited here in favor of turrets and curving walls of glass, arched windows, and a semicircular built-in couch. It's set into the lush hillsides just 20 minutes from San José. See p. 105.
- **Vista del Valle Plantation Inn** (near Grecia; ✆ 450-0800; www.vistadelvalle.com): This is a great choice for those who want something close to the airport but have no need for San José. The separate cabins are influenced by traditional Japanese architecture, with lots of polished woodwork and plenty of light. The gardens are also meticulously tended, and the chef is excellent. There's a nice tile pool and Jacuzzi that look out over a deep river canyon. See p. 108.
- **Sueño del Mar** (Playa Tamarindo; ✆/fax 653-0284; www.sueno-del-mar.com): You might think you're dreaming here. The rooms feature African dolls on the windowsills, Kokopeli candleholders,

and open-air showers with sculpted angelfish, hand-painted tiles, and lush tropical plants. The fabrics are from Bali and Guatemala. Somehow all this works well together. Add in the requisite hammocks under shade trees right on the beach and a new small pool, and you really have something. The breakfasts here are earning local renown; yours comes with the price of your room. See p. 177.

- **Arco Iris Lodge** (Monteverde; © 645-5067; www.arcoirislodge. com): This small lodge is right in Santa Elena, and it's by far the best deal in the Monteverde area. The owners are extremely knowledgeable and helpful. See p. 241.

- **Cabinas Los Cocos** (Playa Zancudo; ©/fax 776-0012; www.los cocos.com): If you've ever dreamed about chucking it all and setting up shop in a simple house right on the beach, you should come here and give it a trial run first. See p. 314.

- **Shawandha Lodge** (Playa Chiquita; © 750-0018; www. shawandhalodge.com): Spacious, individual bungalows set amid flowering gardens and thick jungle make this the most comfortable lodge on the Caribbean coast. Artistic touches abound. See p. 346.

- **Cabinas Casa Verde** (Puerto Viejo; © 750-0015; www. cabinascasaverde.com): This is my favorite budget lodging along the Caribbean coast. The rooms are clean and airy, and have comfortable beds with mosquito nets. The owner is friendly and is always doing some work in the gardens or around the grounds. See p. 344.

11 The Best Restaurants

- **Tin Jo** (San José; © 221-7605): In a city with hundreds of Chinese restaurants, this place stands head and shoulders above the competition. In addition to an extensive selection of Szechuan and Cantonese classics, there are Japanese, Thai, Indian, and Malaysian dishes on the menu. Tin Jo has the most adventurous Asian cuisine in Costa Rica. See p. 111.

- **Grano de Oro Restaurant** (San José; © 255-3322): This elegant little hotel has a similarly elegant restaurant serving delicious Continental dishes and decadent desserts. The open-air seating in the lushly planted central courtyard is delightful, especially for lunch. See p. 114.

- **Bakea** (San José; © 221-1051): The elegant and varied decor of this rambling old colonial home, coupled with the creative fusion cuisine coming out of the kitchen, makes this new place one of the top restaurants in the city. See p. 110.

- **Camarón Dorado** (Playa Brasilito; © 654-4028): Simple, fresh seafood served on plastic lawn furniture set in the sand just steps from the crashing waves makes this place a wonderful spot. The attentive, semiformal service makes it even better. See p. 170.

- **Lazy Wave Food Company** (Tamarindo; © 653-0737): Creative chefs put together an eclectic daily offering of what's fresh and what strikes their fancy. Open-air seating under an old shade tree, reasonable prices, and a relaxed atmosphere all add up to make this my favorite restaurant on the Gold Coast. See p. 180.

- **Playa de los Artistas** (Montezuma; © 642-0920): This place is the perfect blend of refined cuisine and beachside funkiness. There are only a few tables here, so make sure you get here early. Fresh grilled seafood is served in oversize ceramic bowls and on large wooden slabs lined with banana leaves. See p. 201.

- **El Gran Escape** (Quepos; ✆ 777-0395): The prices are right, the portions are generous, and the fish is always fresh and expertly prepared. What more could you ask for from a seafood restaurant in a popular port town? See p. 277.

- **La Pecora Nera** (Puerto Viejo; ✆ 750-0490): I'm not sure that a tiny surfer town on the remote Caribbean coast deserves such fine Italian food, but it's got it. Your best bet here is to allow yourself to be taken on a culinary roller-coaster ride with a mixed feast of the chef's nightly specials and suggestions. See p. 349.

12 The Best Views

- **The Summit of Irazú Volcano** (near San José): On a very clear day, you can see both the Pacific Ocean and the Caribbean Sea from this vantage point. Even if visibility is low and this experience eludes you, you will have a view of the volcano's spectacular landscape, the Meseta Central, and the Orosi Valley. See "Holy Smoke!: Choosing the Volcano Trip That's Right for You" in chapter 4.

- **El Mirador Ehecatl** (✆ 679-9104): This humble little restaurant holds a commanding view of Bahía Salinas. It's not necessarily worth the drive from San José, and the food is basic, at best. But if you're anywhere near La Cruz, this is a must stop for sunset. See "La Cruz" in chapter 5.

- **Iguanazul Hotel** (Playa Junquillal; ✆ 658-8124; www.iguanazul. com): Located on a high bluff above Playa Junquillal, this hotel has a wonderful view of the Pacific and the windswept coastline in either direction. It gets best around sunset, and better yet if you can commandeer one of the hammocks set in a little palapa on the hillside itself. See p. 182.

- **Tabacón Hot Springs Resort & Spa** (near Arenal Volcano; ✆ 256-1500; www.tabacon.com): It seems so close, you'll swear you can reach out and touch the volcano. Unlike on Irazú Volcano (see above), when *this* volcano rumbles and spews, you might have the urge to run for cover. Most rooms here have spectacular views from sheltered private patios or balconies. See p. 221.

- **Villa Caletas** (Playa Hermosa de Jacó; ✆ 637-0606): You'll have a view over the Golfo de Nicoya and the Pacific Ocean beyond. Sunsets at the hotel's outdoor amphitheater are legendary, but it's beautiful here during the day as well. See p. 259.

- **Hotel La Mariposa** (Quepos; ✆ 800/416-2747 or 777-0355; www.lamariposa.com): This place has arguably the best view in Manuel Antonio, and that's saying a lot. Come for breakfast or a sunset drink because, unfortunately, I've had bad luck with dinner here. See p. 271.

- **The Summit of Mount Chirripó** (near San Isidro): What more can one say? At 3,724m (12,215 ft.), this is the highest spot in Costa Rica. On a clear day, you can see both the Pacific Ocean and the Caribbean Sea from here. Even if it isn't clear, you can catch some pretty amazing views and scenery. See "San Isidro de El General: A Base for Exploring Chirripó National Park" in chapter 7.

13 The Best After-Dark Fun

- **Night Tours** (countrywide): Most Neotropical forest dwellers are nocturnal. Animal and insect calls fill the air, and the rustling on the ground all around takes on new meanings. Night tours are offered at most rain- and cloud-forest destinations throughout the country. Many use high-powered flashlights to catch glimpses of various animals. Some even have high-tech night-vision goggles. Some of the better spots for night tours are **Monteverde, Tortuguero,** and the **Osa Peninsula.** Volcano viewing in **Arenal** is another not-to-miss nighttime activity.

- **El Cuartel de la Boca del Monte** (San José; © 221-0327): This is where San José's young, restless, and beautiful congregate. From Wednesday to Saturday, the place is jam-packed. Originally a gay and bohemian hangout, it is now decidedly mixed and leaning toward yuppie. There's frequently live music here. See p. 132.

- **San Pedro** (San José): This is San José's university district, and at night its streets are filled with students strolling among a variety of bars and cafes. If you'd like to join them, keep in mind that **La Villa** (© 281-1571) caters to artists and bohemians, **Mosaikos** (© 280-9541) is popular with young Tico rockers, **Omar Khayyam** (© 253-8455) is a great place to grab an outdoor table and watch the crowds walk by, and **Terra U** (© 225-7249) is the quintessential college bar, attracting a mix of local and foreign exchange students. All of the spots listed above are located in a 3-block stretch that begins 200m (656 ft.) east of the San Pedro Church and heads

north. If you head straight 500m (1,640 ft.) east from the church, you'll come to **Jazz Café** (© 253-8933), which, as its name indicates, often features live jazz. See "San José After Dark" in chapter 4.

- **The Big Bazaar** (Tamarindo): Tamarindo is a rocking surfer beach town, and this is the place to be after dark, especially on Saturday nights, when they light a big bonfire right on the beach. See p. 181.

- **Mar y Sombra** (Manuel Antonio; © 777-0510): Located on the beach a couple of hundred meters from the national park entrance, this is the most happening spot in the Manuel Antonio area. There's a large, open-air dance floor and plenty of tables set in the sand. If the dancing gets too intense, you can always cool your feet in the ocean. See "Manuel Antonio National Park" in chapter 7.

- **San Clemente Bar & Grill** (Dominical; © 787-0055): This is a quintessential surfers' joint, but whether you hang 10 or not, this is where you'll want to hang out in Dominical at night. The fresh seafood and Tex-Mex specialties are hearty, tasty, and inexpensive. And there are pool, Ping-Pong, and foosball tables, as well as televised sporting events and surf videos. See "Dominical" in chapter 7.

- **Johnny's Place** (Puerto Viejo; no phone): Picture yourself sipping a cold beer at a candlelit table set in the sand with the Caribbean lapping at your feet. Could you ask for more? If so, a few steps away there's a steamy dance floor that lets loose to loud reggae. See "Puerto Viejo" in chapter 9.

14 The Best Websites About Costa Rica

- *The Tico Times* (www.ticotimes. net): A selection from the English-language *Tico Times* makes it easy for *norteamericanos* (and other English speakers) to see what's happening in Costa Rica. It prints the top story from its weekly print edition, as well as a daily update of news briefs, a business article, regional news, a fishing column, and travel reviews. There's also a link to current currency-exchange rates.

- **Latin America Network Information Center** (www.lanic.utexas. edu/la/ca/cr): Hosted by the University of Texas Latin American Studies Department, this site houses a vast collection of diverse information about Costa Rica. This is hands-down the best one-stop shop for Web browsing. There are helpful links to a wide range of tourism and general information sites.

- **Maptak** (www.maptak.com): This is the best site I've found for online maps. The site is still expanding and improving, and there's a tiny bit of a learning curve here, but this could become a very valuable resource.

- **Costa Rica Living** (www.costa ricaliving.org): This is the official home page of the best newsgroup dealing with Costa Rica. The active newsgroup deals with a wide range of issues, and its membership includes many long-time residents and bona fide experts. There's plenty of good information in the Clipboard and Files sections.

- *La Nación* **Digital** (www.nacion. com): If you can read Spanish, this is a worthwhile site to browse. The entire content of the country's paper of record is placed online daily, and there's also an extensive searchable archive. It does maintain a small summary of major news items in English, although this section tends to run about a week behind the current events.

Planning Your Trip
to Costa Rica

Costa Rica is one of the fastest-growing and most popular tourist destinations in the Americas, and as the number of visitors increases, so does the need for pretrip planning. When is the best time to go to Costa Rica? The cheapest time? Should you rent a car (or will you need 4WD), and what will it cost? Where should you go in Costa Rica? What are the hotels like? How much should you budget for your trip? These are just a few of the important questions that this chapter answers so that you can be prepared when you arrive in Costa Rica.

1 The Regions in Brief

Costa Rica rightfully should be called "Costas Ricas" because it has two coasts, one on the Pacific Ocean and one on the Caribbean Sea. These two coasts are as different from each other as are the Atlantic and Pacific coasts of North America.

Costa Rica's **Pacific coast** is characterized by a rugged (although mostly accessible) coastline where forested mountains often meet the sea. It can be divided into three distinct regions—Guanacaste and the Nicoya Peninsula, the Central Coast, and the Southern Coast. There are some spectacular stretches of coastline, and most of the country's top beaches are here. This coast varies from the dry, sunny climate of the northwest to the hot, humid rainforests of the south.

The **Caribbean coast** can be divided into two roughly equal stretches, one of which is accessible only by boat or small plane. The remote northeast coastline is a vast flat plain laced with rivers and covered with rainforest. Farther south, along the stretch of coast accessible by car, there are uncrowded beaches and even a bit of coral reef.

Bordered by Nicaragua in the north and Panama in the southeast, Costa Rica is only slightly larger than Vermont and New Hampshire combined. Much of the country is mountainous, with three major ranges running northwest to southeast. Among these mountains are several volcanic peaks, some of which are still active. Between the mountain ranges are fertile valleys, the largest and most populated of which is the Central Valley. With the exception of the dry Guanacaste region, much of Costa Rica's coastal area is hot and humid and covered with dense rainforests.

SAN JOSE & THE CENTRAL VALLEY The Central Valley is characterized by rolling green hills that rise to heights between 900 and 1,200m (2,952–3,936 ft.) above sea level. The climate here is mild and springlike year-round. It's Costa Rica's primary agricultural region, with coffee farms making up the majority of landholdings. The rich volcanic soil of this region makes it ideal for farming. The country's earliest settlements were in this area, and today the Central Valley (which includes San José) is densely populated, with decent roads, and dotted with small towns. Surrounding the Central Valley are high mountains, among which are four volcanic peaks. Two of these, **Poás** and **Irazú,** are still active and have caused extensive damage during cycles of activity in the past 2 centuries. Many of the mountainous regions to the north and to the south of the capital of San José have been declared national parks (Tapantí, Juan Castro, and Braulio Carrillo) to protect their virgin rainforests against logging.

GUANACASTE & THE NICOYA PENINSULA The northwestern corner of the country near the Nicaraguan border is the site of many of Costa Rica's sunniest and most popular **beaches.** Because many Americans have chosen to build beach houses and retirement homes here, Guanacaste, in particular, is experiencing quite a bit of new development. Don't expect a glut of Cancún-style high-rise hotels, but condos, luxury resorts, and golf courses are springing up like mushrooms. That's not to say you'll be towel-to-towel with thousands of strangers. On the contrary, you can still find long stretches of deserted sands. That might not be true for long, however: Now that the new international airport in Liberia is up and running, travelers can get here on a direct flight from North America.

With about 65 inches of rain a year, this region is by far the driest in the country and has been likened to west Texas. Guanacaste province sits at the border of Nicaragua and is named after the shady trees that still shelter the herds of cattle that roam the dusty savanna here. In addition to cattle ranches, Guanacaste boasts semiactive volcanoes, several lakes, and one of the last remnants of tropical dry forest left in Central America. (Dry forest once stretched all the way from Costa Rica up to the Mexican state of Chiapas.).

THE NORTHERN ZONE This region lies to the north of San José and includes rainforests, cloud forests, hot springs, the country's two most active volcanoes (**Arenal** and **Rincón de la Vieja**), **Braulio Carrillo National Park,** and numerous remote lodges. Because this is one of the few regions of Costa Rica without any beaches, it primarily attracts people interested in nature and active sports. **Lake Arenal** boasts some of the best windsurfing in the world, as well as several good mountain-biking trails along its shores. The **Monteverde Cloud Forest,** perhaps Costa Rica's most internationally recognized attraction, is another top draw in this region.

THE CENTRAL PACIFIC COAST Because it's the most easily accessible coastline in Costa Rica, the central Pacific coast boasts the greatest number of beach resorts and hotels. **Playa de Jacó** is the most popular destination here, a beach within a few hours' drive of San José that attracts a large number of Canadian and German charter groups and plenty of Tico tourists on weekends. **Manuel Antonio,** the name of a popular coastal national park as well as the resort area that surrounds it, caters to people seeking a bit more tranquillity and beauty. At the same time, this region is home to the highest peak in Costa Rica—**Mount Chirripó**—where frost is common.

THE SOUTHERN ZONE This hot, humid region is one of Costa Rica's most remote and undeveloped regions. It is characterized by dense rainforests and rugged coastlines. Much of the area is protected in **Corcovado** and **La Amistad** national parks. There is a wealth of wonderful nature lodges spread around the shores of the **Golfo Dulce** and along the **Osa Peninsula.** There's a lot of solitude to be found here, due in no small part to the fact that it's hard to

The Regions in Brief

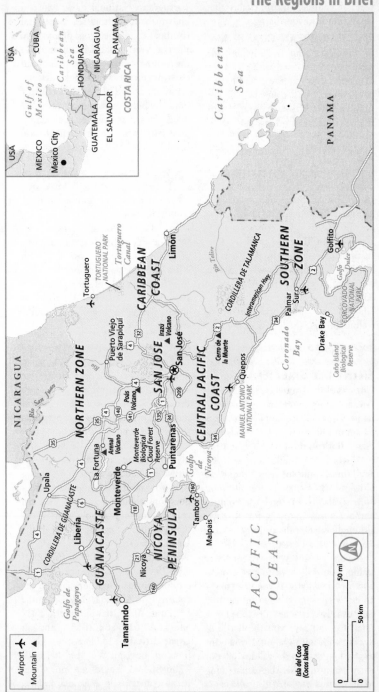

get here and hard to get around. But if you like your ecotourism challenging, you'll find it to your liking.

THE CARIBBEAN COAST   Most of the Caribbean coast is a wide, steamy lowland laced with rivers and blanketed with rainforests and banana plantations. The culture here is predominantly Afro-Caribbean, with many residents speaking English or Caribbean patois. The northern section of this coast is accessible only by boat or small plane and is the site of **Tortuguero National Park,** which is known for its nesting sea turtles and riverboat trips. The towns of **Cahuita, Puerto Viejo,** and **Manzanillo,** on the southern half of the Caribbean coast, are increasingly popular destinations. The coastline here boasts many beautiful beaches and, as yet, few large hotels. However, this area can be rainy, especially between December and April.

2 Visitor Information

In the United States or Canada, you can get a basic packet of information on Costa Rica by contacting the **Costa Rican Tourist Board (ICT,** or Instituto Costarricense de Turismo; ℭ **800/343-6332;** www.visitcosta rica.com). Travelers from the United Kingdom, Australia, and New Zealand will have to rely primarily on this website because the ICT does not have offices or a toll-free number in these countries.

In addition to this official site, you'll be able to find a wealth of Web-based information on Costa Rica with a few clicks of your mouse. See "The Best Websites About Costa Rica" in chapter 1 for some helpful suggestions about where to begin your online search.

3 Entry Requirements & Customs

ENTRY REQUIREMENTS
Citizens of the United States, Canada, Great Britain, and most European nations may visit Costa Rica for a maximum of 90 days. No visa is necessary, but you must have a valid passport, which you should carry with you at all times while you're in Costa Rica. Citizens of Australia, Ireland, and New Zealand can enter the country without a visa and stay for 30 days, although, once in the country, visitors can apply for an extension.

If you overstay your visa or entry stamp, you will have to pay around $45 for an exit visa. If you need to get an exit visa, a travel agent in San José can usually get one for you for a small fee and save you the hassle of dealing with Immigration. If you want to stay longer than the validity of your entry stamp or visa, the easiest thing to do is cross the border into Panama or Nicaragua for 72 hours and then re-enter Costa Rica on a new entry stamp or visa. However, be careful. Periodically, the Costa Rican government has cracked down on "perpetual tourists"; if it notices a continued pattern of exits and entries designed simply to support an extended stay, it might deny you re-entry.

If you need a visa or have other questions about Costa Rica, you can contact any of the following Costa Rican embassies or consulates: in the **United States,** 2112 S St. NW, Washington, DC 20008 (ℭ **202/ 234-2945;** www.costarica-embassy. org for consulate locations around the country); in **Canada,** 325 Dalhousie St., Suite 407, Ottawa, Ontario K1N 5TA (ℭ **613/562-2855**); and in **Great Britain,** 14 Lancaster Gate, London, England W2 3LH (ℭ **020/ 7706-8844**). There are no Costa Rican embassies in Australia or New Zealand, but you could try contacting

> **Tips Lost Documents**
>
> If you lose your passport or need special assistance after you've arrived in Costa Rica, contact your embassy; locations are listed in "Fast Facts: Costa Rica," later in this chapter. Most embassies can replace your passport and help you get an exit visa in about 24 hours.
>
> If your embassy won't get your exit visa for you, see a local travel agent or **OTEC Viajes,** Edificio Ferencz, 2nd floor, Calle 3 between avenidas 1 and 3, almost 3 blocks north of the National Theater (© **256-0633;** www.otec. co.cr). If you try to deal with Immigration yourself, you will face long lines, long waits, and endless frustration. Local travel agents and agencies regularly deal with Immigration and will charge you about $10 to $15 for the service (sometimes they'll do this for free if you ticket with them).

the honorary consul in Sydney, Australia, at Level 11, De La Sala House, 30 Clarence St., Sydney NSW 2000 (© **02/9261-1177**).

To apply for a passport, residents of the **United States** should call © 202/647-0518 or visit http://travel.state. gov; **Canada,** © 800/567-6868 or www.ppt.gc.ca; the **U.K.,** © 0870/521-0410 or www.ukpa.gov.uk; **Ireland,** © 01/671-1633 or www.irl gov.ie/iveagh; **Australia,** © 131-232 or www.passports.gov.au; and **New Zealand,** © 0800/225-050 or 04/474-8100, or www.passports.govt.nz.

CUSTOMS
WHAT YOU CAN BRING TO COSTA RICA
Visitors entering Costa Rica are officially entitled to bring in 500 grams of tobacco, 5 liters of liquor, and US$500 in merchandise. Cameras, computers, and electronic equipment for personal use are permitted duty free. Customs officials in Costa Rica seldom check tourists' luggage.

WHAT YOU CAN TAKE HOME
Returning **U.S. citizens** who have been away for at least 48 hours are allowed to bring back, once every 30 days, $800 worth of merchandise duty free. You'll be charged a flat rate of duty on the next $1,000 worth of purchases. Any dollar amount beyond

that is subject to duty at whatever rates apply. On mailed gifts, the duty-free limit is $200. Be sure to have your receipts or purchases handy to expedite the declaration process. ***Note:*** If you owe duty, you are required to pay on your arrival in the United States, by either cash, personal check, government or traveler's check, or money order, and, in some locations, a Visa or MasterCard. For specifics on what you can bring back, download the invaluable free pamphlet *Know Before You Go* online at **www.cbp.gov**. (Click on "Travel" and then "Know Before You Go! Online Brochure.") Or contact the **U.S. Customs & Border Protection,** 1300 Pennsylvania Ave. NW, Washington, DC 20229 (© **877/287-8667**), and request the pamphlet.

For a clear summary of **Canadian** rules, write for the booklet *I Declare,* issued by the **Canada Border Services Agency** (© **800/461-9999** in Canada, or 204/983-3500; www.cbsa.gc.ca). Canada allows its citizens a C$750 exemption, and you're allowed to bring back duty free one carton of cigarettes, one can of tobacco, 40 imperial ounces of liquor, and 50 cigars. In addition, you're allowed to mail gifts to Canada valued at less than C$60 a day, provided that they're unsolicited and don't contain alcohol or tobacco (write on the package "Unsolicited gift, under $60 value"). All valuables should be declared on the Y-38 form before departure from Canada, including serial numbers of valuables you already own, such as expensive foreign cameras. *Note:* The $750 exemption can be used only once a year and only after an absence of 7 days.

U.K. citizens returning from a non-E.U. country have a customs allowance of 200 cigarettes; 50 cigars; 250 grams of smoking tobacco; 2 liters of still table wine; 1 liter of spirits or strong liqueurs (over 22% volume); 2 liters of fortified wine, sparkling wine or other liqueurs; 60cc (milliliters) perfume; 250cc (milliliters) of toilet water; and £145 worth of all other goods, including gifts and souvenirs. People under 17 cannot have the tobacco or alcohol allowance. For more information, contact HM Customs & Excise at ℂ **0845/010-9000** (from outside the U.K., call 020/8929-0152), or consult the website www.hmce.gov.uk.

The duty-free allowance in **Australia** is A$400 or, for those under 18, A$200. Citizens can bring in 250 cigarettes or 250 grams of loose tobacco, and 1,125 milliliters of alcohol. If you're returning with valuables that you already own, such as foreign-made cameras, you should file form B263. A helpful brochure available from Australian consulates or Customs offices is *Know Before You Go.* For more information, contact the **Australian Customs Service** (ℂ **1300/ 363-263;** www.customs.gov.au).

The duty-free allowance for **New Zealand** is NZ$700. Citizens over 17 can bring in 200 cigarettes, 50 cigars, or 250 grams of tobacco (or a mixture of all three if their combined weight doesn't exceed 250g), plus 4.5 liters of wine and beer, or 1.125 liters of liquor. New Zealand currency does not carry import or export restrictions. Fill out a certificate of export, listing the valuables that you are taking out of the country; that way, you can bring them back without paying duty. Most questions are answered in a free pamphlet available at New Zealand consulates and Customs offices: *New Zealand Customs Guide for Travellers, Notice no. 4.* For more information, contact **New Zealand Customs,** The Customhouse, 17–21 Whitmore St., Box 2218, Wellington (ℂ **04/473-6099** or 0800/ 428-786; www.customs.govt.nz).

4 Money

CASH & CURRENCY

The unit of currency in Costa Rica is the **colón.** In mid-2004, there were approximately 430 colones to the American dollar, but because the colón has been in a constant state of devaluation, you can expect this rate to change. Because of this devaluation and accompanying inflation, *this book lists prices in U.S. dollars only.* To check the very latest exchange rates before you leave home, point your browser to **www.xe.com/ucc.**

The colón is divided into 100 **céntimos.** Currently, two types of coins are in circulation. The older and larger nickel-alloy coins come in denominations of 10, 25, and 50 céntimos and 1, 2, 5, 10, and 20 colones; however, because of their evaporating value, you will probably never see or have to handle céntimos, or anything lower than a 5-colón coin. In 1997, the government introduced gold-hued 5-, 10-, 25-, 50-, 100-, and 500-colón coins. They are smaller and heavier than the older coins, and they will eventually phase out the other currency.

There are paper notes in denominations of 1,000, 2,000, 5,000, and 10,000 colones. You might also encounter a special-issue 5-colón bill that is a popular gift and souvenir. It is valid currency, although it sells for much more than its face value. You might hear people refer to a *rojo* or *tucán,* which are slang terms for the 1,000- and 5,000-colón bills, respectively. One-hundred-colón denominations are called *tejas,* so *cinco tejas* is 500 colones. The 2,000 and 10,000 bills are relatively new, and I've yet to encounter a slang equivalent for them.

In recent years, **forged bills** have become increasingly common. When receiving change in colones, it's a good idea to check the larger-denomination bills, which should have protective bands or hidden images that appear when held up to the light.

If your ATM card doesn't work and you need cash in a hurry, **Western Union** (℅ **800/777-7777** in Costa Rica, or 283-6336; www.western union.com) has numerous offices around San José and in several major towns and cities around the country. It offers a secure and rapid, although pricey, money-wire service and telegram service. A $100 wire costs around $15, and a $1,000 wire costs around $50.

EXCHANGING MONEY

You can change money at all state-owned banks. However, the service at these banks is slow and tedious. This simple transaction can often take as long as an hour and cause unnecessary confusion and anxiety. I don't recommend it.

Fortunately, you don't have to rely on the state's banks. In late 1996, Costa Rica passed a law opening up the state's banking system. Accordingly, private banks have opened around San José and in some of the larger provincial towns and cities. These private banks are kicking the state banks' butts, providing fast service at reasonable commissions, with small or no lines.

Hotels will often exchange money and cash traveler's checks as well; there usually isn't much of a line, but they might shave a few colones off the exchange rate.

Be very careful about exchanging money on the streets; it's extremely risky. In addition to forged bills and short counts, street money-changers frequently work in teams that can leave you holding neither colones nor dollars.

Note: When you change money, ask for some small bills and some 100-colón coins. Petty cash will come in handy for tipping and public transportation. Consider keeping the change separate from your larger bills so that it's readily accessible and so that you're less of a target for theft.

ATMS

ATMs (automated teller machines) are quite common throughout Costa Rica,

The Colón, the U.S. Dollar & the Euro

Colones	U.S. $	E.U. €
10	.02	.02
25	.06	.05
100	.23	.19
500	1.16	.95
5,000	11.63	9.53
10,000	23.25	19.06
25,000	58.15	47.64
50,000	116.28	95.28
100,000	232.50	190.57
500,000	1,163.00	952.86

particularly in San José, and at most major tourist destinations around the country. You'll find them at almost all banks and most shopping centers. Still, make sure you have some cash at the start of your trip, never let yourself run totally out of spending money, and definitely stock up on funds before heading to any of the more remote destinations in the country. Outside San José and any of the more developed beach destinations, it's still best to think of your ATM card as a backup measure because machines are not nearly as readily available or dependable as you might be accustomed to, and you might encounter compatibility problems.

ATMs are linked to a network that most likely includes your bank at home. **Cirrus** (© **800/424-7787**; www.mastercard.com) and **PLUS** (© **800/843-7587**; www.visa.com) are the two most popular networks in the U.S.; call or check online for ATM locations at your destination. Be sure you know your four-digit personal identification number (PIN) before you leave home, and be sure to find out your daily withdrawal limit before you depart. You can also get cash advances on your credit card at an ATM. Keep in mind that credit card companies try to protect themselves from theft by limiting the funds someone can withdraw away from home. Therefore, it's best to call your credit card company before you leave, to provide information on where you're going and how much you plan to spend.

You'll get the best exchange rate if you withdraw money from an ATM, but keep in mind that many banks impose a fee every time a card is used at an ATM in a different city or bank. On top of this, the bank from which you withdraw cash might charge its own fee. Instead of taking out small denominations again and again, and worrying about whether you'll be able to find an ATM in the next small town, it makes sense to take out larger amounts more infrequently.

CREDIT CARDS

Credit cards are invaluable when traveling, and they are widely accepted in Costa Rica (MasterCard and Visa have the greatest coverage, although American Express has relatively wide acceptance and Diners Club is making headway). They are a safe way to carry money and provide a convenient record of all your expenses. You can also withdraw cash advances from your credit cards at most banks (although you'll start paying hefty interest on the advance the moment you receive the cash). At most banks, you don't even need to go to a teller; you can get a cash advance at the ATM if you know your PIN. If you've forgotten yours, or didn't even know you had one, call the number on the back of your credit card and ask the bank to send it to you (allow a week or so for it to arrive by mail). Keep in mind, though, that your credit card company will likely charge a commission (1%–2%) on every foreign purchase you make.

Because credit card purchases are dependent upon phone verifications, some hotels and restaurants in more remote destinations do not accept them. Moreover, many add on a 5% to 10% surcharge for credit card payments. Always check in advance if you're heading to a more remote corner of Costa Rica.

To report a lost or stolen **American Express** card from inside Costa Rica, you can call © **0800/012-3211**; for **MasterCard**, © **0800/011-0184**; for **Visa**, © **0800/011-0130**; and for **Diners Club**, call © **295-9393**. When you contact your bank or issuing company, it might be able to wire you a cash advance off your credit card immediately; in many places, it can deliver an emergency credit card in 1 or 2 days. Odds are that if your

---

Tips **Telephone Access Charges**

I supply local toll-free access numbers to the major international phone carriers on the inside front cover of this guide, but make sure that you know what the charges are for your particular international long-distance provider. Be careful about using these numbers if you're not on a specific plan. If you don't have an international calling plan, charge calls to your credit card only as a very last resort because these calls are usually exorbitantly expensive. If you are making a direct-dial international call from your hotel, always find out what the charges are in advance. A good option is to buy a local international calling card, which will be billed at approximately 50¢ per minute for calls to the U.S. or 70¢ per minute for calls to the rest of the world.

---

wallet is gone, the police won't be able to recover it for you. But your credit card company or insurer might require a police report number, so file a police report anyway (after you cancel your credit cards).

Credomatic (✆ **295-9898**) is the local representative of most major credit cards: American Express, Diners Club, MasterCard, and Visa. It has an office in San José across from the Banco de San José on Calle Central between avenidas 3 and 5. It's open Monday through Friday from 8am to 7pm, and Saturday from 9am to 1pm. You can also call the number above to report all lost or stolen cards 24 hours a day.

TRAVELER'S CHECKS

Traveler's checks are something of an anachronism from the days before the ATM made cash accessible at any time. Traveler's checks used to be the only sound alternative to traveling with dangerously large amounts of cash. They were as reliable as currency but, unlike cash, could be replaced if lost or stolen.

These days, traveler's checks seem less necessary because most cities have 24-hour ATMs that allow you to

withdraw cash as needed. However, you're likely to be charged an ATM withdrawal fee if the bank is not your own, so if you're withdrawing money every day, you might be better off with traveler's checks—provided that you don't mind showing identification every time you want to cash one.

You can get traveler's checks at almost any bank. **American Express** offers denominations of $20, $50, $100, $500, and (for cardholders only) $1,000. You'll pay a service charge ranging from 1% to 4%. You can also get American Express traveler's checks over the phone by calling ✆ **800/221-7282;** Amex gold and platinum cardholders who use this number are exempt from the 1% fee.

Visa offers traveler's checks at Citibank locations nationwide, as well as at several other banks. The service charge ranges between 1.5% and 2%; checks come in denominations of $20, $50, $100, $500, and $1,000. Call ✆ **800/732-1322** for information. AAA members can obtain checks without a fee at most AAA offices. **MasterCard** also offers traveler's checks. Call ✆ **800/223-9920** for a location near you.

5 When to Go

Costa Rica's high season for tourism runs from late November to late April, which coincides almost perfectly with the chill of winter in the United States,

Canada, and Great Britain. The high season is also the dry season. If you want some unadulterated time on a tropical beach and a little less rain during your rainforest experience, this is the time to come. During this period (and especially around the Christmas holidays), the tourism industry operates at full tilt—prices are higher, attractions are more crowded, and reservations need to be made in advance.

In recent years, local tourism operators have begun calling the tropical rainy season (May through mid-Nov) the "green season." The adjective is appropriate. At this time of year, even brown and barren Guanacaste province becomes lush and verdant. I personally love traveling around Costa Rica during the rainy season (but then again, I'm not trying to flee winter in Chicago). It's easy to find or at least negotiate reduced rates, there are far fewer fellow travelers, and the rain is often limited to a few hours each afternoon (although you can occasionally get socked in for a week at a time). A drawback: Some of the country's rugged roads become downright impassable without four-wheel-drive during the rainy season.

CLIMATE

Costa Rica is a tropical country and has distinct wet and dry seasons. However, some regions are rainy all year, and others are very dry and sunny for most of the year. Temperatures vary primarily with elevation, not with season: On the coasts, it's hot all year, while up in the mountains, it can be cool at night any time of year. At the highest elevations (3,000–3,600m/ 9,840–11,808 ft.), frost is common.

Average Daytime Temperatures & Rainfall in San José

	Jan	Feb	Mar	Apr	May	June	July	Aug	Sept	Oct	Nov	Dec
Temp. (°F)	73	75	77	78	78	78	77	77	76	77	75	73
Temp. (°C)	22.8	23.9	25	25.5	25.5	25.5	25	25	24.4	25	23.9	22.8
Days of rain	1	0	1	4	17	20	18	19	20	22	14	4

Generally, the **rainy season** (or "green season") is from May to mid-November. Costa Ricans call this wet time of year their winter. The **dry season,** considered summer by Costa Ricans, is from mid-November to April. In Guanacaste, the dry northwestern province, the dry season lasts several weeks longer than in other places. Even in the rainy season, days often start sunny, with rain falling in the afternoon and evening. On the Caribbean coast, especially south of Limón, you can count on rain year-round, although this area gets less rain in September and October than the rest of the country.

In general, the best time of year to visit weatherwise is in December and January, when everything is still green from the rains, but the sky is clear.

HOLIDAYS

Because Costa Rica is a Roman Catholic country, most of its holidays are church related. The biggies are Christmas, New Year's, and Easter, which are all celebrated for several days. Keep in mind that Holy Week (Easter week) is the biggest holiday time in Costa Rica, and many families head for the beach. (This is the last holiday before school starts.) Also, there is no public transportation on Holy Thursday or Good Friday. Government offices and banks are closed on official holidays, transportation services are reduced, and stores and markets might also close.

Official holidays in Costa Rica include **January 1** (New Year's Day), **March 19** (St. Joseph's Day), Thursday and Friday of Holy Week, **April 11**

(Juan Santamaría's Day), **May 1** (Labor Day), **June 29** (St. Peter and St. Paul Day), **July 25** (annexation of the province of Guanacaste), **August 2** (Virgin of Los Angeles's Day), **August 15** (Mother's Day), **September 15** (Independence Day), **October 12** (Discovery of America/Día de la Raza), **December 8** (Immaculate Conception of the Virgin Mary), **December 24** and **25** (Christmas), and **December 31** (New Year's Eve).

COSTA RICA CALENDAR OF EVENTS

Some of the events listed here might be considered more of a *happening* than an event—there's not, for instance, a Virgin of Los Angeles PR Committee that readily dispenses information. If I haven't listed a contact number, your best bet is to call the **Costa Rican Tourist Board (ICT)** at ✆ **800/ 343-6332** in the U.S., or 223-1733 in Costa Rica, or visit www.visitcostarica.com.

January

Copa del Café (Coffee Cup), San José. Matches for this international event on the junior tennis tour are held at the Costa Rica Country Club (✆ **228-9333**). First week in January.

Fiestas of Palmares, Palmares. Perhaps the largest and best organized of the traditional *fiestas,* it includes bullfights, a horseback parade *(tope),* and a wide range of concerts, carnival rides, and food booths. First 2 weeks in January.

Fiestas of Santa Cruz, Santa Cruz, Guanacaste. This religious celebration honors the Black Christ of Esquipulas (a famous Guatemalan statue), featuring folk dancing, marimba music, and bullfights. Mid-January.

February

Fiesta of the Diablitos, Rey Curré village near San Isidro de El General. Boruca Indians wearing wooden devil and bull masks perform dances representative of the Spanish conquest of Central America; there are fireworks displays and an Indian handicrafts market. Late February.

March

Día del Boyero (Oxcart Drivers' Day), San Antonio de Escazú. Colorfully painted oxcarts parade through this suburb of San José, and local priests bless the oxen. Second Sunday in March.

National Orchid Show, San José. Orchid growers throughout the world gather to show their wares, trade tales and secrets, and admire the hundreds of species on display. Contact the Costa Rican Tourist Board for location and dates in 2005. Mid-March.

April

Holy Week (week before Easter). Religious processions are held in cities and towns throughout the country. March 20 to 27.

Juan Santamaría Day, Alajuela. Costa Rica's national hero is honored with parades, concerts, and dances. April 11.

May

Carrera de San Juan. The country's biggest marathon runs through the mountains, from the outskirts of Cartago to the outskirts of San José. May 17.

July

Fiesta of the Virgin of the Sea, Puntarenas. A regatta of colorfully decorated boats carrying a statue of Puntarenas's patron saint marks this festival. A similar event is held at Playa de Coco. Saturday closest to July 16.

Annexation of Guanacaste Day, Liberia. Tico-style bullfights, folk dancing, horseback parades, rodeos, concerts, and other events celebrate the day when this region became part of Costa Rica. July 25.

August

Fiesta of the Virgin of Los Angeles, Cartago. This is the annual pilgrimage day of the patron saint of Costa Rica. Many people walk from San José 24km (15 miles) to the basilica in Cartago. August 2.

Día de San Ramón, San Ramón. More than two dozen statues of saints from various towns are brought to San Ramón, where they are paraded through the streets. August 31.

September

Costa Rica's Independence Day, celebrated all over the country. Most distinctive are the nighttime parades of children. September 15.

International Beach Clean-Up Day. This is a good excuse to chip in and help clean up the beleaguered shoreline of your favorite beach. Third Saturday in September.

October

Fiesta del Maíz, Upala. At this celebration of corn, local beauty queens wear outfits made from corn plants. October 12.

Limón Carnival/Día de la Raza, Limón. A smaller version of Mardi Gras, complete with floats and dancing in the streets, commemorates Columbus's discovery of Costa Rica. Week of October 12.

November

All Soul's Day/Día de los Muertos, celebrated countrywide. Although it is not as elaborate or ritualized as in Mexico, most Costa Ricans take some time this day to remember the dead with flowers and trips to the cemeteries. November 2.

December

Día de la Pólvora, San Antonio de Belén and Jesús María de San Mateo. Fireworks displays honor Our Lady of the Immaculate Conception. December 8.

Fiesta de los Negritos, Boruca. Boruca Indians celebrate the feast day of their patron saint, the Virgin of the Immaculate Conception, with costumed dances and traditional music. December 8.

Fiesta de la Yeguita, Nicoya. A statue of the Virgin of Guadalupe is paraded through the streets, accompanied by traditional music and dancing. December 12.

Las Posadas. In this countrywide celebration, children and carolers go door to door seeking lodging in a reenactment of Joseph and Mary's search for a place to stay. Begins December 15.

El Tope and Carnival, San José. The streets of downtown belong to horses and their riders in a proud recognition of the country's important agricultural heritage. The next day, those same streets are taken over by carnival floats, marching bands, and street dancers. December 26 and 27.

Festejos Populares, San José. Bullfights and a pretty respectable bunch of carnival rides, games of chance, and fast-food stands are set up at the fairgrounds in Zapote. Last week of December.

6 Health & Insurance

STAYING HEALTHY

Staying healthy on a trip to Costa Rica is predominantly a matter of being a little cautious about what you eat and drink, and using common sense. Know your physical limits, and don't overexert yourself in the ocean, on hikes, or in athletic activities. Respect the tropical sun and protect yourself from it. Limit your exposure to the sun, especially during the first few days of your trip and, thereafter, from 11am to 2pm. Use a sunscreen with a high protection factor, and apply it liberally. Remember that children need more protection than adults do. I recommend buying and drinking bottled water or soft drinks, but the water in San José and in most of the heavily visited spots is safe to drink. The sections below deal with specific health concerns in Costa Rica.

The **U.S. Centers for Disease Control and Prevention** (© 800/ 311-3435; www.cdc.gov) provides up-to-date information on necessary vaccines and health hazards by region or country.

BEFORE YOU GO

In most cases, your existing health plan will provide the coverage you need. But double-check; you might want to buy **travel medical insurance** instead. (See the section on insurance, below.) Bring your insurance ID card with you when you travel.

If you suffer from a chronic illness, consult your doctor before your departure. For conditions such as epilepsy, diabetes, or heart problems, wear a **Medic Alert identification tag** (© 800/825-3785; www.medicalert. org), which will immediately alert doctors to your condition and give them access to your records through Medic Alert's 24-hour hot line.

Pack **prescription medications** in your carry-on luggage, and carry prescription medications in their original containers. Also bring along copies of your prescriptions, in case you lose your pills or run out, and carry the generic name of prescription medicines, in case a local pharmacist is unfamiliar with the brand name. And don't forget an extra pair of contact lenses or prescription glasses.

GENERAL AVAILABILITY OF HEALTH CARE

When you're in Costa Rica, any local consulate can provide a list of area doctors who speak English. The local English-language newspaper, the *Tico Times,* is another good resource. I've listed the best hospitals in San José in "Fast Facts: San José," in chapter 4; they have the most modern facilities in the country. Most state-run hospitals and walk-in clinics around the country have emergency rooms that can treat most conditions, although I highly recommend the private hospitals in San José if your condition is not life threatening and can wait for treatment until you reach one of them.

COMMON AILMENTS

TROPICAL DISEASES Your chance of contracting any serious tropical disease in Costa Rica is slim, especially if you stick to the beaches or traditional spots for visitors. However, malaria, dengue fever, and leptospirosis all exist in Costa Rica, so it's a good idea to know what they are.

Malaria is found in the lowlands on both coasts and in the northern zone. Although it's rarely found in urban areas, it's still a problem in remote wooded regions and along the Caribbean coast. Malaria prophylaxes are available, but several have side effects, and others are of questionable effectiveness. Consult your doctor regarding what is currently considered the best preventive treatment for malaria. Be sure to ask whether a recommended drug will cause you to be hypersensitive to the sun; it would be a shame to come down here for the beaches and then have to hide under an umbrella the whole time. Because malaria-carrying mosquitoes usually come out at night, you should do as much as possible to avoid being bitten after dark. If you are in a malarial area, wear long pants and long sleeves, use insect repellent, and either sleep under a mosquito net or burn mosquito coils (similar to incense, but with a pesticide).

Of greater concern is **dengue fever,** which has had periodic outbreaks in Latin America since the mid-1990s. Dengue fever is similar to malaria and is spread by an aggressive daytime mosquito. This mosquito seems to be most common in lowland urban areas, and Puntarenas, Liberia, and Limón have been the worst-hit cities in Costa Rica. Dengue is also known as "bone-break fever" because it is usually accompanied by severe body aches. The first infection with dengue fever will make you very sick but should cause no serious damage. However, a second infection with a different strain of the dengue virus can lead to internal hemorrhaging and could be life threatening.

Many people are convinced that taking B-complex vitamins daily will help prevent mosquitoes from biting you. I don't think the American Medical Association has endorsed this idea yet, but I've run across it in enough places to think that there might be something to it.

One final tropical fever that I think you should know about (because I got it myself) is **leptospirosis.** There are more than 200 strains of leptospirs, which are animal-borne bacteria transmitted to humans via contact with drinking, swimming, or bathing water. This bacterial infection is easily treated with antibiotics; however, it can quickly cause very high fever and chills, and should be treated promptly.

If you develop a high fever accompanied by severe body aches, nausea, diarrhea, or vomiting during or shortly after a visit to Costa Rica, consult a physician as soon as possible.

Costa Rica has been relatively free of the cholera epidemic that has spread through much of Latin America in recent years. This is largely due to an extensive public-awareness campaign that has promoted good hygiene and increased sanitation. Your chances of contracting cholera while you're here are very slight.

AMOEBAS, PARASITES, DIARRHEA & OTHER INTESTINAL WOES Even though the water in San José and most popular destinations

is generally safe, and even though you've been careful to buy bottled water, order *frescos en leche* (fruit shakes made with milk rather than water), and drink your soft drink warm (without ice cubes—which are made from water, after all), you still might encounter some intestinal difficulties. Most of this is just due to tender northern stomachs coming into contact with slightly more aggressive Latin American intestinal flora. In extreme cases of diarrhea or intestinal discomfort, it's worth taking a stool sample to a lab for analysis. The results will usually pinpoint the amoebic or parasitic culprit, which can then be readily treated with available over-the-counter medicines.

Except in the most established and hygienic of restaurants, it's also advisable to avoid ceviche, a raw seafood salad, especially if it has any shellfish in it. It could be home to any number of bacterial critters.

TROPICAL SUN   Limit your exposure to the sun, especially during the first few days of your trip and, thereafter, from 11am to 2pm. Use a sunscreen with a high protection factor, and apply it liberally. Remember that children need more protection than adults do.

RIPTIDES   Many of Costa Rica's beaches have riptides, strong currents that can drag swimmers out to sea. A riptide occurs when water that has been dumped on the shore by strong waves forms a channel back out to open water. These channels have strong currents. If you get caught in a riptide, you can't escape the current by swimming toward shore; it's like trying to swim upstream in a river. To break free of the current, swim parallel to shore and use the energy of the waves to help you get back to the beach.

BEES, SNAKES & BUGS Although Costa Rica has Africanized bees (the notorious "killer bees" of fact and fable) and several species of venomous snakes, your chances of being bitten are minimal, especially if you refrain from sticking your hands into hives or under rocks in the forest. If you know that you're allergic to bee stings, consult your doctor before traveling.

Snake sightings, much less snakebites, are very rare. Moreover, the majority of snakes in Costa Rica are nonpoisonous. If you do encounter a snake, stay calm, don't make any sudden movements, and do not try to handle it. As recommended above, avoid sticking your hand under rocks, branches, and fallen trees.

Scorpions, black widow spiders, tarantulas, bullet ants, and other biting insects can all be found in Costa Rica. In general, they are not nearly the danger or nuisance most visitors fear. Watch where you stick your hands; in addition, you might want to shake out your clothes and shoes before putting them on, to avoid any unpleasant and painful surprises.

INSURANCE

Check your existing insurance policies and credit card coverage before you buy travel insurance. You might already be covered for lost luggage, canceled tickets, or medical expenses. The cost of travel insurance varies widely, depending on the cost and length of your trip, your age, your health, and the type of trip you're taking.

TRIP-CANCELLATION INSUR-ANCE Trip-cancellation insurance helps you get your money back if you have to back out of a trip, if you have to go home early, or if your travel supplier goes bankrupt. Allowed reasons for cancellation can range from sickness to natural disasters, to the State Department declaring your destination unsafe for travel. (Insurers usually won't cover vague fears, though, as many travelers discovered who tried to cancel their trips in Oct 2001 because

they were wary of flying.) In this unstable world, trip-cancellation insurance is a good buy if you're getting tickets well in advance—who knows what the state of the world, or of your airline, will be in 9 months? Insurance policy details vary, so read the fine print—and especially make sure that your airline or cruise line is on the list of carriers covered in case of bankruptcy. Protect yourself further by paying for the insurance with a credit card—by law, consumers can get their money back on goods and services not received if they report the loss within 60 days after the charge is listed on their credit card statement.

For information, contact one of the following recommended insurers: **Access America** (✆ 866/807-3982; www.accessamerica.com), **Travel Guard International** (✆ 800/826-4919; www.travelguard.com), **Travel Insured International** (✆ 800/243-3174; www.travelinsured.com), and **Travelex Insurance Services** (✆ 888/457-4602; www.travelex-insurance.com).

MEDICAL INSURANCE Most health insurance policies cover you if you get sick away from home—but check, particularly if you're insured by an HMO. For travel overseas, most health plans (including Medicare and Medicaid) do not provide coverage, and the ones that do often require you to pay for services up front and reimburse you only after you return home. Even if your plan does cover overseas treatment, most out-of-country hospitals make you pay your bills up front, and send you a refund only after you've returned home and filed the necessary paperwork with your insurance company. As a safety net, you might want to buy travel medical insurance, particularly if you're traveling to an area where emergency evacuation is a possible scenario. If you require additional medical insurance, try **MEDEX**

Assistance (© 410/453-6300; www. medexassist.com) or **Travel Assistance International** (© 800/821-2828; www.travelassistance.com; for general information on services, call the company's Worldwide Assistance Services, Inc., at © 800/777-8710).

7 Specialized Travel Resources

FOR TRAVELERS WITH DISABILITIES

Although Costa Rica does have a law mandating Equality of Opportunities for People with Disabilities, and facilities are beginning to be adapted, in general, there are relatively few handicapped-accessible buildings. In San José, sidewalks are crowded and uneven. Few hotels offer wheelchair-accessible accommodations, and there are no public buses thus equipped. In short, it's difficult for a person with disabilities to get around in Costa Rica.

However, one local agency specializes in tours for travelers with disabilities and restricted ability. **Vaya Con Silla de Ruedas** (©/fax **454-2810** or 391-5045; www.gowithwheel chairs.com) has a ramp- and elevator-equipped van and knowledgeable bilingual guides. It charges very reasonable prices and can provide anything from simple airport transfers to complete multiday tours. Many travel agencies offer customized tours and itineraries for travelers with disabilities.

The **Costa Rica Deaf Travel Corporation** (© 289-4812; www.cdtcsa. com) is a local travel agency specializing in making group and individual travel arrangements for deaf tourists.

MossRehab (www.mossresourcenet. org) is a great source for information, tips, and resources relating to accessible travel. You'll find links to a number of travel agents who specialize in planning trips for disabled travelers here and through **Access-Able Travel Source** (© 303/232-2979; www. access-able.com), another excellent online source.

You might also want to join a tour catering to travelers with disabilities.

One of the best operators offering tours in Costa Rica is **Flying Wheels Travel** (© 507/451-5005; www. flyingwheelstravel.com).

FOR GAY & LESBIAN TRAVELERS

Costa Rica is a Catholic, conservative, macho country where public displays of same-sex affection are rare and considered somewhat shocking. In 1998, the archbishop of San José publicly denounced homosexuality. There followed two prominent protests in the tourist destinations of Manuel Antonio National Park and Playa Hermosa, Guanacaste, that resulted in some inconvenience for the organizers and participants of openly gay and lesbian group tours. However, gay and lesbian tourism to Costa Rica is quite robust, and gay and lesbian travelers are generally treated with respect and should not experience any harassment.

For a general overview of the current situation, news of any special events or meetings, and up-to-date information, gay and lesbian travelers should check in with the folks at **Uno@Diez,** on Calle 3 between avenidas 5 and 7 in downtown San José (© **258-4561;** www.1en10.com), a coffeehouse, gallery, and Internet cafe.

If you're doing your research online, check out **www.hometown.aol.com/ GayCRica** and **www.gaycostarica. com**. A local tour agency specializing in gay & lesbian travel is **Tiquicia Travel** (www.tiquiciatravel.com). Two other agencies are **Gay Adventure Tours, Inc.** (© 888/206-6523; www. gayadventuretours.com), and **Above and Beyond Tours** (© 800/397-2681; www.abovebeyondtours.com), which offers gay and lesbian tours worldwide and is the exclusive gay and lesbian tour operator for United Airlines.

The **International Gay and Lesbian Travel Association** (© 800/448-8550 or 954/776-2626; www.iglta.org) is the trade association for the gay and lesbian travel industry, and offers an online directory of gay- and lesbian-friendly travel businesses.

FOR SENIORS

Be sure to mention the fact that you're a senior when you first make your travel reservations because many airlines and hotels offer senior discounts. Although it's not common policy in Costa Rica to offer senior discounts, don't be shy about asking for one anyway. You never know. Always carry some kind of identification, such as a driver's license, that shows your date of birth, especially if you've kept your youthful glow.

Members of **AARP** (© 888/687-2277; www.aarp.org) get discounts on hotels (including chains that are represented in Costa Rica), airfares, and car rentals.

If you want something more than the average vacation or guided tour, try **Elderhostel** (© 877/426-8056; www.elderhostel.org), which offers educational travel for seniors. On these escorted tours, the days are packed with seminars, lectures, and field trips, and academic experts lead all the sightseeing. The courses are ungraded, involve no homework, and often focus on the liberal arts. They're not luxury vacations, but they are fun and fulfilling. Elderhostel runs regular educational trips to Costa Rica for travelers age 55 and over (and a spouse or companion of any age). Most tours last about 3 weeks, and many include airfare, accommodations in student dormitories or modest inns, meals, and tuition.

Due to its temperate climate, stable government, low cost of living, and friendly *pensionado* program, Costa Rica is popular with retirees from North America. There are excellent medical facilities in San José and plenty of community organizations to help retirees feel at home. If you would like to learn more about applying for residency and retiring in Costa Rica, contact the **Association of Residents of Costa Rica** in San José (© 221-2053; www.casacanada.net).

FOR FAMILIES

If you have enough trouble getting your kids out of the house in the morning, dragging them thousands of miles away might seem like an insurmountable challenge. But family travel can be immensely rewarding, giving you new ways of seeing the world through smaller pairs of eyes.

Hotels in Costa Rica often give discounts for children under 12, and children under 3 or 4 are usually allowed to stay for free. Discounts for children and the cutoff ages vary according to hotel, but in general, don't assume that your kids can stay in your room for free.

Tips A Note for Female Travelers

For lack of better phrasing, Costa Rica is a typically "macho" Latin American nation. Single women can expect a nearly constant stream of catcalls, hisses, whistles, and car horns, especially in San José. The best advice is to ignore the unwanted attention rather than try to come up with a witty or antagonistic rejoinder. Women should also be careful walking alone at night, both in San José and in other more remote destinations. I definitely don't recommend hitchhiking.

Getting Married in Costa Rica

It's simple and straightforward to get married in Costa Rica. In most cases, all that is required is a current passport. You will have to provide some basic information, including a copy of each passport, your dates of birth, your occupations, your current address, and the names and addresses of your parents. You will also need a copy of your witnesses' passports. Two witnesses are required to be present at the ceremony. If you are traveling alone, your hotel, wedding consultant, or lawyer will provide the required witnesses.

Things are slightly more complicated if one or more of the partners was previously married. In such a case, the previously married partner must provide an official copy of the divorce decree. However, a couple of more draconian requirements exist specifically for recently divorced women. A bride-to-be cannot be remarried in Costa Rica within 300 days of her divorce, and if she was divorced less than 1 year before the current wedding date, she must present a negative pregnancy test.

Most foreigners who come to Costa Rica to get married do so in a civil ceremony officiated by a local lawyer. After the ceremony, the lawyer records the marriage with Costa Rica's National Registry, which issues an official marriage certificate. This process generally takes between 4 and 6 weeks. Most lawyers or wedding coordinators then have the document translated and certified by the Costa Rican Foreign Ministry and at the embassy or consulate of your home country within Costa Rica before mailing it to you. From here, it's a matter of bringing this document to your local civil or religious authorities, if necessary.

Tip: Officially, the lawyer must read all or parts of the Costa Rican civil code on marriage during your ceremony. This is a rather uninspired and

Many hotels, villas, and cabinas come equipped with kitchenettes or full kitchen facilities. These can be a real money-saver for those traveling with children, and I've listed many of these accommodations in the destination chapters that follow.

Hotels offering regular, dependable babysitting service are few and far between. If you will need babysitting, make sure that your hotel offers it, and be sure to ask whether the babysitters are bilingual. In many cases, they are not. This is usually not a problem with infants and toddlers, but it can cause problems with older children.

Recommended family travel websites include **Family Travel Forum** (www.familytravelforum.com), a comprehensive site that offers customized trip planning; **Family Travel Network** (www.familytravelnetwork.com), an award-winning site that offers travel features, deals, and tips; **Traveling Internationally with Your Kids** (www.travelwithyourkids.com), a site offering sound advice for long-distance and international travel with children; and **Family Travel Files** (www.thefamilytravelfiles.com), which offers an online magazine and a directory of off-the-beaten-path tours and tour operators for families.

FOR STUDENTS

Arm yourself with an **international student ID card,** which can offer somewhat dated legal code that, at some weddings, can take as much as 20 minutes to slog through. Most lawyers and wedding coordinators are quite flexible and can work with you to design a ceremony and text that fits your needs and desires. Insist on this.

Most isolated and romantic hotels in Costa Rica have ample experience in hosting weddings, including virtually all of the hotels listed in chapter 1. It's tough to narrow the list, but I'd say your top four choices for a romantic Costa Rican wedding (or honeymoon) are **Hotel Punta Islita** (p. 192), **Villa Caletas** (p. 259), **Makanda-by-the-Sea** (p. 272), and **Flor Blanca Resort** (p. 203). Honorable mentions must be made of La Paloma Lodge (p. 297), Bosque del Cabo Rainforest Lodge (p. 305), Lapa Ríos (p. 305), Finca Rosa Blanca Country Inn (p. 105), the Four Seasons Resort (p. 156), and the Punta Coral private reserve owned by Calypso Tours (✆ **256-8787;** www.calypsotours.com).

Because Costa Rica is more than 90% Roman Catholic, it is usually easy to arrange for a church wedding in all but the most isolated and remote locations. To a lesser extent, a variety of denominational Christian churches and priests are often available to perform or host the ceremony. If you're Jewish, Muslim, Buddhist, Sufi, or Wiccan, it would be best to bring your own officiant.

If you're looking for personalized service beyond what your hotel can offer, or if you want to do it yourself, check out **www.weddingsin costarica.com**, **www.tropicaloccasions.com**, or **www.marcelogalli.com**.

substantial savings on plane tickets, lodging, and entrance fees. It also provides you with basic health and life insurance and a 24-hour help line. The card is available for $22 from **STA Travel** (✆ **800/781-4040;** www. statravel.com), the biggest student travel agency in the world. If you're no longer a student but are still under 26, you can get an **International Youth Travel Card,** which entitles you to some discounts. (*Note:* In 2002, STA Travel bought competitors **Council Travel** and **USIT Campus** after they went bankrupt. It's still operating some offices under the Council name, but it's owned by STA.) **Travel CUTS** (✆ **800/667-2887** or 416/614-2887; www.travelcuts.com) offers similar

services for both Canadians and U.S. residents. Irish students should turn to **USIT** (✆ **01/602-1600;** www. usitnow.ie).

Costa Rica has a network of hostels and budget hotels around the country affiliated with the International Youth Hostel Federation. Check out **Hostelling International Costa Rica** (www.hicr.org), or ask at the **Toruma Youth Hostel,** Avenida Central between calles 29 and 31, San José (✆ **234-8186,** or ✆/fax 224-4085; www.toruma.com). Member hotels give discounts to youth and affiliated travelers, with participating hotels in sites that include Monteverde, La Fortuna, San Isidro, Jacó Beach, Liberia, Tamarindo, Puerto Viejo, Golfito,

Puerto Jiménez, and Rincón de la Vieja National Park.

In San José, there is one travel agency specializing in student and youth travel: **OTEC** (© **256-0633;** www.otec.co.cr; Edificio Ferencz, 2nd floor, Calle 3 between avs. 1 and 3, 275m/10,742 ft. north of the National Theater). If you don't already have an International Student Identity Card, stop by the OTEC office with proof of student status, two passport photos, and a passport or other identification that shows you are under 35 years old; for about $12, you can get an ID card.

8 Planning Your Trip Online

SURFING FOR AIRFARES

The "big three" online travel agencies, **Expedia.com, Travelocity.com,** and **Orbitz.com,** sell most of the air tickets bought on the Internet. (Canadian travelers should try Expedia.ca and Travelocity.ca; U.K. residents can go to Expedia.co.uk and Opodo.co.uk.) Each has different business deals with the airlines and might offer different fares on the same flights, so it's wise to shop around. Expedia and Travelocity will also send you **e-mail notification** when a cheap fare becomes available to your favorite destination. Of the smaller travel agency websites, **Side-Step** (www.sidestep.com) has gotten the best reviews from Frommer's authors. It's a browser add-on that purports to "search 140 sites at once," but in reality it beats competitors' fares only as often as other sites do.

Also remember to check **airline websites.** Even with major airlines, you can often shave a few bucks from a fare by booking directly through the airline and avoiding a travel agency's transaction fee. But you'll get these discounts only by booking online: Most airlines now offer online-only fares that even their phone agents know nothing about. For the websites of airlines that fly to and from your destination, go to "Getting There," below.

Great **last-minute deals** are available through free weekly e-mail services provided directly by the airlines. Most of these are announced on Tuesday or Wednesday and must be purchased online. Most are valid for travel only that weekend, but some can be booked weeks or months in advance. Sign up for weekly e-mail alerts at airline websites, or check megasites that compile comprehensive lists of last-minute specials, such as **Smarter Living** (www.smarterliving.com). For last-minute trips, **site59.com** and **lastminutetravel.com** in the U.S. and **lastminute.com** in Europe often have better air-and-hotel package deals than the major-label sites. A website listing numerous bargain sites and airlines around the world is **www.itravel net.com**.

If you're willing to give up some control over your flight details, use an **opaque fare service** such as **Priceline** (www.priceline.com or www.priceline. co.uk) or **Hotwire** (www.hotwire. com). Both offer rock-bottom prices in exchange for travel on a "mystery airline" at a mysterious time of day, often with a mysterious change of planes en route. The mystery airlines are all major, well-known carriers, and the airlines' routing computers have gotten a lot better than they used to be. But your chances of getting a 6am or 11pm flight are pretty high. Hotwire tells you flight prices before you buy; Priceline usually has better deals than Hotwire, but you have to play their "name our price" game. If you're new at this, the helpful folks at **BiddingForTravel** (www.bidding fortravel.com) do a good job of demystifying Priceline's prices. Priceline and Hotwire are great for flights within North America and between the United States and Europe. But for

Frommers.com: The Complete Travel Resource

For an excellent travel-planning resource, we highly recommend **Frommers.com** (www.frommers.com), voted Best Travel Site by *PC Magazine*. We're a little biased, of course, but we guarantee that you'll find the travel tips, reviews, monthly vacation giveaways, bookstore, and online-booking capabilities thoroughly indispensable. Among the special features are our popular **Destinations** section, where you'll get expert travel tips, hotel and dining recommendations, and advice on the sights to see for more than 3,500 destinations around the globe; the **Frommers.com Newsletter,** with the latest deals, travel trends, and money-saving secrets; our **Community** area featuring **Message Boards,** where Frommer's readers post queries and share advice (sometimes even our authors show up to answer questions); and our **Photo Center,** where you can post and share vacation tips. When your research is done, the **Online Reservations System** (www.frommers.com/book_a_trip) takes you to Frommer's preferred online partners for booking your vacation at affordable prices.

flights to other parts of the world, consolidators will almost always beat their fares.

SURFING FOR HOTELS

Shopping online for hotel deals is much easier in the United States, Canada, and certain parts of Europe than it is in Costa Rica. Also, many smaller hotels and B&Bs don't show up on the big websites at all. Of the "big three" sites, **Expedia** might be the best choice, thanks to its long list of special deals. **Travelocity** runs a close second. Hotel specialist sites **Hotels.com** and **Quikbook.com** are also reliable. An excellent free program, **TravelAxe** (www.travelaxe.net), can help you search multiple hotel sites at once, even ones you might never have heard of.

Your best bet in Costa Rica might be negotiating directly with the hotels themselves, especially the smaller hotels. In this day and age, almost every hotel in Costa Rica has e-mail, if not its own website, and you'll find the contact information right here. However, be aware, that response times might be slower than you'd like, and many of the smaller hotels might have some trouble communicating back and forth in English.

SURFING FOR RENTAL CARS

For booking rental cars online, the best deals are usually found at rental-car company websites, although all the major online travel agencies also offer rental-car reservations services. Priceline and Hotwire work well for rental cars, too; the only "mystery" is which major rental company you get, and for most travelers, the difference among Hertz, Avis, and Budget is negligible.

9 The 21st-Century Traveler

INTERNET ACCESS

WITHOUT YOUR OWN COMPUTER It's hard nowadays to find a city that *doesn't* have a few cybercafes. Although there's no definitive directory for cybercafes, one place to start looking is **www.cybercafe.com**. Most major destinations in Costa Rica have several Internet cafes, and in those destinations that don't, most hotels will let you check your e-mail and surf the Web either for free or for a nominal charge.

To retrieve your e-mail, ask your **Internet service provider (ISP)** if it has a Web-based interface tied to your existing e-mail account. If your ISP doesn't have such an interface, you can use the free **mail2web** service (www. mail2web.com) to view and reply to your home e-mail. For more flexibility, you might want to open a free, Web-based e-mail account with **Yahoo!** (http://mail.yahoo.com) or **Fastmail** (www.fastmail.fm). Your home ISP might be able to forward your e-mail to the Web-based account automatically.

If you need to access files on your office computer, look into a service called **GoToMyPC** (www.gotomypc. com). The service provides a Web-based interface for you to access and manipulate a distant PC from anywhere—even a cybercafe—provided that your "target" PC is on and has an always-on connection to the Internet. The service offers top-quality security, but if you're worried about hackers, use your own laptop rather than a cybercafe to access the GoToMyPC system.

WITH YOUR OWN COMPUTER

Major Internet service providers have **local access numbers** around the world, allowing you to go online by simply placing a local call. Check your ISP's website, or call its toll-free number and ask how you can use your current account away from home, and how much it will cost.

If you're traveling outside the reach of your ISP, the **iPass** network has dial-up numbers in most of the world's countries. You'll have to sign up with an iPass provider, who will then tell you how to set up your computer for your destination. For a list of iPass providers, go to www.ipass.com. One solid provider is **i2roam** (© **866/. 811-6209** or 920/235-0475; www. i2roam.com).

Alternatively, **Racsa,** Avenida 5 and Calle 1 (© **287-0087;** www.racsa.co. cr), the state Internet monopoly, sells prepaid cards in 5-, 10-, and 15-hour denominations for connecting your laptop to the Web via a local phone call. Be sure to factor in the phone call charge if calling from a hotel.

Costa Rica uses standard U.S.-style two- and three- prong electric outlets with 110-volt AC current, and

Online Traveler's Toolbox

Veteran travelers usually carry some essential items to make their trips easier. Following is a selection of online tools to bookmark and use.

- **Foreign Languages for Travelers** (www.travlang.com). Learn basic terms in more than 70 languages, and click on any underlined phrase to hear what it sounds like.
- **Mapquest** (www.mapquest.com). This best of the mapping sites lets you choose a specific address or destination and, in seconds, returns a map and detailed directions.
- **Travel Warnings** (www.travel.state.gov/travel_warnings.html, www. fco.gov.uk/travel, www.voyage.gc.ca, www.dfat.gov.au/consular/ advice). These sites report on places where health concerns or unrest might threaten American, British, Canadian, and Australian travelers. Generally, U.S. warnings are the most paranoid; Australian warnings are the most relaxed.

standard U.S.-style phone jacks. Wherever you go, bring a **connection kit** of the right power and phone adapters, a spare phone cord, and a spare Ethernet network cable.

USING A CELLPHONE

The three letters that define much of the world's wireless capabilities are **GSM** (Global System for Mobiles), a big, seamless network that makes for easy cross-border cellphone use throughout Europe and dozens of other countries worldwide. Costa Rica uses both GSM and TDMA (a separate system and protocol). If your cellphone is on a GSM system and you have a world-capable multiband phone such as many (but not all) Sony Ericsson, Motorola, or Samsung models, you can make and receive calls across much of the globe. Just call your wireless operator and ask for "international roaming" to be activated on your account. Unfortunately, per-minute charges can be high ($1–$5).

Note: So far, GSM world-phone owners cannot use an "unlocked" phone and local chip—no local provider can sell the GSM chip.

Renting a phone in Costa Rica is problematic. Due to a state monopoly on telecommunications, the entire cellphone rental industry exists in an area of legal limbo. Several firms are renting cellphones to visiting tourists and businessmen, but it's probably illegal, and the Costa Rican telecommunications institute could theoretically crack down on them at any time. However, to date, they've been able to go about their business, albeit discreetly. None of the rental companies has a booth or office at the airport, so you'll have to contact them either beforehand or from your hotel. **Cell Service** (© 296-5553; www.cellservice\cr.com) and **Intelicom** (© 283-0102; www.intelicom.co.cr) both rent cellphones. Rates run around $6 per day or $35 per week, with charges of 70¢ per minute for local calls and $2 to $3 per minute for international calls.

10 Getting There

BY PLANE

It takes between 3 and 7 hours to fly to Costa Rica from most U.S. cities, and as Costa Rica becomes more popular with North American travelers, more flights are available into San José's **Juan Santamaría International Airport.** By early 2004, Delta, American, and Continental all had regular nonstop commercial flights to the international airport in Liberia from their hubs in Atlanta, Miami, and Houston, respectively. Liberia is the gateway to the beaches of the Guanacaste region and the Nicoya Peninsula, and a direct flight here eliminates the need for a separate commuter flight in a small aircraft or roughly 5 hours in a car or bus.

THE MAJOR AIRLINES

There is a host of airlines flying into Costa Rica. Be warned that the smaller Latin American carriers tend to make several stops (sometimes unscheduled) en route to San José, thus increasing flying time.

The following airlines currently serve Costa Rica from the United States, using the gateway cities listed. **American Airlines** (© 800/433-7300; www.aa.com) has daily flights from Los Angeles, Miami, New York, and Dallas–Fort Worth. **America West** (© 800/363-2957; www.americawest.com) has one daily direct flight from Phoenix. **Continental** (© 800/525-0280; www.continental.com) offers flights daily from Houston and Newark. **Delta** (© 800/241-4141;

www.delta.com) offers flights from Atlanta. **Mexicana** (© 800/531-7921; www.mexicana.com) offers flights from numerous North American cities, most connecting through the hub in Mexico City. **United Airlines** (© 800/538-2929; www.united.com) has daily flights direct from Washington, D.C., and from Los Angeles, with one stop either in Mexico or Guatemala. **Grupo Taca** (© 800/535-8780; www.grupotaca.com) is a conglomeration of the Central American airlines, with direct flights or connections to and from Boston, Chicago, Los Angeles, San Francisco, Houston, New Orleans, New York, Miami, and Washington.

From Europe, you can take any major carrier to a hub city such as Miami or New York, and then make connections to Costa Rica. Alternately, **Iberia** (www.iberia.com) from Spain, **Lufthansa** (www.lufthansa.com) from Germany, and both **Martin Air** (© 800/627-8462; www.martinairusa.com) and **KLM** (www.klm.com) from Holland have established routes to San José, some direct and others with one connection.

GETTING THROUGH THE AIRPORT

With the federalization of airport security, security procedures at U.S. airports are more stable and consistent than ever. Generally, you'll be fine if you arrive at the airport **1 hour** before a domestic flight and **2 hours** before an international flight; if you show up late, tell an airline employee and she'll probably whisk you to the front of the line.

Bring a **current, government-issued photo ID** such as a driver's license or passport. Keep your ID ready to show at check-in, the security checkpoint, and sometimes even the gate. (Children under 18 do not need government-issued photo IDs for domestic flights, but they do for international flights to most countries.)

The Transportation Security Administration (TSA) has phased out **gate check-in** at all U.S. airports, and **E-tickets** have made paper tickets nearly obsolete. Passengers with E-tickets can beat the ticket-counter lines by using airport **electronic kiosks** or even **online check-in** from your home computer. Online check-in involves logging on to your airlines' website, accessing your reservation, and printing your boarding pass—and the airline might even offer you bonus miles to do so! If you're using a kiosk at the airport, bring the credit card you used to book the ticket or your frequent-flier card. Print your boarding pass from the kiosk, and simply proceed to the security checkpoint with your pass and a photo ID. If you're checking bags or looking to snag an exit-row seat, you will be able to do so using most airline kiosks. Even the smaller airlines are employing the kiosk system, but always call your airline to make sure these alternatives are available. **Curbside check-in** is also a good way to avoid lines, although a few airlines still ban curbside check-in; call before you go.

Security lines can be lengthier in some airports than others. If you have trouble standing for long periods of time, tell an airline employee; the airline will provide a wheelchair. Speed up security by not wearing metal objects such as big belt buckles or clanky earrings. If you've got metallic body parts, a note from your doctor can prevent a long chat with the security screeners. Keep in mind that **only ticketed passengers** are allowed past security, except for folks escorting passengers with disabilities or children.

Federalization has stabilized **what you can carry on** and **what you can't.** The general rule is that sharp things are out, nail clippers are okay, and food and beverages must be passed through the X-ray machine. Bring food in your carry-on rather than checking it; explosive-detection machines used on checked luggage have been known to mistake food (especially chocolate, for some reason) for bombs. Travelers in the United States are allowed one carry-on bag, plus a "personal item" such as a purse, briefcase, or laptop bag. The TSA has issued a list of restricted items; check its website at **www.tsa.gov** for details.

Airport screeners might decide that your checked luggage needs to be searched by hand. You can now purchase luggage locks that allow screeners to open and relock a checked bag if hand searching is necessary; for more details about Travel Sentry certified locks, visit www.travelsentry.org. If you use something other than TSA-approved locks, your lock will be cut off your suitcase if a TSA agent needs to hand-search your luggage.

FLYING FOR LESS: TIPS FOR GETTING THE BEST AIRFARES

Passengers sharing the same airplane cabin rarely pay the same fare. Here are some ways to keep your airfare costs down.

- Passengers who can book their ticket **long in advance,** who can **stay over Saturday night,** or who **fly midweek** or **at less-trafficked hours** often pay a fraction of the full fare. If your schedule is flexible, say so, and ask if you can secure a cheaper fare by changing your flight plans. Also keep an eye out for **promotional specials** and airline **fare wars.**
- Search **the Internet** for cheap fares (see "Planning Your Trip Online," earlier in this chapter).

Tips   What Travel Agents Don't Tell You

You don't have to spend the night in San José. Some travel agents will encourage you to do this so that they can stick you with an unnecessary hotel stay and/or airport transfer fees—twice. But don't listen to them. If your flight arrives in San José early in the day, you should consider heading straight to your first destination. It's easy to catch a domestic flight to many of the more popular beach destinations right from the San José airport. You should definitely book this in advance, and make sure you have enough time to get to the domestic terminal. Moreover, you'll have to carry your bags the 230m (754 ft.) or so between the international and domestic terminals (or take a cab), and you'll also have to use the less reliable carrier Sansa rather than Nature Air for your domestic flight. (Nature Air flights leave from an entirely different airport.) But if this doesn't cause you any grief, you can leave the United States early in the morning and be lounging on the beach before sunset (and, in some cases, by lunchtime).

You can also drive to your first destination if you arrive early enough. However, if the thought of doing a 4-hour drive immediately after your 5-hour flight seems exhausting, my best advice is to head to a hotel such as Vista del Valle Plantation Inn, which is 20 minutes from the airport toward Guanacaste, Monteverde, and Arenal. You'll cut lots of time off your drive the next day. You can either grab your rental car at the airport or have it dropped off at your hotel.

• **Consolidators,** also known as bucket shops, are great sources for international tickets. Start by looking in Sunday newspaper travel sections; U.S. travelers should focus on the *New York Times,* the *Los Angeles Times,* and the *Miami Herald. Beware:* Bucket shop tickets are usually nonrefundable or rigged with stiff cancellation penalties, often as high as 50% to 75% of the ticket price, and some put you on charter airlines, which might leave at inconvenient times and experience delays.

Several reliable consolidators are worldwide and available on the Net. **STA Travel** (*©* 800/ 781-4040; www.statravel.com) is now the world's leader in student travel, thanks to its purchase of Council Travel. It also offers good fares for travelers of all ages. **Flights.com** (*©* 800/TRAV-800; www.eltexpress.com) started in Europe and has excellent fares worldwide. **FlyCheap** (*©* 800/ FLY-CHEAP; www.1800flycheap. com) is owned by package-holiday megalith MyTravel and so has especially good access to fares for sunny destinations. **Air Tickets Direct** (*©* 800/778-3447; www. airticketsdirect.com) is based in Montreal and leverages the currently weak Canadian dollar for low fares.

BY BUS

Bus service runs regularly from Panama City, Panama, and Managua, Nicaragua. If at all possible, it's worth the splurge for a deluxe or express bus. In terms of travel time and convenience, it's always better to get a direct bus rather than one that stops along the way—and you've got a better chance of getting a working restroom in a direct/express or deluxe bus. Some even have television sets showing video movies.

There are several bus lines with regular daily departures connecting the major capital cities of Central America. Call **Panaline** (*©* 255-1205), **Transnica** (*©* 223-4242), **Nicabus** (*©* 223-0293), or **Tica Bus Company** (*©* 221-8954; www.ticabus. com) for further information. All of these lines service Costa Rica directly from Panama City and Managua, with connections to the other principal cities of Central America. None of them will reserve a seat by telephone, and schedules change frequently according to season and demand, so buy your ticket in advance—several days in advance, if you plan to travel on weekends or holidays. From Panama City, it's a 20-hour, 900km (558-mile) trip. The one-way fare is around $20. From Managua, it's 11 hours and 450km (279 miles) to San José, and the one-way fare is around $12.

Whenever you're traveling by bus through Central America, try to keep a watchful eye on your belongings, especially at rest and border stops, whether they're in an overhead bin or stored below decks in a luggage compartment.

BY CAR

It's possible to travel to Costa Rica by car, but it can be difficult, especially for U.S. citizens. After leaving Mexico, the Interamerican Highway (Carretera Interamericana, also known as the Pan-American Hwy.) passes through Guatemala, El Salvador, Honduras, and Nicaragua before reaching Costa Rica. All of these countries can be problematic for travelers for a variety of reasons, including internal violence, crime, corrupt border crossings and visa formalities. If you do decide to undertake this adventure, take the **Gulf coast route** from the border crossing at Brownsville, Texas, because it involves traveling the fewest miles through Mexico. Those planning to travel this route should look through *Driving the Pan-Am Highway to Mexico and Central America,* by Audrey and Raymond Pritchard (Costa Rica Books, 1997), or *You Can Drive To Costa Rica in 8 Days!,* by Dawn Rae Lessler (Harmony Gardens Publishing, 1998). Both are available from the major online bookstores. You can also find a wealth of information online at www.sanbornsinsurance.com and www.drivemeloco.com.

CAR DOCUMENTS   You will need a current driver's license, as well as your vehicle's registration and the original title (no photocopies), to enter the country.

CENTRAL AMERICAN AUTO INSURANCE   Contact **Sanborn's Insurance Company** (© **800/222-0158** or 956/686-0711; www.sanbornsinsurance.com), which has agents at various border towns in the United States. These folks have been servicing this niche for more than 50 years. They can supply you with trip insurance for Mexico and Central America (you won't be able to buy insurance after you've left the U.S.), driving tips, and an itinerary.

CAR SAFETY   It's advisable not to drive at night because of the danger of being robbed by bandits. Also, drink only bottled beverages along the way, to avoid any unpleasant microbes that might be lurking in the local tap water.

BY CRUISE SHIP

More than 100 cruise ships stop each year in Costa Rica, calling at Limón on the Caribbean coast, and at Puerto Caldera and Puntarenas on the Pacific coast. Cruise lines that offer stops in Costa Rica include **Crystal Cruises** (© 800/804-1500; www.crystalcruises.com), **Celebrity Cruises** (© 800/722-5941; www.celebritycruises.com), **Holland America** (© 877/932-4259; www.hollandamerica.com), **Norwegian Cruise Lines** (© 800/327-7030; www.ncl.com), **Princess** (© 800/421-0522; www.princess.com), **Royal Caribbean** (© 800/398-9819; www.rccl.com), and **Radisson Seven Seas Cruises** (© 877/505-5370; www.rssc.com).

It might pay off to book through a travel agency that specializes in cruises; these companies buy in bulk and stay on top of the latest specials and promotions. Try the **Cruise Company** (© **800/289-5505;** www.thecruisecompany.com) or **World Wide Cruises** (© **800/882-9000;** www.wwcruises.com).

11 Package Deals for the Independent Traveler

Before you start your search for the lowest airfare, you might want to consider booking your flight as part of a travel package. Packages are not the same thing as escorted tours. Packages are simply a way to buy the airfare, accommodations, and other elements of your trip (such as car rentals, airport transfers, and sometimes even activities) at the same time and often at discounted prices—kind of like one-stop shopping. Packages are sold in bulk to tour operators—who resell them to the public at a cost that usually undercuts standard rates.

One good source of package deals is the airlines themselves. Most major airlines offer air/land packages, including **American Airlines Vacations** (© 800/321-2121; www.aavacations.com), **Delta Vacations** (© 800/221-6666; www.deltavacations.com), **Continental Airlines Vacations** (© 800/301-3800; www.covacations.com), and **United Vacations** (© 888/854-3899; www.unitedvacations.com). Several big **online travel agencies**—Expedia, Travelocity, Orbitz, Site59, and Lastminute.com—also do a brisk business in packages. In addition, you can check ads in the travel sections of major newspapers or in the national travel magazines, such as *Arthur Frommer's Budget Travel Magazine, Travel & Leisure, National Geographic Traveler,* and *Condé Nast Traveler.* If you're unsure about the pedigree of a smaller packager, check with the Better Business Bureau in the city where the company is based, or go online at www.bbb.org. If a packager won't tell you where it's based, don't fly with it.

Before you book your package through a tour company, remember that with a few phone calls and e-mails, you can often organize the same thing on your own without having to pay the sometimes hefty service fee. This book contains all the information and resources you need to design and book a wonderful trip, tailored to your particular interests and budget. Moreover, package vacations are still a budding industry in Costa Rica and do not offer the kinds of amazing bargains as those to Cancún or the Caribbean. In fact, many come with hidden charges and costs, so shop carefully.

Your best bet is often to do it yourself or to go with a Costa Rican–based specialist; many of these companies emphasize adventure travel or ecotourism and can put together a complete custom itinerary for you. For a complete listing of tour companies servicing Costa Rica, see "Organized Adventure Trips," in chapter 3.

Packages can vary by leaps and bounds. Some offer a better class of hotels than others. Some offer the same hotels for lower prices. Some offer flights on scheduled airlines, while others book charters. Some limit your choice of accommodations and travel days. You are often required to make a large payment up front. On the plus side, packages can save you money, offering group prices but allowing for independent travel. Some even let you add on a few guided excursions or escorted day trips (also at prices lower than if you booked them yourself) without booking an entirely escorted tour.

Before you invest in a package tour, get some answers. Ask about the **accommodations choices** and prices for each. Then look up the hotels' reviews in this guide and check their rates for your specific dates of travel online. You'll also want to find out what **type of room** you get. If you need a certain type of room, ask for it; don't take whatever is thrown your way. Request a nonsmoking room, a quiet room, a room with a view, or whatever you fancy.

Finally, look for **hidden expenses.** Ask whether airport departure fees and taxes, for example, are included in the total cost.

12 Getting Around

BY PLANE

Flying is one of the best ways to get around Costa Rica. Because the country is quite small, flights are short and not too expensive. The domestic airlines of Costa Rica are **Sansa** (© 221-9414; www.flysansa.com), which offers a free shuttle bus from its downtown office to the airport, and **Nature Air** (© 220-3054; www.natureair.com).

I personally recommend Nature Air over Sansa. Sansa has an unfriendly and unwieldy reservation system, it frequently overbooks flights, and it has been known to change schedules with little notice. The one thing Sansa has going for it is that it flies out of the main airport, so it is possible, albeit risky, to make same-day connections with international flights. Flight times are generally between 20 minutes and a little over an hour. Sansa operates from a separate terminal at San José's Juan Santamaría International Airport, while Nature Air operates from **Tobís Bolaños International Airport** in Pavas, 6.4km (4 miles) from San José. The ride from downtown to Pavas takes about 10 minutes, and a metered taxi fare should cost $6 to $8. The ride from the airport to downtown is a different story: Most taxis refuse to use their meter, and the standard fee is set at double the metered rate, around $10 to $12. Recently, Nature Air has begun having some its return flights stop first at the Juan Santamaría International Airport, enabling folks to make an outgoing connection on an international flight.

In the high season (late Nov to late Apr), be sure to book reservations well in advance. For Sansa flights, you don't have to call Costa Rica to make reservations; you can book flights through **Grupo Taca** (© **800/535-8780**; www.grupotaca.com). *But be careful:* I've heard horror stories of ticket vouchers issued in the United States not being accepted in Costa Rica; always reconfirm once you arrive. You can book flights on Nature Air via the Web or e-mail. If you plan to return to San José, buy a round-trip ticket—it's always nice to have a confirmed seat.

Sansa now offers an in-country "air pass" at $250 for 1 week and $300 for 2 weeks; the price is $50 cheaper if you arrive in Costa Rica on Grupo Taca. Theoretically, these allow for unlimited flights inside Costa Rica, although limited seating, overbooking, and preference given to full-price ticket buyers might make these air passes a slightly less appealing bargain.

BY BUS

This is by far the most economical way to get around Costa Rica. Buses are inexpensive and relatively well maintained, and they go nearly everywhere. There are two types: **Local buses** are the cheapest and slowest; they stop frequently and are generally a bit dilapidated. **Express buses** run between San José and most beach towns and major cities; these tend to be newer units and more comfortable, although very few are so new or modern as to have bathroom facilities, and they sometimes operate only on weekends and holidays.

Two companies run regular, fixed schedule departures in passenger vans and small buses to most of the major tourist destinations in the country. **Grayline** (© **220-2126**; www.graylinecostarica.com), run by Fantasy Tours, charges between $21 and $38, depending on your final destination. They have about 10 departures leaving San José each morning and heading or connecting to Jacó, Manuel Antonio, Liberia, Playa Hermosa, La Fortuna, Tamarindo, and playas Conchal and Flamingo. There are return trips to San José every day from these destinations and a variety of interconnecting routes. A similar service, **Interbus** (© **283-5573**; www.costaricapass.com), runs a sliding scale according to destination, with fares between $17 and $38, but with a slightly more extensive route map and more connections. Interbus also offers a month-long "flexipass," which can range in price from $110 for four rides or transfers, to $200 for 10 rides or transfers. *Beware:* Both of these companies offer pickup and drop-off at a wide range of hotels. This means that if you are the first picked up or last dropped off, you might have to sit through a long period of subsequent stops before finally hitting the road or reaching your destination. Moreover, I've heard some horror stories about both lines concerning missed or severely delayed connections and rude drivers. For details on how to get to various destinations from San José, see the "Getting There" sections of the regional chapters that follow.

BY CAR

Renting a car in Costa Rica is no idle proposition. The roads are riddled with potholes, most rural intersections are unmarked, and, for some reason,

Car-Rental Tips

Although it's preferable to use the coverage provided by your home auto-insurance policy or credit card, check carefully to see if the coverage really holds in Costa Rica. Many policies exclude four-wheel-drive vehicles and off-road driving—much of Costa Rica can, in fact, be considered off-road. It's possible at some car-rental agencies to waive the insurance charges, but you will have to pay all damages before leaving the country if you're in an accident. If you do take the insurance, you can expect a deductible of between $750 and $1,500. At some agencies, you can buy additional insurance to lower the deductible. To rent a car in Costa Rica, you must be at least 21 years old and have a valid driver's license and a major credit card in your name. See "Getting Around," in chapter 4, for details on renting a car in San José. You can also rent cars in Quepos, Jacó, Liberia, Playa Conchal, Tamarindo, La Fortuna, and Limón.

sitting behind the wheel of a car seems to turn peaceful Ticos into homicidal maniacs. But unless you want to see the country from the window of a bus (inconvenient) or pay exorbitant amounts for private transfers (expensive), renting a car is still your best option for independent exploring. Four-wheel-drives are particularly useful in the rainy season (May to mid-Nov) and for navigating the bumpy, poorly paved roads year-round.

Be forewarned, however: Although rental cars no longer bear special license plates, they are still readily identifiable to thieves and are frequently targeted. (Nothing is ever safe in a car in Costa Rica, although parking in guarded parking lots helps.) Transit police also seem to target tourists. Never pay money directly to a police officer who stops you for any traffic violation.

Before driving off with a rental car, be sure that you inspect the exterior and point out to the rental-company representative every tiny scratch, dent, tear, or any other damage. It's a common practice with many Costa Rican car-rental companies to claim that you owe payment for minor dings and dents that the company finds when

you return the car. Also, if you get into an accident, be sure that the rental company doesn't try to bill you for a higher amount than the deductible on your rental contract.

These caveats aren't meant to scare you off from driving in Costa Rica. Thousands of tourists rent cars here every year, and the large majority of them encounter no problems. Just keep your wits about you.

Note: It's sometimes cheaper to reserve a car in your home country rather than book when you arrive in Costa Rica. If you know you'll be renting a car, it's always wise to reserve it well in advance for the high season because the rental fleet still can't match demand.

Among the agencies operating in Costa Rica are: **Alamo** (© 800/570-0671 in the U.S., or 441-1260 at Juan Santamaría International Airport; www.alamocostarica.com), **Avis** (© 800/230-4898 in the U.S., or 293-2222 in Costa Rica; www.avis.com), **Budget** (© 800/527-0700 or 441-4444; www.budget.co.cr), **Hertz** (© 800/654-3131 or 441-0097; www.hertz.com), **National** (© 800/328-4567 or 440-0085; www.natcar.com),

Payless (© 800/582-7432 or 443-5286; www.paylesscr.com), and **Thrifty** (© 800/367-2277 or 442-8585; www.thrifty.com). For more listings of Costa Rican car-rental agencies, see "By Car," in "Getting Around," in chapter 4.

GASOLINE Gasoline is sold as "regular" and "super"; both are unleaded. Super is just higher octane. Diesel is available at almost every gas station, as well. Most rental cars run on super, but always ask your rental agent what type of gas your car takes. When going off to remote places, try to leave with a full tank of gas because gas stations can be hard to find. If you need to gas up in a small town, you can sometimes get gasoline from enterprising families who sell it by the liter from their houses. Look for hand-lettered signs that say GASOLINA. At press time, a liter of super cost 280 colones, or roughly $2.50 per gallon.

ROAD CONDITIONS The awful road conditions in San José and throughout the country are legendary, and deservedly so. Despite constant promises to fix the problem, the hot sun, hard rain, and rampant corruption have continued to outpace any progress made toward improving the condition. Even paved roads are often badly potholed, so stay alert. Road conditions get especially tricky during the rainy season, when heavy rains and runoff can destroy a stretch of pavement in the blink of an eye.

Route numbers are rarely used on road signs in Costa Rica, although there are frequent signs listing the number of kilometers to various towns or cities. In recent years, the Transportation Ministry began placing helpful markers at major intersections and turnoffs, but your best bets for on-road directions are still billboards and advertisements for hotels. It's always a good idea to know the names of a few hotels at your destination, just in case your specific hotel hasn't put up any billboards or signs.

RENTER'S INSURANCE Even if you already hold **your own car-insurance policy** at home, coverage doesn't always extend abroad. Be sure to find out whether you'll be covered in Costa Rica, whether your policy extends to all persons who will be driving the rental car, how much liability is covered in case an outside party is injured in an accident, and whether the *type* of vehicle you are renting is included under your contract.

Most **major credit cards** provide some degree of coverage as well—provided that they were used to pay for the rental. Again, terms vary widely, so be sure to call your credit card company directly before you rent. Usually, if you are **uninsured** or are **driving abroad,** your credit card provides primary coverage as long as you decline the rental agency's insurance. This means that the credit card will cover damage or theft of a rental car for the full cost of the vehicle. If you already have insurance, your credit card will provide secondary coverage, which basically covers your deductible. *Credit cards will not cover liability* or the cost of injury to an outside party and/or damage to an outside party's vehicle. If you do not hold an insurance policy, you might seriously want to consider purchasing additional liability insurance from your rental company. Be sure to check the terms, however. Some rental agencies cover liability only if the renter is not at fault; even then, the rental company's obligation varies from state to state.

The basic insurance coverage offered by most car-rental companies, known as the **Loss/Damage Waiver (LDW)** or **Collision Damage Waiver (CDW),** can cost as much as $20 per day. It usually covers the full value of the vehicle, with no deductible if an outside party causes an accident or other damage to the rental car. Liability coverage varies according to the company policy. If you are at fault in an accident, however, you will be covered for the full replacement value of the car, but not for liability. Most rental companies require a police report to process any claims you file, but your private insurer will not be notified of the accident.

MAPS   Car-rental agencies and the ICT information centers (see "Visitor Information," earlier in this chapter) at the airport and in downtown San José have adequate road maps, although the map included with this book is generally better. Other sources in San José for detailed maps include **Seventh Street Books,** Calle 7 between avenidas Central and 1 (✆ 256-8251); **Librería Lehmann,** Avenida Central between calles 1 and 3 (✆ 223-1212); and **Librería Universal,** Avenida Central between calles Central and 1 (✆ 222-2222).

DRIVING RULES   A current foreign driver's license is valid for the first 3 months you are in Costa Rica. Seat belts are required for the driver and front-seat passengers. Motorcyclists must wear a helmet. Highway police use radar, so keep to the speed limit (usually 60–90kmph/37–56 mph) if you don't want to get pulled over. Maybe it just seems this way, but the police seem to target rental cars. Never give the police any money. Speeding tickets can be charged to your credit card for up to a year after you leave the country if they are not paid before departure.

BREAKDOWNS   Be warned that emergency services, both vehicular and medical, are extremely limited once you leave San José, and their availability is directly related to the remoteness of your location at the time of breakdown. You'll find service stations spread over the entire length of the Interamerican Highway, and most of

these have tow trucks and mechanics. The major towns of Puntarenas, Liberia, Quepos, San Isidro, Palmar, and Golfito all have hospitals, and most other moderately sized cities and tourist destinations have some sort of clinic or health-services provider.

If you're involved in an accident, you should contact the **National Insurance Institute (INS)** at ✆ 800/800-8000. You should probably also call the **Transit Police** (✆ 222-9330 or 222-9245); if they have a unit close by, they'll send one. An official transit police report will greatly facilitate any insurance claim. If you can't get help from any of these, try to get written statements from any witnesses. Finally, you can also call ✆ **911,** and they should be able to redirect your call to the appropriate agency.

If the police do show up, you've got a 50/50 chance of finding them helpful or downright antagonistic. Many officers are unsympathetic to the problems of what they perceive to be rich tourists running around in fancy cars with lots of expensive toys and trinkets. Success and happy endings run about equal with horror stories.

If you don't speak Spanish, expect added difficulty in any emergency or stressful situation. Don't expect that rural (or urban) police officers, hospital personnel, service-station personnel, or mechanics will speak English.

If your car breaks down and you're unable to get well off the road, check to see whether there are reflecting triangles in the trunk. If there are, place them as a warning for approaching traffic, arranged in a wedge that starts at the shoulder about 30m (98 ft.) back and nudges gradually toward your car. If your car has no triangles, try to create a similar warning marker using a pile of leaves or branches. Finally, although not endemic, there have been reports of folks being robbed by seemingly friendly Ticos who stop to give assistance. To add insult to injury, there have even been reports of organized gangs who puncture tires of rental cars at rest stops or busy intersections, only to follow them, offer assistance, and make off with belongings and valuables.

BY FERRY

Three different ferries operate across the Gulf of Nicoya. Two are car ferries: one from Puntarenas to Playa Naranjo, and one from Puntarenas to Paquera. The third is a passenger ferry that runs between Puntarenas and Paquera.

BY THUMB

Although buses serve most towns in Costa Rica, service can be infrequent in the remote regions, so local people often hitchhike to get to their destination sooner. If you're driving a car, people will frequently ask you for a ride. In rural areas, a hitchhiker carrying a machete is not necessarily a great danger, but use your judgment. Hitchhiking is not recommended on major roadways or in urban areas. In rural areas it's usually pretty safe. However, women should be extremely cautious about hitchhiking anywhere in Costa Rica. If you choose to hitchhike, keep in mind that if a bus doesn't go to your destination, there probably aren't too many cars going there, either. Good luck.

13 Spanish-Language Programs

As more people travel to Costa Rica with the intention of learning Spanish, the number of options continues to increase. You can find courses of varying lengths and degrees of intensiveness, and many that include cultural activities and day excursions. Many of these schools have reciprocal relationships with U.S. universities, so, in some cases, you can even arrange for college credit. Most Spanish schools can arrange for home stays with a middle-class Tico family for a total-immersion experience. Classes are often small, or even one-on-one, and can last anywhere from 2 to 8 hours a day. Listed below are some of the larger and more established Spanish-language schools, with approximate costs. Most are located in San José, but there are also schools in Heredia, Monteverde, Manuel Antonio, Playa Flamingo, Malpais, Playa Nosara, Montezuma, and Tamarindo. (I'd certainly rather spend 2 weeks or a month in one of these spots than in San José.) Contact the schools for the most current price information.

Centro Lingüístico Conversa ★, A.P. 17-1007, Centro Colón, San José, Costa Rica (© **800/367-7726** in the U.S. and Canada, or 221-7649; www.conversa.net), has classes in both San José and Santa Ana (a suburb of the capital city). A 2-week course here with 4 hours of classes each day, including room and board with a Costa Rican family, costs between $900 and $1,300 for one person, depending on which campus you choose and the level of luxury you're looking for.

Centro Panamericano de Idiomas (CPI) ★, A.P. 151-3007, San Joaquín de Flores, Heredia, Costa Rica (© **888/682-0054** in the U.S., or 265-6306; www.cpi-edu.com), has three campuses: one in the quiet suburban town of Heredia, another in Monteverde, and a new facility in Playa Flamingo. A 1-week program, with 4 hours of class per day and a homestay with a Costa Rican family, costs $365.

Costa Rican Language Academy, A.P. 1966-2050, San José, Costa Rica (© **866/230-6361** in the U.S., or 280-1685; www.spanishandmore.com), has intensive programs with classes only Monday through Thursday, to give students a chance to make longer weekend excursions. The academy also integrates Latin dance and Costa Rican cooking classes into the program. A 2-week class with 4 hours of class per day, plus a homestay, costs $585.

Costa Rica Spanish Institute (COSI), A.P. 1366-2050, San Pedro, Costa Rica (© **800/771-5184** in the U.S., or 234-1001; www.cosi.co.cr), offers small classes in the San Pedro neighborhood of San José, as well as a program at the Pacific beach of Manuel Antonio. The cost is $345 per week with a homestay in San José; at the beach, it's $340, with room and board extra.

Forester Instituto Internacional ★, A.P. 6945-1000, San José, Costa Rica (© **225-3155**, or 225-0135; www.fores.com), is located 75m (246 ft.) south of the Automercado in the Los Yoses district of San José. I've received glowing reports from satisfied customers here. The cost of a 4-week language course with a homestay and excursions is approximately $1,480.

Institute for Central American Development Studies (ICADS) ★★, A.P. 300-2050, San Pedro, Costa Rica (© **225-0508**; www.icadscr.com), not only has one of the best and most extensive fieldwork and volunteer programs in Costa Rica, but it also runs quality Spanish-language immersion programs. A 4-week course with a homestay costs $1,600.

Instituto Británico ★, A.P. 8184-1000, San José, Costa Rica (© **234-9054**; www.institutobritanico.co.cr), is a venerable institution with installations in the Los Yoses neighborhood of San José. A bit more attention seems to be paid to teacher training and selection here than at other institutions around town. A 2-week course with 4 hours of classes per day and a homestay costs $690.

La Escuela Idiomas D'Amore ★, A.P. 67, Quepos, Costa Rica (©/fax **262/367-8598** in the U.S., or ©/fax 777-1143; www.escueladamore.com), is situated in the lush surroundings of Manuel Antonio National Park. A 2-week conversational Spanish course, including a homestay and two meals daily, costs $980. Fifteen percent of your tuition is donated to the World Wildlife Fund. This is a much nicer environment than San José for learning Spanish (for most everything else, too, in fact).

Wayra Instituto de Español (©/fax **653-0359**; www.spanish-wayra.co.cr) is located in the beach town of Tamarindo. A week of classes, 4 hours per day, will run you $200. With a homestay, the cost is $320 to $380.

14 Tips on Accommodations

Tourism insiders had been predicting it for years, and the slowdown following the terrorist attacks of September 11, 2001, has only accelerated the process: A shakedown is in effect. There's a glut of rooms in Costa Rica, and despite the still healthy number of visitors, tough times and fierce competition have begun to take their toll on local hoteliers. When the Costa Rican tourist boom began in the late 1980s, hotels popped up like mushrooms after a few days of rain. In recent years, the country's first true megaresorts have opened, and a couple more are under construction and near completion. The glut is good news for travelers and bargain-hunters. Hotels that

want to survive are being forced to reduce their rates and provide better service.

Glut notwithstanding, there are still few hotels or resorts here offering the sort of luxury you'll find in Hawaii or the Caribbean. Sure, there are hotels that meet international standards, but Costa Rica is not yet a luxury resort destination. (Luckily, prices have remained a whole lot cheaper than those in the Caribbean and Hawaii, too—Costa Rica's hotels are still a bargain, by comparison.) One item that you're likely to want to bring with you is a beach towel. Your hotel might not provide one at all, and even if it does, it might be awfully thin.

Throughout this book, I've separated hotel listings into several broad categories: **Very Expensive,** $150 and up; **Expensive,** $100 to $150; **Moderate,** $50 to $100; and **Inexpensive,** under $50 double. *Rates given in this book do not include the 16.3% room taxes.* These taxes will add considerably to the cost of your room. Also note that with rooms at the beach that cost under $25, you usually don't get hot water.

HOTEL OPTIONS

Upscale travelers are finally starting to get their due in Costa Rica. It has taken time, but spurred on by the example and standards of several international chains, service and amenities have been improving across the board, particularly in the upscale market. The new Four Seasons, along with the Marriott Los Sueños and Paradisus Playa Conchal resorts, is sure to please the demanding luxury traveler, and there are also several wonderful high-end boutique hotels, both in San José and the Central Valley and around the country.

The country's strong suit is its **moderately priced hotels.** In the $50-to-$100 price range, you'll find comfortable and sometimes outstanding accommodations almost anywhere in the country. However, room size and quality vary quite a bit within this price range, so don't expect the kind of uniformity that you find in the United States.

If you're even more budget- or bohemian-minded, there are quite a few good deals for less than $50 per double room. *But beware:* Budget-oriented lodgings often feature shared bathrooms and either cold-water showers or showers heated by electrical

heat-coil units mounted at the showerhead. These are affectionately known as "suicide showers." If your hotel has one, do not try to adjust it while the water is running. Unless specifically noted, all the rooms I've listed in this guide have a private bathroom.

Bed-and-breakfasts have also been proliferating. Although the majority of these are in the San José area, you will now find B&Bs (often gringo-owned and -operated) throughout the country. Another welcome hotel trend in the San José area is the renovation and conversion of old homes into **small hotels.** Most of these hotels are in the Barrio Amón district of downtown San José, which means that you'll sometimes have to put up with noise and exhaust fumes, but these establishments have more character than any other hotels in the country. You'll find similar hotels in the Paseo Colón and Los Yoses districts.

Costa Rica has been riding the ecotourism wave, and there are now small nature-oriented **ecolodges** throughout the country. These lodges offer opportunities to see wildlife (including sloths, monkeys, and hundreds of species of birds) and learn about tropical forests. They range from spartan facilities catering primarily to scientific researchers, to luxury accommodations that are among the finest in the country. Keep in mind that although the nightly room rates at these lodges are often quite moderate, the price of a visit starts to climb when you throw in transportation (often on chartered planes), guided excursions, and meals. Also, just because your

---

⎛Tips Hotel Tip

If you are booking directly with your hotel (either by phone/fax or e-mail), remember that most hotels are accustomed to paying as much as 20% in commission to agents and wholesalers. It never hurts to ask if it will pass some of that on to you. Don't be afraid to bargain.

travel agent can book a reservation at most of these lodges doesn't mean that they're not remote. Be sure to find out how you will be getting to and from your ecolodge and just what tours and services are included in your stay. Then think long and hard about whether you really want to put up with hot, humid weather (cool and wet in the cloud forests); biting insects; rugged transportation; and strenuous hikes to see wildlife.

A couple of uniquely Costa Rican accommodation types that you might encounter are the *apartotel* and the *cabina.* An apartotel is just what it sounds like: an apartment hotel, where you'll get a full kitchen and one or two bedrooms, along with daily maid service. Cabinas are Costa Rica's version of cheap vacation lodging. They're very inexpensive and very basic—often just cinder-block buildings divided into small rooms. Occasionally, you'll find a cabina in which the units are actually cabins, but these are a rarity. Cabinas often have clothes-washing sinks or *pilas,* and some come with kitchenettes; they cater primarily to Tico families on vacation.

15 Tips on Dining

Simply put, Costa Rican cuisine is less than memorable. San José remains the unquestioned gastronomic capital of the country, and here you can find the cuisines of the world served with formal service at moderate prices. At even the more expensive restaurants in San José, it's hard to spend more than $50 per person unless you really splurge on drinks and wine. It gets even cheaper outside the city. There are several excellent French and Italian restaurants around the San José area, as well as Peruvian, Japanese, Swiss, and Spanish establishments.

Costa Rica is a major producer and exporter of beef; consequently, San José has plenty of steakhouses. Unfortunately, quantity doesn't mean quality. Unless you go to one of the better restaurants or steakhouses, you will probably be served rather tough steaks, cut rather thin.

Still, all is not lost. With the increase in international tourism and the need to please a more sophisticated palate, local chefs have begun to create a "nouvelle Costa Rican cuisine," updating timeworn recipes and using traditional ingredients in creative ways.

Outside of the capital and major tourist destinations, your options get very limited, very fast. In fact, many beach resorts are so remote that you have no choice but to eat in the hotel's dining room. Even on the more accessible beaches, the only choices aside from the hotel dining rooms are often cheap local places or overpriced tourist traps serving indifferent meals. At remote jungle lodges, the food is usually served buffet or family style and can range from bland to inspired, depending on who's doing the cooking at the moment, and turnover is high.

If you're looking for cheap eats, you'll find them in little restaurants known as *sodas,* which are the equivalent of diners in the United States. At a soda, you'll have lots of choices: rice and beans with steak, rice and beans with fish, rice and beans with chicken, or, for vegetarians, rice and beans. You get the picture. Rice and beans are standard Tico fare and are served at all three meals a day. Also, although plenty of seafood is available throughout the country, at sodas, it's all too often served fried.

Costa Ricans love to eat, and they love to have a view when they eat. Almost anywhere you go in the country, if there's a view, there will be a restaurant taking advantage of it. These restaurants are often called *miradores.* If you are driving around the country, don't miss an opportunity to dine with a view at some little roadside restaurant. The food might not be fantastic, but the scenery will be.

I have separated restaurant listings throughout this book into three price categories, based on the average cost per person of a meal, including tax and service charge. The categories are **Expensive,** more than $20; **Moderate,** $10 to $20; and **Inexpensive,** less than $10. (Note, however, that individual items in the listings—entrees, for instance—do not include the sales or service taxes.) Keep in mind that there is an additional 13% sales tax, as well as a 10% service charge. Ticos rarely tip, but that doesn't mean that you shouldn't. If the service was particularly good and attentive, you should probably leave a little extra.

16 Tips on Shopping

FOOD FADS Buy coffee. Even if you're not a coffee drinker, you're bound to know someone who is, and coffee is the best buy in Costa Rica. **Café Britt** is the most common brand, sold in hotels and souvenir shops all over the country. Sold in light, dark, and espresso roasts, this is the best widely available brand.

There are several quite good boutique brands and blends available. If you're in Manuel Antonio, pick up your coffee at **Café Milagro** (see chapter 7); and if you're in Monteverde, you can get some excellent fresh-roasted beans at **CASEM** (see chapter 6).

Just be sure you're buying whole beans *(grano entero)* and not ground ones *(molido)*. Packaged Costa Rican grinds are much finer than U.S. grinds and often have sugar mixed right in with the coffee.

Costa Rica also produces its own coffee liqueur (**Café Rica**) and a creme liqueur, both of which are quite inexpensive. These are best purchased in a liquor store or a grocery store. In fact, grocery stores are where I do my best gift shopping.

If you'd like to add a little spice to your life, **Típica Tropical Sauce** produces a line of spicy salsas made from mango, pineapple, passion fruit, and tamarind. A small bottle costs around 75¢ and makes a great gift. **Salsa Lizano,** a flavorful green sauce used the same way we use steak sauce in the United States, is another condiment worth bringing home with you.

HANDICRAFTS Costa Rica is not known for its handicrafts, although it does have a town, **Sarchí,** that's filled with handicraft shops. Sarchí is best known as the home of the colorfully painted Costa Rican oxcart, reproductions of which are manufactured in various scaled-down sizes. These make excellent gifts. (Larger oxcarts can be easily disassembled and shipped to your home.) There's also a lot of furniture made here.

So scant are the country's handicraft offerings that most tourist shops sell Guatemalan clothing, Panamanian appliquéd textiles, El Salvadoran painted wood souvenirs, and Nicaraguan rocking chairs.

The small town of **Guaitíl,** in central Guanacaste, is famous for its pottery. You can find examples of this low-fired simple ceramic work in many gift shops.

There's quite a bit of Costa Rican woodcarving, but it is, for the most part, either tourist-souvenir wooden bowls, napkin holders, and the like, or elegant and expensive art pieces. One exception is the work of **Barry Biensanz,** whose excellent hardwood creations are sold at better gift shops around the country.

COSTA RICAN SPECIALTIES A few other items worth keeping an eye out for include **reproductions of pre-Columbian gold jewelry and carved-stone figurines.** The former are available as either solid gold, silver, or gold-plated. The latter, although interesting, are extremely heavy.

On the streets of San José, you'll see a lot of **hammocks** for sale. I personally find the Costa Rican hammocks a little crude and unstable. The same vendors usually have single-person hanging chairs, which are strung similarly to the full-size hammocks and are a better bet.

Finally, one new item that you'll see at gift shops around the country is **Cuban cigars.** Although these are illegal to bring into the United States, they are perfectly legal and readily available in Costa Rica.

17 Suggested Itineraries

There's a lot to see in Costa Rica. The following itineraries are very rough outlines to help you structure your time and get a taste of some of the country's must-see destinations. Other options include specialized itineraries focused on a particular interest or activity. Bird-watchers could design an itinerary that visits a series of prime bird-watching sites, while volcano enthusiasts could design a route that visits a half-dozen or more of these geological wonders. Those with a general interest in nature will want to try to visit areas of lowland tropical rainforest, cloud forest, coastal mangrove, and perhaps the high-altitude páramo.

Tip: Be sure to bring a disposable waterproof camera or two with you. Whether you use it on a white-water rafting trip, while taking surf lessons, or during a rainforest storm, it's sure to come in handy.

If You Have 1 Week

Day 1 Get settled and visit the museums and the National Theater in San José, if you have time.

Day 2 Make an excursion to Poás Volcano and nearby Waterfall Gardens, or head to the Orosi Valley, Lankester Gardens, and Irazú Volcano. More adventurous souls can go white-water rafting for the day.

Days 3 & 4 Travel to Monteverde and spend some time exploring the cloud forest, or head to Arenal Volcano to enjoy the nightly pyrotechnics, the hot springs, and hikes through the neighboring rainforests.

Days 5 & 6 Head to one of the many Pacific coast beaches. For first-time visitors, I recommend either Tamarindo or Manuel Antonio for their accessibility and range of accommodations and activities.

Day 7 Return to San José.

If You Have 2 Weeks

Spend Days 1 and 2 as in "If You Have 1 Week," above.

Days 3 & 4 Travel to Lake Arenal to see the eruptions of Arenal Volcano, soak in some hot springs, and maybe go to Caño Negro National Wildlife Refuge.

Days 5 & 6 Travel to Monteverde (or another cloud-forest region) and explore the cloud forest.

Days 7 & 8 Explore Rincón de la Vieja or Santa Rosa National Park.

Days 9, 10, 11 & 12 Spend these days relaxing on a beach in Guanacaste, or perhaps exploring a more remote location on the Osa Peninsula or along the Caribbean coast.

Days 13 & 14 Fly to Tortuguero National Park and spend a night there, returning the next day by boat and bus.

18 Recommended Reading

Some of the books mentioned below might be difficult to track down in U.S. bookstores, but you'll find them all in abundance in Costa Rica. A good place to check for most of these titles is **Seventh Street Books,** on Calle 7 between avenidas 1 and Central (℮ **256-8251**).

GENERAL INTEREST For a straightforward, albeit somewhat dry, historical overview, there's *The History of Costa Rica,* by Ivan Molina and Steven Palmer (University of Costa Rica, 2001). For a more readable look into Costa Rican society, check out *The Ticos: Culture and Social Change* ★, by Richard, Karen, and Mavis Biesanz (Lynne Rienner Publishers, 1999), an examination of the country's politics and culture, by the authors of the out-of-print *The Costa Ricans.*

To learn more about the life and culture of Costa Rica's Talamanca coast, an area populated by Afro-Caribbean people whose forebears emigrated from Caribbean islands in the early 19th century, pick up a copy of *What Happen: A Folk-History of Costa Rica's Talamanca Coast* ★, by Paula Palmer. This book is a collection of oral histories taken from a wide range of local characters. A new and improved edition is slated to be published in early 2005 by Distribuidores Zona Tropical.

If you're looking for literature, *Costa Rica: A Traveler's Literary Companion* ★★, edited by Barbara Ras and with a foreword by Oscar Arias Sánchez (Whereabouts Press, 1994), is a collection of short stories by Costa Rican writers, organized by region of the country. If you're lucky, you might find and pick up a copy of *Stories of Tatamundo* (University of Costa Rica Press, 1998), by Fabian Dobles, or *The Lonely Men's Island,* by José León Sánchez (Escritores Unidos, 1997). Sánchez is Costa Rica's "Papillon," and the book details his death-defying escape from San Lucas, a prison island.

Young adults will enjoy Aileen Kilgore Henderson's *The Monkey Thief* ★ (Milkweed Editions, 1997), and Kristin Joy Pratt's *A Walk In The Rainforest* (Dawn Publications, 1992). David Norman publishes a series of coloring books with short descriptive texts, including *Let's Help Costa Rica's Endangered Animals* (WWF, 1998) and *Costa Rican Wildlife* (WWF, 1999).

NATURAL HISTORY I personally that think everyone coming to Costa Rica should read *Tropical Nature* ★★★, by Adrian Forsyth and Ken Miyata (Touchstone Books, 1987). My all-time favorite book on tropical biology, this is a wonderfully written and lively collection of tales and adventures by two Neotropical biologists who spent quite some time in the forests of Costa Rica.

Mario A. Boza's beautiful *Costa Rica National Parks* ★★ (INCAFO, 2004) has been reissued in an elegant coffee-table edition. *Costa Rica's National Parks and Preserves,* by Joseph Franke (The Mountaineers, 1999), is similar, but with fewer photos.

For an introduction to a wide range of Costa Rican fauna, there's *The Field Guide to the Wildlife of Costa Rica* ★★, by Carrol Henderson (University of Texas Press, 2002), which packs a lot of useful information into a concise package. It's a great field guide for amateur naturalists and inquisitive tourists.

A Guide to the Birds of Costa Rica ★★, by F. Gary Stiles and Alexander Skutch (Cornell University Press, 1989), is an invaluable guide to identifying the many birds you'll see during your stay. Most guides and nature lodges have a copy of this book on hand.

Other interesting natural history books that will give you a look at the plants and animals of Costa Rica include *Costa Rica Natural History,* by Daniel Janzen (University of Chicago Press, 1983); the two-volume collection of *Butterflies of Costa Rica,* by Philip DeVries (Princeton University

Press, 1987 and 1997); *The Natural History of Costa Rican Mammals,* by Mark Wainwright (Distruibuidores Zona Tropical, 2003); the new *A Guide to the Amphibians and Reptiles of Costa Rica,* by Twan Leenders (Distruibuidores Zona Tropical, 2001); and the classic *A Neotropical Companion* ✦, by John C. Kricher (Princeton University Press, 1999), which was recently reissued in an expanded edition with color photos.

FAST FACTS: Costa Rica

Addresses See "'I Know There's Got to Be a Number Here Somewhere . . .': The Arcane Art of Finding an Address in San José," on p. 89.

Business Hours Banks are usually open Monday through Friday from 9am to 4pm, although many have begun to offer extended hours. Offices are open Monday through Friday from 8am to 5pm (many close for 1 hr. at lunch). Stores are generally open Monday through Saturday from 9am to 6pm (many close for 1 hr. at lunch). Stores in modern malls generally stay open until 8 or 9pm and don't close for lunch. Most bars are open until 1 or 2am.

Cameras/Film Most types of film are available, as are developing services. However, prices are higher than in the United States, so bring plenty of film with you and wait until you get home for processing.

Drug Laws Drug laws in Costa Rica are strict, so stay away from marijuana and cocaine. Many prescription drugs are sold over the counter here, but often the names are different from those in the United States and Europe. It's always best to have a prescription from a doctor.

Drugstores Called *farmacias* in Spanish, drugstores are quite common throughout the country. Those at hospitals and major clinics are often open 24 hours a day.

Electricity The standard in Costa Rica is the same as in the United States: 110 volts AC (60 cycles). However, three-pronged outlets can be scarce, so it's helpful to bring along an adapter.

Embassies/Consulates The following embassies and consulates are located in San José: **United States Embassy,** in front of Centro Commercial, on the road to Pavas (☏ 220-3939); **Canadian Consulate,** Oficentro Ejecutivo La Sabana, Edificio 5 (☏ 242-4400); and **British Embassy,** Paseo Colón between calles 38 and 40 (☏ 258-2025). There are no Australian or New Zealand embassies in San José.

Emergencies In case of any emergency, dial ☏ **911** (which should have an English-speaking operator); for an ambulance, call ☏ **128;** and to report a fire, call ☏ **118.** If 911 doesn't work, you can contact the police at ☏ **222-1365** or 221-5337, and hopefully they can find someone who speaks English.

Language Spanish is the official language of Costa Rica. *Berlitz Latin American Spanish Phrasebook and Dictionary* (Berlitz Guides, 2001) is probably the best phrase book to bring with you. However, in most tourist areas, you'll be surprised by how well Costa Ricans speak English.

Laundry Dry cleaners and laundromats—be they full-service or self-serve—are few and far between in Costa Rica. Hotel laundry services, which can sometimes be expensive, are far more common. For listings of laundromats, see individual city and town sections.

Liquor Laws Alcoholic beverages are sold every day of the week throughout the year, with the exception of the 2 days before Easter and the 2 days before and after a presidential election. The legal drinking age is 18, although it's almost never enforced. Liquor, everything from beer to hard spirits, is sold in specific liquor stores, as well as at most supermarkets and even convenience stores.

Mail Mail to the United States usually takes a little over a week to reach its destination. The main post office *(correo)* is on Calle 2 between avenidas 1 and 3 (🕾 800/900-2000 toll free in Costa Rica, or 223-9766; www.correos.go.cr), and is open Monday through Friday from 8am to 5:30pm and Saturday from 7:30am to noon. At press time, it cost 110 colones (26¢) to mail a postcard or letter to the United States, and 130 colones (31¢) to Europe. Given the Costa Rican postal service's track record, I recommend paying an extra 400 colones (95¢) to have anything of any value certified. Better yet, use an international courier service or wait until you get home to post it. **DHL,** on Paseo Colón between calles 30 and 32 (🕾 210-3838; www.dhl.com); **EMS Courier,** with desks at the principal metropolitan post offices (🕾 281-0227); **FedEx,** which is based in Heredia but will arrange pickup anywhere in the metropolitan area (🕾 0800/052-1090; www.fedex.com); and **United Parcel Service,** in Pavas (🕾 290-2828; www.ups.com), all operate in Costa Rica. *Note:* Despite what you might be told, packages sent overnight to U.S. addresses tend to take 3 to 4 days to reach their destination.

A post office is called a *correo* in Spanish. You can get stamps at the post office and at some gift shops in large hotels.

If you're sending mail *to* Costa Rica, it generally takes between 10 and 14 days to reach San José, although it can take as much as a month to get to the more remote corners of the country. Plan ahead. Also note that many hotels and ecolodges have mailing addresses in the United States. Always use these addresses when writing from North America or Europe. Never send cash, checks, or valuables through the Costa Rican mail system.

Maps The **Costa Rican Tourist Board** (🕾 800/343-6332; www.visitcosta rica.com) can usually provide you with decent maps of both Costa Rica and San José. See "By Car" in "Getting Around," earlier in this chapter, for names of bookstores that sell good maps.

Newspapers/Magazines There are six Spanish-language dailies in Costa Rica and one English-language weekly, the *Tico Times.* In addition, you can get *Time, Newsweek,* and several U.S. newspapers at some hotel gift shops and a few of the bookstores in San José. If you understand Spanish, *La Nación* is the paper of record. Its "Viva" and "Tiempo Libre" sections list what's going on in the world of music, theater, dance, and more.

Police In most cases, dial 🕾 911 for the police, and you should be able to get someone who speaks English on the line. Other numbers for the **Judicial Police** are 🕾 222-1365 and 221-5337. The numbers for the **Traffic Police (Policía de Tránsito)** are 🕾 222-9330 and 222-9245.

Radio/TV There are about 10 local TV channels; cable and satellite TV from the United States are also common. There are scores of radio stations on the AM and FM dials. In San José, 107.5 FM is my favorite English-language station, with a wide range of musical programming, as well as news and some talk shows.

Restrooms These are known as *sanitarios, servicios sanitarios,* or *baños.* They are marked *damas* (women) and *hombres* or *caballeros* (men). Public restrooms are hard to come by. You will almost never find a public restroom in a city park or downtown area. There are usually public restrooms at most national-park entrances, and much less frequently inside the national park. (There are usually plenty of trees and bushes.) In the towns and cities, it gets much trickier. One must count on the generosity of some hotel or restaurant. Same goes for most beaches. However, most restaurants, and, to a lesser degree, hotels, will let you use their facilities, especially if you buy a soft drink or something. Bus and gas stations often have restrooms, but many of these are pretty grim.

Safety Although most of Costa Rica is safe, crime has become much more common in recent years. San José is known for its pickpockets, so never carry a wallet in your back pocket. A woman should keep a tight grip on her purse. (Keep it tucked under your arm.) Thieves also target gold chains, cameras and video cameras, prominent jewelry, and nice sunglasses. Be sure not to leave valuables in your hotel room. Don't park a car on the street in Costa Rica, especially in San José; there are plenty of public parking lots around the city.

Rental cars generally stick out, and they are easily spotted by thieves, who know that such cars are likely to be full of expensive camera equipment, money, and other valuables. Don't ever leave anything of value in a car parked on the street, not even for a moment. Also be wary of solicitous strangers who stop to help you change a tire or bring you to a service station. Although most are truly good Samaritans, there have been reports of thieves preying on roadside breakdowns.

Public intercity buses are also frequent targets of stealthy thieves. Never check your bags into the hold of a bus if you can avoid it. If this can't be avoided, keep your eye on what leaves the hold. If you put your bags in an overhead rack, be sure you can see the bags at all times. Try not to fall asleep.

Taxes All hotels charge 16.3% tax. Restaurants charge 13% tax and also add on a 10% service charge, for a total of 23% more on your bill.

There is a $26 departure tax for all visitors leaving by air. At press time, the departure tax must be purchased at branches of the Banco Crédito Agrícola de Cartago (BCAC), which has an office in the main terminal at the airport (daily 4am–8pm). The tax can be paid in advance, and I recommend that you do so because the line to purchase it at the airport is sometimes long and slow moving. BCAC has numerous branches around San José and in some of the major tourist towns. The principal office in San José is at Avenida 4, between Calle Central and Calle 2, on the west side of the Parque Central (© 212-7000; www.bancreditocr.com for other branch locations). Not all branches are set up to sell the tax yet, so check in advance. Finally, some local travel agencies have been purchasing the departure tax for tourists. You must give them authorization, as well as your passport number, and pay a small service fee.

Taxis Taxis are common and inexpensive in San José but are harder to find and more expensive in rural areas. In San José, taxis are supposed to charge metered fares. Outside the city and on longer rides, be sure to agree on a price beforehand. For more information on taxis in San José, see "Getting Around," in chapter 4.

Telephones/Faxes Costa Rica has an excellent phone system, with a dial tone similar to that heard in the United States. See "Telephone Tips" on the inside front cover of this book for more information on dialing to, from, and within Costa Rica.

A phone call within Costa Rica costs around 10 colones (3¢) per minute. Pay phones take either a calling card or 5-, 10-, or 20-colón coins. Calling cards are becoming more prominent, and coin-operated phones are getting harder to find. You can purchase calling cards in a host of gift shops and pharmacies. However, there are several competing calling-card companies, and certain cards work only with certain phones. **CHIP** calling cards work with a computer chip and just slide into specific phones, although these phones aren't widely available. A better bet are the **197** and **199** calling cards, which are sold in varying denominations. These have a scratch-off PIN and can be used from any phone in the country. In general terms, the 197 cards are sold in smaller denominations and are used for local calling, while the 199 cards are deemed international and are easier to find in larger denominations. Either card can be used to make any call, however, provided that the card can cover the costs. Another perk of the **199** cards is the fact that you can get the instructions in English. For local calls, it is often easiest to call from your hotel, although you will likely be charged around 100 to 200 colones (25¢–50¢) per call.

You can make international phone calls, as well as send faxes, from the **ICE office,** Avenida 2 between calles 1 and 3, in San José (© **255-0444**). The office is open daily from 7am to 10pm. Faxes cost around $2 per page to the United States. (Many hotels also offer the same service for a fee.) **Radiográfica** (© **287-0087**), at Calle 1 and Avenida 5 in San José, also has fax service.

Note: Numbers beginning with 0800 and 800 within Costa Rica are toll free, but calling an 800 number in the States from Costa Rica is not toll free. In fact, it costs the same as an overseas call.

Time Costa Rica is on Central Standard Time (same as Chicago and St. Louis), 6 hours behind Greenwich mean time. Costa Rica does not use daylight saving time, so the time difference is an additional hour April through October.

Tipping Tipping is not necessary in restaurants, where a 10% service charge is always added to your bill (along with a 13% tax). If service was particularly good, you can leave a little at your own discretion, but it's not mandatory. Porters and bellhops get around 75¢ per bag. You don't need to tip a taxi driver unless the service has been superior; a tip is not usually expected.

Water Although the water in San José is generally safe to drink, water quality varies outside the city. Because many travelers have tender digestive tracts, I recommend playing it safe and sticking to bottled drinks as much as possible. Also avoid ice.

3

The Active Vacation Planner

Although it's possible to come to Costa Rica and stay clean and dry, most visitors want to spend some time getting their hair wet, their feet muddy, and their adrenaline pumping. To many, tropical rainforests and cloud forests are the stuff of myth and legend. Partly because evolution is a slow process, and partly because much of the country's natural landscape is protected in national parks and bioreserves, Costa Rica's primary forests, which are open to adventurous travelers, are still in much the same state as when early explorers such as Columbus found them. And that's not even mentioning the array of lovely tropical beaches.

There are myriad approaches to planning an active vacation in Costa Rica. This chapter lays out your options, from tour operators who run multi-activity package tours that often include stays at ecolodges, to the best places in Costa Rica to pursue active endeavors (with listings of tour operators, guides, and outfitters that specialize in each), to an overview of the country's national parks and bioreserves, with suggestions on how to plan an independent itinerary. I've also listed some educational and volunteer travel options for those of you with a little more time on your hands and a desire to actively assist Costa Rica in the maintenance and preservation of its natural wonders.

1 Organized Adventure Trips

Because many travelers have limited time and resources, organized ecotourism or adventure-travel packages, arranged by tour operators in either the United States or Costa Rica, are a popular way of combining several activities. Bird-watching, horseback riding, rafting, and hiking can be teamed with, say, visits to Monteverde Biological Cloud Forest Reserve and Manuel Antonio National Park.

Traveling with a group has several advantages over traveling independently: Your accommodations and transportation are arranged, and most (if not all) of your meals are included in the cost of a package. If your tour operator has a reasonable amount of experience and a decent track record, you should proceed to each of your destinations quickly without the snags and long delays that those traveling on their own can occasionally face. You'll also have the opportunity to meet like-minded souls who are interested in nature and active sports. Of course, you'll pay more for the convenience of having all your arrangements handled in advance.

In the best cases, group size is kept small (10–20 people), and tours are escorted by knowledgeable guides who are either naturalists or biologists. Be sure to ask about difficulty levels when you're choosing a tour. Although most companies offer "soft adventure" packages that those in moderately good, but not phenomenal, shape can handle, others focus on more hard-core activities geared toward only seasoned athletes or adventure travelers.

U.S.-BASED ADVENTURE TOUR OPERATORS

These agencies and operators specialize in well-organized and coordinated tours that cover your entire stay. Many travelers prefer to have everything arranged and confirmed before arriving in Costa Rica, and this is a good idea for first-timers and during the high season. *Be warned:* Most of these operators are not cheap, with 10-day tours generally costing in the neighborhood of $2,500 per person, not including airfare to Costa Rica.

Abercrombie & Kent ✦ (© 800/323-7308; www.abercrombiekent.com) is a luxury-tour company that offers upscale trips around the globe, and it has several tours of Costa Rica on its menu. It specializes in 9-day highlight tours hitting Monteverde, Arenal, and Tortuguero. Service is relatively personalized and the guides are top-notch. The cost is around $2,500 to $3,000 per adult, not including international airfare.

Butterfield & Robinson ✦ (© 800/678-1147; www.butterfield.com) is another company specializing in the very high-end market. One of its most interesting options is a trip designed for families with children over 8 years old. The trip provides a wealth of activities and adventures for parents and children to enjoy both together and apart. An 8-day/7-night trip costs around $5,000.

Costa Rica Experts ✦ (© 800/827-9046 or 773/935-1009; www.crexpert.com) offers a large menu of a la carte and scheduled departures, as well as day trips and adventure packages.

Overseas Adventure Travel (© 800/493-6824; www.oattravel.com) offers good-value natural history and "soft adventure" itineraries, with optional add-on excursions. Tours are limited to 16 people and are guided by naturalists. All accommodations are in small hotels, lodges, or tent camps. The "Real Affordable Costa Rica" 13-day package lives up to its name at $1,490 per person, including round-trip airfare from Dallas, Houston, or Miami.

Tico Travel ✦ (© 800/493-8426; www.ticotravel.com) has offices in both the United States and Costa Rica. It specializes in surfing and sportfishing packages, but it can put together a wide range of tours arrangements.

In addition to these companies, many environmental organizations, including the **Sierra Club** (© 415/977-5522; www.sierraclub.org), the **Smithsonian Institute** (© 877/338-8687 or 202/357-4700; www.smithsonianjourneys.org), and the **National Audubon Society** (© 800/967-7425 or 212/979-8947; www.audubon.org), periodically offer organized trips to Costa Rica.

COSTA RICAN TOUR AGENCIES

Because many U.S.-based companies subcontract portions of their tours to established Costa Rican companies, some travelers like to set up their tours directly with these companies, thereby cutting out the middleman. That means that these packages are often less expensive than those offered by U.S. companies, but it doesn't mean they are cheap. You're still paying for the convenience of having all your arrangements handled for you.

Scores of agencies in San José offer a plethora of adventure options. These agencies can arrange everything from white-water rafting to sightseeing at one of the nearby volcanoes or a visit to a butterfly farm. Although it's generally quite easy to arrange a day trip at the last minute, other tours are offered only when there are enough interested people or on set dates. It pays to contact a few of the companies before you leave the United States and find out what they might be doing when you arrive.

Coast to Coast Adventures ★★ (© 280-8054; www.ctocadventures.com) has a unique excursion involving no motor vehicles. The company's namesake 2-week trip spans the country, with participants traveling on horses and rafts, by mountain bikes, and on foot. Custom-designed trips (with a minimum of motorized transport) of shorter duration are also available.

Costa Rica Expeditions ★★ (© 257-0766; www.costaricaexpeditions.com) offers everything from 10-day tours covering the whole country, to 3-day/2-night and 2-day/1-night tours of Monteverde Biological Cloud Forest Reserve, Tortuguero National Park, and Corcovado National Park, where they run their own lodges. It also offers 1- to 2-day white-water rafting trips and other excursions. All excursions include transportation, meals, and lodging. Its tours are some of the most expensive in the country, but it is the most consistently reliable outfitter as well (and its customer service is excellent). If you want to go out on your own, Costa Rica Expeditions can supply you with just transportation from place to place.

Costa Rica Sun Tours ★★ (© 296-7757; www.crsuntours.com) offers a wide range of tours and adventures, and specializes in multiday tours that include stays at small country lodges for travelers interested in experiencing nature.

Ecole Travel ★ (© 223-2240; www.ecoletravel.com) offers a range of affordable tours and day trips around the country. Although the company often uses its own guides for longer trips, many of its day trips are subcontracted out. Its tours are popular with students and European travelers, including a fair number of backpackers.

Horizontes ★★ (© 222-2022; www.horizontes.com) is not a specifically adventure-oriented operator, but it offers a wide range of individual, group, and package tours. The company generally hires responsible and knowledgeable guides.

OTEC Viajes (© 256-0633; www.otec.co.cr) offers a range of tour options and specializes in student and discount travel.

Serendipity Adventures ★★ (© 877/507-1358 in the U.S. and Canada, or 558-1000; www.serendipity-costarica.com), an adventure-travel operator, offers everything from ballooning to mountain biking, and sea kayaking to canyoning, as well as most of the popular white-water rafting trips.

2 Activities A to Z

Each listing in this section describes the best places to practice a particular sport or activity and lists tour operators and outfitters. If you want to focus on only one active sport during your Costa Rican stay, these companies are your best bets for quality equipment and knowledgeable service.

Adventure activities and tourism, by their very nature, carry certain risks and dangers. In the past couple of years, there have been several deaths and dozens of minor injuries in activities ranging from mountain biking to white-water rafting, to canopy tours. I try to list only the most reputable and safest of companies. However, if you ever have any doubt as to the safety of the guide, equipment, or activity, it's better to be safe than sorry. Moreover, know your limits and abilities, and don't try to exceed them.

BIKING

There are several significant regional and international touring races in Costa Rica each year, but as a general rule, the major roads are dangerous and inhospitable for cyclists. They're narrow, there's usually no shoulder, and most drivers show little care or consideration for those on two wheels. The options are much more appealing for mountain bikers and off-track riders, however. Fat-tire explorations are relatively new to Costa Rica but are growing fast. If you plan to do a lot of biking and are very attached to your rig, bring your own. However, several companies in San José and elsewhere rent bikes, and the quality of the equipment is improving all the time. I've listed rental shops in each of the regional chapters that follow.

The area around **Lake Arenal** and **Arenal Volcano** wins my vote as the best place for mountain biking in Costa Rica. The scenery's great, with primary forests, waterfalls, and plenty of trails. And nearby Tabacón Hot Springs is a perfect place for those with aching muscles to unwind at the end of the day. See chapter 6 for full details.

TOUR OPERATORS & OUTFITTERS

BiCosta Rica (② 446-7585; www.bruncas.com/bicostarica.html) runs small group tours around the country; it offers some fixed itineraries or can custom-design one around your interests.

Coast to Coast Adventures (② 280-8054; www.ctocadventures.com) offers mountain-biking itineraries, among its many tour options.

Costa Rica Biking Adventures (② 225-6591; www.bikingincostarica.com) is a local outfit offering day trips and multiday excursions around the country using high-quality Trek and Cannondale bikes.

Experience Plus/Specialty Tours ★★ (② 800/685-4565 in the U.S. and Canada; www.experienceplus.com) offers guided group and assisted individual bike tours around the country. This is the only company I know of to use touring bikes. It also offers guided group hiking tours.

Serendipity Adventures (② 877/507-1358 in the U.S. and Canada, or 558-1000; www.serendipity-costarica.com) offers several mountain-biking trips, among its many other expeditions.

BIRD-WATCHING

With more than 850 species of resident and migrant birds identified throughout the country, Costa Rica abounds with great bird-watching sites. Lodges with the best bird-watching include **Savegre Lodge,** in Cerro de la Muerte, off the road to San Isidro de El General (quetzal sightings are almost guaranteed); **La Paloma Lodge** in Drake Bay, where you can sit on the porch of your cabin as the avian parade goes by; **Arenal Observatory Lodge,** on the flanks of Arenal Volcano; **La Selva Biological Station,** in Puerto Viejo de Sarapiquí; **Aviarios del Caribe,** just north of Cahuita; **Lapa Ríos** and **Bosque del Cabo,** on the Osa Peninsula; **Rainbow Adventures,** on Playa Cativa along the Golfo Dulce; **La Laguna del Lagarto Lodge,** up by the Nicaraguan border; and **Tiskita Lodge,** down by the Panamanian border.

⌐Tips A Bird-Watcher's Bible

Serious bird-watchers will find *A Guide to the Birds of Costa Rica,* by F. Gary Stiles and Alexander Skutch (Cornell University Press, 1990), to be essential. For more casual enthusiasts, there's a series of laminated plates covering specific regions that you'll find for sale at many local bookstores and some gift shops. Bird-watchers might also enjoy Dennis Rodgers's *Site Guides: Costa Rica & Panama* (Cinclus Publications, 1997), which details each country's bird-watching bounty by site and region.

Some of the best parks and preserves for serious birders are **Monteverde Biological Cloud Forest Reserve** (for resplendent quetzals and hummingbirds); **Corcovado National Park** (for scarlet macaws); **Caño Negro Wildlife Refuge** (for wading birds, including jabiru storks); **Wilson Botanical Gardens** and the **Las Cruces Biological Station,** near San Vito (the thousands of flowering plants here are bird magnets); **Guayabo, Negritos,** and **Pájaros Islands biological reserves** in the Gulf of Nicoya (for magnificent frigate birds and brown boobies); **Palo Verde National Park** (for ibises, jacanas, storks, and roseate spoonbills); **Tortuguero National Park** (for great green macaws); and **Rincón de la Vieja National Park** (for parakeets and curassows). Rafting trips down the Corobicí and Bebedero rivers near Liberia, boat trips to or at Tortuguero National Park, and hikes in any cloud forest also provide good bird-watching.

In San José, your best bets are to head toward the lush grounds and gardens of the University of Costa Rica, or to Parque del Este, a little farther east in the foothills just outside of town.

U.S.-BASED TOUR OPERATORS

Field Guides (© **800/728-4953** or 512/263-7295; www.fieldguides.com) is a specialty bird-watching travel operator. Its 16-day tour of Costa Rica costs $3,875, not including airfare. Group size is limited to 14 participants.

Wings (© **888/293-6443** or 520/320-9868; www.wingsbirds.com) is also a specialty bird-watching travel operator with more than 27 years of experience in the field. Its 16-day Costa Rica trip covers all the major bird-watching zones in the country and costs around $4,100, not including airfare. Group size is usually between 6 and 14 people.

COSTA RICAN TOUR AGENCIES

In addition to the agencies listed below, check in with the **Birding Club of Costa Rica** ★★ (costaricabirding@hotmail.com), which runs monthly outings and provides you with the opportunity to connect with local English-speaking birders.

Both **Costa Rica Expeditions** ★★ (© **257-0766**; www.costaricaexpeditions. com) and **Costa Rica Sun Tours** ★★ (© **296-7757**; www.crsuntours.com) are well-established companies with very competent and experienced guides who offer a variety of tours to some of the better birding spots in Costa Rica.

BUNGEE JUMPING

Tropical Bungee (© **248-2212**; www.bungee.co.cr) will let you jump off an 80m (262-ft.) bridge over the Río Colorado for $60, including transportation from San José and a video of your jump. A second jump will cost you another $30. The jump site is located on a small bridge over the Río Colorado about 37km (23 miles) northwest of San José, just off the Pan-American Highway. There are obvious and well-placed signs on the highway. Someone should be there from 9am to 3pm every day. They prefer for you to have a reservation, but if you show up on your own, they'll probably let you jump, unless they have huge groups booked ahead of you.

CAMPING

Heavy rains, difficult access, and limited facilities make camping a challenge in Costa Rica. Nevertheless, a backpack and tent will get you far from the crowds and into some of the most pristine and undeveloped nooks and crannies of the country. Those who relish sleeping out on a beach but wouldn't mind a bit more

Where to See the Resplendent Quetzal

Revered by pre-Columbian cultures throughout Central America, the resplendent quetzal has been called the most beautiful bird on earth. Ancient Aztec and Maya Indians believed that the robin-size quetzal protected them in battle. The males of this species have brilliant red breasts; iridescent emerald green heads, backs, and wings; and white tail feathers complemented by a pair of iridescent green tail feathers that are more than .5m (1¾ ft.) long.

The belief that these endangered birds live only in the dense cloud forests cloaking the higher slopes of Central America's mountains was instrumental in bringing many areas of cloud forest under protection as quetzal habitats. (Since then, researchers have discovered that the birds do not, in fact, spend their entire lives here.) After nesting, between March and July, resplendent quetzals migrate down to lower slopes in search of food. These lower slopes have not been preserved in most cases, and now conservationists are trying to salvage enough lower-elevation forests to help the quetzals survive. It is hoped that enough land will soon be set aside to ensure the perpetuation of this magnificent species.

Although for many years **Monteverde Biological Cloud Forest Reserve** was *the* place to see quetzals, throngs of people crowding the reserve's trails now make the pursuit more difficult. Other places where you can see quetzals are in the **Los Angeles Cloud Forest Reserve** near San Ramón, in **Tapantí National Wildlife Refuge,** and in **Chirripó National Park.** Perhaps the best place to spot a quetzal is at one of the specialized lodges located along the Cerro de la Muerte between San José and San Isidro de El General.

luxury (beds, someone to prepare meals for you, and running water) might want to consider staying at the **Corcovado Lodge Tent Camp** on the Osa Peninsula (p. 306) or at the **Almonds & Corals Tent Camp** down in Manzanillo (p. 344). Camping is forbidden in some national parks, so read through the descriptions for each park carefully before you pack a tent.

If you'd like to participate in an organized camping trip, contact **Coast to Coast Adventures** (© 280-8054; www.ctocadventures.com) or **Serendipity Adventures** (© 877/507-1358 in the U.S. and Canada, or 558-1000; www.serendipity-costarica.com).

Another option is to hook up with a **Green Tortoise** (© 800/867-8647 or 415/956-7500 in the U.S.; www.greentortoise.com) tour of Costa Rica. This bus tour/camping outfit runs around five trips each year to Costa Rica, with a 15-day tour of the country costing around $750, not including transportation to Costa Rica.

In my opinion, the best place to pop up a tent on the beach is in **Santa Rosa National Park** or at the Puerto Vargas campsite in **Cahuita National Park.** The best camping trek is, without a doubt, a hike through **Corcovado National Park** or a climb up **Mount Chirripó.**

CANOPY TOURS

Canopy tours are officially all the rage in Costa Rica, largely because they are such an exciting and unique way to experience tropical rainforests. It's estimated that some two-thirds of a typical rainforest's species live in the canopy (the uppermost, branching layer of the forest). From the relative luxury of Rain Forest Aerial Tram's high-tech funicular to the rope-and-climbing-gear rigs of more basic operations, a trip into the canopy will give you a bird's-eye view of a Neotropical forest. There are now canopy-tour operations in or close to nearly every major tourist destination in the country, including Monteverde, Manuel Antonio, La Fortuna, Tabacón, Punta Islita, Villablanca, and Rincón de la Vieja, as well as on Tortuga Island and around Guanacaste and the Osa Peninsula.

Most canopy tours involve strapping yourself into a climbing harness and being winched up to a platform some 30m (98 ft.) above the forest floor, or doing the work yourself. Many of these operations have a series of treetop platforms connected by taut cables. Once up on the first platform, you click your harness into a pulley and glide across the cable to the next (slightly lower) platform, using your hand (protected by a thick leather glove) as a brake. When you reach the last platform, you usually rappel back down to the ground. (Don't worry—they'll teach even the most nervous neophyte.)

Although this can be a lot of fun, do be careful because these tours are popping up all over the place and there is precious little regulation of the activity. Some of the tours are set up by fly-by-night operators. (Obviously, I haven't listed any of those.) Be especially sure that you feel comfortable and confident with the safety standards, guides, and equipment before embarking. The most reputable operator is **The Original Canopy Tours** (see below), but there are other safe, well-run operations around the country. My favorite canopy tours are the Original Canopy Tour's **Kazam Cañon** tour at Rincón de la Vieja, which zigzags back and forth through a deep canyon, and its operation in **Monteverde,** which features an ascent up the hollow interior of a giant strangler fig tree. Before you sign on to any tour, ask whether you have to hoist yourself to the top under your own steam, and then make your decision accordingly. Recently, there has been some controversy: The folks at The Original Canopy Tours were granted a patent by the Costa Rican patent board, and it has been trying to shut down and/or sell licensing to other operators

Another option is to try one of the tram or gondola tours through the canopy. The folks at Rain Forest Aerial Tram (see below) currently have two such operations, and there's yet another ski lift-style gondola ride at the new **Turu BaRi Tropical Park** (© 428-6070; www.turubari.com) outside of San José. See "Side Trips from San José" in chapter 4 for more information.

Rain Forest Aerial Tram Caribbean (© 257-5961; www.rainforest tram.com) is located some 50 minutes from San José. For $50 (transportation extra), this modern tram takes you on a 90-minute trip through the rainforest canopy in the comfort and safety of an enclosed cab. The entrance fee includes an additional guided hike and access to its trail system. The best thing here isn't necessarily the tram ride, which I find somewhat disappointing, but the fact that this makes a good spot for a full-day excursion relatively close to San José. The outfit has a new sister project on the central Pacific coast just outside of Jacó. See "Side Trips from San José" in chapter 4 and "Playa de Jacó" in chapter 7 for more information.

The Original Canopy Tours (© 257-5149; www.canopytour.com) is the largest canopy-tour operator, with sites in Monteverde, Aguas Zarcas,

> **Tips   Beach Blanket, Bingo**
>
> If you plan to spend time at the beach, be sure to pack your own beach towel or mat. Only the more upscale hotels in Costa Rica tend to provide them.

Rincón de la Vieja, Tabacón, and Mahogany Park, as well as along the banks of the Pacuare River.

CRUISING

Cruising options in Costa Rica range from transient cruisers setting up a quick charter business to converted fishing boats taking a few guests out to see the sunset. For information on the major cruise lines that ply the waters off Costa Rica, see "By Cruise Ship" under "Getting There," in chapter 2.

The most popular cruise option in Costa Rica is a day trip from San José (the boats actually leave from Puntarenas) to **Isla Tortuga** in the Nicoya Gulf (see "Side Trips from San José," in chapter 4). Alternately, you can book a cruise to Tortuga from Playa Montezuma at the tip of the Nicoya Peninsula (see chapter 5 for details). It's much cheaper from here (around $40 per person), but the excursion doesn't include the gourmet lunch that's usually featured on cruises leaving from San José.

If diesel fumes and engine noise bother you, the best places to charter a sailboat are in Playa del Coco, Playa Hermosa, and Playa Flamingo in Guanacaste province (see chapter 5); Playa Herradura and Quepos, along the central Pacific coast (see chapter 7); and Golfito, along the southern Pacific coast (see chapter 8). You can get information about sailboat rides and charters at any one of the larger lodgings in these areas. If you're at Flamingo Beach, head to the marina, where you should be able to find a captain who will take you out. My favorite place to charter a sailboat is **Golfito.** From here, it's a pleasant, peaceful day's sail around the Golfo Dulce (see chapter 8).

DIVING & SNORKELING

Many islands, reefs, caves, and rocks lie off the coast of Costa Rica, providing excellent spots for underwater exploration. Visibility varies with season and location. Generally, heavy rainfall tends to swell the rivers and muddy the waters, even well offshore. Banana plantations and their runoff have destroyed most of the Caribbean reefs, although there's still good diving at **Isla Uvita,** just off the coast of Limón, and in **Manzanillo,** down near the Panamanian border. Most divers choose Pacific dive spots such as **Caño Island, Bat Island,** and the **Catalina Islands,** where you're likely to spot manta rays, moray eels, white-tipped sharks, and plenty of smaller fish and coral species. But the ultimate in Costa Rican dive experiences is a week to 10 days spent on a chartered boat, diving off the coast of **Cocos Island** (see "Diving Trips to Isla del Coco" on p. 249).

Snorkeling is not incredibly common or rewarding in Costa Rica. The rain, runoff, and wave conditions that drive scuba divers well offshore tend to make coastal and shallow-water conditions less than optimal. If the weather is calm and the water is clear, you might just get lucky. Ask at your hotel or check the different beach listings to find snorkeling options and operators up and down Costa Rica's coasts. The best snorkeling experience to be had in Costa Rica is on the reefs off **Manzanillo Beach** in the southern Caribbean coast, particularly in the calm months of September and October.

DIVING OUTFITTERS & OPERATORS

In addition to the companies listed below, check the listings at specific beach and port destinations in the regional chapters.

Aggressor Fleet Limited ★★ (© 800/348-2628 or 985/385-2628 in the U.S., or 257-0191; www.aggressor.com) runs the 36m (118-ft.) *Okeanos Aggressor* on regular trips out to Cocos Island.

Diving Mania (© 291-2936; www.divingmania.net) is a San José–based outfit that offers equipment rental, certification classes, and tours.

Diving Safaris de Costa Rica ★ (© 877/853-0538 in the U.S., or 672-0012; www.costaricadiving.net) is perhaps the largest, most professional, and best-established dive operation in the country. Based out of the Sol Playa Hermosa Hotel in Playa Hermosa, this outfitter is also a local pioneer in nitrox diving.

Undersea Hunter ★★ (© 800/203-2120 in the U.S., or 228-6613; www.underseahunter.com) offers the *Undersea Hunter* and its sister ship, the *Sea Hunter,* two pioneers of the live-aboard diving excursions to Cocos Island.

FISHING

Anglers in Costa Rican waters have landed nearly 100 world-record catches, including blue marlin, Pacific sailfish, dolphin, wahoo, yellowfin tuna, guapote, and snook. Whether you want to head offshore looking for a big sail, wrestle a tarpon near a Caribbean river mouth, or choose a quiet spot on Arenal Lake to cast for guapote, you'll find it here. You can land a marlin anywhere along the Pacific coast.

Many of the Pacific port and beach towns—Quepos, Puntarenas, Playa del Coco, Tamarindo, Flamingo, Golfito, Drake Bay, Zancudo—support large charter fleets and have hotels that cater to anglers; see chapters 5, 7, and 8 for recommended boats, captains, and lodges. Costs for fishing trips usually range between $400 and $1,500 per day (depending on the size of the boat) for boat, captain, tackle, drinks, and lunch, so the cost per person depends on the size of the group.

Costa Rica Outdoors ★★ (© 800/308-3394 in the U.S., or 282-6743; www.costaricaoutdoors.com) is a well-established operation run by longtime resident, fisherman, and outdoor writer Jerry Ruhlow that specializes in booking fishing trips around the country.

FISHING LODGES

For more detailed information about these lodges, see their full listings in chapters 8 and 9.

Aguila de Osa Inn ★ (© 296-2190; www.aguiladeosainn.com) is a luxury lodge catering to anglers in Drake Bay. See p. 297.

The **Río Colorado Lodge** (© 800/243-9777 in the U.S. and Canada, or 232-4063; www.riocoloradolodge.com) is located at the Barra del Colorado National Wildlife Refuge. See p. 320.

Roy's Zancudo Lodge (© 877/529-6980 in the U.S., or 776-0008; www.royszancudolodge.com) is located in Playa Zancudo. See p. 314.

Silver King Lodge ★★ (© 800/847-3474 in the U.S., or 381-1403; www.silverkinglodge.com) is a luxury lodge at Barra del Colorado. See p. 321.

GOLF

Costa Rica is not one of the world's great golfing destinations—well, not yet, anyway. There are currently six regulation 18-hole courses open to the public and/or visitors, but several others are either under construction or in the planning stages, with a potential boom shaping up in Guanacaste.

The **Meliá Cariari course** ★★ (© 800/336-3542 in the U.S. and Canada, or 239-0022; www.solmelia.com) is just outside of San José. Greens fees here are

$50, but caddies are mandatory. You should expect to pay your caddy around $20, and pay an extra $25 for a cart. However, you have to be a member or a guest at either the Meliá or Herradura hotels. Another option for golfers staying in the metropolitan area is the 18-hole course **Parque Valle del Sol** ✹ (© 282-9222; www.vallesol.com) in the western suburb of Santa Ana. Greens fees here run $75 for 18 holes, including a cart.

The Meliá chain also runs the **Garra de León course** ✹✹ at the **Paradisus Playa Conchal** resort (© 654-4123; www.solmelia.com) up in Guanacaste. Greens fees here are $140, including a cart. With advance notice and depending on available tee times, this course is currently open to guests at other hotels in the region.

Another major resort course is at the **Los Sueños Marriott Beach & Golf Resort** ✹✹ in Playa Herradura (© 800/228-9290 in the U.S., or 630-9028; www.marriott.com). Greens fees, including a cart, run around $100 for guests of the hotel and $150 for the general public.

Hacienda Pinilla ✹ (© 680-7000; www.haciendapinilla.com) is an 18-hole links-style course located south of Tamarindo. This might just be the most challenging course in the country, and the facilities, though limited, are top-notch. Currently, the course is open to golfers staying at hotels around the area, with advance reservation. Greens fees run around $125 for 18 holes, including a cart.

The newest course to open in Costa Rica is in Guanacaste at the **Four Seasons Resort** (© 212/688-2440 in the U.S., or 696-0098; www.fourseasons.com), but currently it is open only to guests at the hotel.

Golfers who want the most up-to-date information, or those who are interested in a package deal that includes play on a variety of courses, should contact **Costa Rica Golf Adventures** ✹ (© 877/258-2688 in the U.S., or 293-9785; www.golfcr.com).

HANG GLIDING, PARAGLIDING & BALLOONING

Paragliding with a pilot in a tandem rig is taking off (pardon the pun) in the cliff areas around Caldera, just south of Puntarenas. The folks at **Tropical Bungee** (© 248-2212; www.bungee.co.cr) are offering half-hour flights in a tandem rig for $60. They can also offer pilot training classes.

Serendipity Adventures (© 877/507-1358 in the U.S. and Canada, or 558-1000; www.serendipity-costarica.com) will take you up, up, and away in a hot-air balloon on a variety of single- or multiday tours, either in Turrialba, in Naranjo, or near Arenal Volcano. A basic flight costs $900 for up to five people or 800 pounds.

Finally, you can try hang gliding in a tandem rig just outside of Jacó. The folks at **Hang Glide Costa Rica** (© 778-8710; www.hangglidecostarica.com) offer a ride that begins with a tow by an ultralight, followed by a half-hour or so of gentle gliding for $125 per person.

HORSEBACK RIDING

Costa Rica's rural roots are evident in the continued use of horses for real work and transportation throughout the country. Visitors will find that horses are easily available for riding, whether you want to take a sunset trot along the beach, ride through the cloud forest, or take a multiday trek through the northern zone.

Most travelers simply saddle up for a couple of hours, but those looking for a more specifically equestrian-based visit should check in with the following folks.

Coast to Coast Adventures (© 280-8054; www.ctocadventures.com) specializes in 2-week trips spanning the country via horseback, raft, or mountain

---

Tips **Tai Chi in Paradise**

For the past 15 years, tai chi master and two-time U.S. national champion Chris Luth has been leading weeklong retreats to Costa Rica, combining intensive classes in this ancient Chinese martial art with rainforest hikes, river rafting, and just enough beach time. For more information, contact **T'ai Chi in Paradise** (℃ **858/259-1396;** www.taichiinparadise.com).

---

bike, as well as on foot, with no motor vehicles involved. Other trips are also available.

Horseback Ride Costa Rica (℃ **232-3113;** www.horsebackridecostarica.com) puts together custom horseback trips and treks around the country.

Nature Lodge Finca Los Caballos ⋆ (℃/fax **642-0124;** www.nature lodge.net) has the healthiest horses in the Montezuma area. See p. 199 for complete details.

Serendipity Adventures (℃ **877/507-1358** in the U.S. and Canada, or 558-1000; www.serendipity-costarica.com) offers many activities, including horseback treks and tours.

MOTORCYCLES

Visiting bikers can either cruise the highways or try some off-road biking around Costa Rica. All the caveats about driving conditions and driving customs in Costa Rica apply equally for bikers. If you want to rent a Harley-Davidson for cruising around the country, see the folks at **María Alexandra Tours** (℃ **289-5552;** www.mariaalexandra.com). These folks conduct guided bike tours or will rent you a well-equipped late-model Harley by the day or the week. If your tastes run to off-road riding, check in with **Motoadventures** (℃ **228-8494;** www.moto adventuring.com), which runs guided multiday tours on Honda dirt bikes.

ROCK CLIMBING

Although this is a nascent sport in Costa Rica, the possibilities are promising. There are several challenging rock formations close to San José and along the Cerro de la Muerte, as well as great climbing opportunities on Mount Chirripó. The folks at **Tropical Bungee** (℃ **248-2212;** www.bungee.co.cr) are the most dependable operators in this field, and they regularly organize climbing outings. Alternatively, you could stop in at **Mundo Aventura** (℃ **221-6934;** www. maventura.com), an adventure and climbing gear store with an indoor climbing wall and in-house tour company.

SPAS & YOGA RETREATS

Although Costa Rica still doesn't have any world-class destination spas, the conditions here are ripe, and some early efforts are beginning to mature and flourish. I expect the trend to boom here in the coming years.

The **Four Seasons Resort** ⋆⋆ (℃ **800/819-5053** in the U.S., or 696-0098; www.fourseasons.com/costarica) on the Papagayo Peninsula has raised the bar on resort spa experiences in Costa Rica. This new luxury resort has ample facilities and treatment options. See p. 156.

Fusion Natural Spa ⋆, Playa Ocotal, in the Guanacaste region (℃ **670-0914;** www.fusionnaturalspa.com), is a day spa that offers a wide range of massage, aromatherapy, body-wrap, and exfoliating treatments. Half-, full-, and multiday packages are available. See "Playa del Coco & Playa Ocotal," in chapter 5.

Hotel Occidental El Tucano (℗ **460-6000;** www.occidental-hoteles.com), the oldest full-service spa facility in Costa Rica, offers a wide range of treatments in a lush forested setting, with natural hot springs. It's located near Arenal Volcano and La Fortuna. See p. 223.

Samasati 👯, Puerto Viejo de Talamanca (℗ **800/563-9643** in the U.S., or 224-1870; www.samasati.com), is a lovely yoga retreat in some dense forest on a hillside above the Caribbean. Accommodations here range from budget to rustically luxurious. See "Puerto Viejo," in chapter 9.

Serenity Spa 👯 (℗ **643-4094;** serenityspa@racsa.co.cr) started out with a little storefront spa in Jacó but now currently contracts out the spa services at several large resorts up and down the Pacific coast. At last count, it was running the spas at the Marriott Los Sueños, Villas Caletas, Hotel Sí Como No, Hotel Club del Mar, and the San José Marriott, plus its original location in Jacó. See "Playa de Jacó," in chapter 7.

Sueño Azul Resort 👯, Las Horquetas de Sarapiquí (℗ **764-3152;** www. suenoazulresort.com), is a nature lodge and retreat center. This place has close ties to the Omega Institute in Rhinebeck, New York, which brings down a steady stream of visiting teachers and groups for workshops on everything from yoga to meditation to Sufi dancing. See p. 211.

Tabacón Hot Springs Resort & Spa 👯👯, Tabacón (℗ **256-1500;** www. tabacon.com), is currently the country's premier spa, with its spectacular hot springs, lush gardens, and volcano view. A complete range of spa services and treatments are available at reasonable prices. The only downside here is that the volume of daily traffic to the hot springs themselves robs the place of the serenity one would want in a true destination spa. See p. 107.

Xandari Resort & Spa 👯👯, Alajuela (℗ **443-2020;** www.xandari.com), is a unique and distinctive little luxury hotel that has recently added on some top-notch spa facilities and services. This is a good choice if you're looking for a day or 2 of pampering, or for day treatments while staying in San José. See p. 107.

SURFING

When *Endless Summer II,* the sequel to the all-time surf classic, was filmed, the production crew brought its boards and cameras to Costa Rica. Point and beach breaks that work year-round are located all along Costa Rica's immense coastline. **Playas Hermosa, Jacó,** and **Dominical,** on the central Pacific coast, and **Tamarindo** and **Playa Guiones,** in Guanacaste, are becoming mini–surf meccas. **Salsa Brava** in Puerto Viejo is a steep and fast wave that peels off both right and left over shallow coral. It has a habit of breaking boards, but the daredevils keep coming back for more. Beginners and folks looking to learn should stick to the mellower sections of **Jacó** and **Tamarindo**—surf lessons are offered at both beaches. Crowds are starting to gather at the more popular breaks, but you can still stumble onto secret spots on the **Osa** and **Nicoya peninsulas** and along the northern Guanacaste coast. Costa Rica's signature wave is still found at **Playa Pavones,** which is reputed to have one of the longest lefts in the world. The cognoscenti, however, also swear by places such as **Playa Grande, Playa Negra, Matapalo, Malpais,** and **Witch's Rock.** An avid surfer's best bet is to rent a dependable four-wheel-drive vehicle with a rack and take a surfin' safari around the breaks of Guanacaste.

If you're looking for an organized surf vacation, contact **Tico Travel** (℗ **800/ 493-8426** in the U.S.; www.ticotravel.com), or check out **www.crsurf.com**. For swell reports, general surf information, live wave-cams, and great links pages,

In Search of Turtles

Few places in the world have as many sea-turtle nesting sites as Costa Rica. Along both coasts, five species of these huge marine reptiles come ashore at specific times of the year to dig nests in the sand and lay their eggs. Sea turtles are endangered throughout the world due to overhunting, accidental deaths in fishing nets, development on beaches that once served as nesting areas, and the collection and sale (often illegally) of their eggs. International trade in sea-turtle products is already prohibited by most countries (including the U.S.), but sea-turtle numbers continue to dwindle.

Among the species of sea turtles that nest on Costa Rica's beaches are the **olive Ridley** (known for their mass egg-laying migrations, or *arribadas*), **leatherback, hawksbill, green,** and **Pacific green turtle.** Excursions to see nesting turtles have become common, and they are fascinating, but please make sure that you and/or your guide do not disturb the turtles. Any light source (other than red-tinted flashlights) can confuse female turtles and cause them to return to the sea without laying their eggs. In fact, as more development takes place on the Costa Rican coast, hotel lighting might cause the number of nesting turtles to drop. Luckily, many of the nesting beaches have been protected as national parks.

Here are the main places to see nesting sea turtles: **Santa Rosa National Park** (near Liberia), **Las Baulas National Marine Park** (near Tamarindo), **Ostional National Wildlife Refuge** (near Playa Nosara), and **Tortuguero National Park** (on the northern Caribbean coast).

See the regional chapters for a description of the resident turtles and their respective nesting seasons, as well as listings of local tour operators and companies that arrange trips to see sea turtles nesting.

point your browser to **www.surfline.com**. Tico Travel also has a surf break map with descriptions available online at **http://centralamerica.com/cr/surf/surfmap.htm**. Although killer sets are possible at any particular spot at any time of the year, depending upon swell direction, local winds, and distant storms, in broad terms, the northern coast of Guanacaste works best from December to April; the central and southern Pacific coasts work best from April to November; and the Caribbean coast's short big-wave season is December through March.

WHITE-WATER RAFTING, KAYAKING & CANOEING

Whether you're a first-time rafter or a world-class kayaker, Costa Rica's got some white water suited to your abilities. Rivers rise and fall with the rainfall, but you can get wet and wild here even in the dry season. The best white-water rafting ride is still the scenic **Pacuare River,** although, unfortunately, it is slated to be dammed for a hydroelectric project. If you're just experimenting with river rafting, stick to Class II and III rivers, such as the **Reventazón, Sarapiquí, Peñas Blancas,** and **Savegre.** If you already know which end of the paddle goes in the water, there are plenty of Class IV and V sections to run.

Die-hard river rats should try to find a copy of *The Rivers of Costa Rica,* by Michael W. Mayfield and Rafael E. Gallo (Menasha Ridge Press, 1988), which is loaded with technical data and route tips on every rideable river in the country.

Aventuras Naturales ✦ (© **800/514-0411** in the U.S., or 225-3939; www.
toenjoynature.com) is a major rafting operator that runs daily trips on the most
popular rivers in Costa Rica. Its Pacuare Jungle Lodge is a great place to spend
the night on one of its 2-day rafting trips.

Canoe Costa Rica (©/fax **732/350-3963** in the U.S., or 282-3579; www.
canoecostarica.com) is the only outfit I know of that specializes in canoe trips;
it works primarily with custom-designed tours and itineraries, although it does
have several set departure trips each year.

Costa Rica White Water ✦ (© **257-0766;** www.costaricaexpeditions.com)
was the first building block in the Costa Rica Expeditions empire. It remains
one of the best-run rafting operations.

If you're out on the Osa Peninsula, hook up with **Escondido Trex** ✦ (©/fax
735-5210; www.escondidotrex.com).

Rancho Leona (© **841-5341;** www.rancholeona.com) is a small hostel-like
roadside hotel in Heredia that caters to both experienced and beginning kayak-
ers looking to ply the Río Sarapiquí. See chapter 6.

Ríos Tropicales ✦ (© **233-6455;** www.riostropicales.com) is one of the major
operators in Costa Rica, operating on most of the runnable rivers. Lodgings
include a very comfortable lodge on the banks of the Río Pacuare for the 2-day
trips.

WINDSURFING & KITEBOARDING

Windsurfing is not very popular on the high seas here, where winds are fickle
and rental options are limited, even at beach hotels. However, **Lake Arenal** is
considered one of the top spots in the world for high-wind boardsailing. During the winter months, many of the regulars from Washington's Columbia River
Gorge take up residence around the nearby town of Tilarán. Small boards, water
starts, and fancy gibes are the norm. The best time for windsurfing on Lake Arenal is between December and March. The same winds that buffet Lake Arenal
make their way down to **Bahía Salinas** (also known as Bolaños Bay), near La
Cruz, Guanacaste, where you can get in some good windsurfing. Both spots
have also recently seen the opening of operations offering lessons and equipment
rentals in the new high-action sport of kiteboarding. See "La Cruz" in chapter 5
and "Along the Shores of Lake Arenal" in chapter 6 for more information.

3 Costa Rica's Top National Parks & Bioreserves

Costa Rica has 25 national parks, protecting more than 11% of the country.
They range in size from the 212-hectare (524-acre) Guayabo National Monument to the 189,696-hectare (468,549-acre) La Amistad National Park. Many
of these national parks are undeveloped tropical forests, with few services or
facilities available for visitors. Others, however, offer easier access to their wealth
of natural wonders.

Most of the national parks charge a $6-per-person per-day fee for any foreigner,
although some have begun charging slightly more and a few slightly less. Costa
Ricans and foreign residents continue to pay just $1. At parks where camping is
allowed, there is usually an additional charge of around $2 per person per day.

The following section is not a complete listing of all of Costa Rica's national
parks and protected areas, but rather a selective list of those parks that are of
greatest interest and accessibility. They're popular, but they're also among the
best. You'll find detailed information about food and lodging options near some
of the individual parks in the regional chapters that follow. As you'll see from the

descriptions, Costa Rica's national parks vary greatly in terms of attractions, facilities, and accessibility. For a map of the country's parks, see the inside back cover of this guide.

If you're looking for a camping adventure or an extended stay in one of the national parks, I recommend **Santa Rosa, Rincón de la Vieja, Chirripó, Corcovado,** or **Cahuita.** Any of the others are better suited for day trips or guided hikes, or in combination with your travels around the country.

For more information, call the national parks information line at ℭ **192,** or the main office at ℭ **283-8004.** You can also stop by the **National Parks Foundation office** (ℭ **257-2239**) in San José, located between Calle 23 and Avenida 15. Both offices are open Monday through Friday from 9am to 5pm.

SAN JOSE/CENTRAL VALLEY AREA

GUAYABO NATIONAL MONUMENT   This is the country's only significant pre-Columbian archaeological site. It's believed that Guayabo supported a population of about 10,000 people some 3,000 years ago. The park is set in a forested area rich in flora and fauna, although the ruins are quite small and limited when compared to sites in Mexico, Guatemala, and South America. **Location:** 19km (12 miles) northeast of Turrialba, which is 53km (33 miles) east of San José. See "Side Trips from San José," in chapter 4.

IRAZU VOLCANO NATIONAL PARK ⭐   Irazú Volcano is the highest (3,378m/11,080 ft.) of Costa Rica's four active volcanoes and a popular day trip from San José. A paved road leads right up to the crater, and the lookout also allows you a view of both oceans on a clear day. The volcano last erupted in 1963 on the same day U.S. President John F. Kennedy visited the country. There are an information center, picnic tables, restrooms, and a parking area here. **Location:** 55km (34 miles) east of San José. See "Holy Smoke!: Choosing the Volcano Trip That's Right for You," in chapter 4.

POAS VOLCANO NATIONAL PARK ⭐⭐   Poás is the other active volcano close to San José. The main crater is more than 1.6km (1 mile) wide, and it is constantly active with fumaroles and hot geysers. I slightly prefer Poás to Irazú because it is surrounded by dense cloud forests, and there are some nice gentle trails to hike here. Although the area around the volcano is lush, much of the growth is stunted due to the gasses and acid rain. The park sometimes closes when the gases get too feisty. There are nature trails, picnic tables, restrooms, and an information center. **Location:** 37km (23 miles) northwest of San José. See "Holy Smoke!: Choosing the Volcano Trip That's Right for You," in chapter 4.

GUANACASTE & THE NICOYA PENINSULA

BARRA HONDA NATIONAL PARK   Costa Rica's only underground national park, Barra Honda features a series of limestone caves that were once part of a coral reef some 60 million years ago. Today the caves are home to millions of bats and impressive stalactite and stalagmite formations. Only Terciopelo Cave is open to the public. There are a camping area, restrooms, and an information center here, as well as trails through the surrounding tropical dry forest. **Location:** 335km (208 miles) northwest of San José. See "Playa Sámara," in chapter 5.

PALO VERDE NATIONAL PARK   A must for bird-watchers, Palo Verde National Park is one of Costa Rica's best-kept secrets. This part of the Tempisque River lowlands supports a population of more than 50,000 waterfowl and forest bird species. Various ecosystems here include mangroves, savanna brush lands, and evergreen forests. There are camping facilities, an information center, and some nice new accommodations at the Organization for Tropical Studies (OTS) research station here. **Location:** 200km (124 miles) northwest of San José. Be warned that the park entrance is 28km (17 miles) off the highway down a very rugged dirt road; it's another 9km (5½ miles) to the OTS station and campsites. For more information, call the OTS (© **240-6696;** reservas@cro.ots.ac.cr). See "Liberia," in chapter 5.

RINCON DE LA VIEJA NATIONAL PARK ✦✦   This is a large tract of parkland that experiences high volcanic activity. There are numerous fumaroles and geysers, as well as hot springs, cold pools, and mud pots. There are also excellent hikes to the upper craters, as well as to several waterfalls. You should hire a guide for any hot-spring or mud-bath expeditions because inexperienced visitors have been burned. Camping is permitted at two separate sites, each of which has an information center, a picnic area, and restrooms. **Location:** 266km (165 miles) northwest of San José. See "Liberia," in chapter 5.

SANTA ROSA NATIONAL PARK ✦   Occupying a large section of Costa Rica's northwestern Guanacaste province, Santa Rosa contains the country's largest area of tropical dry forest, as well as important turtle-nesting sites and the historically significant La Casona monument. There are also caves for exploring. The beaches here are pristine and have basic camping facilities, and the waves make them quite popular with surfers. An information center, a picnic area, and restrooms are located at the main campsite and entrance. **Location:** 258km (160 miles) northwest of San José. For more information, you can call the park office at © **666-5051.** See "Exploring Santa Rosa National Park," in chapter 5.

THE NORTHERN ZONE

ARENAL NATIONAL PARK ✦✦   This new park, created to protect the ecosystem that surrounds Arenal Volcano, has few services or attractions. Basically, the government has set up a tollbooth on the access road leading to an up-close view of the volcano's lava flows. Most travelers and tour operators choose to forgo the entrance fee and watch the volcano from spots along the dirt road leading to the Arenal Observatory Lodge, or from the road to Tabacón, where the view is just as good as it is inside. However, there are several excellent hiking trails inside the park that explore cooled-off lava flows and the neighboring rainforest. **Location:** 129km (80 miles) northwest of San José. See "Arenal Volcano & La Fortuna," in chapter 6.

BRAULIO CARRILLO NATIONAL PARK   This park, which occupies a large area of the nation's central mountain range, is the park you pass through on your way from San José to the Caribbean coast. A deep rainforest, Braulio Carrillo receives an average of 177 inches of rain per year. There are beautiful rivers, majestic waterfalls, and more than 6,500 species of plants and animals. The park has an information center, picnic tables, restrooms, and hiking trails. Camping is allowed but is not very common or recommended. Be careful here. Make sure you park your car in and base your explorations from the park's main entrance, not just anywhere along the highway. There have been several robberies and attacks against visitors reported at trails leading into the park from the highway. This park also seems to have the highest incidence of lost hikers. **Location:** 22km (14 miles) north of San José. See "Puerto Viejo de Sarapiquí," in chapter 6.

CAÑO NEGRO NATIONAL WILDLIFE REFUGE ✦   A lowland swamp and drainage basin for several northern rivers, Caño Negro is excellent for bird-watching. There are a few basic cabinas and lodges in this area, but the most popular way to visit is on a combined van and boat trip from the La Fortuna/Arenal area. **Location:** 20km (12 miles) south of Los Chiles, near the Nicaraguan border. See "Arenal Volcano & La Fortuna," in chapter 6.

MONTEVERDE BIOLOGICAL CLOUD FOREST RESERVE ★★★　This private reserve might be the most famous patch of forest in Costa Rica. It covers some 26,000 acres of primary forest. Most of it is mid-elevation cloud forest, with a rich variety of flora and fauna. Epiphytes thrive in the cool, misty climate. The most famous resident here is the spectacular resplendent quetzal. There is a well-maintained trail system, as well as some of the best-trained and most experienced guides in the country. Nearby you can visit both the Santa Elena and Sendero Tranquilo reserves. **Location:** 167km (104 miles) northwest of San José. See "Monteverde," in chapter 6.

CENTRAL PACIFIC COAST

CHIRRIPO NATIONAL PARK ★★　Home to Costa Rica's tallest peak, 3,761m (12,336-ft.) Mount Chirripó, Chirripó National Park is a hike, but on a clear day you can see both the Pacific Ocean and the Caribbean Sea from its summit. There are a number of interesting climbing trails here, and camping is allowed. **Location:** 151km (94 miles) southeast of San José. See "San Isidro de El General: A Base for Exploring Chirripó National Park," in chapter 7.

MANUEL ANTONIO NATIONAL PARK ★★　Though relatively small, Manuel Antonio is the most popular national park and supports the largest number of hotels and resorts. This lowland rainforest is home to a healthy monkey population, including the endangered squirrel monkey. The park is best known for its splendid beaches. **Location:** 129km (80 miles) south of San José. See "Manuel Antonio National Park," in chapter 7.

THE SOUTHERN ZONE

CORCOVADO NATIONAL PARK ★★★　The largest single block of virgin lowland rainforest in Central America, Corcovado National Park receives more than 200 inches of rain per year. It's increasingly popular but still very remote. (It has no roads; only dirt tracks lead into it.) Scarlet macaws live here, as do countless other Neotropical species, including two of the country's largest cats, the puma and the endangered jaguar. There are camping facilities and trails throughout the park. **Location:** 335km (208 miles) south of San José, on the Osa Peninsula. See "Puerto Jiménez: Gateway to Corcovado National Park," in chapter 8.

THE CARIBBEAN COAST

CAHUITA NATIONAL PARK ★　A combination land and marine park, Cahuita National Park protects one of the few remaining living coral reefs in the country. The topography here is lush lowland tropical rainforest. Monkeys and numerous bird species are common. Camping is permitted, and there are basic facilities at the Puerto Vargas entrance to the park. If you want to visit for only the day, however, enter from Cahuita village because the local community has taken over that entrance and is asking for only a voluntary donation, in lieu of the normal $6 fee. **Location:** On the Caribbean coast, 42km (26 miles) south of Limón. See "Cahuita," in chapter 9.

TORTUGUERO NATIONAL PARK ★★　Tortuguero National Park has been called the Venice of Costa Rica due to its maze of jungle canals that meander through a dense lowland rainforest. Small boats, launches, and canoes carry visitors through these waterways, where caimans, manatees, and numerous bird

Monkey Business

No trip to Costa Rica would be complete without at least one monkey sighting. Home to four distinct species of primates, Costa Rica offers the opportunity for one of the world's most gratifying wildlife-viewing experiences. Just listen for the deep guttural call of a howler or the rustling of leaves overhead—telltale signs that monkeys are in your vicinity.

Costa Rica's most commonly spotted monkey is the white-faced or **capuchin monkey** (*mono cara blanca* in Spanish), which you might recognize as the infamous culprit from the film *Outbreak*. Contrary to that film's plot, however, these monkeys are native to the New World tropics and do not exist in Africa. Capuchins are agile, medium-size monkeys that make good use of their long, prehensile tails. They inhabit a diverse collection of habitats, ranging from the high-altitude cloud forests of the central region to the lowland mangroves of the Osa Peninsula. It's almost impossible not to spot capuchins at Manuel Antonio (see chapter 7), where the resident white-faced monkeys have become a little too dependent on fruit and junk-food feedings by tourists. Please do not feed wild monkeys (and try to keep your food away from them; they're notorious thieves), and boycott establishments that try to attract both monkeys and tourists with daily feedings.

Howler monkeys (*mono congo* in Spanish) are named for their distinct and eerie call. Large and mostly black, these monkeys can seem ferocious because of their physical appearance and deep, resonant howls that can carry for more than a mile, even in dense rainforest. Biologists believe that male howlers mark the bounds of their territories with these deep, guttural sounds. In the presence of humans, however, howlers are actually a little timid and tend to stay higher up in the canopy than their white-faced cousins. Howlers are fairly common and easy to spot in the dry tropical forests of coastal Guanacaste and the Nicoya Peninsula (see chapter 5).

Even more elusive are **spider monkeys** (*mono araña* in Spanish). These long, slender monkeys are dark brown to black and prefer the high canopies of primary rainforests. Spiders are very adept with their prehensile tails but actually travel through the canopy with a hand-over-hand motion frequently imitated by their less graceful human cousins on playground monkey bars around the world. I've had my best luck spotting spiders along the edges of Tortuguero's jungle canals (see chapter 9), where howlers are also quite common.

The rarest and most endangered of Costa Rica's monkeys is the tiny **squirrel monkey** (*mono tití* in Spanish). These small, brown monkeys have dark eyes surrounded by large white rings, white ears, white chests, and very long tails. In Costa Rica, squirrel monkeys can be found only in Manuel Antonio (see chapter 7) and the Osa Peninsula (see chapter 8). These seemingly hyperactive monkeys are predominantly fruit eaters and often feed on bananas and other fruit trees near hotels in both of the above-mentioned regions. Squirrel monkeys usually travel in large bands, so if you do see them, you'll likely see quite a few.

and mammal species are common. The extremely endangered great green macaw lives here. On the beaches, green sea turtles nest here every year between June and October. The park has a small but helpful information office and some well-marked trails. **Location:** 258km (160 miles) northeast of San José. See "Tortuguero National Park," in chapter 9.

4 Tips on Health, Safety & Etiquette in the Wilderness

Much of what is discussed below is common sense. For more detailed information, see "Health & Insurance," in chapter 2.

Although most tours and activities are safe, there are risks involved in any adventure activity. Know and respect your own physical limits before undertaking any strenuous activity. Be prepared for extremes in temperature and rainfall and for wide fluctuations in weather. A sunny morning hike can quickly become a cold and wet ordeal, so it's usually a good idea to carry along some form of rain gear when hiking in the rainforest, or to have a dry change of clothing waiting at the end of the trail. Be sure to bring along plenty of sunscreen when you're not going to be covered by the forest canopy.

If you do any backcountry packing or camping, remember that it really *is* a jungle out there. Don't go poking under rocks or fallen branches. Snakebites are very rare, but don't do anything to increase the odds. If you do encounter a snake, stay calm, don't make any sudden movements, and *do not* try to handle it. Also avoid swimming in major rivers unless a guide or local operator can vouch for their safety. Although white-water sections and stretches in mountainous areas are generally pretty safe, most mangrove canals and river mouths in Costa Rica support healthy crocodile and caiman populations.

Bugs and bug bites will probably be your greatest health concern in the Costa Rican wilderness, and even they aren't as big of a problem as you might expect. Mostly, bugs are an inconvenience, although mosquitoes can carry malaria or dengue (see "Health & Insurance," in chapter 2, for more information). A strong repellent and proper clothing will minimize both the danger and the inconvenience; you might also want to bring along some cortisone or Benadryl cream to soothe itching. At the beaches, you'll probably be bitten by sand fleas, or *pirujas.* These nearly invisible insects leave an irritating welt. Try not to scratch because this can lead to open sores and infections. Pirujas are most active at sunrise and sunset, so you might want to cover up or avoid the beaches at these times.

And remember: Whenever you enter and enjoy nature, you should tread lightly and try not to disturb the natural environment. There's a popular slogan well known to most campers that certainly applies here: "Leave nothing but footprints; take nothing but memories." If you must take home a souvenir, take photos. Do not cut or uproot plants or flowers. Pack out everything you pack in, and *please* do not litter.

5 Ecologically Oriented Volunteer & Study Programs

Below are some institutions and organizations that are working on ecology and sustainable development projects.

Costa Rica Rainforest Outward Bound School (© **800/676-2018** in the U.S., or 278-6058 in Costa Rica; www.crrobs.org) is the local branch of this well-respected international adventure-based outdoor-education organization. Courses range from 2 weeks to a full semester and cover everything from surfing, kayaking, and tree climbing to learning Spanish.

Earthwatch Institute (© 800/776-0188; www.earthwatch.org) organizes volunteers to go on research trips to help scientists collect data and conduct field experiments in a number of scientific fields and a wide range of settings. Expeditions to Costa Rica range from studies of the nesting habits of leatherback sea turtles to the dry forest ecology of Guanacaste. Fees for food and lodging average around $2,000 for a 2-week expedition, excluding airfare.

Eco Teach (© 800/626-8992; www.ecoteach.com) works primarily in facilitating educational trips for high school and college student groups. Trips focus on Costa Rican ecology and culture. Costs run around $2,200 per person for a 10-day trip, including airfare, lodging, meals, classes, and travel.

Global Volunteers (© 800/487-1074 or 651/407-6100; www.global volunteers.org) is a U.S.-based organization that offers a unique opportunity to travelers who've always wanted a Peace Corps–like experience but couldn't make a 2-year commitment. For 2 to 3 weeks, you can join one of its working vacations in Costa Rica. A certain set of skills, such as engineering or agricultural knowledge, is helpful but by no means necessary. Each trip is undertaken at a particular community's request, to complete a specific project. However, be warned: These "volunteer" experiences do not come cheap. You must pay for your transportation as well as a hefty program fee, around $1,995 for a 2-week program.

Habitat for Humanity International (© 447-2330; www.habitatcostarica. org) has several chapters in Costa Rica and sometimes runs organized Global Village programs here.

The **Institute for Central American Development Studies** ✦ (© 225-0508; www.icads.org) offers internship and research opportunities in the areas of environment, agriculture, human rights, and women's studies. An intensive Spanish-language program can be combined with work-study or volunteer opportunities.

The **Monteverde Institute** (© 645-5053; www.mvinstitute.org) offers study programs in Monteverde and also has a volunteer center that helps in placement and training of volunteers.

The **Organization for Tropical Studies** ✦ (© 240-6696; www.ots.ac.cr) represents several Costa Rican and U.S. universities. This organization's mission is to promote research, education, and the wise use of natural resources in the tropics. Research facilities include La Selva Biological Station near Braulio Carrillo National Park and Palo Verde, and the Wilson Botanical Gardens near San Vito. Housing is provided at one of the research facilities. There's a wide variety of programs, ranging from full-semester undergraduate programs (at around $11,000) to specific graduate courses (of varying duration), to its recently added tourist programs. (These are generally being sponsored/run by established operators such as Costa Rica Expeditions and Elderhostel.) These range in duration from 3 to 10 days, and costs vary greatly. Entrance requirements and competition for some of these courses can be demanding.

Programa Voluntarios para la Conservación del Ambiente (PROVCA) (© 222-7549; mam271@racsa.co.cr) organizes volunteers to work in Costa Rica's national parks. A 14-day minimum commitment is required, as is a basic ability to converse in Spanish. Housing is provided at a basic ranger station, and there is a $15-per-day fee to cover food, which is basic Tico fare.

Vida (© 221-8367; www.vida.org) is a local nongovernmental organization working on sustainable development and conservation issues; it can often place volunteers.

San José

At first blush, San José might seem little more than a chaotic jumble of cars, buses, buildings, and people. The central downtown section of San José is an urban planner's nightmare, where once-quiet streets are now burdened by traffic in a near-constant state of gridlock. Antiquated buses spewing diesel fumes and a lack of emission controls have created a brown cloud over the San José sky. Below the cloud, the city bustles, but it's not particularly hospitable to travelers. Sidewalks are poorly maintained and claustrophobic, and street crime is a problem. Most visitors quickly seek the sanctuary of their hotel room and the first chance to escape the city.

Still, San José is the most cosmopolitan city in Central America. Costa Rica's stable government and the Central Valley's climate have, over the years, attracted people from all over the world. There's a large diplomatic and international business presence here. As a result, there has been a proliferation of small, elegant hotels in renovated historic buildings, as well as innovative new restaurants serving a wide range of international cuisines. Together these hotels and restaurants provide visitors with one of the greatest varieties of options found anywhere between Mexico City and Bogotá.

San José will invariably serve as a default hub or transfer point for all visitors to Costa Rica (at least until the Liberia airport gets more flights). This chapter helps you plan your time in the capital and helps ease your way through the pitfalls inherent in such a rough-and-tumble little city.

IT'S IN THE BEANS San José was built on the profits of the coffee-export business. Between the airport and downtown, you'll pass working coffee farms. Glance up from almost any street in the city and on the surrounding volcanic mountains, and you'll see a patchwork quilt of farm fields, most of which are planted with the *grano de oro* (golden bean), as it's known here. San José was a forgotten backwater of the Spanish empire until the first shipments of the local beans made their way to sleepy souls in Europe late in the 19th century. Soon San José was riding high. Coffee planters, newly rich and craving culture, imposed a tax on themselves to build the Teatro Nacional, San José's most beautiful building. Coffee profits also built the city a university. Today you can wake up and smell the coffee roasting as you wander the streets near the Central Market (Mercado Central), and in any cafe or restaurant you can get a hot cup of sweet, milky *café con leche* to remind you of the bean that built San José.

Why does coffee grow so well around the city? It's the climate. The Central Valley, in which the city sits, has a perfect climate. At 1,125m (3,690 ft.) above sea level, San José enjoys springlike temperatures year-round. The pleasant climate, along with the beautiful views of lush green mountainsides, makes San José a memorable city to visit. All you have to do is glance up at those mountains to know that this is one of the most beautifully situated capitals in Central

America. And if a glance isn't enough for you, you'll find that it's extremely easy to get out into the countryside. Within an hour or 2, you can climb a volcano, go white-water rafting, hike through a cloud forest, and stroll through a butterfly garden—among many, many other activities.

1 Orientation

ARRIVING

BY PLANE

Juan Santamaría International Airport (© 437-2626 for 24-hr. airport information) is located near the city of Alajuela, about 20 minutes from downtown San José. A taxi into town costs between $12 and $15, and a bus is only 60¢. The Alajuela–San José buses run frequently and will drop you off anywhere along Paseo Colón, or at a station near the Parque de la Merced (downtown, between calles 12 and 14 and avs. 2 and 4). There are two separate lines: **Tuasa** buses are red; **Station Wagon** buses are beige/yellow. At the airport, you'll find the bus stop directly in front of the main terminal. Be sure to ask whether the bus is going to San José, or you'll end up in Alajuela. If you have a lot of luggage, you should probably take a cab.

There are quite a few car-rental agencies with desks and offices at the airport, although if you're planning to spend a few days in San José itself, a car is a liability. (If you're heading off immediately to the beach, though, it's much easier to pick up your car here than at a downtown office.) Several car-rental agencies already have desks inside the new terminal, right where passengers exit Customs and Immigration; others are still in limbo awaiting completion of an airport remodeling (see below), so be sure to contact them first to confirm that they will have an agent or an office at the airport when you arrive.

At press time, the airport was still in the midst of a major renovation and expansion. So far, the first phase of the new terminal has been completed, and all of the major airlines have moved their desks into the terminal. The baggage claim and Customs and Immigration areas, which are modern and spacious, are not necessarily fast and efficient. Moreover, despite the major remodeling, chaos and confusion greet arriving passengers the second they step out of the terminal. As in the past, you must abandon the luggage carts just before exiting the building and then face a gauntlet of aggressive taxi drivers and people offering to carry your bags. Fortunately, the official airport taxi service (see below) has set up a kiosk in the relative calm and sanctuary between the exit doors and the clamoring masses. Most porters or skycaps wear a uniform identifying them as such, but sometimes "improvised" porters will try to earn a few dollars here. (Moreover, there's often nowhere for them really to have to carry your bags because the line of waiting taxis and shuttles is just steps away.)

In terms of taxis, you should stick with the official airport taxi service, **Taxis Unidos Aeropuerto** (© 221-6865), which operates a fleet of orange vans and sedans, charging fixed prices according to your destination. Head to its kiosk in the no-man's land just outside the exit door for arriving passengers. Here you can buy a prepaid voucher to the hotel or destination of your choice. Despite the fact that Taxis Unidos has an official monopoly at the airport, you will usually find a handful of regular cabs (in traditional red sedans) and "pirate" cabs, freelance drivers using their own vehicles. You could use either of these latter options, and they tend to charge a dollar or two less, but I recommend using the official service for safety and standardized prices. Keep a very watchful eye on

San José

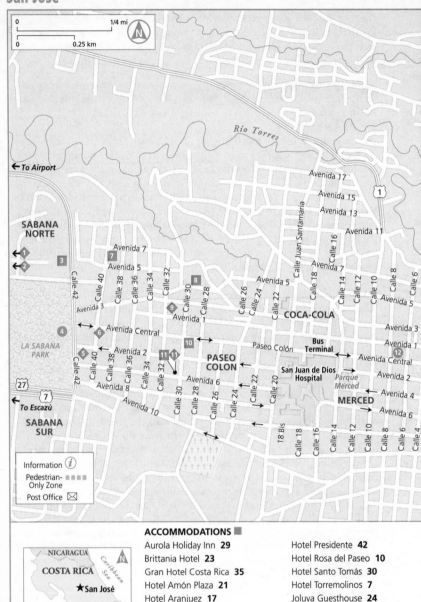

ACCOMMODATIONS ■

Aurola Holiday Inn **29**
Brittania Hotel **23**
Gran Hotel Costa Rica **35**
Hotel Amón Plaza **21**
Hotel Aranjuez **17**
Hotel Cacts **8**
Hotel Del Rey **44**
Hotel Don Carlos **28**
Hotel 1492 Jade y Oro **50**
Hotel Grano de Oro **11**
Hotel Le Bergerac **51**

Hotel Presidente **42**
Hotel Rosa del Paseo **10**
Hotel Santo Tomás **30**
Hotel Torremolinos **7**
Joluva Guesthouse **24**
Pensión de la Cuesta **45**
Radisson Europa Hotel **14**
Raya Vida Villa **18**
Taylor's Inn **22**
Toruma Youth Hostel **48**
Tryp Corobicí **3**

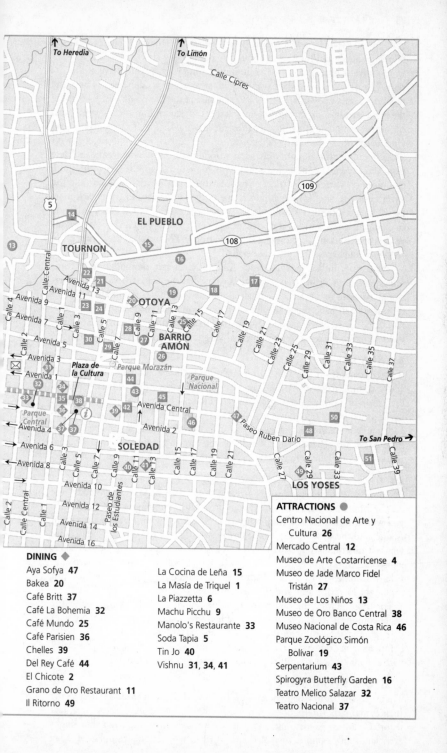

To Heredia

To Limón

Calle Cipres

109

5

14

EL PUEBLO

13

TOURNON

15

108

16

22 21

Avenida 13

Avenida 11

17

Calle 4

Avenida 9

23 24

OTOYA

19

18

Calle 1

Calle 3

Avenida 7

20

Calle 5

Calle 9

Calle 11

Calle 13

25

Calle 15

Calle 17

Calle 19

Avenida 5

30

28

27

BARRIO

Calle 7

29

AMÓN

Calle 21

Calle 23

Calle 25

Calle 31

Calle 33

Calle 35

Calle 2

Avenida 3

26

Calle 29

Calle 37

Avenida 1

Plaza de

la Cultura

Parque Morazán

32

44

Parque

Central

34

43

Parque

Nacional

33

35

38

45

36

39

42

Avenida Central

47

50

i

46

48

Avenida 4

37

31 37

Avenida 2

Paseo Ruben Darío

To San Pedro →

Avenida 6

SOLEDAD

Calle 3

Calle 5

Calle 7

Calle 9

Calle 11

Calle 13

Calle 15

Calle 17

Calle 19

Calle 21

51

Avenida 8

40

41

Calle 27

49

LOS YOSES

Calle 29

Calle 33

Calle 39

Avenida 10

Paseo de los Estudiantes

Calle 2

Calle Central

Calle 1

Avenida 12

Avenida 14

Avenida 16

ATTRACTIONS ●

Centro Nacional de Arte y
Cultura **26**
Mercado Central **12**
Museo de Arte Costarricense **4**
Museo de Jade Marco Fidel
Tristán **27**
Museo de Los Niños **13**
Museo de Oro Banco Central **38**
Museo Nacional de Costa Rica **46**
Parque Zoológico Simón
Bolívar **19**
Serpentarium **43**
Spirogyra Butterfly Garden **16**
Teatro Melico Salazar **32**
Teatro Nacional **37**

DINING ◆

Aya Sofya **47**
Bakea **20**
Café Britt **37**
Café La Bohemia **32**
Café Mundo **25**
Café Parisien **36**
Chelles **39**
Del Rey Café **44**
El Chicote **2**
Grano de Oro Restaurant **11**
Il Ritorno **49**

La Cocina de Leña **15**
La Masía de Triquel **1**
La Piazzetta **6**
Machu Picchu **9**
Manolo's Restaurante **33**
Soda Tapia **5**
Tin Jo **40**
Vishnu **31, 34, 41**

your bags: Thieves have historically preyed on newly arrived passengers and their luggage. You should tip porters about 50¢ per bag.

You have several options for **exchanging money** when you arrive at the airport. There's an ATM in the baggage claim area, which is connected to both the Plus and Cirrus networks. There's also a branch of the **Banco de San José** inside the main terminal, on the second floor across from the airline check-in counters. It's supposed to be open whenever there are arriving flights. If the bank is closed (and even when it's open), there are usually official money-changers (with badges) and unofficial money-changers working just outside the terminal. A few things to note: (1) Although black-market money-changing is illegal, it's quite common; (2) there's never much variance between the official bank rate and the street exchange rate; (3) the airport is one of the safer places to try a black-market exchange, although you should be careful wherever and whenever you decide to change money; and (4) it is increasingly easy to get local currency drawn off your home checking account or credit card from ATMs around the country. See "Money," in chapter 2, for more details.

If you arrive in San José via Nature Air, private aircraft, or another small commuter or charter airline, you might find yourself at the **Tobías Bolaños International Airport** in Pavas. This small airport is located on the western side of downtown San José, about 10 minutes by car from the center. There are no car-rental desks here, however, so unless you have a car or a driver waiting for you here, you will have to take a cab into town, which should cost between $10 and $15.

BY BUS

If you're coming to San José by bus, where you disembark depends on where you're coming from. (The different bus companies have their offices, and thus their drop-off points, all over downtown San José. When you buy your ticket, ask where you'll be let off.) Buses arriving from Panama pass first through Cartago and San Pedro before letting passengers off in downtown San José; buses arriving from Nicaragua generally enter the city on the west end of town, on Paseo Colón. If you're staying here, you can ask to be let off before the final stop.

BY CAR

For those of you intrepid readers arriving by car, you will be entering San José via the Interamerican Highway. If you arrive **from Nicaragua and the north,** you will find that the highway brings you first past the airport and the city of Alajuela, to the western edge of the downtown, right at the end of Paseo Colón, where it hits the Parque Sabana. This area is well marked with large road signs, which will direct you either to the downtown (CENTRO) or to the western suburbs of Rhomerser, Pavas, and Escazú. If you're heading toward downtown, just follow the flow of traffic and turn left on Paseo Colón.

For those of you entering **from Panama and the south,** things get a little more complicated. The Interamerican Highway first passes through the city of Cartago and then through the San José suburbs of Curridabat and San Pedro before reaching downtown. This route is relatively well marked, and if you stick with the major flow of traffic, you should find San José without any problem.

VISITOR INFORMATION

There's an **Instituto Costarricense de Turismo (ICT;** ① **443-2883)** desk at the Juan Santamaría International Airport, located in the baggage claims area, just before Customs. You can pick up maps and browse brochures, and they might even lend you a phone to make or confirm a reservation. It's open Monday

"I Know There's Got to Be a Number Here Somewhere . . .": The Arcane Art of Finding an Address in San José

This is one of the most confusing aspects of visiting Costa Rica in general, and San José in particular. Although there are often street addresses and building numbers for locations in downtown San José, they are almost never used. Addresses are given as a set of coordinates such as "Calle 3 between avenidas Central and 1." It's then up to you to locate the building within that block, keeping in mind that the building could be on either side of the street. Many addresses include additional information, such as the number of meters or *varas* (an old Spanish measurement roughly equal to a yard) from a specified intersection or some other well-known landmark. (These "meter measurements" are not precise but are a good way to give directions to a taxi driver. In basic terms, 100m = 1 block, 200m = 2 blocks, and so on.) These landmarks are what become truly confusing for visitors to the city because they are often simply restaurants, bars, and shops that would be familiar only to locals.

Things get even more confusing when the landmark in question no longer exists. The classic example of this is "the Coca-Cola," one of the most common landmarks used in addresses in the blocks surrounding San José's main market. The trouble is, the Coca-Cola bottling plant that it refers to is no longer there; the edifice is long gone, and one of the principal downtown bus depots stands in its place. Old habits die hard, though, and the address description remains. You might also try to find someplace near the *antiguo higuerón* ("old fig tree") in San Pedro. This tree was felled years ago. In outlying neighborhoods, addresses can become long directions such as "50m/164 ft. south of the old church, then 100m/328 ft. east, then 20m/66 ft. south." Luckily for the visitor, most downtown addresses are more straightforward.

Oh, and if you're wondering how letter carriers manage, well, welcome to the club. Some folks actually get their mail delivered this way, but most people and businesses in San José use a post office box. This is called an *apartado* and is abbreviated "Apdo." or "A.P." in mailing addresses.

through Friday from 9am to 5pm, which is a little bit pathetic because such a large number of flights arrive either on the weekends or after 5pm. If you're looking for the **main ICT visitor information center** in San José, it's located below the Plaza de la Cultura, at the entrance to the Gold Museum, on Calle 5 between avenidas Central and 2 (© **222-1090**). The people here are helpful, although the information they have to offer is rather limited. This office is also open Monday through Friday from 9am to 5pm.

CITY LAYOUT

Downtown San José is laid out on a grid. *Avenidas* (avenues) run east and west, while *calles* (streets) run north and south. The center of the city is at **Avenida**

Central and **Calle Central.** To the north of Avenida Central, the avenidas have odd numbers beginning with Avenida 1; to the south, they have even numbers beginning with Avenida 2. Likewise, calles to the east of Calle Central have odd numbers, and those to the west have even numbers. The main downtown artery is **Avenida 2,** which merges with Avenida Central on either side of the downtown area. West of downtown, Avenida Central becomes **Paseo Colón,** which ends at La Sabana Park and feeds into the highway to Alajuela, the airport, and the Pacific coast. East of downtown, Avenida Central leads to San Pedro and then to Cartago and the Interamerican Highway heading south. **Calle 3** takes you out of town to the north and puts you on the Guápiles Highway out to the Caribbean coast.

THE NEIGHBORHOODS IN BRIEF

San José is sprawling. Today it's divided into dozens of neighborhoods known as *barrios*. Most of the listings in this chapter fall within the main downtown area, but there are a few outlying neighborhoods you'll need to know about.

Downtown In San José's busy downtown, you'll find most of the city's museums, as well as a handful of small urban parks and open-air plazas. There are also many tour companies, restaurants, and hotels here. Unfortunately, traffic noise and exhaust fumes make this one of the least pleasant parts of the city. Streets and avenues are usually bustling and crowded with pedestrians and vehicular traffic, and street crime is most rampant here. Still, the section of Avenida Central between Calle Central and Calle 7 has been converted into a pedestrian mall, slightly improving things on this stretch.

Barrio Amón/Barrio Otoya These two picturesque neighborhoods, just north and east of downtown, are the site of the greatest concentration of historic buildings in San José. Some of these have been renovated and turned into hotels and restaurants. If you're looking for character and don't mind the noise and exhaust fumes from passing cars and buses, this neighborhood makes a good base for exploring the city.

La Sabana/Paseo Colón Paseo Colón, a wide boulevard west of downtown, is an extension of Avenida Central and ends at La Sabana Park. It has several good, small hotels and numerous excellent restaurants. This is also where many of the city's car-rental agencies have their in-town offices.

San Pedro/Los Yoses Located east of downtown San José, Los Yoses is an upper-middle-class neighborhood that is home to many diplomatic missions and embassies. San Pedro is a little farther east and is the site of the University of Costa Rica. There are numerous college-type bars and restaurants all around the edge of the campus, and several good restaurants and small hotels in both neighborhoods.

Escazú/Santa Ana Located in the hills west of San José, Escazú and Santa Ana are two fast-growing suburbs. Although the area is only 15 minutes from San José by taxi, it feels much farther away because of its relaxed atmosphere. This area has a large expatriate community, with many bed-and-breakfast establishments located here.

Heredia/Alajuela/Airport Area Heredia and Alajuela are two colonial-era cities that lie closer to the airport than San José. Alajuela is the closest city to the airport, with Heredia lying about midway between Alajuela and the capital. For more information on these cities, see "Side Trips from San José," later in this chapter. There are several quite nice high-end boutique hotels in this area. There are also several large hotels and one chain hotel located on, or just off, the Interamerican Highway close to the airport.

2 Getting Around

BY BUS

Bus transportation around San José is cheap—the fare is usually somewhere around 15¢ (although the Alajuela/San José buses that run in from the airport cost 60¢). The most important buses are those running east along Avenida 2 and west along Avenida 3. The **Sabana/Cementerio** bus runs from La Sabana Park to downtown and is one of the most convenient buses to use. You'll find a bus stop for the outbound Sabana/Cementerio bus near the main post office on Avenida 3 near the corner of Calle 2, and another one on Calle 11 between avenidas Central and 1. This bus also has stops all along Avenida 2. **San Pedro** buses leave from Avenida Central between calles 9 and 11, in front of the Cine Capri, and take you out of downtown heading east. **Escazú**-bound buses leave from the Coca-Cola bus station, as well as from Avenida 6 and Calle 2, while buses for **Santa Ana** leave only from the Coca-Cola bus station. Alternately, you can pick up both the Escazú and Santa Ana buses, as well as those bound for Alajuela and the airport, from the busy bus stop in front of the Centro Colón shopping center toward the western end of Paseo Colón.

Board buses from the front. The bus drivers can make change, although they don't like to receive large bills. Be especially mindful of your wallet, purse, or other valuables because pickpockets often work the crowded buses.

BY TAXI

Although taxis in San José have meters *(marías),* the drivers sometimes refuse to use them, particularly with foreigners, so you'll occasionally have to negotiate the price. Always try to get them to use the meter first (say *"ponga la maría, por favor"*). The official rate at press time is around 65¢ for the first kilometer (½ mile) and around 35¢ for each additional kilometer. If you have a rough idea of how far it is to your destination, you can estimate how much it should cost from these figures. After 10pm, taxis are legally allowed to add a 20% surcharge. Some of the meters are programmed to include the extra charge automatically, but be careful: Some drivers will use the evening setting during the daytime or (at night) try to charge an extra 20% on top of the higher meter setting. **Tipping** taxi drivers is not expected. It's not uncommon for passengers to sit in the front seat with the driver.

Depending on your location, the time of day, and the weather (rain places taxis at a premium), it's relatively easy to hail a cab downtown. You'll always find taxis in front of the Teatro Nacional (albeit at high prices) and around the Parque Central at Avenida Central and Calle Central. Taxis in front of hotels and the El Pueblo tourist complex usually charge more than others, although this is technically illegal. Most hotels will gladly call you a cab, either for a downtown excursion or for a trip back out to the airport. You can also get a cab by calling **Coopetaxi** (© 235-9966), **Coopeirazu** (© 254-3211), or **Coopeguaria** (© 227-9300).

ON FOOT

Downtown San José is very compact. Nearly every place you might want to go is within a 15-by-4-block area. Because of the traffic congestion, you'll often find it faster to walk than to take a bus or taxi. Be careful when walking th

---

Tips **Car-Rental Advice**

If you know you'll be renting a car, I recommend reserving it in advance from home. All of the major international agencies and many of the local companies have toll-free numbers and websites. Sometimes you can even save a bit on the cost by reserving in advance. Costa Rica's car-rental fleet is not sufficient to meet demand during the high season, and rental cars run at a premium. Sometimes this allows the agencies here on the ground to gouge last-minute car-rental shoppers.

---

streets any time of day or night. Flashy jewelry, loosely held handbags or backpacks, and expensive camera equipment tend to attract thieves. You should also watch your step: Between the earthquakes, wear and tear, and negligence, the sidewalks in San José have become veritable obstacle courses and the cause of more than one sprained ankle.

Avenida Central is a pedestrian-only street for the blocks from Calle Central toward the Cultural Plaza and a little bit beyond. It has been redone with interesting paving stones and the occasional fountain, in an attempt to create a comfortable pedestrian mall.

BY CAR

It will cost you between $35 and $90 per day to rent a car in Costa Rica (the higher prices are for 4WD vehicles). Many car-rental agencies have offices at the airport. If not, they will usually either pick you up or deliver the car to any San José hotel. If you decide to pick up your rental car in downtown San José, be prepared for some very congested streets.

The following companies have desks at Juan Santamaría International Airport, as well as offices downtown: **Alamo** (© 800/462-5266 toll-free within Costa Rica, or 242-7733 central reservations; www.alamocostarica.com), **Adobe Rent A Car** (© 442-2422 at the airport, or 258-4242 in downtown San José; www.adobecar.com), **Avis** (© 800/230-4898 in the U.S., or 293-2222 central reservation number in Costa Rica; www.avis.com), **Budget** (© 800/527-0700 in the U.S., 441-4444 at the airport, or 223-3284 in downtown San José; www.budget.co.cr), **Dollar** (© 443-2950 at the airport, or 257-0671 in downtown San José; www.dollarcostarica.com), **Hertz** (© 800/654-3131 in the U.S., 441-0097 at the airport, or 221-1818 in downtown San José; www.hertz.com), **National Car Rental** (© 800/328-4567 in the U.S., 440-0085 at the airport, or 290-8787 in downtown San José; www.natcar.com), **Payless Rent A Car** (© 800/582-7432 in the U.S., 443-5286 at the airport, or 257-0026 in downtown San José; www.paylesscr.com), **Thrifty** (© 800/367-2277 in the U.S., 442-8585 at the airport, or 257-3434 in downtown San José), and **Toyota Rent A Car** (© 441-1411 at the airport, or 258-5797 in downtown San José; www.toyotarent.com).

There are dozens of other car-rental agencies in San José, and most of them will arrange for airport or hotel pickup or delivery. One of the more dependable agencies is **Hola! Rent A Car,** west of Hotel Irazú, La Uruca, San José (© 231-5666; www.hola.net).

To rent a car in Costa Rica, you must be at least 21 years old and have a valid driver's license and a major credit card. For more advice, see "Getting Around," in chapter 2.

FAST FACTS: San José

American Express American Express Travel Services is represented in Costa Rica by **ASV Olympia**, Oficentro La Sabana, Sabana Sur (© 242-8585; www.asvolympia.com), which can issue traveler's checks and replacement cards, and provide other standard services. To report lost or stolen Amex traveler's checks within Costa Rica, call the number above or © 257-0155.

Bookstores **Seventh Street Books**, Calle 7 between avenidas 1 and Central (© 256-8251), has a wide range of new and used books in English, with an excellent selection of tropical biology, bird, and flora books; it's open daily from 9am to 7pm. For a wide selection of new books in English and Spanish, you can also check out **Librería Internacional** (© 253-9553; www.libreriainternacional.com), which has stores in the Multiplaza mall, as well as locations in Zapote, Alajuela, Rohrmoser, and Barrio Escalante.

Camera Repair **Dima**, Avenida Central between calles 3 and 5 (© 222-3969), is your best bet for any equipment or repair needs.

Car Rentals See "Getting Around," above.

Currency Exchange The best thing to do is to exchange money at your hotel. If the hotel can't do this for you, or if it is giving a very poor rate of exchange, have someone direct you to a private bank or exchange house (*casa de cambio*), where you won't have to stand in line for hours. See "Money" in chapter 2 for more information.

Dentists Call your embassy, which will have a list of recommended dentists. Many bilingual dentists also advertise in the *Tico Times*. Because treatments are so inexpensive in Costa Rica, dental tourism has become a popular option for people needing extensive work.

Doctors Contact your embassy for information on doctors in San José, or see "Hospitals," below.

Drugstores There are countless pharmacies and drugstores in San José. Many of them will deliver at little or no extra cost. The pharmacy at the **Hospital Clínica Bíblica**, Av. 14 between calles Central and 1 (© 257-5252) is open 24 hours every day of the year. The pharmacy (© 208-1080) at the **Hospital CIMA** in Escazú is also open 24 hours every day. **Farmacia Fischel** (© 295-7500; www.fischel.co.cr) has numerous branches around the metropolitan area.

Embassies/Consulates See "Fast Facts: Costa Rica," in chapter 2.

Emergencies In case of any emergency, dial © **911** (which should have an English-speaking operator); for an ambulance, call © **128**; and to report a fire, call © **118**.

Express Mail Services Many international courier and express-mail services have offices in San José, including: **DHL**, on Paseo Colón between calles 30 and 32 (© 210-3838; www.dhl.com); **EMS Courier**, with desks at the principal metropolitan post offices (© 281-0227); **FedEx**, which is based in Heredia but will arrange pickup anywhere in the metropolitan area (© 0800/052-1090; www.fedex.com); and **United Parcel Service**, in Pavas (© 290-2828; www.ups.com). *Beware:* Despite what you might be told, packages sent overnight to U.S. addresses tend to take 3 to 4 days to reach their destination.

Eyeglasses Look for the word *óptica*. **Optica Jiménez** (✆ **257-4658**) and **Optica Vision** (✆ **255-2266**) are two dependable chains with stores around San José. They can do everything from eye exams to repairs.

Hospitals **Clínica Bíblica,** Avenida 14 between calles Central and 1 (✆ **257-5252,** or for emergencies 257-0466; www.clinicabiblica.com), is conveniently located close to downtown and has several English-speaking doctors. The **Hospital CIMA** (✆ **208-1000**; www.hospitalsanjose.net), located in Escazú on the Próspero Fernández Highway, which connects San José and the western suburb of Santa Ana, has the most modern facilities in the country.

Internet Access Internet cafes are popping up around San José at a staggering rate. Rates run between $1 and $3 per hour. Many hotels either have their own Internet cafe or allow guests to send and receive e-mail. If your hotel doesn't provide the service and there's no Internet cafe close by, you can try **Cybercafé Las Arcadas,** at the Las Arcadas shopping center next to the Gran Hotel Costa Rica (✆ **233-3310**), and **Internet Café,** in Plaza San Pedro (✆ **224-7382**; daily 24 hr.), with more offices downtown and around the metropolitan area. All allow Web and e-mail access. Alternatively, **Racsa,** Avenida 5 and Calle 1 (✆ **287-0087**; www.racsa.co.cr), the state Internet monopoly, sells prepaid cards in 5-, 10-, and 15-hour denominations for connecting your laptop to the Web via a local phone call. Some knowledge of configuring your computer's dial-up connection is necessary, and be sure to factor in the phone call charge if calling from a hotel.

Laundry/Dry Cleaning Self-service laundromats are uncommon in Costa Rica, and hotel services can be expensive. **Sixaola** (✆ **240-7667**) and **Tyson** (✆ **225-7549**) are two dependable laundry and dry-cleaning chains with outlets all over town. The latter will even pick up and deliver your clothes free of charge.

Maps The Costa Rican Tourist Board (ICT; see "Visitor Information," earlier in this chapter) can usually provide you with decent maps of both Costa Rica and San José. Other sources in San José are **Seventh Street Books,** Calle 7 between avenidas Central and 1 (✆ **256-8251**); **Librería Lehmann,** Avenida Central between calles 1 and 3 (✆ **223-1212**); and **Librería Universal,** Avenida Central and calles Central and 1 (✆ **222-2222**).

Newspapers & Magazines The *Tico Times* is Costa Rica's principal English-language weekly paper and serves both the expatriate community and visitors. You can also get the *International Herald Tribune,* the *Miami Herald,* the *New York Times, USA Today, Time,* and *Newsweek,* as well as other English-language publications. You'll find these publications in hotel gift shops and in bookstores that sell English-language books. If you understand Spanish, *La Nación* is the leading daily paper. Its "Viva" and "Tiempo Libre" sections have extensive listings of current cultural events.

Photographic Needs Film is generally more expensive in Costa Rica, so bring as much as you will need from home. I also recommend that you wait to have your film processed at home, but if you must develop your prints down here, try **Fuji Foto** (✆ **222-0966**) or **IFSA-Kodak** (✆ **223-1444**), both of which have several storefronts around downtown. For more serious photographic needs (equipment, repairs, and so on), try **Dima,** Avenida Central between calles 3 and 5 (✆ **222-3969**).

Police Dial ⓒ **911** or ⓒ **222-1365** for the police. They should have someone who speaks English.

Post Office The main post office *(correo)* is on Calle 2 between avenidas 1 and 3 (ⓒ **800/900-2000** toll-free in Costa Rica, or 223-9766; www.correos.go.cr), and is open Monday through Friday from 8am to 5:30pm, and Saturday from 7:30am to noon. At press time, it cost 110 colones (26¢) to mail a postcard or letter to the United States, and 130 colones (31¢) to Europe. Given the Costa Rican postal service's track record, I recommend paying an extra 400 colones (95¢) to have anything of any value certified. Better yet, use an international courier service or wait until you get home to post it.

Restrooms These are known as *sanitarios* or *servicios sanitarios.* You might also hear them called *baños.* They are marked *damas* (women) and *hombres* or *caballeros* (men). Public restrooms are rare to nonexistent, but most big hotels and public restaurants will let you use their restrooms. If you're downtown, there are public restrooms at the entrance to the Gold Museum.

Safety Pickpockets and purse slashers are rife in San José, especially on public buses, in the markets, on crowded sidewalks, and near hospitals. Leave your passport, money, and other valuables in your hotel safe, and carry only as much as you really need when you go out. It's a good idea to make a photocopy of your passport's opening pages and carry that with you. If you do carry anything valuable with you, keep it in a money belt or special passport bag around your neck. Day packs are a prime target of brazen pickpockets throughout the city. One common scam involves someone dousing you or your pack with mustard or ice cream. Another scamster (or two) will then quickly come to your aid—they are usually much more interested in cleaning you out than cleaning you up.

Stay away from the red-light district northwest of the Central Market. Also, be advised that the Parque Nacional is not a safe place for a late-night stroll. Other precautions include walking around corner vendors, not between the vendor and the building. The tight space between the vendor and the building is a favorite spot for pickpockets. Never park a car on the street, and never leave anything of value in a car, even if it's in a guarded parking lot. Don't even leave your car unattended by the curb in front of a hotel while you dash in to check on your reservation. With these precautions in mind, you should have a safe visit to San José. Also, see "Safety" in "Fast Facts: Costa Rica," in chapter 2.

Taxes All hotels charge 16.3% tax. Restaurants charge 13% tax and also add on a 10% service charge, for a total of 23% more on your bill. There is an airport departure tax of $26.

Taxis See "Getting Around," above.

Telegrams/Faxes You can send telegrams and faxes from the **ICE office** on Avenida 2 between calles 1 and 3 (www.grupoice.com; daily 7am–10pm), as well as from most **post office** branches (ⓒ **800/900-2000** toll-free in Costa Rica; www.correos.go.cr).

Telephones See "Telephones/Faxes" in "Fast Facts: Costa Rica," in chapter 2. There are no city or area codes to dial from within Costa Rica; use the country code, 506, only when dialing a San José number from outside

Costa Rica. (To call San José from the U.S., dial the international access code [011], then 506, and then the seven-digit number.)

Time Zone San José is on Central Standard Time (same as Chicago and St. Louis), 6 hours behind Greenwich mean time.

Useful Telephone Numbers For directory assistance, call 𝄢 **113**; for international directory assistance, call 𝄢 **124**; and for the exact time (in Spanish), call 𝄢 **112**.

Water The water in San José is perfectly fine to drink. Nonetheless, travelers sometimes experience stomach discomfort during their first few days in Costa Rica. If you want to be cautious, drink bottled water and *frescos* made with milk instead of water. *Sin hielo* means "no ice," and this is what you'll want to say if you're nervous about the water—just because it's frozen doesn't mean it's not water.

Weather The weather in San José (including the Central Valley) is usually temperate, never getting extremely hot or cold. May through November is the rainy season, although the rain usually falls only in the afternoon and evening.

3 Where to Stay

Not long ago, hotels were popping up all over downtown San José. Well, the boom has stopped and there's a distinct glut of accommodations. This can be good for you, the visitor, because it's created a healthy degree of competition— it pays to shop around for special packages or promotions when you plan to visit. However, there's been a significant weeding-out process, and the better-run establishments (including those recommended here) are often booked well in advance during the high season.

In San José, your choices range from luxury resorts to budget pensions charging only a few dollars a night. However, these two extremes are the exceptions, not the norm. The vast number of accommodations, and the best deals, are to be found in the $60-to-$120 price range. Within this relatively moderate bracket, you'll find restored homes that have been turned into small hotels and bed-and-breakfasts, modern hotels with swimming pools and exercise rooms, and older downtown business hotels.

CHOOSING WHERE TO STAY **Downtown hotels,** many of which are in beautifully restored homes, are convenient to museums, restaurants, and shopping, but they can be noisy. Many people are also bothered by the exhaust fumes that permeate downtown streets. Moreover, because the streets of downtown are not especially safe, particularly at night, you will often be taking taxis whether you stay downtown or in a close-by neighborhood or suburb. **Barrio Amón** is the downtown neighborhood with the most character and remnants of colonial architecture. If you want clean air and a peaceful night's sleep, consider staying out in the suburbs. **Escazú** and **Santa Ana** are both quiet yet modern suburbs, and many of the hotels here have great views. Heading east from downtown, **Los Yoses** is fairly close to the center of the action yet is still quiet. If you've rented a car, make sure your hotel provides secure parking, or you'll have to find (and pay for) a nearby lot. If you plan to take some day tours, you can just as easily arrange these from a hotel situated outside the downtown area.

If you're heading out to Guanacaste, the central Pacific, or the northern zone, you might consider a hotel or bed-and-breakfast either near or beyond the airport. Sure, you give up proximity to downtown, but you can cut as much as an hour off your travel time to any of these destinations. Many car-rental companies will even deliver to or pick up cars from these establishments.

ALTERNATIVES TO HOTELS   If you plan to be in town for a while or are traveling with family or several friends, you might want to consider staying in an *apartotel*, a cross between an apartment complex and a hotel. You can rent by the day, week, or month, and you get a furnished apartment with a full kitchen, plus housekeeping and laundry service. Options include **Apartotel El Sesteo** (℗ **296-1805;** fax 296-1865; www.sesteo.com), **Apartotel La Sabana** (℗ **220-2422;** fax 231-7386; www.apartotel-lasabana.com), **Apartotel María Alexandra** (℗ **228-1507;** fax 289-5192; www.mariaalexandra.com), and **Apartotel Los Yoses** (℗ **225-0033;** fax 225-5595; www.apartotel.com).

DOWNTOWN SAN JOSE/BARRIO AMON
VERY EXPENSIVE

Radisson Europa Hotel ★★   This hotel is geared primarily to business travelers, but it's a good choice for anyone looking for a big, dependable luxury hotel near downtown San José. Wooden headboards and angular window nooks and other small architectural details give these rooms an edge over those in the Aurola Holiday Inn (see below), although it's not as convenient for walking around downtown. An extra $20 buys you an executive room, which is basically a standard room with a coffeemaker, a scale, terry-cloth bathrobes, and an extra telephone in the bathroom. The junior suites, called CEO Club rooms here, are in an isolated wing with its own comfortable lounge and honor bar. They come with all the above amenities, as well as a desk and chair, in-room fax machine, and small balcony. The hotel features a well-equipped gym that is part of the local Multispa chain.

Calle Blancos, behind La República building (A.P. 538-2120), San José. ℗ 800/333-3333 in the U.S., or 257-3257. Fax 257-8221. www.radisson.com. 107 units. $170–$200 double; $250 junior suite; $700 presidential suite. AE, DC, MC, V. Free parking. **Amenities:** 2 restaurants; bar; lounge; outdoor pool; gym; tour desk; car-rental agency; full-service business center; small shopping arcade; limited room service; massage; laundry service; nonsmoking rooms. *In room:* A/C, TV, dataport, minibar, hair dryer, iron, safe.

EXPENSIVE

Aurola Holiday Inn ★   Situated directly across the street from the attractive downtown Parque Morazán, this is San José's only high-rise deluxe hotel. The rooms are everything you might expect in this price range—but nothing more. The hotel has been around for quite a few years, and the age shows. Moreover, I've found that the service can be somewhat hit-or-miss. Still, the location is great for exploring downtown on foot, and if you get one of the upper-floor rooms on the north side, you'll have one of the best views in the city.

Av. 5 and Calle 5 (A.P. 7802-1000), San José. ℗ 800/465-4329 in the U.S. and Canada, or 222-2424. Fax 255-1171. www.aurola-holidayinn.com. 200 units. $125–$150 double; $150 junior suite; $225–$450 suite. AE, DC, MC, V. Free parking. **Amenities:** 2 restaurants; bar; indoor pool and poolside snack bar; exercise room; Jacuzzi; sauna; tour desk; car-rental desk; well-appointed business center; limited room service (6am–midnight); laundry service; nonsmoking rooms. *In room:* A/C, TV, dataport, minibar, coffeemaker, hair dryer, iron, safe.

Hotel Amón Plaza ★   Located on the north edge of the historic Barrio Amón neighborhood, this hotel is larger and more luxurious than most of the area's smaller hotels. There's nothing particularly distinctive about the property or rooms here; however, in terms of service, amenities, location, and price, this hotel gets my nod over the nearby Holiday Inn. The rooms are all spacious and well kept, and you are close to several good restaurants.

Av. 11 and Calle 3 bis (A.P. 4192-1000), San José. ℂ **258-8782**. Fax 257-0284. www.hotelamonplaza.com. 90 units. $120 double; $145–$225 suite. AE, DC, MC, V. Free parking. **Amenities:** Restaurant; bar; small exercise room; Jacuzzi; sauna; tour desk; modest business center; laundry service; nonsmoking rooms. *In room:* A/C, TV, coffeemaker, hair dryer, safe.

MODERATE

Britannia Hotel ★★ *Finds*   This is the most luxurious choice among the many hotels that have been created from restored old houses in downtown San José. Built in 1910, the large, low building, with its wraparound veranda, is certainly one of the most attractive in the neighborhood. In the lobby, tile floors, large stained-glass picture windows, a brass chandelier, and reproduction Victorian decor all help set a tone of tropical luxury. Along with restoring the old home, the owners have built a four-story addition, which is separated from the original building by a narrow atrium. Rooms in the original home have hardwood floors and furniture; high ceilings and fans help keep them cool. In the deluxe rooms and junior suites, you get air-conditioning. Although the street-side rooms have double glass, light sleepers will still want to avoid them. The quietest rooms are those toward the back of the addition. In what was once the wine cellar, you'll find a casual restaurant. The buffet breakfast is served in the adjacent skylit room. Afternoon tea and happy-hour drinks are also served.

Calle 3 and Av. 11 (A.P. 3742-1000), San José. ℂ **800/263-2618** in the U.S., or 223-6667. Fax 223-6411. www.hotelbritanniacostarica.com. 23 units. $89–$105 double; $117 junior suite. AE, MC, V. Parking nearby. **Amenities:** Restaurant; bar; tour desk; limited room service; laundry service; nonsmoking rooms. *In room:* TV, safe.

Gran Hotel Costa Rica   Although the Gran Hotel Costa Rica can claim the best location of any downtown hotel (bordering the National Theater and the Plaza de la Cultura), it does not, unfortunately, offer rooms to match the prestigious location or name. Most of the guest rooms here are fairly large, but they have not been well maintained over the decades; there's an adequate but rather run-down feel, especially in the bathrooms. The Café Parisien is the hotel's greatest attribute, and it's memorable not so much for its food as for its atmosphere—it's an open-air patio that overlooks the National Theater, street musicians, and all the activity of the Plaza de la Cultura.

Av. 2, between calles 1 and 3, San José. ℂ **221-4000**. Fax 221-3501. www.granhotelcr.com. 110 units. $60–$75 double; $85–$150 suite. Rates include breakfast buffet. AE, DC, MC, V. Free parking. **Amenities:** 2 restaurants; bar; tour desk; 24-hr. room service; laundry service. *In room:* TV.

Hotel Del Rey   You can't miss the Del Rey; it's a massive pink corner building with vaguely colonial styling. The lobby continues the facade's theme with pink-tile floors and stone columns. Inside, a carved hardwood door marks every guest room. The rooms vary in size and comfort: There are quiet interior rooms that have no windows, and larger rooms with windows (but also street noise). Try for a sixth-floor room with a balcony. The hotel's 24-hour Del Rey Café serves respectable U.S.-style deli sandwiches, seafood, steaks, and pasta dishes. Much of the first floor is taken up with a lively casino and the neighboring Blue Marlin Bar, which is very popular with tourists, expatriates, and prostitutes.

Av. 1 and Calle 9 (A.P. 6241-1000), San José. ℂ **888/972-7272** in the U.S., or 257-7800. Fax 221-0096. www. hoteldelrey.com. 104 units. $68–$85 double; $135 suite. AE, MC, V. Parking nearby. **Amenities:** Restaurant; bar; tour desk; 24-hr. room service; laundry service. *In room:* A/C, TV, minibar, hair dryer, safe.

Hotel Don Carlos ★ *Finds* If you're looking for a small hotel that is unmistakably Costa Rican and hints at the days of the planters and coffee barons, this is the place for you. Located in an old residential neighborhood, only blocks from the business district, the Don Carlos is popular with both vacationers and businesspeople. A large reproduction of a pre-Columbian carved-stone human figure stands outside the front door of this gray inn, which was a former president's mansion. Inside you'll find many more such reproductions, as well as orchids, ferns, palms, paintings, and parrots. After a day of exploring the capital, there's nothing like settling down in the lounge, the small courtyard, or the sunny deck, where the wicker furniture, bubbling fountain, and tropical breezes will make you think you're Hope or Crosby on the road to somewhere. The rooms are distinct and vary greatly in size, so be specific when you reserve, or ask if it's possible to see a few when you check in. There's a soothing 10-person Jacuzzi and an outdoor orchid garden and atrium where breakfast is served. The gift shop here is one of the largest in the country, and guests have free use of the hotel's Internet access.

779 Calle 9, between avs. 7 and 9, San José. ✆ **221-6707.** Fax 255-0828. www.doncarloshotel.com. 33 units. $65–$75 double. Rates include continental breakfast. AE, MC, V. Free parking. **Amenities:** Restaurant; bar; Jacuzzi; tour desk; limited room service (7am–9pm); laundry service. *In room:* TV, hair dryer, iron, safe.

Hotel Presidente This modern business-class hotel is a good midrange option in the heart of downtown. Although the hotel's eight stories practically qualify it for skyscraper status, very few of the rooms have any view to speak of; those with north-facing windows are your best bet. Rooms are all clean and modern, and feature the basic amenities you'd expect. Most rooms come with one double and one single bed. If you want more space, opt for one of the junior suites or the suites. The master suite is a massive two-bedroom affair, featuring a wide-screen TV in the living room and a private eight-person Jacuzzi. There's a very popular casual cafe-style restaurant just off the street.

Av. Central and Calle 7 (A.P. 2922-1000), San José. ✆ **222-3022.** Fax 221-1205. www.hotel-presidente.com. 100 units. $75 double; $105–$250 suite. Rates include full breakfast buffet. AE, MC, V. Free parking. **Amenities:** Restaurant; bar; rooftop Jacuzzi and sauna; tour desk; limited room service (6am–10pm); babysitting; laundry service. *In room:* A/C, TV, safe.

Hotel Santo Tomás ★★ *Value* Even though it's on a busy downtown street, this converted mansion is a quiet oasis inside. Built 100 years ago by a coffee baron, the house has been lovingly restored and maintained by its owner, Thomas Douglas. Throughout the hotel you'll enjoy the deep, dark tones of well-aged and well-worked wood. The rooms vary in size, but most are fairly spacious and have a small table and chairs. Skylights in some bathrooms will brighten your morning, and firm beds provide a good night's sleep. There are a couple of patio areas, as well as a lounge and combination breakfast room and outdoor bar. There's also a small kidney-shape outdoor pool with a Jacuzzi above it; the two are solar heated and connected by a tiny waterslide. The staff and management are extremely helpful with tour arrangements and any other needs or requests, and the restaurant here is excellent.

Av. 7, between calles 3 and 5, San José. ✆ **255-0448.** Fax 222-3950. www.hotelsantotomas.com. 20 units. $65–$100 double. Rates include breakfast buffet. MC, V. Parking nearby. **Amenities:** Restaurant; bar; lounge; small outdoor pool; exercise room; Jacuzzi; tour desk; laundry service; nonsmoking rooms. *In room:* TV.

Raya Vida Villa ★ Located behind a big iron gate at the end of a narrow, dead-end lane, this little bed-and-breakfast is so secluded that it seems to be in a world all its own, yet it's in downtown San José. Behind the gate, in a shady old garden, is a miniature villa. The restored old stucco home is furnished with the owners' eclectic collection of crafts from around the world, and in the living room you'll find a grand piano and fireplace. Guest rooms are all different. The upstairs rooms have the largest bathrooms, and one even has a Jacuzzi tub. However, I like the downstairs room that opens onto a small open-air patio with a fountain.

A.P. 2209-2100, San José (mailing address: P.O. Box 025216-1638, Miami, FL 33102-5216). © 223-4168. Fax 223-4157. www.rayavida.com. 4 units. $95 double. Rates include full breakfast and round-trip airport transfer. Rates lower in the off season. MC, V. Free parking. *In room:* TV, no phone.

Taylor's Inn Here's yet another lovely converted home turned bed-and-breakfast. The rooms are all arranged around the interior courtyard, which features flowering ginger and other tropical flora—a perfect place for breakfast. Most rooms have one single and one double bed, although a few have sleeping lofts and are good for families. All are very clean and feature artwork from prominent Costa Rican artists. The suite is a bit bigger, with a 20-inch television. Don't expect a sense of hermetic privacy here, though—most of the rooms open onto the courtyard, and the old wooden construction guarantees that you hear every footfall and conversation of other guests passing by your door. The hotel has a helpful tour desk.

Av. 13, between calles 3 and 3 bis (A.P. 531-1000), San José. © 257-4333. Fax 221-1475. www.catours. co.cr. 10 units. $60 double. Rates include buffet breakfast. Rates slightly lower in the off season. AE, MC, V. **Amenities:** Lounge; tour desk; laundry service; nonsmoking rooms. *In room:* TV, safe, no phone.

INEXPENSIVE

In addition to the places listed below, **Casa Ridgeway** (© 233-6168) is a quaint little guesthouse run by a local Quaker group at Calle 15 and Avenida 6 bis, near the downtown courts. Other good options include **Kap's Place** (© 221-1169; www.kapsplace.com), located just across from the Hotel Aranjuez on Calle 19 between avenidas 11 and 13, and **Hotel Doña Ines** (© 222-7443; www. donaines.com).

Finally, real budget hounds might want to look into either **Tranquilo Back-packers** (© 223-3189; www.tranquilobackpackers.com), on Calle 7 between avenidas 9 and 11, or **Costa Rica Backpackers** (© 221-6191; www.costarica backpackers.com), on Avenida 6 between calles 21 and 23.

Hotel Aranjuez *Value* This is probably the best and deservedly most popular budget option close to downtown. Located on a quiet and safe street in the Barrio Amón neighborhood, this humble hotel is made up of five contiguous houses. The rooms are all simple and clean, although some are little dark. Both the rooms and bathrooms vary greatly in size, so be very specific when reserving, or ask to see a few rooms when you arrive. The nicest features here, aside from the convivial hostel-like atmosphere, are the lush and shady gardens; the hanging orchids, bromeliads, and ferns decorating the hallways and nooks; and the numerous open lounge areas furnished with chairs, tables, and couches—great for lazing around and sharing travel tales with your fellow guests. The hotel has a couple of computers and offers guests free Internet and e-mail services.

Calle 19, between avs. 11 and 13 (A.P. 457-2070), San José. © 877/898-8663 in the U.S., or 256-1825. Fax 223-3528. www.hotelaranjuez.com. 35 units, 6 with shared bathroom. $24 double with shared bathroom; $35–$38 double with private bathroom. Rates include breakfast buffet. V. Free parking. **Amenities:** Bar; several lounge areas; tour desk; laundry service. *In room:* TV, safe.

Joluva Guesthouse Although you can find a less expensive hotel, few in this price range offer the old-fashioned architectural detail of the Joluva, with old-tile and hardwood floors throughout and high ceilings (one room offers beautiful plasterwork on the ceiling). The hotel is located in the heart of Barrio Amón. Still, the rooms are small and a bit dark, and only two have windows that open onto the small courtyard. The breakfast room has skylights, which help brighten it a bit. This hotel caters to a gay clientele, but all guests are welcome. All rooms are nonsmoking.

936 Calle 3B, between avs. 9 and 11, San José. © 223-7961. Fax 257-7668. www.joluva.com. 7 units, 6 with private bathroom. $25 double without bathroom; $50 double with bathroom. Rates include continental breakfast. AE, MC, V. Parking nearby. **Amenities:** Tour desk; laundry service; nonsmoking rooms. *In room:* TV, safe, no phone.

Pensión de la Cuesta *(Value* If you don't mind a clean communal bathroom down the hall from your room, this little bed-and-breakfast on the hill leading up to the Parque Nacional is a real bargain and definitely worth considering. It was once the home of Otto Apuy, a well-known Costa Rican artist, and original artwork abounds. The building itself is a classic example of a tropical wood-frame home and has been painted an eye-catching pink with blue-and-white trim. Some of the rooms can be a bit dark and are very simply furnished, but there's a sunny and cheery sunken lounge/courtyard area in the center of the house. Most of the rooms have one double and a set of bunk beds. Overall, the place feels a lot like a hostel. The owners give you free run of the kitchen and even offer free use of their Internet connection.

1332 Cuesta de Núñez, Av. 1 between calles 11 and 15, San José. © 256-7946 or ©/fax 255-2896. www. suntoursandfun.com. 9 units, none with private bathroom. $27–$35 double. Rates include continental breakfast. Children under 12 stay free in parent's room. AE, MC, V. Parking nearby. **Amenities:** Lounge w/cable TV; tour desk; laundry service. *In room:* No phone.

LA SABANA/PASEO COLON
MODERATE
In addition to the hotels listed below, business travelers looking for a modern, comfortable business-class hotel in this area could check into the **Palma Real** (© 290-4160; www.hotelpalmareal.com), although I think you get more amenities and options at the Tryp Corobicí (see below), for a similar price.

Hotel Grano de Oro ★★ *Finds* San José boasts dozens of old homes that have been converted into hotels, but few offer the luxurious accommodations or professional service that can be found at the Grano de Oro. Located on a quiet side street off Paseo Colón, this small hotel offers a variety of room types to fit most budgets and tastes. Personally, I prefer the patio rooms, which have French doors opening onto private patios. However, if you want a room with plenty of space, ask for one of the deluxe rooms, which have large, modern, tiled baths with big tubs. All rooms are nonsmoking.

Throughout all the guest rooms, you'll find attractive hardwood furniture, including old-fashioned wardrobes in some rooms. For additional luxuries, you can stay in one of the suites, which have whirlpool tubs. The Vista de Oro suite is the hotel's crown jewel, with its own private staircase and wonderful views of the city and surrounding mountains. If you don't grab a suite, you still have access to the hotel's two rooftop Jacuzzis. The hotel's patio-garden restaurant serves excellent international cuisine and some of the best desserts in the city.

Calle 30, no. 251, between avs. 2 and 4, 150m (492 ft.) south of Paseo Colón, San José (mailing address: SJO 36, P.O. Box 025216, Miami, FL 33102). © 255-3322. Fax 221-2782. www.hotelgranodeoro.com. 35 units. $90–$125 double; $150–$255 suite. AE, MC, V. Free parking. **Amenities:** Restaurant; lounge; 2 rooftop Jacuzzis; concierge; tour desk; limited room service (6am–10pm); laundry service; nonsmoking rooms. *In room:* TV, minibar, safe.

Hotel Rosa del Paseo ✦   This hotel is housed in one of San José's most beautiful old stucco homes, right on busy Paseo Colón. However, the rooms are all located away from the street and are well insulated against the noise. Built more than 110 years ago, this old home underwent a complete renovation and modernization a few years ago and is now richly appointed and surprisingly evocative of 19th-century Costa Rica. The rooms are all quite comfortable; the master suite even comes with its own balcony and Jacuzzi. I'd definitely try to grab one of the rooms on the second floor, which feature wooden floors and front doors that open onto the open-air central courtyard. There are beautiful details throughout the hotel: transoms, ornate stucco doorframes, and polished hardwood floors.

2862 Paseo Colón, between calles 28 and 30 (A.P. 287-1007, Centro Colón), San José. ✆ **257-3225.** Fax 223-2776. www.rosadelpaseo.com. 18 units. $70 double; $85–$100 suite. Rates include continental breakfast. AE, DC, MC, V. Limited free parking. **Amenities:** Bar; lounge; tour desk; babysitting; laundry service; nonsmoking rooms. *In room:* TV, safe.

Hotel Torremolinos   If you want to be close to downtown, have some of the trappings of a modern business-class hotel, and not spend a fortune, this is a good choice. Located at the west end of Paseo Colón, the Torremolinos is on a fairly quiet street and is built around a colorful and well-tended garden that makes the hotel's pool a wonderful place to while away an afternoon. The rooms are simply furnished and have plenty of space.

Calle 40 and Av. 5 bis (A.P. 434-1150, La Uruca), San José. ✆ **222-5266.** Fax 255-3167. www.occidental-hoteles.com. 84 units. $75 double. Rates include breakfast. AE, MC, V. Free parking. **Amenities:** Restaurant; bar; small outdoor pool; tour desk; modest business center; limited room service; laundry service. *In room:* TV, coffeemaker, hair dryer, safe.

Tryp Corobicí ✦   Located just past the end of Paseo Colón and on the edge of Parque La Sabana, the Corobicí offers all the amenities you would expect at a large airport hotel, with one added bonus: It's much closer to downtown. The lobby is a vast expanse of marble floor faced by blank walls, although the Art Deco furnishings lend a bit of character. Guest rooms are modern and comfortable, with good beds and walls of glass through which, on most floors, you get good views of the valley and surrounding mountains. Joggers will enjoy the nearby Parque La Sabana. The Corobicí claims to have the largest health spa in Central America; I'm not sure that this is still true, but you will find a well-equipped exercise room and aerobics classes. The Fuji restaurant here is one of the best Japanese and sushi restaurants in San José.

Autopista General Cañas, Sabana Norte (A.P. 2443-1000), San José. ✆ **888/485-2676** in the U.S., or 232-8122. Fax 231-5834. www.solmelia.com. 203 units. $90–$120 double; $120–$160 suite. AE, MC, V. Free parking. **Amenities:** 2 restaurants; bar; lounge; midsize outdoor pool; health club and spa; Jacuzzi; sauna; tour desk; car-rental desk; business center; shopping arcade; salon; 24-hr. room service; in-room massage; babysitting; laundry service; nonsmoking rooms. *In room:* A/C, TV, minibar, hair dryer, safe.

INEXPENSIVE

Hotel Cacts   This is one of the more interesting and unusual budget hotels I've ever seen. It's housed in an attractive tropical contemporary home on a business and residential street. The current complex is a maze of rooms and hallways on several levels. Rooms vary considerably in size, so it's always best to check out a few first, if possible. The deluxe rooms here come with televisions and telephones, whereas the older standard rooms lack both of these amenities. There are also four budget rooms that share a couple of common bathrooms. The third-floor open terrace serves as the breakfast area. The staff here is very helpful, and the hotel will receive mail and faxes, change money, and store baggage for guests. By the time you read this, they might just have added an outdoor pool.

Av. 3 bis, no. 2845, between calles 28 and 30 (A.P. 379-1005), San José. © **221-2928** or 221-6546. Fax 221-8616. hcacts@sol.racsa.co.cr. 25 units. $35 double with shared bathroom; $35–$50 double with private bathroom. Rates include breakfast buffet. AE, MC, V. Free parking. **Amenities:** Lounge; tour desk; laundry service; nonsmoking rooms. *In room:* No phone.

SAN PEDRO/LOS YOSES
MODERATE

Hotel 1492 Jade y Oro ★   Housed in a restored old home on a quiet street in the heart of the Barrio Escalante neighborhood just east of the city center, this little bed-and-breakfast makes a good base for exploring the city or this side of town. The rooms are simple and tastefully done with locally crafted wooden furniture, plenty of light, and a homey feel. Breakfast is served in an open-air rancho overlooking a lovely little garden. The hotel is run by a Costa Rican family, and you really get the feel that you are staying in a local joint.

Av. 1, no. 2985, between calles 31 and 33, Barrio Escalante. © **256-5913.** Fax 280-6206. www.hotel1492.com. 10 units. $70–$80 double. Rates include full breakfast. AE, MC, V. Free parking. **Amenities:** Laundry service; nonsmoking rooms. *In room:* TV.

Hotel Le Bergerac ★★ *(Finds)*   With all the sophistication and charm of a small French inn, the Hotel Le Bergerac has ingratiated itself with business travelers and members of various diplomatic missions. These visitors have found a tranquil environment in a quiet suburban neighborhood, spacious and comfortable accommodations, personal service, and gourmet meals. The hotel is composed of three houses with courtyard gardens in between. Almost all of the rooms are quite large, and each is a little different. My favorite rooms are those with private patio gardens. Some rooms have king-size beds and refrigerators, and in the old master bedroom you'll find a little balcony.

In the evenings, candlelight and classical music set a relaxing and romantic mood. The long-standing L'Ile de France restaurant has set up shop here, and gourmet French and Continental dinners are available for guests and by reservation.

Calle 35, no. 50 (A.P. 1107-1002), San José. © **234-7850.** Fax 225-9103. www.bergerachotel.com. 24 units. $68–$95 double. Rates include full breakfast. AE, DC, MC, V. Free parking. **Amenities:** Restaurant; lounge; concierge; tour desk; business and secretarial services; laundry service. *In room:* TV, hair dryer, safe.

INEXPENSIVE

Toruma Youth Hostel *(Value)*   This attractive old building, with its long veranda, is the largest hostel in Costa Rica's system of official youth hostels. Although it's possible to find other accommodations around town in this price range, none would likely be as clean. The atmosphere here is convivial and will be familiar to anyone who has hostelled in Europe. There's a large lounge in the center of the building with a high ceiling and a great deal of light. The dorms have four to six beds per room, although three rooms here actually are classified as doubles and are rented out on a first-come, first-served basis to couples. All rooms are nonsmoking. The staff here can help you arrange stays at other hostels and trips around the country, and they'll even watch some of your bags for you for free.

Av. Central, between calles 29 and 31 (A.P. 1355-1002), San José. © **234-8186** or ©/fax 224-4085. www.toruma.com. 95 beds, all with shared bathroom. $10–$22 per person per night with IYHF card; $18–$25 general public. Rates include continental breakfast. MC, V. Free parking. *In room:* No phone.

ESCAZU & SANTA ANA

Located about 15 minutes west of San José and about the same distance from the international airport, these affluent suburbs have experienced rapid growth in recent years, as the metropolitan area continues its urban sprawl. Both Escazú and Santa Ana are popular with the Costa Rican professional class and North American retirees and expatriates, and quite a few hotels have sprung up to cater to their needs. It's relatively easy to commute between Escazú or Santa Ana and downtown via bus or taxi. Taxi fare should run around $8 to $10 (each way). A bus costs around 30¢.

VERY EXPENSIVE

Hotel Alta ★★   This small boutique hotel is infused with old-world charm. Curves and high arches abound. My favorite touch is the winding interior alleyway that snakes down from the reception through the hotel. Most of the rooms here have wonderful views of the Central Valley from private balconies; the others have nice garden patios. The rooms are all up to modern resort standards, although some have cramped bathrooms. The suites are considerably larger, each with a separate sitting room with its own television, as well as large Jacuzzi-style tubs (no jets, though) in spacious bathrooms; they're definitely worth the slight splurge. If you opt to rent the entire upper floor, the penthouse becomes a three-bedroom, full-floor extravaganza, with a massive living room and open-air rooftop patio. The hotel's La Luz restaurant (p. 116) is one of the more elegant and creative in the Central Valley.

Alto de las Palomas, old road to Santa Ana. ✆ 888/388-2582 in the U.S. and Canada, or 282-4160. Fax 282-4162. www.thealtahotel.com. 23 units. $155 double; $185 junior suite; $350 master suite; $790 penthouse. Rates include continental breakfast and complimentary airport shuttle. Rates lower in the off season. AE, DC, MC, V. Free parking. **Amenities:** Restaurant; bar; midsize pool; exercise room; Jacuzzi; sauna; concierge; tour desk; secretarial services; limited room service (7am–10pm); in-room massage; laundry service. *In room:* A/C, TV, dataport, minibar, coffeemaker, hair dryer, iron, safe.

Real InterContinental San José ★★   This is a modern and luxurious large-scale business-class hotel. Three five-story wings radiate off a central hub. The large, open lobby has a flagstone-and-mosaic floor. The rooms are all well appointed, with either one king-size or two double beds, a working desk, a sitting chair and ottoman, and a large armoire housing a 25-inch television. For an extra $30, you can stay on the Club InterContinental floor and enjoy personalized concierge and butler services, a separate check-in area, an on-floor buffet breakfast, and an assortment of refreshments, sweets, hors d'oeuvres, and drinks throughout the day. This floor is where the junior and master suites are located.

The hotel is just across from a large, modern shopping-mall complex, which is nice if you want access to the shopping, restaurants, and a six-plex movie theater. Overall, the InterContinental offers many of the same features and amenities as the Marriott (p. 106), although the latter gets the nod in terms of service, restaurants, and ambience.

Autopista Próspero Fernández, across from the Multiplaza mall, Escazú. ✆ 289-7000. Fax 289-8930. www.gruporeal.com. 260 units. $180–$260 double; $500–$1,000 suite. AE, MC, V. Free parking. **Amenities:** 2 restaurants; 2 bars; lounge; large free-form pool; outdoor tennis court; modest health club and spa; Jacuzzi; concierge; tour desk; car-rental desk; well-appointed business center; small shopping arcade; salon; 24-hr. room service; in-room massage; laundry service; nonsmoking rooms. *In room:* A/C, TV, minibar, coffeemaker, hair dryer, safe.

MODERATE

In addition to the hotels listed below, the **Courtyard San José** (✆ 888/236-2427 in the U.S. and Canada, or 208-3000; www.marriott.com) and **Comfort Hotel Real Santa Ana** (✆ 204-6700; www.choicehotels.com) are both modern business-class hotels that have recently opened within a few miles of each other, right on the western Próspero Fernández Highway connecting Santa Ana and Escazú with San José.

Casa de las Tías *(Finds)*   This converted Victorian-style home is comfortable and brimming with local character. The rooms are homey and simply decorated in a sort of Costa Rican country motif. The hotel has a wonderful covered veranda for sitting and admiring the well-tended gardens, as well as a TV room and common areas inside the house. The owners live on-site and are extremely helpful and friendly. Located on a quiet side street, Casa de las Tías is nonetheless just a block away from a busy section of Escazú, where you'll find scores of restaurants and shops. The hotel is located 100m (328 ft.) south and 150m (492 ft.) east of El Cruce de San Rafael de Escazú.

San Rafael de Escazú. © **289-5517.** Fax 289-7353. www.hotels.co.cr. 5 units. $65–$77 double. Rates include full breakfast. AE, MC, V. **Amenities:** Tour desk; laundry service.

Hotel Mirador Pico Blanco   There's nothing fancy about the rooms here, but most offer absolutely fabulous views. Some rooms have high ceilings, creating an appearance of spaciousness, and almost all of them have balconies (albeit small ones). A few resident macaws fly around the hillsides during the day but come home here each evening. The restaurant is a popular and inexpensive spot, probably the cheapest "view" restaurant in the valley; the bar has been getting bigger and more popular over the years as well.

1km (½ mile) south of the church in San Antonio de Escazú (A.P. 900), Escazú. © **228-1908.** Fax 289-5189. www.hotelpicoblanco.com. 25 units. $48–$70 double. MC, V. Free parking. **Amenities:** Restaurant; bar; tour desk; limited room service (8am–10pm); babysitting; laundry service. *In room:* TV, no phone.

HEREDIA & ALAJUELA (AIRPORT AREA)

Alajuela and Heredia are two colonial-era cities that lie much closer to the airport than San José. Alajuela is the closest city to the airport, with Heredia lying about midway between Alajuela and the capital. These are two great places to find small, distinct, and charming hotels. If you'd like to learn more about either of these cities, see "Side Trips from San José," later in this chapter. If your plans are to get yourself to a remote beach or rainforest lodge as quickly as possible and to use San José and the Central Valley purely as a transportation hub, or if you just detest urban clutter, noise, and pollution, you might do well to choose one of the hotels listed below.

VERY EXPENSIVE

Finca Rosa Blanca Country Inn ★★★ *(Finds)*   Finca Rosa Blanca is an eclectic architectural confection set amid the lush, green hillsides of a coffee plantation. Square corners seem to have been prohibited in the design of this beautiful home. There are turrets and curving walls of glass, arched windows, and a semi-circular built-in couch. Everywhere the glow of polished hardwood blends with blindingly white stucco walls and brightly painted murals.

Inside there's original artwork everywhere, and each room is decidedly unique. There's the black-and-white room with a patio and bed made from coffee-tree wood. Another room has a bed built into a corner and a handmade tub with windows on two sides. The view is fabulous. If breathtaking bathrooms are your idea of the ultimate luxury, consider splurging on the master suite, which has a stone waterfall that cascades into a tub in front of a huge picture window. This suite also has a spiral staircase that leads to the top of the turret. The two separate villas have the same sense of eclectic luxury, with small kitchenettes and quite a bit of space and privacy. All rooms are nonsmoking.

A four-course gourmet dinner served in the small dining room will run you $32 per person. Be sure to reserve early because there's limited seating. In a tiny space off the living room, there's an honor bar tucked into a reproduction of a typical Costa Rican oxcart.

Santa Bárbara de Heredia (mailing address: SJO 3475, P.O. Box 25369, Miami, FL 33102). ℂ **269-9392.** Fax 269-9555. www.fincarosablanca.com. 7 units, 2 villas. $180–$270 double. Extra person $30. Rates include breakfast. AE, MC, V. Free parking. **Amenities:** Restaurant; small honor bar; lounge; small free-form outdoor pool set in the hillside; small exercise room; Jacuzzi; concierge; tour desk; limited room service; in-room massage; babysitting; laundry service; nonsmoking rooms. *In room:* Minibar, safe.

Marriott Costa Rica Hotel ★★★ For my money, the Marriott is the only luxury resort hotel in the San José area that gets almost everything right. Amenities are plentiful, and service here reaches a level of attention to detail uncommon in Costa Rica. The hotel is designed in a mixed colonial style, with hand-painted Mexican tiles, antique red-clay roof tiles, weathered columns, and heavy wooden doors, lintels, and trim. The centerpiece is a large open-air interior patio, which somewhat replicates Old Havana's Plaza de Armas. The rooms are all comfortable and well appointed, with either a king-size or two double beds, two telephones, a working desk, an elegant wooden armoire holding a large television, plenty of closet space, a comfortable sitting chair and ottoman, and a small "Juliet" balcony. The bathrooms are up to par but seem slightly small for this price. The casual Villa Hermosa restaurant serves well-prepared "nouvelle Costa Rican" and international dishes, and there's a more upscale Spanish restaurant and tapas bar in a faux wine cellar. The large lobby-level bar features daily piano music and weekend nights of jazz, with both indoor and patio seating.

San Antonio de Belén (A.P. 502-4005). ℂ **888/236-2427** in the U.S. and Canada, or 298-0844. Fax 298-0033. www.marriott.com. 252 units. $230 double; $260 executive level; $500 master suite; $1,000 presidential suite. Rates lower in the off season. AE, DC, MC, V. Free valet parking. **Amenities:** 3 restaurants; bar; lounge; 2 outdoor pools; golf driving range; 3 outdoor tennis courts; small but well-appointed health club and sauna; Jacuzzi; concierge; tour desk; car-rental desk; free airport and downtown shuttle; business center and secretarial services; small shopping arcade; salon; 24-hr. room service; in-room massage; babysitting; laundry service; nonsmoking rooms. *In room:* A/C, TV, dataport, minibar, coffeemaker, hair dryer, iron, safe.

Meliá Cariari ★★ *Kids* With its use of stone walls, an open-air lobby, and lush garden plantings, the Cariari has more of a tropical feel than the two luxury hotels mentioned above. Over the past few years, the guest rooms have been remodeled, and all now have plenty of space and comfort. The rooms, which are done in rich dark tones, have either one king-size bed or two double beds, although I find most of the bathrooms a bit small. The suites are more spacious and similarly appointed. The Cariari has a massive pool, tennis, and spa complex. The Cariari is also the only hotel in the Central Valley with its own golf course (although guests at the Herradura have access to the course, tennis courts, and spa as well), along with a sister course at the Paradisus Playa Conchal resort, which makes this a good choice for golfers looking for a package tour.

Autopista General Cañas, Ciudad Cariari (A.P. 737-1007, Centro Colón), San José. ℂ **888/956-3542** in the U.S. and Canada, or 239-0022. Fax 239-2803. www.solmelia.com. 220 units. $120–$150 double; $200–$400 suite. AE, DC, MC, V. Free valet parking. **Amenities:** 3 restaurants; 2 bars; lounge; Olympic-size pool divided into lanes for training, as well as another large pool w/swim-up bar; 18-hole golf course and pro shop; 12 tennis courts; health club w/saunas and Jacuzzis; game room; concierge; tour desk; car-rental desk; complimentary airport and downtown shuttle; business center; salon; 24-hr. room service; in-room massage; babysitting; laundry service; nonsmoking rooms. *In room:* A/C, TV, dataport, minibar, coffeemaker, hair dryer, iron, safe.

Peace Lodge ★★ *(Finds)*   The rooms at this outgrowth of the popular La Paz Waterfall Gardens just might be some of the most impressive in the country—and the bathrooms in the deluxe units easily earn that distinction. The rooms are quite large and feature sparkling wood floors and trim, handcrafted four-poster beds, beautiful stone fireplaces, intricately sculpted steel light fixtures, and a host of other creative touches and details. Every room has a private balcony fitted with a mosaic-tiled Jacuzzi. The aforementioned deluxe bathrooms come with a second oversize Jacuzzi set under a skylight in the middle of an immense room that features a full interior wall planted with ferns, orchids, and bromeliads, and fed by a functioning waterfall system. Guests here have full access to all the tours and attractions of the La Paz Waterfall Gardens (p. 122) during normal operating hours and beyond. So far, only 10 rooms have been opened here, but the plan is for a total of 40. The lodge is located about 45 minutes from the airport and makes a good first stop if your itinerary takes you next to La Fortuna and Arenal volcano, or to the Puerto Viejo de Sarapiqui region.

6km (3¾ miles) north of Varablanca on the road to San Miguel. © 482-2720 or 225-0643. www.waterfall gardens.com. 10 units. $185–$215 double; $295 villa. Rates include breakfast and entrance to La Paz Waterfall Gardens. Rates lower in the off season. AE, MC, V. **Amenities:** Restaurant; bar; laundry service. *In room:* A/C, TV, stocked minibar, coffeemaker, safe.

Xandari Resort & Spa ★★ *(Finds)*   Xandari is yet another architecturally stunning small hotel not far from the airport. Set on a high hilltop above the city of Alajuela, Xandari commands wonderful views of the surrounding coffee farms and the Central Valley below. The villas are huge private affairs with high-curved ceilings, stained-glass windows, and handmade fine furniture. All come with both an outdoor patio with a view and a private covered palapa, as well as a smaller interior terrace with chaise longues. Most have king-size beds; the rest have two queens. There are spacious living rooms with rattan sofas and chairs, as well as small kitchenettes. The owners are artists, and their original works and innovative design touches abound. The hotel grounds contain several miles of trails that pass by at least five jungle waterfalls, as well as lush gardens and fruit orchards. The adjacent "spa village" features a series of private thatch-roofed treatment rooms, many with their own Jacuzzi, and most with stunning views. A wide range of spa and beauty treatments is offered, in addition to yoga and other fitness classes.

A.P. 1485-4050, Alajuela (mailing address: Box 1449, Summerland, CA 93067). © 800/686-7879 in the U.S., or 443-2020. Fax 442-4847. www.xandari.com. 18 villas. $180–$260 villa for 2. Rates include continental breakfast and airport shuttle. $20 for extra person over 12; $10 for children 3–11; children under 3 stay free in parent's room. Rates lower in the off season. AE, MC, V. **Amenities:** Restaurant; bar; lounge; 2 lap pools; small outdoor exercise room; several Jacuzzis; spa; in-room massage; laundry service. *In room:* Kitchenette, minibar, safe.

EXPENSIVE
Hampton Inn & Suites   If familiarity, basic comfort, and proximity to the airport are important to you, then the Hampton Inn is your best bet. The rooms are what you'd expect from a well-known chain, and because the hotel is relatively new, they don't show much wear and tear. There are actually two separate buildings: The one closest to the highway holds the hotel rooms, while set farther back is a separate building of one- and two-bedroom suites. Aside from being more spacious, the suites come with a minifridge and microwave oven. Breakfast is served, but there are no other dining options right on the premises, although there is a Costa Rican fast-food chicken joint just across the parking

lot. This is a good choice if your plane arrives very late or leaves very early, and you don't plan to spend any time in San José.

Autopista General Cañas, by the airport (A.P. 195-4003), San José. ☎ **800/426-7866** in the U.S., or 443-0043. Fax 442-9532. www.hamptoninn.com. 100 units. $110 double; $132 suite. Rates include continental breakfast and airport shuttle. AE, DC, MC, V. Free parking. **Amenities:** Bar; small outdoor pool; small exercise room; tour desk; business center; babysitting; laundry service; nonsmoking rooms. *In room:* A/C, TV, coffeemaker, hair dryer, iron, safe.

Vista del Valle Plantation Inn ★★ *Finds*　If you have little need for San José and would like a comfortable base for exploring the rest of Costa Rica, consider this fine little country inn. It began as a converted private home, and the owners have been adding elegant little cottages around their grounds, which command an impressive view over the Río Grande and its steep-walled canyon. The architecture here has a strong Japanese influence. Most of the accommodations are in independent or duplex cottages or villas. The cottages are open and airy, with lots of windows letting in lots of light. You'll also find plenty of varnished woodwork, small kitchenettes (in some), and comfortable wraparound decks. My favorites are the Mona Lisa and Ylang-Ylang suites, which are octagonal affairs set on the edge of the bluff with great views, and featuring private outdoor showers.

The grounds are wonderfully landscaped, with several inviting seating areas set among a wealth of flowering tropical plants. Meals are served on the poolside terrace's dining area. The dinner menu varies nightly, featuring fine Continental cuisine prepared with fresh local ingredients. The hotel is located 20 minutes north of the Juan Santamaría Airport, and staying here can cut as much as an hour off your travel time to the Pacific coast beaches, Arenal Volcano, and the Monteverde Cloud Forest.

A.P. 185-4003, Alajuela (mailing address: SJO 1994, P.O. Box 025216, Miami, FL, 33102). ☎ **450-0800** or ☎/fax 451-1165. www.vistadelvalle.com. 12 units. $90 double in the main house; $140–$160 villa. Rates include full breakfast. Rates lower in the off season. AE, MC, V. **Amenities:** Restaurant; midsize tile pool w/an interesting little fountain/waterfall; tennis court; Jacuzzi; laundry service. *In room:* Fridge, no phone.

MODERATE

Hotel Bougainvillea ★ *Value*　The Hotel Bougainvillea is an excellent choice—a great value if you're looking for a hotel in a quiet residential neighborhood not far from downtown. It offers most of the amenities of the more expensive resort hotels around the Central Valley, but it charges considerably less. The views across the valley from this hillside location are wonderful, and the gardens are beautifully designed and well tended. In fact, the bird-watching is pretty good in the hotel's relatively expansive gardens. Rooms are carpeted and have small triangular balconies oriented to the views. Although there is no air-conditioning, there are fans, and temperatures rarely get too hot here. A complimentary hourly downtown shuttle bus will take you in and out of town.

In Santo Tomás de Santo Domingo de Heredia, 100m (328 ft.) west of the Escuela de Santo Tomás (A.P. 69-2120), San José. ☎ **244-1414.** Fax 244-1313. www.bougainvillea.co.cr. 81 units. $78–$100 double. AE, DC, MC, V. Free parking. **Amenities:** Restaurant; bar; midsize outdoor pool in attractive garden; 2 outdoor lighted tennis courts; Jacuzzi; sauna; tour desk; business center; limited room service; babysitting; laundry service; nonsmoking rooms. *In room:* TV, hair dryer.

Orquídeas Inn　This little boutique inn is just 10 minutes from the airport on the road heading out of Alajuela to Grecia and the Poás Volcano. The rooms are all spacious and comfortable, with tile floors, private bathrooms, and colorful Guatemalan bedspreads. The deluxe rooms are in a separate building up on a hill, and most of these offer wonderful views, particularly those with balconies facing one of the nearby volcanoes. There are a few larger minisuites located around the small pool, as well as a separate geodesic dome with a king-size bed in a loft reached by a spiral staircase, a large sunken tub in the bathroom, and a full kitchen and living-room area. The entire grounds are lush and tropical. The Marilyn Monroe bar serves up good drinks, *bocas*, and some seriously spicy buffalo wings.

A.P. 394, Alajuela. © **433-9346.** Fax 433-9740. www.orquideasinn.com. 27 units. $65–$99 double; $89–$150 suite. Rates include breakfast buffet. AE, MC, V. No children under 10. **Amenities:** Restaurant; bar; 2 midsize outdoor pools; tennis court; concierge; tour desk; laundry service.

4 Where to Dine

In broad terms, Costa Rican cuisine is easily disparaged and dismissed. Rice and beans are served at nearly every meal, the selection of other dishes is minimal, and Ticos generally don't go for spicy food—or so the criticism goes. In recent years, though, some contemporary and creative chefs have been trying to educate and enlighten the Costa Rican palate, particularly in San José, and the early results are promising. Still, most visitors to the capital city quickly tire of Tico fare, even in its more chichi incarnations, and start seeking out the many local restaurants serving international cuisines. They are richly rewarded.

San José has a rather amazing variety of restaurants serving cuisines from all over the world, and you'll never pay much even at the best restaurants. In fact, you really have to work at it to spend more than $40 per person for even the most extravagant meal (not including liquor). Most restaurants fall into the moderate price range. Service can be indifferent at many restaurants because the gratuity is already tacked onto the check, and tipping is not common among locals.

LOCAL CUISINE   If you'd really like to sample the local flavor, head to a *soda*, the equivalent of a diner in the United States, where you can get good, cheap, and filling Tico food. Rice and beans are the staples here and show up at breakfast, lunch, and dinner (when mixed together, they're called *gallo pinto*). For breakfast, they're garnished with everything from fried eggs to steak. At lunch and dinner, rice and beans are the main components of a *casado* (which means "married"), the Costa Rican equivalent of a "blue-plate special." A *casado* generally is served with a salad of cabbage and tomatoes, fried bananas, and steak, chicken, or fish. A plate of *gallo pinto* might cost $2, and a *casado* might cost $2.50 to $4, usually with a *fresco* (a fresh fruit drink) thrown into the bargain.

While in Costa Rica, be sure to taste a few of these *frescos*. They're a bit like a fresh-fruit milkshake without the ice cream, and when made with mangoes, papayas, bananas, or any of the other delicious tropical fruits of Costa Rica, they're pure ambrosia. *Frescos* can be made with water *(con agua)* or with milk *(con leche)*, and preferences vary. Certain fruits such as carambola (star fruit), *maracuyá* (a type of passion fruit), and *cas* (you'll just have to try it) are used only with water. But remember, although the water in Costa Rica is generally very safe to drink, those with tender stomachs or intestinal tracts should stick to *frescos* made with milk because it's pasteurized.

FRUIT VENDORS   There's a fruit vendor on almost every street corner in downtown San José. If you're lucky enough to be in town between April and June, you can sample more varieties of mangoes than you ever knew existed. I like buying them already cut up in a little bag; they cost a little more this way, but you don't get nearly as messy. Be sure to try a green mango with salt and

---

Tips   Shameless Plug

If you want a more comprehensive guide to the restaurant scene in San José and around the country, pick up a copy of my recently released *Tico Times Restaurant Guide to Costa Rica,* which features reviews of more than 300 restaurants around Costa Rica, indexed by location, cuisine type, and overall quality. The guide is available in local bookstores, supermarkets, gift shops, and the airport.

---

chile peppers—guaranteed to wake up your taste buds. Another common street food that you might be wondering about is called *pejibaye,* a bright orange palm nut about the size of a plum. They're boiled in big pots on carts, you eat them in much the same way you eat an avocado, and they taste a bit like squash.

LATE-NIGHT BITES   San José has quite a few **all-night restaurants.** The best of these is the **Café Parisien,** which is described below. Another popular place, which is quite a bit seedier, is **Chelles,** on Avenida Central and Calle 9 (see "San José After Dark," later in this chapter, for more information). The **Del Rey Café,** at the Hotel Del Rey (p. 98), is also open 24 hours. Finally, there's a **Denny's (***©* **231-3500),** located at the Best Western Irazú, on the highway out to the airport.

DOWNTOWN SAN JOSE

In addition to the places listed below, the restaurant in the **Hotel Santo Tomás** (*©* **255-0448;** p. 99) is making its mark on the local scene with well-prepared and very reasonably priced international and Continental fare.

MODERATE

Bakea *★★* *Finds* INTERNATIONAL   This new restaurant is eclectic across the board, from its architecture to its cuisine. Housed in an old historic downtown home, it has one room with a plexiglass floor and underfoot lighting revealing the original joists and foundations. There's also a separate intimate dining room, a courtyard patio done in a postmodern industrial chic style, and a main dining room that is both casual and elegant. The owner-chef is trained in classical French cooking, which she has updated with a host of modern and local flourishes. I particularly like the *filete multicolor,* a tenderloin cut bathed in a guava glaze served over polenta and accompanied by caramelized tomatoes. The signature *cahuita y caramelo* dessert is a standout chocolate-banana tart with a molten chocolate center and macadamia pieces thrown in for good measure.

Av. 7 and Calle 11, Casa 956. *©* **248-0303.** Reservations recommended. Main courses $8–$18. AE, MC, V. Tues–Sat noon–midnight.

Café La Bohemia *★* *Finds* INTERNATIONAL   This restaurant occupies the space of the old landmark *soda* La Perla, adjoining the Teatro Melico Salazar. High ceilings, marble-topped tables, and formally dressed waiters give this simple European-style cafe an air of elegance that is hard to find or top in the downtown area. The menu is strong on crepes, quiches, sandwiches, and other light lunchtime fair, although you can get a hearty plate of pasta or a pepper steak. There's also a good variety of desserts and coffee drinks. The walls here usually feature rotating exhibits of local painters and photographers.

Av. 2 and Calle Central. *©* **258-8465.** Reservations recommended. Main courses $7–$17. AE, MC, V. Mon–Sat 10am–10pm; Sun 11am–11pm when there are performances at the Teatro Melico Salazar.

Café Mundo ★ *Finds* INTERNATIONAL   This was one of the first places in San José to mix creative cuisine with an ambience of casual elegance, and it's still one of the best of the bunch. Wood tables and Art Deco wrought-iron chairs are spread spaciously around several rooms in this former colonial mansion. There's additional seating on the open-air veranda and in the small gardens both front and back. The food here follows the modern trend toward fusion cuisine. The appetizers include vegetable tempura, crab cakes, and chicken satay alongside more traditional Tico standards such as *patacones* and fried yuca. There's a long list of pastas and pizzas, as well as more substantial main courses. There are nightly specials and delicious desserts. One room here is a lively bar with colorful wall murals by Costa Rican artist Miguel Cassafont that has become the popular hangout for a broad mix of San José's gay, bohemian, theater, arts, and university crowds.

Calle 15 and Av. 9, 200m (656 ft.) east and 100m (328 ft.) north of the INS building. ℭ **222-6190.** Reservations recommended. Main courses $6–$18. AE, MC, V. Mon–Thurs 11am–11pm; Fri 11am–midnight; Sat 5pm–midnight.

Café Parisien INTERNATIONAL   The Gran Hotel Costa Rica is hardly the best hotel in San José, but it does have a picturesque and popular patio cafe right on the Plaza de la Cultura. A wrought-iron railing, white columns, and arches create an old-world atmosphere; on the plaza in front of the cafe, a marimba band performs and vendors sell handicrafts. It's open 24 hours a day and is one of the best spots in town to people-watch. Stop by for the breakfast and watch the plaza vendors set up their booths, or peruse the *Tico Times* over coffee while you have your shoes polished. The menu is basic and the food is unspectacular, but there isn't a better place downtown to bask in the tropical sunshine while you sip a beer or have a light lunch. This is also a great place to come just before or after a show at the National Theater.

In the Gran Hotel Costa Rica (p. 98), Av. 2 between calles 1 and 3. ℭ **221-4011.** Sandwiches $3–$6; main courses $5–$21. AE, DC, MC, V. Daily 24 hr.

La Cocina de Leña COSTA RICAN   Located in the El Pueblo shopping, dining, and entertainment center, La Cocina de Leña ("The Wood Stove") is designed to create a rustic feel. There are stacks of firewood on shelves above the booths, long stalks of bananas hanging from pillars, tables suspended from the ceiling by heavy ropes, and, most unusual of all, menus printed on paper bags. If you're adventurous, you could try some of the more unusual dishes—perhaps oxtail stew served with yuca and *plátano* might appeal to you. If not, there are plenty of steaks and seafood dishes on the menu. *Chilasuilas* are delicious tortillas filled with fried meat. Black-bean soup with egg is a Costa Rican standard and is mighty fine here; the corn soup with pork is equally satisfying. For dessert, there's *tres leches* cake as well as the more unusual sweetened *chiverre*, which is a type of squash that looks remarkably like a watermelon.

Centro Comercial El Pueblo. ℭ **255-1360** or 223-3704. Reservations recommended. Main courses $6–$22. AE, MC, V. Daily 11am–11pm.

Tin Jo ★★ *Finds* CHINESE/PAN-ASIAN   San José has hundreds of Chinese restaurants, but most simply serve up tired takes on chop suey, chow mein, and fried rice. In contrast, Tin Jo has a wide and varied menu, with an assortment of Cantonese and Szechuan staples, as well as a range of Thai, Japanese, and Malaysian dishes, and even some Indian food. This is a true Pan-Asian restaurant. The mu shu is so good that you'll forgive the fact that the pancakes are actually thin flour tortillas. Some of the dishes are served in edible rice-noodle bowls, and the pineapple shrimp in coconut-milk curry is served in the hollowed-out half of a fresh pineapple. Other dishes not to miss include the salt-and-pepper shrimp, beef teriyaki, and Thai curries. Tin Jo is also a great option for vegetarians. For dessert, try the sticky rice with mango, or banana tempura. The waiters here are some of the most attentive in Costa Rica. The decor features artwork and textiles from across Asia, and you'll have real tablecloths and cloth napkins.

Calle 11, between avs. 6 and 8. © 221-7605 or 257-3622. Main courses $5–$12. AE, MC, V. Mon–Sat 11:30am–3pm and 5:30–10pm (Fri–Sat kitchen open till 11pm); Sun 11:30am–10pm.

INEXPENSIVE

In addition to the places listed below, **Aya Sofya** (© 221-7185), a simple Turkish restaurant and cafeteria on Avenida Central and Calle 21, is a great place for a light, quick bite.

Café Britt ⭐ CONTINENTAL/COFFEEHOUSE   The folks at Café Britt have been running the in-house restaurant at the Teatro Nacional for a few years now, to good effect. Even if there's no show on during your visit, you can enjoy a light meal, sandwich, dessert, or a cup of coffee here, while soaking up the neo-classical atmosphere. The theater was built in the 1890s from the designs of European architects, and the Art Nouveau chandeliers, ceiling murals, and marble floors and tables are pure Parisian. There are also plenty of desserts and a wide range of coffee drinks. The ambience is French-cafe chic, but the marimba music drifting in from outside the open window and the changing art exhibits by local artists will remind you that you're still in Costa Rica. On sunny days, there's outdoor seating at wrought-iron tables on the side of the theater.

In the Teatro Nacional, Av. 2 between calles 3 and 5. © 221-3262. Sandwiches $3–$5; main courses $5–$12. AE, MC, V. Mon–Sat 10am–6pm.

Manolo's Restaurante COSTA RICAN   This roomy restaurant, spread out over three floors on a busy corner of Avenida Central, is popular with Ticos and travelers alike. You can grab a first-floor table to check out the action passing by on the street, or catch the live folk-dance performances that are staged nightly upstairs. The open kitchen serves up steaks and fish, but there's also a popular buffet that includes several typical Costa Rican dishes, such as *plátanos*-and-black-bean soup, for about $5. The ground floor has the feel of a diner. It's a good place for a quick sandwich or perhaps a fried-dough *churro* and a shot of espresso. There's another Manolo's located on Avenida Central and Calle 11.

Av. Central, between calles Central and 2. © 221-2041. All items $3–$12. AE, MC, V. Daily 11:30am–10pm upstairs, 24 hr. downstairs.

Vishnu VEGETARIAN   Vegetarians will most certainly find their way here. There are booths for two or four people and photomurals on the walls. The vibe here's a little too plastic, too loud, and too brightly lit for my tastes in a vegetarian joint. However, most people just come for the filling *plato del día* that includes soup, salad, veggies, an entree, and dessert for around $3. There are also bean burgers and cheese sandwiches on whole-wheat bread. At the cashier's counter, you can buy natural cosmetics, honey, and bags of granola. This restaurant is part of the Vishnu chain; there are eight sister restaurants spread over the city.

Av. 1, between calles 1 and 3. © 256-6063. Main courses $3–$8. MC, V. Daily 8am–9:30pm.

Moments Only in the Central Valley: Dining Under the Stars on a Mountain's Edge

Although there are myriad unique experiences to be had in Costa Rica, one of my favorites is dining on the side of a volcano, with the lights of San José shimmering below. These hanging restaurants, called *miradores*, are a resourceful response to the city's topography. Because San José is set in a broad valley surrounded on all sides by volcanic mountains, people who live in these mountainous areas have no place to go but up—so they do, building roadside cafes vertically up the sides of the volcanoes.

The food at most of these establishments is not usually spectacular, but the views often are, particularly at night, when the whole wide valley sparkles in a wash of lights. The town of **Aserri,** 10km (6¼ miles) south of downtown San José, is the king of miradores, and **Mirador Ram Luna** (𝄐 **230-3060;** closed Mon) is the king of Aserri. Grab a window seat and, if you've got the fortitude, order a plate of *chicharrones* (fried pork rinds). There's often live music. You can hire a cab for around $9, or take the Aserri bus at Avenida 6 between calles Central and 2. Just ask the driver where to get off.

There are also miradores in the hills above Escazú and in San Ramón de Tres Ríos and Heredia. One of the best of this bunch is **Le Monestère** (𝄐 **289-4404;** closed Sun), an elegant converted church serving somewhat overrated French and Belgian cuisine in a spectacular setting above the hills of Escazú. I recommend coming here just for the less formal **La Cava Grill,** which often features live music.

LA SABANA/PASEO COLON
EXPENSIVE

La Masía de Triquel ⭐ SPANISH   Despite relocation, a healthy field of competitors, and the death of founding chef Francisco Triquel, La Masía de Triquel is still San José's finest Spanish restaurant. Francisco Triquel Jr. has seen to that. Service is extremely formal, and the regular clientele includes most of the city's upper crust. Although Costa Rica is known for its beef, here you'll also find wonderfully prepared lamb, quail, and rabbit. Seafood dishes include the usual shrimp and lobster, but also squid and octopus. However, there is really no decision to be made when perusing the menu: Start with a big bowl of gazpacho and then spend the rest of the evening enjoying all the succulent surprises you'll find in a big dish of paella.

Sabana Norte, 50m (164 ft.) west and 175m (574 ft.) north of the Burger King in La Sabana. 𝄐 **296-3528.** Reservations recommended. Main courses $10–$22. AE, MC, V. Mon–Sat 11:30am–2pm and 6:30–10:30pm.

La Piazzetta ⭐ ITALIAN   With an amazingly long menu and service by waiters in suits and bow ties, this restaurant harks back to the Italian restaurants of old in the United States, when southern Italian cooking was still an exotic ethnic cuisine. The menu includes quite a few risotto dishes, as well as several lobster offerings. The veal scaloppine in a truffle sauce is excellent. Salads are colorful and artistically arranged. For dessert, sample a classic chocolate mousse or tiramisu. The wine list is quite extensive, with good and reasonably priced offerings from Italy.

Paseo Colón near Calle 40 (opposite Banco de Costa Rica). © **222-7896.** Reservations recommended. Main courses $6–$26. AE, MC, V. Mon–Fri noon–2:30pm and 6:30–11pm; Sat 6:30–11pm.

MODERATE

El Chicote ☆ COSTA RICAN/STEAKHOUSE   This is one of San José's most popular steakhouses. The large room is divided by half-walls planted with tropical flora and a bevy of hanging ferns. There are heavy wooden beams and plenty of varnished-wood accents all around. True meat aficionados should order the imported rib-eye or pound-and-a-half T-bone. There's an extensive selection of fish and poultry dishes as well. Everything comes with a choice of baked or mashed potatoes, black beans, and fresh tortillas. The wine list features a broad range of Italian, Spanish, French, and Californian wines. Waiters wear black jackets, white shirts, and black bow ties, and service is unusually formal for Costa Rica.

Av. Las Américas, 400m (1,312 ft.) west of the ICE building, Sabana Norte. © **232-0936** or 232-3777. Reservations recommended. Main courses $8–$23. AE, MC, V. Mon–Fri 11am–3pm and 6–11pm; Sat–Sun 11am–midnight.

Grano de Oro Restaurant ☆☆ *Finds* CONTINENTAL   The small restaurant located just off the central courtyard of this wonderful downtown hotel is both elegant and relaxed. The menu features a wide range of meat and fish dishes. The *lomito piemontes* is two medallions of filet mignon stuffed with Gorgonzola cheese in a sherry sauce, while the *lomito Diana* comes with fresh pears and a thick brandy reduction. If you opt for fish, I recommend the macadamia-encrusted corvina, which is served with a light and tangy orange sauce. Be sure to save room for the "Grano de Oro pie," a decadent dessert with various layers of chocolate and coffee mousses and creams. When the weather's nice, you can grab a table in the courtyard. This is a particularly nice option for lunch.

Calle 30, no. 251, between avs. 2 and 4, 150m (492 ft.) south of Paseo Colón. © **255-3322.** Reservations recommended. Main courses $8–$20. AE, MC, V. Daily 6am–10pm.

Machu Picchu ☆ PERUVIAN/CONTINENTAL   Machu Picchu is an unpretentious little restaurant that has become one of the most popular places in San José. One of my favorite entrees is the *causa limeña,* lemon-flavored mashed potatoes stuffed with shrimp. The ceviche here is excellent, as is the *ají de gallina,* a dish of shredded chicken in a fragrant cream sauce, and octopus with garlic butter. For main dishes, I recommend *corvina a lo macho,* sea bass in a slightly spicy tomato-based seafood sauce. Be sure to ask for a pisco sour, a classic Peruvian drink made from *pisco,* a grape liquor. These folks have a sister restaurant (© **283-3679**) over in San Pedro.

Calle 32, between avs. 1 and 3, 150m (492 ft.) north of the KFC on Paseo Colón. © **222-7384.** Reservations recommended. Main courses $4–$15. AE, DC, MC, V. Mon–Sat 11am–3pm and 6–10pm.

INEXPENSIVE

Soda Tapia COSTA RICAN   The food is unspectacular, dependable, and quite inexpensive at this very popular local diner. There's seating inside the brightly lit dining room, as well as on the sidewalk-style patio fronting the parking area. Dour but efficient waitstaff take the order you mark down on your combination menu/bill. This is a great place for late-night eats, or for before or after a visit to La Sabana Park or Museo de Arte Costarricense.

Calle 42 and Av. 2, across from the Museo de Arte Costarricense. © **222-6734.** Sandwiches $2.50–$3.50; main dishes $4–$7. MC, V. Sun–Thurs 6am–2am; Fri–Sat 24 hr.

SAN PEDRO/LOS YOSES

In addition to the restaurants listed below, local and visiting vegetarians swear by the little **Restaurante El Vegetariano San Pedro** (✆ 224-1163), located 125m (410 ft.) north of the San Pedro Church. You might also want to check out **Sabor y Sueños** (✆ 257-4148), an elegant, yet bohemian little restaurant in an artistically decorated old mansion tucked away in a quiet residential section of Barrio Escalante. Despite the massive size and popularity of **Il Pomodoro,** I prefer **Pane E Vino** (✆ 280-2869), an excellent pasta-and-pizza joint on the eastern edge of San Pedro.

Finally, if you continue a little farther east to Curridabat, you'll find **Matsuri** (✆ 280-5522), a simple little restaurant in a somewhat desultory little strip mall that just might be the best sushi joint in the city.

MODERATE

Ambrosia ✪ CONTINENTAL   This elegant little restaurant is a good choice for lunch or dinner. Greek and Latin mythology make their way onto the menu: Seafood dishes are named after Ulysses, Circe, and Poseidon; Zeus, Apollo, and Orion provide namesakes for the different steaks; and the pasta selections are anchored by Ravioli Romulus. Behind the mythology, you'll find well-prepared meals made with fresh ingredients and interesting spices. The Crepe Aphrodite is a delicate crepe filled with chunks of fish and shrimp in a Gouda cheese sauce. The Corvina Cassiopeia is a grilled sea-bass filet topped with a light almond sauce. The ambience is relaxed, and the service can be a bit inattentive. There's a small bar at the center of the restaurant, and live piano music is sometimes offered in the evenings.

Centro Comercial Calle Real. ✆ 253-8012. Sandwiches and salads $3–$6; main courses $5–$15. AE, DC, MC, V. Mon–Sat 11:30am–10:30pm; Sun 11:30am–4pm.

Il Ritorno ✪ ITALIAN   The name of this restaurant translates as "The Return," and it's the not-very-humble, yet arguably deserved, announcement of chef and owner Tony D'Alaimo's comeback after leaving the longstanding and popular Il Ponte Vecchio and Costa Rica for several years. The menu features a wide selection of antipasti, pastas, main dishes, and thin-crust wood-oven baked pizzas. I like the *vitello il ritorno,* delicate cuts of veal in a cognac-based sauce. Service is semiformal and attentive. There are a few specials each evening, and Tony's mother's recipe for fresh ravioli in a cream sauce flavored with nutmeg is usually available.

Barrio California, 200m (656 ft.) south of KFC. ✆ 225-0543. Main courses $6–$16. AE, MC, V. Mon–Sat 11:30am–2:30pm and 6–10pm.

Olio ✪ (Value) MEDITERRANEAN   The exposed brick walls, dark wood wainscoting, and stained-glass lamps imbue this place with character and romance. Couples might want to grab a table in a quiet nook, while groups tend to dominate the large main room or crowd the bar. The extensive tapas menu features traditional Spanish fare, as well as bruschetta, antipasti, and a Greek *mezza* plate. For a main dish, I recommend the chicken Vesubio, which is marinated first in a balsamic vinegar reduction and finished with a creamy herb sauce; or the *arrollado siciliano,* which is a thin filet of steak rolled around spinach, sun-dried tomatoes, and mozzarella cheese and topped with a pomodoro sauce. The midsize wine list features modestly priced wines from Italy, France, Spain, Germany, Chile, Greece, and even Bulgaria.

Barrio California, 200m (656 ft.) north of Bagelman's. ✆ 281-0541. Main courses $5–$12. AE, DC, MC, V. Mon–Sat noon–4pm and 6pm–midnight.

INEXPENSIVE

Whappin' ★ *Finds* COSTA RICAN/CARIBBEAN   You don't have to go to Limón or Cahuita to get good home-cooked Caribbean food anymore. Although they seldom have *rondon,* you can always get the classic rice and beans cooked in coconut milk, as well as a range of fish and chicken dishes from the coastal region. I personally like the whole red snapper covered in a spicy sauce of sautéed onions. There's a small bar at the entrance and some simple tables spread around the restaurant, with an alcove here and there. Everything is very simple, and the prices are quite reasonable. After a dinner of fresh fish, with rice, beans, and patacones, the only letdown is that the beach is some 4 hours away.

Barrio Escalante, 200m (656 ft.) east of El Farolito. ℂ 283-1480. Main courses $4–$11. AE, MC, V. Mon–Sat noon–3pm and 6–11pm.

ESCAZU & SANTA ANA

These two suburbs on the western side of town have the most vibrant restaurant scene in San José. Although there's high turnover and sudden closings, this remains a good area to check out for a variety of dining experiences. In addition to the places mentioned below, **Il Panino** (ℂ 228-3126) is an upscale sandwich shop and cafe, located in the Centro Comercial El Paco, and **Taj Mahal** (ℂ 228-0980) serves respectable Indian fare about 1km (½ mile) farther west on the old road to Santa Ana. **Santa Ana Tex Mex** (ℂ 282-6342) is one of the most popular places on this side of town. Located a half block north of the main church in Santa Ana, it serves up Tex-Mex cuisine in a lively atmosphere.

Finally, a good one-stop option to consider is the Plaza Itskatzu shopping center located just off the highway and sharing a parking lot with the Courtyard San José. Here you'll find a wide variety of moderately priced restaurant options, including **Tutti Li** (ℂ 289-8768), a good Italian restaurant and pizzeria; **Fresk Co.** (ℂ 228-2279), a salad bar and lunch joint; **Icarus** (ℂ 215-2079), an upscale Continental restaurant (and a bit more expensive than the others); **Chancay** (ℂ 289-6964), which serves Peruvian and Peruvian/Chinese cuisine; **La Guagua** (ℂ 288-5112), serving up tasty Cuban food; **Las Tapas de Manuel** (ℂ 288-1633); and an **Outback Steakhouse** (ℂ 288-0511) franchise.

EXPENSIVE

La Luz ★★ CALIFORNIAN/FUSION   La Luz serves up some of the more adventurous food in Costa Rica, mixing fresh local ingredients with the best of a whole host of international ethnic cuisines. The fiery garlic prawns are sautéed in ancho-chile oil and sage and served over a roasted-garlic potato mash. Then the whole thing is served with a garnish of fried leeks and a tequila-lime butter and cilantro-oil sauce. I also enjoy the beef tenderloin in a strawberry-balsamic reduction, served over a champagne-infused risotto. On top of all this, there are nightly specials, such as fresh-baked rolls and breads, and a wide selection of inventive appetizers and desserts. The glass-walled dining room is one of the most elegant in town, with a view of the city lights. The waitstaff is attentive and knowledgeable. La Luz is also open for breakfast and lunch.

In the Hotel Alta (p. 104), on the old road to Santa Ana. ℂ 282-4160. Reservations recommended. Main courses $6–$24. AE, DC, MC, V. Daily 7am–3pm and 6–10pm.

MODERATE

Barbecue Los Anonos ★ COSTA RICAN/STEAKHOUSE   Good steaks and well-prepared Costa Rican cuisine have made this simple restaurant something of an institution. Most of the seating here is at simple wooden tables covered with red-and-white checkered tablecloths, and long and rustic booths set under the shelter of low interior red-tile roofs. Aged Angus beef is served here, and this is *the* place to come if you're craving a 16-ounce T-bone. There are a host of chicken, pork, and fish options here; I recommend the mixed grilled plate for two, which comes with a little bit of everything.

600m (1,968 ft.) west of the Los Anonos bridge in San Rafael de Escazú, next to the Sarretto Market. ⓒ 228-0180. Reservations recommended. Main courses $7–$25. AE, MC, V. Tues–Sat noon–3pm; Tues–Thurs 6–10pm; Fri–Sat 6–11pm; Sun 11:30am–9pm.

5 What to See & Do

Most visitors to Costa Rica try to get out of the city as fast as possible so they can spend more time on the beach or off in the rainforests. But if you'll be in San José for longer than an overnight stay, there are a few attractions to keep you busy. Some of the best and most modern museums in Central America are here, with a wealth of fascinating pre-Columbian artifacts. Some of the best include the recently remodeled Jade Museum and the centrally located National Arts Center, featuring yet another museum and several performing-arts spaces. There are also several great things to see and do just outside San José in the Central Valley. If you start doing day trips out of the city, you can spend quite a few days in this region.

ORGANIZED TOURS   There really isn't much reason to take a tour of San José. It's so compact that you can easily visit all the major sights on your own, as described below. However, if you want to take a city tour, which will run you between $15 and $35, here are some companies: **Horizontes Travel** ⓐ, Calle 32 between avenidas 3 and 5 (ⓒ **222-2022;** www.horizontes.com); **Grayline Tours,** Avenida 7 between calles 6 and 8, with additional offices at the Hampton Inn and Best Western Irazu (ⓒ **220-2126;** www.graylinecostarica.com); and **Swiss Travel Service** (ⓒ **282-4898;** www.swisstravelcr.com). These same companies also offer a whole range of day trips out of San José (see "Side Trips from San José," later in this chapter). Almost all of the major hotels have tour desks, and most of the smaller hotels will also help arrange tours and day trips.

SUGGESTED ITINERARIES

If You Have 1 Day

Start your day on the Plaza de la Cultura. Visit the Gold Museum and see if you can get tickets for a performance that night at the Teatro Nacional. From the Plaza de la Cultura, stroll up Avenida Central to the Museo Nacional. After lunch, head over to the neighboring National Arts Center (if you have the energy for another museum). After all this culture, some shopping at the open-air stalls at the Plaza de la Democracia is in order. Try dinner at either Café Mundo or El Chicote before going to the Teatro Nacional. After the performance, you can have a cup of coffee or a nightcap on the outdoor patio of the Café Parisien before calling it a night.

If You Have 2 Days

On day 2, you're probably best off taking one of the day trips outside of San José described below. Alternatively, you could spend the day further exploring the capital. Start by heading out on Paseo Colón to the Museo de Arte Costarricense and La Sabana Park. Intrepid travelers can do some shopping at the Mercado Central. If you've brought kids along, you'll want to visit the Children's Museum or the Spyrogyra Butterfly Garden.

If You Have 3 Days

On day 3, head out to the Poás Volcano and then visit the La Paz Waterfall Gardens, returning through the hills of Heredia, with a stop at INBio Park if you've got the time and energy. Alternatively you could head to the Irazú Volcano, the Orosi Valley, Lankester Gardens, and Cartago. Start your day at the volcano and work your way

back toward San José. If you want to try an organized tour, try a cruise to Isla Tortuga in the Gulf of Nicoya, a white-water rafting trip on the Pacuare River, or a visit to the Rain Forest Aerial Tram Caribbean.

If You Have 4 Days or More

Get out of San José. Do a 1- or 2-night trip to Tortuguero, Monteverde, Manuel Antonio, or Arenal.

THE TOP ATTRACTIONS

Centro Nacional de Arte y Cultura ★★ *Finds*   Occupying a full city block, this was once the National Liquor Factory (FANAL). Now it houses the offices of the Cultural Ministry, several performing-arts centers, and the Museum of Contemporary Art and Design. The latter has done an excellent job of promoting cutting-edge Costa Rican and Central American artists, while also featuring impressive traveling international exhibits, including large retrospectives by Mexican painter José Cuevas and Ecuadorian painter Oswaldo Guayasamín. If you're looking for modern dance, experimental theater, or a lecture on Costa Rican video, this is the place to check. Allow around 2 hours to take in all the exhibits here.

Calle 13 between avs. 3 and 5. © **257-7202** or 257-9370. www.madc.ac.cr. Admission $1. Museum Tues–Sat 10am–5pm. Bus: Any downtown bus.

Museo de Arte Costarricense ★   This small museum at the end of Paseo Colón in Parque La Sabana was formerly an airport terminal. Today it houses a collection of works in all media by Costa Rica's most celebrated artists. On display are some exceptionally beautiful pieces in a wide range of styles, demonstrating how Costa Rican artists have interpreted and imitated the major European movements over the years. In addition to the permanent collection of sculptures, paintings, and prints, there are regular temporary exhibits. If the second floor is open during your visit, be sure to go up and have a look at the conference room's bas-relief walls, which chronicle the history of Costa Rica from pre-Columbian times to the present with evocative images of its people. The newest addition here is a nascent sculpture garden. So far, only a few major pieces have been placed here, but the outdoor setting is lovely, and the collection should grow with time. You can easily spend an hour or two here—more if you take a stroll through the neighboring park.

Calle 42 and Paseo Colón, Parque La Sabana Este. © **222-7155**. Admission $1.50 for adults, free for children and students. Tues–Sun 10am–4pm. Bus: Sabana–Cementerio.

Museo de Jade Marco Fidel Tristán ★   Jade was the most valuable commodity among the pre-Columbian cultures of Mexico and Central America, worth more than gold. This modern museum displays a huge collection of jade artifacts dating from 500 B.C. to A.D. 800. Most are large pendants that were parts of necklaces and are primarily human and animal figures. A fascinating display illustrates how the primitive peoples of this region carved this extremely hard stone.

There is also an extensive collection of pre-Columbian polychromed terracotta vases, bowls, and figurines. Some of these pieces are amazingly modern in design and exhibit a surprisingly advanced technique. Particularly fascinating is a vase that incorporates real human teeth, and a display that shows how jade was embedded in human teeth merely for decorative reasons. Most of the identifying labels and explanations are in Spanish, but there are a few in English. Before you leave, be sure to check out the splendid view of San José from the lounge area.

Av. 7 between calles 9 and 9B, 11th floor, INS Building. ℂ 287-6034. Admission $2 for adults, free for children under 12. Mon–Fri 8:30am–3:30pm. Bus: Any downtown bus.

Museo de Los Niños *Kids*   A former barracks and then prison, this museum houses an extensive collection of exhibits designed to edify and entertain children of all ages. Experience a simulated earthquake, or make music by dancing across the floor. Many of the exhibits encourage hands-on play. If you're traveling with children, you'll definitely want to come here, and you might want to visit even if you don't. This museum sometimes features limited shows of "serious" art and is also the home of the National Auditorium. You can spend anywhere from 1 to 4 hours here, depending on how much time your children spend at each exhibit. Be careful, though: The museum is large and spread out, and it's easy to lose track of a family member or friend.

This museum is located a few blocks north of downtown, on Calle 4. It's within easy walking distance, but you might want to take a cab because you'll have to walk right through the worst part of the red-light district.

Calle 4 and Av. 9. ℂ 258-4929. www.museocr.com. Admission $2 for adults, $1.50 for students and children under 18. Tues–Fri 8am–4pm; Sat–Sun 10am–5pm. Bus: Any downtown bus.

Museo de Oro Banco Central ★★   Located directly beneath the Plaza de la Cultura, this unusual underground museum houses one of the largest collections of pre-Columbian gold in the Americas. On display are more than 20,000 troy ounces of gold in more than 2,000 objects. The sheer number of small pieces can be overwhelming and seem redundant, but the unusual display cases and complex lighting systems show off every piece to its utmost. This museum complex also includes a gallery for temporary art exhibits, separate numismatic and philatelic museums (coins and stamps, for us regular folks), a modest gift shop, and a branch of the Costa Rican Tourist Institute's information center. Plan to spend between 1 and 2 hours here.

Calle 5, between avs. Central and 2, underneath the Plaza de la Cultura. ℂ 243-4214. www.museosdel bancocentral.org. Admission $4 for adults, $1.50 for students, 75¢ for children under 12. Tues–Sun 10am–4:30pm. Bus: Any downtown bus.

Museo Nacional de Costa Rica ★   Costa Rica's most important historical museum is housed in a former army barracks that was the scene of fighting during the civil war of 1948. You can still see hundreds of bullet holes on the turrets at the corners of the building. Inside this traditional Spanish-style courtyard building, you will find displays on Costa Rican history and culture from pre-Columbian times to the present. In the pre-Columbian rooms, you'll see a 2,500-year-old jade carving that is shaped like a seashell and etched with an image of a hand holding a small animal.

Among the most fascinating objects unearthed at Costa Rica's numerous archaeological sites are many *metates*, or grinding stones. This type of grinding stone is still in use today throughout Central America; however, the ones on display here are more ornately decorated than those that you will see anywhere else. Some of the metates are the size of a small bed and are believed to have been part of funeral rites. A separate vault houses the museum's collection of pre-Columbian gold jewelry and figurines. In the courtyard, you'll be treated to a wonderful view of the city and see some of Costa Rica's mysterious stone spheres. It takes about 2 hours to take in the lion's share of the collection here.

Calle 17, between avs. Central and 2, on the Plaza de la Democracia. ℂ 257-1433. www.museocostarica. com. Admission $4 for adults, $2 for students and children under 12. Tues–Sat 8:30am–4pm; Sun 9am–4pm. Closed Dec 25 and 31. Bus: Any downtown bus.

Parque Zoológico Simón Bolívar *Kids*   This zoo has received some upkeep and renovation in recent years. But although it no longer suffers from an over-whelming sense of neglect and despair, the whole thing is still slightly lackluster. Why spend time here when you could head out into the forests and jungles? You won't see the great concentrations of wildlife available in one stop here at the zoo, but you'll see the animals in their natural habitats, not yours. The zoo is really geared toward locals and school groups, with a collection that includes Asian, African, and Costa Rican animals. There's a children's discovery area, a snake-and-reptile house, and a gift shop. You can easily spend a whole morning or afternoon here.

Av. 11 and Calle 7, in Barrio Amón. ℂ 256-0012. Admission $2 for adults, free for children under 3. Mon–Fri 8am–4pm; Sat–Sun 9am–5pm. Bus: Any downtown bus.

Serpentarium *Kids*   Reptiles and amphibians abound in the tropics, and the Serpentarium offers a good introduction to all that slithers and hops through the jungles of Costa Rica. The live snakes, lizards, and frogs are kept in terrariums that simulate their natural environments. Poisonous snakes make up a large part of the collection, with the dreaded fer-de-lance pit viper eliciting gasps from enthralled visitors. Also fascinating to see are the tiny, brilliantly colored poison arrow frogs. Iguanas and Jesus Christ lizards are two of the more commonly spot-ted of Costa Rica's reptiles, and both are represented here. If you show up around 3pm, you might catch them feeding the piranhas and perhaps some of the snakes. It takes only about 30 to 40 minutes to run through this small serpentarium.

Av. 1, between calles 9 and 11. ℂ 255-4210. Admission $5 for adults, $1.50 for children under 13. Mon–Fri 9am–6pm; Sat–Sun 10am–5pm. Bus: Any downtown bus.

Spirogyra Butterfly Garden   This butterfly garden is smaller and less elab-orate than Butterfly Farm (see below), but it provides a good introduction to the life cycle of butterflies. Moreover, it's a calm and quiet oasis in a noisy and crowded city, quite close to downtown. Visitors spend anywhere from a half-hour to several hours here, depending on whether they have lunch or refresh-ments at the small coffee shop and gallery. You'll be given a self-guided tour booklet when you arrive, and there's an 18-minute video shown continuously throughout the day. You'll find Spyrogyra near El Pueblo, a short taxi ride from the center of San José.

100m (328 ft.) east and 150m (492 ft.) south of El Pueblo Shopping Center. ℂ/fax 222-2937. www.info costarica.com/butterfly. Admission $6. Daily 8am–4pm (cafe open till 7:30pm). Bus: Calle Blancos bus from Calle 3 and Av. 5.

OUTSIDE SAN JOSE

The **Juan Santamaría Historical Museum,** Avenida 3 between calles Central and 2 (ℂ 441-4775; www.museojuansantamaria.go.cr), isn't worth a trip of its own, but if you're looking to make an afternoon of it in Alajuela, you might want to make a stop here before or after Zoo Ave. (p. 122). The museum com-memorates Costa Rica's national hero, who gave his life defending the country against a small army led by William Walker, a U.S. citizen who invaded Costa

Travel Tip: He who finds the best hotel deal has more to spend on facials involving knobbly vegetables.

Hello, the Roaming Gnome here. I've been nabbed from the garden and taken round the world. The people who took me are so terribly clever. They find the best offerings on Travelocity. For very little cha-ching. And that means I get to be pampered and exfoliated till I'm pink as a bunny's doodah.

travelocity®

1-888-TRAVELOCITY / travelocity.com / America Online Keyword: Travel

Plan your vacation

- flights, hotels, car rentals
- cruises & vacation packages
- destination guides
- fare alerts
- go to yahoo.com, click travel

DO YOU YAHOO!?

Rica in 1856, attempting to set up a slave state. The museum is open Tuesday through Sunday from 10am to 6pm; admission is free.

To locate the attractions below, see "The Central Valley" map on p. 135.

Butterfly Farm ★   At any given time, you might see around 30 of the 80 different species of butterflies raised at this butterfly farm south of Alajuela. The butterflies live in a large enclosed garden similar to an aviary and flutter about the heads of visitors during tours of the gardens. You should be certain to spot glittering blue morphos and a large butterfly that mimics the eyes of an owl.

The admission includes a 2-hour guided tour. In the demonstration room, you'll see butterfly eggs, caterpillars, and pupae. There are cocoons trimmed in a shimmering gold color and cocoons that mimic a snake's head to frighten away predators. The last guided tour of the day begins at 3pm.

If you reserve in advance, the Butterfly Farm has three daily bus tours that run from many major San José hotels, the cost, including round-trip transportation and admission to the garden, is $25 for adults, $20 for students, and $13 for children under 12. Buses pick up passengers at more than 20 different hotels in the San José area.

In front of Los Reyes Country Club, La Guácima de Alajuela. 🄲 **438-0400.** www.butterflyfarm.co.cr. Admission $15 for adults, $10 for students, $7 for children 5–12, and free for children under 5. Daily 8:30am–5pm.

Café Britt Farm ★   Although bananas are the main export of Costa Rica, most people are far more interested in the country's second most important export crop: coffee. Café Britt is one of the leading brands here, and the company has put together an interesting tour and stage production at its farm, which is 20 minutes outside of San José. Here, you'll see how coffee is grown. You'll also visit the roasting plant to learn how a coffee "cherry" is turned into a delicious roasted bean. Tasting sessions are offered for visitors to experience the different qualities of coffee. There is also a restaurant and a store where you can buy coffee and coffee-related gift items. The entire tour, including transportation, takes about 3 to 4 hours. The folks here offer several full-day options that combine a visit to the Britt Farm with a stop at Poás Volcano, the Butterfly Farm (see above), or the Rain Forest Aerial Tram Caribbean.

North of Heredia on the road to Barva. 🄲 **277-1600.** www.coffeetour.com. Admission $26 per person, including transportation from downtown San José. 3 tours daily: 9, 11am, and 3pm during the high season; reduced schedule in the off season. Store open daily 8:30am–5pm year-round.

INBio Park ★★ *Kids*   Run by the National Biodiversity Institute (Instituto Nacional de Biodiversidad, or INBio), this place is part museum, part educational center, and part nature park. In addition to watching a 15-minute informational video, visitors can tour two large pavilions explaining Costa Rica's biodiversity and natural wonders, and hike on trails that re-create the ecosystems of a tropical rainforest, dry forest, and premontane forest. A 2-hour guided hike is included in the entrance fee, and self-guided tour booklets are also available. There's a good-size butterfly garden, as well as a plexiglass viewing window into the small lagoon. One of my favorite attractions here is the series of wonderful animal sculptures donated by one of Costa Rica's premiere artists, José Sancho. There's a simple cafeteria-style restaurant here for lunch, as well as a coffee shop and gift shop. You can easily spend 2 to 3 hours here.

400m (1,312 ft.) north and 250m (820 ft.) west of the Shell station in Santo Domingo de Heredia. 🄲 **507-8107.** www.inbio.ac.cr. Admission $15 for adults, $8 for children under 13. Rates slightly lower in the off season. Daily 7:30am–4pm. INBio Park can arrange round-trip transportation from downtown for $10 per person.

Lankester Gardens ★★ There are more than 1,400 varieties of orchids in Costa Rica, and no fewer than 800 species are on display at this botanical garden in Cartago province. Created in the 1940s by English naturalist Charles Lankester, the gardens are now administered by the University of Costa Rica. The primary goal is to preserve the local flora, with an emphasis on orchids and bromeliads. Paved trails meander from open, sunny gardens into shady forests. In each environment, different species of orchids are in bloom. There's an information center and gift shop, and the trails are well tended and well marked.

Plan to spend between 1 and 3 hours here if you're interested in flowers and gardening; you could run through it more quickly if you're not. You can easily combine a visit here with an enjoyable tour of Cartago and/or the Orosi Valley and Irazú Volcano. See "Side Trips from San José," later in this chapter.

Paraíso de Cartago. ✆ 552-3247. Admission $5 adults, $1 children. Daily 8:30am–3:30pm. Closed all national holidays. Take the Cartago bus from San José, and then the Paraíso bus from a stop 1 block south and ¾ block west of the Catholic church ruins in Cartago (ride takes 30–40 min.).

La Paz Waterfall Gardens ★★ *Kids* The namesake attraction here consists of a series of trails through primary and secondary forest alongside the La Paz River, with lookouts over a series of powerful falls, including the namesake La Paz Fall. There's also an orchid garden, a hummingbird garden, and a huge butterfly garden—in fact, they claim it's the largest in the world. I find the admission fee a little steep, but everything is wonderfully done and the trails and waterfalls are beautiful. A buffet lunch will run you an extra $10 at the large cafeteria-style restaurant. This is a good stop after a morning visit to the Poás Volcano. Plan to spend between 2 and 4 hours here. The hotel rooms here (Peace Lodge; p. 107) are some of the nicest in the country. When I last visited they were planning to add horseback-riding tours and trout fishing.

6km (3¾ miles) north of Varablanca on the road to San Miguel. ✆ 482-2720 or 225-0643. www.waterfall gardens.com. Admission $21 for adults, $10 for children and students with valid ID. Daily 8:30am–5:30pm. Take a Puerto Viejo de Sarapiquí bus from Calle 12 and Av. 9 (make sure it passes through Varablanca and La Virgen), and ask to be let off at the entrance. These buses are infrequent, and coordinating your return can be difficult, so it's best to come in a rental car or arrange transport.

Zoo Ave. ★ Dozens of scarlet macaws, reclusive owls, majestic raptors, several different species of toucans, and a host of brilliantly colored birds from Costa Rica and around the world make this one exciting place to visit. Bird-watching enthusiasts will be able to get a closer look at birds they might have seen in the wild. There are also large iguana, deer, and monkey exhibits—and look out for the 3.6m (12-ft.) crocodile. Zoo Ave. houses only injured, donated, or confiscated animals. It takes about 2 hours to walk the paths and visit all the exhibits here.

La Garita, Alajuela. ✆ 433-8989. www.zooave.org. Admission $9 for adults, $2 for children under 12. Daily 9am–5pm. Catch one of the frequent Alajuela buses on Av. 2 between calles 12 and 14. In Alajuela, transfer to a bus for Atenas and get off at Zoo Ave. before you get to La Garita. Fare is 55¢.

6 Outdoor Activities & Spectator Sports

Due to the chaos and pollution, you'll probably want to get out of the city before undertaking anything too strenuous. But if you want to brave the elements, there are a few activities in and around San José.

La Sabana Park (at the western end of Paseo Colón), formerly San José's international airport, is the city's center for active sports and recreation. Here you'll find everything from jogging trails, soccer fields, and a few public tennis courts to the National Stadium. All the facilities are free and open to the public.

Families gather for picnics, people fly kites, and there's even an outdoor sculpture garden. If you really want to experience the local culture, try getting into a pickup soccer game here. However, be careful in this park, especially at dusk or after dark, when it becomes a favorite haunt for youth gangs and muggers.

For information on horseback riding, hiking, and white-water rafting trips from San José, see "Side Trips from San José," later in this chapter.

BIRD-WATCHING   Serious birders will certainly want to head out of San José, but it is still possible to see quite a few species in the metropolitan area. Two of the best spots for urban bird-watching are the campus at the **University of Costa Rica,** in the eastern suburb of San Pedro, and **Parque del Este** ✸, located a little farther east on the road to San Ramón de Tres Ríos. To get to the university campus, take any San Pedro bus from Avenida Central between calles 9 and 11. To get to Parque del Este, take the San Ramón/Parque del Este bus from Calle 9 between avenidas Central and 2. If you want to hook up with fellow birders, e-mail the **Birding Club of Costa Rica** ✸✸ (costaricabirding@ hotmail.com), which frequently organizes expeditions around the Central Valley and beyond.

BULLFIGHTING   Although I hesitate to call it a sport, **Las Corridas a la Tica** (Costa Rican bullfighting) is a popular and frequently comic stadium event. Instead of the blood-and-gore/life-and-death confrontation of traditional bullfighting, Ticos just like to tease the bull. In a typical *corrida,* anywhere from 50 to 150 *toreadores improvisados* (literally, "improvised bullfighters") stand in the ring waiting for the bull. What follows is a slapstick scramble to safety whenever the bull heads toward a crowd of bullfighters. The braver bullfighters try to slap the bull's backside as the beast chases down one of his buddies.

You can see a bullfight during the various Festejos Populares (City Fairs) around the country. The country's largest Festejos Populares are held in Zapote, a suburb east of San José. The corridas run all day and well into the night during Christmas week and the first week in January here. Admission is $2 to $5. Take the Zapote bus from Calle 1 between avenidas 4 and 6. If you're in Costa Rica during the holidays but can't make it out to the stadium, don't despair— the local TV stations show nothing but live broadcasts from Zapote. This is a purely seasonal activity and occurs in San José only during the Festejos. However, there are yearly *festejos* in nearly every little town around the country. Ask at your hotel; if your timing's right, you might be able to take one of these in.

GOLF & TENNIS   If you want to play tennis or golf in San José, your options are limited. Your best bet is to stay at the Meliá Cariari (p. 106). Tennis players looking for a real local experience on some rough concrete courts can take a racket and some balls down to **Parque La Sabana.** Golfers can try the 18-hole course **Parque Valle del Sol** ✸ (© 282-9222; www.vallesol.com), in the western suburb of Santa Ana. This course is open to the public. Greens fees are $75 for 18 holes, including a cart. The course at the Meliá Cariari is not technically open to the public, but if there's room, they'll generally let guests at other hotels tee off with advance notice.

HOTEL SPAS & WORKOUT FACILITIES   Most of the higher-end hotels have some sort of pool and exercise facilities. You'll find the best of these at the Marriott Costa Rica Hotel (p. 106), Tryp Corobicí (p. 102), and Meliá Cariari (p. 106). The Meliá Cariari has the nicest (really the only) Olympic-size lap pool, in addition to 11 tennis courts and a well-equipped exercise room. If you're looking for a good, serious workout, I recommend the **Multispa** ✸ (© 231-5542), located in the Tryp Corobicí. Even if you're not a guest at the hotel, you can use the facilities here and join in any class for $12 per day. Multispa has five other locations around the Central Valley.

JOGGING Try **La Sabana Park,** mentioned above, or head to **Parque del Este,** which is east of town, in the foothills above San Pedro. Take the San Ramón/Parque del Este bus from Calle 9 between avenidas Central and 2. It's never a good idea to jog at night, on busy streets, or alone. Women should be particularly careful about jogging alone. And remember, Tico drivers are not accustomed to sport joggers on residential streets, so don't expect drivers to give you much berth.

SOCCER/FUTBOL Ticos take their *fútbol* seriously. Costa Rican professional soccer is some of the best in Central America, and the national team, or *Sele (selección nacional),* qualified for the 2002 World Cup, for the second time in the country's history. The soccer season runs from September to June, with the finals spread out over several weeks in late June and early July.

You don't need to buy tickets in advance. Tickets generally run between $2 and $15. It's worth paying a little extra for *sombra numerado* (reserved seats in the shade). This will protect you from both the sun and the more rowdy aficionados. Costa Rican soccer fans take the sport seriously, and several violent incidents both inside and outside the stadiums have marred the sport in recent years, so be careful. Other options include *sombra* (general admission in the shade), *palco* and *palco numerado* (general admission and reserved mezzanine), and *sol general* (general admission in full sun).

The main San José team is Saprissa (affectionately called El Monstruo, or "The Monster"). **Saprissa's stadium** is in Tibás (take any Tibás bus from Calle 2 and Av. 5). Games are often held on Sunday at 11am, but occasionally they are scheduled for Saturday afternoon or Wednesday evening. Check the local newspapers for game times and locations.

SWIMMING If you aren't going to get to the beach anytime soon and your hotel doesn't have a pool, you can use the pool at the Multispa facility at the hotel **Tryp Corobicí** (② **231-5542**) for $12. Alternately, for a real Tico experience, head to **Ojo de Agua** (② **441-2808**), on the road between the airport and San Antonio de Belén. The spring-fed waters are cool and refreshing, and even if it seems a bit chilly in San José, it's always several degrees warmer out here. This place is very popular with Ticos and can get quite crowded on weekends. Unfortunately, you have to keep an eye on your valuables here, and the place feels a little rundown. Admission is $2.50. Buses leave almost hourly for Ojo de Agua from Avenida 2 and Calle 12.

7 Shopping

Serious shoppers will be disappointed in Costa Rica. Aside from coffee and oxcarts, there isn't much that's distinctly Costa Rican. To compensate for its own relative lack of goods, Costa Rica does a brisk business in selling crafts and clothes imported from Guatemala, Panama, and Ecuador.

THE SHOPPING SCENE San José's central shopping corridor is bounded by avenidas 1 and 2, from about Calle 14 in the west to Calle 13 in the east. For several blocks west of the Plaza de la Cultura, **Avenida Central** is a pedestrian-only street mall where you'll find store after store of inexpensive clothes for men, women, and children. Depending on the mood of the police that day, you might find a lot of street vendors as well.

Tips   Joe to Go

Two words of advice: Buy coffee. Lots of it.

Coffee is the best shopping deal in all of Costa Rica. Although the best Costa Rican coffee is supposedly shipped off to North American and European markets, it's hard to beat the coffee that's roasted right in front of you here. Best of all is the price: One pound of coffee sells for around $3. It makes a great gift and truly is a local product.

Café Britt is the big name in Costa Rican coffee. These folks have the largest export business in the country, and, although high-priced, its blends are very dependable. My favorites, however, are the coffees roasted and packaged in Manuel Antonio and Monteverde, by **Café Milagro** and **Café Monteverde**, respectively. If you're going to either of these places, definitely pick up their beans.

The best place to buy coffee is in any supermarket. Why pay more at a gift or specialty shop? You can also try **Café Trébol**, on Calle 8 between avenidas Central and 1 (on the western side of the Central Market; © 221-8363). It's open Monday through Saturday from 7am to 6:30pm, and Sunday from 8:30am to 12:30pm.

Be sure to ask for whole beans; Costa Rican grinds are often too fine for standard coffee filters. The store will pack the beans for you in whatever size bag you want. If you buy prepackaged coffee in a supermarket in Costa Rica, the whole beans will be marked either *grano* (grain) or *grano entero* (whole bean). If you opt for ground varieties *(molido),* be sure the package is marked *puro;* otherwise, it will likely be mixed with a good amount of sugar, the way Ticos like it.

One good coffee-related gift to bring home is a coffee sock and stand. This is the most common mechanism for brewing coffee beans in Costa Rica. It consists of a simple circular stand, made out of wood or wire, that holds a sock. Put the ground beans in the sock, place a pot or cup below, and pour boiling water through. You can find the socks and stands at most supermarkets and in the Mercado Central. In fancier crafts shops, you'll find them made out of ceramic. Depending on its construction, a stand will cost you between $1.50 and $15; socks run around 30¢, so buy a few spares.

Most shops in the downtown district are open Monday through Saturday from about 8am to 6pm. Some shops close for lunch, while others remain open (it's just the luck of the draw for shoppers). When you do purchase something, you'll be happy to find that the sales and import taxes have already been figured into the display price.

International laws prohibit trade in endangered wildlife, so don't buy any plants or animals, even if they're readily for sale. Do not buy any kind of sea-turtle products (including jewelry); wild birds; lizard, snake, or cat skins; corals; or orchids (except those grown commercially). No matter how unique, beautiful, insignificant, or inexpensive it might seem, your purchase will directly contribute to the further hunting of endangered species.

It's especially hard to capture the subtle shades and colors of the rain and cloud forests, and many a traveler has gone home thinking that his or her undeveloped film contained the full beauty of the jungle, only to return from the photo developer with 36 bright-green blurs. To avoid this heartache, you might want to pick up some postcards of the sights you want to remember forever and send them to yourself.

MARKETS   There are several markets near downtown, but by far the largest is the **Mercado Central,** located between avenidas Central and 1 and calles 6 and 8. Although this dark maze of stalls is primarily a food market, inside you'll find all manner of vendors, including a few selling Costa Rican souvenirs, crude leather goods, and musical instruments. Be especially careful about your wallet or purse and any prominent jewelry because very skilled pickpockets frequent this area. All the streets surrounding the Mercado Central are jammed with produce vendors selling from small carts or loading and unloading trucks. It's always a hive of activity, with crowds of people jostling for space on the streets. Your best bet is to visit on Sunday or on weekdays; Saturdays are particularly busy. In the hot days of the dry season, the aromas can get quite heady. If you have a delicate constitution, don't eat any fruit that you don't peel yourself (oranges, bananas, mangoes, and so on).

There is also a daily street market on the west side of the **Plaza de la Democracia.** Here you'll find two long rows of outdoor stalls selling T-shirts, Guatemalan and Ecuadorian handicrafts and clothing, small ceramic *ocarinas* (a small musical wind instrument), and handmade jewelry. The atmosphere here is much more open than at the Mercado Central, which I find just a bit too claustrophobic. You might be able to bargain prices down a little bit, but bargaining is not a traditional part of the vendor culture here, so you'll have to work hard to save a few dollars.

Finally, two other similar options downtown include **La Casona,** Calle Central between avenidas Central and 1 (© **222-7999**), a three-story warren of crafts and souvenir shops; and **El Pueblo,** a tourism complex built in the style of a mock colonial-era village, with a wide range of restaurants, gift shops, art galleries, bars, and discos.

MODERN MALLS   With globalization and modernization taking hold in Costa Rica, much of the local shopping scene has shifted to large megamalls. Modern multilevel affairs with cineplexes, food courts, and international brand-name stores are becoming more ubiquitous. The biggest and most modern of these malls include the **Mall San Pedro, Multiplaza, Terra Mall,** and **Mall Real Cariari.** Although they lack the charm of small shops found around San José, they are a reasonable option for one-stop shopping; most contain at least one or two local galleries and crafts shops, along with a large supermarket, which is always the best place to stock up on local coffee, hot sauces, liquors, and other non-perishable foodstuffs.

SHOPPING A TO Z
ART GALLERIES

Arte Latino   This gallery carries original artwork in a variety of media, featuring predominantly Central American themes. Some of it is pretty gaudy, but this is a good place to find Nicaraguan and Costa Rican "primitive" paintings. The gallery also has storefronts in the Multiplaza Mall in Escazú and at the Mall Cariari, which is located on the Interamerican Highway, about halfway between the airport and downtown, across the street from the Hotel Herradura. Calle 5 and Av. 1. © **258-3306.**

Galería Andrómeda This small, personal gallery features contemporary national artists of good quality. There are usually prints and paintings by several artists on display, and prices are very reasonable. Calle 9 at Av. 9. © 223-3529.

Galería 11–12 ★ This outstanding gallery deals mainly in high-end Costa Rican art, from neoclassical painters such as Teodorico Quirós to modern masters such as Francisco Amighetti and Paco Zuñiga, to current stars such as Rafa Fernández, Fernando Carballo, and Fabio Herrera. Av. 15 and Calle 35, Casa 3506, in Barrio Escalante (from the Farolito, 200m/656 ft. east and 100m/328 ft. north). © 280-8441. www.galeria11-12.com.

Galería Jacobo Karpio This excellent gallery handles some of the more adventurous modern art to be found in Costa Rica. Karpio has a steady stable of prominent Mexican, Cuban, and Argentine artists, as well as some local talent. Av. 1, between calles 11 and 13. © 257-7963.

Galería Kandinsky Owned by the daughter of one of Costa Rica's most prominent modern painters, Rafa Fernandez, this small gallery usually has a good selection of high-end contemporary Costa Rican paintings, be it the house collection or some specific temporary exhibit. Centro Comercial Calle Real, San Pedro. © 234-0478. galkandinsky@yahoo.com.

HANDICRAFTS

As I've said, the quality of Costa Rican handicrafts is generally very low, and the offerings are limited. The most typical items you'll find are hand-painted wooden **oxcarts.** These come in a variety of sizes, and the big ones can be shipped to your home for a very reasonable price. If you want to stick to downtown San José, try the outdoor market on the **Plaza de la Democracia,** although prices here tend to be high and bargaining can be difficult. If you prefer to do your crafts shopping in a flea-market atmosphere, head over to **La Casona** on Calle Central between avenidas Central and 1.

Notable exceptions to the generally meager crafts offerings include the fine wooden creations of **Barry Biesanz** ★★ (© 289-4337; www.biesanz.com). His work is sold in many of the finer gift shops around, but beware: Biesanz's work is often imitated, so make sure that what you buy is the real deal (he generally burns his signature into the bottom of the piece). **Lil Mena** is a local artist who specializes in working with and painting on handmade papers and rough fibers. You'll find her work in a number of shops around San José.

You might also run across **carved masks** made by the indigenous Boruca people of southern Costa Rica. These full-size balsa-wood masks come in a variety of styles, both painted and unpainted, and run anywhere from $10 to $70, depending on the quality of workmanship. **Cecilia "Pefi" Figueres** ★★ makes practical ceramic ware that is lively and fun. Look for her brightly colored abstract and figurative bowls, pitchers, coffee mugs, and more at some of the better gift shops around the city.

Scores of shops around San José sell a wide variety of crafts, from the truly tacky to the divinely inspired. Here are some that sell more of the latter and fewer of the former.

Angie Theologos's Gallery Angie makes sumptuous handcrafted jackets from hand-woven and embroidered Guatemalan textiles. Her work also includes bolero jackets, plus T-shirts made with Panamanian *molas* (appliquéd panels). San Pedro (call for appointment and directions). © 225-6565.

Biesanz Woodworks ★ *Finds* Biesanz makes a wide range of high-quality items, including bowls, jewelry boxes, humidors, and some wonderful sets of wooden chopsticks. It recently moved to a new showroom, with the woodshop out back. Biesanz Woodworks is actively involved in reforestation, so you can even pick up a hardwood seedling here. Bello Horizonte, Escazú. © 289-4337. www.biesanz.com. Call for directions and off-hour appointments.

Boutique Annemarie ★★ Occupying two floors at the Hotel Don Carlos, this shop has an amazing array of wood products, leather goods, papier-mâché figurines, paintings, books, cards, posters, and jewelry. You'll see most of this stuff at the other shops, but not in such quantities or in such a relaxed and pressure-free environment. Don't miss this shopping experience. At the Hotel Don Carlos, Calle 9, between avs. 7 and 9. © 221-6063.

Galería Namu ★★ This shop has some very high-quality arts and crafts, including excellent Boruca and Huetar carved masks and "primitive" paintings, many painted by rural women. It also carries a good selection of the ceramic work of Cecilia "Pefi" Figueres. This place organizes tours to visit various indigenous tribes and artisans as well. Av. 7 between calles 5 and 7. © 256-3412. www.galeria namu.com.

Las Garzas Handicraft Market This is the most appealing artisans' market close to San José. (It's a short ride out of town.) It includes more than 25 shops selling wood, metal, and ceramic crafts, among a large variety of other items. There's a huge selection, and you can get some really good buys here. It's open daily. In Moravia, 100m (328 ft.) south and 50m (164 ft.) east of the Red Cross Station. © 236-0037. Ask a taxi driver to take you to Las Garzas Mercado de Artesanía in Moravia.

Suraska Among the selections here are ceramics, mobiles, and jewelry. This store tends to carry higher-quality items than most gift shops downtown. Be warned, however, that the prices here are accordingly more expensive. Calle 5 and Av. 3. © 222-0129.

JEWELRY

Plaza Esmeralda Part working jewelry factory, part shopping center, part tourist trap, this is still a good place to come to buy replicas of pre-Columbian jewelry. The several shops here carry a wide range of typical tourist souvenirs and locally produced arts and craftworks at fair prices. Visitors are treated to a 15-minute guided tour where you can see some of the jewelry being manufactured. Sabana Norte. 800m (2,624 ft.) north of Jack's in Pavas. © 296-0312. www.plaza-esmeralda.com.

LEATHER GOODS

In general, Costa Rican leather products are not of the highest grade or quality, and prices are not particularly low—but take a look and see for yourself. In addition to the shop listed below, **Del Río** (© 262-1415) is a local leather goods manufacturer, with stores in most of the city's modern malls. It also offers free hotel pickup and transfer to its factory outlet in Heredia.

Malety This is one of the outlets in San José where you can shop for locally produced leather bags, briefcases, purses, wallets, and other such items. A second store is located on Calle 1 between avenidas Central and 2. Av. 1 between calles 1 and 3. © 221-1670.

LIQUOR

The national drink is *guaro,* a rough, clear liquor made from sugar cane. The most popular brand is **Cacique,** which you'll find at every liquor store and most supermarkets. Costa Ricans drink their *guaro* straight or mixed with club soda or Fresca. When drinking it straight, it's customary to follow a shot with a bite into a fresh lime covered in salt.

Costa Ricans also drink a lot of rum. The premier Costa Rican rum is **Centenario,** but I recommend that you opt for the Nicaraguan **Flor de Caña** or Cuban **Havana Club,** which are both far superior rums.

Several brands and styles of coffee-based liqueurs are also produced in Costa Rica. **Café Rica** is similar to Kahlúa, and you can also find several types of coffee cream liqueurs. The folks at **Café Britt** produce their own line of coffee liqueurs, which are quite good. You can buy them in most supermarkets, liquor stores, and tourist shops, but the best prices I've seen are at the supermarket chain Mas X Menos. There is a **Mas X Menos** store on Paseo Colón and another on Avenida Central at the east end of town, just below the Museo Nacional de Costa Rica.

MUSIC

A CD of Costa Rican music makes a great souvenir. Many gift shops around the country carry a small selection of Costa Rican music. **Editus** is an inventive trio (guitar, violin, and percussion) that has a several albums out. They've won two Grammy awards for their collaborations with Rubén Blades on the albums *Tiempos* and *Mundo.* You should also see discs by **Cantoamérica,** which plays upbeat dance music ranging from salsa to son to calypso to merengue. Jazz pianist **Manuel Obregón** has several excellent albums out, including *Simbiosis,* on which he improvises along with the sounds of Costa Rica's wildlife, waterfalls, and weather; as well as his work with the *Papaya Orchestra,* a collaboration and gathering of musicians from around Central America. Finally, there's a new label, Papaya Music (www.papayamusic.com), that produces and distributes an excellent range of local music, including everyone from Obregon to **Malpais,** a local pop-rock band, to a broad selection of traditional folk music, including one of my favorite local discs, *Dr. Bombodee,* by the Costa Rican–born calypsonian Walter "Gavitt" Ferguson.

8 San José After Dark

Catering to a mix of tourists, college students, and just generally party-loving Ticos, San José has a host of options to meet the nocturnal needs of visitors and residents alike. You'll find plenty of interesting clubs and bars, a wide range of theaters, and some very lively discos and dance salons.

To find out what's going on in San José while you're in town, pick up a copy of the *Tico Times* (English) or *La Nación* (Spanish). The former is a good place to find out where local expatriates are hanging out; the latter's "Viva" and "Tiempo Libre" sections have extensive listings of discos, movie theaters, and live music.

THE PERFORMING ARTS

Theater is very popular in Costa Rica, and downtown San José is studded with small theaters. However, tastes tend toward the burlesque, and the crowd pleasers are almost always simplistic sexual comedies. The **National Theater Company** is one major exception, tackling works from Lope de Vega to Lorca, to Mamet. Almost all of the theater offerings are in Spanish, although the **Little Theater Group** is a long-standing amateur group that periodically stages works in English. Check the *Tico Times* to see if anything is running during your stay.

Costa Rica has a strong modern dance scene. Both the **University of Costa Rica** and the **National University** have modern-dance companies that perform regularly in various venues in San José. In addition to the university-sponsored companies, there's a host of smaller independent companies worth catching. **Los Denmedium** and **Diquis Tiquis** are particularly good.

The **National Symphony Orchestra** is a respectable orchestra by regional standards, although its repertoire tends to be rather conservative. The symphony season runs March through November, with concerts roughly every other weekend at the **Teatro Nacional,** Avenida 2 between calles 3 and 5 (© 221-3756), and the **Auditorio Nacional** (© 222-7647), located at the Museo de Los Niños (p. 119). Tickets cost between $3 and $15 and can be purchased at the box office.

Visiting artists also stop in Costa Rica from time to time. Recent concerts have featured pop star Alanis Morisette, reggae legends Steel Pulse, Spanish singer Alejandro Sanz, Argentine legend Charly García, Chilean rockers La Ley, and salsa star Oscar De León. Many of these concerts and guest performances take place in San José's two historic theaters, the Teatro Nacional (see above) and the **Teatro Melico Salazar,** Avenida 2 between calles Central and 2 (© 221-4952), as well as at the **Auditorio Nacional** (see above). Really large shows are sometimes held at soccer stadiums or at the amphitheater at the Hotel Herradura.

Costa Rica's cultural panorama changes drastically every March, when the country hosts large arts festivals. In odd-numbered years, **El Festival Nacional de las Artes** reigns supreme, featuring purely local talent. In even-numbered years, the month-long fete is **El Festival Internacional de las Artes,** which offers a nightly smorgasbord of dance, theater, music, and monologue from around the world. Most nights of the festival, you will have between 4 and 10 shows to choose from. Many are free, and the most expensive ticket is $5. For exact dates and details of the program, you can contact the Ministry of Youth, Culture, and Sports (© 255-3188), although you might have trouble getting any information if you don't speak Spanish.

THE CLUB, MUSIC & DANCE SCENE

You'll find plenty of places to hit the dance floor in San José. Salsa and merengue are the main beats that move people here, and many of the dance clubs, discos, and salons feature live music on the weekends. You'll find a pretty limited selection, though, if you're looking to catch some small-club jazz, rock, or blues.

The daily "Viva" and Thursday's "Tiempo Libre" sections of *La Nación* newspaper have weekly performance schedules. Some dance bands to watch for are Pimienta Negra, Kalua, and Los Brillanticos. El Guato, Ghandi, Inconsciente Colectivo, Kadeho, Malpais, and Suite Doble are popular local rock groups, Marfil is a good cover band, and both Mr. Jones Blues Band and the Blind Pig Blues Band are electric blues outfits. If you're looking for jazz, check out Jazz Expresso, Editus, El Sexteto de Jazz Latino, or pianist Manuel Obregón. Two very good local bands that don't seem to play that frequently are Cantoamérica and Adrian Goizueta's Grupo Experimental.

A good place to sample a range of San José's nightlife is in **El Pueblo,** a shopping, dining, and entertainment complex done up like an old Spanish village. It's just across the river to the north of town. The best way to get there is by taxi; all the drivers know El Pueblo well. Within the alleyways that wind through El Pueblo are a dozen or more bars, clubs, and discos—there's even an indoor soccer playing field. **Cocoloco** (© 222-8782) features nightly "fiestas," **Discoteque Infinito** (© 223-2195) has three different environments under one roof, and **Twister** (© 222-5746) and **Friends** (© 223-5283) are happening party spots. Across the street you'll find **La Plaza** (© 257-1077), one of my favorite dance spots.

Most of the places listed below charge a nominal cover charge; sometimes it includes a drink or two.

Club Bash ⭐ Housed in the old Cine California movie theater, this place is huge, with high ceilings and a bare-bones industrial feel to it. The music tends toward a modern mix of trance, house, and techno. Club Bash draws a wide range of dancers mixing all-out ravers with teenie boppers and hard-core late-night partiers. Av. 1 between calles 23 and 25, in the old Cine California. ✆ 221-9978.

El Tobogán ⭐⭐ *(Finds)* The dance floor in this place is about the size of a football field, yet it still fills up. This is a place where Ticos come with their loved ones and dance partners. The music is mix of classic Latin dance rhythms—salsa, cumbia, merengue, and son. It's open only on the weekends (till about 2am), but there's always a live band here, and sometimes it's very good. 200m (656 ft.) north and 100m (328 ft.) east of the La República main office, off the Guápiles Hwy. ✆ 223-8920.

La Plaza ⭐ This large, open, upscale disco seems to be the favored dance venue for the young and beautiful of San José. The interior is designed to resemble a colonial plaza. Tunes come in sets that can range from salsa to merengue to reggae to electronic. This place pulls a younger crowd than many of the other spots around town; the party here is Wednesday through Saturday nights till around 4am. Admission is around $3. Across from the El Pueblo shopping center. ✆ 257-1077.

Salsa 54 This is the place to go to watch expert salsa dancers and to try some yourself. You can take formal Latin dance classes here, or you might learn something just by watching. This place is popular with Ticos, and tourists are a rare commodity here—tourists who can really dance salsa even more so. It's open daily till 4am. Calle 3 between avs. 1 and 3. ✆ 233-3814.

THE BAR SCENE

There seems to be something for every taste here. Lounge lizards will be happy in most hotel bars in the downtown area, while students and the young at heart will have no problem mixing in at the livelier spots around town. Sports fans can find plenty of places to catch the most important games of the day, and there are even a couple of brewpubs that are drastically improving the quality and selection of the local suds.

The best part of the varied bar scene in San José is something called a *boca,* the equivalent of a tapa in Spain: a little dish of snacks that arrives at your table when you order a drink. Although this is a somewhat dying tradition, especially in the younger, hipper bars, you will still find *bocas* alive and well in the older, more traditional Costa Rican drinking establishments. In most, the *bocas* are free, but in some, where the dishes are more sophisticated, you'll have to pay for the treats. You'll find drinks reasonably priced, with beer costing around $2 a bottle, and mixed drinks costing $2 to $4.

Café Expresivo ⭐ Laid back and funky, this cafe and gallery features live performances most evenings. The gigs range from open-mike sessions to storytelling marathons, to folk and jazz concerts featuring some of the country's top talent. It's open Tuesday through Friday from noon to midnight, and Saturday and Sunday from 5pm to midnight. 375m (1,230 ft.) east of the Santa Teresita Church, Barrio Escalante. ✆ 224-1202.

Café Loft ⭐ This is another good place to come for electronic music, trance, house, and trip-hop. The vibe here is postmodern chic, with a heavy European influence. There's a decent menu of nouveau French and international cuisine to munch on, and usually a DJ spinning existential electronic music. Grab a table at the quieter restaurant area, sit on a comfortable couch in one of the many nooks, or mingle at the lively bar. It's open Tuesday through Saturday from 7pm to 2am. Av. 11 and Calle 3. © **221-2302**.

Chelles *Finds* This classic downtown bar and restaurant makes up for its lack of ambience with plenty of tradition and its diverse and colorful clientele. The lights are bright, the chairs surround simple Formica-topped card tables, and mirrors adorn most of the walls. Simple sandwiches and meals are served, and pretty good *bocas* come with the drinks. It's open daily, 'round the clock. Av. Central and Calle 9. © **221-1369**.

El Cuartel de la Boca del Monte ★★ This popular bar, one of San José's best, began life as an artist-and-bohemian hangout, and over the years it has evolved into the leading meat market for the young and well heeled. However, artists still come, as do foreign exchange students, visitors, and, for some reason, many of the river-rafting guides, so there's always a diverse mix. There's usually live music here on Monday, Wednesday, and Friday nights, and when there is, the place is packed shoulder to shoulder. From Monday to Friday, it's open for lunch and again in the evenings; on weekends, it opens at 4pm. On most nights, it's open till about 1am, although the revelry might continue till about 3am on Friday or Saturday. Av. 1 between calles 21 and 23 (50m/164 ft. west of the Cine Magaly). © **221-0327**.

Key Largo ★ *Finds* Following a meticulous restoration, San José's most popular prostitute pickup bar is back in business and looking better than ever. Housed in a beautiful old building just off Parque Morazán in the heart of downtown, Key Largo is worth a visit if just to take in the scene and admire the dark-stained carved wood ceilings. There are a couple of pool tables in one room, and there's usually a live band. Calle 7 between avs. 1 and 3. © **221-0277**.

Meridiano al Este ★★ This new club, restaurant, and performance space might just become the best spot in San José to catch live music. Owned by some of the members of the Grammy award-winning group Editus, this place actually took acoustic and sight-line considerations into account during the design phase, unlike most other bars that host live music in town. The food is simple, with a selection of sandwiches, pizzas, and international fare. It's open daily from 11:30am until around 2am, depending on the crowd. Av. Central, across from La Bomba La Primavera, Barrio California. © **256-2705**.

Rio This bar and restaurant is close to the University of Costa Rica and, consequently, attracts a younger clientele. At night, Rio is usually packed to overflowing with a rowdy college-age crowd. It's open daily till 1am. Av. Central, Los Yoses. © **225-8371**.

Shakespeare Bar Located next to the Sala Garbo movie theater, this quiet and classy little spot is a good place to meet after a movie or a show at the Sala Garbo or Laurence Olivier Theater next door. It recently started having live music again regularly, featuring local jazz, folk, and blues outfits. It's open daily till midnight. Av. 2 and Calle 28. © **258-6787**.

HANGING OUT IN SAN PEDRO

The funky 2-block stretch of **San Pedro** ★★ just south of the University of Costa Rica has been dubbed La Calle de Amargura, or the "Street of Bitterness," and it's the heart and soul of this eastern suburb and college town. Bars and cafes are mixed in with bookstores and copy shops. After dark, the streets here are packed with teens, punks, students, and professors barhopping and just hanging around. You can walk the strip until someplace strikes your fancy—you don't need a travel guide to find **Omar Khayyam** (© 253-8455) or **Pizza Caccio** (© 224-3261), which lie at the heart of this district—or you can try one of the places listed below.

Hard rockers, metal freaks, ravers, and rowdy young crowds tend to congregate at the **Sand Bar** (© 225-9229), in the Centro Comercial Cocorí, and **El Yos** (© 280-1139), located 75m (246 ft.) west of the Automercado in Los Yoses. The latter club often has live music or DJs.

You can get here by heading out (east) on Avenida 2, following the flow of traffic. You will first pass through the neighborhood of Los Yoses before you reach a big traffic circle with a big fountain in the center (La Fuente de la Hispanidad). The Mall San Pedro is located on this traffic circle. Heading straight through the circle (well, going around it and continuing on what would have been a straight path), you'll come to the Church of San Pedro, about 4 blocks east of the circle. The church is the major landmark in San Pedro. You can also take a bus here from downtown.

Jazz Café ★★ (Finds) Opened by one of the former owners of the popular but now defunct La Maga, the Jazz Café has quickly become one of the more happening spots in San Pedro and one of my favorites. Wrought-iron chairs, sculpted busts of famous jazz artists, and creative lighting give the place ambience. There's live music here most nights, and visiting artists have included Chucho Valdés and Tony Pérez. It's open daily till about 2am. Next to the Banco Popular on Av. Central. © 253-8933.

La Villa (Finds) This converted Victorian house holds the ghosts of Che Guevara and Camilo Cienfuegos, although they've taken down the posters of these and other Latin American revolutionaries on the walls and painted over all the graffiti. Around the tables you'll find poets and painters mixing with a new generation of student activists, all in a convivial college-town atmosphere. Consistent with the revolutionary ethos, everything is priced reasonably and, when there's no live music, a battered sound system plays a steady stream of Silvio Rodríguez, Mercedes Sosa, and other *Nueva Trova* stalwarts. It's open Monday through Saturday from 11am to 1am, and Sunday from 7pm to 1am. 200m (656 ft.) east and 125m (410 ft.) north of the Church in San Pedro. © 281-1571.

Mosaikos The entrance to this popular nightspot is a long, narrow corridor/bar that is generally packed solid. In the back there's a larger room, with another bar, some tables, and some funky art. The crowd here is young and can get quite rowdy. Most recently they've added DJs and a move toward house, techno, and trance-style dance music, although you're also just as likely to hear reggae, ska, or hip-hop tunes blasting. It's open Monday through Saturday from 11am to 2am, and Sunday from 5pm to 2am. 200m (656 ft.) east and 150m (492 ft.) north of the Church in San Pedro. © 280-9541.

Planet Mall This place is on the fourth floor of the Mall San Pedro. There are a couple of quiet nooks and corners, but most of the action takes place under the neon lights on and around the immense dance floor, which sometimes features live music. Depending on what's going on here, the cover can be as much $10, sometimes even more. It's open Thursday through Saturday evenings till 2am. In the San Pedro Mall. © 280-4693.

Terra U Set on a busy corner in the heart of the University district, this place is quickly becoming one of the most popular bars in the area. Part of this is due to the inviting open-air street-front patio area, which provides a nice alternative to the all-too-common smoke-filled rooms found at most other trendy spots. It's open Monday through Saturday evenings till 2am. 200m (656 ft.) east and 150m (492 ft.) north of the Church in San Pedro. ⓒ **225-7249.**

THE GAY & LESBIAN SCENE

Because Costa Rica is such a conservative Catholic country, the gay and lesbian communities here are rather discreet. Homosexuality is not generally under attack, but many gay and lesbian organizations guard their privacy, and the club scene is changeable and not well publicized. For a general overview of the current situation, news of any special events or meetings, and up-to-date information, gay and lesbian travelers should check in at **Uno@Diez,** on Calle 3 between avenidas 5 and 7 (ⓒ **258-4561;** www.1en10.com), a downtown coffeehouse, gallery, and Internet cafe.

The most established and happening gay and lesbian bars and dance clubs in San José are **Déjà Vu,** Calle 2 between avenidas 14 and 16 (ⓒ **223-3758**), and **La Avispa,** Calle 1 between avenidas 8 and 10 (ⓒ **223-5343;** www.laavispa. co.cr). The former is predominantly a guys' bar; the latter is popular with both men and women, although it sometimes sets aside certain nights of the week or month for specific persuasions. There's also **Buenas Vibraciones** (ⓒ **223-4573**), out on Paseo de los Estudiantes; **Pucho's Bar** (ⓒ **256-1147**), on Calle 11 and Avenida 8; and **El Bochinche** (ⓒ **221-0500**), on Calle 11 between avenidas 10 and 12.

CASINOS

Gambling is legal in Costa Rica, and there are casinos at virtually every major hotel. However, as in Tico bullfighting, there are some idiosyncrasies involved in gambling *a la Tica.*

If blackjack is your game, you'll want to play "rummy." The rules are almost identical, except that the house doesn't pay 1½ times on blackjack—instead, it pays double on any three of a kind or three-card straight flush.

If you're looking for roulette, what you'll find here is a bingolike spinning cage of numbered balls. The betting is the same, but some of the glamour is lost.

You'll also find a version of five-card-draw poker, but the rule differences are so complex that I advise you to sit down and watch for a while and then ask some questions before joining in. That's about all you'll find. There are no craps tables or baccarat.

There's some controversy over slot machines—one-armed bandits are currently outlawed—but you will be able to play electronic slots and poker games. Most of the casinos here are quite casual and small by international standards. You might have to dress up slightly at some of the fancier hotels, but most are accustomed to tropical vacation attire.

9 Side Trips from San José

San José makes an excellent base for exploring the beautiful Central Valley and the surrounding mountains. For first-time visitors, the best way to make the most of these excursions is usually to take a guided tour, but if you rent a car, you'll have greater independence. Some day trips also can be done by public bus.

GUIDED TOURS & ADVENTURES

A number of companies offer a wide variety of primarily nature-related day tours out of San José. The most reputable include **Costa Rica Expeditions** ★★

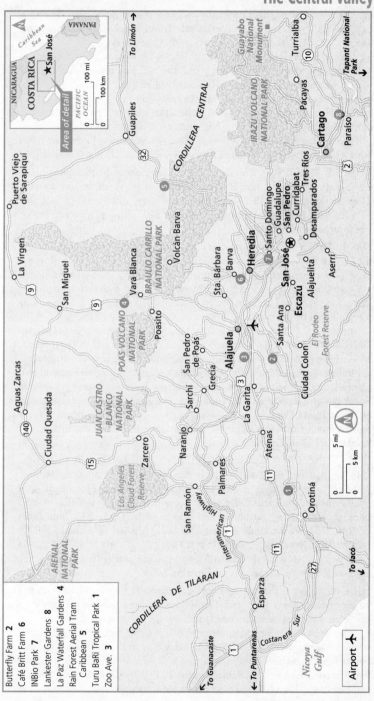

Caribbean Sea

NICARAGUA

COSTA RICA

★San José

PACIFIC OCEAN

Area of detail

PANAMA

0   100 mi
0   100 km

To Limón →

Guayabo National Monument

Turrialba

(10)

Tapanti National Park →

IRAZÚ VOLCANO NATIONAL PARK

Pacayas

CORDILLERA CENTRAL

Cartago

8

Paraíso

Guápiles

(32)

Puerto Viejo de Sarapiquí

Tres Ríos

(2)

Curridabat

Desamparados

Guadalupe

San Pedro

Santo Domingo

La Virgen

5

BRAULIO CARRILLO NATIONAL PARK

Volcán Barva

Sta. Bárbara

Barva

Heredia

7

San José

✪

Aserrí

La Paz Waterfall Gardens

San Miguel

(9)

Vara Blanca

6

Alajuelita

(9)

POÁS VOLCANO NATIONAL PARK

4

Poasito

San Pedro de Poás

Alajuela

3

Santa Ana

Escazú

Ciudad Colón

El Rodeo Forest Reserve

Aguas Zarcas

JUAN CASTRO BLANCO NATIONAL PARK

Grecia

3

La Garita

2

Sarchi

Ciudad Quesada

(140)

Zarcero

Naranjo

Atenas

(11)

(15)

Los Ángeles Cloud Forest Reserve

Palmares

1

Orotina

San Ramón

Interamerican Highway

(1)

To Jacó ↓

ARENAL NATIONAL PARK

CORDILLERA DE TILARAN

Esparza

(27)

(1)

Costanera Sur

(11)

Nicoya Gulf

← To Guanacaste

← To Puntarenas

Legend

Butterfly Farm **2**
Café Britt Farm **6**
INBio Park **7**
Lankester Gardens **8**
La Paz Waterfall Gardens **4**
Rain Forest Aerial Tram Caribbean **5**
Turu BaRi Tropical Park **1**
Zoo Ave. **3**

0   5 mi
0   5 km

Airport ✈

(© 257-0766; www.costaricaexpeditions.com), **Costa Rica Sun Tours** ★ (© 296-7757; www.crsuntours.com), **Ecole Travel** (© 223-2240), **Horizontes Tours** ★ (© 222-2022; www.horizontes.com), **Otec Tours** (© 257-0166; www. otec.co.cr), and **Swiss Travel Service** (© 282-4898; www.swisstravelcr.com).

Before signing on for a tour of any sort, find out how many fellow travelers will be accompanying you, how much time will be spent in transit and eating lunch, and how much time will actually be spent doing the primary activity. I've had complaints about tours that were rushed, that spent too much time in a bus or on secondary activities, or that had a cattle-car, assembly-line feel to them.

The tours below are arranged by type of activity. In addition to these are many other tours, some of which combine two or three different activities or destinations.

BUNGEE JUMPING   There's nothing unique about bungee jumping in Costa Rica, but the site here is quite beautiful. If you've always had the bug, **Tropical Bungee** (© **248-2212;** www.bungee.co.cr) will let you jump off an 80m (262-ft.) bridge for $60; two jumps cost $90. Transportation is provided free from San José twice daily.

DAY CRUISES   Several companies offer cruises to the lovely Tortuga Island in the Gulf of Nicoya. These full-day tours generally entail an early departure for the 2½-hour chartered bus ride to Puntarenas, where you board your vessel for a 1½-hour cruise to Tortuga Island. Then you get several hours on the uninhabited island, where you can swim, lie on the beach, play volleyball, or try a canopy tour, followed by the return journey.

The original and most dependable company running these trips is **Calypso Tours** ★ (© **256-2727;** www.calypsotours.com). The tour costs $99 per person and includes round-trip transportation from San José, a basic continental breakfast during the bus ride to the boat, all drinks on the cruise, and an excellent buffet lunch on the beach at the island. The Calypso Tours main vessel is a massive motor-powered catamaran. A second runs a separate tour to a private nature reserve at **Punta Coral** ★. The beach is much nicer at Tortuga Island, but the tour to Punta Coral is much more intimate, and the restaurant, hiking, and kayaking are all superior here.

EXPLORING PRE-COLUMBIAN RUINS   Although Costa Rica lacks the kind of massive pre-Columbian archaeological sites found in Mexico, Guatemala, or Honduras, it does have **Guayabo National Monument** ★, a small excavated town that today is just a small collection of building foundations, cobbled streets, aqueducts, and a small plaza. **Costa Rica Sun Tours** (© **296-7757;** www.crsuntours.com) offers a day trip here for around $125 per person. If you have a car or are an intrepid bus hound, you can do this tour on your own. Admission to the park is $4, and you can usually find a guide at the entrance for $5. See the section on Turrialba, below.

HIKING   Most of the tour agencies listed above offer 1-day guided hikes to a variety of destinations. In general, I recommend taking guided hikes to really see and learn about the local flora and fauna.

If you don't plan to visit Monteverde or one of Costa Rica's other cloud-forest reserves (see chapter 6), consider doing a day tour to the **Los Angeles Cloud Forest Reserve** ★. This full-day excursion and guided walk through the cloud forest is operated by the **Villablanca Hotel** (© **228-4603;** www.villablanca-costarica.com). The cost is $77, which includes transportation, breakfast, and lunch. It also offers horseback riding and canopy-tour options.

HORSEBACK RIDING   Options are nearly endless outside of San José, but it's more difficult to find a place to saddle up in the metropolitan area. The **La Caraña Riding Academy** (℡ 282-6106) is located in Santa Ana and offers riding classes as well as some guided trail rides.

MOUNTAIN BIKING   The best bicycle riding is well outside of San José—on dirt roads where you're not likely to be run off the highway by a semi, or run head-on into someone coming around a blind curve in the wrong lane. Several companies run a variety of 1-day and multiday tours out of San José. The 1-day tours usually involve a round-trip bus or van ride out of downtown to the primary destination. These destinations include the towns of Sarchí and Turrialba, as well as the Irazú and Poás volcanoes. Several of these tours are designed to be either entirely or primarily descents. **Costa Rica Biking Adventure** (℡ 225-6591; www.bikingincostarica.com) offers a variety of mountain-biking tours using high-end bikes and gear. A 1-day trip should cost between $70 and $120 per person.

Another company offering mountain-biking trips is **Coast to Coast Adventures** (℡ 280-8054; www.ctocadventures.com), which, in addition to its 2-week namesake adventure, also designs customized mountain-biking trips of shorter duration.

RAFTING, KAYAKING & RIVER TRIPS   Cascading down Costa Rica's mountain ranges are dozens of tumultuous rivers, several of which have become very popular for white-water rafting and kayaking. If I had to choose just one day trip to do out of San José, it would be a white-water rafting trip. For between $75 and $95, you can spend a day rafting through lush tropical forests; multiday trips are also available. Some of the most reliable rafting companies are **Aventuras Naturales** ⭑ (℡ 800/514-0411 in the U.S., or 225-3939), **Costa Rica White Water** ⭑ (℡ 257-0766), and **Ríos Tropicales** ⭑ (℡ 233-6455).

These companies all ply a number of rivers of varying difficulties, including the popular Pacuare and Reventazón rivers. For more information, see "White-Water Rafting, Kayaking & Canoeing," in chapter 3.

The Sarapiquí River is also a popular waterway for day trips out of San José. **Ecoscapes Highlights Tour** (℡ 297-0664; www.ecoscapetours.com) runs a jam-packed trip here that combines a stop at the La Paz waterfall, a visit to a banana plantation, a rainforest hike, and a boat ride on the river for $79 per person, including round-trip transportation, breakfast, and lunch.

Perhaps the best-known river tours are those that go up to **Tortuguero National Park** ⭑⭑. Although it's possible to do this tour as a day trip out of San José, it's a long, tiring, and expensive day. You're much better off doing it as a 1- or 2-night trip. See chapter 9 for details.

CANOPY TOURS & AERIAL TRAMS   Getting off the ground and up into the tree tops is the latest fad in Costa Rican tourism, and there are scores of such tours around the country. You have several options relatively close to San José. The folks at the **Original Canopy Tours** ⭑⭑ (℡ 257-5149; www.canopy tour.com) have their **Mahogany Park** operation, located about one hour outside of San José. The tour here features 10 platforms, and at the end, you have the choice of taking a cable to a ground station or doing a 18m (60-ft.) rappel down to finish off. The tour takes about 2 hours and costs $45.

A less adventurous option is the **Rain Forest Aerial Tram Caribbean** ⭑ (℡ 257-5961; www.rainforesttram.com), built on a private reserve bordering Braulio Carillo National Park. This pioneering tramway is the brainchild of rainforest researcher Dr. Donald Perry, whose cable-car system through the forest canopy at Rara Avis helped establish him as an early expert on rainforest

Holy Smoke!: Choosing the Volcano Trip That's Right for You

Poás, Irazú, and Arenal volcanoes are three of Costa Rica's most popular destinations, and the first two are easy day trips from San José (see below). Although numerous companies offer day trips to Arenal, I don't recommend them because there's at least 3½ hours of travel time in each direction. You usually arrive when the volcano is hidden by clouds and leave before the night's darkness shows off its glowing eruptions. For more information on Arenal Volcano, see chapter 6.

Tour companies offering trips to Poás and Irazú include **Costa Rica Expeditions** ✦✦ (📞 257-0766), **Costa Rica Sun Tours** ✦✦ (📞 296-7757), **Horizontes** ✦ (📞 222-2022), and **Swiss Travel Service** (📞 282-4898). Prices range from $25 to $35 for a half-day trip, and from $50 to $90 for a full-day trip.

The 3,378m (11,080-ft.) **Irazú Volcano** ✦ is historically one of Costa Rica's more active volcanoes, although it's relatively quiet these days. It last erupted on March 19, 1963, on the day that President John F. Kennedy arrived in Costa Rica. There's a good paved road right to the rim of the crater, where a desolate expanse of gray sand nurtures few plants and the air smells of sulfur. The landscape here is often compared to that of the moon. There are magnificent views of the fertile Meseta Central and Orosi Valley as you drive up from Cartago, and if you're very lucky, you might be able to see both the Pacific Ocean and the Caribbean Sea. Clouds usually descend by noon, so get here as early in the day as possible.

There's a visitor center up here with information on the volcano and natural history. A short trail leads to the rim of the volcano's two craters, their walls a maze of eroded gullies feeding onto the flat floor far below. This is a national park, with an admission fee of $6 charged at the gate. Dress in layers; this might be the tropics, but it can be cold up at the top if the sun's not out. The park restaurant, at an elevation of 3,022m (9,912 ft.), with walls of windows looking out over the valley far below, claims to be the highest restaurant in Central America.

If you don't want to take an organized tour, buses leave for Irazú Volcano Saturday, Sunday, and holidays at 8am from Avenida 2 between

canopies. The tramway takes visitors on a 90-minute ride through the treetops, where they have the chance to glimpse the complex web of life that makes these forests unique. There are also well-groomed trails through the rainforest and a restaurant on-site, so a trip here can easily take up a full day. In fact, if you want to spend the night, there are 10 simple but clean and comfortable bungalows here, which cost $80 per person per day (double occupancy), including three meals, taxes, and unlimited use of the tram and facilities.

The cost for tours, including transportation from San José and either breakfast or lunch, is $79. Alternatively, you can drive or take one of the frequent Guápiles buses—they leave every half-hour throughout the day and cost $2—from the new Caribbean bus terminal (Gran Terminal del Caribe) on Calle Central, 1 block north of Avenida 11. Ask the driver to let you off in front of the *teleférico*.

calles 1 and 3 (in front of the Gran Hotel Costa Rica). The fare is $5 round-trip, with the bus leaving the volcano at 1pm. To make sure that the buses are running, call © **272-0651**. If you're driving, head northeast out of Cartago toward San Rafael, and then continue driving uphill toward the volcano, passing the turnoffs for Cot and Tierra Blanca en route.

Poás Volcano ★★ is 37km (23 miles) from San José on narrow roads that wind through a landscape of fertile farms and dark forests. As at Irazú, there's a paved road right to the top, although you'll have to hike in about 1km (½ mile) to reach the crater. The volcano stands 2,640m (8,659 ft.) tall and is located within a national park, which preserves not only the volcano but also dense stands of virgin forest. Poás's crater, said to be the second largest in the world, is more than a mile across. Geysers in the crater sometimes spew steam and muddy water 180m (590 ft.) into the air, making this the largest geyser in the world. There's an information center where you can see a slide show about the volcano, and there are marked hiking trails through the cloud forest that rings the crater. About 15 minutes from the parking area, along a forest trail, is an overlook onto beautiful Botos Lake, which has formed in one of the volcano's extinct craters.

Be prepared when you come to Poás: This volcano is often enveloped in dense clouds. If you want to see the crater, it's best to come early and during the dry season. Moreover, it can get cool up here, especially when the sun isn't shining, so dress appropriately. Admission to the national park is $6 at the gate.

In case you don't want to go on a tour, there's a daily bus (© **442-6900**) from Avenida 2 between calles 12 and 14 that leaves at 8:30am and returns at 2pm. The fare is $2.50 round-trip. The bus is often crowded, so arrive early. If you're driving, head for Alajuela and continue on the main road through town and follow signs for Fraijanes. Just beyond Fraijanes, you will connect with the road between San Pedro de Poás and Poasito; turn right toward Poasito and continue to the rim of the volcano.

If you're driving, head out on the Guápiles Highway as if driving to the Caribbean coast. Watch for the tram's roadside welcome center—it's hard to miss. For walk-ins, the entrance fee is $50; students and anyone under 18 pay $25. Because this is a popular tour for groups, I highly recommend that you have an advance reservation in the high season and, if possible, a ticket; otherwise, you could end up waiting a long time for your tram ride or even be shut out. The tram can handle only about 80 passengers per hour, so scheduling is tight; the folks here try to schedule as much as possible in advance.

Finally, the new **Turu BaRi Tropical Park** (© **428-6070;** www.turubari.com) is aiming to cover as many bases as possible. Located about 90 minutes outside of San José, this park features a series of gardens, trails, and exhibits set in a deep valley that you can reach by means of a gondola-style ski lift, by cable and zip-line canopy tour, or on horseback. Down in the valley, you can wander around the botanical gardens, orchid gardens, and butterfly gardens, or grab a bite at the typical Costa Rican restaurant. The gondola ride here actually features enclosed cabin cars (with windows that open) and doesn't provide nearly the sense of intimacy or contact with the forest that the Aerial Tram does. Admission is $55 for adults and $40 for students and children.

CARTAGO & THE OROSI VALLEY

These two regions southeast of San José can easily be combined into a day trip. You might also squeeze in a visit to the Irazú Volcano (see "Holy Smoke!: Choosing the Volcano Trip That's Right for You," above, for details).

CARTAGO

Located about 24km (15 miles) southeast of San José, **Cartago** ✦ is the former capital of Costa Rica. Founded in 1563, it was Costa Rica's first city—and was, in fact, its *only* city for almost 150 years. Irazú Volcano rises up from the edge of town, and although it's quiet these days, it has not always been so peaceful. Earthquakes have damaged Cartago repeatedly over the years, so today few of the old colonial buildings are left standing. In the center of the city, a public park winds through the ruins of a large church that was destroyed in 1910 before it could be finished. Construction was abandoned after the quake, and today the ruins sit at the heart of a neatly manicured park, with quiet paths and plenty of benches. The ruins themselves are closed off, but the park itself is lovely.

Cartago's most famous building is the **Basílica de Nuestra Señora de los Angeles (Basilica of Our Lady of the Angels),** which is dedicated to the patron saint of Costa Rica and stands on the east side of town. Within the walls of this Byzantine-style church is a shrine containing the tiny figure of **La Negrita,** the Black Virgin, which is nearly lost amid its ornate altar. Legend has it that La Negrita first revealed herself on this site to a peasant girl in 1635. Miraculous healing powers have been attributed to La Negrita, and, over the years, thousands of pilgrims have come to the shrine seeking cures for their illnesses and difficulties. The walls of the shrine are covered with a fascinating array of tiny silver images left as thanks for cures effected by La Negrita. Amid the plethora of diminutive silver arms and legs, there are also hands, feet, hearts, lungs, kidneys, eyes, torsos, breasts, and—peculiarly—guns, trucks, beds, and planes. There are even dozens of sports trophies that I assume were left in thanks for helping teams win big games. Outside the church, vendors sell a wide selection of these trinkets, as well as little candle replicas of La Negrita. August 2 is the day dedicated to La Negrita; on this day, tens of thousands of people walk to Cartago from San José and elsewhere in the country, in devotion to this powerful statue.

More than 1km (½ mile) east of Cartago, on the road to Paraíso, you'll find **Lankester Gardens** ✦✦ (© 552-3247; p. 122), a botanical garden known for its orchid collection.

GETTING THERE   Buses (© 233-5350) for Cartago leave San José every 10 minutes between 5am and midnight from Calle 5 between avenidas 18 and 20. You can also pick up one en route at any of the little covered bus stops along Avenida Central in Los Yoses and San Pedro. The length of the trip is 45 minutes; the fare is about 45¢.

OROSI VALLEY

The Orosi Valley, southeast of Cartago and visible from the top of Irazú on a clear day, is generally considered one of the most beautiful valleys in Costa Rica.

The Reventazón River meanders through this steep-sided valley until it collects in the lake formed by the Cachí Dam. There are scenic overlooks near the town of Orosi, which is at the head of the valley, and in Ujarrás, which is on the banks of the lake. Near Ujarrás are the ruins of Costa Rica's oldest church (built in 1693), whose tranquil gardens are a great place to sit and gaze at the surrounding mountains. In the town of Orosi itself, there is yet another colonial church, built in 1743. A small museum here displays religious artifacts. Near the town of Cachí, you'll find **La Casa del Soñador (The House of the Dreamer;** ✆ **577-1047)**, which is the home and gallery of the late sculptor Macedonio Quesada and his sons, who carry on the family tradition.

From the Orosi Valley, it's a quick shot to the entrance to the **Tapantí National Park** 🐾, where you'll find some gentle and beautiful hiking trails, as well as riverside picnic areas. The park is open daily from 8am to 4pm; admission is $6.

GETTING THERE   If you're driving, take the road to Paraíso from Cartago, head toward Ujarrás, continue around the lake, and then pass through Cachí and on to Orosi. From Orosi, the road leads back to Paraíso. It is difficult to explore this whole area by public bus because this is not a densely populated region and the connections are often infrequent or unreliable. However, there are regular buses from Cartago to the town of Orosi. These buses run roughly every half-hour and leave the main bus terminal in Cartago. The trip takes 30 minutes, and the fare is 55¢. There are also guided day tours of this area from San José (call any of the companies listed under "Guided Tours & Adventures," earlier in this section).

TURRIALBA

This attractive little town 53km (33 miles) east of San José is best known as the starting point and home base for many popular white-water rafting trips. However, it's also worth a visit if you have an interest in pre-Columbian history or tropical botany.

Guayabo National Monument 🐾 is one of Costa Rica's only pre-Columbian sites that has been excavated and is open to the public. It's located 19km (12 miles) northeast of Turrialba and preserves a town site that dates from between 1000 B.C. and A.D. 1400. Archaeologists believe that Guayabo might have supported a population of as many as 10,000 people, but there is no clue yet to why the city was eventually abandoned only shortly before the Spanish arrived in the New World. Excavated ruins at Guayabo consist of paved roads, aqueducts, stone bridges, and house and temple foundations. There are also gravesites and petroglyphs. The monument is open daily from 8am to 4pm. This is a national park, and admission is $6 at the gate. For more information, see "Costa Rica's Top National Parks & Bioreserves," in chapter 3.

Botanists and gardeners will want to pay a visit to the **Center for Agronomy Research and Development (CATIE;** www.catie.ac.cr), which is located 5km (3 miles) southeast of Turrialba on the road to Siquirres. This center is one of the world's foremost facilities for research into tropical agriculture. Among the plants on CATIE's 2,000 acres are hundreds of varieties of cacao and thousands of varieties of coffee. The plants here have been collected from all over the world. In addition to trees used for food and other purposes, there are plants grown strictly for ornamental purposes. CATIE is open Monday through Friday from 7am to 4pm. Guided tours are available with advance notice for $10 per person, with a four-person minimum. Call ✆ **556-6431** for reservations.

While you're in the area, don't miss an opportunity to spend a little time at **Turrialtico (**✆ **538-1111;** www.turrialtico.com), a rustic yet beautiful open-air restaurant and small hotel high on a hill overlooking the Turrialba Valley. The view from here is one of the finest in the country, with lush greenery far below and volcanoes in the distance. Meals are quite inexpensive; a room will cost you around $52, with breakfast. This place is popular with rafting companies that bring groups here for meals and for overnights before, during, and after multi-day rafting trips. You'll find Turrialtico about 10km (6¼ miles) out of Turrialba on the road to Siquirres.

If you're looking for some luxury in this area, check out **Casa Turire** ⭑ (© **531-1111;** www.hotelcasaturire.com), where well-appointed rooms and suites in an elegant country mansion run between $130 and $240. The hotel is set on the banks of the lake formed recently by the Angostura dam project, and you can take a kayak or paddleboat out on the lake here.

GETTING THERE   Buses (© **556-4233**) leave San José hourly for Turrialba throughout the day from Calle 13 between avenidas 6 and 8. The fare is $1.75. If you're driving, take the road from Cartago to Paraíso, then through Juan Viñas, and on to Turrialba. It's pretty well marked. (Alternatively you can head toward the small town of Cot, on the road to Irazú Volcano, and then through the town of Pacayas on to Turrialba, another well-marked route.)

Turrialba itself is a bit of a jumble, and you will probably have to ask directions to get to locations out of town. Guayabo is about 20km (12 miles) beyond Turrialba on a road that is paved the entire way except for the last 3km (1¾ miles). There are also around three buses daily to Guayabo from the main bus terminal in Turrialba.

HEREDIA, GRECIA, SARCHI & ZARCERO

All of these cities and towns are northwest of San José and can be combined into a long day trip (if you have a car), perhaps in conjunction with a visit to Poás Volcano and/or the Waterfall Gardens. The scenery here is rich and verdant, and the small towns and scattered farming communities are truly representative of Costa Rica's agricultural heartland and campesino tradition. This is a great area to explore on your own in a rental car, if you don't mind getting lost a bit—the roads are narrow, winding, and poorly marked. If you're relying on buses, you'll be able to visit any of the towns listed below, but probably just one or two per day.

The road to Heredia turns north off the highway from San José to the airport. If you're going to Sarchí, take the highway west toward Puntarenas. Turn north to Grecia and then west to Sarchí. There'll be plenty of signs.

HEREDIA

Set on the flanks of the impressive Barva Volcano, this city was founded in 1706. Heredia is affectionately known as "The City of Flowers." A colonial church inaugurated in 1763 stands in the central park. The stone facade leaves no questions as to the age of the church, but the altar inside is decorated with neon stars and a crescent moon surrounding a statue of the Virgin Mary. In the middle of the palm-shaded park is a music temple, and across the street, beside several tile-roofed municipal buildings, is the tower of an old Spanish fort. Of all the cities in the Meseta Central, Heredia has the most colonial feel to it—you'll still see adobe buildings with Spanish tile roofs along narrow streets. Heredia is also the site of the **National Autonomous University,** so you'll find some nice coffee shops and bookstores near the school.

Surrounding Heredia is an intricate maze of picturesque villages and towns, including Santa Barbara, Santo Domingo, Barva, and San Joaquín de Flores. The newest attraction up here is the **INBio Park** ⭑⭑ (© **507-8107;** p. 121). Located on 5 hectares (12 acres) in Santo Domingo de Heredia, this place is part museum, part educational center, and part nature park. On the road to Barva, you'll find the small **Museo de Cultura Popular** (✆ **260-1619**), which is open Monday through Friday from 8am to 4pm, and Saturday and Sunday from 10am to 5pm; admission is $2. If you make your way to San Pedro de Barva de Heredia, stop in at **La Lluna de Valencia** (✆ **269-6665**), a delightful rustic Spanish restaurant with amazing paella, delicious sangria, and a very amiable host.

Buses leave for Heredia almost every 10 minutes from Calle 12 and Avenida 2, and from Calle 1 between avenidas 7 and 9. Bus fare is 45¢.

GRECIA

The picturesque little town of Grecia is noteworthy for its unusual metal church, which is painted a deep red and has white gingerbread trim. Just off the central park, next to the Palacio Municipal, you'll find the humble **Grecia Regional Museum** (✆ **494-6767**), which has some simple exhibits and information about the town's history. About 1km (½ mile) outside of Grecia, on the old road to Alajuela, you will find the **World of Snakes** (✆ **494-3700**). Open daily from 8am to 4pm, this serpentarium has more than 150 snakes representing more than 50 species. Although the $11 admission includes a guided tour, I find it a bit steep for this type of attraction.

Buses leave San José every half-hour for Grecia from Avenida 3 between calles 16 and 18. The road to Sarchí is to the left as you face the church in Grecia, but due to all the one-way streets, you'll have to drive around it.

SARCHÍ ✿

Sarchí is Costa Rica's main artisan town. The colorfully painted miniature **oxcarts** that you see all over the country are made here. Oxcarts such as these were once used to haul coffee beans to market. Today, although you might occasionally see oxcarts in use, most are purely decorative. However, they remain a well-known symbol of Costa Rica. In addition to miniature oxcarts, many carved wooden souvenirs are made here with rare hardwoods from the nation's forests. There are dozens of shops in town, and all have similar prices.

Aside from handicrafts, the other reason to visit Sarchí is to see its unforgettable **church.** Built between 1950 and 1958, the church is painted pink with aquamarine trim and looks strangely like a child's birthday cake. About five buses leave San José for Sarchí from Avenida 3 between calles 16 and 18. Alternately, you can take any Grecia bus from this same station. In Grecia they connect with the Alajuela-Sarchí buses, which leave every 30 minutes from Calle 8 between avenidas Central and 1 in Alajuela. The fare is 75¢.

ZARCERO

Beyond Sarchí, on picturesque roads lined with cedar trees, you'll find the town of Zarcero. In a small park in the middle of town is a **menagerie of sculpted shrubs** that includes a monkey on a motorcycle, people and animals dancing, an ox pulling a cart, a man wearing a top hat, and a large elephant. Behind all the topiary is a wonderful rural **church.** It's almost worth the drive just to see this park, but it's best to take in Zarcero as a quick stop on the way to La Fortuna and Arenal Volcano.

Buses (✆ **255-4318**) for Zarcero leave from San José hourly from the Atlántico del Norte bus station at Avenida 9 and Calle 12. This is actually the Ciudad Quesada–San Carlos bus. Just tell the driver that you want to get off in Zarcero, and keep an eye out for the topiary.

Guanacaste & the Nicoya Peninsula: The Gold Coast

Guanacaste province is Costa Rica's hottest and driest region. The rainy season starts later and ends earlier here, and overall it's more dependably sunny in this region than in other parts of the country. Combine this climate with a coastline that stretches from the Nicaraguan border to the southern tip of the Nicoya Peninsula, and you have an equation that yields beach bliss.

Beautiful beaches abound along this coastline. Some are pristine and deserted, some are dotted with new luxury resorts, and others are backed by little villages where you can still get a clean double room for less than $30 a night. These beaches vary from long, straight stretches of sand to tiny coves bordered by rocky headlands. Whatever your preference is in beaches, you're likely to find something that comes close to perfection.

This is Costa Rica's most coveted vacation region and the site of its greatest tourism development. The change is dramatic and ongoing. Large resorts have sprung up, and more are in the works. So far, four regulation golf courses have opened, and several more are under construction. The long-awaited international airport in Liberia is finally getting on its feet, and it is now possible to fly from major U.S. and Canadian hub cities directly in and out of Liberia—and on to any one of the numerous beaches below—without having to go through San José.

There is one caveat: During the dry season (mid-Nov to Apr), when sunshine is most reliable, the hillsides in Guanacaste turn browner than the chaparral of southern California. Dust from dirt roads blankets the trees in many areas, and the vistas are far from tropical. Driving these dirt roads without air-conditioning and hermetically sealed windows can be extremely unpleasant. But if you can't tolerate the least bit of rain during your holiday in the sun, the beaches up here are where you'll want to be.

On the other hand, if you happen to visit this area in the rainy season (May to mid-Nov), the hillsides are a beautiful, rich green, and the sun usually shines all morning, giving way to an afternoon shower—just in time for a nice siesta.

Guanacaste is also Costa Rica's "Wild West," a dry landscape of cattle ranches and cowboys, who are known here as *sabaneros,* a name that derives from the Spanish word for "savanna" or "grassland." This is big country, with big views and big sky. If it weren't for those rainforest-clad volcanoes in the distance, you might swear you were in Texas. However, Guanacaste hasn't always looked this way. At one time, this land was covered with a dense, although fairly dry, forest that was cut for lumber and to create pasturelands for grazing cattle. Today that dry tropical forest exists only in remnants preserved in several national parks. Up in

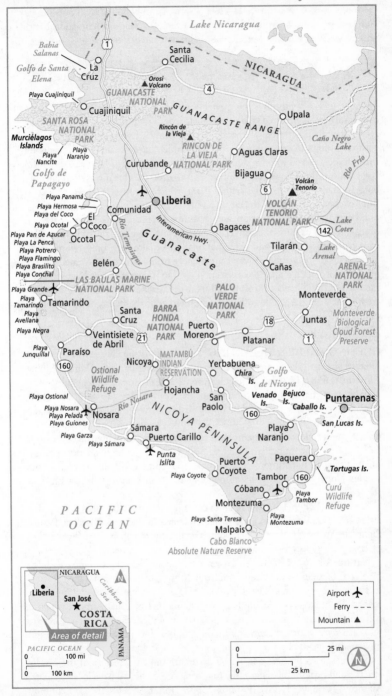

Lake Nicaragua

Bahía Salanas

Golfo de Santa Elena

La Cruz

Santa Cecilia

NICARAGUA

▲ Orosi Volcano

GUANACASTE NATIONAL PARK

Playa Cuajiniquil

Cuajiniquil

GUANACASTE RANGE

Upala

SANTA ROSA NATIONAL PARK

Rincón de la Vieja ▲

RINCON DE LA VIEJA NATIONAL PARK

Caño Negro Lake

Murciélagos Islands

Playa Nancite

Playa Naranjo

Curubande

Aguas Claras

Bijagua

Río Frio

Golfo de Papagayo

Volcán Tenorio ▲

✈ Liberia

Playa Panamá
Playa Hermosa
Playa del Coco
Playa Ocotal

Comunidad

El Coco

VOLCÁN TENORIO NATIONAL PARK

142

Lake Coter

Playa Pan de Azúcar
Playa La Penca
Playa Potrero
Playa Flamingo
Playa Brasilito
Playa Conchal

Ocotal

Bagaces

Interamerican Hwy.

Guanacaste

Río Tempisque

Tilarán

Lake Arenal

Belén

Cañas

ARENAL NATIONAL PARK

Playa Grande ✈

LAS BAULAS MARINE NATIONAL PARK

PALO VERDE NATIONAL PARK

Monteverde

Playa Tamarindo
Playa Avellana

Tamarindo

Santa Cruz

BARRA HONDA NATIONAL PARK

Puerto Moreno

Juntas

Monteverde Biological Cloud Forest Preserve

Playa Negra

Veintisiete de Abril

21

Platanar

18

Playa Junquillal

Paraíso

MATAMBÚ INDIAN RESERVATION

Nicoya

Yerbabuena

Chira Is.

Golfo de Nicoya

1

160

Ostional Wildlife Refuge

Río Nosara

Hojancha

San Paolo

Venado Is.

Bejuco Is.

Puntarenas

Caballo Is.

Playa Ostional
Playa Nosara
Playa Pelada
Playa Guiones

Nosara ✈

NICOYA PENINSULA

San Lucas Is.

Playa Garza

Sámara

Puerto Carillo

Playa Naranjo

160

Playa Sámara

✈ Punta Islita

Puerto Coyote

Paquera

Tortugas Is.

Playa Coyote

Tambor

160

Cóbano ✈

Curú Wildlife Refuge

PACIFIC OCEAN

Montezuma

Playa Tambor

Playa Santa Teresa

Malpais

Playa Montezuma

Cabo Blanco Absolute Nature Reserve

NICARAGUA

N

Caribbean Sea

● Liberia

San José ★

COSTA RICA

Airport ✈

Ferry — — —

Mountain ▲

Area of detail

PACIFIC OCEAN

PANAMA

| 0 | 100 mi |

| 0 | 100 km |

| 0 | 25 mi |

| 0 | 25 km |

N

the mountains, in **Rincón de la Vieja National Park** 🌟🌟, you'll find not only forests and wildlife, but also hot springs and bubbling mud pots similar to those in Yellowstone National Park in the United States.

1 Liberia

217km (135 miles) NW of San José; 132km (82 miles) NW of Puntarenas

Founded in 1769, Liberia is the capital of Guanacaste province, and although it can hardly be considered a bustling metropolis, it does boast more colonial atmosphere than almost any other city in the country. Its narrow streets are lined with charming old adobe homes, many of which have ornate stone accents on their facades, carved wooden doors, and aged red-tile roofs. Many have beautiful large, shuttered windows (some don't even have iron bars for protection) opening onto the narrow streets. The central plaza, which occupies 2 square blocks in front of the church, is still the city's social hub and principal gathering spot.

Liberia is best looked upon as a base for exploring this region or as an overnight stop as part of a longer itinerary. From here, it's possible to do day trips to nearby beaches and three national parks, although only two of them have facilities for visitors. Several moderately priced hotels are located on the outskirts of Liberia at the intersection of the Interamerican Highway and the road to the Nicoya Peninsula and its many beaches. Still, all things considered, it's usually preferable to base yourself either at the beach or at one of the mountain lodges in the area.

ESSENTIALS

GETTING THERE & DEPARTING   By Plane   It finally seems as if regular direct flights to Liberia are—forgive the pun—taking off. The Daniel Oduber Airport (© **668-1117**) in Liberia now receives a steady stream of scheduled commercial and charter flights throughout the year. **Delta** (© **800/241-4141;** www.delta.com) has five weekly direct flights between its Atlanta hub and Liberia, **American Airlines** (© **800/433-7300;** www.aa.com) offers three weekly direct flights between Miami and Liberia, and **Continental** (© **800/ 525-0280;** www.continental.com) has three weekly direct flights between Houston and Liberia. In addition, there are numerous commercial charter flights from various North American cities throughout the high season. Check with your travel agent.

Sansa (© **221-9414;** www.flysansa.com) has one daily flight to Liberia that leaves at 11:50am from San José's Juan Santamaría International Airport. Return flights depart for San José at 12:50pm. The fare for the 50-minute flight is $71 each way.

Nature Air (© **220-3054;** www.natureair.com) has three flights daily to Liberia at 8:30 and 11am, and 2pm from Tobías Bolaños International Airport in Pavas. Return flights leave Liberia at 5:35 and 9:55am, and 12:25pm. The 5:35am flight stops first at the Juan Santamaría International Airport, which is convenient for those departing on an international flight that same day. Fares are $80 each way. During the low season, the number of flights is often reduced and the schedule changes.

If you plan to fly here and rent a car to continue on to one of the nearby beaches and explore the region, the following companies all have local agencies: **Alamo** (© **668-1111**), **Avis** (© **666-7585**), **Dollar** (© **668-1061**), **Economy Rent A Car** (© **666-2816**), **Payless** (© **667-0511**), **Sol Rent A Car** (© **666-2222**), and **Toyota Rent A Car** (© **666-7193**). You can also reserve

⌒ **Finds** **An Interesting Stop on Your Way to Liberia**

If you're driving to or from Guanacaste, be sure to take a brief break to check out the **Catholic Church** ✦ in Cañas. Well-known painter, installation artist, and local prodigal son Otto Apuy has designed and directed the envelopment of the entire church in colorful mosaic. The work uses whole and broken tiles in glossy, vibrant colors to depict both religious and abstract themes. The church is located in the center of town, just a few blocks off the highway.

with these and most major international car-rental companies via their San José and international offices (see "Getting Around," in chapter 4).

By Car   Take the Interamerican Highway west from San José, and follow the signs for Nicaragua and the Guanacaste beaches. It takes approximately 3½ to 4 hours to drive to Liberia.

By Bus   Express buses (✆ **222-1650,** or 666-0458 in Liberia) leave **San José** roughly every hour between 6am and 8pm from Calle 24 between avenidas 5 and 7. The ride to Liberia is 4 hours. A one-way fare costs $4.50.

Grayline (✆ **220-2126;** www.graylinecostarica.com) has a daily bus that leaves San José for Liberia at 7am; the fare is $25. **Interbus** (✆ **283-5573;** www.costaricapass.com) has two daily buses that leave San José for Liberia at 7:30am and 2pm; the fare is $25 to Liberia. The 7:30am bus has connections to Rincón de la Vieja and Santa Rosa national parks. Both companies will pick you up at most San José–area hotels.

Buses depart for San José and most of the area beaches and national parks from the Liberia bus station on the edge of town, 200m (656 ft.) north and 100m (328 ft.) east of the main intersection on the Interamerican Highway. Express buses for San José leave roughly every hour between 5am and 8pm. For information on getting to the various beaches, see the sections below.

FAST FACTS   If you need a taxi, dial ✆ **666-0073.** If you want to check e-mail or surf the Web, check in at **Cibermania** (✆ **666-7240**), which is located on the street fronting the north side of the central park.

EXPLORING THE TOWN

The central plaza in Liberia is a great place to people-watch, especially in the early evenings and on weekends. Grab a seat on one of the many concrete benches, or join the families and young lovers as they leisurely stroll around. If you venture off for a few blocks in any direction, you'll see fine examples of the classic Spanish colonial architecture—adobe buildings with ornate wooden doors, heavy beams, central courtyards, and faded, sagging, red-tile roofs—that abound in this small city.

It's not much, but you might want to check out the tiny **Sabanero Museum** (✆ **665-0135**), which has a small collection of photos and exhibits depicting the life and times, and tools of the trade of the colonial and postcolonial residents of this horse and cattle country. The museum, which doubles as a basic information center for the city and region, is located about 3 blocks south of the church. It's ostensibly open Monday through Saturday from 8am to 5pm, with an hour-long break for lunch; admission is 50¢. However, because demand is so low, this place is often closed without warning or according to the staff's whims.

Finally, the newest development here is the opening of a modern shopping mall on the southern outskirts of town. This is the place to come if you desperately need a food court fix or want to catch a semi-late-run movie at the local multiplex.

OUTDOOR ADVENTURES NEAR LIBERIA
EXPLORING RINCON DE LA VIEJA NATIONAL PARK 𝅘𝅥𝅘𝅥
This national park begins on the flanks of the Rincón de la Vieja Volcano and includes this volcano's active crater. Down lower, you'll find an area of geothermal activity similar to that of Yellowstone National Park in the United States. Fumaroles, geysers, and hot pools cover this small area, creating a bizarre, otherworldly landscape. In addition to hot springs and mud pots, you can explore waterfalls, a lake, and volcanic craters. The bird-watching here is excellent, and the views across the pasturelands to the Pacific Ocean are stunning.

The main entrance is 25km (16 miles) northeast of Liberia, down a badly rutted dirt road. The park entrance fee is $6 per person per day. Camping will cost you an extra $2 per person per day. There are actually two entrances and camping areas here, the **Santa María** and **Las Pailas** (© 661-8139) ranger stations. The latter is by far the more popular and accessible, and it's closer to the action. Here you'll find two small camping areas near each other. I recommend the one closer to the river, although the bathroom and shower facilities are about 90m (295 ft.) away, at the other site. For those seeking a less rugged tour of the park, there are several lodges located around the perimeter of the park; all offer guided hikes and horseback rides into the park.

GETTING THERE   To reach the Las Espuelas entrance, drive about 5km (3 miles) north of Liberia and turn right on the dirt road to the park. The turnoff is well marked. In about 12km (7½ miles), you'll pass through the small village of Curubandé. Continue on this road for another 6km (3¾ miles) until you reach the Hacienda Lodge Guachipelin. The lodge is private property, and the owners have been charging vehicles a $2 toll to pass through their gate and continue on to the park. I'm not sure if this is legal or mandatory, but it's not worth the hassle to protest. Pay the toll, pass through the lodge's gate, and continue for another 4km (2½ miles) until you reach the park entrance.

There are two routes to the **Santa María entrance.** The principal route heads out of the northeastern end of Liberia toward the small village of San Jorge. This route is about 25km (16 miles) long and takes roughly 45 minutes. A four-wheel-drive vehicle is required. Alternatively, you can reach the Santa Maria entrance from a turnoff from the Interamerican Highway at Bagaces. From here, head north through Guayabo, Aguas Claras, and Colonia Blanca. The road is paved up to Colonia Blanca, but again, a four-wheel-drive vehicle is required for the final, very rough 10km (6¼ miles) of gravel road.

HIKING IN THE PARK   There are several excellent trails inside the Rincón de la Vieja National Park. More energetic hikers can tackle the 8km (5 miles) up to **the summit** and explore the several craters and beautiful lakes up here. On a clear day, you'll be rewarded with a fabulous view of the plains of Guanacaste and the Pacific Ocean below. The easiest hiking is the gentle **Las Pailas loop** 𝅘𝅥. This 3km (1¾-mile) trail is just off the Las Espuelas park entrance and passes by several bubbling mud pots and steaming fumaroles. This trail crosses a river, so you'll have to either take off your shoes or get them wet. The whole loop takes around 2 hours.

My favorite hike here is to the **Blue Lake** and **La Cangrejo Waterfall** ✶✶. This 5km (3-mile) trail passes through several different life zones, including dry forest, transitional moist forest, and open savanna. A variety of birds and mammals are commonly sighted. Pack a lunch; at the end of your 2-hour hike in, you can picnic at the aptly named Blue Lake, where a 30m (98-ft.) waterfall empties into the small pond whose crystal-blue hues are amazing.

BIRDING

The **Río Tempisque Basin** ✶, southwest of town, is one of the best places in the country to spot marsh and stream birds by the hundreds. This area is an important breeding ground for gallinules, jacanas, and limpkins, as well as a common habitat for numerous heron and kingfisher species.

Several tour operators offer excursions and a wide range of tours in the region from Liberia. **Swiss Travel Services** (✆ 282-4898; www.swisstravelcr.com) is the largest and most reliable of the major tour operators in the region.

One of the most popular tours is a boat tour down the Bebedero River to **Palo Verde National Park** ✶, which is south of Cañas and is best known for its migratory bird populations. Some of the best bird-watching requires no more than a little walking around the Biological Station in the park.

RAFTING TRIPS

Leisurely raft trips (with little white water) are offered by **Safaris Corobicí** (✆/fax **669-6191;** www.nicoya.com), about 40km (25 miles) south of Liberia. It has 2-hour ($37), 3-hour ($45), and half-day ($60) trips that are great for families and bird-watchers. Along the way, you might see many of the area's more exotic animal residents: howler monkeys, iguanas, caimans, coatimundis, otters, toucans, parrots, motmots, trogons, and many other species of birds. Aside from your binoculars and camera, a bathing suit and sunscreen are the only things you'll need. Safaris Corobicí is based on the main highway, just before the Restaurant Rincón Corobicí (p. 151). It also runs trips on the Bebedero River.

SHOPPING

On the road to the beaches, just west of the airport are several large souvenir shops. These are popular stopping points on organized tours throughout this region. The best of the bunch for a one-stop shop is **Kaltak Arts & Craft Market** (✆ **667-0696**). However, you might find better selection and prices, especially for Guaitil pottery, at some of the smaller makeshift roadside kiosks that line the road between Liberia and the Guanacaste beaches.

WHERE TO STAY
IN TOWN
Moderate

Best Western El Sitio Hotel & Casino   Located just out of town, about 75m (246 ft.) west of the main intersection on the road to Santa Cruz and the beaches, this hotel has a basic Spanish-influenced hacienda style, with an open and modern feel. Throughout the hotel, there are cool tile floors and original paintings of local Guanacaste scenes. There's a rancho-style bar/restaurant beside the large, shady pool, as well as a relatively well-equipped little gym. This hotel is popular with Costa Ricans as both a conference site and a weekend getaway. This is the closest thing to a modern, midrange resort hotel in Liberia and is a decent deal.

Liberia (A.P. 134-5000), Guanacaste. ✆ **666-1211**. Fax 666-2059. www.bestwestern.com. 52 units. $65 double. Rates include full breakfast. AE, MC, V. **Amenities:** 2 restaurants; 2 bars; large outdoor pool; exercise room; tour desk; car-rental desk; laundry service. *In room:* A/C, TV.

Inexpensive

Hotel Boyeros (*Value*)   This economical hotel isn't quite as modern or well appointed as the El Sitio Hotel, but it's clearly the most comfortable budget option in town. Arches with turned wooden railings and a red-tile roof give this two-story motel-style building a Spanish feel. The best and coolest rooms are on the second floor of the east wing. There's a large central courtyard, with the swimming pools, some basic playground equipment, and a massive shade tree.

Liberia (A.P. 85-5000), Guanacaste. ℂ 666-0995 or 666-0809. Fax 666-2529. www.hotelboyeros.com. 70 units. $40 double; $48 triple. AE, MC, V. **Amenities:** 24-hr. restaurant; bar; midsize pool and children's pool; game room; limited room service (6am–10pm); laundry service. *In room:* A/C, TV, safe.

Hotel Guanacaste   This basic, economical little choice is primarily a hostel catering to young travelers on a tight budget. In addition to the small and simply furnished rooms—almost all of which have bunk beds with thin foam mattresses—there's a basic *soda* serving cheap Tico meals. The management here can help arrange trips to nearby national parks and tell you about other budget accommodations, including campgrounds, in the area. The two newest rooms are doubles with air-conditioning; these cost slightly more.

A.P. 251-5000 (25m/82 ft. west of the bus station; 1 block north and 2 blocks east of the intersection of the Interamerican Hwy. and the road to the beaches), Liberia, Guanacaste. ℂ 666-0085. Fax 666-2287. htlguana@racsa.co.cr. 30 units. $20–$30 double. Discounts for students and those holding a valid hostel ID. AE, MC, V. **Amenities:** Restaurant; bike rental; laundry service. *In room:* No phone.

Posada del Tope   This humble little pension is nothing fancy, but the rooms and shared bathrooms are clean, the owners are friendly and helpful, and it's a real bargain. Only a couple of rooms have double beds; the rest have one, two, or three single beds. The nicest thing about Posada del Tope is that it's housed in a wonderfully restored traditional colonial home, with high ceilings, big shuttered windows facing the street, and hefty wooden trim all around. There's safe parking and Internet access, and a few of the rooms even have televisions. These folks also run another simple hotel in another old home, Casa Real, located directly across the street. This annex has more rooms and a basic restaurant serving inexpensive Tico cuisine.

Calle Real (1½ blocks south of the central park), Liberia, Guanacaste. ℂ/fax 666-3876. 15 units, all with shared bathroom. $12 double; $18 triple. AE, MC, V. Free parking. **Amenities:** Restaurant; bike rental; tour desk. *In room:* TV in some units, no phone.

NEAR RINCON DE LA VIEJA NATIONAL PARK

In addition to the hotels listed below, there are a couple of other good choices. Located on the Cañas Dulces road, **Buena Vista Lodge** (ℂ 661-8156; www. buenavistacr.com) is set on the edge of the national park and offers a wide range of activities and attractions. The delightful **La Carolina Lodge** (ℂ 380-1656; www.lacarolinalodge.com) is on a working farm, next to a clear flowing river. This place is located on the road between the Interamerican Highway and Upala, and it affords excellent access to the Tenorio Volcano and Río Celeste Falls.

Hacienda Lodge Guachipelin   Located 23km (14 miles) northeast of Liberia on the edge of Rincón de la Vieja National Park, this lodge is centered on a 19th-century ranch house and a still-operational cattle and horse ranch. Most of the rooms are housed in rows of buildings just off the old ranch house. The new rooms are quite spacious and modern, and come with either a private patio or a wide shared veranda. Those in the older buildings are still clean and comfortable but much more rustic in feel.

This is one of the closest lodges to the thermal springs (10km/6¼ miles) and bubbling mud pots (5km/3 miles) of Rincón de la Vieja National Park. Horseback rides can be arranged to the geothermal areas, as well as to various lakes, the top of a nearby dormant volcano, and some beautiful waterfalls. There's a good-size kidney-shape pool right by the lodge and a couple of natural swimming holes in nearby creeks and rivers. It isn't easy to get to the lodge, so plan to take all your meals here and go on a few guided tours. These folks work together with the Original Canopy Tour and the neighboring **Kazam Canyon attraction** ★★ ($45 per person); you can sign up for an adventure in which you strap on a climbing harness and ride back and forth over a deep canyon while hanging from a cable—it's one of my favorite "canopy tours" in the country.

Rincón de la Vieja (A.P. 636-4050, Alajuela). ℂ **442-2818** or 666-8075. Fax 442-1910. www.guachipelin. com. 40 units. $110 double. Rates include 3 meals and taxes. AE, MC, V. Follow the directions/signs to Curubandé and Rincón de la Vieja National Park. A 4WD vehicle is required in the rainy season (May to mid-Nov) and strongly recommended at other times. **Amenities:** Restaurant; outdoor pool; laundry service. *In room:* No phone.

Rincón de la Vieja Mountain Lodge   This is the closest lodge to the Las Pailas mud pots and the Azufrale hot springs. Rooms vary in size, and the nicest are the individual cabins, which come with hammocks on their private balconies. In all rooms, the furnishings and decor are simple and rustic. Quite a few come with one queen-size and one set of bunk beds. Meals are served in a large open-air rancho in the middle of the complex. The lodge offers numerous day-long tours either on foot, by mountain bike, or on horseback. It also runs an extensive canopy tour, which takes you on a high-wire ride over a couple dozen different treetop platforms, beginning with a manual ascent up a towering ceiba tree. This place is geared toward rustic adventurers, backpackers, students, and nature enthusiasts.

Rincón de la Vieja (A.P. 164-5000, Liberia), Guanacaste. ℂ/fax 661-8198. www.rincondelaviejalodge.com. 42 units. $58–$70 double. Student discounts and off-season rates available. AE, MC, V. If you're driving, follow the directions to the Hacienda Lodge Guachipelin and continue driving on this dirt road for another 7km (4⅓ miles), bearing right at the turnoff for the park entrance. **Amenities:** Restaurant; bar; small pool; laundry service. *In room:* No phone.

WHERE TO DINE

There are plenty of standard Tico dining choices in Liberia. In town, the most popular alternatives are **Pizzería Pronto** (ℂ **666-2098**), which is located 100m (328 ft.) north of the visitor information center, and **Pizzería da Beppe** (ℂ **666-0917**), located near the highway on the road that leads into central Liberia. Both serve a wide range of pizzas and assorted pasta dishes. Just south of Liberia, on the opposite side of the road from Las Espuelas, you'll find thick cuts and fresh meat at the **Steakhouse La Tablita** (ℂ **666-7122**). Another alternative is to choose one of the *sodas* around the central park. The best of these is **Restaurante Paseo Real** (ℂ **666-3455**). If you want fast food, you can find both **Burger King** and **Papa John's** in a small shopping complex on the northwest corner of the main intersection of the Interamerican Highway and the road to the beaches, as well as an even bigger food court with more fast-food options at the new mall on the southern outskirts of town.

Restaurant Rincón Corobicí COSTA RICAN/INTERNATIONAL   The food here has actually improved here in recent years, and the setting on the banks of the Corobicí river is wonderful. Although there's plenty of covered seating in the main open-air dining room, you'll want to choose a table on the wooden deck overlooking the river. The sound of rushing water tumbling over the rocks in the riverbed is a soothing accompaniment to the simple but filling meals. The whole fried fish is your best choice here, although you can also have steaks, lobster, shrimp, sandwiches, and even a couple of lamb dishes. This restaurant makes an ideal lunch stop if you're heading to or coming from Liberia, or if you have just done a rafting trip on the Corobicí River. Be sure to try the fried yuca chips—you might never go back to french fries.

Interamerican Hwy., 5km (3 miles) north of Cañas. © 669-6262. Main courses $4–$22. AE, DC, MC, V. Daily 8am–9pm.

2 La Cruz

277km (172 miles) NW of San José; 59km (37 miles) NW of Liberia; 20km (12 miles) S of Peñas Blancas

La Cruz is a tiny hilltop town near the Nicaraguan border. The town itself has little to offer beyond a fabulous view of Bahía Salinas, but it does serve as a gateway to the nearly deserted beaches down below, a few mountain lodges bordering the nearby Santa Rosa and Guanacaste national parks, and the Nicaraguan border crossing at Peñas Blancas.

There's not really much to do in La Cruz except catch a sunset and some ceviche at the **El Mirador Ehecatl** (© 679-9104). This humble little restaurant holds a commanding view of Bahía Salinas and serves up hearty Tico standards at only slightly inflated prices. Similarly, there's not really much reason to stay in La Cruz, but if you must, check out **Amalia's Inn** (©/fax 679-9181), which is a simple little hotel with a small pool and good views of the bay. (Instead of staying in town, check out the listings I've given below for places to stay in the environs of La Cruz.)

ESSENTIALS
GETTING THERE & DEPARTING **By Plane** The nearest airport with regularly scheduled service is in Liberia (see "Liberia," earlier in this chapter).

By Car Take the Interamerican Highway west from San José and follow the signs for Nicaragua and the Guanacaste beaches. When you reach Liberia, head straight through the major intersection, following signs to Peñas Blancas and the Nicaraguan border. Allow approximately 5 hours to get from San José to La Cruz.

By Bus Buses (© 256-9072) leave San José daily for **Peñas Blancas** at 5, 7, 7:45, and 10:30am, and 1:30 and 4pm from Calle 16 between avenidas 3 and 5, 1 block north of the Coca-Cola bus terminal. These buses stop in La Cruz and will also let you off at the entrance to Santa Rosa National Park. The ride to La Cruz takes 6 hours; a one-way fare costs $5. More buses often are added on weekends.

Buses leave Liberia for Peñas Blancas at 5:30, 8:30, and 11am, and 2 and 4:30pm. The ride to La Cruz takes about 1 hour and costs $2.

Buses depart for San José from Peñas Blancas daily at 5, 7:15, and 10:30am, noon, and 1:30 and 3:30pm, passing through La Cruz about 20 minutes later. Buses leave Liberia for San José roughly every hour between 5am and 8pm.

ORIENTATION The highway passes slightly to the east of town. You'll pass the turnoffs to Santa Rosa National Park, Playa Caujiniquil, and Los Inocentes Lodge before you reach the town. To reach the beaches of Bahía Salinas, head into La Cruz to El Mirador Ehecatl and then follow the signs down to the water.

EXPLORING SANTA ROSA NATIONAL PARK
Best known for its remote, pristine beaches (reached by several kilometers of hiking trails or a 4WD vehicle), **Santa Rosa National Park** ✦ (© 666-5051)

is a great place to camp on the beach, surf, or (if you're lucky) watch sea turtles nest. Located 30km (19 miles) north of Liberia and 21km (13 miles) south of La Cruz on the Interamerican Highway, Costa Rica's first national park blankets the Santa Elena Peninsula. Unlike other national parks, it was founded not to preserve the land, but to save a building, known as **La Casona,** that played an important role in Costa Rican independence. It was here, in 1856, that Costa Rican forces fought the decisive Battle of Santa Rosa, forcing the U.S.-backed soldier of fortune William Walker and his men to flee into Nicaragua. La Casona was completely destroyed by arson in 2001, but it has already been rebuilt and again houses a small museum.

It costs $6 per person to enter the park. Camping is allowed at several sites within the park. A campsite costs $2 per person per day. There's camping near the entrance and principal ranger station, as well as near La Casona and down by playas Naranjo and Nancite.

THE BEACHES ★★   Eight kilometers (5 miles) west of La Casona, down a rugged road that's impassable during the rainy season (it's rough on 4WD vehicles even in the dry season), is **Playa Naranjo.** Four kilometers (2½ miles) north of Playa Naranjo, along a hiking trail that follows the beach, you'll find **Playa Nancite. Playa Blanca** is 21km (13 miles) down a dirt road from Caujiniquil, which itself is 20km (12 miles) north of the park entrance. None of these three beaches has shower or restroom facilities. (Playa Nancite does have some facilities, but they're in a reservation-only camping area.) Bring along your own water, food, and anything else you'll need, and expect to find things relatively quiet and deserted.

Playa Nancite is known for its *arribadas* ("arrivals," grouped egg-layings) of Olive Ridley sea turtles, which come ashore to nest by the tens of thousands each year in October. Playa Naranjo is legendary for its perfect surfing waves. In fact, this spot is quite popular with day-trippers who come in by boat from the Playa del Coco area to ride the waves that break around Witch's Rock, which lies just offshore.

On the northern side of the peninsula is **Playa Blanca,** a beautiful, remote white-sand beach with calm waters. This beach is reached by way of the small village of Caujiniquil and is accessible only during the dry season.

If you reach Caujiniquil and then head north for a few kilometers, you'll come to a small annex to the national park system at **Playa Junquillal (© 679-9692),** not to be confused with the more-developed beach of the same name farther south in Guanacaste. This is a lovely little beach that is also often good for swimming. You'll have to pay the park entrance fee ($4) to use the beach, and $2 more to camp here. There are basic bathroom and shower facilities.

FUN ON & OVER THE WAVES

The waters of Bahía Salinas are buffeted by serious winds from mid-November through mid-May, and this area is a prime spot for windsurfing. The folks at **Tico Wind** (www.ticowind.com) have an operation during the windy season at the **Ecoplaya Beach Resort** (see below). If you want to try your hand at the new sport of kiteboarding, check in with the folks at **Kitesurfing Center (© 826-5221;** www.suntoursandfun.com), who set up shop each year at Playa Copal, on the shores of Bahía Salinas.

WHERE TO STAY NEAR LA CRUZ

Ecoplaya Beach Resort ★   This is by far the most comfortable, dare I say luxurious, beach hotel in the area. (However, aside from a facile attempt to cash in on a trend, I see no reason to use "eco" in the name.) The rooms are classified as either studios or junior, master, or luxury suites. Definitely opt for one of the suites because the studios are a bit cramped. The wide range in prices here reflects the wide range of room sizes. Inside they all have high ceilings, tile floors, and plenty of varnished wood accents. The beach here is calm and attractive, although the winter winds really howl. To take advantage of this, the hotel features a fully equipped windsurf and kiteboard center, offering rentals and classes. This is also a good option if you're looking to combine some beach time with excursions to Santa Rosa National Park, Los Inocentes Lodge, and/or neighboring Nicaragua. But if you're just looking for a beach-resort vacation, I recommend heading to one of the beaches farther south in Guanacaste.

La Coyotera Beach, Salinas Bay. (℃ **228-7146.** Fax 289-4536. www.ecoplaya.com. 16 units. $88–$160 double. Rates lower in the off season, higher during peak weeks. AE, MC, V. From La Cruz, take the dirt road that passes to the right of El Mirador Ehecatl restaurant (as you face the water) and then follow signs to the hotel. **Amenities:** Restaurant; bar; midsize outdoor pool; 2 Jacuzzis; watersports equipment rental; tour desk; laundry service. *In room:* A/C, TV, kitchenette, fridge, coffeemaker.

Los Inocentes Lodge ✦   Set on a ranch 14km (8¾ miles) from La Cruz, near the Nicaraguan border and bordering Guanacaste National Park, Los Inocentes is popular with naturalists interested in exploring the nearby dry and transitional forests. Horseback riding through the ranch is the most popular activity; the ranch does a brisk business in day trips by visitors staying at other hotels.

The rooms are located in the main lodge building, which dates back to 1890. Some have high ceilings, and most open onto large verandas with hammocks and wicker rocking chairs. Each room has access to a private bathroom, but most are not attached to the room (some folks on the 2nd floor even have to go downstairs to their bathroom on the 1st floor). The cabins, which are located about 90m (295 ft.) away from the main lodge, are two-bedroom affairs and are generally reserved for families and small groups. Meals are simple but filling. There's a great view of Orosi Volcano from the lodge, and the bird-watching here is excellent.

On the flanks of the Orosi Volcano (A.P. 228-3000, Heredia). (℃ **679-9190.** Fax 679-9224. www.losinocentes lodge.com. 11 units, 12 cabins. $48 per person. Rates include all meals and taxes. AE, MC, V. **Amenities:** Restaurant; small pool; Jacuzzi; tour desk; laundry service. *In room:* No phone.

3 Playa Hermosa, Playa Panamá & Papagayo ✦

258km (160 miles) NW of San José; 40km (25 miles) SW of Liberia

A good destination for families with kids, **Playa Hermosa** ✦ means "beautiful beach," which is an appropriate name for this crescent of sand. Surrounded by steep forested hills, this curving gray-sand beach is long and wide and rarely crowded. Fringing the beach is a swath of trees that stays surprisingly green right through the dry season. The shade provided by these trees, along with the calm protected waters, is a big part of the beach's appeal. Rocky headlands jut out into the surf at both ends of the beach, and at the base of these rocks you'll find fun tide pools to explore.

Beyond Playa Hermosa, you'll find the still underdeveloped **Playa Panamá** and, farther on, the calm waters of **Bahía Culebra** ✦. Lack of facilities and misuse by campers and day visitors has turned Playa Panamá, another calm and protected stretch of sand, into one of the worst garbage dumps on the coast. However, things are a bit different along the shores of Bahía Culebra, a large protected bay dotted with small, semiprivate patches of beach and ringed with mostly intact dry forest.

Around the north end of Bahía Culebra is the rapidly developing **Papagayo Peninsula** and development. Currently the home to two large all-inclusive resorts and one championship golf course, this area is slated to expand and develop even more in the coming years. This peninsula has a half-dozen or so small to midsize beaches, the nicest of which might just be **Playa Nacascolo** 👫👫, which is the domain of the new Four Seasons Resort here—but all beaches in Costa Rica are public, so you cannot be denied entry.

ESSENTIALS

GETTING THERE & DEPARTING   By Plane   The nearest airport with regularly scheduled service is in Liberia. From here you can arrange a taxi to bring you the rest of the way. The ride takes about 25 minutes and should cost $20 to $25.

By Car   Follow the directions for getting to Liberia (see earlier in this chapter), and then head west toward Santa Cruz. The turnoff for the Papagayo Peninsula is prominently marked 8km (5 miles) south of the Liberia airport. At the corner here, you'll see a massive Do It Center hardware store and lumber yard. If you're going on to Playa Hermosa and Playa Panamá, continue on a little farther and, just past the village of Comunidad, turn right. In about 11km (6¾ miles), you'll come to a fork in the road; take the right fork. These roads are relatively well marked, and a host of prominent hotel billboards should make it easy enough to find the beach. The drive takes about 4½ hours from San José.

By Bus   Express buses (© 221-7202) leave San José daily at 3:20pm from Calle 20 between avenidas 3 and 5, stopping first at Playa Hermosa and next at Playa Panamá, 3km (1¾ miles) farther north. One-way fare for the 5-hour trip is $5.

Grayline (© 220-2126; www.graylinecostarica.com) has a daily bus that leaves San José for all the beaches in this area at 7am; the fare is $25. **Interbus** (© 283-5573; www.costaricapass.com) has two daily buses that leave San José for all the beaches in this area at 7:30am and 2pm; the fare is $25. Both companies will pick you up at most San José–area hotels.

Alternatively, you can take a bus from San José to Liberia (see earlier in this chapter for details) and then take a bus from Liberia to Playa Hermosa and Playa Panamá. Buses (© 666-0042) leave Liberia for these two beaches daily at 5, 7:30, and 11:30am, and 3:30 and 5:30pm. The trip lasts 40 minutes because the bus stops frequently to drop off and pick up passengers. The one-way fare costs $1.25. These bus schedules change frequently, so it's always best to check in advance. During the high season and on weekends, extra buses from Liberia are sometimes added. Alternatively, you can take a bus to Playa del Coco, from which playas Hermosa and Panamá are a relatively quick taxi ride away. Taxi fare should run between $5 and $8.

One direct bus departs for San José daily at 4:30am from Playa Panamá, with a stop in Playa Hermosa along the way. Buses to Liberia leave Playa Panamá at 6 and 10am, and 2, 5, and 7pm, stopping in Playa Hermosa a few minutes later. Ask at your hotel where to catch the bus.

ORIENTATION   There are no real towns here, just a few houses and hotels on and near the beach. From the turnoff for the Papagayo Peninsula, a paved road leads around to the Allegro Papagayo and Four Seasons resorts. There is a new connecting road between the Papagayo Peninsula road and Playa Panamá. This 11km (6¾-mile) stretch of road is unpaved but well maintained. If you continue on to the beaches a little farther south, you'll come to Playa Hermosa first, followed by Playa Panamá a few kilometers farther along the same road. The road ends at the Fiesta Premier Resort & Spa.

Playa Hermosa is about a 450m (1,476-ft.) stretch of beach, with all the hotels laid out along this stretch. From the main road, which continues on to Playa Panamá, there are about three access roads heading off toward the beach. All the hotels are well marked, with signs pointing guests down the right access road.

FUN ON & UNDER THE WATER

Most of the beaches up here are usually quite calm and good for swimming.

If you want to do some diving, check in with **Diving Safaris de Costa Rica** ★ (© 877/853-0538 in the U.S., or 672-0012; www.costaricadiving.net), which is headquartered on the principal access road into Playa Hermosa, about 137m (450 ft.) before you hit the beach. This is a long-established and respected dive opera- tion. It has a large shop and offers a wide range of trips to numerous dive spots, and it also offers night dives, multiday packages, certification classes, and Nitrox dives. Alternatively, you can check out **Resort Divers** (© 672-0106; www.resort divers-cr.com), which has set up shop at several of the hotels in this area. A two- tank dive should run between $65 and $125 per person, depending primarily on the distance traveled to the dive sites.

In the middle of Playa Hermosa, you'll find **Aqua Sport** (© 672-0050), which is the principal watersports equipment rental center for Playa Hermosa. Kayaks, sailboards, canoes, bicycles, beach umbrellas, snorkel gear, and parasails are all available for rental at fairly reasonable rates. This is also where you'll find the local post office, some public phones, a small supermarket, and a restaurant.

Because the beaches in this area are relatively protected and generally flat, surfers should look into boat trips to nearby Witch's Rock and Ollie's Point. **Diving Safaris de Costa Rica** (© 672-0012), **Hotel Finisterra** (© 670-0293), and **Aqua Sport** (© 672-0050) all offer trips for up to six surfers for around $250, including lunch. All of these companies also offer fishing trips for between $250 and $1,200 for groups of two to four anglers.

If you're interested in wind power, you can take a 6-hour cruise on the 11m (36-ft.) catamaran *Spanish Dancer* (© 841-5604). The cost is $60 per person, including lunch and drinks. A shorter sunset tour costs $45 per person.

OTHER OPTIONS

Other activities in the area include horseback riding, all-terrain quad tours, canopy tours, and trips to other major attractions in the Guanacaste region. **Swiss Travel Service** (© 668-1020) has operations in the area and offers a wide range of activities and tours, including trips to Santa Rosa or Rincón de la Vieja national parks, and rafting on the Corobicí River. These folks have desks at many of the hotels around here and will pick you up at any hotel in the area.

If you want to try one of the zip-line canopy tours, your best bet in this area is to head to the **Witch's Rock Canopy Tour** (© 666-7546), located just before the Allegro Papagayo Resort. The 2½-hour tour covers 3km (1¾ miles) of cables touching down on 24 platforms, and costs $40.

WHERE TO STAY
VERY EXPENSIVE

Four Seasons Resort Costa Rica ★★★ (Kids)   Set near the very end of a long peninsula on a narrow spit of land between two white-sand beaches, this is easily the most luxurious and impressive large-scale resort in Costa Rica. The majority of the rooms are in three long, four-story, oceanfront buildings. The architecture here is quite stunning, with most buildings featuring flowing roof designs and other touches imitating the forms of turtles, armadillos, and butterflies.

All of the rooms are very spacious, with wood floors, rich wood furnishings, tasteful fixtures and decorations from around the world, marble bathrooms with a deep tub and separate shower, and luscious cotton sheets and bathrobes. The rooms on the third and fourth floors have the best views and are priced accordingly. The others have either garden views or partial ocean views, even though every room faces the sea. All have a large private balcony with a futon sofa, a table and a couple of chairs, and a smooth-working roll-up screen system. On the rocky hill at the very end of the peninsula are the resort's suites and villas. These are all similarly appointed, but with even more space and often either a private pool, a Jacuzzi, or an open-air gazebo for soaking in the views. The resort also features the Four Seasons' renowned service (including family-friendly amenities such as kid-size bathrobes and childproof rooms), and one of the best-equipped full-service spas in the country.

Papagayo Peninsula, Guanacaste. (C) **800/819-5053** or 212/688-2440 in the U.S., or 696-0098. Fax 696-0010. www.fourseasons.com/costarica. 153 units. $395–$495 double; $895 executive suite; $1,050–$4,500 suites and villas. Rates lower in the off season, higher during peak weeks. Children stay free in parent's room. AE, DC, DISC, MC, V. **Amenities:** 3 restaurants; 2 bars; lounge; 3 free-form pools; championship 18-hole golf course; 2 tennis courts; modern, full-service spa; watersports equipment; children's programs; tour desk; concierge; 24-hr. room service; massage; babysitting; laundry service; nonsmoking rooms. *In room:* A/C, TV/DVD, dataport, hair dryer, safe.

EXPENSIVE

Allegro Papagayo Resort ★★ *Kids*   If you're looking for an all-inclusive vacation at a large modern resort with a wide range of facilities and activities, this is your best choice in the region. The rooms are all identical in size—comfortable enough, but by no means extravagant—and housed in 14 different three-story buildings spread over a steep hillside overlooking the sea. Obviously, the rooms on the upper floors in the buildings higher up the hill have the best views. All come with two queen-size beds or one king-size bed, a small private balcony, and the full complement of modern amenities. The beach is an isolated patch of hard-packed salt-and-pepper sand that almost disappears at high tide. The waters here are very protected, and the drop-off is very gradual. However, most folks will want to spend their beach time at the hotel's "Fun Club" on a beautiful nearby white-sand beach. A regular boat shuttle brings folks to and fro, and at the site there's a snack bar/grill and a whole host of watersports equipment and activities.

Playa Manzanillo, Guanacaste (A.P. 434-1150, La Uruca). (C) **248-2323.** Fax 221-9095. www.occidental-hoteles.com. 300 units. $190–$320 double. Rates include food, drinks, a range of activities, and taxes. AE, DC, MC, V. **Amenities:** 2 restaurants; 3 bars; large free-form pool; small fitness center; 2 Jacuzzis; watersports equipment; children's programs; tour desk; massage; babysitting; laundry service. *In room:* A/C, TV, fridge, coffeemaker, hair dryer, safe.

Fiesta Premier Resort & Spa ★★ *Kids*   This was the first all-inclusive resort in the Guanacaste region. It has changed its name and management at least three times, but it seems to have settled down and been put into the best shape of its career. Most of the duplex villas can be separated into two rooms or shared by a family or two couples. Inside, one room is equipped with a king-size bed; the other has two queen-size beds. All rooms have marble floors, large bathrooms, and small private patios or balconies. The resort is quite spread out, so if you don't want to do a lot of walking or wait for the minivan shuttles, ask for a room near the main pool and restaurants. If you want a good view, ask for one on the hill overlooking the bay. For those seeking more isolation, there are rooms located in the dry forest behind the resort. The hotel has a host of organized sports and activities, including daily programs for children. The hotel has its own small crescent-shape swath of beach, which is very calm and protected for swimming. The hotel's dinner theater and disco complex offers up nightly entertainment revues and late-night dancing, and there's also a small casino on-site.

Playa Panamá, Guanacaste. ⓒ 296-6263 or 672-0000. Fax 220-3409. www.fiestapremier.com. 160 units. $240–$360 double. Rates include food, drinks, activities, and taxes. Rates lower in the off season, higher during peak weeks. AE, MC, V. **Amenities:** 3 restaurants; 3-tiered main pool, a small lap pool, and a resistance lap pool; outdoor tennis court; well-equipped spa and fitness center w/Jacuzzis and sauna; watersports equipment; children's programs; tour desk; car-rental desk; shopping arcade; salon; babysitting; laundry service. *In room:* A/C, TV, minibar, hair dryer, coffeemaker, safe.

Villas Sol Hotel & Villas Beach Resort ⭐   Set on a steep hillside at the north end of the beach, the Villas Sol is the latest incarnation of a large and longstanding project that has changed hands several times, divided and grown over the past years. The hotel is at the top of the hill, about 270m (886 ft.) from the beach—you'll need to be in good shape to stay here, or else you can spend some time waiting for the sporadic jitney service. Luckily, the two pools are both at the top of the hill if you want to opt out of the trip to and from the beach. The hotel rooms are all well maintained and quite standard for this price range; most have excellent views. The villas are new units located just off the entrance. All have kitchens, satellite TVs, and modern furnishings. About a third of them have their own small swimming pool or Jacuzzi, and only a few of the newest villas, built high on the hill, have really worthwhile views. Just so you don't get too confused: This whole complex was formerly the Condovac Hotel and Villas, and later the Sol Playa Hermosa.

Playa Hermosa, Guanacaste. ⓒ 257-0607. Fax 223-3086. www.villassol.com. 54 units, 106 villas. $123 double; $242–$309 villa. Rates lower during the off season, higher during peak weeks. AE, DC, MC, V. **Amenities:** 2 restaurants; 2 bars; 2 outdoor pools; 2 lighted outdoor tennis courts; limited watersports equipment rental; tour desk; laundry service. *In room:* A/C, TV, coffeemaker, hair dryer, safe.

MODERATE

El Velero Hotel ⭐   This small hotel is the best choice right on the beach in Playa Hermosa. White walls and polished tile floors give El Velero a Mediterranean flavor. The guest rooms are large, and those on the second floor have high ceilings. The furnishings are simple, though, and some of the bathrooms are a bit small. All the rooms have air-conditioning, but the fans alone are often enough to keep things cool. The hotel has its own popular little restaurant, which offers a good selection of meat, fish, and shrimp dishes, as well as weekly barbecue fests. Various tours, horseback riding, and fishing trips can be arranged through the hotel; however, the most popular excursions are the full-day and sunset cruises on the hotel's namesake sailboat.

Playa Hermosa (A.P. 49-5019), Guanacaste. ⓒ/fax 672-0016. www.costaricahotel.net. 22 units. $72 double. Rates lower in the off season, higher rates during peak periods. AE, MC, V. **Amenities:** Restaurant; bar; small pool by the beach; tour desk; laundry service. *In room:* A/C, coffeemaker, safe.

Hotel Finisterra   This hillside hotel offers clean, spacious accommodations on the southern end of Playa Hermosa. The rooms are all located on the second floor and come with either one queen-size bed or two double beds. Large picture windows face either a forested hillside or the Pacific Ocean. A large open-air restaurant and lounge takes up most of the first floor, and there's a refreshing little pool with good views. The restaurant here serves a nightly mix of fresh seafood, steaks, and chicken prepared with fusion flare. The owners have a van

for beach transfers (the beach is about 270m/886 ft. away, down the steep driveway), as well as a couple of boats for fishing and tours.

Playa Hermosa, Guanacaste. © 672-0293. Fax 672-0227. www.finisterra.net. 10 units. $59 double. Rates include full breakfast. Rates lower in the off season, higher during peak periods. MC, V. **Amenities:** Restaurant; bar; small pool; tour desk; babysitting; laundry service. *In room:* No phone.

Villa del Sueño Hotel ★ Value   Although this hotel is not right on the beach (it's about 90m/295 ft. from the sand), its well-groomed lawns and gardens feel like an oasis in the dust and heat of a Guanacaste dry season. Villa del Sueño offers clean and comfortable rooms at a good price, and the Villa del Sueño Restaurant here is one of the best in Playa Hermosa (p. 160). All of the rooms have cool tile floors, high hardwood ceilings, ceiling fans, and well-placed windows for cross ventilation. The second-floor superior rooms have more space, larger windows, and air-conditioning. There's a small pool and open-air bar in the center courtyard. Meals are served in the main building's open-air restaurant, which even has a stage and features live music during much of the high season. The folks here manage a neighboring condominium development, which has additional apartment and efficiency units available for nightly and weekly rental.

Playa Hermosa, Guanacaste (mailing address: Interlink 2059, P.O. Box 025635, Miami, FL 33102). ©/fax 672-0026. www.villadelsueno.com. 15 units. $59–$89 double. Rates lower in the off season, higher during peak periods. AE, MC, V. **Amenities:** Restaurant; bar; small pool; tour desk; laundry service. *In room:* A/C in some units, no phone.

INEXPENSIVE

Hotel Playa Hermosa   Tucked away under shady trees, this sprawling beachfront spread is under new ownership and is in the process of receiving a major remodel and upgrade. The remodeled rooms have been entirely redone, with new tile floors and contemporary furniture and fixtures. By the time you read this, all of the rooms should be up-to-date. The open-air restaurant has a rustic tropical feel, with unfinished tree trunks holding up the roof, and serves a range of Tico and international dishes. This hotel has a prime location, with plenty of beachfront on the quiet southern end of Playa Hermosa.

Playa Hermosa, Guanacaste. © 672-0046. Fax 672-0019. 22 units. $45–$65 double. Rates lower in the off season, higher during peak periods. MC, V. Turn left at the 1st road into Playa Hermosa; the hotel's white archway gate is about 1km (½ mile) down this dirt road. **Amenities:** Restaurant; bar; laundry service. *In room:* A/C in some units, no phone.

DINING & AFTER-DARK DIVERSIONS

For nightlife, see whether there's any live music at Villa del Sueño Restaurant (see below), or head to the **Monkey Bar** (© 672-0267), which is inland, off the main road to Playa Panamá; has a pool table and a satellite TV; and serves U.S.-style bar food.

In addition to the place listed below, you'll find good restaurants at both the **El Velero Hotel** and the **Hotel Finisterra** (see "Where to Stay," above).

Puesta de Sol INTERNATIONAL   This place has a fabulous setting, slightly uphill and just off the beach. A half-dozen or so rustic wooden tables sit on a red-tile floor under spinning ceiling fans and a rustic red-tile roof supported by posts made from the twisted trunks of strangler fig trees. A few lengths of heavy rope strung between these posts are all there is for walls. This is a great place for a lunch break without sacrificing too much beach time. The restaurant's name translates as "Sunset," and its modest hillside perch gives it a good view of the nightly spectacle. This place recently changed hands, but the food is

still hearty and well prepared, with an emphasis on fresh fish and American-style pub food.

On the beach toward the north end of Playa Hermosa. ℰ 672-0103. Main courses $5–$12. AE, MC, V. Daily noon–midnight.

Villa del Sueño Restaurant ❋ CONTINENTAL   There's a mellow yet refined atmosphere under the slow-turning ceiling fans at this simple open-air restaurant. In addition to the regular items on the menu, there's a small selection of nightly specials on a chalkboard. If you venture away from the fresh fish, there are well-prepared pasta dishes, as well as meat and poultry options. There's a stage and a small lounge at one end of the dining room, and there's live music here most evenings during the high season.

At the Villa del Sueño Hotel. ℰ 672-0026. Main courses $8–$18. AE, MC, V. Daily 7am–10pm.

4 Playa del Coco & Playa Ocotal

253km (157 miles) NW of San José; 35km (22 miles) W of Liberia

Playa del Coco is one of the most easily accessible beaches in Guanacaste, with a paved road running right down to the water; it has long been a popular destination with middle-class Ticos and weekend revelers from San José. It's also a prime scuba-diving spot. The beach, which has grayish-brown sand, is quite wide at low tide and almost nonexistent at high tide. In between high and low tides, it's just right. The crowds that come here like their music loud and constant, so if you're in search of a quiet retreat, stay away from the center of town. Still, if you're looking for a beach with a wide range of inexpensive hotels, lively nightlife, and plenty of cheap food and beer close at hand, you'll enjoy Playa del Coco.

Better still, if you have a car, head over to **Playa Ocotal** ❋, which is a couple of kilometers to the south. This tiny pocket cove features a small salt-and-pepper beach bordered by high bluffs, and is quite beautiful. When it's calm, there's good snorkeling around some rocky islands close to shore here.

ESSENTIALS

GETTING THERE & DEPARTING   By Plane   The nearest airport with regularly scheduled flights is in Liberia. From there you can arrange for a taxi to take you to Playa del Coco or Playa Ocotal, which is about a 25-minute drive, for $20 to $25.

By Car   From Liberia, head west toward Santa Cruz. Just past the village of Comunidad, turn right. In about 11km (6¾ miles), you'll come to a fork in the road. Take the left fork. It takes about 4½ hours from San José.

By Bus   Express buses (ℰ 222-1650) leave San José for Playa del Coco at 8am and 2 and 4pm daily from Calle 24 between avenidas 5 and 7. Allow 5 hours for the trip. A one-way ticket is $5. From Liberia, buses to Playa del Coco leave at 5:30, 7, 9, and 11am, and 12:30, 2:30, 4:30, and 6:30pm. A one-way ticket for the 40-minute trip costs $1.50. These bus schedules change frequently, so it's always best to check in advance. During the high season and on weekends, extra buses from Liberia are sometimes added.

Grayline (ℰ 220-2126; www.graylinecostarica.com) has a daily bus that leaves San José for Playa del Coco at 7am; the fare is $25. **Interbus** (ℰ 283-5573; www.costaricapass.com) has two daily buses that leave San José for Playa del Coco at 7:30am and 2pm; the fare is $25. Both companies will pick you up at most San José–area hotels.

The direct bus for San José leaves Playa del Coco daily at 4 and 8am and 2pm. Buses for Liberia leave at 6, 9, and 11am, and 1, 3, and 6pm.

Depending on demand, the Playa del Coco buses sometimes go as far as Playa Ocotal; it's worth checking beforehand, if possible. Otherwise, a taxi should cost around $5.

ORIENTATION   Playa del Coco is a small but busy beach town. Most of its hotels and restaurants are either on the water, on the road leading into town, or on the road that heads north, about 100m (328 ft.) inland from and parallel to the beach. Playa Ocotal, which is south of Playa del Coco on a paved road that leaves the main road about 183m (600 ft.) before the beach, is a small collection of vacation homes, condos, and a couple of hotels. It has one bar and one restaurant on the beach.

FAST FACTS   There's a branch of the state-run **Banco Nacional** (✆ **670-0801**) on the main road into town, about 300m (984 ft.) before you hit the beach. If you can't flag down a **taxi** easily on the street, call ✆ **670-0408.** For the local **police,** dial ✆ **670-0258;** for the local **health clinic,** call ✆ **670-0987.**

FUN ON & OFF THE BEACH

Plenty of boats are anchored here at Playa del Coco, and that means plenty of opportunities to go fishing, diving, or sailing. However, the most popular activities, especially among the hordes of Ticos who come here, are hanging out on the beach, hanging out in the *sodas,* and cruising the bars and discos at night. If you're interested, you might be able to join a soccer match. (The soccer field is in the middle of town.) It's also possible to arrange horseback rides; ask at your hotel.

SCUBA DIVING   Scuba diving is the most popular watersport in the area, and dive shops abound. **Ocotal Diving** (✆ **670-0321;** www.ocotaldiving.com) and **Rich Coast Diving** (✆ **800/434-8464** in the U.S. and Canada, or 670-0176 in Costa Rica; www.richcoastdiving.com) are the most established and offer equipment rentals and dive trips. A two-tank dive, with equipment, should cost between $75 and $125 per person, depending on the distance to the dive site. Both also offer PADI certification courses.

SPORTFISHING   Full- and half-day sportfishing excursions can be arranged through **Agua Rica Yacht Charters** (✆ **877/589-0539** in the U.S. and Canada, or 670-0805 in Costa Rica; www.aguaricacharters.com) or **Papagayo Sportfishing** (✆/fax **670-0354**). A half-day of fishing, with boat, captain, food, and tackle, should cost between $200 and $550 for two to four passengers; a full day should run between $500 and $1,200.

SURFING   There's no surf whatsoever in Playas del Coco. But this is a popular jumping-off point for daily boat trips to Witch's Rock and Ollie's Point (named after Oliver North, who was allegedly running some of the Contra War from these parts) up in Santa Rosa National Park. Most of the abovementioned sportfishing and dive operations also offer trips to ferry surfers up to these two isolated surf breaks. A boat that carries six surfers for a full day, including lunch and beer, should run around $300. In late 2003, the Costa Rican government began regulating access to both Witch's Rock and Ollie's Point, which are technically within the Santa Rosa National Park. Permits were sometimes required, and boats were sometimes turned away. For the most current information, you should ask at your hotel or check in with **Witch's Rock Surf Camp** (✆ **829-0249;** www.witchesrocksurfcamp.com), which caters to hard-core surfers.

A DAY SPA AT THE BEACH   If you're in the mood for any spa treatments while in this area, definitely head to **Fusion Natural Spa** ✦ (© **670-0914**; www.fusionnaturalspa.com), which is located on the hillside above Playa Ocotal. The folks here offer a wide range of massage, aromatherapy, body-wrap, and exfoliating treatments. Individual treatments run from $40 to $80, or you could opt for a multitreatment or multiday package.

WHERE TO STAY
EXPENSIVE

El Ocotal Beach Resort ✦   This is the most luxurious hotel in the Playa del Coco area. The guest rooms vary in size, styling, and age. The least expensive rooms are closest to the beach, and the six duplex bungalows are strung along the hillside that climbs toward the reception. In both cases, the rooms are showing their age, although the bungalows are quite spacious. The rooms with the best views and greatest comfort are at the top of the hill, overlooking a dramatic stretch of rocky coastline. These rooms feature pastel-wash painted walls and colorful floral bedspreads. The third-floor suite, no. 520, is the best room in the whole joint, with a large wraparound balcony and private Jacuzzi. *Note:* It's a steep, vigorous hike from top to bottom. Scuba diving and sportfishing are the main draws here, and package tours are available. Diminutive Playa Ocotal is one of the prettiest beaches along this stretch of coast and offers good swimming.

El Ocotal's **hilltop restaurant** is one of its greatest assets. The large open-air dining room opens onto an expansive, multilevel deck that has more seating, as well as a stunning view of Playa Ocotal and miles of coastline. This is a great place to come for sunset and a drink, and the meals are pretty good as well.

Playa del Coco (A.P. 1), Guanacaste. © **670-0321** or 248-0098. Fax 670-0083. www.ocotalresort.com. 59 units, 12 bungalows, 5 suites. $125 double; $180–$235 bungalow; $235 suite. Rates include full breakfast. Rates lower in the off season, higher during peak weeks. AE, DC, MC, V. **Amenities:** 2 restaurants; 3 small pools; lighted outdoor tennis court; exercise room; Jacuzzi; tour desk; laundry service. *In room:* A/C, TV, coffeemaker, hair dryer, safe.

MODERATE

In addition to the places listed below, **Villa Flores B&B** (© **670-0269**; www. hotel-villa-flores.com) is a good option in this price range, located north of downtown in Playas del Coco and just off the beach.

Best Western Coco Verde   This two-story hotel is the biggest thing in Playa del Coco and is a good bet if you're looking for a clean, comfortable, modern room close to the beach and all the action. The rooms are identical in size but come equipped with a variety of bedding options for singles, couples, and families. They all share a common veranda, which gets blasted by the hot afternoon Guanacaste sun. The casino here is the liveliest in Playas del Coco. You can't miss this green-and-white building on your right, on the main road into Playa del Coco, about 200m (656 ft.) before you hit the beach.

Playa del Coco (A.P. 61), Guanacaste. © **670-0494**. Fax 670-0555. 33 units. $80–$110 double. Rates include breakfast. Rates lower in the off season. V. **Amenities:** Restaurant; bar; small pool; petite spa; tour desk; limited room service; laundry service. *In room:* A/C, TV, coffeemaker, hair dryer, safe.

Hotel Villa Casa Blanca ✦   With friendly, helpful owners, beautiful gardens, and attractive rooms, this bed-and-breakfast inn is one of my favorite options in the area. Located about 500m (1,640 ft.) inland from the beach at Playa Ocotal, it's built in the style of a Spanish villa. All the guest rooms feature fine furnishings and are well kept. Some are a tad small, but others are quite roomy and even have kitchenettes. The suites are higher up and have ocean views. My favorite has a secluded patio with lush flowering plants all around.

A little rancho serves as an open-air bar and breakfast area, and beside this is a pretty little lap pool with a bridge over it. Another separate rancho serves as a sort of lounge/recreation area and has a satellite television. There's also an inviting hot tub and sitting area near the pool. Villa Casa Blanca manages several rental houses and condos in the area, so if you plan to stay for a week or more, or if you need lots of room, ask about these.

Playa Ocotal (A.P. 176-5019), Playa del Coco, Guanacaste. $\textcircled{C}$ **670-0518.** Fax 670-0448. www.costa-rica-hotels-travel.com. 15 units. $80 double; $105–$125 suite. Rates include breakfast buffet. Rates lower in the off season. AE, MC, V. **Amenities:** Outdoor lounge and bar; small pool; Jacuzzi; tour desk; laundry service. *In room:* A/C, no phone.

Villa del Sol B&B   This small bed-and-breakfast, located 1km (½ mile) north of Playa del Coco village, is a friendly family-run joint. There are seven rooms in the original building here. All are spacious and clean and receive plenty of light. Several have the option of air-conditioning for an extra $5. The most interesting room has a round queen-size bed, high ceilings, and views of the gardens. Still, the nicest rooms here are the six studios, each with a small kitchenette, a private bathroom, air-conditioning, a television, and a telephone. Those on the second floor even have a bit of ocean view from their shared veranda. There's an inviting small pool with a covered barbecue area. Tasty dinners are prepared nightly for guests from a small menu of European-influenced dishes. For me, the hotel's greatest attribute is its location on the quiet northern end of Playa del Coco. To find the hotel, just turn onto the dirt road just beyond the Hotel Coco Verde, before you hit the beach.

Playa del Coco, Guanacaste. $\textcircled{C}$ **866/815-8902** in U.S., or $\textcircled{C}$/fax 670-0085. www.villadelsol.com. 13 units, 11 with private bathroom. $50 double; $60 studio apt. Rates include full breakfast for rooms only, not studio apts. Rates lower in the off season, higher during peak periods. AE, MC, V. **Amenities:** Restaurant; small pool; tour desk. *In room:* No phone.

WHERE TO DINE

There are dozens of cheap open-air *sodas* at the traffic circle in the center of El Coco village. These restaurants serve Tico standards, with an emphasis on fried fish. Prices are quite low—and so is the quality, for the most part.

For views and sunsets, you can't beat the restaurant at **El Ocotal Beach Resort** (p. 162), although food and service are inconsistent. For better food and a good, albeit lower, view of the sea, the same folks run the beachside **Father Rooster Bar and Restaurant,** in Playa Ocotal.

In addition to the places listed below, you can get excellent Italian food at the Sol y Luna restaurant of the **Hotel La Puerta del Sol,** located 200m (656 ft.) north and 100m (328 ft.) east of the main road at the turnoff just beyond the Hotel Coco Verde, before you hit the beach. For a simple sandwich, salad, or fresh fruit juice, check out **Chile Dulce** on the main road in Playas del Coco.

Finally, when I last visited, the former owners and chefs at the Puesta del Sol in Playa Hermosa were setting up shop in a new restaurant to be called **Picante,** at the Bahía Pez Vela condo complex in Playa Ocotal. They promised to be serving up some creative international fusion cuisine at their new digs.

Chef Bob's Louisiana Bar & Grill ★★ SEAFOOD/CAJUN   This place is a definite notch above the rest of the options in town. In addition to the daily catch cooked to order and a host of Cajun specialties, you can get seared yellowfin tuna with a ginger-sesame sauce, blackened mahimahi, or broiled grouper with Veracruz sauce. There are several types of jambalaya, some pasta dishes, and a full complement of meat and poultry selections. The choicest tables are on the second-floor open-air deck overlooking the main street of Playa del Coco, although there are tables nearby in an enclosed little dining room.

200m (656 ft.) before the beach on the main road. 𝒞 **670-0882.** Main courses $7–$24. AE, MC, V. Daily 11am–10pm.

Pato Loco ITALIAN/PASTA   This small Italian-run restaurant and hotel serves up the best pasta in these parts. Choose spaghetti, penne, linguine, or fettuccine in one of its innumerable fresh sauces, or opt for the nightly special. For vegetarians, the penne *melanzana* (with eggplant) on the regular menu is a standout. Service is friendly and informal at the six tables spread out underneath the exposed red-tile roof. You'll even find a good selection of Italian wines at fair prices here.

800m (2,624 ft.) before the beach on the main road. 𝒞 **670-0145.** Main courses $5–$16. V. Fri–Wed 6–9pm.

Tequila Bar & Grill ★ MEXICAN   This is a simple and rustic joint that serves good Mexican food and magnificent margaritas—in fact, there are 20 different types of margaritas on the menu here. Because this is a fishing town, I recommend the seafood tacos and fajitas, although they both come in chicken and beef varieties. Main-course meals include pork chops in a chipotle barbecue sauce and grilled chicken with tomatillo and lime, as well some fish dishes. Definitely grab one of the open-air streetside tables, if you get here early enough to snag one.

150m (492 ft.) before the beach on the main road. 𝒞 **670-0741.** Main courses $5–$14. No credit cards. Thurs–Tues 11am–10pm.

PLAYA DEL COCO AFTER DARK

Playa del Coco is one of Costa Rica's liveliest beach towns after dark. On the road into town, you'll find **Banana Surf Bar** (𝒞 **670-0605**), a comfortable second-floor affair with good *bocas* (appetizers) and some outdoor tables on the veranda overlooking Coco's main street. Lately they've been getting folks dancing to a modern mix of hip-hop, trance, and other dance rhythms. Closer to the beach is the **Lizard Lounge** (𝒞 **670-0525**), which has a popular pool table and a laid-back tropical vibe. Alternatively, you can head across the park to the **El Bohio Bar & Yacht Club** (𝒞 **670-0447**), which is popular with expatriates and often shows sporting events on its TV. **Cocomar** (no phone) is the main disco in town. It's located just off the little park right on the beach. (If these directions don't get you there, just follow the loud music.)

Finally, if you want to test your luck, head to the casino at either the **Best Western Coco Verde** (𝒞 **670-0494**) or the **Hotel La Flor de Itabo** (𝒞 **670-0292**).

5 Playas Flamingo, Potrero, Brasilito & Conchal

280km (174 miles) NW of San José; 66km (41 miles) SW of Liberia

These beaches were among the first in Costa Rica to attract international attention, and are the heart of Guanacaste's "Gold Coast." Still, with attention and development shifting toward the Papagayo Gulf a little farther north, along with the amazing boom in Tamarindo to the south, this has become a great place to find desolate stretches of beautiful beach and isolated hotels in a wide range of price categories.

Playa Conchal ★★ is the first in a string of beaches stretching north along this coast. The 310-room **Paradisus Playa Conchal** (p. 167) is one of the premier large-scale luxury resorts in Costa Rica. For decades this was the semiprivate haunt

the Flamingo Marina, still manages a fleet of boats. Contact him via his company, **Oso Viejo** (© 654-5201; www.flamingobeachcr.com). A full-day fishing excursion can cost between $500 and $1,600, depending on the size of the boat. Half-day trips cost between $250 and $750.

Alternatively, you can contact the **Edge Adventure Company** (© 654-4946) or the **Flamingo Marina Resort Hotel and Club.**

If you're looking for a full- or half-day sail or sunset cruise, check in with **Oso Viejo** (see above) to see what boats are available, or ask about the 52-foot cutter *Shannon.* Prices range from around $50 to $125 per person, depending on the length of the cruise. Multiday trips are also available.

GOLF   The **Paradisus Playa Conchal** ★★ (© 654-4123) is home to an excellent golf course featuring a few wonderful views of the ocean. This Robert Trent Jones–designed resort course is currently still open to the walk-in public, but as the all-inclusive resort itself gets more popular, it might restrict public access. Currently, it costs $140 in greens fees for as many rounds as you can squeeze into one day, including a cart. If you tee off after 1pm, it's just $90.

HORSEBACK RIDING   You can arrange a horseback ride with the **Flamingo Equestrian Center** (© 654-4089) or **Brasilito Excursions** (© 654-4237). This last place works out of the Hotel Brasilito. Depending on the size of your group, it should cost between $10 and $20 per person per hour.

OTHER ADVENTURE TOURS   In addition to the above-mentioned activities, you can rent a sea kayak from **The Edge Adventure Company** (© 654-4946). Alternatively, check in with the tour desk at the **Flamingo Marina Resort Hotel and Club,** which offers a host of tours to other nearby destinations, as well as hiking and rafting trips.

LEARN THE LANGUAGE   The **Centro Panamericano de Idiomas** (© 654-5002; www.cpi-edu.com), which has schools in San José and Monteverde, recently opened a branch in Flamingo, across from the Flamingo Marina, facing Potrero Bay. A 1-week course with 4 hours of classes per day, including a homestay, costs $365. Longer course options are available.

WHERE TO STAY

If you plan to be here for a while or are coming down with friends or a large family, you might want to consider renting a condo or house. For information and reservations, contact the folks at the **Marina Trading Post** (© 654-4004; www.marinatradingpost.com) or **Emerald Shores Realty** (© 654-4554; www. emeraldshoresrealty.net).

VERY EXPENSIVE

Paradisus Playa Conchal ★★★   This sprawling hotel is the largest and most luxurious all-inclusive resort in Costa Rica. From the massive open-air reception building down to the free-form swimming pool (the largest in Central America), everything here is on a grand scale. There's a small-village feel to the layout; guest rooms are located in 30 separate two-story buildings, reached by way of constantly circulating shuttles. All rooms are suites and come with either one king-size bed or two double beds in a raised bedroom nook. Down below, there's a comfortable sitting area, with a couch, coffee table, and chairs with ottomans. The bathrooms are large and modern, with marble tiles, full tubs, bidets, and even a telephone. Each unit has a garden patio or a small balcony. Although the rooms are exactly the same, the Royal level suites come with private butler service and general VIP attention. Only three of the building units actually front the ocean, and two of these contain the Presidential suites, which have double the living area of the standard suites and even more luxurious appointments. Unlike most all-inclusives, only one of the restaurants here is buffet; the rest are sit-down a la carte affairs, although they are still decidedly mediocre.

The hotel has a beautiful **golf course** ⭐⭐⭐, with broad, open holes; rolling hills; and the occasional sea view. Because of the golf course and its ponds and wetlands, there's good bird-watching here, with healthy populations of parrots, roseate spoonbills, and wood storks. Because the hotel owns so much land behind Playa Conchal, guests here have almost exclusive access to this crushed-seashell beach.

Playa Conchal (A.P. 499-4005, San Antonio de Belén), Guanacaste. 𝒞 **888/336-3542** in the U.S., or 654-4123. Fax 654-4181. www.paradisusplayaconchal.com. 310 suites. $398–$598 double; $498–$898 Royal suites; $1,300–$1,700 Presidential suite. Rates include all meals, drinks, taxes, a wide range of activities, and use of nonmotorized land and watersports equipment. Golf and spa services extra. AE, MC, V. **Amenities:** 5 restaurants; 3 bars; 2 lounges; massive free-form pool w/several Jacuzzis; Robert Trent Jones–designed 18-hole golf course and pro shop; 4 lighted tennis courts; exercise room; modest spa and exercise facilities; watersports equipment rental; bike rental; children's programs; concierge; tour desk; car-rental desk; modest business center; shopping arcade; 24-hr. room service; in-room massage; babysitting; laundry service; nonsmoking rooms. In room: A/C, TV, minibar, fridge, coffeemaker, hair dryer, safe.

EXPENSIVE

Flamingo Beach Resort Formerly a Holiday Inn, this hotel, located right across the road from the beach at Playa Flamingo, is a large, modern facility with a great location. It has suffered years of neglect and mismanagement, and although my most recent visit showed some promise, I'm not sure that it's out of the woods yet. The hotel is constructed in a horseshoe shape around a large pool and opens out on the ocean. Half of the rooms have clear views of the ocean across a narrow dirt road. All the rooms are clean and cool, with tile floors and comfortable bathrooms. The pool- and beachview rooms are slightly nicer, and you'll pay a little more for them. The suites each have a sitting room, a wet bar, and a VCR. The hotel also rents some slightly less expensive (and much less attractive) rooms in a new annex behind the main building.

Playa Flamingo, Guanacaste. 𝒞 **888/500-9090** in the U.S. and Canada, or 654-4444 in Costa Rica. Fax 654-4060. www.resortflamingobeach.com. 91 units. $120–$140 double; $200–$280 suite. Rates lower in the off season. AE, MC, V. **Amenities:** 2 restaurants; 2 bars; large outdoor pool; outdoor tennis court; exercise room; game room; tour desk; laundry service. In room: A/C, TV, fridge, hair dryer, coffeemaker, safe.

Hotel Sugar Beach ⭐ As the name implies, the Hotel Sugar Beach is located on the white sands about a 15-minute drive north of Playa Potrero along a rough dirt road. It's one of the only hotels in the area, and that's what gives it most of its charm, in my opinion—lots of seclusion and privacy. The beach is on a small cove surrounded by rocky hills. The hotel itself is perched above the water. Nature lovers will be thrilled to find wild howler monkeys and iguanas almost on their doorsteps. Snorkelers should be happy here, too; this cove has some good snorkeling in the dry season. The rooms, which come in a variety of sizes and configurations, have received a good amount of remodeling and upgrading in recent years. Tile floors, wicker furniture, beautiful carved doors, and big bathrooms all add up to first-class comfort. Hammocks under the trees provide a great place to while away a hot afternoon.

Playa Pan de Azúcar (A.P. 90, Santa Cruz), Guanacaste. 𝒞 **654-4242.** Fax 654-4239. www.sugar-beach.com. 28 units. $110–$138 double; $165–$190 suite. Rates lower in the off season. AE, MC, V. **Amenities:** Restaurant;

bar; small kidney-shape pool set on the hillside; watersports equipment rental; tour desk; laundry service. *In room:* A/C, TV, minifridge, safe.

MODERATE

Flamingo Marina Resort Hotel and Club ⭐   Located up the hill from the beach, the Flamingo Marina Hotel is a midsize resort with a good mix of facilities and amenities. This place was built in several phases, and there's no real sense of coherence or grand plan here. The rooms vary greatly in size, age, comfort, and furnishings. Standard rooms have tile floors and lots of wood accents. The suites have wet bars in the seating area, minifridges, and private whirlpool tubs. Newer condo units have full kitchenettes. All the rooms have patios or balconies, and most have pretty good bay views. This place caters to fishermen and scuba divers, and a whole host of tours and adventures is offered here.

Playa Flamingo (A.P. 321-1002, San José), Guanacaste. © 800/276-7501 in the U.S. and Canada, or 654-4141. Fax 654-4035. www.flamingomarina.com. 45 units, 44 apts. $85 double; $145 suite; $180–$280 apt. Rates lower in the off season, slightly higher during peak periods. Breakfast included for rooms and suites. AE, DC, MC, V. **Amenities:** Restaurant; snack bar; 2 bars; 4 small pools; outdoor tennis court; exercise room; 2 Jacuzzis; watersports equipment rental; tour desk; laundry service. *In room:* A/C, TV, safe.

Mariner Inn *Value*   This small hotel is located close to the marina and is definitely the best bargain in Playa Flamingo. The rooms are cool and comfortable, if a tad on the small side. Most of the rooms come with just one double bed. But all come with air-conditioning, a small television, and a desk. There's one larger two-bedroom "efficiency" unit with a private balcony. The Spreaders Bar and small restaurant here are both quite popular with the local expat community.

Playa Flamingo. © 654-4081. Fax 654-4024. 12 units. $40–$70 double. AE, MC, V. **Amenities:** Restaurant; bar; small pool. *In room:* A/C, TV.

INEXPENSIVE

There is a string of inexpensive *cabinas* on the main road leading into Brasilito, just before you hit the beach. The best of these has consistently been **Cabinas Conchal** (© 654-4257), but it's worthwhile to pop in at a couple and see a few rooms before choosing. It's also possible to camp on playas Potrero and Brasilito. At the former, contact **Maiyra's** (© 654-4213); at the latter, try **Camping Brasilito** (© 654-4452), which recently added some budget rooms as well. Each charges around $3 to $5 per person to make camp and use the basic bathroom facilities, or around $10 per person to stay in a basic cabin.

Cabinas Cristina *Value*   This little place is located on Playa Potrero, across the bay from Playa Flamingo and a few kilometers north of Brasilito. Although Cabinas Cristina isn't on the beach, it's a great budget option in this area. The rooms are spacious and very clean. You can opt for a simple room with a couple of beds, a desk, and a fan, or a two-bedroom apartment with a kitchenette and air-conditioning. All rooms have small verandas with large rocking chairs. There's a small pool in the middle of a grassy green yard and a thatch-roofed palapa. Playa Potrero is a 5-minute walk down a dirt road.

Playa Potrero (A.P. 121, Santa Cruz), Guanacaste. © 654-4006. Fax 654-4128. www.cabinascristina.com. 6 units. $30–$60 double. V. **Amenities:** Small pool. *In room:* No phone.

Hotel Brasilito *Value*   This hotel, right in Brasilito, and just across a sand road and steps from the beach, offers basic small rooms that are quite clean and well maintained. There's also a bar and a big open-air restaurant that serves economical meals. Even with Playa Brasilito's glut of budget options, this is one of the best values in town and is the closest to the water. The higher-priced rooms have nice balconies and ocean views. The hotel rents snorkeling equipment, kayaks, body boards, and horses, and can arrange a variety of tours.

Playa Brasilito, Santa Cruz, Guanacaste. (C) 654-4237. Fax 654-4247. www.brasilito.com. 15 units. $20–$35 double. V (6% surcharge). **Amenities:** Restaurant; watersports equipment rental; tour desk; laundry service. *In room:* No phone.

WHERE TO DINE

In addition to the places listed below, you'll find good fresh seafood and authentic Spanish cuisine at **Rancho Grande** ((C) 654-4494), which is in Flamingo, on the inland road connecting Playa Potrero and Brasilito.

Amberes CONTINENTAL   Not only is this the most upscale restaurant outside of a hotel, but it also boasts a bar, an open-air disco, and even a tiny casino. You can come for dinner and make it an evening. Although the menu changes nightly, you'll always find a wide selection, with an emphasis on seafood. Fresh fish served either meunière or Provence style is the best dish here. Unfortunately, the music can become way too loud at dinner, but if you dine early, it should be no problem—the disco doesn't usually get cranking until 10pm.

Playa Flamingo, near the Flamingo Marina Hotel. (C) 654-4001. Reservations recommended in high season. Main courses $6–$22. AE, MC, V. Daily 5–10pm.

Camarón Dorado ★★ *Finds* SEAFOOD   With a series of tables and kerosene torches set right in the sand just steps from the crashing surf, this is one of my favorite restaurants in the area. There are more tables in a simple, open-air dining room, for those who don't want sand in their shoes. The service is semiformal, with the attentive waitstaff bringing a bowl of flower-infused water to wash your hands even before you order. The seafood is fresh, wonderfully prepared, and reasonably priced. When I asked to see the wine list, two waiters came over carrying about 12 different bottles between them.

Playa Brasilito (C) 654-4028. Reservations recommended in high season. Main courses $5–$21. MC, V. Daily 11am–10pm.

Marie's ★ COSTA RICAN/SEAFOOD   This is a great little place for a quick bite or a leisurely sit-down meal. The menu has grown over the years, although the best option here is always some simply prepared fresh fish, chicken, or meat. Check the blackboard for the daily specials, which usually highlight the freshest catch, such as mahimahi (dorado), marlin, and red snapper. You'll also find such Tico favorites as *casados* and ceviche, as well as burritos and quesadillas. Tables in the open-air restaurant are made from slabs of tree trunks.

Playa Flamingo. (C) 654-4136. Sandwiches $3–$6; main courses $5–$20. V. Daily 6:30am–9:30pm.

PLAYA FLAMINGO AFTER DARK

If you don't head to the disco and casino at Amberes, check out the poolside bar at the **Mariner Inn** ((C) 654-4081), which seems to be the liveliest spot in town. In Brasilito, **The Happy Snapper** ((C) 654-4413) is a great place for sunsets, drinks, and a meal.

6 Playa Tamarindo ★★ & Playa Grande ★★

295km (183 miles) NW of San José; 73km (45 miles) SW of Liberia

Tamarindo is a boomtown—perhaps too much of a boomtown. So far, the development remains a mixture of predominantly small hotels in a variety of price ranges and an eclectic array of restaurants. Ongoing development continues

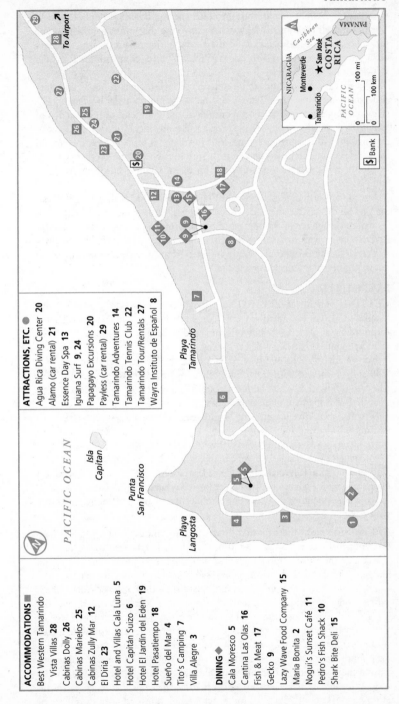

Tamarindo

ACCOMMODATIONS ■

Best Western Tamarindo
Vista Villas **28**
Cabinas Dolly **26**
Cabinas Marielos **25**
Cabinas Zully Mar **12**
El Diriá **23**
Hotel and Villas Cala Luna **5**
Hotel Capitán Suizo **6**
Hotel El Jardín del Eden **19**
Hotel Pasatiempo **18**
Sueño del Mar **4**
Tito's Camping **7**
Villa Alegre **3**

DINING ◆

Cala Moresco **5**
Cantina Las Olas **16**
Fish & Meat **17**
Gecko **9**
Lazy Wave Food Company **15**
Maria Bonita **2**
Nogui's Sunset Café **11**
Pedro's Fish Shack **10**
Shark Bite Deli **15**

ATTRACTIONS, ETC. ●

Agua Rica Diving Center **20**
Alamo (car rental) **21**
Essence Day Spa **13**
Iguana Surf **9, 24**
Papagayo Excursions **20**
Payless (car rental) **29**
Tamarindo Adventures **14**
Tamarindo Tennis Club **22**
Tamarindo Tour/Rentals **27**
Wayra Instituto de Español **8**

PACIFIC OCEAN

Isla
Capitán

Punta
San Francisco

Playa
Langosta

Playa
Tamarindó

To Airport

$ Bank

Caribbean
Sea

NICARAGUA

Monteverde

San José ★ COSTA
RICA

PANAMA

PACIFIC
OCEAN

Tamarindo

0   100 mi
0   100 km

to spread up the hills inland from the beach and south beyond Punta Langosta. The beach itself is a long, wide swath of white sand that curves gently from one rocky headland to another. Behind the beach are low, dry hills that can be a dreary brown in the dry season but that instantly turn green with the first brief showers of the rainy season.

Two midsize resorts and an abundance of stylish smaller hotels and very dependable surf have made Tamarindo one of the most popular beaches on this coast. Fishing boats bob at their moorings at the south end of the beach, and brown pelicans fish just outside the breakers. A sandy islet offshore makes a great destination if you're a strong swimmer; if you're not, it makes a great foreground for sunsets. Tamarindo is popular with surfers, who ply the break right here or use the town as a jumping-off place for playas Grande, Langosta, Avellana, and Negra.

Just to the north of Tamarindo lies **Playa Grande,** one of the principal nesting sites for the giant leatherback turtle, the largest turtle in the world. This beach is often too rough for swimming, but the well-formed and consistent beach break is very popular with surfers here as well. I almost hate to mention places to stay in Playa Grande because the steady influx of tourists and development could doom this beach as a turtle-nesting site.

ESSENTIALS

GETTING THERE & DEPARTING **By Plane** **Sansa** (© 221-9414; www. flysansa.com) flies to Tamarindo from San José's Juan Santamaría International Airport daily at 5:15, 8:30, and 11:50am, and 1, 2:30, and 3:50pm. The flight takes 55 minutes. The fare is $71 each way.

Nature Air (© 220-3054; www.natureair.com) flies to Tamarindo daily at 8:30 and 11am, and 4pm from Tobías Bolaños International Airport in Pavas. The fare is $80 each way. The flight takes 55 minutes. During the low season, the number of flights is often reduced and the schedule changes.

Whether you arrive on Sansa or Nature Air, there are always a couple of cabs or minivans waiting for arriving flights. It costs around $5 for the ride into town.

Sansa flights leave Tamarindo for San José at 6:20 and 9:35am, and 12:55, 2:15, 3:40, and 4:55pm daily. Nature Air flights leave for San José at 6 and 9:30am, and noon. The 6am flight stops first at the Juan Santamaría International Airport, which is convenient for those making a connection to an international flight that same day.

By Car The most direct route is by way of the Tempisque River bridge. Take the Interamerican Highway west from San José. Forty-seven kilometers (29 miles) past the turnoff for Puntarenas, you'll see signs for the turnoff to the bridge. After crossing the river, follow the signs for Nicoya and Santa Cruz. Continue north out of Santa Cruz, until just before the village of Belén, where you will find the turnoff for Tamarindo. In another 20km (12 miles), take the left fork for Playa Tamarindo at Huacas and continue on until the village of Villareal, where you make your final turn into Tamarindo. The trip should take around 4½ hours. You can save a little time, especially in the dry season, by taking a more direct but rougher route: To take this route, you turn left just after passing the main intersection for Santa Cruz at the turnoff for Playa Junquillal and Ostional. The road is paved until the tiny village of Veintesiete de Abril. From here, it's about 20km (12 miles) on a rough dirt road until the village of Villareal, where you make your final turn into Tamarindo.

Alternatively, you can drive here via Liberia. When you reach Liberia, turn west and follow the signs for Santa Cruz and the various beaches. Just beyond the town of Belén, take the turnoff for playas Flamingo, Brasilito, and Tamarindo. From here, follow the directions for the second option above. This route takes around 5½ hours.

By Bus Tracopa express buses (© 222-2666) leave San José daily for Tamarindo at 11am and 3:30pm, departing from Calle 14 between avenidas 3 and 5. The trip takes 5 hours; the one-way fare is $6.

Alternatively, you can catch a bus to Santa Cruz from the same station, or from the **Tralapa** station (© 221-7202) at Calle 20 between avenidas 3 and 5. Buses leave both stations for Santa Cruz roughly every hour between 6am and 6pm. The trip's duration is 4 hours; the one-way fare is around $5. Buses leave Santa Cruz (© 680-0392) for Tamarindo roughly every 1½ hours between 6am and 6pm; the one-way fare is $1.50.

Grayline (© 220-2126; www.graylinecostarica.com) has a daily bus that leaves San José for Tamarindo at 7am; the fare is $25. **Interbus** (© 283-5573; www.costaricapass.com) has two daily buses that leave San José for Tamarindo at 7:30am and 2pm; the fare is $25. Both companies will pick you up at most San José–area hotels.

Direct buses leave Tamarindo for San José daily at 5:45am and 3:30pm. Buses to Santa Cruz leave roughly every 1½ hours between 6am and 6pm. In Santa Cruz, you can transfer to one of the frequent San José buses.

ORIENTATION   The road leading into town runs parallel to the beach and ends in a small cul-de-sac just past Cabinas Zully Mar. A couple of side roads off this main road lead farther on, to playas Langosta, Avellana, and Negra. You'll find several of the newer hotels mentioned below off these side roads.

FAST FACTS   The local **police** can be reached at © 653-0283. You'll find the **Mariposa Laundry** (no phone) just past the turnoff for Playa Langosta.

GETTING AROUND   **Payless** (© 653-0015) has an office at the Pueblo Dorado Hotel. **Alamo** (© 653-0727), **Budget** (© 653-4381), and **Economy Rent A Car** (© 653-0752) all have offices on the main road into Tamarindo. Moreover, most of the agencies listed in "Liberia," earlier in this chapter, will arrange delivery and pickup in Tamarindo. You can call **a taxi** at © 653-0751 or 653-0586.

FUN ON & OFF THE BEACH

Tamarindo is a long beach, and although it can sometimes be great for swimming, it's often too rough. You also have to be careful when and where you swim. There are rocks just offshore in several places, some of which are exposed only at low tide. An encounter with one of these rocks could be nasty, especially if you're bodysurfing. You should also avoid swimming near the estuary mouth, where the currents can carry you out away from the beach. That said, the best swimming is always down at the southern end of the beach, toward Punta Langosta.

If you just want to laze on the beach, you can pick up beach chairs, umbrellas, and mats at **Tamarindo Tour/Rentals** (©/fax 653-0078), located on the right as you come into town. It's open daily. There's a little storefront and gift shop here, which doubles as a local information center and clearinghouse for condo and apartment rentals around the area.

If you get sore and worn out from all the activities listed below or just want some pampering, call Shannon Vacca at the **Essence Day Spa** (© 653-0291)

Tips **Yo Quiero Hablar Español**

If you want to try an intensive immersion program or just brush up on your rusty high school Spanish, check in with the folks at **Wayra Instituto de Español** (©/fax **653-0359;** www.spanish-wayra.co.cr). This place is located up a side street from Iguana Surf.

for professional sports and/or Swedish massage. The spa is located next to the Cabinas Coral Reef, but with advance notice, a therapist can come to any hotel in the area. A 1-hour massage costs $65; half-hour, $30. For some more active rejuvenation, you can check into the regular yoga, martial arts, and aerobics classes offered at **Cabinas Arco Iris** (© **653-0330;** www.hotelarcoiris.com).

BIKING   Bikes are available for rent at several locations in Tamraindo. Check around; I like the bikes at **Iguana Surf** (© **653-0148;** www.iguanasurf.net). These folks have a shop on the main road into Tamarindo, but their main office is a little bit out of "downtown" Tamarindo, on the road to Playa Langosta. They also have a third office at the Barceló Playa Langosta resort on Playa Langosta. This outfit rents gear for other active pursuits, too; see "Watersports," below.

FOUR-WHEELING   Tamarindo Adventures (© **653-0108;** www.tamarindo adventures.net) has a fleet of four-wheel-drive all-terrain vehicles. They're available for the day ($85) and half-day ($60). A variety of guided ATV tours range in duration from 1 to 8 hours and in price from $40 to $110 per person. This company also rents snorkel equipment, surf and boogie boards, and jet skis, and offers a full menu of other guided tours around the region.

GOLF   Hacienda Pinilla (© **680-7000;** www.haciendapinilla.com) is a beautiful 18-hole links-style course located south of Tamarindo. This might just be the most challenging course in the country, and the facilities, although limited, are top-notch. Currently, the course is accepting golfers staying at hotels around the area, with advance reservation. Greens fees run around $125 for 18 holes, including a cart. Many folks staying in Tamarindo also play at the **Paradisus Playa Conchal** ★★, an excellent resort course (p. 167).

HORSEBACK RIDING   You'll probably see plenty of horses and riders running up and down the beach. You can flag down one of these and ask about rates, or set up a riding date with **Casagua Horses** ★ (© **653-8041),** **Tamarindo Adventures** (© **653-0108;** www.tamarindoadventures.net), or **Papagayo Excursions** (©/fax **653-0254;** www.papagayoexcursions.com). Rates for horse rental, with a guide, are around $10 to $15 per hour.

SAILBOAT CHARTERS   The 52-foot ketch *Samonique III* (© **388-7870;** www.costarica-sailing.com) is available for anything from sunset cruises to weeklong trips out to Cocos Island. A half-day cruise costs $60 per person, and a full day is $95 per person. This includes an open bar and snacks on the half-day cruise, and lunch on the full-day trip. Beyond this, it runs a sunset cruise for $45 per person; charter rates are around $250 per person per day, including board, and vary, depending on the size of your group.

SCUBA DIVING   If you want to do any scuba diving or snorkeling while you're here, check in with **Agua Rica Diving Center** (© **653-0094;** www.aguarica.net), which you'll find in the tiny shopping center across from El

Diriá resort. It has a full-service dive shop and offers day trips, multiday dive cruises, and the standard resort and full-certification courses.

SPORTFISHING   A host of captains offer anglers here a chance to go after the "big ones" that abound in the waters offshore. From the Tamarindo estuary, it takes only 20 minutes to reach the edge of the continental shelf, and the waters are preferred by marlin and sailfish. Although fishing is good all year, the peak season for billfish is between mid-April and August. You can contact **Tamarindo Sportfishing** (𝒸 653-0090; www.tamarindosportfishing.com), **Warren Sellers Sportfishing** (𝒸 653-0186; www.wssportfishing.com), or **Capullo Sportfishing** (𝒸 837-3130; www.capullo.com). All offer half-day trips for between $300 and $600, and full-day trips for between $500 and $1,600.

TENNIS   You can rent court time and equipment at the **Tamarindo Tennis Club** (𝒸 653-0898), which features two lighted outdoor courts located on the back road on the way to the Hotel El Jardín del Edén. It is open from 6am to 10pm, and court time runs $15 per hour.

TOURS GALORE   **Tamarindo Adventures, Papagayo Excursions,** and **Iguana Surf** all offer a host of tour and activity options. Papagayo Excursions probably offers the widest selection of full- and multiday trips, including outboard or kayak tours through the nearby estuary and mangroves, excursions to Santa Cruz and Guaitíl, raft floats on the Corobicí River, and tours to Palo Verde and Rincón de la Vieja national parks. Rates run between $30 and $95, depending on the length of the tour and group size.

There are a couple of zip-line canopy tours in the area. Probably the best, and certainly the closest, is the **Tamarindo Canopy Tour** (𝒸 653-0597), which is located just on the outskirts of town. It features four cables connecting seven platforms and offers excellent views of the ocean and surrounding landscape ($35).

WATCHING NESTING SEA TURTLES   On nearby **Playa Grande,** leatherback sea turtles nest between late September and late February. The turtles come ashore to lay their eggs only at night. During the nesting season, you'll be inundated with opportunities to sign up for the nightly tours, which usually cost around $35 to $45 per person. No flash photography is allowed because any sort of light can confuse the turtles and prevent them from laying their eggs; guides must use red-tinted flashlights.

Note: Turtle nesting is a natural, unpredictable, and increasingly rare event. You might have to wait your turn for hours, hike quite a ways, and even accept the possibility that no nesting mothers will be spotted that evening. Moreover, with the vast development in this area, the number of nesting turtles has dropped and the number of tourists has skyrocketed. Do not expect an intimate experience.

If your hotel can't set it up for you, you'll see signs all over town offering tours. Make sure you go with someone licensed and reputable. The best tours these days are run through and include a stop at **El Mundo de la Tortuga,** a small turtle museum/exhibit at Playa Grande. At the museum, visitors take the half-hour self-guided tour by picking up a cassette player and choosing a tour cassette in English, Spanish, German, or Italian. Afterward, you can watch television while waiting for your group to head out to the beach. The museum opens each afternoon at 4:30pm and stays open until the turtle tours are done for the night.

Do-it-yourselfers can drive over to Playa Grande and book a tour directly with either **El Mundo de la Tortuga** (𝒸/fax 653-0471; cost $25) or the **National Parks Service** (𝒸 653-0470; $13). The Parks Service operates out of a small shack next to the turtle museum and opens each evening at around 6pm to begin taking reservations. Whomever you decide to go with, try to make a reservation in advance because only a limited number of people are allowed on the beach at one time. Spots fill up fast, and if you don't have a reservation, you might have to wait until really late, or you might not be able to go out onto the beach.

WATERSPORTS If you want to try snorkeling, surfing, or sea kayaking while in Tamarindo, **Iguana Surf** and **Tamarindo Adventures** both rent snorkeling equipment, boogie boards, sea kayaks, and surfboards. They have half-day and hourly rates for many of these items. You can also rent similar equipment of slightly lesser quality and at slightly lower rates from **Tamarindo Tour/Rentals.**

If you want to learn to catch a wave while in Tamarindo, check in with the **Tamarindo Surf School** (© 653-0923; www.tamarindosurfschool.com).

WHERE TO STAY

In addition to the hotels listed below, Tamarindo and Playa Grande have a wide range of beach houses and condos for rent by the night, the week, or the month. For more information on this option, check out **Remax Tamarindo** (© 653-0073; www.remax-oceansurf-cr.com) or **Century 21** (© 653-0030; www.c21tamarindo.com).

IN TOWN
Very Expensive

Hotel and Villas Cala Luna ★★ If you're looking for serious luxury in Tamarindo, stay in one of the two- or three-bedroom villas here, which are the size of a small home and just as well equipped. The living rooms are huge, with high-peaked ceilings, couches, tables and chairs, satellite televisions, and complete sound systems. The full kitchens come with microwave ovens and cappuccino machines—even washing machines. If this isn't enough, each villa has its own private swimming pool. The bedrooms are spacious and elegant, with either a king-size bed or two double beds. Everything is done in soft pastels with handpainted accents, and the red-tile roofs and Mexican tile floors add elegance while keeping things cool. Rooms in the hotel are spacious and similarly well done, with their own terraces, but you'll have to share the hotel's main swimming pool with the rest of the guests. The hotel isn't right on the beach; you have to cross the street and walk a short path to reach the ocean.

Playa Tamarindo, Guanacaste. © 653-0214. Fax 653-0213. www.calaluna.com. 20 units, 19 villas. $140–$170 double; $250–$420 villa. Rates include continental breakfast. Rates slightly higher during peak weeks. AE, MC, V. **Amenities:** Restaurant; bar; large free-form pool w/poolside bar; watersports equipment rental; bike rental; tour desk; limited room service (6am–10pm); in-room massage; babysitting; laundry service. *In room:* A/C, TV, hair dryer, safe.

Expensive

El Diriá ★ This is Tamarindo's oldest and largest beachfront resort. Constant remodeling and new construction has kept it in good shape. Wedged into a narrow piece of land planted with tropical gardens and palm trees, the Diriá has an enviable spot, smack dab in the middle of Tamarindo's long beach. The newest addition rises three stories over the main entrance and lobby. The rooms are done in contemporary pastel colors with red-tile floors. Some have separate seating areas, and most have minibars, hair dryers, and a basket of toiletries in the small bathroom. I especially recommend the second- and third-floor "sunset deluxe" rooms, which feature oceanview private balconies. The central location and modern rooms make this an excellent choice in town.

Playa Tamarindo (A.P. 476-1007, San José), Guanacaste. © 653-0031. Fax 653-0848. www.eldiria.com.
127 units. $137–$180 double. Rates include breakfast buffet. Rates lower in the off season. AE, MC, V.
Amenities: 2 restaurants; 2 bars; 2 outdoor pools; watersports equipment rental; game room; tour desk;
car-rental desk; laundry service. *In room:* A/C, TV, fridge, safe.

Hotel Capitán Suizo ★★ *Kids*   This well-appointed beachfront hotel is
located on the quiet southern end of Tamarindo. The rooms are located in a
series of two-story buildings. The lower rooms have air-conditioning and private
patios; the upper units have plenty of cross ventilation and small balconies. All
have large bathrooms and sitting rooms with fold-down futon couches. In effect,
all the rooms are really suites, with their separate sitting/living room area. The
spacious bungalows are spread around the shady grounds; these all come with a
tub in the bathroom and an inviting outdoor shower among the trees.

The hotel's free-form pool is quite nice. The shallow end slopes in gradually,
imitating a beach, and there's also a separate children's pool. Perhaps this hotel's
greatest attribute is the fact that it's just steps from one of the calmer and more
isolated sections of Playa Tamarindo.

Playa Tamarindo, Guanacaste. © 653-0353 or 653-0075. Fax 653-0292. www.hotelcapitansuizo.com.
22 units, 8 bungalows. $125–$145 double; $175 bungalow. Rates include continental breakfast. Rates lower
in the off season, higher during peak periods. AE, MC, V. **Amenities:** Restaurant; bar; midsize outdoor pool
and children's pool; small exercise room; tour desk; laundry service. *In room:* Fridge, safe.

Hotel El Jardín del Edén ★   It isn't right on the beach, but this is one of the
most luxurious and comfortable hotels in Tamarindo. The French owners bring
a touch of sophistication that's often lacking at beach hotels in Costa Rica. There
are splendid views from many of the guest rooms, which are in Mediterranean-
style buildings on a hill 136m (446 ft.) from and high above the beach. Almost
all have balconies or private terraces with views of the Pacific. The large stone-
tiled terraces, in particular, give you the sense that you're staying at your own private villa. The honeymoon room has a large bathroom with a tub; other rooms
have showers only.

Playa Tamarindo, Guanacaste. © 653-0137. Fax 653-0111. www.jardindeleden.com. 18 units, 2 apts.
$100–$120 double. Rates include full breakfast. Rates lower in the off season, higher during peak weeks.
AE, MC, V. **Amenities:** Restaurant; bar; 2 small adjoining pools; small exercise room; Jacuzzi; tour desk; limited room service (8am–5pm); laundry service. *In room:* A/C, TV, minibar, hair dryer, safe.

Sueño del Mar ★ *Finds*   Located at the south end of Tamarindo Beach on
Punta Langosta, Sueño del Mar has charming little touches and innovative
design: four-poster beds made from driftwood, African dolls on the windowsills,
Kokopeli candleholders, and open-air showers with sculpted angelfish, hand-
painted tiles, and lush tropical plants. Fabrics are from Bali and Guatemala.
Somehow all of this works well together, and the requisite chairs and lounges
nestled under shade trees right on the beach add the crowning touch.

The two casitas have their own kitchens, veranda, and sleeping loft. The honeymoon suite is a spacious second-floor room, with wraparound screened-in
windows, a delightful open-air bathtub and shower, and an ocean view. The
beach right out front is rocky and a bit rough, but it does reveal some nice, quiet
tidal pools at low tide; it's one of the better sunset-viewing spots in Costa Rica.
Breakfasts are huge and elaborate. No children under 12 are allowed unless your
party rents out the whole hotel.

Playa Tamarindo, Guanacaste. ©/fax 653-0284. www.sueno-del-mar.com. 4 units, 2 casitas. $155 double;
$170–$195 suite or casita. Rates include full breakfast. Rates lower in the off season, higher during peak
periods. MC, V. **Amenities:** Small pool; free use of snorkel equipment and boogie boards; tour desk. *In room:*
A/C, safe.

Villa Alegre ✦   This small bed-and-breakfast on Playa Langosta is a well-run and homey option. The owners' years of globetrotting have inspired them to decorate each room in the theme of a different country. The Guatemalan and United States rooms share a large bathroom; however, these can easily be joined to form one larger suite. Each room has its own private patio. The villas are quite spacious and luxurious, with kitchenettes. My favorite is the Japanese unit, with its subtle design touches and great woodwork. The Russian villa and Mexican room are truly wheelchair-accessible and -equipped. The beach is just 91m (298 ft.) or so away through the trees. Breakfasts are delicious and abundant.

Playa Tamarindo, Guanacaste. ℭ 653-0270. Fax 653-0287. www.villaalegrecostarica.com. 5 units, 3 with private bathroom; 2 villas. $110–$125 double; $175 villa. Rates include full breakfast. Rates lower in the off season. AE, MC, V. **Amenities:** Small pool. *In room:* A/C, safe, no phone.

Moderate

Best Western Tamarindo Vista Villas   This place was originally conceived of as a condo project, and then converted into a hotel and taken over by the Best Western chain. Nevertheless, it overwhelmingly attracts and caters to surfers. There's a wide range of accommodations here, from the simple gardenview rooms to the Tropical and Corona suites. The former are basic budget motel-like affairs. The latter are split-level one-bedroom affairs with full kitchens, large living rooms (with two couches that can double as single beds), and either a private patio or a balcony with fabulous views of the Pacific Ocean. This hotel really caters to surfers, and there is a lively, beach-party atmosphere around the pool and at the bar here.

Playa Tamarindo, Guanacaste. ℭ 800/536-3241 in the U.S. and Canada, or 653-0114 in Costa Rica. Fax 653-0115. www.tamarindovistavillas.com. 32 units. $99–$119 double; $139–$219 suite. AE, DC, MC, V. **Amenities:** Restaurant; bar; midsize free-form pool w/swim-up bar and a waterfall that is sometimes turned on; tour desk; laundry service. *In room:* A/C, TV/VCR, safe.

Hotel Pasatiempo ✦   A dependable midrange option, this hotel is set back from the beach a couple of hundred meters in a grove of shady trees. Most of the rooms are housed in duplex buildings, but each room has its own private patio with a hammock or chairs. There's plenty of space in every room, and some even sleep five people. The two new suites are quite comfortable. Each room bears the name of a different beach, and the bedroom walls feature hand-painted murals. A small yet very inviting pool sits in the center of the complex.

The restaurant here serves excellent fresh fish, as well as pizza and Tex-Mex specialties. This popular rancho-style affair also has a pool table, a nightly happy hour, cable television with live sporting events, good snacks, and occasional live music.

Playa Tamarindo, Santa Cruz, Guanacaste. ℭ 653-0096. Fax 653-0275. www.hotelpasatiempo.com. 14 units. $69–$85 double. Rates slightly lower in the off season, slightly higher during peak periods. AE, MC, V. **Amenities:** Popular restaurant; bar; midsize pool; exercise room; tour desk; laundry service. *In room:* A/C, no phone.

Inexpensive

In addition to the *cabinas* listed below, there's **Tito's Camping,** located out toward the Hotel Capitán Suizo in Tamarindo. It costs $2.50 per person. Moreover, on my last visit, **Cabinas Arco Iris** (ℭ 653-0330; www.hotelarcoiris.com) was looking pretty good as a slightly inland option. **Cabinas Dolly** (ℭ 653-0017), a perennial budget favorite, still has the best location right on the beach in the center of town.

Cabinas Marielos   This place is located down a palm-shaded driveway across the road from the beach. Rooms are clean and fairly well maintained, although they're small and simply furnished. Patios have tile floors and wooden chairs.

Some of the bathrooms are quite small, but they're clean. There's a kitchen that guests can use, and the garden provides a bit of shade. Prices have increased rather dramatically here in recent years, and I'm not sure that it's quite justified. Although this is still a good, comfortable budget option, true backpackers will probably be happier at Cabinas Dolly (see above); Zully Mar also gives you a little bit more for your money in this price range.

Playa Tamarindo, Guanacaste. ℗/fax **653-0141**. cabinasmarielos@hotmail.com. 20 units. $45–$55 double. AE, MC, V (7% surcharge). **Amenities:** Tour desk; surfboard rentals. *In room:* No phone.

Cabinas Zully Mar The Zully Mar has long been a favorite of budget travelers. The best rooms here are in a two-story, white-stucco building with a wide, curving staircase on the outside. They have air-conditioning, tile floors, long verandas, overhead or standing fans, large bathrooms, and doors that are hand-carved with pre-Columbian motifs. The older, less expensive rooms are smaller and darker, and have soft foam mattresses. There is a small free-form pool that's refreshing if you don't want to walk across the street to the beach, although there's not much landscaping or shade around it.

Tamarindo, Guanacaste. ℗ **653-0140**. Fax 653-0028. zullymar@racsa.co.cr. 40 units. $43–$61 double. Rates lower in the off season. AE, MC, V. **Amenities:** Restaurant; small outdoor pool; laundry service. *In room:* No phone.

IN PLAYA GRANDE

Hotel El Bucanero This hotel is a decent but slightly overpriced choice in Playa Grande, about 91m (298 ft.) from the beach. The rooms are all clean and cool, with tile floors and private bathrooms. The rooms come in several sizes and a mix of bed arrangements. The hotel's restaurant and bar, which is located on the second floor of the octagonal main building, serves reasonably priced seafood dishes, burgers, and sandwiches, and Tico standards. The bar has a lively American surfer/sports bar feel to it, but the best part about it is the fact that it's an open-air affair and gets a nice breeze.

Playa Grande, Guanacaste. ℗/fax **653-0480**. www.elbucanero.com. 7 units. $38–$75 double. Rates lower in the off season. V (6% surcharge). **Amenities:** Restaurant; bar. *In room:* A/C, no phone.

Las Tortugas Hotel ★ *Finds* Playa Grande is best known for the leatherback turtles that nest here, and much of the beach is now part of Las Baulas National Park, which was created to protect the turtles. However, this beach is also very popular with surfers, who make up a large percentage of the clientele at this beachfront hotel. Several of the rooms are quite large, and most have interesting stone floors and shower stalls. The upper suite has a curving staircase that leads to its second room. A few canoes on the nearby estuary are available for gentle paddling among the mangroves.

The owners led the fight to have the area declared a national park and continue to do everything possible to protect the turtles. As part of the hotel's turtle-friendly design, a natural wall of shrubs and trees shields the beach from the restaurant's light and noise, and the swimming pool is fittingly shaped like a turtle.

Playa Grande (A.P. 164, Santa Cruz), Guanacaste. ℗ **653-0423** or ℗/fax 653-0458. www.cool.co.cr/usr/ turtles. 11 units. $45–$65 double; $85–$90 suite. Rates lower in the off season, slightly higher during peak weeks. V (5% surcharge). **Amenities:** Restaurant; bar; small pool; Jacuzzi. *In room:* A/C, no phone.

WHERE TO DINE

In addition to the restaurants listed below, **Nogui's Sunset Café** is one of the most popular places in town—and rightly so. This simple open-air cafe just off the beach on the small traffic circle serves hearty breakfasts and well-prepared salads, sandwiches, and quiche for lunch. The **Shark Bite Deli,** located at the crossroads to Playa Langosta, is another great place for sandwiches and light lunches. The **Cala Moresco** restaurant, at the Hotel and Villas Cala Luna (p. 176), is the place to go if you're looking for some good Italian and Mediterranean cuisine served up in an elegant open-air atmosphere. Out in Playa Langosta, I've gotten good reports about the new **Maria Bonita** restaurant, which features international fare with an emphasis on Latin American and Caribbean cuisine. Finally, **Fish & Meat** is yet another new restaurant specializing in both sushi and grilled meats.

Cantina Las Olas ★ *Value* MEXICAN   A Tamarindo favorite, this casual open-air restaurant is painted in light blue pastel, with bright geometric designs for trim. There's a large and popular bar in the back and a pool table off to the side. Dining is at one of the three wooden picnic tables or several smaller bare-wood tables. The tacos, burritos, and fajitas are all well-prepared Tex-Mex standards and come with a very spicy hot sauce on the side. There are even several vegetarian entrees. I recommend the fish burritos, but ask about the nightly specials, which might feature blackened fish tacos or shrimp enchiladas. Wash the whole thing down with some mango margaritas. Because this is a surfer hangout, you can expect surf videos and loud rock 'n' roll or reggae music, and the occasional live band.

On the side road toward Punta Langosta before Iguana Surf. ℂ **653-0862.** Main courses $3–$9. No credit cards. Mon–Sat 6pm–midnight (kitchen closes at 10pm). Closed Oct.

Gecko ★ SEAFOOD/INTERNATIONAL   This place serves up a mix of Mediterranean-inspired seafood and pasta dishes in a casual open-air setting. The menu changes periodically and is displayed on a big blackboard. I had a wonderful seared tuna with wasabi and red onions served over a fresh salad. Blackened snapper, freshly baked mussels, and mahimahi in a Dijon-mustard sauce were also on the menu.

At Iguana Surf, on the road to Playa Langosta. ℂ **653-0334.** Reservations not accepted. Main courses $7–$18. No credit cards. Wed–Sun 5:30–9:30pm.

Lazy Wave Food Company ★★ *Finds* SEAFOOD/FUSION   Serving an eclectic selection of daily specials and decadent baked goods, this has quickly become one of the favorite spots in Tamarindo. All of the seating is open-air, on a raised wooden deck under a tentlike awning supported by an old Almedro tree. The chalkboard usually offers up a selection of about a half dozen each of appetizers and entrees. There's almost always some fresh wasabi-crusted tuna, and other options could range from shrimp-and-smoked-sausage jambalaya to chile-garlic beef pepper pot.

Just before Hotel Pasatiempo. ℂ **653-0737.** Reservations not accepted. Main courses $7–$12. No credit cards. Mon–Sat 7am–10pm; Sun 6–10pm.

Pedro's Fish Shack SEAFOOD/COSTA RICAN   This place started out literally as a shack on the beach. Popularity and renovations have spiffed it up some, but this remains a simple, open-air beachfront seafood joint, with rustic wooden tables and chairs. The fish is still caught fresh every day, and your best bet is to get it grilled or fried. However, when they have it, it's definitely worth starting things off with a plate of tuna sashimi.

On the beach, just beyond Nogui's Sunset Café. No phone. Main courses $4–$17. No credit cards. Daily 11:30am–10pm.

TAMARINDO AFTER DARK

As a popular surfer destination, Tamarindo has a sometimes raging nightlife. On Saturday nights, the place to be is **The Big Bazaar,** which hosts a massive beach party, replete with a raging bonfire. Other popular spots that go off throughout the week include **La Bodega,** located on the little traffic circle, the **Crazy Monkey Bar** at the Best Western Vista Villas, and the bar at the Hotel Pasatiempo (p. 178), which sometimes features live music.

For those looking for some gaming, there are two casinos in town, one across from the El Diriá hotel, and another out in Playa Langosta at the Barceló Playa Langosta resort.

EN ROUTE SOUTH: PLAYA AVELLANAS & PLAYA NEGRA

As you head south from Tamarindo, you'll come to several as-yet-underdeveloped beaches, most of which are quite popular with surfers. Beyond Tamarindo and Playa Langosta are **Playa Avellanas** and then **Playa Negra,** both of which have a few basic *cabinas* catering to surfers.

WHERE TO STAY

Cabinas Las Olas   This collection of duplex cabins is a popular surf lodge. The entire complex is set in the shade of some tall trees, a couple hundred meters inland from the beach and bordering a mangrove reserve. The rooms are simple but clean and are a good value. Each comes with a private little veranda with a table and some chairs and a hammock. The beach here is a long stretch of almost always uncrowded white sand. There are good beach breaks for surfers up and down the shoreline, especially toward the northern end and the Langosta estuary. Mountain bikes and sea kayaks are available here for rent.

Playa Avellanas, Santa Cruz, Guanacaste. © 658-8315. Fax 658-8331. www.cabinaslasolas.co.cr. 10 units. $65 double. Rates lower in the off season. MC, V. **Amenities:** Restaurant; bar; laundry service. *In room:* No phone.

Hotel Playa Negra   This collection of thatch-roofed bungalows is right in front of the famous Playa Negra point break. Even if you're not a surfer, the beach and coast along this area are beautiful, with coral and rock outcroppings and calm tide pools. The round bungalows each have one queen-size and two single beds, two desks, a ceiling fan, and a private bathroom. Although they have concrete floors, everything is painted in contrasting pastels and feels quite comfortable. The restaurant is close to the ocean in a large open-air rancho and serves as a social hub for guests and surfers staying at more basic *cabinas* inland from the beach.

Playa Negra (A.P. 31-5150, Santa Cruz), Guanacaste. © 658-8034. Fax 658-8035. www.playanegra.com. 10 bungalows. $55–$66 double. AE, MC, V. **Amenities:** Restaurant; bar; midsize oval pool; laundry service. *In room:* No phone.

7 Playa Junquillal ⟨★⟩

30km (19 miles) W of Santa Cruz; 20km (12 miles) S of Tamarindo

Playa Junquillal (pronounced "hoon-kee-*yal*") is a long, windswept beach that, for most of its length, is backed by grasslands. This gives it a very different feel from other beaches on this coast. There's really no village to speak of here, so if you're heading out this way, plan to get away from it all. In fact, if you're looking to leave the madding crowds behind and want some unfettered time on a nearly deserted beach, this is a great choice. The long stretch of sand is great for strolling, and the sunsets are superb. When the waves are up and the sea is rough, this beach can be a little dangerous for swimming. When it's calm, jump right on in.

ESSENTIALS

GETTING THERE & DEPARTING **By Plane** The nearest airport with regularly scheduled flights is in Tamarindo (see above). You can arrange a taxi from the airport to Playa Junquillal. The ride should take around 40 minutes and cost about $35 to $40.

By Car Take the Interamerican Highway from San José. Forty-seven kilometers (29 miles) past the turnoff for Puntarenas, you'll see signs and the turnoff for the new Tempisque River bridge. After crossing the river, follow the signs for Nicoya and Santa Cruz. Just after leaving the main intersection for Santa Cruz, you'll see a marked turnoff for Playa Junquillal, Ostional, and Tamarindo. The road is paved for 14km (8½ miles), until the tiny village of Veintesiete de Abril. From here, it's another rough 18km (11 miles) to Playa Junquillal.

By Bus To get here by bus, you must first head to Santa Cruz and, from there, take another bus to Playa Junquillal. Buses depart San José for Santa Cruz roughly every hour between 6am and 6pm from the **Tralapa** bus station (© 221-7202) at Calle 20 between avenidas 3 and 5, and from the **Tracopa** bus station (© 222-2666) at Calle 14 between avenidas 3 and 5. Trip duration is around 4 hours; the fare is $5. Buses leave Santa Cruz for Junquillal at 10:30am, and 2:30 and 4pm. The ride takes about 1 hour, and the one-way fare is $1.50. Buses depart Playa Junquillal for Santa Cruz daily at 6am, noon, and 5:30pm. If you miss the connection, you can hire a taxi for the trip to Junquillal for around $30.

WHAT TO DO IN JUNQUILLAL

Other than walking on the beach, swimming when the surf isn't too strong, and exploring tide pools, there isn't much to do here—which is just fine with me. This beach is ideal for anyone who wants to relax without any distractions. Bring a few good books. You can rent bikes at the Iguanazul Hotel, which is a good way to get up and down to the beach; horseback-riding tours are also popular.

If you're a surfer, the beach break right in Junquillal is sometimes pretty good. I've also heard that if you look hard enough, there are a few hidden reef and point breaks around.

Several sportfishing boats operate out of Playa Junquillal. Inquire at your hotel, or ask at the Iguanazul Hotel (see below). If you want to rent a mountain bike, you can also check in at the Iguanazul.

Finally, if you want to do some diving, check in with Micke and Maarten at **El Lugarcito** (©/fax **658-8436;** lugarcito@racsa.co.cr). These folks offer day trips to the Catalina Islands, as well as resort and full-certification courses.

WHERE TO STAY & DINE

Most of the hotels listed below have their own restaurants. You can also get good pizza, homemade pasta, and fresh seafood at **Pizzería Tatanka** (© **658-8426**), which is located on your left as you come into Junquillal. This place also offers simple rooms at reasonable rates.

MODERATE

Iguanazul Hotel ✦ Set on a windswept, grassy bluff above a rocky beach, Iguanazul is far from the crowds. Originally catering to surfers, this is definitely the place in Junquillal for sun worshipers who like to have a good time; the clientele tends to be young and active. The pool is large, as is the surrounding patio area, and there's a volleyball court. If you're feeling mellow, head down to one of the quiet coves or grab a hammock set in a covered palapa on the hillside. Guest rooms are spacious and nicely decorated with basket lampshades, wicker furniture, red-tile floors, high ceilings, and blue-and-white–tile bathrooms. The higher prices are for air-conditioned rooms, and a few of these even have televisions. Even if you're not staying here, this is a good place to dine; the food is excellent and the sunset views are phenomenal. When I last visited, work had just begun on a neighboring condominium project.

Playa Junquillal (A.P. 130-5150, Santa Cruz), Guanacaste. © 658-8124 or ©/fax 658-8123. www.iguanazul. com. 24 units. $70–$90 double; $80–$100 triple. Rates include continental breakfast. Rates lower in the off season. AE, MC, V. **Amenities:** Recommended restaurant; bar; outdoor pool; watersports equipment rental; bike rental; game room; tour desk; laundry service. *In room:* A/C and TV in some units, no phone.

INEXPENSIVE

In addition to the lodgings listed below, **Camping Los Malinches** (© 658-8429) has wonderful campsites on fluffy grass amid manicured gardens set on a bluff above the beach. Camping will run you $5 per person, and the fee entitles you to bathroom and shower privileges. You'll see a sign on the right as you drive toward Playa Junquillal, a little bit beyond the Iguanazul Hotel. The campground is located about 1km (½ mile) down this dirt road. You'll also find very basic rooms just steps from the beach at **Hotel Playa Junquillal** (© 888/666-2322 in the U.S., or 658-8432 in Costa Rica; www.playa-junquillal.com).

Hibiscus Hotel *Value*   Although the accommodations here are very simple, the friendly German owner makes sure that everything is always clean and in top shape. The grounds are pleasantly shady, with plenty of flowering tropical flora, and the beach is just across the road. The rooms have cool Mexican-tile floors and firm beds. The service and ambience here are excellent for the price range. The restaurant serves very well-prepared international cuisine and fresh seafood at reasonable prices.

Playa Junquillal (A.P. 163-5150, Santa Cruz), Guanacaste. ©/fax **658-8437.** www.adventure-costarica. com/hibiscus. 5 units. $42 double; $52 triple. Rates include full breakfast. V. **Amenities:** Restaurant; laundry service. *In room:* No phone.

Hotel El Castillo Divertido   This fanciful hotel, built by a young German, is a tropical rendition of a classic medieval castle (well, sort of). Ramparts and a turret with a rooftop bar certainly grab the attention of passersby. Guest rooms here are fairly small, although rates are certainly fair. Ask for an upstairs room with a balcony. If you don't get one of these, you'll still have a good view from the hotel's rooftop bar, which sometimes features live music. The hotel is about 500m (1,640 ft.) from the beach.

Playa Junquillal, Santa Cruz, Guanacaste. ©/fax **658-8428.** 7 units. $30–$40 double. Rates lower in the off season. AE, MC, V. **Amenities:** Restaurant; bar. *In room:* No phone.

8 Playa Nosara ✶✶

55km (34 miles) SW of Nicoya; 266km (165 miles) W of San José

Playa Nosara is actually several beaches, almost all of which are nearly deserted most of the time. Because the village of Nosara is several kilometers from the beach, and because most of the land near the beach has been zoned primarily as a residential community, Nosara has been spared the sort of ugly, uncontrolled growth characteristic of many other Guanacaste beaches. All of the hotels here are small and spread out, with most tucked away down side roads. There's none of the hotels-piled-on-top-of-hotels feeling that you get at playas Flamingo, Tamarindo, and Coco. In fact, on first arriving here, it's hard to believe there are any hotels around at all. Nosara has long been popular with North American retirees and a handful of Hollywood celebs, and they, too, have made sure that their homes are not crammed cheek-by-jowl in one spot, hiding them instead among the profusion of trees that make Nosara one of the greenest spots on the Nicoya Peninsula. If you're looking for reliably sunny weather and a bit of tropical greenery, this is a good bet.

The best way to get to Nosara is to fly, but, with everything so spread out, that makes getting around difficult after you've arrived. The roads to and in Nosara are in horrendous shape, and though there has long been talk of some sections being widened and paved, it will probably still be quite a few years before the blacktop reaches here.

ESSENTIALS

GETTING THERE & DEPARTING **By Plane** Sansa (© 221-9414; www.flysansa.com) has two flights daily to Nosara, departing from San José's Juan Santamaría International Airport at 8:10am and 1:50pm. The fare for the 50-minute flight is $71 each way. **Nature Air** (© 220-3054; www.natureair. com) also has two flights daily that leave at 8:30am and 1pm from Tobías Bolaños International Airport in Pavas. The fare is $80 each way. Taxis are waiting for every arrival; fares range between $4 and $7 to most hotels.

The return Sansa flights to San José depart Nosara daily at 9:15am and 12:55pm, and the Travelair flights leave at 9:45am and 2pm.

By Car   Follow the directions for getting to Playa Sámara (see "Playa Sámara," below), but watch for a well-marked fork in the road a few kilometers before you reach that beach. The right-hand fork leads to Nosara over another 22km (14 miles) of terrible road.

By Bus   An express bus (© 222-2666) leaves San José daily at 6am from Calle 14 between avenidas 3 and 5. The trip's duration is 5½ hours; the one-way fare is $6.

You can also take a bus from San José to Nicoya (see below for details) and then catch a second bus from Nicoya to Nosara. Buses leave Nicoya for Nosara daily at 5 and 10am, and 2pm. Trip duration is 2 hours; the one-way fare is $1.25.

The bus to San José leaves daily at 12:30pm. Buses to Nicoya leave Nosara daily at 6am and 12:15 and 3pm. Buses leave Nicoya for San José roughly every hour between 5am and 5pm.

Interbus (© 283-5573; www.costaricapass.com) runs a bus from San José to Playa Nosara at 8:30am; the fare is $38. A minimum of two passengers is required.

ORIENTATION   The village of Nosara is about 5km (3 miles) inland from the beach. The small airstrip ends practically in town; however, most of the hotels listed here are on or near the beach itself. You'll find the **post office** and **police station** right at the end of the airstrip. If you need a **taxi,** call © 682-0142. There's an **Internet cafe** in the village and others at Café de Paris and Harbor Reef Lodge (p. 186).

FUN ON & OFF THE BEACH

There are several beaches at Nosara, including the long, curving **Playa Guiones** ✦✦, **Playa Nosara** ✦, and, my personal favorite, diminutive **Playa Pelada** ✦✦. Pelada is a short white-sand beach with three deep scallops, backed by sea grasses and mangroves. There isn't too much sand at high tide, so you'll want to hit the beach when the tide's out. At either end of the beach there are rocky outcroppings that reveal tide pools at low tide. Surfing and bodysurfing are both good here, particularly at Playa Guiones, which is garnering quite a reputation as a consistent and rideable beach break. Because the village of Nosara is several miles inland, these beaches are very clean, secluded, and quiet.

With miles of excellent beach breaks and relatively few crowds, this is a great place to learn how to surf. If you want to try to stand up for your first time, check in with the folks at **Safari Surf School** (℃ 682-0573; www.safarisurf school.com).

BIRD- & SEA TURTLE–WATCHING   Bird-watchers should explore the mangrove swamps around the estuary mouth of the Río Nosara. Just walk north from Playa Pelada and follow the riverbank; explore the paths into the mangroves.

If you time your trip right, you can do a night tour to nearby **Playa Ostional** to watch nesting Olive Ridley sea turtles. These turtles come ashore by the thousands in a mass egg-laying phenomenon known as an *arribada*. These *arribadas* take place 4 to 10 times between July and November; each occurrence lasts between 3 and 10 days. Consider yourself very lucky if you happen to be around during one of these fascinating natural phenomena. Even if it's not turtle-nesting season, you might want to look into visiting Playa Ostional, just to have a long, wide expanse of beach to yourself. However, be careful swimming here because the surf and riptides can be formidable. During the dry season (mid-Nov to Apr), you can usually get here in a regular car, but during the rainy season you'll need four-wheel-drive. This beach is part of Ostional National Wildlife Refuge. At the northwest end of the refuge is **India Point,** which is known for its tide pools and rocky outcrops.

The *arribadas* are so difficult to predict that no one runs regularly scheduled turtle-viewing trips, but when the *arribada* is in full swing, several local tour guides and agencies offer tours. Your best bet is to ask the staff at your hotel or check in with **Iguana Expeditions** (℃ 682-0450; www.iguanaexpeditions.com).

FISHING CHARTERS & OTHER OUTDOOR ACTIVITIES   All of the hotels in the area can arrange fishing charters for $250 to $500 for a half-day, or $450 to $1,100 for a full day. These rates are for one to four people and vary according to boat size and accouterments.

HORSEBACK RIDING   The folks at **Casa Río Nosara Excursions** (℃ 682-0117) have a large stable of well-cared-for horses and a range of beach, jungle, and waterfall rides to choose from. Rates run around $15 to $20 per hour per person.

KAYAK TOURS   Based out of the Gilded Iguana hotel and restaurant, **Iguana Expeditions** ⊛ (℃ 682-0450; www.iguanaexpeditions.com) offers a range of full- and half-day tours around the area. Explore the inland coastal mangroves, or combine some open-water paddling with a snorkel break at San Juanillo. A half-day tour with picnic lunch costs around $45; full-day tours run between $60 and $90. These folks can also arrange inexpensive fishing outings in a *panga,* or small craft, with a local fisherman.

YOGA & MORE   If you want to spend some time getting mind and body together, check in with the **Nosara Wellness Center** (℃ 682-0360; www. nosarawellness.com), which offers yoga classes, massage therapy, and a host of custom-designed "retreat" options.

WHERE TO STAY

In addition to the places listed below, **The Gilded Iguana** (© 682-0259; www. gildediguana.com) has comfortable rooms in several different price ranges and has recently added a pool.

Almost Paradise *Value*   Located on the hill above Playa Pelada, this delightful little hotel is aptly named. This older wood building is a welcome relief from all the concrete and cinder block that is so common in Costa Rican construction. The rooms are simple and clean, and feature colorful local artwork; most have some ocean view. My favorites are those just off the restaurant, which have access to a broad, inviting covered veranda with hammocks, sitting chairs, and a great view. Breakfast is served in a common area that acts as the hotel's bar and lounge at night. These folks also rent a separate fully equipped apartment, which is great for longer stays.

Playa Nosara (A.P. 15-5233), Guanacaste. ©/fax **682-0173**. 5 units. $45–$50 double. Rates lower in the off season, higher during peak weeks. V (6% surcharge). **Amenities:** Bar; small plunge pool; laundry service. *In room:* No phone.

Café de Paris ⭐   Located on the main road into Nosara, where it branches off to Playa Guiones, this popular little bakery and bistro has some equally popular rooms out back, set behind the restaurant and pool in a series of duplex buildings. All have high ceilings and plenty of room; about half have kitchenettes. A few shady ranchos are spread around the grounds for afternoon lazing. These folks also rent a couple of luxury villas with fabulous views atop a steep hill across the street.

Playa Nosara, Guanacaste. © **682-0087**. Fax 682-0089. www.cafedeparis.net. 14 units. $39–$79 double; $120 villa. Rates include continental breakfast. AE, MC, V. **Amenities:** Restaurant; bar; small pool; game room; tour desk; laundry service. *In room:* A/C, no phone.

Harbor Reef Lodge ⭐   This hotel caters to both surfers and fishermen, with clean, spacious rooms close to the beach (about 182m/597 ft. inland from Playa Guiones). In fact, these are probably the most comfortable rooms close to the beach in Nosara. The suites come with separate sitting rooms, and a couple even have kitchenettes. There's a cool, oasislike feel to the lush grounds. The hotel offers surf lessons and sportfishing outings, and even has a small general store and Internet cafe on the grounds.

Playa Nosara, Guanacaste. © **682-0059**. Fax 682-0060. www.harborreef.com. 16 units. $74 double; $90–$110 suite. AE, MC, V. **Amenities:** Restaurant; bar; small pool; watersports equipment rental; bike rental; tour desk; laundry service. *In room:* A/C, fridge, coffeemaker, no phone.

Hotel Villa Taype   This sprawling hotel is located down a side road that leads from the main road to Playa Guiones and is the closest thing to a resort in this neck of the woods. The room decor is simple but attractive, with white-tile floors, high ceilings, overhead fans, and well-designed bathrooms. All the rooms have patios, but the bungalows are a little larger, and each has its own little *ranchito*, with a sitting area and hammock. Best of all, the beach is only about 90m (295 ft.) away. During the high season, it even opens a small disco here, which can get quite lively.

Playa Nosara (A.P. 8-5233), Guanacaste. © **682-0333**. Fax 682-0187. www.villataype.com. 12 units, 10 bungalows. $60–$80 double; $115–$135 bungalow. Rates include breakfast buffet. Rates lower in the off season. AE, MC, V. **Amenities:** Restaurant; bar; midsize pool w/swim-up bar and children's pool; outdoor lighted tennis court; watersports equipment rental; game room; tour desk; laundry service. *In room:* A/C, TV.

Tips Yo Quiero Hablar Español

You can brush up on or start up your Spanish at the **Rey de Nosara Language School** (℗/fax **682-0215**; www.reydenosara.itgo.com). It offers group and private lessons according to demand, and can coordinate week or multiweek packages.

Lagarta Lodge   Located on a hillside high over the Nosara River, this small lodge is an excellent choice for bird-watchers and other travelers who are more interested in the flora and fauna than the beach. The rooms are spartan but acceptable. The lodge borders its own private reserve, which has trails along the riverbank and through the mangrove and tropical humid forests here. There are spectacular views from the restaurant and most rooms over the river and surrounding forest, with the beaches of Nosara and Ostional in the distance. You'll want to have your own vehicle if you're staying here: The beach is a good 10- to 15-minute hike away, and it's uphill on the way back.

Playa Nosara (A.P. 18-5233), Guanacaste. ℗ **682-0035**. Fax 682-0135. www.lagarta.com. 7 units. $65 double. Rates lower in the off season. AE, MC, V. **Amenities:** Restaurant; bar; midsize outdoor pool; tour desk; laundry service. *In room:* No phone.

Nosara Beach Hotel   Perched high on a hill above both Playa Pelada and Playa Guiones, this hotel has the best views in the area, if not necessarily the best accommodations. In the 12 years I've been visiting, the place has always had the feeling of someone's unfinished backyard project, and it still does. There's a six-story tower with an onion dome on top, looking something like "Gaudí Goes Russian Orthodox." Although this is the best place to take in the amazing sunsets, it's not yet finished, and service can be spotty. The large kidney-shape pool is open, but work is still ongoing on most of the rooms and surrounding landscaping. Most of the rooms have balconies overlooking either Playa Guiones or Playa Pelada. They are simple and clean, and most are quite spacious.

Playa Nosara (A.P. 4-5233), Guanacaste. ℗ **682-0121**. Fax 682-0123. www.nosarabeachhotel.com. 20 units. $30–$60 double. No credit cards. **Amenities:** Bar; midsize outdoor pool; tour desk; laundry service. *In room:* No phone.

DINING & AFTER-DARK DIVERSIONS

In addition to the places mentioned below, **Marlin Bill's** (℗ **682-0458**) is a popular and massive open-air haunt on the hillside on the main road, just across from Café de Paris (below). You can expect to get good, fresh seafood and American classics here. Also, **La Dolce Vita** (℗ **682-0107**) is located on the road to Playa Samara and serves up excellent Italian fare nightly.

When evening rolls around, don't expect a major party scene. Nightlife near the beach seems to center on the Café de Paris, Marlin Bill's, and the Gilded Iguana. In "downtown" Nosara, you'll probably want to check out either **Las Iguanas Locas** (℗ **682-0161**), a German-run restaurant/bar, or **Tropicana** (℗ **682-0140**), the town's disco. Both are on the streets fronting the soccer field.

Café de Paris ✦ *Finds* BAKERY/BISTRO   This popular little place has wonderful fresh-baked goods and a wide assortment of light bites and full-on meals. You can get pizza or nachos or filling sandwiches on fresh baguettes. There are also hearty salads, as well as fish, meat, and chicken dishes. I enjoy stopping in for a cup of espresso and a fresh almond croissant. Sporting events or movie videos are shown nightly, and there's even a pool table and Internet cafe here.

On the main road into Nosara. © **682-0087.** Baked goods 50¢–$4; main courses $4–$15. AE, MC, V. Daily 7am–11pm.

Doña Olga's COSTA RICAN   Little more than a roof over a concrete slab, Olga's is still one of the most popular restaurants in Nosara. Gringos and Ticos alike hang out here, savoring fried-fish *casados,* sandwiches, and breakfasts that include huge helpings of bacon. The restaurant is located right on the beach, where the road ends at Playa Pelada, and is just a stone's throw from the water.

On the beach at Playa Pelada. No phone. Main courses $3–$15. No credit cards. Daily 6:30am–10pm.

The Gilded Iguana ★ SEAFOOD/GRILL   This simple restaurant serves fish so fresh that it's still wiggling: The owner's husband, Chiqui, is a local fisherman. There are also great burgers, Costa Rican *casados,* and a short list of nightly specials. If you're in town fishing yourself, they'll cook your catch. Sporting events are shown on a not-quite-big-enough television. Overall, the vibe is sociable and lively.

About 90m (295 ft.) inland from the beach at Playa Guiones. © **682-0259.** Main courses $4–$14. V. Daily 7am–9:30am, 11am–2pm, and 5–10pm.

9 Playa Sámara ★

35km (22 miles) S of Nicoya; 245km (152 miles) W of San José

Playa Sámara is a pretty beach on a long, horseshoe-shape bay. Unlike most of the rest of the Pacific coast, the water here is excellent for swimming, because an offshore island and rocky headlands break up most of the surf. Because Playa Sámara is easily accessible along a well-paved road, and because there are quite a few cheap *cabinas, sodas,* and raging discos here, this beach is popular both with families seeking a quick and inexpensive getaway and with young Ticos out for a weekend of beach partying. Given this heavy traffic and party atmosphere, this isn't my first choice for a relaxing beach getaway. Still, the calm waters and steep cliffs on the far side of the bay make this a very attractive spot, and the beach is long, wide, and protected. Moreover, if you drive along the rugged coastal road in either direction, you'll come to some truly spectacular beaches.

ESSENTIALS

GETTING THERE & DEPARTING   By Plane   Sansa (© **221-9414;** www. flysansa.com) flies to Carillo (15 min. south of Sámara) daily at 8:10am and 11:50am from San José's Juan Santamaría International Airport. The flight might stop first at either Punta Islita or Nosara and takes approximately 1 hour; the fare is $71 each way.

Nature Air (© **220-3054;** www.natureair.com) flies to Carillo daily at 1pm from Tobías Bolaños International Airport in Pavas. The flight stops first in Nosara and takes 1 hour and 10 minutes; the fare is $80 each way.

Most hotels will arrange to pick you up in Carillo. If not, you'll have to hire a cab for between $8 and $10.

Sansa flights leave Carillo for San José at 9:15am and 12:55pm. Nature Air flies out of Carillo daily at 2:15pm.

By Car   Take the Interamerican Highway from San José. Forty-seven kilometers (29 miles) past the turnoff for Puntarenas, you'll see signs and the turnoff for the new Tempisque River bridge. After crossing the bridge, continue north to Nicoya.

In Nicoya, head more or less straight through town until you see signs for Playa Sámara. From here, it's a paved road almost all the way to the beach.

By Bus Express buses (© **222-2666**) leave San José daily at 12:30 and 6:15pm from Calle 14 between avenidas 3 and 5. The trip lasts 5 hours; the one-way fare is $6. Extra buses are sometimes added on weekends and during peak periods, so it's always wise to check.

Alternatively, you can take a bus from this same San José station to Nicoya and then catch a second bus from Nicoya to Sámara. Buses leave San José for Nicoya roughly every hour throughout the day between 5am and 5pm. The trip takes 4 hours; the fare is $4. Buses leave Nicoya for Sámara and Carillo daily at 6, 8, and 10am; noon; and 3, 4:30, and 6pm. The trip's duration is 1½ hours. The fare to Sámara is $1.50; the fare to Carillo is $2.

Express buses to San José leave daily at 4:30 and 8:45am. Buses for Nicoya leave daily at 5:30, 6, 7, 8:45, and 11:30am, and 1:15, 4:30, and 5:30pm. Buses leave Nicoya for San José roughly every hour between 5am and 5pm.

Grayline (© **220-2126;** www.graylinecostarica.com) has a daily bus that leaves San José for Playa Sámara at 7am; the fare is $25. **Interbus** (© **283-5573;** www.costaricapass.com) has a daily bus that leaves San José for Playa Sámara at 8:30am; the fare is $30. Both companies will pick you up at most San José–area hotels.

ORIENTATION   Sámara is a busy little town at the bottom of a steep hill. The main road heads straight into town, passing the soccer field before coming to an end at the beach. Just before the beach is a road to the left that leads to most of the hotels listed below. This road also leads to Playa Carillo (see below) and Hotel Punta Islita (p. 192).

FUN ON & OFF THE BEACH

Aside from sitting on the sand and soaking up the sun, the main activities in Playa Sámara seem to be hanging out in the bars and *sodas* and dancing into the early-morning hours. But if you're looking for something more, there's horse-back riding, either on the beach or through the bordering pastureland and forests. Other options include sea kayaking in the calm waters off of Playa Sámara, sportfishing, snorkeling and scuba diving, boat tours, mountain biking, and tours to Playa Ostional to see the mass nestings of Olive Ridley sea turtles. You can inquire about and book any of these tours at your hotel.

You'll find that the beach is nicer and cleaner down at the south end. Better yet, head about 8km (5 miles) south to **Playa Carillo** ✸✸, a long crescent of soft, white sand. There's almost no development here, so the beach is almost always deserted and there are loads of palm trees providing shade. If you've got a good four-wheel-drive vehicle, ask for directions at your hotel and set off in search of the hidden gems of **Playa Buena Vista** ✸ and **Playa Barrigona** ✸✸, which are north of Sámara, less than a half-hour drive away. A taxi to Playa Carillo should cost about $5 to $6 each way. Because it's a bit farther and the roads are a little rougher, expect to pay a little more to reach Playa Buena Vista, and even more for Playa Barrigona.

Cavers will want to head 62km (38 miles) northeast of Playa Sámara on the road to the Tempisque bridge. If you don't have a car, your best bet is to get to Nicoya, which is about a half-hour away by bus, and then take a taxi to the park, which should cost about $10. Here, at **Barra Honda National Park** ✸ (© **686-6760**), there's an extensive system of caves, some of which reach more than 200m (656 ft.) in depth. Human remains and indigenous relics have been found in other caves, but these are not open to the public. Because this is a national park, you'll have to pay the $6 entrance fee. If you plan to descend the one publicly accessible cave, you'll also need to rent (or bring your own) equipment and hire a local guide at the park entrance station. Depending upon your group size and bargaining abilities, expect to pay $12 to $30 per person for a visit to the Terciopelo Cave, including the guide, harness, helmet, and flashlight. Furthermore, the cave is open only during the dry season (mid-Nov to Apr). Inside you'll see plenty of impressive stalactites and stalagmites while visiting several chambers of varying sizes. Even if you don't descend, the trails around Barra Honda and its prominent limestone plateau are great for hiking and birdwatching. There's a simple bunkhouse here offering basic accommodations for around $5 per person, camping is permitted for $2 per person, and a simple *soda* offers up filling, inexpensive meals right on-site.

The folks at **Wingnuts Canopy Tours** (© 656-0153) offer one of the popular zip-line and harness "canopy tours." The 2-hour outing costs $40 per person. You'll find their office by the giant strangler fig tree, or *matapalo,* toward the southern end of the beach.

Almost every hotel in the area can arrange sportfishing trips, or you could contact **Kingfisher** (© 656-0091; www.costaricabillfishing.com).

If you want to check out the surrounding hillsides or pedal yourself to one of the nearby beaches recommended above, **Bike Costa Rica** (© 656-0120) has a fleet of modern Trek mountain bikes that rent for $3.75 per hour or $25 per day. It also offers guided half- and full-day tours.

Finally, if you want to acquire or polish some language skills while here, check in with the **Samara Language School** (© 656-0127). These folks offer a range of programs and private lessons, and can arrange for a homestay with a local family.

WHERE TO STAY
EXPENSIVE

In addition to the places listed below, **Hacienda Dorada** (© 866/430-7232 in the U.S., or 255-0932 in Costa Rica; www.dorada.com) rents three large and luxurious fully equipped villas on a hillside above and behind Playa Buenavista.

Villas Playa Sámara   Located toward the southern extreme of Playa Sámara, right on the beach, this place has the nicest setting and grounds around, if not the best facilities. Built to resemble a small village, the hotel consists of numerous villas varying in size from one to three bedrooms. White-stucco exterior walls and red-tile roofs give the whole thing a Mediterranean look, and the whole complex is set right off a nice, quiet, and calm section of beach. The spacious rooms are outfitted with bamboo furniture and have tiled bathrooms. All the villas have kitchens and patios, and are finished with colorful bedspreads and artwork, basket lampshades, and vertical blinds on the windows; most have airconditioning. This place has many of the facilities and amenities one would expect at a midsize beach resort. However, the upkeep and maintenance have been spotty, and service can be downright bad.

Playa Sámara (A.P. 111-1007, Centro Colón, San José), Guanacaste. © 256-8228 or 656-0372. Fax 220-3348. www.villasplayasamara.com. 57 units. $90–$125 double; $175–$245 2- to 3-room villa. Rates lower in the off season, higher during peak weeks. AE, MC, V. **Amenities:** Restaurant; bar; midsize outdoor pool; exercise room; Jacuzzi; bike rental; tour desk; laundry service. *In room:* No phone.

MODERATE
Hotel Las Brisas del Pacífico ✦   Located on the southern stretch of Playa Sámara, this hotel is set amid very shady grounds right on a quiet section of the

beach, and backs up on a steep hill. Most of the rooms are found in the three-story building, up a long and steep flight of stairs at the top of the hill. These have comfortable balconies and walls of glass that provide an excellent view of the bay. The third-floor rooms are the largest here, but the second-floor rooms actually have the best views. At the base of the hill are rooms in stucco duplexes with steeply pitched tile roofs and red-tile patios. The range in prices reflects the range in room size, location, and amenities. Depending on the season and demand, either one or both of the restaurants here will be open. Regardless, you'll find excellent fresh seafood and perfectly prepared Italian pastas and entrees.

Playa Sámara (A.P. 11917-1000, San José), Guanacaste. © 656-0250. Fax 656-0248. www.brisas.net. 34 units. $70–$105 double. Rates lower in the off season, higher during peak weeks. AE, MC, V. **Amenities:** 2 restaurants; 2 bars; 2 midsize outdoor pools; 2 unheated Jacuzzis; limited watersports equipment rental; tour desk; laundry service. In room: A/C in some units, safe, no phone.

INEXPENSIVE

In addition to the places listed below, I like the tidy, German-run **Hotel Belvedere** (© 656-0213; www.belvederesamara.net), located on the hill overlooking the beach.

You'll find a slew of very inexpensive places to stay along the road into town and around the soccer field. Many of the rooms at these places are less accommodating than your average jail cell. As an alternative, you can pitch a tent right by the beach for a few dollars at either **Camping Coco's** (© 656-0496) or **Camping Río Lagarto** (© 656-0028). Both have basic showers and bathrooms. You'll find Camping Coco's several hundred meters south of the downtown, but I prefer Rio Lagarto, which is about a half-kilometer north of the center of town. It can be reached from the beach or from the beach-access road beside the defunct Hotel Isla Chora.

Casa del Mar   Located on the inland side of the beach-access road, 1 block south of "downtown," Casa del Mar is just 50m (164 ft.) from the beach. The rooms here are immaculate, and most of them are quite spacious. The place feels like a cool oasis from the harsh Guanacaste sun, with its open-air restaurant, shady central courtyard, and small pool/Jacuzzi. Although the units with shared bathrooms are the best bargains here, I'd opt for a second-floor room with a private bathroom. Several rooms come with air-conditioning, and a few even have small fridges.

Playa Sámara, Nicoya, Guanacaste. © 656-0264. Fax 656-0129. www.casadelmarsamara.com. 17 units, 11 with private bathroom. $35–$50 double. Rates include continental breakfast. Rates lower in the off season. $10 extra for air-conditioning. AE, MC, V. **Amenities:** Restaurant; bar; unheated pool/Jacuzzi; tour desk; laundry service. In room: No phone.

Casa Valeria   This is the best beachfront super-budget option in town. The rooms are quite basic and much more rustic than those at either Giada or Casa del Mar, but they are just steps away from the sand and surf. The best bets here are the four individual bungalows. There's a basic restaurant, as well as some tables, chairs, and hammocks set in the shade of some tall coconut palms. This place is popular with European backpackers, and there's a hostel feel to the whole operation.

Playa Sámara, Nicoya, Guanacaste. © 656-0511. Fax 656-0317. 9 units. $30–$40 double. Rates include breakfast. V. **Amenities:** Restaurant. In room: No phone.

Hotel Giada *Value*   This neat little Italian-owned hotel is located on the left-hand side of the main road into town, about 150m (492 ft.) before the beach. The rooms are all very clean and comfortable, and even have a small balcony.

Breakfast is served in a cool, shady central gazebo. The management is very helpful and can arrange diving or fishing expeditions and horseback-riding trips.

Playa Sámara, Nicoya, Guanacaste. ℂ 656-0132. Fax 656-0131. www.hotelgiada.net. 13 units. $48 double. Rates include breakfast. Rates lower in the off season, higher during peak periods. AE, DC, MC, V. **Amenities:** Restaurant; bar; small pool; tour desk; laundry service. *In room:* A/C, TV, no phone.

A NEARBY LUXURY HOTEL

Hotel Punta Islita ★★★ *(Finds)* This is one of the most exclusive and romantic luxury resorts in Costa Rica. It's isolated on a high bluff between two mountain ridges that meet the sea. The rooms here are done in a Santa Fe style, with red Mexican floor tiles, neo-Navajo-print bedspreads, and adobe-colored walls offset with sky-blue doors and trim. Each room has a king-size bed and a private patio with a hammock; a few of these also have a Jacuzzi. The suites come with a separate sitting room and a private two-person plunge pool or Jacuzzi; the villas have two or three bedrooms, their own private swimming pools, and full kitchens.

The beach below the hotel is a small crescent of gray-white sand with a calm, protected section at the northern end. It's about a 10-minute hike, but the hotel will shuttle you up and back if you don't feel like walking. You can take the hotel's small "canopy tour," which leaves from just below the small exercise room and ends just steps from the beach. There's a rancho bar and grill down there for when you get hungry or thirsty, and a new lap pool for when the waves are too rough. Recent improvements here include beefed-up spa services and facilities and a few new villas.

Although most guests opt to fly into the nearby airstrip, it's possible to drive here. Punta Islita is just two beaches south of Sámara. If you do drive, it's best to come over on the new Tempisque River bridge, follow the directions to Playa Sámara, and continue south.

Playa Islita (A.P. 242-1225, Plaza Mayor, San José), Guanacaste. ℂ 231-6122. Fax 231-0715. www. hotelpuntaislita.com. 32 units, 8 villas. $198–$275 double; $330–$385 suite; $450–$700 villa. Rates include breakfast. AE, MC, V. **Amenities:** 2 restaurants; bar; small tile pool and lap pool; driving range; 2 tennis courts; small spa and exercise room; Jacuzzi; watersports equipment, bike, horse, and 4×4 rentals; game room; free beach shuttle; tour desk; in-room massage; laundry service. *In room:* A/C, TV, minibar, coffeemaker, hair dryer, safe.

DINING & AFTER-DARK DIVERSIONS

There are numerous inexpensive *sodas* in Sámara, and most of the hotels have their own dining rooms. If you want to eat overlooking the water, check out either **El Ancla** or **El Delfín** for seafood and Tico cuisine. These two places are right next to each other on the beach, a little bit to the left (or south) of where the main road dead-ends at the beach. For Italian cuisine, check out the new **Terra Nostra,** next to the soccer field.

After dark, the most happening place in town is **La Góndola Bar,** which has a pool table, dartboards, and board games. Still, my favorite evening activity is walking the long, wide expanse of beach and watching the stars.

Las Brasas ☆ SPANISH/SEAFOOD This two-story, open-air affair serves authentic Spanish cuisine and well-prepared fresh seafood. The whole fish *a la catalana* is excellent, as is the paella, but my favorite dish here is the gazpacho Andaluz, a refreshing lunch choice on a hot afternoon. There's a good selection of Spanish wines, a rarity in Costa Rica. Service is attentive yet informal.

On the main road into Sámara, about 90m (295 ft.) before the beach. ℂ 656-0546. Reservations recommended in the high season. Main courses $7–$20. V. Daily noon–11pm. Closed Mon in the off season.

10 Playa Tambor

150km–168km (93–104 miles) W of San José (not including ferry ride); 20km (12 miles) S of Paquera; 38km (24 miles) S of Naranjo

Playa Tambor itself is a long scimitar of beach protected on either end by rocky headlands. These headlands give the waters a certain amount of protection from Pacific swells, making this a good beach for swimming. This beach and the two hotels listed below were chosen as the prime locations for Fox television's *Temptation Island 2*. However, the sand is a rather hard-packed, dull gray-brown color, which often receives a large amount of flotsam and jetsam brought in by the sea. I find this beach much less attractive than those located farther south along the Nicoya Peninsula. There has been a bit of development here, with Costa Rica's first all-inclusive beach resort, the Barceló Playa Tambor Beach Resort, which opened in 1993, followed by a sister condominium project and a nine-hole golf course. But despite this development, the Tambor has a forgotten, isolated feel.

Both the hotels listed below offer horseback riding and tours around this part of the peninsula and can arrange dive trips.

Curú Wildlife Refuge ★, 16km (10 miles) north of Tambor (© **710-8236**), is a private reserve that has several pretty, secluded beaches, as well as forests and mangrove swamps. This area is extremely rich in wildlife. Howler and white-faced monkeys are often spotted here, as are quite a few species of birds. Admission for the day is $6 per person. There are some rustic cabins available with advance notice for around $30 per person per day, including the entrance and three square meals. If you don't have a car, you should arrange pickup with the folks who manage this refuge. Or, you could hire a taxi in Paquera to take you there for around $6.

ESSENTIALS

GETTING THERE & DEPARTING By Plane Sansa (© **221-9414;** www.flysansa.com) flies twice daily to Tambor from San José's Juan Santamaría International Airport at 10:25am and 4:25pm. These flights depart for San José at 11am and 5:05pm. Flight duration is 30 minutes; the fare is $58 each way.

Nature Air (© **220-3054;** www.natureair.com) flies to Tambor daily at 8:30am and 1pm from Tobías Bolaños International Airport in Pavas. Flight duration is 30 minutes; the fare is $66 each way. The return flights leave at 9:10am and 1:40pm.

By Car The traditional route here is to take the Interamerican Highway from San José to Puntarenas and catch the ferry to either Naranjo or Paquera. Tambor is about 45 minutes south of Paquera and 2 hours south of Naranjo. The road from Paquera to Tambor was upgraded when the resort was built, and taking the Paquera ferry will save you time and some rough, dusty driving. The road from Naranjo to Paquera is all dirt and gravel and in very bad shape.

Two companies are running a car ferry between Puntarenas and Paquera, and this has eased some of the load. However, I still recommend arriving early during the peak season and on weekends because lines can be quite long; if you miss the next ferry, you'll have to wait around 2 hours or more for the next one. **Ferries to Paquera** (Naviera Tambor: © **661-2084;** Paquera Ferry: © **641-0515**) leave roughly every 2 hours between 5am and 8:15pm. The trip takes 1½ hours. The fare is around $10 for a car and driver, $1.50 for additional adults,

$4 for adults in first class, $1 for children, and $2 for children in first class. The ferry schedule changes frequently, with extra ferries often added to meet demand. It is always best to check in advance.

The **Naranjo ferry** (*©* **661-1069**) leaves daily at 3, 7, and 10:50am, and 2:50 and 7pm. The trip takes 1½ hours. The fare is $12 for cars, $2 for adults, and 75¢ for children.

However, following the opening of the Tempisque River bridge, there is another option. Although heading farther north and crossing the bridge is more circuitous, you will be driving the whole time, which is quite a bit faster than taking a seaborne ferry. Moreover, you will not be at the whim of the ferry schedule and the sometimes sold-out boats. To go this route, take the Interamerican Highway west from San José. Forty-seven kilometers (29 miles) past the turnoff for Puntarenas, turn left for the Tempisque River bridge. After you cross the Tempisque River, head to Quebrada Honda and then south to route 21, following signs for San Pablo, Jicaral, Lepanto, Playa Naranjo, and Paquera. This route is recommended if you foresee waiting more than 2 hours for a ferry.

The car ferry from Paquera to Puntarenas leaves roughly every 2 hours between 6am and 9pm.

By Bus & Ferry   If you're traveling from San José by public transportation, it takes two buses and a ferry ride to get to Tambor.

Express buses (*©* **222-0064**) leave for Puntarenas from San José daily every 30 minutes between 6am and 9pm from Calle 16 and Avenida 12. Trip duration is 2½ hours; the fare is $3.

From Puntarenas, you can take one of the car ferries mentioned above or the passenger launch *Paquereña* (*©* **641-0515**), which leaves from the pier behind the market at 6:30 and 10:30am, and 3:30pm. Ferry-trip duration is 1½ hours; the fare is $2. A bus south to Montezuma (this will drop you off in Tambor) will be waiting to meet the ferry when it arrives in Paquera. The bus ride takes about 45 minutes; the fare is $2. Be careful not to take the Naranjo ferry because it does not meet with regular onward bus transportation to Tambor.

When you're ready to head back, the Paquera bus, which originates in Montezuma, passes through Tambor at approximately 6, 9, and 11am, and 12:45, 3, and 5pm to meet the various ferries heading to Puntarenas. The Paquereña ferry returns for Puntarenas at 8:30am, and 1 and 5pm. Total trip duration is 3½ hours. Buses to San José leave Puntarenas daily every 30 minutes between 5:30am and 8pm.

ORIENTATION   Although there's a small village of Tambor, through which the main road passes, the hotels themselves are scattered along several kilometers. You'll see signs for these hotels as the road circles around Playa Tambor.

WHERE TO STAY

Aside from the hotels listed here, there are a few inexpensive *cabinas* available near the town of Tambor, at the southern end of the beach. Of these, your best bet is **Hotel Dos Largatos** (*©*/fax **683-0236**), located right on the beach next to Tambor Tropical.

The **Barceló Playa Tambor Beach Resort** was Costa Rica's first all-inclusive resort, but its beach is mediocre, at best, and the Barceló company has been accused of violating Costa Rica's environmental laws, ignoring zoning regulations, and mistreating workers. So although this resort is a major presence here, I don't recommend it; there are much better all-inclusive options available farther north in Guanacaste.

Tambor Tropical This is one of the more architecturally interesting hotels around. The rooms here are located in five two-story octagonal cabins, and the whole place is an orgy of varnished hardwoods, with purpleheart and cocobolo offsetting each other at every turn. The rooms are enormous and come with large, complete kitchens and a spacious sitting area. The walls are, in effect, nothing but shuttered picture windows, which give you the choice of gazing out at the ocean or shutting in for a bit of privacy. The upstairs rooms have large wraparound verandas, and the lower rooms have garden-level decks. The beach is only steps away. Plenty of coconut palms and flowering plants provide a very tropical feel.

Tambor, Puntarenas (mailing address: 867 Liberty St. NE, Salem, OR 97301). ⓒ **866/890-2537** in the U.S., or 683-0011 in Costa Rica. Fax 683-0013. www.tambortropical.com. 10 units. $150–$175 double. Rates include continental breakfast. AE, MC, V. No children under 16. **Amenities:** Restaurant; bar; small free-form tile pool and Jacuzzi; tour desk; laundry service. *In room:* Kitchenette, fridge, coffeemaker, iron, no phone.

Tango Mar Resort Tango Mar was *the* original luxury resort in this neck of the woods, and it's still a great place to get away from it all. With only 18 rooms and scattered suites and villas, there are never any crowds. The water is wonderfully clear, and the beach is fronted by coconut palms and luxuriant lawns. If you choose to go exploring, you'll find seaside cliffs and a beautiful nearby waterfall that pours into a tide pool. The hotel rooms all have big balconies and glass walls to soak up the ocean views; some even have their own Jacuzzis. The suites are set back among shade trees and flowering vegetation. Most come with carved four-poster canopy beds and indoor Jacuzzis. The villas are all different, but all are spacious and relatively secluded. Some of the suites and villas are a bit far from the beach and main hotel, so you'll need either your own car or one of the hotel's gas-powered golf carts. The suites closest to the beach are the five octagonal Tiki suites. The newest addition here is a small spa and yoga space above the main lodge and reception area.

Playa Tambor, Puntarenas. ⓒ **683-0001.** Fax 683-0003. www.tangomar.com. 18 units, 17 suites, 3 villas. $165 double; $165–$210 suite; $450–$1,000 villa. Rates include breakfast. Rates slightly lower during the off season, higher during peak weeks. AE, DC, MC, V. **Amenities:** Restaurant; bar; 3 small pools; 9-hole par-3 golf course ($25 full-day greens fee) w/wonderful sea views; 2 lighted tennis courts; limited watersports equipment rental; bike rental; tour desk; limited room service; in-room massage; laundry service. *In room:* A/C, TV, minibar, safe.

11 Playa Montezuma

166km–184km (103–114 miles) W of San José (not including the ferry ride); 36km (22 miles) SE of Paquera; 54km (33 miles) S of Naranjo

For years, Montezuma has enjoyed near-legendary status among backpackers, UFO seekers, hippie expatriates, and European budget travelers. Although it still maintains its alternative vibe, Montezuma is a great destination for all manner of travelers looking for a quiet beach retreat surrounded by some stunning scenery. Today the town has a well-tended, somewhat booming feel to it, and there are lodgings of value and quality in all price ranges. After all, it's the natural beauty, miles of almost abandoned beaches, rich wildlife, and jungle waterfalls that first made Montezuma famous, and they continue to make this one of my favorite beach towns in Costa Rica.

ESSENTIALS

GETTING THERE & DEPARTING   By Plane   The nearest airport is in Tambor, 17km (11 miles) away (see "Playa Tambor," above, for flight details). Some of the hotels listed below might be willing to pick you up in Tambor for a reasonable fee. If not, you'll have to hire a taxi, which could cost anywhere between $10 and $20. **Taxis** are generally waiting to meet most regularly scheduled planes, but if they aren't, you can call Gilberto Rodríguez (© **642-0241**) for a cab.

By Car   The traditional route here is to take the Interamerican Highway from San José to Puntarenas and catch the ferry to either Naranjo or Paquera. Montezuma is about 50 minutes south of Tambor, 1½ hours south of Paquera, and 2¾ hours south of Naranjo. The road from Paquera to Tambor is paved, and taking the Paquera ferry will save you time and some rough, dusty driving. The road from Naranjo to Paquera is all dirt and gravel and is in very bad shape.

Two companies are running a car ferry between Puntarenas and Paquera, and this has eased some of the load. However, I still recommend arriving early during the peak season and on weekends because lines can be quite long; if you miss the next ferry, you'll have to wait around 2 hours or more for the next one. **Ferries to Paquera** (Naviera Tambor: © **661-2084;** Paquera Ferry: © **641-0515**) leave roughly every 2 hours between 5am and 8:15pm. The trip takes 1½ hours. The fare is around $10 for a car and driver, $1.50 for additional adults, $4 for adults in first class, $1 for children, and $2 for children in first class. The ferry schedule changes frequently, with extra ferries often added to meet demand. It is always best to check in advance.

The **Naranjo ferry** (© **661-1069**) leaves daily at 3, 7, and 10:50am, and 2:50 and 7pm. The trip takes 1½ hours. The fare is $12 for cars, $2 for adults, and 75¢ for children.

However, with the opening of the Tempisque River bridge, there is another option. Although heading farther north and crossing the bridge is more circuitous, you will be driving the whole time, which is quite a bit faster than taking a seaborne ferry. Moreover, you will not be at the whim of the ferry schedule and the sometimes sold-out boats. To go this route, take the Interamerican Highway west from San José. Forty-seven kilometers (29 miles) past the turnoff for Puntarenas, turn left for the Tempisque River bridge. After you cross the Tempisque River, head to Quebrada Honda and then south to route 21, following signs for San Pablo, Jicaral, Lepanto, Playa Naranjo, and Paquera. This route is recommended if you foresee waiting more than 2 hours for a ferry.

The car ferry from Paquera to Puntarenas leaves roughly every 2 hours between 6am and 9pm.

By Bus & Ferry   If you're traveling from San José by public transportation, it takes two buses and a ferry ride to get to Montezuma.

Express buses (© **222-0064**) leave for Puntarenas from San José daily every 30 minutes between 6am and 9pm from Calle 16 and Avenida 12. Trip duration is 2½ hours; the fare is $3.

From Puntarenas, you can take one of the car ferries mentioned above or the passenger launch *Paquereña* (© **641-0515**), which leaves from the pier behind the market at 6:30 and 10:30am, and 3:30pm. Ferry-trip duration is 1½ hours; the fare is $2. The bus south to Montezuma will be waiting to meet the ferry when it arrives in Paquera. The bus ride takes 1½ hours; the fare is $3. Be careful not to take the Naranjo ferry because it does not meet with regular onward bus transportation to Montezuma.

Buses these days are met by hordes of locals trying to corral you to one of the many budget hotels. Remember, they are getting a commission for every body they bring in, so their information is biased.

When you're ready to return, buses for Paquera leave Montezuma daily at 5:30, 8:15, and 10am; noon; and 2 and 4pm to connect with the various ferries back to Puntarenas. The Paquereña ferry leaves for Puntarenas at 8:30am and 1 and 5pm. Buses to San José leave Puntarenas daily every 30 minutes between 5:30am and 8pm.

ORIENTATION   As the winding mountain road that descends into Montezuma bottoms out, you turn left onto a small dirt road that defines the village proper. On this 1-block road, you will find El Sano Banano Village Cafe and, across from it, a small park with its own brand-new basketball court and children's playground. The bus stops at the end of this road. From here, hotels are scattered up and down the beach and around the village's few sand streets. If you're looking for Internet access, try the high-speed satellite connections offered at El Sano Banano's Internet cafe.

FUN ON & OFF THE BEACH

In Montezuma, mostly you just hang out at the beach, at a restaurant, at a bar, or in a hammock. The ocean here is a gorgeous royal blue, and beautiful beaches stretch out along the coast on either side of town. Be careful, though: The waves can occasionally be too rough for casual swimming, and you need to be aware of stray rocks at your feet. Be sure you know where the rocks and tide are before doing any bodysurfing. The best places to swim are a couple hundred meters north of town in front of **El Rincón de los Monos,** or several kilometers farther north at Playa Grande.

If you're interested in more than just hanging out, head for the **waterfall** 🏵 just south of town—it's one of those tropical fantasies where water comes pouring down into a deep pool. It's a popular spot, but it's a bit of a hike up the stream. There are actually a couple of waterfalls up this stream, but the upper falls are by far the more spectacular. You'll find the trail to the falls just over the bridge south of the village (on your right just past Las Cascadas restaurant). At the first major outcropping of rocks, the trail disappears and you have to scramble up the rocks and river for a bit. A trail occasionally reappears for short stretches. Just stick close to the stream, and you'll eventually hit the falls.

HORSEBACK RIDING   Several people around the village will rent you horses for around $8 to $10 an hour, although most people choose to do a guided 4-hour horseback tour for $30 to $40. The longer rides usually go to a second waterfall 8km (5 miles) north of Montezuma. Dubbed **El Chorro** 🏵🏵, this waterfall cascades straight down into a deep tide pool at the edge of the ocean. The pool here is a delightful mix of fresh- and seawater, and you can bathe while gazing out over the sea and rocky coastline. When the water is clear and calm, this is one of my favorite swimming holes in all of Costa Rica. However, the pool here is dependent upon the tides—it disappears entirely at very high tide. Luis, whose rental place is down the road that leads from town out to the beach, is a reliable source for horses, as is "Roger the horse guy"—any local can direct you to him. However, you'll find the best-cared-for and -kept horses at **Finca Los Caballos** 🏵 (✆ **642-0124**), which is located up the hill on the road leading into Montezuma.

Tips **Buy the Book . . . or Just Borrow It**

If you came unprepared or run out of reading material, check in at **Librería Topsy** (✆ **642-0576**), which, in addition to selling books, runs a lending library.

OTHER ACTIVITIES   There are some rental shops in the center of the village where you can rent a bicycle by the day or hour, as well as boogie boards and snorkeling equipment (although the water must be very calm for snorkeling).

A range of guided tour and adventure options is available in Montezuma. **Cocozuma Traveler** (© 642-0911; www.cocozuma.com) and **Montezuma Travel Adventures** (© 823-6111; www. montezumatraveladventures.com) can both arrange horseback riding, boat tours, and rafting trips; car and motorcycle rentals; airport transfers; international phone, fax, and Internet service; and currency exchange.

Cabo Blanco Divers (©/fax 642-0482; www.caboblancodivers.com) has set up shop across the street from Chico's Bar and offers most of the same tours as the places mentioned above, as well as diving trips and certification classes. One of the more popular excursions is a day trip to Tortuga Island ($40, including lunch). Most hotels can also arrange most of these tours and services.

You might want to stop and visit the **Solera Botanical Gardens** (© 642-0469). You can spend a very pleasant hour or so strolling through the gardens (essentially a nursery) and admiring the tropical flora. This place is located a bit outside of Cóbano, on the way to Tambor. Admission is $3.

One popular new tour option here is the **Waterfall Canopy Tour** (★ (© 823-6111), which is built right alongside Montezuma's famous falls. The tour, which features 9 cables connecting 11 platforms, includes a swim at the foot of the falls and costs $30 per person.

AN EXCURSION TO CABO BLANCO NATURE RESERVE

As beautiful as the beaches around Montezuma are, the beaches at **Cabo Blanco Absolute Nature Reserve** ★★, 11km (6¾ miles) south of the village, are even more stunning. Located at the southernmost tip of the Nicoya Peninsula, Cabo Blanco is a national park that preserves a nesting site for brown pelicans, magnificent frigate birds, and brown boobies. The beaches are backed by lush tropical forest that is home to howler monkeys. You can hike through the preserve's lush forest right down to the deserted, pristine beach, which is 4km (2½ miles) away. Or, you can take a shorter 2km (1¼-mile) loop trail through the primary forest here. This is Costa Rica's oldest official bioreserve and was set up thanks to the pioneering efforts of conservationists Karen Mogensen and Nicholas Wessberg. Admission is $6; the reserve is closed on Monday and Tuesday.

On your way out to Cabo Blanco, you'll pass through the tiny village of **Cabuya.** Some very basic *cabinas* and hotels have sprung up out here, and there are a couple of hidden patches of beach to discover if you poke around some of the deserted dirt roads.

Shuttle buses head from Montezuma to Cabo Blanco roughly every 2 hours beginning at 8am, and then turn around and bring folks from Cabo Blanco to Montezuma; the last one leaves Cabo Blanco around 4pm. The fare is $2 each way. These shuttles usually don't run during the low season. Alternatively, you can share a taxi: The fare is around $12 per taxi, which can hold four or five passengers. Taxis tend to hang around Montezuma center. One dependable *taxista* is **Gilberto Rodríguez** (© 642-0241).

WHERE TO STAY

In addition to the places listed below, the **Hotel El Jardín** (© 642-0548; www.hoteleljardin.com), located right at the crossroads to town at the bottom of the hill, has recently upgraded its rooms and added a swimming pool. The rooms here are spread up a steep hillside, and some require a short but vigorous hike to reach.

MODERATE

Amor de Mar ✶   It would be difficult to imagine a more idyllic spot in this price range—or in *any* price range. With its wide expanse of neatly trimmed grass sloping down to the sea, tide pools (one of which is as big as a small swimming pool), and hammocks slung from the mango trees, this is the perfect place for anyone who wants to do some serious relaxing. The rooms are all housed in a beautifully appointed two-story building, which abounds in varnished hardwoods. Most of the rooms have plenty of space and receive lots of sunlight. The big porch on the second floor is a great place for reading or just gazing out to sea. Only breakfast and lunch are served here, but they are served on a beautiful open-air patio overlooking the sea. The breakfast specialties include big banana pancakes and fresh homemade whole-wheat French bread.

Montezuma, Cóbano de Puntarenas. ©/fax 642-0262. www.amordemar.com. 11 units, 9 with private bathroom. $35–$45 double with shared bathroom; $55–$80 double with private bathroom. Rates lower in the off season. V (7% surcharge). **Amenities:** Restaurant; laundry service. *In room:* No phone.

El Sano Banano Beach Resort ✶✶ *(Finds*   This place is the sort of tropical retreat many travelers dream about finding. Set in a lush patch of forest just steps away from the sand, the hotel offers rooms that are about a 15-minute walk northeast of town along the beach. (*Note:* Don't try to drive up the beach, even if you have a 4WD vehicle—seclusion and quiet are the main offerings of this place, and cars would ruin the atmosphere. If you don't want to carry all your bags, the hotel staff will be pleased to bring them to your room.) Coco Joe's Rancho is the largest cabin and features a luscious wraparound balcony and a small sleeping loft. But I also like the smaller cabins, which are yellow ferroconcrete geodesic domes that look like igloos. Some of the showers are outdoor garden affairs, which match the surroundings perfectly. There are also three spacious suites with private balconies and sleeping lofts in a separate building, with three standard rooms on the ground floor below them. Many guests opt for extended stays. There's a beautiful little swimming pool with a sculpted waterfall, and the whole operation is set amid lush gardens planted with lots of banana, heliconia, and elephant-ear plants.

These folks also run an in-town B&B, located just off their popular restaurant (see below). The rooms here feature air-conditioning and satellite televisions; because of the design, you are basically forced to use the air-conditioning.

Montezuma, Cóbano de Puntarenas. © 642-0638. Fax 642-0631. www.elbanano.com. 15 units, 8 bungalows, 3 suites. $55 double in-town; $105 double beach room; $130–$150 bungalow or suite; $180 Coco Joe's Rancho. Rates in town include full breakfast; rates at the beach resort include breakfast and dinner. Rates lower in the off season. AE, MC, V. **Amenities:** 2 restaurants (1 in town, about a 15-min. walk away; p. 201); tour desk; in-room massage; laundry service. *In room:* Fridge, coffeemaker, safe, no phone.

Nature Lodge Finca Los Caballos ✶   This remote lodge is located on a high ridge about 3km (1¾ miles) above Montezuma. The rooms are in two separate concrete-block buildings. Each room has one double or one double and one single bed, a private bathroom, and polished cement floors. Spanish-style tile roofs, hardwood trim, and some nice paintings add accents. I prefer the end rooms of each building because they have open gables (screened, of course) that allow for more cross ventilation. Every room has a small patio, and there are plenty of hammocks strung around. There's a small pool here, with a wonderful view of rolling hills down to the Pacific Ocean. The restaurant serves creative, well-prepared meals using fresh and natural ingredients.

Finca Los Caballos translates to "horse ranch," and riding is taken seriously here. The owners have 16 hectares (40 acres) of land and access to many neighboring ranches and trail systems. The horses are well tended and trained. The standard trips to Montezuma's waterfalls are available, as are a host of other adventure-tour options.

Cóbano de Puntarenas (A.P. 22). ℂ 642-0664 or ℂ/fax 642-0124. www.naturelodge.net. 8 units, 1 apt. $57–$70 double. V. **Amenities:** Restaurant; small pool; tour desk; laundry service. *In room:* No phone.

INEXPENSIVE

Now that camping on the beach is discouraged (although many folks still get away with it), most campers make do at **El Rincón de los Monos** (ℂ 642-0048), which is about 90m (295 ft.) north of town along the beach. It charges about $3 per tent and provides showers and bathrooms. Others head south toward Cabuya and Cabo Blanco. **El Pargo Feliz** (ℂ 642-0064) and **Cabinas Mar y Cielo** (ℂ 642-0261) are two good budget options right in the center of town.

Hotel La Aurora   Just to the left as you enter the village of Montezuma, you'll find this longstanding budget hotel. The rooms are spread out over two neighboring buildings fronting the village's small park and playground. The newer rooms here are clean and modern but have a tad less character than the older rooms, which are located in a spacious three-story wooden building. There's even a two-room apartment on the third floor here, with a private balcony and a bit of an ocean view through the treetops. The hotel also features a small lending library, some hammocks and comfortable chairs, a communal kitchen, and flowering vines growing up the walls. In fact, there are plants and vines all over La Aurora, which keeps things cool and gives the place a fitting tropical feel. Fresh coffee, tea, and hearty breakfasts are served each morning.

Montezuma (A.P. 2), Cóbano de Puntarenas. ℂ/fax 642-0051. hotelaurora@racsa.co.cr. 16 units, 13 with private bathroom. $21 double with shared bathroom; $30–$50 double with bathroom. Rates lower in the off season. AE, MC, V. **Amenities:** Laundry service. *In room:* No phone.

Hotel Los Mangos   Situated across the road from the water a bit before the waterfall on the road toward Cabo Blanco, this place takes its name from the many mango trees under which the bungalows are built. (If mango is your passion, come in May, when it's in season.) The rooms are fairly basic, but they are a good value and you get access to the pool, to boot. However, the octagonal bungalows built of Costa Rican hardwoods are the nicest accommodations here. Each has a small porch with rocking chairs, a thatched roof, a good amount of space, and ceiling fans. The swimming pool is built to resemble a natural pond—there's even an artificial waterfall flowing into it—and there's a separate Jacuzzi. The old restaurant here has been converted into a yoga studio, and daily yoga classes are offered.

Montezuma, Cóbano de Puntarenas. ℂ 642-0076. Fax 642-0259. www.hotellosmangos.com. 10 units, 6 with private bathroom; 9 bungalows. $30 double with shared bathroom; $60 double with private bathroom; $70 bungalow. Rates lower in the off season. V. **Amenities:** Small pool; Jacuzzi; laundry service. *In room:* No phone.

Hotel Lucy *(Value*   Situated on a pretty section of beach a bit south of town, in front of Los Mangos, this converted two-story home has the best location of any budget lodging in Montezuma. If you can snag a second-floor room with an ocean view, you'll be in budget heaven. A recent remodeling has even spruced things up a bit and added some rooms with private bathrooms. The beach here is a bit rough and rocky for swimming, but the sunbathing and sunsets are beautiful. There's a small restaurant here serving Tico standards and fresh seafood at very reasonable prices all day long.

Montezuma, Cóbano de Puntarenas. (C) 642-0273. 16 units, 7 with bathroom. $12 double with shared bathroom; $20 double with private bathroom. No credit cards. **Amenities:** Restaurant; laundry service. *In room:* No phone.

WHERE TO DINE

In addition to the places listed below, you'll find several basic *sodas* and casual restaurants right in the village. My favorite of these is the simple **Restaurante Lucy,** which has a few tables set on the sand a few feet from the ocean, right next to the Hotel Lucy. There's also **Pizzería Angulo Etrusco,** which is located at the crossroads into town and serves good thin-crust pizzas, calzones, and pastas.

El Sano Banano Village Cafe ★★ VEGETARIAN/INTERNATIONAL Delicious vegetarian meals, including nightly specials, sandwiches, and salads, are the specialty of this ever-popular Montezuma restaurant, although there's also a variety of fish and chicken dishes. Lunches feature hefty sandwiches on whole-wheat bread, pita pizzas, and filling fish and vegetarian *casados* for around $5. The yogurt fruit shakes are fabulous, but I like to get a little more decadent and have one of the mocha shakes.

El Sano Banano also doubles as the local movie house. Nightly DVD releases are projected on a large screen; the selection ranges from first-run to quite artsy, and there's a constantly growing library of more than 800 movies. The movies begin at 7:30pm and require a minimum purchase of $5.

On the main road into the village. (C) 642-0638. Main courses $5–$14. AE, MC, V. Daily 7am–9:30pm.

Las Cascadas COSTA RICAN/SPANISH This little open-air restaurant is built on the banks of the stream just outside of the village, and it takes its name from the nearby waterfalls. The owners are Catalans, and the menu features plenty of Spanish and Catalan classics, including *gazpacho, zarzuela,* and *paella.* A standout opener is the salad of avocado, hearts of palm, and home-smoked, locally caught tuna. For entrees, I'd stick to the fresh fish, although there are some meat dishes and even a few vegetarian options. Be sure to finish things off with the crema Catalan, the Spanish take on crème brûlée. This is one of the more enjoyable places in Montezuma to have a meal—you can sit for hours beneath the thatched roof listening to the stream rushing past.

On the road out of town toward Cabo Blanco. (C) 642-0057. Main courses $4–$17. V. Daily 7am–10pm.

Playa de los Artistas ★★ *Finds* ITALIAN/MEDITERRANEAN This popular open-air restaurant is beside an old house fronting the beach, and there are only a few tables, so arrive early. If you don't get a seat and you feel hearty, try the low wooden table surrounded by tatami mats on the sand. Meals are served in large, broad wooden bowls set on ceramic-ringed coasters and come with plenty of fresh bread for soaking up the sauces. The menu changes nightly but always features several fish dishes. The fresh grouper in a black-pepper sauce is phenomenal. The new outdoor grill is great for grilled fish and seafood.

Across from Hotel Los Mangos. (C) 642-0920. Reservations recommended. Main courses $7–$21. No credit cards. Mon–Sat 5–10:30pm.

MONTEZUMA AFTER DARK

Montezuma has had a tough time coming to terms with its nightlife. For years, local businesses had banded together to force most of the loud, late-night activity out of town. This has eased somewhat, and there's currently quite an active nightlife in Montezuma proper. The local action seems to base itself either at **Chico's Bar** or at the bar at the **Hotel Moctezuma.** Both are located on the main strip in town facing the water. For real raging nightlife, some folks head to the large disco at the **Barceló Playa Tambor Beach Resort,** located on the main road between Paquera and Cobano, about 20km (12 miles) south of Paquera and about 16km (10 miles) north of Montezuma. Playa Tambor Beach Resort has even been known to offer free round-trip taxi service to lure partiers. If your evening tastes are mellower, **El Sano Banano Village Cafe** (p. 201) doubles as the local movie house.

12 Malpais/Santa Teresa ★★

150km (93 miles) W of San José; 12km (7½ miles) S of Cóbano

Malpais (or Mal País) translates as "badlands," and I can't decide whether this is an accurate description or a deliberate local ploy to keep this place private—if the latter, it has officially failed. The beach here is a long, wide expanse of light sand dotted with rocky outcroppings. Sure, it can get rough here, but the surfers seem to like it. The road out here from Cóbano used to be even rougher than the surf, but it's gradually being tamed. This place is Costa Rica's hottest new hot spot, and hotels and restaurants are opening up at an increasing pace. Still, it should take some time before this area becomes yesterday's news. What you'll find in Malpais and Santa Teresa today is a scattering of beach hotels and simple restaurants, miles of nearly deserted beach, and easy access to some nice jungle and the nearby **Cabo Blanco Reserve** (p. 198).

If you decide to do anything here besides sunbathe on the beach and play in the waves, your options include nature hikes, horseback riding, and scuba diving and snorkeling, which most hotels can help arrange.

ESSENTIALS

GETTING THERE & DEPARTING   By Car   Follow the directions above to Montezuma (see "Playa Montezuma," earlier in this chapter). At Cóbano, follow the signs to Malpais and Playa Santa Teresa. It's another 12km (7½ miles) or so down a very rough dirt road that pretty much requires four-wheel drive year-round and is sometimes impassable during the rainy season. However, if you're heading out this way, check with your hotel because there are perennial rumors that this road might someday be paved.

By Bus & Ferry   Follow the directions above for getting to Montezuma, but get off the Montezuma bus in Cóbano. From Cóbano, there are buses daily for Malpais and Santa Teresa at 10:30am and 1:30pm (the fare is $1.50). Buses return daily to Cóbano at 7 and 11:45am. *Be forewarned:* These bus schedules are subject to change according to demand, road conditions, and the whim of the bus company. Moreover, as the popularity of this destination grows, more buses are occasionally added, so it pays to check with your hotel in advance.

If you miss the bus connection, you can hire a cab for around $12.

ORIENTATION   Malpais and Santa Teresa are two tiny beach villages. As you reach the ocean, the road forks; Playa Carmen is straight ahead, Malpais is to your left, and Santa Teresa is to your right. If you continue beyond Santa Teresa, you'll come to the even more deserted beaches of Playa Hermosa and Manzanillo (not to be confused with beaches of the same names to be found elsewhere in the country).

FUN ON & OFF THE BEACH

Surfing is the main draw here, but as the area opens to a broader range of tourists, a whole host of activities is also becoming available. Still, if you want to rent a board or take a lesson, check out the **Santa Teresa Surf School** (© 640-0106; www.santateresasurfschool.com).

If you want to go scuba diving, contact **Pacific Divers** (© 640-0187; www.pacificdivers-costarica.com), which offers daily boat dives into the rich waters off the Cabo Blanco reserve.

You can also try a canopy adventure here at **Canopy del Pacífico** (© 640-0071), which is located toward the southern end of Malpais and inland. A 2-hour tour over the nearly 1km (½ mile) of cables touches down on eight platforms, features two rappels, and offers good views of both the forest and the ocean below. The cost is $35.

If the waves aren't happening, or if you just want to complement your new-found surfing skills with some linguistic maneuvering, contact the folks at the **Santa Teresa Beach Spanish School** (© 640-0049), who run week-long total immersion classes with or without lodging.

Finally, any hotel in the area can arrange a horseback riding–trip into the hills and along the beaches of this region, or a sportfishing excursion out onto the high seas.

WHERE TO STAY
VERY EXPENSIVE

Flor Blanca Resort ★★ *Finds*   This intimate resort hotel is, hands down, the most luxurious option in this neck of the woods and one of the most luxurious boutique hotels in the country. The individual villas are huge, with a vast central living area opening onto a spacious veranda. The furnishings, decorations, and architecture boast a mix of Latin American and Asian influences, with some African adornments thrown in for good measure. Most overlook the lush gardens here, and about half have views through these to the sea. Every unit features a large open-air bathroom with a garden shower and teardrop-shape tub set amid flowering tropical foliage. You can opt for either the one-bedroom villas with a four-poster king-size bed in the main bedroom, or a two-bedroom, two-bathroom villa better suited to families, with two twin beds in a separate upstairs bedroom. You'll find several examples of the resort's namesake tree planted around the grounds.

The restaurant here features wonderfully prepared creative fusion cuisine. There's a full-size and active dojo on grounds, where yoga, kickboxing, and cardio-workout classes are regularly offered. The free-form pool is on two levels, with a sculpted waterfall connecting them and a shady Indonesian-style gazebo off to one side for lounging around in. Flor Blanca is located toward the northern end of Playa Santa Teresa. The resort doesn't allow children under 6.

Playa Santa Teresa, Cóbano, Puntarenas. © 640-0232. Fax 640-0226. www.florblanca.com. 10 units. $290–$340 double; $490–$540 2-bedroom villa for 4. Rates include full breakfast. Rates lower during the off season, higher during peak weeks. AE, DC, MC, V. No children under 6. **Amenities:** Restaurant; bar; pool; small open-air gym; watersports equipment rental; bike rental; laundry service. *In room:* A/C, kitchenette, coffeemaker.

MODERATE

In addition to the hotel listed below, the four bungalows at **The Place** (©/fax 640-0001; www.theplacemalpais.com) are quite stylish and reasonably priced.

Trópico Latino Lodge 🏖️   One of the first hotels out here, this beachfront spread is still a good choice. The nicest accommodations here are the two new private bungalows, which have artistic tile work and finishings and views of the ocean. The original rooms here are housed in four duplex bungalows. These are huge—the king-size bamboo bed barely makes a dent in the floor space. There's also a separate sofa bed, as well as a small desk, a wall unit of shelves, and closet space galore. Although none of the older rooms has any ocean view to speak of, they all have private patios with a hammock. The shady grounds are rich in the native pochote tree, which is known for its spiky trunk. The small restaurant here has excellent fresh fish and plenty of pasta dishes, probably just to please the palate of the Italian owners. A wide range of tours and activities can be arranged, as can transport to Cóbano or the Tambor airport.

Playa Santa Teresa, Cóbano, Puntarenas. ✆ 640-0062. Fax 640-0117. www.hoteltropicolatino.com. 10 units. $85–$95 double. Rates lower in the off season. No credit cards. **Amenities:** Restaurant; bar; small free-form pool; Jacuzzi; laundry service. *In room:* A/C in some units, safe, no phone.

INEXPENSIVE

In addition to the hotels listed below, budget travelers can check out **Cabinas Bosque Mar** (✆ 640-0074), which is on the Malpais road and has a few basic rooms and has a swimming pool. You can also pitch a tent at several spots along the beaches here. Look for camping signs; you should get bathroom and shower access for a few bucks.

Frank's Place   Building on the perennial popularity of their long-standing restaurant, the folks here have added a hodge-podge of rooms in a variety of styles, price ranges, and configurations. Nine rooms are very basic and feature a shared bathroom; four units come with private bathrooms, a minifridge, and a tiny television set. Only four rooms here feature double beds, although a few come with complete kitchenettes, and some have air-conditioning. Although the midrange rooms are a decent value and the hotel is well located, I don't think the higher priced rooms here are worth it—you can certainly do better for the money. There's a small pool at the center of the complex, as well as an unheated Jacuzzi. The restaurant here is a glorified *soda,* but it does serve good Costa Rican cuisine, fresh fish, and a smattering of international dishes. It's also one of the most popular hangouts in Malpais. This place is located at the crossroads of Malpais and Playa Carmen, just as you enter town.

Malpais, Cóbano de Puntarenas. ✆/fax 640-0071. www.malpais.net. 23 units, 9 with shared bathroom. $24 double with shared bathroom; $28–$85 double with private bathroom. AE, MC, V. **Amenities:** Restaurant; bar; small pool; Jacuzzi; watersports equipment rental; bike rental; tour desk; laundry service. *In room:* No phone.

Mal País Surf Camp & Resort   There's a wide range of accommodations here, reflected in the equally wide range of prices. The most basic rooms are open-air ranchos with gravel floors, lathe-and-bamboo walls, bead curtains for a door, and shared bathrooms. From here, your options get progressively more comfortable, ranging from shared-bathroom bunk-bed rooms to new deluxe poolside villas, to private houses with all the amenities. You can also pitch a tent. There's a refreshing free-form tile pool in the center of the complex, and the large, open main lodge area serves as a combination restaurant, bar, lounge, and surfboard-storage area. There's satellite TV with surf videos playing most of the day, as well as pool, Ping-Pong, and foosball tables. As the name implies, this place is run by and caters to surfers. The overall vibe here is loose and funky, as it should be. The restaurant serves filling, fresh, and, at times, quite creative cuisine, depending on how accomplished the itinerant surf-chef-of-the-month is. Surf rentals, lessons, and video sessions are all available.

Malpais, Cóbano de Puntarenas. ©/fax **640-0061.** www.malpaissurfcamp.com. 16 units, 8 with shared bathroom. $20–$25 double with shared bathroom; $35–$65 double with private bathroom; $7 per person camping. AE, MC, V. **Amenities:** Restaurant; bar; midsize pool; small exercise room; watersports equipment rental; bike rental; game room; tour desk; babysitting; laundry service. *In room:* Safe, no phone.

WHERE TO DINE

In addition to the place listed below, you might try **La Bella Napoli** (© **640-0073**), a homey Italian restaurant located across the street from Cabinas Bosque Mar, or **Mary's** (© **640-0153**), which features wood-oven baked pizzas and is located toward the northern end of Malpais.

Finally, one of the best restaurants in town is the elegant **Nectar** (© **640-0232**), at the Flor Blanca Resort (p. 203).

Soda Piedra Mar *Finds* COSTA RICAN/SEAFOOD   This simple open-air restaurant is set on a rocky outcropping just steps away from the sea. The place is little more than a zinc-roofed shack that seems as if a stiff breeze would quickly level it. There are only a few tables here under the low roof; weather permitting, more tables are set in the sand under the sun or stars. The fare is simple, but the fish is guaranteed fresh, the portions are hearty, the lobster is very reasonably priced, and the setting and sunsets are wonderful.

On the beach in Malpais. © **640-0069.** Main courses $3–$12. No credit cards. Daily 7am–10pm.

6

The Northern Zone: Mountain Lakes, Cloud Forests & a Volcano

The northern zone, roughly defined as the area north of San José, between Guanacaste province on the west and the lowlands of the Caribbean coast on the east, is a naturalist's dream come true. Small, isolated lodges abound, and the sheer diversity of terrain, flora, and fauna is astounding. Slight changes in elevation create unique microclimates and ecosystems throughout the region. There are rainforests and cloud forests, jungle rivers, mountain lakes, lowland marshes, and an unbelievable wealth of birds and other wildlife.

In addition to its reputation for muddy hiking trails and crocodile-filled rivers, the northern zone claims one of the best windsurfing spots in the world (on **Lake Arenal** ★, which is free of crocodiles, by the way) and Costa Rica's most active volcano. **Arenal Volcano** ★★, when free of clouds, puts on spectacular nighttime light shows. Adding a touch of comfort to a visit to the northern zone are several hot springs and a variety of hotel options that vary in their levels of luxury.

1 Puerto Viejo de Sarapiquí ★

82km (51 miles) N of San José; 102km (63 miles) E of La Fortuna

The Sarapiquí region, named for the river that drains this area, lies at the foot of the Cordillera Central mountain range. To the west is the rainforest of **Braulio Carrillo National Park,** and to the east are **Tortuguero National Park** ★★ and **Barra del Colorado National Wildlife Refuge** ★. In between these protected areas lay thousands of acres of banana, pineapple, and palm plantations. Here you can see the great contradiction of Costa Rica: On the one hand, the country is known for its national parks, which preserve some of the largest tracts of rainforest left in Central America; on the other hand, nearly every acre of land outside of these parks, save a few private reserves, has been clear-cut and converted into plantations—and the cutting continues.

Within the remaining rainforest are several lodges that attract naturalists (both amateur and professional). Two of these lodges, La Selva and Rara Avis, have become well known for the research that's conducted on their surrounding reserves. Bird-watching and rainforest hikes are the primary attractions, but more adventure-oriented travelers will find plenty of activities available here, including canopy tours and boating and rafting trips along the Sarapiquí River.

ESSENTIALS

GETTING THERE & DEPARTING   By Car   The Guápiles Highway, which leads to the Caribbean coast, heads north out of downtown San José on Calle 3 before heading east. Turn north before reaching Guápiles on the road to

The Northern Zone

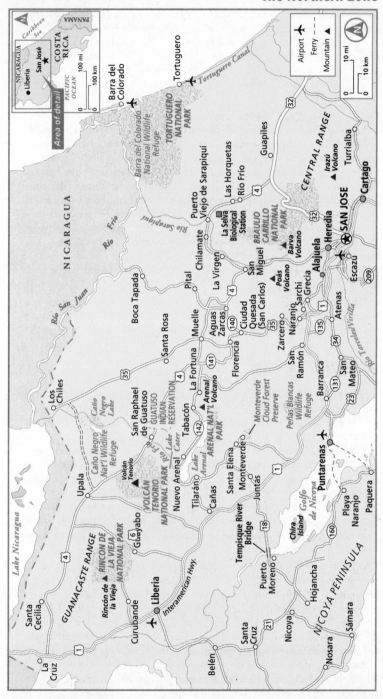

Río Frío, and continue north through Las Horquetas, passing the turnoffs for Rara Avis, La Selva, and El Gavilán lodges before reaching Puerto Viejo.

A more scenic route goes through Heredia, Barva, Varablanca, and San Miguel before reaching Puerto Viejo. This route passes very close to the Poás Volcano and directly in front of the La Paz waterfall. If you want to take this route, head west out of San José, and then turn north to Heredia and follow the signs for Varablanca.

By Bus   Buses (© 257-6854) leave San José roughly every hour between 6am and 6pm from the **Gran Terminal del Caribe,** on Calle Central, 1 block north of Avenida 11. The buses are marked RIO FRIO, PUERTO VIEJO, or both. There are two routes to Puerto Viejo de Sarapiquí. The faster route heads out on the Guápiles Highway, through Braulio Carrillo National Park and then past Las Horquetas. The slower but more scenic route heads out through Heredia, Varablanca, and La Virgen, passing between the Barva and Poás volcanoes. If you're heading to La Selva, Rara Avis, or El Gavilán lodges, be sure you're on a bus going through Braulio Carrillo and Las Horquetas. The trip takes between 2 and 4 hours, depending on the route taken, the condition of the roads, and the frequency of stops; the fare is around $2.50.

Buses for San José leave Puerto Viejo (© 766-6740) roughly every hour between 6am and 6pm.

ORIENTATION   Puerto Viejo is a small town, at the center of which is a soccer field. If you continue past the soccer field on the main road and stay on the paved road, and then turn right at the Banco Nacional, you'll come to the Río Sarapiquí and the dock, where you can look into arranging a boat trip.

WHAT TO SEE & DO

BOAT TRIPS   For the adventurous, Puerto Viejo is a jumping-off point for trips down the Río Sarapiquí to Barra del Colorado National Wildlife Refuge and Tortuguero National Park on the Caribbean coast. A boat for up to 10 people will cost you around $200 to $250 to Barra del Colorado, and $250 to $350 to Tortuguero. If you're interested in this trip, it's worth checking at your hotel or with **Oasis Nature Tours** (© 766-6108; www.oasisnaturetours.com). Alternatively, you can head down to the town dock on the bank of the Sarapiquí and see if you can arrange a less expensive boat trip on your own by tagging along with another group or, better yet, with a bunch of locals.

In addition to the longer trips, you can take shorter trips on the river for between $15 and $20 per person per hour. A trip down the Sarapiquí, even if it's for only an hour or two, provides opportunities to spot crocodiles, caimans, monkeys, sloths, and dozens of bird species.

RAFTING & KAYAKING   If you want a faster, wilder ride on the river, check in with **Aguas Bravas** (© 292-2072; www.aguas-bravas.co.cr) or **Aventuras del Sarapiquí** (© 766-6768; www.sarapiqui.com). Both companies run trips on a variety of sections of the Sarapiquí River, ranging from Class III to Class V. Trips cost between $50 and $75 per person. Both Aguas Bravas and Aventuras del Sarapiquí also run mountain-biking tours in the area, and they rent kayaks and offer kayak trips for more experienced and/or daring river rats.

Another option is to take a kayak trip with the folks at **Rancho Leona,** in La Virgen de Sarapiquí (© 841-5341; www.rancholeona.com). Rancho Leona is a small stained-glass workshop, kayaking center, and rustic guesthouse on the banks of the Río Sarapiquí in the village of La Virgen. Its trips are offered as a package that includes 2 nights of lodging in simple dormitory-style accommodations and an all-day kayak trip with some basic instruction and lunch on the river. The cost for the 2-day trip is $75 per person. No experience is necessary, and the river here is very calm. Trips for experienced kayakers can be arranged.

TWO MAJOR ATTRACTIONS EN ROUTE If you're driving to Puerto Viejo de Sarapiquí via the Guápiles Highway, you might want to stop at the **Aerial Tram** 🐸. You'll see the entrance to the Aerial Tram on your right shortly after passing through the Zurquí tunnel. If you're traveling via Varablanca and La Virgin, you'll want to visit the **La Paz Waterfall Gardens** 🐸🐸, which is right on the winding road to Puerto Viejo de Sarapiquí, about 6km (3¾ miles) beyond Varablaca. For more information, see "What to See & Do" and "Side Trips from San José," in chapter 4.

HIKING & GUIDED TOURS Anyone can take advantage of the 56km (35 miles) of well-maintained **trails at La Selva** (p. 211). If you're not staying there, however, you'll have to take a guided hike, led by experienced and well-informed naturalists. Half- and full-day hikes ($26 and $36, respectively) are offered daily, but you must reserve in advance (📞 **766-6565;** laselva@sloth. ots.ac.cr). The half-day tours leave at 8am and 1:30pm daily.

My favorite hike starts off with the Cantarrana ("singing frog") trail, which includes a section of low bridges over a rainforest swamp. From here, you can join up with either the near or far circular loop trails—**CCC** and **CCL.**

Another good hiking option are the trails and suspended bridges at the **Centro Neotrópico Sarapiquís** (p. 211).

Finally, if you want to visit the Sarapiquí region on a day trip from San José, call either **Costa Rica Fun Adventures** (📞 **290-6015;** www.crfunadventures.com) or **Ecoscapes Highlights Tour** (📞 **297-0664;** www.costaricasbesttour.com), which run jam-packed day trips up here that combine a bus ride and stop at the La Paz waterfall, a visit to a coffee farm, a rainforest hike, and a boat ride on the river for around $80 per person.

BUGGING OUT Located at the La Quinta de Sarapiquí Country Inn (p. 212), entomologist Richard Whitten's **Jewels of the Rainforest insect museum** is a lively, educational, and aesthetic display of part of his massive collection of insect species from around the world. The hotel also has a modest set of historical items and displays, a butterfly garden, and a frog farm. The $9 admission fee gets you into all of these attractions.

A NATURAL HISTORY THEME PARK IN THE MAKING The **Centro Neotrópico Sarapiquís** (p. 211) is working toward the creation of one of the most unique natural-history projects in the region. The Alma Ata Archaeological Park is basically an ongoing dig of a modest pre-Columbian gravesite; so far, 12 graves, some petroglyphs, and numerous pieces of ceramic and jewelry have been unearthed. Plans for the park include the reconstruction of a small indigenous village. The hotel also has a small museum that displays examples of the ceramics, tools, clothing, and carvings found here, as well as other natural-history exhibits. Just across the hotel's driveway, you'll find the Chester Field Biological Gardens, which feature well-tended and displayed examples of local medicinal and ornamental plants and herbs, as well as food crops. Admission to the archeological park, museum, and gardens costs $19. If you just want to visit the small archeological site, the cost is $7. A self-guided walk through the botanical gardens is free.

Across the Sarapiquí River from the Centro Neotrópico is the 300-hectare (741-acre) private **Tirimbina Biological Reserve** 🐸 (📞 **761-1579;** www. tirimbina.org), which features a small network of trails and several impressive suspension bridges, both over the river and through the forest canopy. A self-guided walk of the bridges and trails of the reserve costs $10 per person, and a 2-hour guided tour costs just $15 per person—definitely worth the extra $5.

WHERE TO STAY & DINE

All of the lodges listed below arrange excursions throughout the region, including boat trips on the Sarapiquí, guided hikes in the rainforest, and horseback or mountain-bike rides. Also note that the rates for all of lodges in the "Expensive" category include all meals, taxes, and usually a tour or two, greatly reducing their real cost.

EXPENSIVE

Rara Avis   Once the exclusive stomping grounds of scientists and students, Rara Avis is one of the first, most responsible, biologically rich, and isolated ecolodge operations in Costa Rica. There are several lodging options here, but the Waterfall Lodge is by far the most comfortable and popular. It has rustic but comfortable rooms in a two-story building near the main lodge and dining room, and just a couple hundred meters from its namesake two-tiered waterfall. Each unit here is a corner room with a wraparound porch. For those who want closer communion with nature, Rara Avis has a two-room cabin set deep in the forest beside a river, about a 10-minute hike from the main lodge, as well as three more rustic two-bedroom cabins with shared bathrooms, located in a small clearing about a 5-minute walk from the lodge. Meals are basic Tico-style dishes with lots of beans and rice.

The grounds of Rara Avis are adjacent to Braulio Carrillo National Park, and together the two areas have many miles of trails for you to explore. Bird-watchers, take note: More than 362 species of birds have been sighted here.

When making reservations, be sure to get directions for how to get to Las Horquetas, and information on coordinating your ride on the lodge's tractor. The tractor leaves around 9am each day for the 3-hour ride to the lodge.

15km (9⅓ miles) from Las Horquetas (A.P. 8105-1000, San José). © 253-0844 or 764-3131. Fax 257-0438. www.rara-avis.com. 16 units, 10 with private bathroom. $45 per person with shared bathroom; $140–$160 double with private bathroom. Rates include transportation from Las Horquetas (you can't get here by car), guided hikes, all meals, and taxes. AE, MC, V. **Amenities:** Restaurant. *In room:* No phone.

Selva Verde Lodge ♠   This long-standing rainforest lodge is one of the original ecotourist ventures in Costa Rica. Expansion and remodeling have kept things comfortable and up-to-date. The lodge buildings are all made of varnished hardwoods inside and out, and are built on pilings so that the rooms are on the second floor. They're all connected by covered walkways that keep you dry even though this area receives more than 150 inches of rain each year. The bungalows are located across the road and 500m (1,640 ft.) into the forest; they're not nearly as comfortable as the rooms in the main compound, but they do offer somewhat more privacy. Most meals are served buffet style in a beautiful large dining room that overlooks the river. Selva Verde is located right between the main road (a few kilometers west of Puerto Viejo) and by the Río Sarapiquí. Across the river is a large rainforest preserve. There are several trails on the grounds, a wonderful suspension bridge, and a separate little zip-line adventure across the Sarapiquí River to more trails, a nice little swimming hole on the river, and modest butterfly and botanical gardens.

Chilamate (A.P. 55-3069), Sarapiquí. © 800/451-7111 in the U.S. and Canada, or 766-6800. Fax 766-6011. www.selvaverde.com. 45 units, 5 bungalows. $144 double; $180 triple. Rates include 3 meals daily and taxes. Rates lower in the off season (May–Nov). AE, DC, MC, V. **Amenities:** 2 restaurants; bar; tour desk; laundry service. *In room:* Hair dryer, safe.

MODERATE

Centro Neotrópico Sarapiquís ✿   Located on a high bluff fronting the Sarapiquí River, this complex is the most unique project in the Sarapiquí region. The deluxe rooms are housed in three large, round buildings, or *palenques*. Based on the traditional pre-Columbian constructions of the area, each of the three palenques has a towering thatch roof rising some 18m (59 ft.). The rooms are all comfortable and spacious, although a little dark, and each has a door leading out to the shared veranda that encircles the building. The 12 standard rooms are all housed in the main lodge building and are somewhat smaller and less luxurious, and lack the veranda.

The hotel has several interesting attractions, including a small natural history museum, an on-site excavation of a pre-Columbian graveyard, and a well-marked botanical garden. Just across the river lies the 300-hectare (741-acre) Tirimbina Biological Reserve, with a small network of trails and several impressive suspension bridges, both over the river and through the forest canopy. Tours of the museum and reserve cost extra and are open to guests at other hotels in the area.

No smoking is permitted in any of the rooms, or on any of the terraces, although smokers can light up in the bar and restaurant.

A.P. 86-3069, La Virgen de Sarapiquí. ✆ **761-1004.** Fax 761-1415. www.sarapiquis.org. 36 units. $82–$90 double. Rates lower in the off season. V. **Amenities:** Restaurant; bar; tour desk; limited room service; babysitting; laundry service; nonsmoking rooms.

La Selva Biological Station ✿   Located a few kilometers south of Puerto Viejo, La Selva Biological Station caters primarily to students and researchers but also accepts visitors seeking a rustic rainforest adventure. The atmosphere is definitely that of a scientific research center. La Selva, which is operated by the Organization for Tropical Studies (OTS), covers 1,480 hectares (3,656 acres) and is contiguous with Braulio Carrillo National Park. There are miles of well-maintained hiking trails to explore. Researchers estimate that more than 2,000 species of flora exist in this private reserve, and 400-plus species of birds have been identified here, making this a great choice if you want to do some serious bird-watching. Rooms are basic but large, and the high ceilings help keep them cool. Most have bunk beds, and all share bathrooms. The dining hall is a big, bright place where students and scientists swap data over fried chicken or fish with rice and beans.

Because scientific research is the primary objective of La Selva, researchers receive priority over casual, short-term visitors. However, very informative guided tours are available most days, even if you are staying at another hotel in the area. Call the local number (✆ **766-6565**) at least a day in advance to arrange one of these. If you want to stay overnight at La Selva, you should have a reservation with the San José office—they try to discourage walk-in traffic. Moreover, because there are very few rooms here, it pays to book in advance. The rates here are quite high for the actual accommodations, but you can take some solace in the fact that you're helping to support valuable and valiant research and conservation efforts.

Puerto Viejo (A.P. 676-2050, San Pedro, Costa Rica; mailing address in the U.S.: Box 90630, Durham, NC 27708). ✆ **240-6696** or 766-6565. Fax 240-6783. www.ots.ac.cr. 10 units, all with shared bathroom. $68 per person double occupancy. Rates include all meals, a half-day tour, and taxes. Lower rates for researchers and student groups. MC, V. **Amenities:** Restaurant; kayak rentals; laundry service. *In room:* No phone.

Sueño Azul Resort ✿   This nature lodge and wellness retreat offers the nicest accommodations in the area. Set at the juncture of two rivers and backed by rainforest and forested mountains, the setting's pretty darn nice as well. The rooms are all spacious, with high ceilings, two double beds, large bathrooms, and a private porch overlooking either one of the rivers or a small lake. Ten of the rooms come with air-conditioning, and there's one large junior suite with its own outdoor Jacuzzi. Meals are served in an open-air dining room set to take in the view, and there are a pool, Jacuzzi, bar, and rancho down by the rivers' edge.

A wide range of tours and activities is offered, including rainforest hikes, horseback riding, mountain biking, and fly-fishing, as well as trips to the area's major attractions. Sueño Azul also has a good-size spa and yoga facility. This place has been chosen as the main base of operations for a series of workshops and retreats to be conducted by the well-known and respected Omega Institute.

Las Horquetas de Sarapiquí (A.P. 3630-1000, San José). © 764-4244. Fax 764-3129. www.suenoazulresort. com. 45 units. $86–$105 double, $125 suite. Rates lower in the off season. MC, V. **Amenities:** Restaurant; small pool; activities desk; laundry service. *In room:* Hair dryer, no phone.

INEXPENSIVE

In addition to the places listed below, budget travelers might want to check out the **Posada Andrea Cristina** (© 766-6265; www.andreacristina.com), which is located just on the outskirts of Puerto Viejo and is run by Alex Martínez, an excellent local guide and pioneering conservationist in the region.

Gavilán Sarapiquí River Lodge   Located on the banks of the Río Sarapiquí just south of Puerto Viejo on the road to Río Frío, Gavilán is surrounded by 100 hectares (247 acres) of forest reserve (secondary forest) and 14 hectares (35 acres) of gardens planted with lots of flowering ginger, heliconia, orchids, and bromeliads. Guest rooms are basic and simply furnished, and the beds are a bit soft for my taste. Still, all have fans and hot water, and there are always fresh-cut flowers. Most have one single and one double bed, but there are variations. What Gavilán lacks in luxurious comfort, it makes up for in friendliness and attentive service. There's an unheated Jacuzzi in the garden and several open-air ranchos, some of which have hammocks strung up for afternoon siestas. Tico and Continental meals are served buffet style, and there are always plenty of fresh fruits and juices. Lunch will run you $10; dinner costs $12. Guided hikes through the forest, horseback rides, and river trips are all offered for around $20 per person.

Puerto Viejo de Sarapiquí (A.P. 445-2010, San José). © 234-9507 or 766-6743. Fax 253-6556. www.gavilan lodge.com. 13 units. $50 double. Rates include breakfast. Rates lower in the off season. MC, V. **Amenities:** Restaurant; bar; Jacuzzi; laundry service. *In room:* No phone.

La Quinta de Sarapiquí Country Inn *(Value)*   This small, family-run lodge makes a good base for exploring the Sarapiquí region. Located on the banks of the Sardinal River about 15 minutes west of Puerto Viejo, La Quinta caters primarily to nature lovers and bird-watchers. The rooms are located in a half-dozen buildings dispersed around the grounds among richly flowering gardens and connected by covered walkways. They're simple but clean, with good lighting and comfortable bathrooms. Each room has a small patio with a sitting chair or two for gazing out into the garden. There's a small pool, and it's even safe to swim in the river. In addition to the Jewels of the Rainforest museum here, there's also a small gift shop, a butterfly garden, a frog garden, and a vegetable garden and reforestation project on hand. If you don't have a car, call the hotel to see if you can arrange a pickup in Puerto Viejo. Meals are served either buffet or family style in the main lodge and will run you an extra $25 per day.

Chilamate (A.P. 11021-1000, San José), Sarapiquí. © 761-1300. Fax 761-1395. www.laquintasarapiqui.com. 23 units. $50 double. Children under 12 stay free in parent's room. AE, MC, V. **Amenities:** Restaurant; bar; small pool; tour desk; laundry service.

A REMOTE NATURE LODGE

La Laguna del Lagarto Lodge ☆ *Finds*   It's hard to get much more remote than this. Located near the Nicaraguan border, La Laguna del Lagarto Lodge is bordered by more than 480 hectares (1,186 acres) of virgin rainforest that is home to a rich variety of tropical flora and fauna. The accommodations are simple yet comfortable. Most rooms open onto a balcony or veranda with sitting chairs and hammocks. Meals, which will run you around $30 per person per day, are served family style in the open-air dining room and are filling affairs.

The hotel is named after the two man-made lagoons that sit below the lodge buildings; canoes are available for paddling around these and several other nearby jungle waterways. There are more than 10km (6¼ miles) of well-maintained hiking trails, and the lodge offers trips on the San Carlos River ($25). More than 350 species of birds have been spotted here, and the hotel is involved in efforts to preserve the rare great green macaw, two of which I spotted soon after my arrival. In addition to the rainforest, the lodge sits on a small pepper plantation and has other lands planted with palmito, pineapple, and other tropical fruits.

To get here, you head first to Pital and then continue on dirt roads to the town of Boca Tapada. It's another 6km (3¾ miles) to the lodge on more bumpy dirt roads. It's also possible to get here on public transportation (call for directions), or you can arrange for the lodge to handle your transportation from San José. The lodge's transfers cost $200 round-trip for two people, or $70 per person for more than three. But anyone with a four-wheel-drive can make the trip here independently, so you're best off driving on your own.

Boca Tapada (A.P. 995-1007, San José). ⓒ **289-8163.** Fax 289-5295. www.lagarto-lodge-costa-rica.com. 20 units, 18 with private bathroom. $48 double with shared bathroom; $58 double with private bathroom. AE, MC, V (5% surcharge). **Amenities:** Restaurant; bar. *In room:* No phone.

2 Arenal Volcano & La Fortuna ☆☆

140km (87 miles) NW of San José; 61km (38 miles) E of Tilarán

If you've never experienced them firsthand, the sights and sounds of an active volcano erupting are awesome. **Arenal** is one of the world's most regularly active volcanoes. In July 1968, the volcano, which had lain dormant for hundreds of years, surprised everybody by erupting with sudden violence. The nearby village of Tabacón was destroyed, and nearly 80 of its inhabitants were killed. Since that eruption, 1,607m (5,271-ft.) Arenal has been Costa Rica's most active volcano. Frequent powerful explosions send cascades of red-hot lava rocks tumbling down the western slope, and during the day, the lava flows steam and rumble. However, at night the volcano puts on its most mesmerizing show. If you are lucky enough to be here on a clear and active night, you'll see the night sky turned red by lava spewing from Arenal's crater. In the past few years, the forests to the south of the volcano have been declared Arenal National Park. Eventually, this park should stretch all the way to Monteverde Biological Cloud Forest Reserve.

Lying at the eastern foot of this natural spectacle is the tiny farming community of **La Fortuna.** In recent years, this town has become a magnet for volcano watchers from around the world. There's a host of moderately priced hotels in and near La Fortuna, and from here you can arrange night tours to the best volcano-viewing spots, which are 17km (11 miles) away on the western slope, past Tabacón Hot Springs.

ESSENTIALS

GETTING THERE & DEPARTING   By Car   There are several routes to La Fortuna from San José. The most popular is to head west on the Interamerican Highway and then turn north at Naranjo, continuing north through Zarcero to Ciudad Quesada. From Ciudad Quesada, one route goes through Jabillos, while the other goes through Muelle. The former route is better marked, more popular, slightly shorter, and generally better maintained, but the severe weather and heavy traffic quickly take their toll, and the roads up here can be notoriously bad for long stretches. This route offers wonderful views of the San Carlos valley as you come down from Ciudad Quesada, and Zarcero, with its topiary gardens and quaint church, makes a good place to stop, stretch your legs, and snap a few photos (see "Side Trips from San José," in chapter 4, for more information).

You can also stay on the Interamerican Highway until San Ramón (west of Naranjo) and then head north through La Tigra. This route is also very scenic and passes the hotels Villablanca and Valle Escondido. The travel time on any of the above routes is between 3 and 4 hours.

Finally, if you're combining your visit here with a stop at the Poás Volcano and La Paz waterfall, or if you're staying at one of the lodges closer to Aguas Zarcas, you can go first to Alajuela or Heredia and then head north to Varablanca before continuing on to San Miguel, where you turn west toward Río Cuarto and Aguas Zarcas. From Aguas Zarcas, continue west through Muelle to the turnoff for La Fortuna. This is the longest route.

By Bus   Buses (© 255-4318) leave San José for La Fortuna roughly every hour between 5am and 7:30pm from the **Atlántico del Norte** bus station at Avenida 9 and Calle 12. The trip's duration is 4½ hours; the fare is $3. The bus you take might be labeled TILARAN. Make sure it is passing through Ciudad Quesada. If it is, you're in luck because it will also pass through La Fortuna. If it's not, you'll end up in Tilarán via the Interamerican Highway, passing through the Guanacaste town of Cañas.

Alternatively, you can take a bus from the same station to Ciudad Quesada and transfer there to another bus to La Fortuna. These buses also depart roughly every hour between 5am and 7:30pm. The fare for the 2½-hour trip is $2.50. Local buses between Ciudad Quesada and La Fortuna run regularly through the day, although the schedule changes frequently, depending on demand. The trip lasts 1 hour; the fare is $1.50.

Buses depart **Monteverde/Santa Elena** for Tilarán every day at 7am. This is a journey of only 35km (22 miles), but the trip lasts 2½ hours because the road is in such horrendous condition. Pregnant women and people with bad backs should think twice about making this trip, especially by bus. The return bus from Tilarán to Santa Elena leaves at 1pm. The fare is $2. Buses from Tilarán to La Fortuna depart daily at 7am and 12:30pm (hence, a person coming from Monteverde would have to wait for the 12:30pm bus) and make the return trip at 8am and 2:30pm. The trip is 3 to 4 hours; the fare is $2.50.

Buses depart La Fortuna for San José roughly every hour between 5am and 7:30pm; in some instances, you might have to transfer in Ciudad Quesada. From there, you can catch one of the frequent buses to San José.

Grayline (© 220-2126; www.graylinecostarica.com) has a daily bus that leaves San José for La Fortuna at 8am; the fare is $25. **Interbus** (© 283-5573; www.costaricapass.com) has a daily bus that leaves San José for La Fortuna at 8am, also for $25. Both companies will pick you up at most San José–area

> ## _Tips_ Boats, Horses & Taxis
>
> You can travel between La Fortuna and Monteverde by boat and taxi, or on a combination boat, horseback, and taxi trip. A 10- to 20-minute boat ride across Lake Arenal cuts out hours of driving around its shores. From La Fortuna to the put-in point is about a 25-minute taxi ride. It's about a 1½-hour four-wheel-drive taxi ride between the Río Chiquito dock on the other side of Lake Arenal and Santa Elena. These trips can be arranged in either direction for between $25 and $35 per person, all-inclusive.
>
> You can also add on a horseback ride on the Santa Elena/Monteverde side of the lake. There are several routes and rides offered. The steepest and most adventurous heads up the mountains and through the forest to the town of San Gerardo, which is only a 30-minute car ride from Santa Elena. Other routes throw in mellower and shorter sections of horseback riding along the lakeside lowlands. With the horseback ride, this trip runs around $55 to $65 per person.
>
> _Be forewarned:_ The riding is often rainy, muddy, and steep. Many find it much more arduous than awe-inspiring. Moreover, I've received numerous complaints about the condition of the trails and the treatment of the horses, so be very careful and demanding before signing on for this trip. Find out what route you will be taking, as well as the condition of the horses, if possible. **Desafío Expeditions (© 479-9464; www.desafiocostarica.com)** is one of the more reputable operators. They will even drive your car around for you while you take the scenic (and sore) route.

hotels. Both companies also run routes from La Fortuna with connections to most other major destinations in Costa Rica.

ORIENTATION & FAST FACTS   As you enter La Fortuna, you'll see the massive volcano directly in front of you. La Fortuna is only a few streets wide, with almost all the hotels, restaurants, and shops clustered along the main road that leads out of town toward Tabacón and the volcano. There are several small information and tour-booking offices, as well as a laundromat, on the streets that surround the small central park that fronts the Catholic church. There's a Banco de Costa Rica as you enter La Fortuna, just over the Río Burío bridge, and a Banco Nacional in the center of town, across the park from the church. Both have ATMs.

GETTING AROUND   If you don't have a car, you'll need to either take a cab or go on an organized tour if you want to visit the hot springs or view the volcano eruption. There are tons of taxis in La Fortuna (you can flag one down practically anywhere), and there is always a line of them ready and waiting along the main road beside the central park. A taxi between La Fortuna and Tabacón should cost around $5. Another alternative is to rent a car when you get here. **Alamo (© 479-9090)** and **Poás (© 479-9400; www.carentals.com)** both have offices in La Fortuna.

WHAT TO SEE & DO
EXPERIENCING THE VOLCANO ⭐⭐

The first thing you should know is that Arenal Volcano borders a region of cloud and rainforests, and the volcano's cone is often socked in by fog. Many people come to Arenal and never get to see the exposed cone. Moreover, the volcano does go through periods when it is relatively quiet.

The second thing you should know is that you can't climb Arenal Volcano; it's not safe due to the constant activity. Several foolish people who have ignored this warning have lost their lives, and others have been severely injured. The most recent fatalities occurred in August 2000.

Still, waiting for and watching Arenal's regular eruptions is the main activity in La Fortuna and is best done at night when the orange lava glows against the starry sky. Although it's possible simply to look up from the middle of town and see Arenal erupting, the view is best from the north and west sides of the volcano along the road to Tabacón and toward the national park entrance. If you have a car, you can drive along this road, but if you've arrived by bus, you will need to take a taxi or tour.

Arenal National Park constitutes an area of more than 2,880 hectares (7,114 acres), which includes the viewing and parking areas closest to the volcano. The park is open daily from 8am to 10pm and charges $6 admission per person. The trails through forest and over old lava flows inside the park are gorgeous and fun. (Be careful climbing on those volcanic boulders.) However, at night, the view from inside the park is no better than on the roads just outside it.

If you don't have a car and are staying in La Fortuna, every hotel in town and several tour offices offer night tours to the volcano. (They don't actually enter the park; they stop on the road that runs between the park entrance and the Arenal Observatory Lodge.) These tours generally cost between $7 and $15 per person. Often these volcano-viewing tours include a stop at one of the local hot springs, and the price goes up accordingly (see "Taking a Soothing Soak in Hot Springs," below, for a description of the different options and fees).

OTHER ADVENTUROUS PURSUITS IN THE AREA

Aside from the impressive volcanic activity, the area around Arenal Volcano is packed with other natural wonders.

LA FORTUNA FALLS   Leading the list of side attractions in the area is the impressive **Río Fortuna waterfall** ⭐, located about 5.5km (3½ miles) outside of town in a lush jungle setting. There's a sign in town to indicate the road that leads out to the falls. You can drive or hike to just within viewing distance. When you get to the entrance to the lookout, you'll have to pay a $3 entrance fee to actually check out the falls. It's another 15- to 20-minute hike down a steep and often muddy path to the pool formed by the waterfall. You can swim, but stay away from the turbulent water at the base of the falls—several people have drowned here. Instead, check out and enjoy the calm pool just around the bend, or join the locals at the popular swimming hole under the bridge on the paved road, just after the turnoff for the road up to the falls. The trail to the falls is open daily from 8am to 4pm.

HIKING & HORSEBACK RIDING   Horseback riding is a popular activity in this area, and there are scores of good rides on dirt back roads and through open fields and dense rainforest. Volcano and lake views come with the terrain on most rides. Horseback trips to the Río Fortuna waterfall are perhaps the most popular tours sold, but remember, the horse will get you only to the entrance;

Taking a Soothing Soak in Hot Springs

Arenal Volcano has bestowed a terrific fringe benefit on the area around it: several naturally heated thermal springs. Located at the site of the former village that was destroyed by the 1968 eruption, **Tabacón Hot Springs Resort & Spa**★★★ (© 256-1500; www.tabacon.com) is the most extensive and luxurious spot to soak your tired bones. A series of variously sized pools, fed by natural springs, are spread out among lush gardens. At the center is a large, warm, spring-fed swimming pool with a slide, a swim-up bar, and a perfect view of the volcano. One of the stronger streams flows over a sculpted waterfall, with a rock ledge underneath that provides a perfect place to sit and receive a free hydraulic shoulder massage. The resort also has a spa on the grounds offering professional massages, mud masks, and other treatments at reasonable prices. (Make appointments in advance.)

In addition to the poolside swim-up bar, there's a restaurant and separate snack bar and grill here. You can sign a credit card voucher when you enter and charge your food and drinks throughout your stay. This sure beats pulling soggy bills from your bathing suit.

Entrance fees are $29 for adults and $17 for children under 9. The hot springs are open daily from noon to 10pm (spa treatments can actually be scheduled as early as 8am, and guests at the hotel here can enter at 10am). The management recently instituted a policy of limiting the number of visitors at any one time, so reservations are recommended during the high season (late Nov to late Apr).

Across the street from the resort and down a gravel driveway are **Las Fuentes Termales,** another bathing spot fed by the same springs and run by the same folks. You'll find several large pools here, but far more basic facilities and no view. Admission is $10. There are changing rooms and showers, but you won't find the Disneyland atmosphere, pampering spa treatments, or magnificent gardens that prevail at the Tabacón resort.

Baldi Termae (© 479-9652), next to the Volcano Look Disco, are the first hot springs you'll come to as you drive from La Fortuna toward Tabacón; however, I find this place far less attractive than the options mentioned above. The main attraction here is the swim-up bar set in the center of the circular concrete pool. Admission is $10.

However, just across the street from Baldi Termae is the unmarked entrance of a new hot spring option, **Eco Termales** ★★ (© 479-8484). Smaller and more intimate than Tabacón, this series of pools set amid lush forest and gardens is almost as picturesque and luxurious, although the spa services are much less extensive and there is no view of the volcano. Reservations are absolutely necessary here. Admission is $14.

from there, you'll have to hike a bit. A horseback ride to the falls should cost between $25 and $30, including the entrance fee.

One popular and strenuous hike is to **Cerro Chato,** a dormant volcanic cone on the flank of Arenal. There's a pretty little lake up here. **Desafío Expeditions** ★

(© 479-9464; www.desafiocostarica.com) leads this 4-hour hike for $45, including lunch.

Aventuras Arenal (© 479-9133; www.arenaladventures.com), **Desafío Expediciones** ✦ (© 479-9464; www.desafiocostarica.com), and **Sunset Tours** ✦ (© 479-9800) are the main tour operators in the area. In addition to the above tours, each of these companies offers most of the tours listed below, as well as fishing trips and sightseeing excursions on the lake.

CANOPY TOURS & CANYONING   The **Original Canopy Tour** ✦ company (© 257-5149; www.canopytour.com) has an operation set up right at the Tabacón Hot Springs Resort & Spa. The 2-hour tour ($45 per person) leaves right from the hot springs and includes the entrance to the **Las Fuentes Termales** pools. You strap on a climbing harness, ascend more than 30m (98 ft.) to a treetop platform, and careen from tree to tree while hanging from a pulley on a skinny cable. This same company has another canopy tour at **Termales del Bosque** (p. 224) just outside of Aguas Zarcas.

You can also hike the trails and bridges of **Arenal Hanging Bridges** (© 253-5080; www.hangingbridges.com). Located just over the Lake Arenal dam, this attraction is a complex of gentle trails and suspension bridges through a beautiful tract of primary forest. It's open daily from 7am to 4pm; admission is $20. Guided tours and night tours are also available.

If you'd like a bigger rush than the canopy tours offer, you could go "canyoning" with **Pure Trek Canyoning** ✦✦ (© 479-9940; www.puretrek.com). This new adventure sport is a mix of hiking through and alongside a jungle river, punctuated with periodic rappels through and alongside the faces of four waterfalls. The largest rappel is 50m (164 ft.). The tour is wet and adventurous, and costs $80 per person, including lunch.

WHITE-WATER RAFTING & CANOEING   For adventurous tours of the area, check out **Desafío Expeditions** ✦ (© 479-9464; www.desafiocostarica.com) or **Aguas Bravas** (© 292-2072; www.aguas-bravas.co.cr). Both of these companies offer daily raft rides of Class I to II, III, and IV to V on different sections of the Toro, Peñas Blancas, and Sarapiquí rivers. A half-day trip on the Peñas Blancas leaving from La Fortuna costs around $45 per person; a full day of rafting costs $60 to $70 per person, depending on what section of what river you ride. Both of these companies also offer mountain biking and most of the standard local guided trips.

A more laid-back alternative is to take a canoe tour with **Canoa Aventura** (© 479-8200; www.canoaaventura.cr.gs), which offers half-, full-, and multiday excursions on a variety of rivers in the region.

FISHING   With Lake Arenal just around the corner, fishing is a popular activity here. The big action is *guapote,* a Central American species of rainbow bass. However, you can also book fishing trips to Caño Negro, where snook, tarpon, and other game fish can be stalked. Most hotels and adventure-tour companies can arrange fishing excursions. Costs run around $100 to $200 for a half-day, and $200 to $400 for a full day.

ATV   If you want to try riding a four-wheel ATV (all-terrain vehicle), check in with the folks at **Fourtrax Adventures** (© 479-8444; www.fourtraxadventure.com). Their principal tour is a 4-hour adventure through the nearby back roads, fruit orchards, and secondary forest. The tour includes either breakfast or lunch, and stops at a beautiful swimming hole and a local butterfly farm. Cost is $75 per ATV, which can hold up to two people.

SIDE TRIPS FROM LA FORTUNA

La Fortuna is a great place from which to make a day trip to the **Caño Negro National Wildlife Refuge** ☆. This vast network of marshes and rivers (particularly the Río Frío) is 100km (62 miles) north of La Fortuna near the town of Los Chiles. This refuge is best known for its amazing abundance of bird life, including roseate spoonbills, jabiru storks, herons, and egrets, but you can also see caimans and crocodiles. Bird-watchers should not miss this refuge, although keep in mind that the main lake dries up in the dry season (mid-Apr to Nov), which reduces the number of wading birds. Full-day tours to Caño Negro average between $40 and $60 per person. However, most of the tours run out of La Fortuna that are billed as Caño Negro never really enter the refuge, but instead ply sections of the nearby Río Frio, featuring similar wildlife and ecosystems. If you're interested in staying in this area and really visiting the refuge, check out the **Caño Negro Natural Lodge** (see "Where To Stay & Dine Farther Afield," below).

You can also visit the **Venado Caverns,** a 45-minute drive away. In addition to plenty of stalactites, stalagmites, and other limestone formations, you'll see bats and cave fish. Tours here cost $35 to $45.

Aventuras Arenal, Sunset Tours, and **Desafío Expeditions** all offer trips to Caño Negro and Venado Caverns. Check in with these folks (see "Hiking & Horseback Riding," above), or ask at your hotel for more information.

Kids and the young at heart might enjoy the pool, fountain, and water slide at **Jungla y Senderos Los Lagos** (© 479-8000; www.hotelloslagos.com). I personally come here more for the network of trails and small lakes that are also on this property. It recently added a small crocodile hatchery and tilapia farm, a canopy tour, and some basic hot springs. They've also got rooms and cabins that range widely in size, amenities, and price. You'll find Los Lagos on the road to Tabacón, a few kilometers out of La Fortuna. It charges $10 for daily use of its facilities.

WHERE TO STAY IN LA FORTUNA

La Fortuna is a tourist boomtown; basic hotels have popped up here at a phenomenal rate. Right in La Fortuna you'll find a score of budget options. If you have time, it's worth walking around and checking out a couple. If you have a car, drive a little bit out of town toward Tabacón, and you'll find several more basic cabins, some that even offer views of the volcano. There are a couple places both in town and right on the outskirts of La Fortuna that allow camping, with access to basic bathroom facilities, for around $5 to $7 per person per night.

Hotel La Fortuna   Located 1 block south of the gas station, this perennial budget travelers' favorite has risen from the ashes. A 1997 fire destroyed most of the original hotel, but reconstruction was quick. Accommodations are very basic, but what do you expect at these prices? At least the rooms are clean and have private bathrooms. There is a popular open-air restaurant at the front of the hotel, and the helpful owners can arrange a wide variety of tours.

La Fortuna, San Carlos. ©/fax 479-9197. 13 units. $10–$15 per person. Rates include breakfast. V. **Amenities:** Restaurant; tour desk. *In room:* No phone.

Hotel Las Colinas   This three-story building in the center of town offers clean but basic rooms. You'll need to be in good shape if you stay in one of the third-floor rooms, but it's worth it if you can snag room no. 33, which has a private balcony and an unobstructed view of the volcano. However, most of the other rooms are much less desirable, considering the wear and tear they've received over the years, so try to have a look at one or two before settling in.

There are a few rooms on the ground floor, but they don't even have windows to the outside and are very dark.

La Fortuna (A.P. 06), San Carlos. ©/fax **479-9305**. www.lascolinasarenal.com. 19 units. $30 double; $45 triple. Rates lower in the off season. MC, V. *In room:* No phone.

Hotel San Bosco *Value* Located a block off La Fortuna's main street, the San Bosco offers the best rooms to be found right in town. The hotel actually has two styles of rooms. The older units are all well maintained and feature tile floors and fans. However, these are standard budget hotel affairs. The newer and slightly more expensive rooms are much more attractive and have stone walls, tile floors, reading lights, televisions, and benches on the veranda in front. There's an observation deck for volcano viewing on the top floor of the hotel, as well as a helpful front desk staff.

La Fortuna, San Carlos (200m/656 ft. north of the central park). © **479-9050**. Fax 479-9109. www.arenal-volcano.com. 34 units. $40–$50 double. Rates lower in the off season. AE, MC, V. **Amenities:** Small outdoor pool and separate children's pool; small exercise room; Jacuzzi; tour desk; laundry service. *In room:* A/C, no phone.

Luigi's Hotel This small in-town hotel has a lively, hostel-like atmosphere. The rooms are all comfortable and clean; those on the second floor have the best views of the volcano, although those on the first floor have higher ceilings. All open onto a long shared veranda or porch, and some come with small televisions. Despite the name and the fact that the restaurant here is a pizza and pasta joint, the owners are actually Costa Rican, not Italian.

La Fortuna, San Carlos. ©/fax **479-9898**. www.luigislodge.com. 20 units. $50–$65 double. Rates include breakfast. MC, V. **Amenities:** Restaurant; bar; small outdoor pool; gym; Jacuzzi; tour desk; laundry service. *In room:* A/C, TV in some units, coffeemaker, hair dryer, no phone.

WHERE TO DINE IN & AROUND LA FORTUNA

Dining in La Fortuna is nowhere near as spectacular as volcano viewing, although, given the area's popularity, there's no lack of options. Most folks either eat at their hotel or go to any one of a number of basic *sodas* serving Tico standards. The favorite meeting places in town are the **El Jardín Restaurant** (© 479-9360), **Luigi's Pizza** (© 479-9636), and **Lava Rocks** (© 479-8039); all are on the main road, right in the center of La Fortuna. Other choices include **La Choza de Laurel** (© 479-9231), **Rancho La Cascada** (© 479-9145), and **La Pradera** (© 479-9597). For basic Mexican fare, try **Las Brasitas** (© 479-9819).

Heading out of town, you'll find **El Vagabundo** (© 479-9565), an Italian pizza and spaghetti joint. After dark, the area's biggest attraction is the volcano, but the **Volcano Look Disco** (© 479-9616) on the road to Tabacón is trying to compete. If you get bored of the eruptions and seismic rumbling, head here for heavy dance beats and mirrored disco balls. Right in town, the folks at Luigi's Hotel have opened a midsize **casino** just next door to their hotel and restaurant.

On my last visit, the **Mirador Arenal Kioro** (© **356-1491**) was just getting up and running. This restaurant and lookout features a commanding view of the volcano, with a series of private dining tents, and plans for some volcano-view Jacuzzis and hot springs.

El Novillo ★ *Finds* STEAKHOUSE/COSTA RICAN This place is the definition of "nothing fancy." In fact, it's just some lawn furniture (tables and chairs) set on a concrete slab underneath a high, open zinc roof. Still, it has garnered a well-deserved reputation as the best steakhouse in the area. The steaks are big and tender and well prepared. The chicken and fish dishes are huge as well and also nicely done. Meals come with garlic bread, fries, and some slaw. If you want a real local treat, order some fried yuca as a side. If the night is clear, you can get a good view of any volcanic activity from the parking lot here.

On the road to Tabacón, 10km (6¼ miles) outside of La Fortuna. © **460-6433**. Main courses $5–$9. No credit cards. Daily 10am–midnight.

WHERE TO STAY NEAR THE VOLCANO
EXPENSIVE
Tabacón Hot Springs Resort & Spa ★★ This is by far the most upscale option in the Arenal area. Steady improvements in service and amenities have only made this a better option. Many rooms here have excellent, direct views of the volcano. However, quite a few of the rooms have obstructed, or no, view; unfortunately, it's often the luck of the draw whether you will get a room with a view. Those on the upper floors of the 300-block building have the best vistas. Although the hotel allows you to request a view when making a reservation, they have the unenviable reputation not only of not honoring these requests, but also of regularly overbooking during the high season.

All rooms are spacious, with nice wooden furniture; each has a private terrace or balcony with a table and a couple of chairs for volcano viewing. Nine of the rooms here are truly designed to be accessible to travelers with disabilities, and 11 are suites, with separate sitting rooms and many with a private volcano-view Jacuzzi. Guests here enjoy privileges at the spectacular hot springs complex and spa across the street (see "Taking a Soothing Soak in Hot Springs" on p. 217), including slightly extended hours. There's a large hot spring–fed pool and separate Jacuzzi right at the hotel as well.

As you drive along the main road between La Fortuna and Lake Arenal, you'll see the resort on your right. About 90m (295 ft.) or so later, around a sharp bend, the hot springs and spa will be on your left.

On the main road between La Fortuna and Lake Arenal, Tabacón (P.O. Box 181-1007, Centro Colón, San José). © **256-1500**. Fax 221-3075. www.tabacon.com. 106 units. $139–$159 double; $189–$299 suite. Rates include buffet breakfast. AE, DC, MC, V. **Amenities:** 2 restaurants; 2 bars; large pool w/swim-up bar; extensive hot springs and spa facilities; exercise room; Jacuzzi; bike rental; tour desk; in-room massage; laundry service. *In room:* A/C, TV, coffeemaker, hair dryer, safe.

MODERATE
In addition to the places listed below, there has been a real boom of construction going on along the entire length of the road between La Fortuna and Tabacón. If you have a car and some time, you might want to stop and check out any new or interesting hotels or cabins that strike your fancy along the way.

Arenal Lodge ★ Located high on a hillside above Lake Arenal, this lodge has a direct view of Arenal Volcano (some 9.5km/6 miles away) over a forested valley. Although it's not as close to the volcano as some of the other lodges mentioned below, the view is still stunning. The standard rooms, although attractively decorated, have no views at all. The best rooms here are the junior suites, which have two queen-size beds, balconies, large picture windows, and lots of space. The matrimonial suite comes with its own private Jacuzzi. Five separate buildings on a hill behind the main building house the 10 chalet rooms; these rooms all have plenty of space, small kitchenettes, and good views from their balconies or patios, although they feel too spartan for my taste.

Meals are served in a dining room with a glass wall facing the volcano. After dinner, you can retire to the library, where there's a huge stone fireplace and a pool table, or soak in the outdoor Jacuzzi. A separate lounge has a TV and VCR. Situated on a macadamia plantation between two strips of virgin forest, the lodge has several trails that are great for bird-watching.

Lake Arenal (A.P. 2495-2050, San Pedro). ℂ 253-5080 or 460-1881. Fax 253-5016. www.arenallodge.com. 35 units. $69 double; $117–$147 suites and chalet rooms. Rates include buffet breakfast and mountain-bike tour. AE, MC, V. Drive west from La Fortuna past Tabacón and the National Park entrance. About 200m (656 ft.) past the dam over Lake Arenal, you'll see a steep driveway. The lodge is a couple of kilometers up the driveway. **Amenities:** Restaurant; bar; Jacuzzi; bike rental; tour desk; free shuttle to Tabacón Hot Springs 4 times daily; laundry service. *In room:* Fridge, coffeemaker, no phone.

Arenal Observatory Lodge ⭐⭐

This once-rustic lodge was originally built for the use of volcanologists from the Smithsonian Institute but has long been one of my favorite options in the Arenal area. The hotel is only 4km (2½ miles) from the volcano and is built on a high ridge, with a spectacular view of the cone. Lying in bed at night listening to the eruptions, it's easy to think you're in imminent danger (don't worry—you're not). The best rooms here are the five junior suites built below the restaurant and main lodge, as well as the four rooms in the Observatory Block. The "Smithsonian" rooms feature massive picture windows, with a direct view of the volcano. The standard rooms are simple and rustic affairs with no volcano views just off the main lodge, and the most basic rooms are housed in the original *casona* (big house) and are located about 500m (1,640 ft.) from the main lodge.

The lodge offers a number of guided and unguided hiking options, including a free morning trip to one of the cooled-off lava flows, as well as a wide range of other tours. Meals are served in a well-placed dining room, with a full wall of glass facing the volcano. This is one of the better nature lodges for travelers with disabilities, with five rooms truly equipped for wheelchair access and a paved path extending almost a kilometer (½ mile) into the rainforest. When you're not hiking or touring the region, you can hang by the volcano-view swimming pool and Jacuzzi. The only downside here is that due to the shifting of vents and a major blowout on the side of the main crater, you now get better views of lava flows from the Tabacón side of the volcano.

To get here, head to the national park entrance, stay on the dirt road past the entrance, and follow the signs to the Observatory Lodge. A four-wheel-drive vehicle used to be required for the 9km (5½-mile) dirt road up to the lodge, but two bridges now eliminate the need to ford any major rivers, and a traditional sedan will usually make it even in the rainy season—although you'll always be better off with the clearance afforded by a four-wheel-drive vehicle.

On the flanks of Arenal Volcano (A.P. 13411-1000, San José). ℂ 290-7011 or 695-5033. Fax 290-8427. www.arenal-observatory.co.cr. 35 units. $56–$80 standard double; $107 Smithsonian; $122 junior suite. Rates include breakfast buffet. Rates lower in the off season. AE, MC, V. **Amenities:** Restaurant; bar; outdoor pool; Jacuzzi; tour desk; laundry service. *In room:* No phone.

Montaña de Fuego Inn ⭐

This place started out as a small collection of cabins with a great view and great prices. As its popularity has grown, the prices and a whole host of new cabins have quickly gone up. Inside, the cabins are all varnished wood, with sparse appointments. Still, there's no denying that the rooms here have amazing volcano views from their spacious glass-enclosed porches. The junior suites all have air-conditioning and minifridges, and some even have back balconies overlooking a forested ravine, in addition to the volcano-facing front porch. There's a large, glass-walled restaurant, Acuarelas, that serves Continental cuisine that I consider overpriced. Behind the hotel are some rolling hills that lead down to a small river surrounded by patches of gallery forest, where they conduct an adventurous horseback, hiking, rappel, and kayak loop tour.

If this place is full, check next door at the **Cabañas Arenal Paraíso** (© 460-5333; www.arenalparaiso.com), which has very similar accommodations and is run by the same family. (The owners of the two lodges are brothers.) Both of these hotels are located 8km (5 miles) outside La Fortuna on the road to Tabacón.

La Palma de la Fortuna (A.P. 82-4417), San Carlos. © 460-1220. Fax 460-1455. www.montanadefuego.com. 50 units. $90–$110 double. Rates include breakfast. MC, V. **Amenities:** Restaurant; 2 bars; small pool; small spa; 2 Jacuzzis; tour desk; massage; laundry service. *In room:* TV, coffeemaker.

Volcano Lodge   This lodge is a collection of duplexes across the road from and facing the volcano. All of the rooms come with two double beds, a private bathroom, two wicker chairs inside, and a small terrace with a couple of wooden rocking chairs for volcano viewing outside. The appointments are simple, but the rooms are spacious and get plenty of light through big picture windows. Room nos. 1 through 12 have the best views. A wide range of tours is available.

La Fortuna de San Carlos. © 460-6080 or 460-6022. Fax 460-6020. www.volcanolodge.com. 40 units. $78 double. Rates include continental breakfast. Rates lower in the off season. AE, MC, V. **Amenities:** Restaurant; bar; small free-form outdoor pool; Jacuzzi; tour desk; free shuttle to Tabacón Hot Springs; laundry service. *In room:* A/C, no phone.

INEXPENSIVE

In addition to the options in La Fortuna, if you've got a car, **Cabinas Los Guayabos** (©/fax 460-6644) offers five simple rooms, with the views and the location of the more expensive lodgings listed above.

WHERE TO STAY & DINE FARTHER AFIELD

All of the hotels listed in the following two sections are at least a half-hour drive from La Fortuna and the volcano. Most, if not all, offer both night and day tours to Arenal and Tabacón, but they also hope to attract you with their own natural charms.

EAST OF LA FORTUNA

Hotel La Garza ⋆   This comfortable, small nature lodge is set on a large working ranch just south of Muelle. La Garza means "the egret," and you'll see plenty of these birds here because they roost nearby. Also, the ranch includes 300 hectares (741 acres) of primary rainforest, where many other species of birds can be spotted. Built on the banks of the San Carlos River, the hotel consists of six duplex bungalows, each of which has a deck overlooking the river. Large trees provide shade, and the sound of the river lulls you to sleep at night. High ceilings and overhead fans help keep the rooms cool, and all the rooms are attractively decorated and have views of Arenal Volcano in the distance. The hotel's restaurant and bar are reached via a small suspension bridge over the lazy little river that runs through the property. You can arrange tours of the region or wander around the ranch observing the day-to-day activities.

Plantanar, San Carlos. © 475-5222. Fax 475-5015. www.hotellagarza.com. 12 units. $80 double. Rates include breakfast. Rates lower in the off season. AE, DC, MC, V. **Amenities:** Restaurant; bar; small outdoor pool; outdoor tennis court; Jacuzzi; tour desk; laundry service. *In room:* A/C.

Hotel Occidental El Tucano   El Tucano is one of the oldest and more extensive spa facilities in Costa Rica, with natural hot springs, indoor and natural steam rooms, and a wide range of massage and spa treatments. The resort is located in a steep-walled valley and faces a lush rainforest. The rooms are set into the hillside and are connected by narrow, winding alleys and stairways. Most rooms are rather unspectacular but are comfortable enough. The two presidential suites have private terraces, in-room Jacuzzis, and large-screen TVs. This place has never really taken off as a destination spa. Instead, it's a popular weekend retreat for Costa Ricans, and there can be a real party atmosphere around the pools and poolside bars, especially on weekends.

There are hiking trails on the property, and you can arrange a variety of tours around the region, including some on horseback. Just hanging around, you should see plenty of colorful toucans, the hotel's namesake, as well as many other birds. The dining room is large and features international cuisine. The best tables here are on an outdoor balcony overlooking the river. El Tucano is located 8.5km (5¼ miles) north of Ciudad Quesada (San Carlos) on the road to Aguas Zarcas.

Aguas Calientes de San Carlos (A.P. 434-1150, La Uruca, San José). ✆ 460-6000. Fax 460-1692. www.occidental-hoteles.com. 90 units. $90 double; $120–$150 suite. Rates include breakfast buffet. AE, MC, V. **Amenities:** Restaurant; bar; large natural spring–heated outdoor pool and several smaller pools; minigolf course; 2 outdoor tennis courts; small gym; spa; Jacuzzi; sauna; tour desk; salon; limited room service; massage; laundry service. *In room:* TV, hair dryer, safe.

Termales del Bosque *(Finds)*   This place packs a lot of ecotourism punch for the buck. Most of the rooms are in duplex buildings set on a small hill. Each comes with two double beds or a double and a single, and front and back patios. The rooms are clean and spacious. There is also a three-bedroom bungalow with a shared bathroom and kitchenette.

It's nowhere near as extensive as the neighboring El Tucano Resort, but Termales del Bosque does have some truly wonderful **natural hot springs** ★★ set in rich rainforest. The series of sculpted pools is set on the banks of a small river. Down by the pools, there's a natural steam room (scented each day with fresh eucalyptus), a massage room, and a snack-and-juice bar. The trail down here winds through the thick forest, and, if you want to keep on walking, you can take guided or self-guided tours on a network of well-marked trails. You can rent horses right at the lodge, and there's even a canopy tour. If you aren't staying here, you can use the pools and hike the trails for $8, or do the canopy tour for $45. You'll find Termales del Bosque on the road from San Carlos to Aguas Zarcas, just before El Tucano.

Ciudad Quesada (A.P. 243-4400), San Carlos. ✆ 460-4740. Fax 460-1356. www.termalesdelbosque.com. 25 units. $45 double. Rates include full breakfast. AE, DC, MC, V. **Amenities:** Restaurant; several hot-spring pools set beside a forest river; tour desk; massage; laundry service. *In room:* TV, no phone.

Tilajari Resort Hotel ★ *(Kids)*   This sprawling 12-hectare (30-acre) resort just outside the farming community of Muelle (28km/17 miles from La Fortuna) makes a good base for exploring this area and offers terrific bird-watching. Built on the banks of the San Carlos River, the Tilajari offers some of the more luxurious accommodations in the region. Most of the rooms have views of the river (some even have balconies), while others open onto rich flowering gardens. Each suite comes with a separate living room and sitting area. Large iguanas are frequently sighted on the grounds, and crocodiles live in the San Carlos River. There's also an orchid garden, a tropical fruit-and-vegetable garden, a medicinal herb garden, and a well-maintained butterfly garden. The large open-air dining room has both formal and informal sections and a bar.

Tilajari is quite popular with Tico families, especially on weekends. This is a great place for your kids to have a chance to interact and play with their Costa Rican counterparts. The lodge arranges tours around the region, including trips to Caño Negro, Arenal Volcano and Tabacón Hot Springs, and Fortuna Falls, for around $45 per person. Trips into the nearby rainforest (on foot, on horseback, or by tractor), can also be arranged, as can gentle floats on the Peñas Blancas River. Tennis is quite popular and important here, and the hotel frequently hosts local tournaments.

Tilajari is almost directly between La Fortuna, Aguas Zarcas, and Ciudad Quesada, and there are roads leading here from each of these towns.

Muelle (A.P. 81-4400), San Carlos. ☎ 469-9091. Fax 469-9095. www.tilajari.com. 76 units. $85–$93 double; $93–$109 suite. Rates include full breakfast. Rates lower in the off season. AE, MC, V. **Amenities:** Restaurant; bar; large outdoor pool; 6 lighted tennis courts (2 indoors); exercise room; Jacuzzi; sauna; bike rental; game room; tour desk; laundry service. In room: A/C, TV, hair dryer, safe.

NORTH OF LA FORTUNA

Caño Negro Natural Lodge ★   This small nature lodge is the nicest option in the tiny village of Caño Negro. If you really want to visit the Caño Negro Wildlife Refuge, either for bird-watching and wildlife viewing or for fishing, this is a good choice. The rooms, housed in a series of duplex buildings, are all simple but roomy, clean, and comfortable. They all come with "swamp coolers," small electric units that use evaporation as a cooling mechanism and that are advertised here as "air-conditioning." Although they make a dent in the predominately hot and humid climate—especially when combined with the overhead ceiling fans—it might not be enough for some folks. The hotel has spacious grounds full of flowering plants, tropical palms, and fruit trees.

To get here, drive toward Los Chiles; several kilometers before Los Chiles, you'll see signs for this hotel and the wildlife refuge. From here, it's 18km (11 miles) on a flat dirt road to the village, refuge, and hotel.

Caño Negro. ☎ 471-1426. Fax 471-1100. www.canonegrolodge.com. 10 units. $90 double; $100 triple. Rates include continental breakfast. Rates lower in the off season. AE, DC, MC, V. **Amenities:** Restaurant; bar; midsize outdoor pool; tour desk; game room; laundry service. In room: Safe.

SOUTH OF LA FORTUNA

Villablanca Hotel   Owned and operated by a former president of Costa Rica and his family, this lodge consists of a series of Tico-style casitas surrounded by 800 hectares (1,976 acres) of farm and forest. Each casita is built of adobe and has traditional tile floors and whitewashed walls with deep-blue trim. (This is the classic color scheme of 19th-century adobe homes throughout the country.) Inside you'll find a rounded fireplace in one corner, window seats, comfortable hardwood chairs, colorful curtains, and two twin beds covered with colorful bedspreads. The suites have two bedrooms and two baths. Most rooms come with electric teapots, and some have small refrigerators. In several rooms, the bathrooms have tubs that look out through a wall of windows onto lush gardens.

The dining room, which offers a simple but filling buffet, is in the hacienda-style main lodge. A central atrium garden, library, TV room/lounge, gift shop, and small bar round out the hotel. Villablanca is off the beaten track, but it is relatively close to San José, and if you're interested in bird-watching or exploring a cloud forest and want to avoid the crowds of Monteverde, this is a good choice.

Adjacent to the lodge are 11km (6¾ miles) of trails through the **Los Angeles Cloud Forest Reserve.** Admission to the reserve is $24 per person and includes a guided hike. You can also rent horses ($12 per hour) or take an adventurous swing through the canopy on a canopy tour ($39). If you're driving, head west out of San José to San Ramón and then head north, following the signs to Villablanca. Or you can take a public bus from San José to San Ramón and then take a taxi for around $15.

San Ramón (A.P. 247-1250), Alajuela. ℂ 800/289-8687 in the U.S. and Canada, or 228-4603 or 661-1600 in Costa Rica. Fax 228-4004. www.villablanca-costarica.com. 52 units. $99 double; $120–$164 suite. Rates include buffet breakfast. AE, DC, MC, V. **Amenities:** Restaurant; bar; laundry service. *In room:* Fridge in some units, no phone.

3 Along the Shores of Lake Arenal ✶

200km (124 miles) NW of San José; 20km (12 miles) NW of Monteverde; 70km (43 miles) SE of Liberia

This remains one of the least-developed tourism regions in Costa Rica, but not for lack of resources or charms. It does, after all, have Lake Arenal, a man-made lake with an area of 86 sq. km (34 sq. miles), making it the largest lake in Costa Rica, surrounded by rolling hills that are partly pastured and partly forested. The perfect cone of Arenal Volcano lies at the opposite (east) end of the lake from the small towns of Tilarán and Nuevo Arenal. The volcano's barren slopes are a stunning sight from here, especially when reflected in the waters of the lake. The northwest side of Lake Arenal is a dry region of rolling hills and pastures, distinctly different from the more lush landscape near La Fortuna.

People around here used to curse the winds, which often come blasting across this end of the lake at 60 knots or greater. However, because the first sailboarders caught wind of Lake Arenal's combination of warm, fresh water, steady blows, and spectacular scenery, things have been changing quickly. Although the towns of Tilarán and Nuevo Arenal are little more than quiet rural communities, hotels are proliferating all along the shores of the lake. Even if you aren't a fanatical sailboarder, you might enjoy hanging out by the lake, hiking in the nearby forests, and catching glimpses of Arenal Volcano.

The lake's other claim to fame is its rainbow-bass fishing. These fighting fish are known in Central America as *guapote* and are large members of the cichlid family. Their sharp teeth and fighting nature make them a real challenge.

ESSENTIALS
GETTING THERE & DEPARTING   By Car   From San José, take the Interamerican Highway west toward Puntarenas, and then continue north on this road to Cañas. In Cañas, turn east toward Tilarán. The drive takes 4 hours. If you're continuing on to Nuevo Arenal, follow the signs in town, which will put you on the road that skirts the shore of the lake. Nuevo Arenal is about a half-hour drive from Tilarán. You can also drive here from La Fortuna, along a scenic road that winds around the lake. From La Fortuna, it's approximately 1 hour to Nuevo Arenal and 1½ hours to Tilarán.

By Bus   Express buses (ℂ 222-3854) leave San José for Tilarán daily at 7:30 and 9:30am, and 12:45, 3:45, and 6:30pm from Calle 12 between avenidas 7 and 9. The trip lasts from 4 to 5½ hours, depending on road conditions; the fare is $3.

There are also morning and afternoon buses from **Puntarenas** to Tilarán. The ride takes about 3 hours; the fare is $2.50. (For details on getting to Puntarenas, see "Puntarenas," in chapter 7.) From **Monteverde** (Santa Elena), there is a bus daily at 7am. The fare for the 3-hour trip is $2. Buses from **La Fortuna** leave for Tilarán daily at 8am and 2:30pm, returning at 7am and 12:30pm. The trip is 3 to 4 hours; the fare is $2.50.

From Tilarán, direct buses to San José leave daily at 5, 7, and 9:30am, and 2 and 5pm. Buses to Puntarenas leave at 6am and 1pm daily. The bus to Santa

Elena (Monteverde) leaves daily at 1pm. Buses also leave regularly for Cañas, where you can catch buses north or south along the Interamerican Highway. Buses for La Fortuna, at the south end of Lake Arenal, leave daily at 7am and 3pm.

ORIENTATION & FAST FACTS   Tilarán is about 5km (3 miles) from Lake Arenal. All roads into town lead to the central park, which is Tilarán's main point of reference for addresses. If you need to exchange money, check at one of the hotels listed here, or go to the Banco Nacional. If you need a taxi to get to a lodge on Lake Arenal, call **Taxis Unidos Tilarán** (© **695-5324**).

WHAT TO SEE & DO

WINDSURFING & KITEBOARDING   If you want to try windsurfing, you can rent equipment from **Tilawa Windsurfing Center** (© **695-5050;** www.windsurfcostarica.com), which has its facilities on one of the lake's few accessible beaches, about 8km (5 miles) from Tilarán on the road along the west end of the lake. Boards rent for around $50 per day, and lessons are also available. These folks are also offering classes and rentals for the new high-octane sport of kiteboarding. Another option that is especially popular with serious sailboarders is **Tico Wind** (© **692-2002;** www.ticowind.com), which sets up shop on the shores of the lake each year from December 1 to the end of April, when the winds blow. Rates run around $65 per day, including lunch, with multiday packages available. If you can't reach them via the phone or website, the folks at either **Mystica** or **Rock River Lodge** (see "Where to Stay," below) can hook you up.

SWIMMING & HIKING   Up above Lake Arenal on the far side of the lake from Tilarán, you'll find the beautiful little heart-shape **Lake Coter.** This lake is surrounded by forest and has good swimming. (UFO watchers also claim that this is a popular pit stop for extraterrestrials.) A taxi to Lake Coter costs around $12.

If you feel like strapping on your boots, there are some hiking trails on the far side of Lake Arenal, near the smaller Lake Coter.

MOUNTAIN BIKING   This is a great area to explore on a mountain bike. **Rock River Lodge** has some high-end mountain bikes, which will run you around $35 per day. You can also rent bikes from the **Hotel Tilawa** (see "Where to Stay," below) or in the town of Tilarán at **La Carreta** hotel & restaurant (© **695-6593**).

FISHING   Ask at your hotel if you want to try your hand at fishing for *guapote*. A half-day fishing trip should cost around $150 per boat, and a full day goes for around $250. The boats used will usually accommodate up to three people fishing.

HORSEBACK RIDING   Any of the hotels in the area can hook you up with a horseback-riding tour for around $10 to $15 per hour.

A PRIVATE GARDEN   Continuing clockwise on the road around the lake will bring you to the town of Nuevo Arenal, where the pavement ends. If you continue another 4km (2½ miles) on the dirt road, you'll come to the **Arenal Botanical Gardens & Butterfly Sanctuary** ⚘ (© **694-4305;** open Nov–May daily 9am–5pm; $8 admission). This private garden was started only in 1991, but it's already quite beautiful and extensive. Not only are there many tropical plants and flowers to be seen, but the butterfly garden also is quite large and well stocked, and there are usually scores of hummingbirds here.

ARTS, CRAFTS & DOWN-HOME COOKING   If you're in the area, don't miss **Toad Hall** ⚘⚘ (© **692-8020**). Located 9km (5½ miles) outside of Nuevo

Arenal, toward La Fortuna, this roadside gallery and cafe serves up excellent breakfasts, light lunches, and a wide range of coffee drinks and desserts. It also has one of the better-stocked galleries in the country. You'll find the works of Lil Mena, Cecilia Figueres, Patricia Erickson, and Barry Biesanz, among others, as well as a good selection of craftworks.

You'll find **The Lucky Bug Gallery** ⭐, another excellent little roadside arts and crafts and souvenir shop, attached to Willy's Caballo Negro restaurant (p. 230).

WHERE TO STAY

In addition to the places listed below, the **Ceiba Tree Lodge** (ℂ **692-8050;** www.ceibatree-lodge.com) is a small, simple lodge with a beautiful view and lovely gardens, located on a hill above the lake. **La Mansion Inn Arenal** (ℂ **692-8018;** www.lamansionarenal.com) is the most upscale option in this area; although the hotel is very nice, I'm not sure the rates are fully justified.

MODERATE

Chalet Nicholas *(Value)* This friendly American-owned bed-and-breakfast is located 2.5km (1½ miles) west of Nuevo Arenal and sits on a hill above the road. There are great views from the garden, and all three rooms have a view of Arenal Volcano in the distance. This converted home is set on 6 hectares (15 acres) and has pretty flower gardens, an organic vegetable garden, and an orchid garden. Behind the property are acres of forest through which you can hike in search of birds, orchids, butterflies, and other tropical beauties. The upstairs loft room is the largest unit, with its own private deck. No smoking is allowed in the house or on the grounds. A 3-hour horseback-riding tour costs $25 per person. Owners John and Catherine Nicholas go out of their way to make their guests feel at home, although their four Great Danes might intimidate you when you first drive up. All around, it's a really good deal.

Tilarán (A.P. 72-5710), Guanacaste. ℂ **694-4041.** www.chaletnicholas.com. 3 units. $59 double. Rates include full breakfast. No credit cards. *In room:* No phone.

Hotel Tilawa ⭐ *(Kids)* Built to resemble the Palace of Knossos on the island of Crete, the Hotel Tilawa sits high on the slopes above the lake and has a sweeping vista down to the water. It's primarily a windsurfers' and kiteboarders' hangout. Unusual colors and antique paint effects give the hotel a weathered look; inside there are wall murals and other artistic paint treatments throughout. Rooms have dyed cement floors, Guatemalan bedspreads, and big windows. Some have kitchenettes. Tilawa can arrange windsurfing, kiteboarding, mountain biking, horseback riding, and fishing trips. It also offers a 5-hour tour by boat across the lake, with a visit to Tabacón Hot Springs, for $50. There's even a small skate park for radical skateboarders and BMX freestyle bikers, which makes this a good place to bring teenagers. The hotel has recently been taken over by new management, and so far there have been some promising improvements.

Tilarán (A.P. 92-5710), Guanacaste. ℂ **695-5050.** Fax 695-5766. www.hotel-tilawa.com. 28 units. $61–$82 double; $92–$113 suite. Rates lower in the off season, higher during peak periods. MC, V. **Amenities:** Restaurant; brewpub; small outdoor pool; outdoor tennis court; sailboard, kiteboard, and bike rental nearby; tour desk; laundry service.

Mystica ⭐ *(Value)* Set on a high hill above Lake Arenal (about midway between Nuevo Arenal and Tilarán), this establishment has simple but spacious and cheery rooms. The painted cement floors are kept immaculate, and the rooms get good ventilation from their large windows. All units open onto a long and broad shared veranda with a great view of the lake. The owners here can help you book a wide range of adventures and tours. Perhaps the star attraction here is the hotel's excellent little Italian restaurant and pizzeria by the same name (p. 230).

On the road between Tilarán and Nuevo Arenal (A.P. 29-5710, Tilarán). ✆ **692-1001.** Fax 692-1002. www.mysticalodge.com. 6 units. $60 double. Rates include continental breakfast. V. **Amenities:** Restaurant; bar; laundry service. *In room:* No phone.

Rock River Lodge ★ *Value*   Set high on a grassy hill above the lake, this small lodge is *the joint* for serious windsurfers. The rooms are in a long, low lodge set on stilts. Walls and floors are made of hardwood, and there are bamboo railings along the veranda. Wind chimes let you know when the breezes are kicking up, and there are sling chairs on the porch. Rooms are midsize; each has one double bed and a bunk bed, and a small tiled bathroom. Although it is fairly simple in style, this is one of the most attractive lodges in the area. The newer bungalows, which are farther up the hill, offer more privacy and space and have small sculpted bathtubs in larger bathrooms. It's a long walk down to the lake (not to mention the walk back up), so a car is recommended. Meals are served in the spacious open-air restaurant, where there's a large stone fireplace. When the wind isn't up, owner Norman List offers mountain-biking trips and horseback and hiking adventures around the region.

Tilarán (A.P. 95), Guanacaste. ✆/fax **692-1180.** www.rockriverlodge.com. 6 units, 8 bungalows. $45 double; $65 bungalow for 2. Extra person $12. V (6% surcharge). **Amenities:** Restaurant; bar; sailboard and bike rental; laundry service. *In room:* No phone.

Villa Decary ★ *Finds*   Named after a French explorer (and a rare palm species that he discovered and named), this small bed-and-breakfast is nestled on a hill above Lake Arenal, midway between the town of Nuevo Arenal and the Arenal Botanical Gardens. Each room comes with one queen-size and one twin bed, large picture windows, and a spacious private balcony with a lake view. The rooms get plenty of light, and the bright Guatemalan bedspreads and white-tile floors create a vibrant look. The separate casitas have full kitchens, more room, and even better views of the lake from their slightly higher perches. Breakfasts are extravagant and memorable, with a steady stream of fresh fruits; fresh juice; strong coffee; homemade pancakes, waffles, or muffins; and usually an excellent omelet or soufflé. There's great bird-watching on the hotel grounds, and howler monkeys are common guests here as well.

Nuevo Arenal, 5717 Tilarán, Guanacaste. ✆ **383-3012,** or ✆/fax 694-4330. www.villadecary.com. 5 units, 3 casitas. $89 double; $109–$129 casita for 2. Rates include full breakfast. Extra person $15. No credit cards. *In room:* No phone.

INEXPENSIVE

Cabinas Mary   Located right on Tilarán's large and sunny central park, Cabinas Mary is a very basic but fairly clean lodging. It's upstairs from the restaurant of the same name and has safe parking in back. Rooms are large, and most have plenty of windows. You even get hot water here, which is a surprise at this price. The restaurant downstairs is a popular hangout.

Tilarán (A.P. 89), Guanacaste. ✆/fax **695-5479.** 18 units. $22 double. V. **Amenities:** Restaurant; bar. *In room:* No phone.

Hotel Naralit   This budget hotel is a good bet in Tilarán. The rooms are clean and comfortable, and some even come with cable TV, albeit with very small television sets. There are three second-floor rooms that have a nice shared balcony, more natural light, and views of the town's church.

Tilarán, Guanacaste. ✆ **695-5393.** Fax 695-6767. 26 units. $18–$30 double. V. *In room:* No phone.

WHERE TO DINE

There are numerous inexpensive places to eat in Tilarán, including the restaurant at Cabinas Mary, as well as **La Carreta** (© 695-6593), a popular restaurant and bar around the corner, which has recently added some hotel rooms. If you're staying outside of town, you'll likely eat in your hotel's dining room because there are few restaurants around the shores of the lake.

In Nuevo Arenal, try the pizzas and pastas at **Tramonti** (© 694-4282). For breakfast, snacks, and fresh-baked goods, check out **Tom's Pan German Bakery** (© 694-4547). Also worth mentioning is **Equus BBQ** (© 692-1101), a small open-air restaurant in front of Xiloe Lodge that has a view of the lake. It specializes in roast chicken and steaks.

Mystica ✪ PIZZA/ITALIAN   The restaurant in this Italian-run hotel has a wonderful setting high on a hill overlooking the lake. The large dining room features rustic wooden chairs and tables, varnished wood floors, colorful tablecloths, and abundant flower arrangements. The most striking features, aside from the view, are the large open fireplace on one end and the large brick oven, in the shape of a small cottage, on the other that turns out pizzas. The pastas and delicious main dishes are authentically northern Italian. Whenever possible, Mystica uses fresh ingredients from its own garden.

On the road between Tilarán and Nuevo Arenal. © 692-1001. Main courses $3–$9. MC, V. Daily 7:30am–9pm.

Willy's Caballo Negro ✪ (Finds) GERMAN/EUROPEAN   The German owners of this attractive little roadside cafe serve up three different types of schnitzel, both chicken and veal cordon bleu, and a host of other old-world meat dishes. Try the Zigeuner Schnitzel, a tender veal cutlet in a slightly spicy sauce of onions and bell peppers, served with spätzle. Despite the emphasis on meats and sausages, vegetarians will find several tasty and filling options here, including stuffed potatoes and eggplant Parmesan. Wooden tables are set around the edges of the round dining room, with a high peaked roof. Candles and creative lighting give the place a cozy and warm feel. There's a small, picturesque lake behind the restaurant and the very interesting Lucky Bug Gallery, run by the owner's triplet daughters.

Nuevo Arenal (about 3km/1¾ miles out of town on the road to Tilarán). © 694-4515. Main courses $4–$12. MC, V. Daily 8am–8pm.

4 Monteverde ★/★

167km (104 miles) NW of San José; 82km (51 miles) NW of Puntarenas

Next to Manuel Antonio, this is Costa Rica's most internationally recognized tourist destination. The fame and accompanying traffic have led some to dub it the Monteverde Crowd Forest. Nevertheless, the reserve itself and the extensive network of private reserves around it are incredibly rich in biodiversity, and a well-organized infrastructure helps guarantee a rewarding experience for both first-time and experienced ecoadventurers.

Monteverde translates as "green mountain," and that's exactly what you'll find at the end of the steep and windy rutted dirt road that leads here. Along the way, you'll pass through mile after mile of often dry, brown pasturelands. All of these pastures were once covered with dense forest, but now only small pieces of that original forest remain.

Monteverde

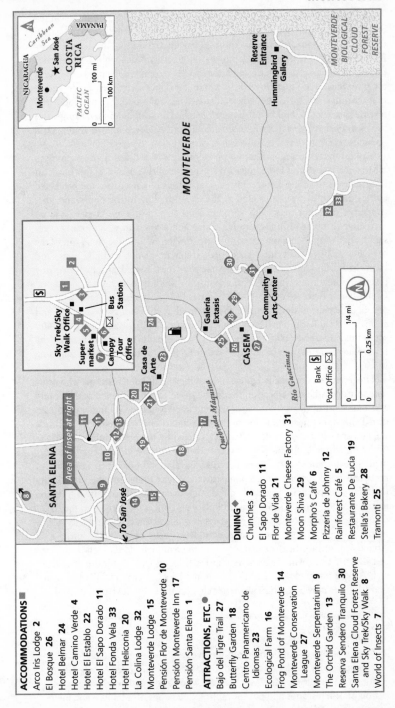

ACCOMMODATIONS ■
Arco Iris Lodge **2**
El Bosque **26**
Hotel Belmar **24**
Hotel Camino Verde **4**
Hotel El Establo **22**
Hotel El Sapo Dorado **11**
Hotel Fonda Vela **33**
Hotel Heliconia **20**
La Colina Lodge **32**
Monteverde Lodge **15**
Pensión Flor de Monteverde **10**
Pensión Monteverde Inn **17**
Pensión Santa Elena **1**

ATTRACTIONS, ETC. ●
Bajo del Tigre Trail **27**
Butterfly Garden **18**
Centro Panamericano de
  Idiomas **23**
Ecological Farm **16**
Frog Pond of Monteverde **14**
Monteverde Conservation
  League **27**
Monteverde Serpentarium **9**
The Orchid Garden **13**
Reserva Sendero Tranquilo **30**
Santa Elena Cloud Forest Reserve
  and Sky Trek/Sky Walk **8**
World of Insects **7**

DINING ◆
Chunches **3**
El Sapo Dorado **11**
Flor de Vida **21**
Monteverde Cheese Factory **31**
Moon Shiva **29**
Morpho's Café **6**
Pizzería de Johnny **12**
Rainforest Café **5**
Restaurante De Lucía **19**
Stella's Bakery **28**
Tramonti **25**

231

The village of Monteverde was founded in 1951 by Quakers from the United States who wanted to leave behind a constant fear of war as well as an obligation to support continued militarism through paying U.S. taxes. They chose Costa Rica primarily because it had no standing army. Although Monteverde's founders came here to farm the land, they wisely recognized the need to preserve the rare cloud forest that covered the mountain slopes above their fields, and to that end they dedicated the largest adjacent tract of cloud forest as the Monteverde Biological Cloud Forest Reserve. Perched on a high mountain ridge, this tiny, scattered village and surrounding cloud forest are well known among both scientific researchers and ecotravelers.

Cloud forests are a mountaintop phenomenon. Moist, warm air sweeping in off the nearby ocean is forced upward by mountain slopes, and as this moist air rises, it cools, forming clouds. The mountaintops of Costa Rica are blanketed almost daily in dense clouds, and as these clouds cling to the slopes, moisture condenses on forest trees. This constant level of moisture has given rise to an incredible diversity of innovative life forms and a forest in which nearly every square inch of space has some sort of plant growing. Within the cloud forest, the branches of huge trees are draped with epiphytic plants: orchids, ferns, and bromeliads. This intense botanic competition has created an almost equally diverse population of insects, birds, and other wildlife. Monteverde Biological Cloud Forest Reserve covers 10,400 hectares (25,688 acres) of forest, including several different life zones that are characterized by different types of plants and animals. Within this small area are more than 2,000 species of plants, 400 species of birds, and 100 different species of mammals. It's no wonder that the reserve has been the site of constant scientific investigations since its founding in 1972.

The reserve was originally known only to the handful of researchers who came here to study different aspects of life in the cloud forest. However, as the beauty and biological diversity of the area became known outside of academic circles, casual visitors began arriving. For many, the primary goal was a chance to glimpse the rare and elusive **quetzal,** a bird once revered by the pre-Columbian peoples of the Americas. As the number of visitors began to grow, lodges began opening, word spread, more lodges opened, and so on. Today Monteverde is a place of great and fragile beauty whose popularity threatens to destroy the very beauty that draws people to it. That said, and despite the hordes of ecotourists traipsing its trails, Monteverde is still a beautiful place and offers a glimpse into the life of one of the world's most threatened ecosystems. However, if your primary goal is to sight a quetzal, you should also consider visiting other cloud forest areas around Costa Rica. In particular, consider the San Gerardo de Dota and Cerro de la Muerte areas, which have several specialty lodges (see "San Isidro de El General: A Base for Exploring Chirripó National Park" in chapter 7), where you'll find far fewer crowds and usually better chances of seeing the famed quetzal.

Tips A Good Read

If you want an in-depth look into the lives and history of the local Quaker community, try to pick up a copy of the *Monteverde Jubilee Family Album.* Published in 2001 by the Monteverde Association of Friends, this collection of oral histories and photographs is 260 pages of local lore and memoirs, well worth the $20 price.

ESSENTIALS

GETTING THERE & DEPARTING   By Car   Take the Interamerican Highway toward Nicaragua. About 20km (12 miles) past the turnoff for Puntarenas there will be a marked turnoff for Sardinal, Santa Elena, and Monteverde. From this turnoff, the road is paved almost as far as the tiny town of Guacimal. From here it's another 20km (12 miles) to Santa Elena. It should take you a little over 2 hours to reach the turnoff and another 1½ hours or so from there.

An alternative route is to continue on the Interamerican Highway until just before the Río Lagarto Bridge. This turnoff isn't always well marked. From the Río Lagarto turnoff, it's 38km (24 miles) to Santa Elena and Monteverde.

Whichever route you take, the final going is slow because the roads into Santa Elena are rough, unpaved dirt and gravel affairs. Many people are told that these roads are not passable without four-wheel-drive, but I've been driving them in regular cars for years, albeit in the dry season. Don't try it in the rainy season (mid-Apr to Nov) unless you have four-wheel-drive.

> **Tips   Driving Note**
>
> All roads to and around Monteverde are rugged. Pregnant women and people with bad backs should think twice before embarking on these painful, poorly maintained roads. It's usually possible to make the trip in a standard two-wheel-drive vehicle in the dry season (Dec–Mar), but even so, you might want the extra clearance afforded by four-wheel-drive. In the rainy season (Apr–Nov), four-wheel-drive is a must.

Just before you enter the town of Santa Elena, you'll be stopped at a little tollbooth collecting 200 colones. The money is ostensibly going to maintain the road, and payment is actually optional.

By Bus   Express buses (© **222-3854** or 645-5159) leave San José daily at 6:30am and 2:30pm from Calle 12 between avenidas 7 and 9. The trip takes around 4 hours; the fare is $6.

There's also a daily bus that departs Puntarenas for Santa Elena, only a few kilometers from Monteverde, at 2pm. The bus stop in Puntarenas is across the street from the main bus station. The fare for the 2½-hour trip is $2.50.

There is a daily bus from Tilarán (Lake Arenal) at 1pm. Trip duration, believe it or not, is 2 hours (for a 40km/25-mile trip); the fare is $2.

Grayline (© **220-2126**; www.graylinecostarica.com) has a daily bus that leaves San José for Monteverde at 7am; the fare is $38. **Interbus** (© **283-5573**; www.interbusonline.com) has a daily bus that leaves San José for Monteverde at 9am; the fare is $30. Another option is to take **Costa Rica Expeditions'** van (© **257-0766**; www.costaricaexpeditions.com) from San José; the fare is $40. Any of the above companies will pick you up at most San José–area hotels.

The express bus departs for San José daily at 6:30am and 2:30pm. The bus from Santa Elena to Puntarenas leaves daily at 6am. If you are heading to Manuel Antonio, take the 6am Santa Elena/Puntarenas bus and transfer in Puntarenas. To reach Liberia, take any bus down the mountain and get off at the Río Lagarto Bridge, where you hit the paved road. You can then flag down a bus bound for Liberia (almost any bus heading north). The Santa Elena/Tilarán bus leaves daily at 7am. Both **Grayline** and **Interbus** offer routes with connections to most major destinations in Costa Rica.

> ## Tips   Alternative Transport
>
> You can travel between Monteverde and La Fortuna by boat and taxi, or on a combination boat, horseback, and taxi trip. See "Boats, Horses & Taxis" on p. 215 for more information. Any of the trips described there can be done in the reverse direction departing from Monteverde. Most hotels and **Desafío Expeditions** (© 645-5874; www.monteverdetours.com) can arrange this trip for you. Desafío also offers multiday hikes from Monteverde to Arenal; you spend the night in rustic research facilities inside the Bosque Eterno de los Niños.

GETTING AROUND   There are two buses daily between the town of Santa Elena and the Monteverde Biological Cloud Forest Reserve. The buses leave Santa Elena for the reserve at 6:15am and 1pm, returning at noon and 4pm. Fare is $1.50. There's also periodic van transportation between the town of Santa Elena and the Santa Elena Cloud Forest Reserve. Ask around town, and you should be able to find the current schedule and book a ride for around $2 per person. A taxi (© **645-6969** or 645-5148) between Santa Elena and either the Monteverde Reserve or the Santa Elena Cloud Forest Reserve costs around $8 for up to four people. Count on paying between $4 and $8 for the ride from Santa Elena to your lodge in Monteverde. Finally, several places around town rent ATVs, or all-terrain vehicles, for around $60 per day. Hourly rates and guided tours are also available.

ORIENTATION   As you approach Santa Elena, take the right fork in the road if you're heading directly to Monteverde. If you continue straight, you'll come into the little village of **Santa Elena,** which has a bus stop, a health clinic, a bank, a general store, a laundromat, and a few simple restaurants, budget hotels, a souvenir shop, and tour offices.

Monteverde, on the other hand, is not a village in the traditional sense of the word. There's no center of town—only dirt lanes leading off from the main road to various farms. This main road has signs for all the hotels and restaurants mentioned here, and it dead-ends at the reserve entrance.

FAST FACTS   The telephone number for the **local clinic** is © **645-5076;** for the **Red Cross,** © **645-6128;** and for the **local police,** © **911** or **645-5127.** There's a 24-hour gas station located about halfway between the town of Santa Elena and the Monteverde Biological Cloud Forest Reserve.

EXPLORING THE MONTEVERDE BIOLOGICAL CLOUD FOREST RESERVE ✦✦✦

The Monteverde Biological Cloud Forest Reserve (© **645-5122;** www.cct.or.cr) is one of the most developed and well-maintained natural attractions in Costa Rica. The trails are clearly marked, regularly traveled, and generally gentle in terms of ascents and descents. The cloud forest here is lush and largely untouched. Still, keep in mind that most of the birds and mammals you've been reading about are rare, elusive, and nocturnal. Moreover, to all but the most trained of eyes, those thousands of exotic ferns, orchids, and bromeliads tend to blend into one large mass of indistinguishable green. However, with a guide hired through your hotel, or on one of the reserve's official guided 2- to 3-hour hikes, you can see and learn far more than you could on your own. At $15 per person, the reserve's tours might seem like a splurge, especially after you pay the entrance fee, but I strongly recommend that you go with a guide.

Perhaps the most famous resident of the cloud forests of Costa Rica is the quetzal, a robin-size bird with iridescent green wings and a ruby-red breast, which has become extremely rare due to habitat destruction. The male quetzal also has two long tail feathers that can reach nearly .6m (2 ft.) in length, making it one of the most spectacular birds on earth. The best time to see quetzals is early morning to midmorning, and the best months are February through April (mating season).

Other animals that have been seen in Monteverde, although sightings are extremely rare, include jaguars, ocelots, and tapirs. After the quetzal, Monteverde's most famous resident was the golden toad (*sapo dorado*), a rare native species. However, the golden toad has disappeared from the forest and is feared extinct. Competing theories of the toad's demise include adverse effects of a natural drought cycle, the disappearing ozone layer, pesticides, and acid rain. Photos of the golden toad abound in Monteverde. (I particularly like the shots of amphibian group sex.) I'm sure you'll be as saddened as I was by the disappearance of such a beautiful creature.

ADMISSION, HOURS & TOURS   The reserve is open daily from 7am to 4pm, and the entrance fee is $12 for adults and $6.50 for students and children. Because only 120 people are allowed into the reserve at any one time, you might be forced to wait for a while. Most hotels can reserve a guided walk and entrance to the reserve for the following day for you, or you can get tickets in advance directly at the reserve entrance.

Some of the trails can be very muddy, depending on the season, so ask about current conditions. If the mud is heavy, you can rent rubber boots at the reserve entrance for $2 per day. They might make your hike much more pleasant.

Before venturing into the forest, have a look around the information center. There are several guidebooks available, as well as posters and postcards of some of the reserve's more famous animal inhabitants.

Night tours of the reserve leave every evening at 7:15pm. Reservations are not necessary; just show up at the reserve entrance around 7pm. The cost is $13, including admission to the reserve, a 2-hour hike, and, most important, a guide with a high-powered searchlight.

WHAT TO SEE & DO OUTSIDE THE RESERVE
BIRD-WATCHING & HIKING
Ample bird-watching and hiking opportunities can also be found outside the reserve boundaries. You can avoid the crowds at Monteverde by heading

---

Tips **Seeing the Forest for the Trees, Bromeliads, Monkeys, Hummingbirds . . .**

Because the entrance fee to Monteverde is valid for a full day, I recommend taking an early-morning walk with a guide and then heading off on your own either directly after that hike or after lunch. A guide will certainly point out and explain a lot, but there's also much to be said for walking quietly through the forest on your own or in very small groups. This will also allow you to stray from the well-traveled paths in the park.

5km (3 miles) north from the village of Santa Elena to the **Santa Elena Cloud Forest Reserve** ✮✮ (© 645-5390). This 360-hectare (889-acre) reserve has a maximum elevation of 1,680m (5,510 ft.), which makes it the highest cloud forest in the Monteverde area. There are 13km (8 miles) of hiking trails, as well as an information center. Because it borders the Monteverde Reserve, a similar richness of flora and fauna is to be found here, although quetzals are not nearly as common. The $8 entry fee at this reserve goes directly to support local schools. The reserve is open daily from 7am to 4pm. Guided tours are available for $15 per person, not including the entrance fee. (Call the number above to make a reservation for the tour.) A night tour is also offered each evening at 7pm.

Sky Walk ✮✮ (© 645-5238; www.skywalk.co.cr) is a network of forest paths and suspension bridges that provides visitors with a view previously reserved for birds, monkeys, and the much more adventurous traveler. The bridges reach 39m (128 ft.) above the ground at their highest point, so acrophobia could be an issue. The Sky Walk and its sister attraction, **Sky Trek** (see "Canopy Tours," below), are located about 3.5km (2¼ miles) outside of the town of Santa Elena, on the road to the Santa Elena Cloud Forest Reserve. The Sky Walk is open daily from 7am to 4pm; admission is $15. For an extra $10, a knowledgeable guide will point out the diverse flora and fauna on the walk. For $45 per person, you can do the Sky Trek canopy tour and then walk the trails and bridges of the Sky Walk. Reservations are recommended for the Sky Trek. These folks will provide round-trip transportation from Santa Elena for just $2 per person.

To learn even more about Monteverde, stop in at the **Monteverde Conservation League** (© 645-5003; www.acmonteverde.com), which administers the 21,600-hectare (53,352-acre) private reserve **Bosque Eterno de Los Niños (Children's Eternal Forest),** as well as the Bajo del Tigre Trail. The Conservation League has its office on the Cerro Plano road, 50m (164 ft.) before the Butterfly Garden. In addition to being a good source for information, it also sells books, T-shirts, and cards, and all proceeds go to purchase more land for the Bosque Eterno de Los Niños. The **Bajo del Tigre Trail** ✮ is a 3.5km (2¼-mile) trail that's home to several different bird species not usually found within the reserve. You can take several different loops, lasting anywhere from 1 hour to several hours. The trail starts a little past the CASEM artisans' shop (see "Shopping," below) and is open daily from 8am to 5pm. Admission is $5 general and $2 for students.

You can also go on guided 3-hour hikes at the **Reserva Sendero Tranquilo** ✮ (© 645-5010), which has 80 hectares (198 acres) of land, two-thirds of which is in virgin forest. This reserve is located up the hill from the cheese factory, charges $20 for its tours, and is open daily from 7am to 3pm seasonally.

Finally, you can walk the trails and grounds of the **Ecological Farm** ✮ (© 645-5554; www.fincaecologicamonteverde.com), a family-run wildlife refuge and private reserve located down the Cerro Plano road. This place has four main trails through a variety of ecosystems, and wildlife viewing is often quite good here. There are a couple of pretty waterfalls off the trails, and sometimes night tours are offered. It's open daily from 7am to 5pm; admission is $7.

CANOPY TOURS

One of the oldest canopy tours in the country is run by **The Original Canopy Tour** ✮✮ (© 645-5243; www.canopytour.com), which has an office right in the center of Santa Elena. This is of the more interesting canopy tours in Costa Rica because the initial ascent is made by climbing up the hollowed-out interior of a giant strangler fig. This tour was recently expanded and now has 11 platforms and two rappels, making it the most adventurous such option in

Monteverde. The 3-hour tours run three times daily and cost $45 for adults, $35 for students, and $25 for children under 12.

Another popular option is offered by the folks at **Sky Trek** ★★ (© 645-5238; www.skytrek.com), a growing complex of aerial adventures and hiking trails. This is one of the more extensive canopy tours in the country, with two very long cables to cross. The longest of these is some 700m (2,296 ft.) long, high above the forest floor. There are no rappel descents here, and you brake using the pulley system for friction. This tour costs $40.

There's actually a glut of canopy tours in the Monteverde area, and I personally can recommend only the two mentioned above. Anybody in average physical condition can do any of the canopy tours in Monteverde, but they're not for the faint-hearted or acrophobic. Try to book directly with the companies listed above or through your hotel. Beware of touts on the streets of Monteverde, who make a small commission and frequently try to steer tourists to the operator paying the highest percentage.

HORSEBACK RIDING

Meg's Riding Stables (© 645-5560), **La Estrella Stables** (© 645-5075), **Palomina Horse Tours** (© 645-5479), and **Sabine's Smiling Horses** (© 645-5051; www.horseback-riding-tour.com) are the more established operators, offering guided rides for around $10 per hour. As I mentioned earlier in "Boats, Horses & Taxis" (p. 215), there are horseback/boat trips linking Monteverde/Santa Elena with La Fortuna. This is certainly an exciting and adventurous means of connecting these two popular destinations, but I've received numerous complaints about the state of the trails and the treatment of the horses, so be very careful before undertaking this trip.

Another option is to set up a day tour and sauna at **El Sol** ★ (© 645-5838; www.elsolnuestro.com). Located about a 10-minute car ride down the mountain from Santa Elena, these folks take you on a roughly 3-hour ride either to San Luis or to an isolated little waterfall with an excellent swimming hole. After the ride back, you'll find the wood-burning traditional Swedish sauna all fired up, with a refreshing and beautiful little pool beside it. The tour costs around $50 per person, including lunch. These folks also have two very rustically luxurious private cabins ($60–$80 double), with excellent views.

OTHER ATTRACTIONS IN MONTEVERDE

Birds are not the only colorful fauna in Monteverde. Butterflies abound here, and the **Butterfly Garden** ★ (© 645-5512), located near the Pensión Monteverde Inn, displays many of Costa Rica's most beautiful species. Besides the hundreds of preserved and mounted butterflies, there's a garden and a greenhouse where you can watch live butterflies. The garden is open daily from 9:30am to 4pm, and admission is $9 for adults and $6 for students and children, including a guided tour. The best time to visit is between 9:30am and 1pm, when the butterflies are most active.

If your taste runs toward the slithery, you can check out the **Monteverde Serpentarium** (© 645-5238; www.snaketour.com), on the road to the reserve. This place was recently remodeled and the new enclosures and informative displays are a vast improvement. It's open daily from 9am to 8pm and charges $7 for admission. The **Frog Pond of Monteverde** (© 645-6320), located a couple of hundred meters north of the Monteverde Lodge, is probably a better bet. The $8 entrance gets you a 45-minute tour, and your ticket is good for 2 days. A variety of species populate a series of glass terrariums. This place is open daily from

> **Tips** **Music in Monteverde**
>
> Each year, throughout much of the high season, the **Monteverde Institute** (© 645-5053; www.mvinstitute.org) hosts the annual **Monteverde Music Festival.** There's a different concert every Thursday, Friday, and Saturday evening. Featuring mostly Costa Rican groups, the programming ranges from folk to jazz to classical. Admission is $10 for adults and $5 for students. Given the success of this annual event, the Institute is planning to extend its programming throughout much of the year.

9am to 8:30pm. I especially recommend that you stop by at least once after dark, when the tree frogs are active. The newest entry in this field is the **World of Insects** (© 645-6859), which features a couple dozen terrariums filled with some of the area's more interesting creepy crawlers. My favorites are the giant horned beetles. This place is located 300m (984 ft.) west of the supermarket in Santa Elena. It's open daily from 8am to 9pm; admission is $7.

Because the vegetation in the cloud forest is so dense, most of the forest's animal residents are rather difficult to spot. If you were unsatisfied with your sightings, even with a naturalist guide leading you, you might want to consider attending a slide show of photographs taken in the reserve. There is a host of daily slide shows around Monteverde. The longest running of these takes place at the **Monteverde Lodge, Hotel El Sapo Dorado, Hotel Belmar** (see "Where to Stay," below, for phone numbers), and **Hummingbird Gallery** (see "Shopping," below). Dates, show times, and admissions vary, so inquire at your hotel or one of the places mentioned above.

If you've had your fill of birds, snakes, frogs, bugs, and butterflies, you might want to stop at the **Orchid Garden** ★ (© 645-5510), on the main road toward the reserve. This small botanical garden boasts more than 400 species of orchids. Admission is $5 for adults and $3 for students. It's open daily from 8am to 5pm.

The **Centro Panamericano de Idiomas** ★ (© 888/682-0054 in the U.S. and Canada, or 645-5441; www.spanishlanguageschool.com) offers immersion language classes in a wonderful setting. A 1-week program, with 4 hours of class per day and a homestay with a Costa Rican family, costs $365.

Almost all of the area hotels can arrange a wide variety of other tours and activities, including guided night tours of the cloud forest and night trips to the Arenal Volcano (a tedious 4-hr. ride, each way).

SHOPPING

Perhaps the best-stocked gift shop in Monteverde is the **Hummingbird Gallery** (© 645-5030). You'll find the gallery just outside the reserve entrance. Hanging from trees around it are several hummingbird feeders that attract more than seven species of these tiny birds. At any given moment, there might be several dozen hummingbirds buzzing and chattering around the building and your head. Inside you will, of course, find a lot of beautiful color prints of hummingbirds and other local flora and fauna, as well as a wide range of craft items, T-shirts, and other gifts. The Hummingbird Gallery is open daily from 8:30am to 4:30pm.

Another good option is **CASEM** (© 645-5190), located on the right side of the main road, just across from Stella's Bakery. This crafts cooperative sells embroidered clothing, T-shirts, posters, and postcards with photos of the local flora and fauna, Boruca weavings, locally grown and roasted coffee, and many other items to remind you of your visit to Monteverde. CASEM is open Monday through Saturday from 8am to 5pm, and Sunday from 10am to 4pm (closed Sun May–Oct). There is also a well-stocked **gift shop** at the entrance to the Monteverde Biological Cloud Forest Reserve. You'll find plenty of T-shirts, postcards, and assorted crafts here, as well as a well-stocked selection of science and natural-history books.

Over the years, Monteverde has developed a nice little community of artists. Around town, you'll see paintings by local artists such as Paul Smith and Meg Wallace, whose works are displayed at the Fonda Vela Hotel and Stella's Bakery, respectively. You might also check out **Galería Extasis** ★ (© 645-5548), which sells the intriguing wooden sculptures of artist Marco Tulio Brenes, or the new **Casa de Arte** ★ (© 645-5275), which has a mix of arts and crafts in many media. Both of these are located just off the main road to the reserve. Another nice place to visit is the **Community Arts Center,** which is located just beyond the Cheese Factory (see below) on the right hand side of the road. In addition to studio space, there's a small gallery and gift shop here selling the work of local artists and artisans.

Finally, it's also worth stopping by the **Monteverde Cheese Factory** to pick up some of the best cheese in Costa Rica. (You can even watch it being processed and get homemade ice cream.) The cheese factory is located right on the main road about midway between Santa Elena and the Reserve. It's open Monday through Saturday from 7:30am to 4pm, and Sunday from 7:30am to noon.

WHERE TO STAY

When choosing a place to stay in Monteverde, be sure to check whether the rates include a meal plan. In the past, almost all the lodges included three meals a day in their prices, but this practice is waning. Check before you assume anything.

MODERATE

In addition to the hotels listed below, **Hotel Poco a Poco** (© 645-6000; www.hotelpocoapoco.com) is yet another comfortable option in this price range. Or you can try **El Sol** ★ (© 645-5838; www.elsolnuestro.com), which is located about 10 minutes south of Santa Elena, on the road to the Interamerican Highway.

Hotel Belmar ★   You'll think you're in the Alps when you stay at this beautiful Swiss chalet–style hotel. Set on the top of a grassy hill, the Belmar has stunning views of the Nicoya Gulf and the Pacific. Afternoons in the dining room or lounge are idyllic, with bright sunlight streaming in through a west-facing glass wall. Sunsets are spectacular. Most of the guest rooms are fitted with wood paneling, French doors, and little balconies that open onto splendid views. There are actually two buildings here. My favorite rooms are in the main building; those in the Chalet building are a bit smaller. The restaurant serves a mix of well-prepared Tico and international cuisine. The Belmar is up a dirt road that passes to the left of the gas station as you come into the village of Monteverde.

Monteverde (A.P. 17-5655), Puntarenas. © 645-5201. Fax 645-5135. www.hotelbelmar.net. 32 units. $70–$80 double. Rates lower in the off season. V. **Amenities:** Restaurant; bar; Jacuzzi; game room; tour desk; laundry service. *In room:* No phone.

Hotel El Establo ★   This place has undergone a major transformation. From a working stable with some budget rooms, it has morphed into what could prove to be the most luxurious and comfortable hotel in Monteverde. The original hotel and budget rooms still stand down by the road, and a massive block of newer suites is located a couple hundred meters inland and up a steep hill, giving them all great views. These rooms are quite large, have private balconies or patios, and a tub, and separate shower, and are supposed to have a full plate of modern amenities: television, telephone, minibar, and hair dryer. However, the owners have put the purchase and installation of these final features on hold, and there's no telling when they will finally finish these rooms. In the meantime, they have set up seven different lounge areas with televisions. Up by the new wing, you'll find a pretty good-size heated swimming pool and sauna. The older budget rooms are still available, although they are no longer budget priced. Of these, the second-floor rooms are my favorites; those on the end of the hall have a bit more light than others. El Establo owns 48 hectares (119 acres) of land backing the hotel, and half of that is primary forest.

Monteverde (A.P. 549-2050, San Pedro). © **645-5110**. Fax 645-5041. www.hotelelestablo.com. 22 units. $72 standard double; $129–$172 suite double. AE, MC, V. **Amenities:** Restaurant; bar; outdoor pool; sauna; tour desk; babysitting; laundry service.

Hotel El Sapo Dorado ★★ *Finds*   Located on a steep hill between Santa Elena and the reserve, El Sapo Dorado (named for Monteverde's famous golden toad) offers some of the most charming and comfortable accommodations in Monteverde. The spacious cabins are built of hardwoods both inside and out and are surrounded by a grassy lawn. Big windows let in lots of light, and high ceilings keep the rooms cool during the day. Some of the older cabins have fireplaces, which are a welcome feature on chilly nights and during the peak parts of the rainy season. My favorite rooms are the sunset suites, which have private terraces with views to the Gulf of Nicoya and wonderful sunsets.

There's an excellent restaurant here (see "Where to Dine," below), and the quiet yet jovial bar stays open until 10pm. The hotel has a combination conference/game room, where it sometimes shows slide shows at night. Not only does El Sapo Dorado own and manage the Reserva Sendero Tranquilo, but it also has a network of well-maintained trails into primary forest on-site. To find the hotel and restaurant, watch for the sign on the left-hand side of the main road to the reserve, a few hundred yards outside of the town of Santa Elena.

Monteverde (A.P. 9-5655), Puntarenas. © **645-5010**. Fax 645-5180. www.sapodorado.com. 30 units. $89–$99 double. AE, MC, V. **Amenities:** Restaurant; bar; tour desk; massage; laundry service.

Hotel Fonda Vela ★★   Although it's one of the older hotels here, Fonda Vela is still one of the top choices in Monteverde. Moreover, this is one of the closer lodges to the Cloud Forest Reserve, an easy 15-minute walk away. Guest rooms are in nine separate buildings scattered among the forests and pastures of this former farm, and most have views of the Nicoya Gulf. Lots of hardwood has been used throughout. The junior suites all come with cable television. The newer junior suites, some of which have excellent views, are the best rooms in the house, and I prefer them to the older and larger junior suites. The dining room has great sunset views, and it sometimes even features live music. There's a popular bar here, as well as a small system of private trails. Meals will run you around $36 per person per day. Throughout the hotel, you'll see paintings by co-owner Paul Smith, who also handcrafts violins and cellos and is a musician himself.

Monteverde (A.P. 70060-1000, San José). © **257-1413** or 645-5125. Fax 257-1416. www.fondavela.com. 40 units. $85 double; $94 junior suite. Extra person $9. AE, MC, V. **Amenities:** Restaurant; bar; horse rental; tour desk; shuttle to the reserve; babysitting; laundry service. *In room:* Stocked minibar.

Hotel Heliconia ★   The Heliconia is another comfortable and semiluxurious hotel. The newer main lodge building is a three-story behemoth, located high on a hill behind the rest of the hotel's several buildings. Here you'll find most of the suites and junior suites, which are immense rooms featuring varnished wood walls, carpeted floors, two king-size beds, and huge private balconies. All of the rooms on the second and third floors here get great sunset views. Rooms in the older buildings down by the road are also done in floor-to-ceiling hardwoods that give them the rustic feel of a mountain resort. Some of these have large picture windows facing dense forest. All around, there are paths that lead through attractive gardens and to a hot tub in a bamboo grove; additional trails lead from the hotel up to and through a 240-hectare (593-acre) private reserve of virgin forest with scenic views of the Nicoya Gulf.

Monteverde (A.P. 10921-1000, San José). (℃) **645-5109.** Fax 645-5007. 32 units. $80 double; $90 junior suite; $106 suite. V. **Amenities:** Restaurant; bar; Jacuzzi; tour desk; laundry service. *In room:* Safe.

Monteverde Lodge ★★ *(Kids)* Operated by Costa Rica Expeditions, the Monteverde Lodge was one of the first ecolodges in Monteverde, and it remains one of the most popular. It's located 5km (3 miles) from the reserve entrance in a secluded setting near Santa Elena. Guest rooms are large and comfortable, and have recently received some much-needed remodeling. Most feature angled walls of glass with chairs and a table placed so that avid bird-watchers can do a bit of birding without leaving their rooms. The gardens and secondary forest surrounding the lodge have some gentle groomed trails and are also home to quite a few species of birds. Perhaps the lodge's most popular attraction is the large hot tub in a big atrium garden just off the lobby. After hiking all day, you can soak your bones under the stars.

The hotel's dining room offers great views, good food, and excellent formal service provided by bow-tied waiters. The adjacent bar is a popular gathering spot, and there are regular evening slide shows focusing on the cloud forest. Scheduled bus service to and from San José is available ($40 each way), as is a shuttle to the reserve ($6 each way), horseback riding, and a variety of optional tours. The excellent guides here have lots of experience with family groups.

Monteverde (mailing address: Dept. 235, P.O. Box 025216, Miami, FL 33102-5216). (℃) **257-0766** or 645-5057. Fax 257-1665. www.costaricaexpeditions.com. 27 units. $99 double. Rates slightly lower in the off season. AE, MC, V. **Amenities:** Restaurant; bar; Jacuzzi; tour desk; laundry service. *In room:* Coffeemaker, safe.

INEXPENSIVE

In addition to the hotels listed below, there are quite a few pensiónes and backpacker specials in Santa Elena and spread out along the road to the reserve. The best of these are **Hotel Camino Verde** (℃ 645-6296; fax 645-5916), **Pensión Flor de Monteverde** (℃ 645-5236), **Pensión Monteverde Inn** (℃ 645-5156), and **Pensión Santa Elena** (℃ 645-5051; www.monteverdeinfo.com). All charge around $8 to $10 per person.

One option at the higher end of this price range worth checking out is **Claro de Luna** (℃ 645-5269; www.claro-de-luna.com), which has beautiful, spacious rooms in a new house located off the main road just beyond the tollbooth before entering Santa Elena.

Finally, it is possible to stay in one of the very basic dormitory rooms right at the **Monteverde Biological Cloud Forest Reserve** (℃ 645-5122; www.cct.or.cr). A bunk bed and three meals per day here run $26 per person. Admission to the reserve is extra.

Arco Iris Lodge ★ *(Finds)* This is by far the nicest hotel right in Santa Elena and is a great value. In fact, it's one of the nicest hotels in the area, regardless of price. The rooms are spread out in eight separate buildings (so, in effect, most are individual cabins). All have wood or tile floors and plenty of wood accents. My favorite is the "honeymoon cabin," which has its own private balcony with a forest view and good bird-watching. Budget travelers can inquire about the two rooms here equipped with bunk beds (for $19 single, $28 double). The management here is extremely helpful, speaks five languages, and can arrange a wide variety of tours. Although they've recently stopped serving lunch and dinner, there's a breakfast buffet for $6.50; beer, wine, and other refreshments are available throughout the day and evening.

Monteverde (A.P. 003-5655), Puntarenas. © 645-5067. Fax 645-5022. www.arcoirislodge.com. 12 units. $42–$55 double. AE, MC, V. **Amenities:** Tour desk; laundry service. *In room:* No phone.

El Bosque   Hidden down the hill behind El Bosque restaurant (on the main road to the reserve) is one of Monteverde's better values. Although the rooms are very basic, they're clean and fairly large and have high ceilings, picture windows, and double beds. The cement floors and simple furnishings help keep the rates down, while the varnished wood paneling give the place a touch of style. The rooms are arranged in a semicircle around a minimally landscaped garden. The hotel's restaurant is some 90m (295 ft.) up a dirt road and down a path that crosses a junglelike ravine by footbridge, which turns going for breakfast into a morning bird-watching trip.

Monteverde (A.P. 27-5655), Puntarenas. © 645-5221 or 645-5158. Fax 645-5129. elbosque@racsa.co.cr. 28 units. $32–$42 double. AE, DC, MC, V. **Amenities:** Restaurant; bar; tour desk; laundry service. *In room:* No phone.

La Colina Lodge *Value*   One of the oldest lodges in Monteverde, the former Flor Mar Pension has changed hands a couple of times in recent years but has also gotten some much-needed attention and renovation. The rooms are housed in two separate buildings. Everything is still quite simple here but is much, much nicer than before, and far more appealing than most budget options around. Most rooms have one double and one single bed, although a couple still have bunk beds. The restaurant area is warm and cozy, with a big fireplace, and there's a separate common lounge area with satellite television. Service is friendly and attentive, and they even allow camping here, with access to the shared bathrooms. The lodge is pretty close to the reserve, which is a plus for budget travelers without a car.

Monteverde. © 645-5009. Fax 645-5580. www.lacolinalodge.com. 11 units, 6 with private bathroom. $36 double with shared bathroom; $42 double with private bathroom; $5 per person camping. Rates include full breakfast; except for campers. V. **Amenities:** Restaurant; laundry service. *In room:* No phone.

WHERE TO DINE

Most lodges in Monteverde have their own dining rooms, and these are the most convenient places to eat, especially if you don't have a car. Because most visitors want to get an early start, they usually grab a quick breakfast at their hotel. It's also common for people to have their lodge pack them a bag lunch to take with them to the reserve, although there's now a decent little *soda* at the reserve entrance. If you're in the mood to eat out, there are several inexpensive restaurants scattered along the road between Santa Elena and Monteverde.

A popular choice for lunch is **Stella's Bakery** (© 645-5560; www.stellasbakery. com), across the road from the CASEM gift shop. Stella's is open daily from 6am to 6pm and has a small cafe and a few outdoor tables, where you can pile your plate with an assortment of fresh foods served cafeteria style. The selection changes but might include vegetarian quiche, eggplant parmigiana, and different salads. It

Tips Take a Break

If all of the activities in Monteverde have worn you out, stop in at **Flor de Vida** ⚘ (✆ **645-6081**), a delightful coffeehouse and restaurant located about midway between Santa Elena and the Monteverde Cloud Forest Reserve. These folks have bagels, homemade granola, and omelets for breakfast; delicious and decadent baked goods; and an interesting range of daily specials for lunch and dinner. There are always a few vegetarian items as well.

In downtown Santa Elena, you could try the **Rainforest Café** (✆ **645-5841**) or **Chunches** (✆ **645-5147**), a bookstore with a small coffee shop and espresso bar that also doubles as a laundromat.

also has freshly baked breads and muffins and a daily supply of other decadent baked goods.

In addition to the places listed below, you can get good pizzas and pastas at **Tramonti** (✆ **645-6120**), the sister restaurant to the popular Tramonti in Nuevo Arenal, which has set up shop in the restaurant attached to the Hotel El Bosque. Also, the restaurant at the **Hotel Poco a Poco** (✆ **645-6000**) has been getting good marks with a wide range of international dishes, including some Chinese and Japanese fare. Finally, on my last visit, **Moon Shiva** (✆ **645-6270**) had opened 100m (30 ft.) up the hill across from CASEM.

El Sapo Dorado ⚘⚘ INTERNATIONAL   Located high on a hill above the main road, El Sapo Dorado provides great sunsets and good food. The menu is a little bit more imaginative than at most restaurants in Monteverde, which makes it well worth a visit even if you miss the sunset. The regularly changing menu might include grilled corvina in heart-of-palm sauce, shrimp in a Sambucca mushroom sauce, or filet mignon in pepper-cream sauce. The emphasis is on fresh ingredients and healthful preparation, and there are always vegetarian and vegan options as well. If you come for lunch or a sunset dinner, definitely grab a table in the large, covered dining room, which has full walls of picture windows for taking in the views.

On the left as you go from Santa Elena toward the reserve. ✆ 645-5010. Reservations recommended during high season. Main courses $10–$20. AE, MC, V. Daily 7–10am, noon–3pm, and 6–9pm.

Morpho's Café COSTA RICAN/INTERNATIONAL   Probably the best and most popular restaurant in the town of Santa Elena, this simple second-floor affair serves up hearty and economical meals. There are soups, sandwiches, and _casados_ for lunch and dinner, and delicious fresh fruit juices, ice-cream shakes, and home-baked desserts throughout the day. The tables and chairs are made from rough-hewn lumber and whole branches and trunks, and the place brims with a light convivial atmosphere. This place is a very popular hangout for backpackers and budget travelers.

In downtown Santa Elena, across from the supermarket. ✆ 645-5607. Main courses $3–$8. MC, V. Daily 11am–10pm.

Pizzería de Johnny PIZZA/ITALIAN ⚘   This popular pizza joint has grown from a little hole-in-the-wall to a near institution here in Monteverde. The thin-crust wood-oven pizzas are delicious, and there's a large menu of meat, chicken, and pasta dishes as well. You can start things off with a bruschetta or mussels

Parmesan. The signature pizza Traviesa comes with artichoke hearts, onions, mushrooms, garlic, and marinated tomatoes. There's a modest little gift shop and a quiet bar off the large open dining room, but the nicest tables are on the covered veranda out back.

On the road to the reserve, a little beyond El Sapo Dorado, on your right. ℭ **645-5066.** Reservations recommended during high season. Small pizzas $4–$7, medium pies $8–$14, large pies $14–$22; other main courses $5–$14. MC, V. Daily 11am–10pm.

Restaurante De Lucía COSTA RICAN/INTERNATIONAL   In just a few years here, De Lucía's has earned some local renown. There's really no menu, but your waiter will bring out a platter with the nightly selection of meats and fresh fish, which are then grilled to order. One of the more interesting dishes is the chicken in orange sauce. All meals come with fresh homemade tortillas and a full accompaniment of side orders and vegetables. The sweet *plátanos* prepared on the open grill are delicious. Service is informal and friendly. The heavy wood tables and chairs are spread comfortably around the large dining room.

On the road down to the Butterfly Farm, on your right. ℭ **645-5337.** Reservations recommended during high season (late Nov to late Apr). Lunch $3–$8; main courses $8–$14. AE, MC, V. Daily 7am–9pm.

MONTEVERDE AFTER DARK

The most popular after dark-activities in Monteverde are night hikes in one of the reserves and a natural history slide show (see "Other Attractions in Monteverde," earlier in this chapter). However, if you want a taste of the local party scene, head to either **La Taberna,** which is just outside of downtown Santa Elena before the Serpentarium, or the **La Cascada Disco,** which is located on the road toward the reserve, beside a jungle river and small waterfall. Both of these attract a mix of locals and tourists, crank music loud, and get people dancing. Alternatively, the **Flor de Vida** and **Moon Shiva** sometimes feature live music or open-mic jam sessions.

7

The Central Pacific Coast:
Where the Mountains
Meet the Sea

The central Pacific coast is home to some of the most accessible beaches in Costa Rica. They range from the somewhat seedy Puntarenas and the cut-rate, fun-in-the-sun Jacó, to the jungle-clad hillsides of Manuel Antonio and Dominical. For the most part, this coast is not as spectacular or varied as that of the Nicoya Peninsula and Guanacaste, but on the bright side, in the dry season, it doesn't get as brown and desolate looking. The climate here is considerably more humid than that farther north, but it's not nearly as steamy as along the south Pacific or Caribbean coasts.

Jacó and Manuel Antonio are Costa Rica's two most developed beaches, while Puntarenas, a former seaport, offers the most urban beach setting in the country. (It's just a short day

trip from San José). If you're looking to get away from it all without traveling too far or spending too much, **Dominical** ☆ should be your top choice on this coast.

This is also where you'll find some of Costa Rica's most popular and spectacular national parks and biological reserves: **Manuel Antonio National Park** ☆☆, home of three-toed sloths and white-faced monkeys; **Chirripó National Park** ☆☆, a misty cloud forest that becomes a barren *páramo* (a region above 3,000m/9,840 ft.) at the peak of its namesake, Mount Chirripó; and **Carara Biological Reserve** ☆☆, one of the last places in Costa Rica where you can see the disappearing dry forest join the damp, humid forests that extend south down the coast. You might even glimpse a scarlet macaw.

1 Puntarenas

115km (71 miles) W of San José; 191km (118 miles) S of Liberia; 75km (47 miles) N of Playa de Jacó

Some see Puntarenas as a fallen jewel with vast potential; others see nothing more than a run-down, rough-and-tumble port town best seen through a rearview mirror. I tend to hold the latter view.

A 16km (10-mile) spit of land jutting into the Gulf of Nicoya, Puntarenas was once Costa Rica's busiest port, but that changed drastically when the government inaugurated nearby Puerto Caldera, a modern container port facility. After losing its shipping business, the city survived primarily on commercial fishing. Watching the tourist boom bring big bucks to other cities, Puntarenas decided to try to grab its piece of the pie. After decades of decay and neglect, Puntarenas has definitely received some long-overdue attention; however, it still needs some work. In 1998, Puntarenas initiated a large public works and renovation project that has so far yielded a new cruise-ship docking facility, a convention and recreation center, a modest maritime museum, and an artisans' row where visitors can stock up on regional arts and crafts.

There's a good highway leading all the way from San José, so Puntarenas can be reached (on a good day, with no traffic) in a little more than 2 hours by car, which makes it one of the closest beaches to San José(at least in elapsed time, if not in actual mileage. Because Puntarenas is a city, a former port town, and a commercial fishing center, this beach has a very different character from any other in Costa Rica. A long, straight stretch of sand with gentle surf, the beach is backed for most of its length by the **Paseo de los Turistas (Tourist Walk).** Across a wide boulevard from the paseo are hotels, restaurants, bars, discos, and shops. The sunsets and the views across the Gulf of Nicoya are quite beautiful, and there's usually a cooling breeze blowing in off the water. All around town you'll find unusual old buildings, reminders of the important role that Puntarenas once played in Costa Rican history. It was from here that much of the Central Valley's coffee crop was once shipped, and while the coffee barons in the highlands were getting rich, so were the merchants of Puntarenas.

Still, Puntarenas is primarily a place to spend the night during transit. Here you must pick up the ferries to the southern Nicoya Peninsula, and many folks like to arrive the night before and get an early start. It's also a good place to break up the longer trip up to or back from Guanacaste. Puntarenas is also popular as a weekend holiday spot for Ticos from San José and is at its liveliest on weekends.

ESSENTIALS

GETTING THERE & DEPARTING   By Car   Head west out of San José on the Interamerican Highway, passing the airport and Alajuela, and follow the signs to Puntarenas. The drive takes between 2 and 2½ hours.

By Bus   Express buses (© **222-0064**) leave San José daily every hour between 6am and 9pm from Calle 16 and Avenida 12. Trip duration is 2½ hours; the fare is $3.

The main Puntarenas bus station is cater-cornered to the main pier on the Paseo de los Turistas. Buses to **San José** leave daily every hour between 5:30am and 8pm. The bus to **Santa Elena** leaves daily at 2pm from a stop across the railroad tracks from the main bus station. Buses to **Quepos** (Manuel Antonio) leave daily at 5 and 11am, and 2:30 and 4:30pm.

By Ferry   See "Playa Tambor" or "Playa Montezuma," in chapter 5, for information on crossing to and returning from Puntarenas from Paquera or Naranjo on the Nicoya Peninsula.

ORIENTATION   Puntarenas is built on a long, narrow sand spit that stretches 16km (10 miles) out into the Gulf of Nicoya and is marked by only five streets at its widest. The ferry docks for the Nicoya Peninsula are near the far end of town, as are the bus station and market. The north side of town faces an estuary, and the south side faces the mouth of the gulf. The Paseo de los Turistas is on the south side of town, beginning at the pier and extending out to the point.

⟨Moments   A Colorful Festival

If you're in Puntarenas on the Saturday closest to July 16, you can witness the **Fiesta of the Virgin of the Sea.** During this festival, a regatta of colorfully decorated boats carries a statue of Puntarenas's patron saint.

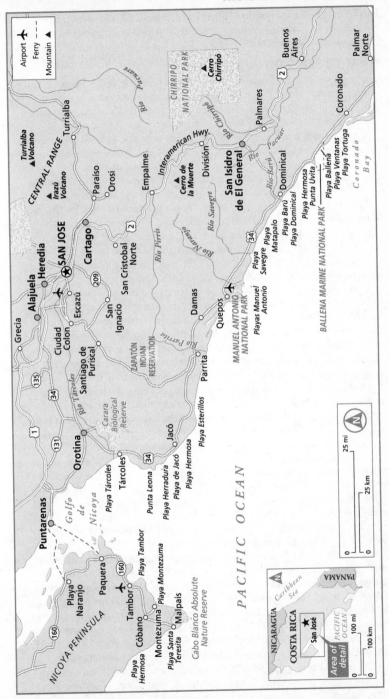

Airport ✈
Ferry − − −
Mountain ▲

CHIRRIPÓ NATIONAL PARK

▲ Cerro Chirripó

Buenos Aires

Palmar Norte

Río Pacuare

Turrialba Volcano ▲
Turrialba

CENTRAL RANGE

Irazú Volcano ▲

Paraíso
Orosi

Empalme

Interamerican Hwy.

Cerro de la Muerte ▲
División

Palmares

Río Chirripó

Río General

Coronado

Río Savegre

San Isidro de El General

34

Playa Ballena
Playa Ventanas
Playa Tortuga

Dominical

Coronado Bay

Río Barú
Río Pacuar

SAN JOSE
Cartago
Heredia
Alajuela

209

2

San Cristobal Norte

Río Pirris

Playa Savegre
Playa Matapalo
Playa Barú
Playa Dominical

Playa Hermosa
Punta Uvita

BALLENA MARINE NATIONAL PARK

Grecia

Escazú
San Ignacio

Ciudad Colon

Santiago de Puriscal

ZAPATÓN INDIAN RESERVATION

Damas

Quepos

MANUEL ANTONIO NATIONAL PARK

Playas Manuel Antonio

135

34

Río Tárcoles

Carara Biological Reserve

Río Parrita

Parrita

1

131

Orotina

Playa Estrellos

Playa Tárcoles
Tárcoles

34

Jacó

Playa de Jacó
Playa Hermosa

Punta Leona
Playa Herradura

Puntarenas

Golfo de Nicoya

Golfo de Nicoya

160

Paquera

Playa Tambor

PACIFIC OCEAN

Playa Naranjo

Tambor
Cóbano
Montezuma
Malpaís

Playa Montezuma

Playa Santa Teresita

Cabo Blanco Absolute Nature Reserve

Playa Hermosa

NICOYA PENINSULA

160

25 mi

25 km

N

Area of detail

NICARAGUA

COSTA RICA
★ San José

PACIFIC OCEAN

PANAMA

Caribbean Sea

100 mi

100 km

FAST FACTS   Check out the **Millennium Cibercafé** (© 661-4759), right on the Paseo de los Turistas, if you need to send or check e-mail. If you need a taxi, call **Coopetico** (© 663-2020).

WHAT TO SEE & DO

Take a walk along the **Paseo de los Turistas,** which feels rather like a Florida beach town out of the 1950s. The hotels across the street range in style from converted old wooden homes with bright gingerbread trim to modern concrete monstrosities, to tasteful Art Deco relics that need a new coat of paint.

If you venture into the center of the city, be sure to check out the **central plaza around the Catholic Church.** The church itself is interesting because it has portholes for windows, reflecting the city's maritime tradition. Here you'll also find the city's cultural center, **La Casa de la Cultura** (© 661-1394), and a small museum with exhibits in both English and Spanish. Admission is free.

The newest attraction in town is the **Parque Marino del Pacífico (Pacific Marine Park;** © 661-5272), a modest collection of saltwater aquariums highlighting the sea life of Costa Rica. There are 28 separate tanks, with the largest dedicated to re-creating the undersea environment of Cocos Island. This modest aquarium is located 2 blocks east of the main cruise-ship terminal and is open Tuesday through Sunday from 9am to 4pm. Admission is $7.

If you want to go swimming, the ocean waters are now said to be perfectly safe (pollution was a problem for many years), although the beach is still not very attractive. Your best bet is to head back down the spit; just a few kilometers out of town, you'll find **Playa Doña Aña,** a popular beach with picnic tables, restrooms and changing rooms, and a couple of *sodas.* If you head a little farther south, you will come to **Playa Tivives,** which is virtually unvisited by tourists but quite popular with Ticos, many of whom have beach houses up and down this long, brown sand beach. Surfers can check out the beach break here or head to the mouth of the Barranca River, which boasts an amazingly long left break. Still, surfers and swimmers should be careful; there are crocodiles in both the Barranca and Tivives river mouths, and, despite improvements, I'd be wary of pollution in the waters emptying out of the rivers here.

Puntarenas isn't known as one of Costa Rica's prime sportfishing ports, but there are usually a few charter boats available. Check at your hotel or near the docks, or call **Latii Express Travel** (© 877/575-3277 in the U.S., or 296-1146; www.costaricalatiiexpress.com), which maintains a fleet here in Puntarenas and also operates out of the new marina at the Marriott Los Sueños resort. Rates are usually between $400 and $600 for a half-day and between $800 and $1,400 for a full day (these rates are for up to six people).

You can also take a yacht cruise through the tiny, uninhabited islands of the Guayabo, Negritos, and Pajaros Islands Biological Reserve. These cruises include a lunch buffet and a relaxing stop on beautiful and undeveloped **Tortuga Island** ✦, where you can swim, snorkel, and sunbathe. The water is clear blue, and the sand is bright white. However, this trip has surged in popularity, and the tours have begun to have a cattle-car feel. Several San José–based companies offer these excursions, with round-trip transportation from San José, but if you're already in Puntarenas, you might receive a slight discount by boarding here.

Calypso Tours ✦ (© 256-8787; www.calypsotours.com) is the most reputable company that cruises out of Puntarenas. In addition to Tortuga Island trips, Calypso Tours takes folks to its own private nature reserve at Punta Coral and even on a sunset cruise that includes dinner and some guided stargazing.

Diving Trips to Isla del Coco (Cocos Island)

This little speck of land located some 480km (300 miles) off the Pacific coast was a prime pirate hideout and refueling station. Robert Louis Stevenson most likely modeled *Treasure Island* on Cocos. Sir Francis Drake, Captain Edward Davis, William Dampier, and Mary Welch are just some of the famous corsairs who dropped anchor in the calm harbors of this Pacific pearl. They allegedly left troves of buried loot, although scores of treasure-hunters over several centuries have failed to unearth more than a smattering of the purported bounty. The Costa Rican flag was first raised here on September 15, 1869. Throughout its history, Cocos Island has provided anchorage and fresh water to hundreds of ships and has entertained divers and dignitaries. (Franklin Delano Roosevelt visited it three times.) In 1978, it was declared a national park and protected area.

The clear, warm waters around Cocos are widely regarded as one of the most rewarding **dive destinations** ★★★ on this planet. This is a prime place to see schooling herds of scalloped hammerhead sharks. On a recent shallow-water checkout dive—normally, a perfunctory and uninspiring affair—I spotted my first hammerhead lurking just 4.5m (15 ft.) below me within 15 seconds of flipping into the water. Soon there were more, and soon they came much, much closer.

Other denizens of the waters around Cocos Island include white- and silver-tipped reef sharks; marbled, manta, eagle, and mobula rays; moray and spotted eels; octopi; spiny and slipper lobsters; hawksbill turtles; squirrel fish, trigger fish, and angelfish; surgeon fish, trumpet fish, grouper, grunts, snapper, jack, tangs; and more. Two of the more spectacular underwater residents here include the red-lipped batfish and the frogfish.

Most diving at Cocos is relatively deep (26–35m/85–115 ft.), and there are often strong currents and choppy swells to deal with—not to mention all those sharks. This is not a trip for novice divers.

The perimeter of Cocos Island is ringed by steep, forested cliffs punctuated by dozens of majestic waterfalls cascading down in stages or steady streams for hundreds of feet. The island itself has a series of trails that climb its steep hills and wind through its rainforested interior. There are several endemic bird, reptile, and plant species here, including the ubiquitous Cocos finch, which I spotted soon after landing onshore, and the wild Cocos Island pig.

With just a small ranger station housing a handful of national park guards, Cocos Island is essentially uninhabited. Visitors these days come on private or charter yachts, fishing boats, or one of the few live-aboard dive vessels that make regular voyages out here. It's a long trip: Most dive vessels take 30 to 36 hours to reach Cocos. Sailboats are even slower.

Both the **Aggressor Fleet Limited** (© 800/348-2628 or 985/385-2628 in the U.S. and Canada, or 257-0191; www.aggressor.com) and **Undersea Hunter** (© 800/203-2120 in the U.S., or 228-6613; www.underseahunter. com) regularly run dive trips to Cocos Island from Puntarenas.

Any of these cruises will run you $99 per person, whether you join them in San José or Puntarenas. If you check down at the docks, you might find some other boats that ply the waters of the Nicoya Gulf. Some of these companies also offer sunset cruises with live music, snacks, and a bar.

WHERE TO STAY
MODERATE

Hotel Las Brisas   Out near the end of the Paseo de los Turistas, you'll find this clean hotel with large air-conditioned rooms, a small pool out front, and the beach right across the street. All the rooms have tile floors, double or twin beds, and small televisions and tables. Large picture windows keep the rooms sunny and bright during the day. There's complimentary coffee and a secure parking lot. The hotel's small open-air restaurant serves a wide range of international cuisine. There's always a Greek-style fish special or homemade moussaka on the menu, as well as some Mexican dishes and more traditional Continental fare.

Paseo de los Turistas (A.P. 83-5400), Puntarenas. ℂ 661-4040. Fax 661-2120. 20 units. $65–$85 double. Rates include breakfast. Rates lower in the off season. AE, DC, MC, V. **Amenities:** Restaurant; bar; small pool. *In room:* A/C, TV, safe.

Hotel Tioga   This 1950s modern-style hotel is probably your best choice on the Paseo de los Turistas. The beach is across the street, and there are plenty of nearby restaurants. When you walk through the front door, you enter a court-yard with a pool that's been painted a brilliant shade of blue. In the middle of the pool, there's a tiny island with a palm tree growing on it. Rooms vary in size and view. The larger, most expensive rooms are attractive, with huge closets, modern bathrooms, and private balconies with a view of the ocean. The smaller, less-expensive rooms have louvered, frosted-glass windows to let in lots of light and air while maintaining some privacy. The garden-sector rooms, however, have only cold-water showers.

Paseo de los Turistas (A.P. 96-5400), Puntarenas. ℂ 661-0271 or 255-3115. Fax 661-0127. www.hoteltioga. com. 46 units. $63–$126 double. Rates include breakfast. Rates lower in the off season and for extended stays. AE, DC, MC, V. **Amenities:** Restaurant; bar; small pool. *In room:* A/C, TV.

INEXPENSIVE

In addition to the hotel listed below, the **Hotel La Punta** (ℂ/fax **661-0696**) is a decent option located very close to the ferry docks.

Hotel Ayi Con   Centrally located near the market and close enough to the fer-ryboat docks, the Ayi Con is your basic low-budget Tico accommodation. It's above a row of shops in a very busy shopping district of Puntarenas and is fre-quented primarily by Costa Ricans. Backpackers will find that this is probably the best and the cleanest of the very cheap hotels in Puntarenas. If you're just passing through and have to spend a night in town, this place is acceptable.

Puntarenas (50m/164 ft. south of the market). ℂ 661-0164 or 661-1477. 44 units, 22 with private bath-room. $12 double with shared bathroom; $20 double with private bathroom; $25 double with private bathroom and A/C. No credit cards. *In room:* No phone.

WHERE TO DINE

Because you're in a seaport, try some of the local catch. Corvina (sea bass) is the most popular offering, and it's served in various forms and preparations. My favorite dish on a hot afternoon is ceviche, and you'll find that just about every restaurant in town serves this savory marinated seafood concoction.

The most economical option is to pull up a table at one of the many open-air snack bars *(sodas)* along the Paseo de los Turistas. They serve everything from sandwiches, drinks, and ice cream to ceviche and fish meals. Sandwiches are priced at around $2, and a fish filet with rice and beans should cost around $4. If you want some seafood in a slightly more formal atmosphere, try the **Caribbean Breeze** or **Capitán Moreno,** or the open-air **Restaurant Aloha,** all located on the Paseo de los Turistas.

La Yunta Steakhouse ⭐ *Finds* STEAKS/SEAFOOD   This airy place bills itself as a steakhouse, but it has an ample menu of seafood dishes as well. Most of the tables are located on a two-tiered covered veranda at the front of the restaurant, overlooking the street and the ocean just beyond. Overall, this restaurant has the nicest ambience in town. The portions are immense, and the meat is tender and well prepared.

Paseo de los Turistas. ℂ **661-3216.** Reservations recommended in high season and on weekends. Main courses $4–$21. AE, MC, V. Daily 10am–midnight.

2 Playa de Jacó ⭐

117km (73 miles) W of San José; 75km (47 miles) S of Puntarenas

Playa de Jacó is the closest thing in Costa Rica to Daytona Beach during spring break. This long stretch of beach is strung with a dense hodgepodge of hotels in all price categories, cheap souvenir shops, seafood restaurants, pizza joints, and even a miniature-golf course. The number-one attraction is the surf, and this is definitely a surfer-dominated beach town. Surfers love the consistent beach break here (and at neighboring Playa Hermosa). However, the beach here is not particularly appealing. It's made of dark-gray sand with lots of little rocks, and it's often very rough. Canadian charter flights keep this town pretty full during the northern winter months, and Jacó is also gaining popularity with German tourists and young Ticos. This is the most touristy beach in Costa Rica and is a prime example of what happens when rapid growth hits a beach town. However, on the outskirts of town and close to the beach, there's still plenty of greenery to offset the excess of cement and chaotic jumble of the town's main street. In fact, after the dryness of Guanacaste, this is the first beach on the Pacific coast to have a tropical feel. The humidity is palpable, and the lushness of the tropical forest is visible on the hillsides surrounding town. In hotel gardens, flowers bloom profusely throughout the year.

ESSENTIALS

GETTING THERE & DEPARTING   By Car   There are several routes to Jacó. The most popular one is a narrow and winding two-lane road, the "old highway," over and through mountains. This road is equal parts scenic and harrowing—it's not uncommon to encounter buses and trucks passing on blind curves, or to find yourself at the back of a long line of cars stuck behind a slow-moving truck crawling up one of the steep hills. Begin this route by taking the Interamerican Highway west out of San José and exiting just west of Alajuela near the town of Atenas. Follow any of the numerous signs to any hotel in Jacó or Manuel Antonio. The old highway meets the Costanera highway a few kilometers west of Orotina. From here it's a straight and flat shot down the coast to Jacó.

Alternatively, it's possible to head out of San José on the highway to Escazú and Santa Ana. Continue on to the town of Ciudad Colón. From Ciudad Colón, follow signs to Puriscal and then Orotina. This is a similarly scenic and winding route through the mountains, with the same caveats, but it is less traveled and slightly more direct than the more popular route mentioned above.

Finally, an easier, although longer, route is to take the Interamerican Highway west out of San José and get off at the Puntarenas exit. From here, head south on the Costanera.

By Bus   Express buses (© 223-1109 or 643-3135) leave San José daily at 7:30 and 10:30am, and 1, 3:30, and 6:30pm from the Coca-Cola bus terminal at Calle 16 between avenidas 1 and 3. The trip takes between 2½ and 3 hours; the fare is $2.50. On weekends and holidays, extra buses are often added, so it's worth calling to check.

Grayline (© 220-2126; www.graylinecostarica.com) has a daily bus that leaves San José for Jacó at 8:30am; the fare is $21. Interbus (© 283-5573; www.costaricapass.com) has two daily buses that leave San José for Jacó at 9am and 1:30pm; the fare is $17. Both companies will pick you up at most San José–area hotels.

Buses from San José to **Quepos** and Manuel Antonio also pass by Jacó. (They let passengers off on the highway about 1km/½ mile from town). These buses leave San José daily at 6, 7, and 10am; noon; and 2, 4, 6, and 7:30pm. Trip duration is 2½ to 3 hours; the fare to Jacó is $3 on the indirect bus to Quepos and $5 on the direct bus to Manuel Antonio. However, during the busy months, some of these buses will refuse passengers getting off in Jacó or will accept them only if they pay the full fare to Quepos or Manuel Antonio.

From **Puntarenas,** there are buses daily to Jacó at 5 and 11am and 2:30 and 4:30pm, or you can catch Quepos-bound buses daily at 5, 8, and 11am, and 3:30pm, and get off in Jacó. Either way, the trip's duration is 1 hour; the fare is $1.50.

The Jacó bus station is at the north end of town, at a small mall across from the Jacó Fiesta Hotel. Buses for San José leave daily at 5, 7:30, and 11am, and 3 and 5pm. Buses returning to San José from Quepos pass periodically and pick up passengers on the highway. Because schedules can change, it's best to ask at your hotel about current departure times.

ORIENTATION   Playa de Jacó is a short distance off the southern highway. One main road runs parallel to the beach, with a host of arteries heading toward the water; off these roads you'll find most of the hotels and restaurants.

GETTING AROUND   Almost everything is within walking distance in Jacó, but you can rent a bicycle or scooter from several shops on the main street or call **Jacó Taxi** (© 643-3030). A bike rental should run you around $8 to $12 per day, and a scooter should cost between $30 and $45 per day. For longer excursions, you can rent a car from **Budget** (© 643-2265), **Economy** (© 643-1719), **National** (© 643-1752), **Payless** (© 643-3224), or **Zuma** (© 643-3207). Expect to pay approximately $50 for a 1-day rental. You might also consider talking to any of the local taxi drivers, who would probably take you wherever you wanted to go for the same $50 per day, thus saving you some hassle and headache.

FAST FACTS   Both the **Banco Nacional** (© 643-3072) and the **Banco de Costa Rica** (© 643-3695) have branches in town on the main road and are open Monday through Friday from 8:30am to 3pm. There's a well-stocked **Farmacia Fischel** (© 643-2683) in the El Galeone shopping center, as well as the **Farmacia Jacó** (© 643-3205); both are on the main road through town. There's a gas station out on the main highway, between Playa Herradura and Jacó, and another at the south end of town. The **health center** (© 643-3667) and **post office** (© 643-3479) are at the Municipal Center at the south end of town, across from El Naranjal restaurant.

A **public phone office,** from which you can make international calls, is located in the ICE building on the main road. This office is open Monday through Saturday from 8am to noon and 1 to 5pm. There are a half-dozen or more **Internet cafes** in town, as well as several inexpensive full-service laundromats. There's a **Western Union office** in a small strip mall across from La Hacienda restaurant.

FUN ON & OFF THE BEACH

Unfortunately, this beach has a nasty reputation for riptides (as does most of Costa Rica's Pacific coast). Even strong swimmers have been known to drown in the power rips. At times, storms far offshore cause huge waves to pound on the beach, making it impossible to go into the water much beyond your waist. If this is the case, you'll have to be content with the hotel pool.

After you've spent some time on Playa de Jacó, you might want to visit some of the other nearby beaches. **Playa Hermosa,** 10km (6¼ miles) southeast of Jacó, where sea turtles lay eggs from July to December, is also well known for its great surfing waves. **Playa Herradura,** about 6.5km (4 miles) northwest of Jacó, is a hard-packed brown-sand-and-rock beach ringed by lush hillsides. For years, this was an almost deserted beach with just a few basic cabins and campgrounds. Now it's home to the Marriott Los Sueños Ocean & Golf Resort. However, the Marriott occupies only one end of the beach here; despite its presence, Playa Herradura still feels a lot more isolated and deserted than Jacó. All of these beaches are easily reached by car, moped, or bicycle—if you've got a lot of energy. **Playa Esterillos,** 22km (14 miles) southeast of Jacó, is long and wide and almost always nearly deserted. All are signposted, so you'll have no trouble finding them. Finally, Punta Leona, which is a cross between a hotel, a resort, and a private country club, has some of the nicer beaches in the area. Although they effectively have restricted access to their beaches for years, this is technically illegal in Costa Rica, and lawsuits are seeking to open public access to **playas Manta** and **Blanca,** two very nice white-sand beaches inside the Punta Leona complex.

If you try to do any shopping in Jacó, you'll be overrun with shops selling T-shirts, cut-rate souvenirs, and handmade jewelry and trinkets. Two exceptions are **Guacamole** ✴ (© **643-1120**), a small clothing store that produces its own line of batik beachwear, and **La Galería Heliconia** ✴ (© **643-3613**), which carries a good selection of artworks and pottery.

BIKING   You can rent a bike for around $8 to $12 per day or $1.50 per hour. Bikes are available from a slew of shops along the main road. Shop around, and make sure you get a bike that is in good condition and that is comfortable to ride.

CANOPY TOURS   The newest entry in this growing field is the **Rain Forest Aerial Tram Pacific** (© **257-5961;** www.rainforestram.com). A sister project to the original Rain Forest Aerial Tram, this attraction features modified ski-lift type gondolas that take you through and above the transitional forests here bordering Carara National Park. The $55 entrance fee includes the guided 40-minute tram ride, as well as a guided 45-minute hike on a network of trails. You can also hike the company's trails at your leisure for as long as you like. The Aerial Tram is located a few kilometers inland from an exit just north of the first entrance into Jacó.

Villa Lapas (p. 259) has two different tours through the treetops outside of Jacó. The better option, for my money, is a guided hike on its network of trails and five suspended bridges ($20 per person). The operator also has a relatively low-adrenaline zip-line canopy tour ($35 per person), with seven platforms connected by six cables. **Chiclets Tree Tour** (📞/fax **643-1879**) offers up a canopy adventure ($60 per person) just outside Jacó in nearby Playa Hermosa. This is a little more adventurous tour, with 13 platforms set in transitional forest, with some sweeping views of the Pacific.

Finally, Jacó is also a good jumping-off point for a trip to the **Original Canopy Tour's Mahogany Park** (📞 **257-5149**; www.canopytour.com) in San Mateo, or to the new **Turu BaRi Tropical Park** (📞 **428-6070**; www.turubari.com), near Orotina. See chapters 3 and 4 for more details.

HORSEBACK RIDING Horseback-riding tours give you a chance to get away from all the development in Jacó and see a bit of nature. Contact **Happy Trails** (📞 643-1894) or **Hermanos Salazar** (📞 643-3203) to make a reservation. Down in Playa Hermosa, check in with **Diana's Trail Rides** (📞 643-3808). Over in Playa Herradura, you can try the **Jacó Equestrian Center** (📞 643-1569). Tours lasting 3 to 4 hours cost anywhere from $35 to $65.

KAYAKING **Kayak Jacó** (📞 **643-1233**; www.kayakjaco.com) runs a couple of different trips. Tours range from gentle paddles and floats on the Tulin River to combination ocean-kayaking/snorkel trip on calm Herradura Bay, to full-on kayak surfing at one of the local beach breaks. You can also do some moderate white-water kayaking in easy-to-use inflatable kayaks, or try your hand in the ocean on one of the eight-person outrigger canoes. Most options run around 4 hours and include transportation to and from the put-in, as well as fresh fruit and soft drinks during the trip. The tours cost between $50 and $80 per person, depending on the particular trip and group size.

A SPA The **Serenity Spa** ⭐ (📞 **643-4094**) offers massage, as well as mud packs, face and body treatments, and manicures and pedicures. The spa's Jacó branch is located on the first floor, among a tiny little cul-de-sac of shops next to Zuma Rent-A-Car. These folks also have operations at the Marriott Los Sueños resort, Villa Caletas, and Club del Mar Condominiums & Resort.

SPORTFISHING, SCUBA DIVING & SEABORNE FUN With the opening of the Marriott Los Sueños resort (p. 258) and its adjacent 250-slip marina, much of the local maritime activity has shifted over here. If you're interested in doing some sportfishing, scuba diving, or any other waterborne activity, I recommend that you check with your hotel or at the marina. One dependable operator that is already set up here is **Bobcat & Spanish Fly Sportfishing** (📞 **866/888-6426** in the U.S., or 637-8824 in Costa Rica; www.spanishflysportfishing.com). Alternatively, you can ask at **Club del Mar Condominiums & Resort** (📞 643-3194). A half-day fishing trip for four people costs around $250 to $500, and a full day costs between $550 and $1,200.

SURFING The same waves that often make Playa de Jacó dangerous for swimmers make it one of the most popular beaches in the country with surfers. Nearby **Playa Hermosa** and **Playa Escondida** are also excellent surfing beaches. Those who want to challenge the waves can rent surfboards for around $3 an hour or $10 to $15 per day, and boogie boards for $2 an hour, from any one of the numerous surf shops along the main road. If you want to learn how to surf, check in at the **Surfing Academy of Costa Rica** (📞 643-1948; acasurf45@hotmail.com).

ORGANIZED TOURS FARTHER AFIELD If you'll be spending your entire Costa Rican visit in Jacó but would like to see some other parts of the country, you can arrange tours through the local offices of **Grayline Tours** (📞 643-3231), which operates out of the Best Western Jacó Beach Hotel (p. 257), or **Explorica**

(© 643-3586). Both of these companies offer day tours to Arenal, Poás, and Irazú volcanoes; white-water rafting trips; cruises to Tortuga Island; and trips to Braulio Carrillo National Park and other places. Rates range from $35 to $110 for day trips. Overnight trips are also available. Thanks to improvements to the road, you can now reach Manuel Antonio in about 1 hour from Jacó. In addition to the abovementioned companies, many local operators offer a variety of tour options in Manuel Antonio, including trips to the national park, the Rainmaker Nature Refuge, and the Isla Damas estuary.

CARARA BIOLOGICAL RESERVE ★★

A little more than 15km (9⅓ miles) north of Jacó is Carara Biological Reserve, a world-renowned nesting ground for **scarlet macaws.** It has a few kilometers of trails open to visitors. There's a loop trail that takes about an hour, and another trail that's open only to tour groups. The macaws migrate daily, spending their days in the park and their nights among the coastal mangroves. It's best to view them in the early morning when they arrive, or around sunset when they head back to the coast for the evening, but a good guide can usually find them for you during the day. Whether or not you see them, you should hear their loud squawks. Among the other wildlife that you might see here are caimans, coatimundis, armadillos, pacas, peccaries, river otters, kinkajous, and, of course, hundreds of species of birds.

Be sure to bring along insect repellent, or, better yet, wear light cotton long sleeves and pants. (I was once foolish enough to attempt a quick hike while returning from Manuel Antonio, still in beach clothes and flip-flops—not a good idea.) The reserve is open daily from 8am to 4pm. Admission is $6 per person at the gate.

Several companies offer tours to Carara Biological Reserve for around $30 to $40. Check at your hotel or contact **Explorica Tours** (© 643-3586) for schedules and more information. If you're looking for a more personalized tour, check out Lisa Robertson, a knowledgeable and amiable guide who runs **Happy Trails** (© 643-1894). You can hike the trails of Carara independently, but my advice is to take the guided tour; you'll learn a lot more about your surroundings.

The muddy banks of the Tárcoles River are home to a healthy population of American crocodiles, and just north of the entrance to the Carara Biological Reserve is a bridge that's a prime spot for viewing both the crocs and the macaw migrations. It's worth a stop, but be careful: Thieves and pickpockets have traditionally worked this spot. There's now a police kiosk here, and the situation has improved dramatically. Still, don't leave your car or valuables unguarded for long, and be wary if yours is the only car parked here.

When you're in Jacó, you'll find several operators who run daily crocodile tours on the Tárcoles River. These are simple tours in open skiffs or Boston Whalers. Most of these companies bring along plenty of freshly killed chicken to attract the reptiles and pump up the adrenaline. Don't expect a highly trained naturalist guide or any semblance of respect for the natural world. Do expect to pay between $30 and $45 per person for the trip.

Finally, just beyond Carara National Park on the Costanera Sur in the direction of Jacó, you'll find a turnoff for some spectacular waterfalls (including a 180m/590-ft. fall) around the town of **Bijagual.** There are several ways to visit these falls and people run tours from Jacó or from entrances both at the top and bottom of the falls. At the top, a local family runs the **Complejo Ecológico La Catarata** (© 661-8263), which features a basic restaurant and a campground.

They run horseback tours down to the falls for around $35. Alternatively, you can hike in from an entrance lower down. The hike takes about 45 minutes each way, and the entrance is $10 per person. Finally, while you're in this area, you can visit the **Pura Vida Botanical Gardens** (© 200-5040). Entrance to the gardens is a bit steep, at $15. To get here, turn off at the signs for Hotel Villa Lapas. From here, it's a rough 8km (5 miles) up to the top of the falls.

WHERE TO STAY IN PLAYA DE JACÓ

Because Punta Leona, Playa Herradura, and Playa Hermosa de Jacó (not to be confused with Playa Hermosa in Guanacaste) are close, many people choose accommodations in these beach towns as well. Selected listings for these towns follow this section.

EXPENSIVE

Club del Mar Condominiums & Resort ★★ (Kids)   This has long been my favorite Playa de Jacó hotel because of its location, friendly owners, and attractively designed rooms. A major expansion and remodeling has only made it an even better option. Club del Mar is at the far southern end of the beach, where the rocky hills meet the sand. Most of the rooms are actually one- or two-bedroom condo units, with full kitchens. All are spacious and feature private balconies or porches. There are also eight rooms on the second floor of the large main building, as well as two huge and luxurious penthouse suites up on the third floor. All units come with an ocean view, although some are more open and expansive than others. The grounds are lush and chock-full of flowering heliconia and ginger. There's a good open-air restaurant, as well as some modest spa facilities.

Playa de Jacó (A.P. 107-4023), Puntarenas. © 643-3194. Fax 643-3550. www.clubdelmarcostarica.com. 32 units. $120 double; $175–$250 condo; $500 penthouse. Rates lower in the off season. AE, DC, MC, V. **Amenities:** Restaurant; bar; midsize free-form pool; small spa; tour desk; concierge; limited room service (8am–9pm); in-room massage; babysitting. *In room:* A/C, TV, fridge, safe.

MODERATE

In addition to the places listed below, the oceanfront **Apartotel Girasol** ★ (© 800/923-2779 in the U.S. and Canada, or 643-1591; www.girasol.com), with 16 fully equipped one-bedroom apartments, is a good option in this category, especially for longer stays.

Apartotel Flamboyant (Value)   Don't let the name fool you: The Flamboyant is actually rather quiet and intimate. The rooms are arranged around a small swimming pool and are only a few steps from the beach. They're all spacious, with simple furnishings, and most have kitchenettes. The more expensive rooms have air-conditioning, televisions, and private balconies. You'll find the hotel down a narrow lane toward the ocean, down from the Wishbone Cafe, which is on the main road in the middle of Jacó.

Playa de Jacó (A.P. 18), Puntarenas. © 643-3146. Fax 643-1068. flamboya@racsa.co.cr. 15 units. $60–$80 double. AE, MC, V. **Amenities:** Outdoor pool; unheated Jacuzzi. *In room:* A/C, TV, and kitchenette in some units, safe, no phone.

Arenal Pacífico ★   This is probably the best midrange option in town, and it's right on the beach, to boot. The rooms are nothing special—and almost none offers an ocean view—but they are clean and cool, and most are pretty spacious. The three superior rooms come with cable television, an unstocked minifridge, a microwave, and a coffeemaker. The grounds are pretty lush for Jacó, and you even have to cross a shady bridge over a little stream to get from the parking lot and reception to the rooms and restaurant. There's a small pool, with a little waterfall filling it, and a separate unheated Jacuzzi. Beside the pool, a few hammocks are hung in the shade. The restaurant serves standard Tico and international fare, but it is set right up against the sand and just steps from the sea.

Playa de Jacó (A.P. 962-1000, San José), Puntarenas. © 253-5080 or 643-3419. Fax 253-5016. www.arenal pacifico.com. 16 units. $80–$95 double. Rates include continental breakfast. Rates lower in the off season. **Amenities:** Restaurant; bar; pool; Jacuzzi; bike rental; tour desk; laundry service. *In room:* A/C, TV, safe.

Best Western Jacó Beach Hotel   This has long been Jacó's most popular resort hotel. Situated right on the beach, this five-story hotel offers all the amenities and services you could want at this price. The hotel is often packed throughout the high season, and a party atmosphere pervades the place. The open-air lobby is surrounded by lush gardens, and covered walkways connect the hotel's buildings. Rooms are adequate and have tile floors and walls of glass facing balconies; however, not all of the rooms have good views (some face another building), and many of them show the wear and tear of age and heavy occupancy. Ask for a view room on a higher floor and with an ocean view, if possible. Bathrooms tend to be a bit battered, but they do have bathtubs. Lately, a large percentage of guests opts for an all-inclusive package.

Playa de Jacó (A.P. 962-1000, San José), Puntarenas. © 800/528-1234 in the U.S. and Canada, or 643-1000. Fax 643-3246. www.bestwesterncostarica.com. 120 units. $85–$110 double. AE, DC, MC, V. **Amenities:** 2 restaurants; 2 bars; too-small circular pool; outdoor tennis court; watersports equipment rental; complimentary bike use; tour desk; limited room service (7am–9pm); laundry service. *In room:* A/C, TV, safe.

Hotel Cocal ★   Located right on the beach, the building is done in colonial style, with arched porticos surrounding a courtyard that contains two medium-size pools, a few palapas for shade, and a thatch-roofed bar. Each guest room is of good size, with a tile floor, a double and a single bed, a desk, and a porch or a balcony. The beachfront location here and the modest array of amenities are the hotel's greatest attributes. The Cocal is on one of the nameless streets leading down to the beach from the main road through Jacó; watch for its sign in the middle of town.

Playa de Jacó (A.P. 54), Puntarenas. © 800/732-9266 in the U.S., or 643-3067. Fax 643-1201. www.hotel cocalandcasino.com. 43 units. $80–$118 double. Rates include breakfast. Rates lower in the off season. AE, MC, V. **Amenities:** 2 restaurants; 2 bars; 2 small pools; laundry service. *In room:* A/C in some units, safe, no phone.

Pochote Grande   Named for a huge old pochote tree on the grounds, this well-kept and attractive hotel is located right on the beach at the far north end of Jacó. The grounds are shady and lush, and there's a refreshing little pool. All of the rooms are quite large, although sparsely furnished, and have white-tile floors, one queen-size and one single bed, a small fridge, and a balcony or patio. I prefer the second-floor rooms, which are blessed with high ceilings. The modest restaurant and snack bar serve a mixture of Tico, German, and American meals. (The owners are German by way of Africa.)

Playa de Jacó (A.P. 42), Puntarenas. © 643-3236. Fax 220-4979. www.hotelpochotegrande.com. 24 units. $55 double; $70 triple. Add $5 for a room with A/C. Rates lower in the off season. AE, MC, V. **Amenities:** Restaurant; bar; pool. *In room:* Fridge, safe, no phone.

INEXPENSIVE

There are several campgrounds in or near Playa de Jacó. **Madrigal** (© **643-3851**), at the south end of town at the foot of some jungly cliffs, is my favorite. You can also try **El Hicaco** (© **643-3004**), which is close to the beach but also pretty close to the Disco La Central, so don't expect to get much sleep if you stay here. Campsites run between $2 and $5 per night.

Hotel Mar de Luz ★ *Value* This is one of Playa de Jacó's best deals and a comfortable alternative to the typical string of cut-rate *cabinas* you'll find crowding this popular beach town. All the rooms are immaculate and comfortable. Some feature stone walls, small sitting areas, and one or two double beds placed on a raised sleeping nook. My only complaint is that the windows are too small and mostly sealed, so you're forced to use the air-conditioning. In the gardens just off the pools are a couple of grills available for guest use. There is also a comfortable common sitting area, with a selection of magazines and books in several languages. Dutch owners Victor and Carmen Keulen seem driven to offer as much comfort, quality, and service as they can for the price. You'll find the hotel 50m (164 ft.) east of the Hotel Tangeri, right in the center of Jacó.

Playa de Jacó (A.P. 143), Puntarenas. ©/fax **643-3259**. www.mardeluz.com. 29 units. $50 double. Rates lower in the off season. V. **Amenities:** 2 small-to-midsize adult pools and children's pool; Jacuzzi; game room; tour desk; babysitting; laundry service; nonsmoking rooms. *In room:* A/C, TV, kitchenette in some units, minifridge, coffeemaker, safe, no phone.

Hotel Zabamar The Zabamar is set back from the beach in a shady compound. The older rooms have red-tile floors, small refrigerators, ceiling fans, hammocks on their front porches, and showers in enclosed private patios. There are also 10 newer rooms with air-conditioning. There are even *pilas* (laundry sinks) in little gravel-and-palm gardens behind the older rooms. Some have rustic wooden benches and chairs. The shallow swimming pool stays quite warm. Travelers on tight budgets will appreciate the size of the older, less-expensive rooms.

Playa de Jacó, Puntarenas. ©/fax **643-3174**. 20 units. $35 double; $50 double with A/C. Rates include breakfast. Rates lower in the off season; discounts for long-term stays. AE, MC, V. **Amenities:** Restaurant; bar; small outdoor pool; laundry service. *In room:* No phone.

WHERE TO STAY JUST NORTH OF PLAYA DE JACO
VERY EXPENSIVE

Marriott Los Sueños Ocean & Golf Resort ★★★ *Kids* This is the closest large-scale resort to San José and is one of the nicest in the country. The hotel is a massive, four-story horseshoe facing the beach. The whole thing is done in a Spanish colonial style, with stucco walls, heavy wooden doors, and red-clay roof tiles. The rooms are all spacious and tastefully done. They come with one king-size or two queen-size beds, a large armoire, a desk, and a sitting chair with an ottoman. The bathrooms are large and have plenty of counter space. Every room has a balcony, but all are not created equal. Most have only small Juliet-style balconies. Those facing the ocean are clearly superior, and a few of the ocean-facing rooms even have large, comfortable balconies with chaise longues and tables and chairs. (You'll have to specifically request these.)

The expansive lobby area opens out on a large terrace and the Puesta del Sol bar, with its panoramic views of the beach and the bluffs bordering Playa Herradura. The pool is a vast, intricate maze built to imitate the canals of Venice (in miniature), with private nooks and grottos; kids love exploring it. The beach here is calm and good for swimming, although it's one of the least attractive beaches on this coast, with a mix of rocks and hard-packed, dark-brown sand. The Ted Robinson–designed 18-hole golf course winds through some of the neighboring forest and is an excellent, if not particularly challenging, resort course. The Stellaris casino is the largest and most comfortable I've found at a beach resort in Costa Rica.

Playa Herradura (A.P. 502-4005), San Antonio de Belén. © **888/236-2427** in the U.S., 298-0844, or 630-9000. Fax 630-9090. www.marriott.com. 211 units. $170–$395 double; $650 suite, $1,100 presidential suite. Rates lower in the off season. AE, MC, V. **Amenities:** 4 restaurants; coffee shop; 2 bars; lounge; large outdoor pool;

golf course and pro shop; 4 outdoor tennis courts; health club and spa; watersports equipment rentals; children's program; game room; concierge; tour desk; car-rental desk; salon; 24-hr. room service; in-room massage; babysitting; laundry service; nonsmoking rooms. *In room:* A/C, TV, minibar, coffeemaker, hair dryer, iron, safe.

Villa Caletas ★★★ *(Finds)*   It's hard to find a luxury hotel in Costa Rica with a more spectacular setting. Perched 350m (1,148 ft.) above the sea, Villa Caletas enjoys commanding views of the Pacific over forested hillsides. The regular rooms are all elegantly appointed and spacious, but you'll definitely want to stay in a villa or suite here. Each individual villa is situated on a patch of hillside facing the sea or forests. Inside you'll find a main bedroom with a queen-size bed and a comfortable sitting room with couches that convert into two single beds. The villas feature white-tile floors, modern bathrooms, and a private terrace for soaking up the views. The junior suites are even larger and come with their own outdoor Jacuzzi. The suites and master suites are larger still—and even come with their own private swimming pools. There are only two master suites here, and one is a vigorous hike downhill from the main hotel building and restaurants. The same is true of some of the villas and juniors.

Although most guests are happy to lounge around and swim in the free-form "infinity" pool that seems to blend into the sea below and beyond, Villa Caletas offers hourly shuttle service to its own little private beach, as well as a host of tour options. There's also a Greek-style amphitheater that hosts periodic sunset concerts of jazz or classical music.

A.P. 12358-1000, San José. © **637-0606.** Fax 637-0404. www.hotelvillacaletas.com. 35 units. $140–$170 double; $180 villa; $235–$350 suite. Rates slightly lower in the off season. Extra person $35. AE, MC, V. **Amenities:** 2 restaurants; bar; midsize pool w/spectacular view; spa; concierge; tour desk; beach shuttle; in-room massage; laundry service. *In room:* A/C, TV, minibar, coffeemaker, hair dryer, safe.

MODERATE

Villa Lapas ★   Located on a lush piece of property along the Río Tarcolitos and bordering Carara National Park, Villa Lapas is a good choice if you're looking to combine a bit of ecoadventure and bird-watching with some beach time. The rooms here are spacious, with two double beds, cool red-clay tile floors, air-conditioning, ceiling fans, and a shady veranda with wooden benches for taking in the scenery. The hotel's nicest feature is its massive, open-air restaurant and deck overlooking the river where buffet-style meals are served. Villa Lapas has 217 hectares (536 acres) of land with excellent trails, a series of suspended bridges crossing the river, and its own canopy tour. The newest addition here is a small re-creation of a typical Costa Rican rural village of times gone by. This riverside attraction features a massive gift shop, a restaurant, and an open-air bar. You'll see the signs for Villa Lapas on the left, just after passing Carara National Park. The hotel is about 15 to 20 minutes from the beaches of Jacó, Hermosa, and Herradura.

Tárcoles (A.P. 419-4005, San Antonio de Belén). © **637-0232.** Fax 637-0227. www.villalapas.com. 55 units. $80–$110 double. AE, MC, V. **Amenities:** 2 restaurants; 2 bars; small pool; 2 Jacuzzis; laundry service. *In room:* A/C, safe.

WHERE TO DINE

Playa de Jacó has a wide range of restaurants. Many cater to surfers and budget travelers. Budget travelers who really want to save money on meals can always stay at a hotel that provides kitchenettes for its guests, shop at the local *supermercado,* and fix their own meals. Even the most inexpensive lodgings have restaurants, so if you don't want to cook, you won't have to venture far.

In addition to the places listed below, if you're looking for simply prepared fresh seafood, **El Barco de Mariscos** (© 643-2831) and **Restaurante Santimar**

(© 643-3605) are both good bets that serve standard Tico beach fare—fresh seafood, sandwiches, chicken, and steak. For a filling American-style breakfast, try **Chatty Cathy's** (© 643-1039) or the **Sunrise Breakfast Place** (© 643-3361). For a coffee break, cappuccino, and fresh pastries and breads, head to either **Pachi's Pan** (© 643-1153) or **Café del M@r** (© 643-1250). **Monica's Pasta** (© 643-1776) is another popular spot for simple pastas and pizzas.

Chef Kent Green is serving up excellent Pacific-Rim fusion cuisine at the **Pacific Bistro** ★ (© 643-3771) in a new location right on the strip in downtown Jacó. I've also received good reports about similar fusion fare being served up at the small **Hotel Poseidon** (© 643-1642). And although the place lacks ambience, sushi lovers should head to **Tsunami Sushi** (© 368-7003), inside the El Galeone strip mall.

On the main road to Jacó, at the first main entrance into town, you'll find **The Lighthouse** (© 643-3083), a steakhouse, seafood restaurant, and raw bar, which is open 24 hours daily and also has an extensive gift shop. **Steve & Lisa's** (© 637-0594), located several miles outside of town, around Tárcoles, is a good place for lunch. The food here is standard Tico fare, but the ocean-side setting and views set it apart from other simple *sodas*.

Caliche's Wishbone ★ Finds SEAFOOD/MEXICAN

This casual spot that is popular with surfers offers Tex-Mex standards and homemade pizzas. However, you can also get excellent fresh fish and perfectly prepared seafood dishes, as well as hearty stuffed potatoes and a variety of sandwiches served in homemade pita bread. The portions are huge. It almost always has fresh tuna lightly seared and served with a soy-wasabi dressing. The nicest tables are street-side on a covered veranda. Inside are more tables, as well as a bar with television sets showing surf videos.

On the main road in Jacó. © **643-3406.** Main courses $4–$15. V. Thurs–Tues 11:30am–3pm and 5:30–10pm.

El Hicaco ★ SEAFOOD/COSTA RICAN

This is probably the best of all the simple Costa Rican seafood joints in Jacó. The food is good but not outstanding, but the setting is simply wonderful: right on the edge of the beach, with the majority of the tables outdoors under the stars, tall palm trees, and some interesting lighting. Stick with the freshly caught grilled seafood or lobster, although there are plenty of meat and chicken selections on the menu as well.

On the beach in downtown Jacó. © **643-3226.** Reservations recommended during high season. Main courses $5–$18. V. Daily 11am–11pm.

El Nuevo Latino ★★ LATIN FUSION

This restaurant offers creative and modern takes on local and regional dishes. The dozen or so tables are set in a narrow room that features a glass wall running its length, fronting a gorgeous pool fed by a series of spouts from a story-high aqueduct. The service and setting are semiformal, but there's no dress code—they realize that you're at the beach and on vacation here. Standout dishes include the plantain-crusted red snapper and the guava-glazed baby-back ribs. Be sure to start things off with the lamb empanadas, small Argentine pastries stuffed with minced lamb and served with several tasty sauces, or the lobster-and-shrimp croquettes, which come with a roasted-corn and pepper salsa.

At the Marriott Los Sueños resort (p. 258). © **630-9000.** Reservations recommended. Main courses $18–$38. AE, MC, V. Daily 6–11pm. Closed Mon during the low season.

Rioasis PIZZA/MEXICAN

Rioasis serves hearty burritos, simple pasta dishes, and a wide array of freshly baked wood-oven pizzas. My favorite item is the Greek pizza, with olives, feta cheese, and anchovies, but the barbecue chicken pizza is also delicious. There is both indoor and terrace seating, as well as a bar area, complete with a pool table, dartboards, and a couple of TVs for sports events and surf videos.

On the main road in Jacó. © 643-3354. Main courses $4–$12. V. Wed–Mon noon–midnight.

PLAYA DE JACO AFTER DARK

Playa de Jacó is the central Pacific's party town. There are tons of bars and several discos. The **Disco La Central** is packed every night of the high season and every weekend during the off season. La Central is right on the beach near the south end of town. There's a huge open-air hall that features the requisite 1970s flashing lights and suspended mirrored ball, as well as a garden bar in a thatch-roofed building that's a slightly quieter place to have a drink. The disco charges a nominal cover charge. For a more casual atmosphere, head to either the **Beatle Bar** or **Onyx Bar.** Both are located right on the main drag in town. *Note:* There's a fair amount of prostitution in Jacó. It's not uncommon to find working women at any of the abovementioned places, as well as cruising other bars around town.

If you're looking for a surfer hangout, check out **La Hacienda,** a second-floor bar with a laid-back feel, a beat-up pool table, a dartboard, and surf videos on the TVs. Lately, live rock bands have been performing here on weekends. La Hacienda is located on the main drag toward the north end of town.

Sports freaks can catch the latest games at **Hotel Copacabana** or **El Zarpe.** The latter serves up good, reasonably priced burritos, burgers, and other assorted bar food.

EN ROUTE SOUTH TO MANUEL ANTONIO: PLAYA HERMOSA

Playa Hermosa is the first beach you'll hit as you head south from Playa de Jacó. This is primarily a surfers' beach, but it is still a lovely spot to spend some beach time. In fact, even though the surf conditions here can be rather rough and unprotected, and the beach is made of dark volcanic sand, I find Playa Hermosa much more attractive than Jacó. In addition to the hotels listed below, there are a host of simple hotels and *cabinas* catering to surfers. Prices, conditions, and upkeep can vary greatly. If you've got the time, your best bet is to visit a few until you find the best deal on the cleanest room.

If you're looking for something even more remote and undeveloped, head farther south to Playa Esterillos Este for the **Auberge du Pélican** (© 778-8105; www.aubergepelican.com).

At night, most folks in Playa Hermosa find their way to **The Backyard** (© 643-3936), a lively surfer bar with a pool table, darts, and hearty food.

WHERE TO STAY

In addition to the places mentioned below, **Costa Nera** (© 643-1942) is an attractive little Italian-run bed-and-breakfast that offers rooms for between $40 and $55 double. A couple of these rooms even front the ocean.

The Backyard ✪ This perennially popular bar and restaurant also has some of the most modern and comfortable rooms in Playa Hermosa, although they're pretty pricey for what you get. The two-story building features spacious rooms with dark red terra-cotta tile floors and simple furnishings. The second-floor rooms are definitely nicer than those on the ground floor. The oceanfront end units are classified as suites. They are a bit bigger and do have excellent ocean views. The small pool features a little sculpted rock waterfall and is quite refreshing on the hot days here. Despite the physical upgrade, this place is still quintessentially a surfer joint.

Playa Hermosa de Jacó (A.P. 132), Jacó, Puntarenas. ℂ/fax **643-1311**. www.backyardhotel.com. 8 units. $100–$145 double. Rates lower in the off season. AE, MC, V. **Amenities:** Restaurant; bar; small outdoor pool; laundry service. *In room:* A/C, TV, safe.

Cabinas Las Olas Playa Hermosa is a renowned surfing beach, and this has historically been its most popular surfer hotel. The main building is on a hill by the road. The rooms are all basic but comfortable. The nicest room here is the "Skybox Suite," located on the top floor, with a great view. Closer to the beach are three A-frame cabins or *ranchos,* each of which has a roomy bedroom on the second floor (in the peak of the A) and a single bed, a bunk bed, a kitchenette, and a bathroom on the ground floor. Between the main building and the cabins is a pool with a small stone waterfall. Out by the ocean there's a restaurant that serves breakfast and dinner daily.

Playa Hermosa (A.P. 258-4023), Jacó, Puntarenas. ℂ/fax **643-3687.** www.amerisol.com/costarica/lasolas. 8 units. $40–$60 double. AE, MC, V. **Amenities:** Restaurant; bar; surf- and boogie-board rental; tour desk; laundry service. *In room:* Fridge, safe, no phone.

Terraza del Pacífico ✦ Located just over the hill at the start of Playa Hermosa, this hotel has a wonderful setting on a mostly undeveloped section of beach. In recent years, it's received major renovations and repairs, and it finally seems to be getting into shape. In the middle of the complex is a circular pool with a swim-up bar and plenty of chaise longues for sunbathing and siestas. Red-tile roofs and faux-stucco walls give the buildings a Mediterranean look, and hardwood balcony railings add a touch of the tropics. Each guest room has two double beds, a private bathroom, and either a patio or balcony. A couple of suites are considerably larger and even include a kitchenette. The hotel's restaurant and open-air bar are located within a few feet of the high-tide mark. The hotel offers a range of tours, including a nearby canopy tour. Surfing is still the major draw here, and the Terraza has even installed klieg lights on the beach for night surfing.

Playa Hermosa de Jacó (A.P. 168-4023), Jacó, Puntarenas. ℂ **643-3222.** Fax 643-3424. www.terraza-del-pacifico.com. 43 units. $100 double. Rates include breakfast buffet. Rates lower in the off season. AE, MC, V. **Amenities:** Restaurant; bar; outdoor pool w/swim-up bar; laundry service. *In room:* A/C, TV, safe.

3 Manuel Antonio National Park ✦✦

140km (87 miles) SW of San José; 69km (43 miles) S of Playa de Jacó

No other destination in Costa Rica has received more international attention than Manuel Antonio. Many first-time visitors to Costa Rica plan their vacation around seeing it, and it's no surprise why: The views from the hills overlooking Manuel Antonio are spectacular, the beaches (particularly those inside the national park) are idyllic, and its jungles are crawling with white-faced and squirrel monkeys, among other forms of exotic wildlife. The flip side is that you'll have to pay more to see it, and you'll have to share it with more fellow travelers than on other parts of this coast. Moreover, development here is leaving a noticeable footprint. What was once a smattering of small hotels tucked into the forested hillside has become a long string of lodgings along the 7km (4⅓ miles) of road between Quepos and the national park entrance. Hotel roofs now regularly break the tree line, and there are numerous architectural and environmental anomalies, including a retired cargo plane recently converted into a roadside bar, a terrible eyesore.

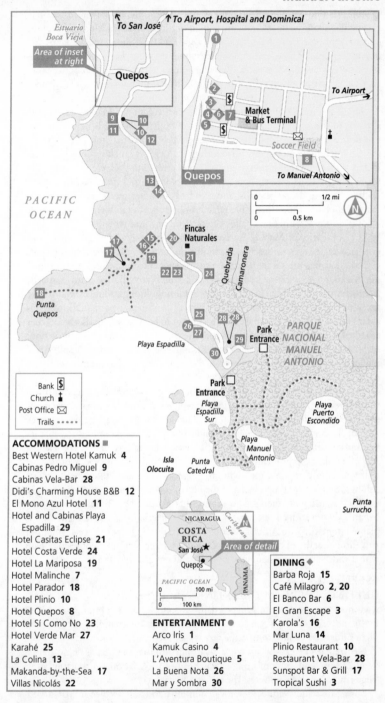

Estuario
Boca Vieja

To San José ↑ To Airport, Hospital and Dominical

Area of inset
at right

Quepos

1

2
3
$
4 6 7
5
$

Market
& Bus Terminal

To Airport →

9
11
10
10
12

Soccer Field

8

✝

Quepos

To Manuel Antonio ↘

PACIFIC
OCEAN

0   1/2 mi
0   0.5 km

N

13
14

17
16
17
15
19
20
21
22 23
24

Fincas
Naturales

Quebrada Camaronera

18

Punta
Quepos

25
26
28 28
27
30
29

Park
Entrance

PARQUE
NACIONAL
MANUEL
ANTONIO

Playa Espadilla

Bank $
Church ✝
Post Office ✉
Trails ·····

Park
Entrance
Playa
Espadilla
Sur

Playa
Puerto
Escondido

Playa
Manuel
Antonio

Isla
Olocuita

Punta
Catedral

Punta
Surrucho

NICARAGUA
COSTA
RICA
San José ★
Quepos
PACIFIC OCEAN
Caribbean Sea
Area of detail
PANAMA
0   100 mi
0 100 km

ACCOMMODATIONS ■
Best Western Hotel Kamuk **4**
Cabinas Pedro Miguel **9**
Cabinas Vela-Bar **28**
Didi's Charming House B&B **12**
El Mono Azul Hotel **11**
Hotel and Cabinas Playa
  Espadilla **29**
Hotel Casitas Eclipse **21**
Hotel Costa Verde **24**
Hotel La Mariposa **19**
Hotel Malinche **7**
Hotel Parador **18**
Hotel Plinio **10**
Hotel Quepos **8**
Hotel Sí Como No **23**
Hotel Verde Mar **27**
Karahé **25**
La Colina **13**
Makanda-by-the-Sea **17**
Villas Nicolás **22**

ENTERTAINMENT ●
Arco Iris **1**
Kamuk Casino **4**
L'Aventura Boutique **5**
La Buena Nota **26**
Mar y Sombra **30**

DINING ◆
Barba Roja **15**
Café Milagro **2, 20**
El Banco Bar **6**
El Gran Escape **3**
Karola's **16**
Mar Luna **14**
Plinio Restaurant **10**
Restaurant Vela-Bar **28**
Sunspot Bar & Grill **17**
Tropical Sushi **3**

Still, this remains one of the most beautiful locations in the entire country. Gazing down on the blue Pacific from high on the hillsides of Manuel Antonio, it's almost impossible to hold back a gasp of delight. Offshore, rocky islands dot the vast expanse of blue, and in the foreground, the rich, deep green of the rainforest sweeps down to the water. Even cheap Instamatics regularly produce postcard-perfect snapshots. It's this superb view that the numerous hotels at Manuel Antonio sell and that keeps people transfixed on decks, patios, and balconies.

One of the most popular national parks in the country, Manuel Antonio is also one of the smallest, covering fewer than 680 hectares (1,680 acres). Its several nearly perfect small beaches are connected by trails that meander through the rainforest. The mountains surrounding the beaches quickly rise as you head inland from the water; however, the park was created to preserve not its beautiful beaches, but its forests, home to endangered squirrel monkeys, three-toed sloths, purple-and-orange crabs, and hundreds of other species of birds, mammals, and plants. Once this entire stretch of coast was a rainforest teeming with wildlife, but now only this small rocky outcrop of forest remains.

The popularity of Manuel Antonio has brought increased development and ever-growing crowds of beachgoers. In just the last few years, these factors have turned what was once a remote and pristine spot into an area full of overflowing parking areas, overpriced hotels, and noisy crowds. In many respects, Manuel Antonio has been victimized by its adoring throngs, some of whom have taken to feeding the wild animals (monkeys and pizotes, in particular), which is a dangerous distortion of what ecotourism should be. On weekends, the beaches are filled with people, and the disco near the park entrance blares its music until early morning. A jumble of snack shacks, souvenir stands, and makeshift parking lots line the beach road just outside the park, making the entrance road look more like a slum than a national park.

Those views that are so bewitching also have their own set of drawbacks. If you want a great view, you aren't going to be staying on the beach—in fact, you probably won't be able to walk to the beach. This means that you'll be driving back and forth, taking taxis, or riding the public bus a lot. Also keep in mind that it's hot and humid here, and it rains a lot. However, the rain is what keeps Manuel Antonio lush and green, and this wouldn't be the tropics if things were otherwise.

If you're traveling on a rock-bottom budget or are mainly interested in sportfishing, you might end up staying in the nearby town of **Quepos,** which was once a quiet banana port; the land to the north was used by Chiquita to grow its bananas. Disease wiped out most of the banana plantations, and now the land is planted primarily with African oil-palm trees. To reach Quepos by road, you must pass through miles of these oil-palm plantations. Increasingly, Quepos is filling up with a wide variety of restaurants, souvenir and crafts shops, and lively bars.

ESSENTIALS

GETTING THERE & DEPARTING By Plane Sansa (© **221-9414;** www.flysansa.com) flies to Quepos daily at 7:45, 8:50, and 11am, and 12:50, 2:40, and 4:25pm from San José's Juan Santamaría International Airport. The flight's duration is 30 minutes; the fare is $44 each way.

Nature Air (© **220-3054;** www.natureair.com) flies to Quepos daily at 7:35, 9, and 11am, and 4:30pm from Tobías Bolaños International Airport in Pavas. Flight duration is 30 minutes; the fare is $50 each way.

Both Sansa and Nature Air provide airport-transfer service coordinated with their arriving flights. The service costs around $4 per person each way, depending

> **Tips Travel Tips**
>
> Despite the aforementioned caveats, Manuel Antonio is still a fabulous destination with a wealth of activities and attractions for all types and all ages. If you plan carefully, you can avoid many of the problems that detract from its appeal. If you steer clear of the peak months (Dec–Mar), you'll miss most of the crowds. If you must come during the peak months, try to avoid weekends, when the beach is packed with families from San José. If you visit the park early in the morning, you can leave when the crowds begin to show up at midday. In the afternoon, you can lounge by your pool or on your patio. If you stay at a hotel partway up the hill from the park entrance, you'll have relatively easy access to the beach, you might get a view, and, best of all, you'll be out of earshot of the disco.

on where exactly your hotel is located. Speak to your airline's agent when you arrive to confirm your return flight and coordinate a pickup at your hotel for that day, if necessary. Taxis occasionally meet incoming flights as well. Expect to be charged between $8 and $12 per car for up to four people, depending on the distance to your hotel and your bargaining abilities.

When you're ready to depart, **Sansa** (© 777-0683 in Quepos) has daily flights to San José that leave at 8:30, 9:30, and 11:45am, and 1:35, 3:25, and 5:10pm.

Nature Air flights leave for San José daily at 8:35 and 11:10am, and 1:25 and 5:30pm. The 8:35am flight makes a stop to drop off passengers at the Juan Santamaría International Airport.

By Car   From San José, the most popular route is to take the narrow and winding old highway, which turns off the Interamerican Highway just west of Alajuela near the town of Atenas and joins the Costanera near Orotina. Just follow the many signs to hotels in either Jacó or Manuel Antonio. When you reach Jacó, it's a straight shot and another hour to Manuel Antonio.

You can also take the Interamerican Highway west to the Puntarenas turnoff and head south on the Costanera, the coastal road through Jacó. This is your best bet if you are heading to Manuel Antonio from Puntarenas or any point north.

Finally, you could try the more rugged route beginning in Ciudad Colón, a western suburb of San José, and then head out to Puriscal and join the Costanera near Parrita. This is the shortest route, but some sections are not paved and others are in rough shape. Nevertheless, locals often use it, especially during the dry season. Four-wheel-drive vehicles are recommended, but normal two-wheel-drive sedans can usually make it.

By Bus   **Express buses** (© 223-5567) to Manuel Antonio leave San José daily at 6am, noon, and 6 and 7:30pm from the Coca-Cola bus terminal at Calle 16 between avenidas 1 and 3. Trip duration is 3½ hours; the fare is $5. These buses go all the way to the park entrance and will drop you off at any of the hotels along the way.

Regular buses (© 223-5567) to Quepos leave San José daily at 7 and 10am, and 2 and 4pm. Trip duration is 4½ hours; the fare is $4. These buses stop in Quepos. From here, if you're staying at one of the hotels on the road to Manuel Antonio, you must take a local bus or taxi to your hotel.

Grayline (© 220-2126; www.graylinecostarica.com) has a daily bus that leaves San José for Quepos and Manuel Antonio at 8:30am; the fare is $25.

Interbus (© 283-5573; www.costaricapass.com) has two daily buses that leave San José for Quepos and Manuel Antonio at 9am and 1:30pm; the fare is $25. Both companies will pick you up at most San José–area hotels.

Buses leave **Puntarenas** for Quepos daily at 5 and 11am, and 2:30 and 4:30pm. The ride takes 2½ hours; the fare is $3.

Many of the buses for Quepos stop to unload and pick up passengers in **Playa de Jacó.** If you're in Jacó heading toward Manuel Antonio, you can try your luck at one of the covered bus stops out on the Interamerican Highway (see "Playa de Jacó," earlier in this chapter).

From Quepos, buses leave for Manuel Antonio daily, roughly every half-hour, from 6am to 7pm, with one late bus at 10pm. The fare is 35¢. The ride takes about 15 minutes.

When you're ready to depart, the Quepos bus station (© 777-0101) is next to the market, which is 3 blocks east of the water and 2 blocks north of the road to Manuel Antonio. Express buses to San José leave daily at 6 and 9:30am, noon, and 3 and 5pm. Local buses to San José (duration is 4 hr.) leave at 5 and 8am, and 2 and 4pm.

In the busy winter months, tickets sell out well in advance, especially on weekends; if you can, purchase your ticket several days in advance. However, you must buy your Quepos-bound tickets in San José and your San José return tickets in Quepos. If you're staying in Manuel Antonio, you can buy your return ticket for a direct bus in advance in Quepos and then wait along the road to be picked up. There is no particular bus stop; just make sure you are out to flag down the bus and give it time to stop—you don't want to be standing in a blind spot when the bus comes flying around some tight corner.

Buses for **Puntarenas** leave daily at 4:30, 7:30, and 10:30am, and 3pm. Any bus headed for San José or Puntarenas will let you off in Playa de Jacó.

ORIENTATION   Quepos is a little port town at the mouth of the Boca Vieja Estuary. After crossing the bridge into town, take the lower road (to the left of the high road). In 4 blocks, turn left; you'll be on the road to Manuel Antonio. This road winds through town a bit before starting over the hill to all the hotels and the national park.

GETTING AROUND   A taxi from Quepos to Manuel Antonio (or any hotel along the road toward the park) costs between $2 and $4. The return trip from the park to your hotel should cost only 75¢ per person. I know that this system doesn't make much sense, but this is a fixed price, so watch out for drivers who try to charge more. At night, or if the taxi must leave the main road (for hotels such as La Mariposa, El Parador, and Makanda), the charge is a little higher. If you need to call a taxi, dial © 777-1695 or 777-0425.

The bus between Quepos and Manuel Antonio takes 15 minutes each way and runs roughly every half-hour from 6am to 7pm daily, with one late bus leaving Quepos at 10pm and returning from Manuel Antonio at 10:25pm. The buses, which leave from the main bus terminal in Quepos, near the market, go all the way to the National Park entrance before turning around and returning. You can flag down these buses from any point on the side of the road. The fare is 35¢.

You can also rent a car from **Adobe** (© 777-4242), **Alamo** (© 777-3344), **Economy** (© 777-5353), or **Payless Rent-a-Car** (© 777-0115) for around $50 a day. All have offices in downtown Quepos, but with advance notice, someone will meet you at the airport with your car for no extra charge.

If you rent a car, never leave anything of value in it unless you intend to stay within sight of the car at all times. Car break-ins are common here. There are now a couple of parking lots just outside the park entrance that cost around $3 for the whole day. You should definitely keep your car in one of these while exploring the park or soaking up sun on the beach. And although these lots do offer a modicum of protection and safety, you should still not leave anything of value exposed in the car. The trunk is probably safe.

FAST FACTS   The telephone number of the **Quepos Hospital** is ℭ 777-0922; for the **local police,** call ℭ 777-2117. There are several pharmacies in Quepos, as well as a pharmacy at the hospital. There are also a half-dozen or so laundromats and laundry services in town. For film, batteries, and any urgent developing, try **Todo Foto Quepos** (ℭ 777-1442).

There are a handful of **Internet cafes** around Quepos and along the road to Manuel Antonio, and many hotels are providing this service as well.

EXPLORING THE NATIONAL PARK

Manuel Antonio is a small park with only three major trails. Most visitors come primarily to lie on one of the beaches and check out the white-faced monkeys, which sometimes seem as common as tourists. A guide is not essential here, but as I've said before, unless you're experienced in rainforest hiking, you'll see and learn a lot more with one. A 2- or 3-hour guided hike should cost between $25 and $35 per person. Almost any of the hotels in town can help you set up a tour of the park. If you decide to explore the park on your own, a basic map is usually available at the park entrance for $1.

ENTRY POINT, FEES & REGULATIONS   The park is closed on Monday but is open Tuesday through Sunday from 8am to 4pm year-round. You'll find the principal park entrance at **Playa Espadilla,** the beach at the end of the road from Quepos. To reach the park station, you must cross a small, sometimes polluted stream that's little more than ankle-deep at low tide but that can be knee- or even waist-deep at high tide. For years there has been talk of building a bridge over this stream; in the meantime, you'll have to either wade it, or pay a boatman a buck or two for the very quick crossing. Just over the stream, you'll find the small ranger station. This is where you can pick up the small map of the park I mentioned above. You can also enter the park at an inland entrance located at the end of the side road that leads off perpendicular to **Playa Espadilla** just beyond Marlin Restaurant. Whichever entrance you choose, you will have to pay a fee of $6 per person to enter. The Parks Service allows only 600 visitors to enter each day, which could mean that you won't get in if you arrive in midafternoon during the high season. Camping is not allowed.

THE BEACHES   **Playa Espadilla Sur** (as opposed to Playa Espadilla, which is just outside the park; see "Hitting the Water," below) is the first beach within the actual park boundaries. It's usually the least-crowded beach in the park and one of the best places to find a quiet shade tree to plant yourself under. If you want to explore further, you can walk along this soft-sand beach or follow a trail through the forest parallel to the beach. **Playa Manuel Antonio,** which is the most popular beach inside the park, is a short, deep crescent of white sand backed by lush rainforest. The water here is sometimes clear enough to offer good snorkeling along the rocks at either end. At low tide, Playa Manuel Antonio shows a very interesting relic: a circular stone turtle trap left by its pre-Columbian residents. From Playa Manuel Antonio, there's another slightly longer trail to **Puerto Escondido,** where there's a blowhole that sends up plumes of spray at high tide.

Tips **Helping Out**

If you want to help efforts in protecting the endangered squirrel monkey *(mono tití)*, make a donation to **ASCOMOTI** (© 224-5703; www.ascomoti. org), which is working in conjunction with a host of local tourism businesses to protect this pint-size primate.

THE HIKING TRAILS   From either Playa Espadilla Sur or Playa Manuel Antonio, you can take a circular hike around a high promontory bluff. The farthest point on this hike, which takes about 25 minutes round-trip, is **Punta Catedral** ★★, where the view is spectacular. The trail is a little steep in places, but anybody in average shape can do it. I have done it in sturdy sandals, but you might want to wear good hiking shoes. This is a good place to spot monkeys, although you're more likely to see a white-faced monkey than a rare squirrel monkey.

Another good place to see monkeys is the **trail inland** from Playa Manuel Antonio. This is a linear trail and mostly uphill, but not too taxing. It's great to spend hours exploring the steamy jungle and then take a refreshing dip in the ocean.

Finally, there's a trail that leads first to Puerto Escondido (see above) and **Punta Surrucho,** where there are some sea caves. Be careful when hiking beyond Puerto Escondido: What seems like easy beach hiking at low tide becomes treacherous to impassable at high tide. Don't get trapped.

HITTING THE WATER

BEACHES OUTSIDE THE PARK   **Playa Espadilla,** the gray-sand beach just outside the park boundary, is often perfect for board surfing and bodysurfing. At times, it can be a bit rough for casual swimming, but because there's no entrance fee, it's the most popular beach with locals and visiting Ticos. Some shops by the water rent boogie boards, beach chairs, and beach umbrellas. A full-day rental of a beach umbrella and two chaise longues costs around $10. (These are not available inside the park.)

BOATING, KAYAKING, RAFTING & SPORTFISHING TOURS   **Iguana Tours** (© 777-1262; www.iguanatours.com) is the most established and dependable tour operator in the area; it offers river rafting, sea kayaking, mangrove tours, and guided hikes. These folks have an office on the main road, just as you begin to head out of Quepos toward Manuel Antonio. One of its offerings, among my favorite tours in the area, is a mangrove estuary tour of Damas Island with Jorge Cruz. These trips generally include lunch, a stop on Damas Island, and roughly 3 to 4 hours of cruising the waterways. You'll see loads of wildlife. The cost is $60.

Several rafting companies in Quepos ply the same rivers. Among them are **Iguana Tours** (see above), **H2O Adventures** (© 777-4092; www.riostropicales. com), and **Amigos del Río** (© 777-0082; www.amigosdelrio.com). All offer full-day rafting trips for around $85 to $100. Large multiperson rafts are used during the rainy season, and single-person "duckies" are broken out when the water levels drop. Both of the above companies also offer half-day rafting adventures and sea-kayaking trips for around $65.

Among the other boating options available around Quepos/Manuel Antonio are excursions in search of dolphins and sunset cruises. In addition to **Iguana Tours** (see above), **Sunset Sails** (© 777-1304) and **Planet Dolphin** (©/fax 777-2137; www.planetdolphin.com) offer these tours for between $40 and $65 per person. The latter uses a 20-seater powerboat, so don't sign up expecting a leisurely sail. However, the tour does include a snorkel break and frequent dolphin sightings. **Waverunner Safaris** (✆ **777-1706**) offers 2-hour Jet Ski tours for $99 per person. This tour plies the same waters and includes some snorkeling and the possibility of a dolphin encounter.

Quepos is one of Costa Rica's billfish centers, and sailfish, marlin, and tuna are all common in these waters. In the past year or so, fresh and brackish water fishing in the mangroves and estuaries has also become popular. If you're into sportfishing, try hooking up with **Blue Fin Sportfishing** (✆ 777-1676; www.bluefinsportfishing.com), **Blue Water** (✆ 800/807-1585 in the U.S. and Canada, or 777-1596; www.sportfishingincostarica.com), **High Tec Sportfishing** (✆ 777-3465), or **Poseidon Adventures** (✆ 777-0935; cksibus@racsa.co.cr). A full day of fishing should cost between $450 and $1,500, depending on the size of the boat. There's a lot of competition here, so it pays to shop around and investigate.

SCUBA DIVING **Costa Rica Adventure Divers** (✆ **777-2273;** www.costarica diving.com) offers two-tank dive trips for $85 per person, including equipment, as well as certification and resort courses. Because most of the diving is close to shore, dive trips are offered only December through May, when there is less runoff from the rains, although visibility here is still quite variable. Dive courses can be conducted throughout the year, with advance notice.

OTHER ACTIVITIES IN THE AREA

ATV   If you want to try riding a four-wheel ATV (all-terrain vehicle), check in with the folks at **Fourtrax Adventures** (✆ **777-1825;** www.fourtraxadventure. com). Their principal tour is a 4-hour adventure through African palm plantations, rural towns, and secondary forest to a jungle waterfall, where you stop for a dip. You cross several rivers and a long suspension bridge. Either breakfast or lunch is served, depending on the timing. Cost is $95 per ATV, which can hold one or two people.

BIKING   If you want to do some mountain biking while you're here, check in with **Estrella Tour** (✆/fax **777-1286;** estrellatour@hotmail.com), in downtown Quepos. Well-maintained bikes rent for around $20 per day. You can also do a number of different guided tours according to skill level for between $45 and $95 per day, as well as multiday expeditions.

BUTTERFLY GARDEN **Fincas Naturales/The Nature Farm Reserve** (✆ **777-0850;** www.butterflygardens.co.cr) is just across from (and run by) Hotel Sí Como No. A lovely bi-level **butterfly garden** ✫ is the centerpiece attraction here, but there is also a private reserve and a small network of well-groomed trails through the forest. A 1-hour guided tour of the butterfly garden costs $15 per person, or $25 when combined with a 1-hour guided hike through the forest.

CANOPY ADVENTURES About 20 minutes outside of Quepos is **Rainmaker Nature Refuge** (✆ **777-3565;** www.rainmakercostarica.com). The main attraction here is a system of connected suspension bridges strung through the forest canopy, crisscrossing a deep ravine. There are six bridges; the longest is 90m (295 ft.) across. There's also a small network of trails and some great swimming holes. A half-day tour, including a light breakfast, a buffet lunch, round-trip transportation from Quepos, and a guide, costs $65 per person. Tours leave every morning, and most hotels in the area can book them for you.

There are also several canopy tours in the area. The most adventurous are offered by **Canopy Safari** ✫ (✆ **777-0100;** www.canopysafari.com) and

---

Tips Yo Quiero Hablar Español

La Escuela de Idiomas D'Amore (©/fax **777-1143**; www.escueladamore.com)
runs language-immersion programs out of a former hotel with a fabulous
view, on the road to Manuel Antonio. A 2-week conversational Spanish
course, including a homestay and two meals daily, costs $980. Or you can try
the **Costa Rica Spanish Institute (COSI; © 800/771-5184** in the U.S. and
Canada; 234-1001 or 777-0021 in Costa Rica; www.cosi.co.cr), which charges
$340 per week, with room and board extra.

Dream Forest Canopy Tour (© 777-3030). Both consist of a series of platforms connected by zip lines. Adventurers use a harness-and-pulley system to
"zip" between platforms, using a leather-gloved hand as their only brake. The
Titi Canopy Tour (© 777-1020) is a similar but mellower setup. A canopy tour
should run you between $45 and $65 per person.

HORSEBACK RIDING   If your tropical fantasy is to ride a horse down a
beach between jungle and ocean, contact **Stable Equus** (© 777-0001), which
charges $35 for a 2-hour ride in Manuel Antonio. This stable allegedly treats its
animals more humanely than other stables in the area and is also concerned with
keeping horse droppings off the beaches. **Brisas del Nara** (© 779-1235;
www.horsebacktour.com) offers full- and half-day horseback excursions that
pass through both primary and secondary forest and feature a swimming stop at
a jungle waterfall. A full-day tour with these folks, including breakfast and
lunch, costs $55 per person ($45 half-day).

SOOTHE YOUR BODY & SOUL   There are quite a few massage therapists
around Manuel Antonio and a couple of day spas. The best of these are **Sea
Glass Spa** ⋆ (© 777-2607; www.seaglassspa.com), located down a winding
road on the ocean side just before Villas Nicolás, and **Serenity Spa** ⋆ (© 777-
0777), located in the Hotel Sí Como No. A wide range of treatments, wraps,
and facials are available.

SHOPPING

If you're looking for souvenirs, you'll find plenty of beach towels, beachwear, and
handmade jewelry in a variety of small shops in Quepos and at impromptu stalls
down near the national park. For a good selection in one spot, try **La Buena
Nota** (© 777-1002), which is on the road to Manuel Antonio, right near the
Karahé hotel (p. 275). This shop is jam-packed with all sorts of beachwear, souvenirs, used books, and U.S. magazines and newspapers. It also has a few basic
rooms located above the store, and if you'd like to find out about renting a
house, this is a good place to ask.

   If you're looking for higher-end gifts, check out **L'Aventura Boutique** (© 777-
1019), on Avenida Central in Quepos. This small shop has a nice collection of
woodwork by Barry Biesanz, banana-fabric works by Lil Mena, and pottery by
Cecilia "Pefi" Figueres.

   The Hotel Sí Como No's **Regálame** gift shop is pretty well stocked and now has
two locations: one at the small shopping center in front of the hotel, and another
down in Quepos, on the main road just as you cross the bridge into town.

   One of my favorite hangouts has always been **Café Milagro** ⋆⋆ (© 777-
1707; www.cafemilagro.com), a homey coffeehouse and gift shop with two locations in the area. The folks here roast their own beans and also have a mail-order

service to keep you in Costa Rican coffee year-round. The menu includes a daily selection of freshly baked sweets, simple sandwiches and breakfast items, and a wide range of coffee drinks. You'll find local art for sale on the walls and a good selection of Cuban cigars and international newspapers, too. The original store-front, just over the bridge on your left as you enter Quepos, has recently been expanded, and there's another branch on the main road to Manuel Antonio right across from the turnoff for Hotel La Mariposa.

WHERE TO STAY

Take care when choosing your accommodations in Quepos/Manuel Antonio. There are very few true beachfront hotels in Manuel Antonio, so you won't have much luck finding a hotel where you can walk directly out of your room and onto the beach. In fact, most of the nicer hotels here are 1km (½ mile) or so away from the beach, high on the hill overlooking the ocean.

If you're traveling on a rock-bottom budget, you'll get more for your money by staying in Quepos and taking the bus to the beaches at Manuel Antonio every day. The rooms in Quepos might be small, but they're generally cleaner and more appealing than those available in the same price category closer to the park.

VERY EXPENSIVE

If you're coming for an extended stay with your family or a large group, you might look into the **Escape Villas** (© **866/839-5526** in the U.S., or 777-5258 in Costa Rica; www.vivalasvillas.com), which rents out a handful of very large and luxurious private villas with all the amenities and some of the best views in Manuel Antonio.

Hotel La Mariposa ★   La Mariposa has been transformed from an intimate and elegant boutique hotel, with just 10 large villas set discreetly into the hillside, into a hodgepodge of rooms, suites, and villas crowned by an awkward behemoth of a building towering over everything in sight. Although this is still one of Manuel Antonio's premier accommodations, I think the expansion and growth have cost this place much of its charm. Perched on a ridge at the top of the hill between Quepos and Manuel Antonio, La Mariposa (The Butterfly) commands a mountains-to-the-sea vista of more than 270 degrees. Needless to say, the sunsets here are knockouts, and the daytime views are pretty captivating themselves.

The nicest accommodations are the Premier Suites, housed in two newer three-story buildings constructed over the foundation of a couple of the original villas. These rooms are large, well equipped, and tastefully decorated, with excellent views. Most of surviving older villas have been split into separate junior suites and deluxe rooms. The junior suites each have a Jacuzzi out on the small balcony or just inside its sliding glass door. There are rooms in the four-story addition to the hotel's main building; they're quite spacious and have great views, but they don't have much charm or personality. There are also a few standard rooms, which are certainly comfortable but have no view to speak of.

Manuel Antonio (A.P. 4, Quepos). © 800/416-2747 in the U.S., or 777-0355. Fax 777-0050. www.lamariposa. com. 60 units. $155–$175 double; $215–$310 suite or villa; $375 penthouse suite. Rates lower in the off season. Extra person $40. AE, MC, V. **Amenities:** Restaurant; bar; 3 small pools; concierge; tour desk; complimentary shuttle to and from the national park; in-room massage; babysitting; laundry service. *In room:* A/C, minibar, safe.

Hotel Parador ★★   This hotel is spread out over more than 4¾ hectares (12 acres) of land on a low peninsula, down a dirt road from Hotel La Mariposa. Its design aims to imitate Spanish Mediterranean grandeur, and the main building is loaded with antiques, including 17th-century Dutch and Flemish oil paintings, a 300-year-old carved wooden horse, and 16th-century church and castle doors.

The standard rooms are well appointed but far too small for this price range. All have private patios, but few have any view to speak of. Deluxe rooms offer slightly more space, and the second-floor units have private balconies.

The spacious junior suites are located on the top of a hill, giving a good view of the sea and Cathedral Point in the distance. Note that it's a bit of a hike up to these units, although the hotel offers an on-call golf-cart shuttle service. The premium rooms, located in a three-story building built on a high spot on the grounds, have the best views and are my first choice here. The hotel runs a shuttle van to the national park, and there's a small, secluded beach about 500m (1,640 ft.) from the hotel.

Manuel Antonio (A.P. 284, Quepos). © 777-1414. Fax 777-1437. www.hotelparador.com. 108 units. $175 standard double; $200–$230 deluxe double; $260–$290 premium double; $305 junior suite; $700 presidential suite. Rates include breakfast buffet. Rates slightly higher during peak weeks, significantly lower in the off season. AE, MC, V. **Amenities:** 2 restaurants; 2 bars; large free-form pool w/swim-up bar and central fountain; outdoor tennis court; modest gym and spa; Jacuzzi; concierge; tour desk; room service; in-room massage; babysitting; laundry service. *In room:* A/C, TV, minibar, coffeemaker, hair dryer, safe.

Hotel Sí Como No ★★ *Finds* *Kids*   Owner Jim Damalas has done a great job of creating a lively, upscale midsize resort that blends in with and respects the rainforests and natural wonders of Manuel Antonio. Sí Como No offers an array of facilities and modern amenities, with an ecologically conscious attitude.

All the wood used is farm grown, and although all the rooms have energy-efficient air-conditioning units, guests are urged to use them only when necessary. The standard rooms (housed in the hotel's main building or in the ground floor of a villa) are quite acceptable, but it's worth the modest splurge for a superior or deluxe room or a suite. Most of these are on the top floors of the two- to three-story villas, with spectacular treetop views out over the forest and onto the Pacific. These rooms all have a bedroom with an adjoining living room area, a private balcony, and either a kitchenette or a wet bar. There are a series of deluxe suites with lots of space and large garden bathrooms, some of which have private Jacuzzis. A separate building set on a high patch of land has a more Art Deco style to it. This building features a penthouse suite with a very romantic outdoor Jacuzzi. There are two pools, including one reserved for adults, a full-service spa, and an expanded restaurant area. They also have a wonderful little butterfly garden just across the street. A wide range of tours is available. This is a place equally suited to families traveling with children and to couples looking for a romantic getaway.

Manuel Antonio (mailing address: Mail Stop SJO 297, P.O. Box 025216, Miami, FL 33102). © 777-0777. Fax 777-1093. www.sicomono.com. 60 units. $160–$250 double. Rates include breakfast. Rates lower in the off season. Extra person $30. Children under 6 stay free in parent's room. AE, MC, V. **Amenities:** 2 restaurants; 2 bars; 2 midsize pools, including 1 w/small waterslide; modest spa; 2 outdoor Jacuzzis; concierge; tour desk; free beach shuttle; in-room massage; babysitting; laundry service. *In room:* A/C, minibar, coffeemaker, hair dryer, iron, safe.

Makanda-by-the-Sea ★★ *Finds*   Located halfway down the road to Hotel El Parador and Punta Quepos, Makanda is a wonderfully luxurious collection of studio apartments and private villas. Each is individually decorated with flair and a sense of style. If you combine villa no. 1 with the three studios, you get one very large four-bedroom villa, great for a family or a small group (although children under 16 are not allowed, unless you rent out the whole hotel). Every choice comes with a full kitchenette and either a terrace or a balcony. The grounds are well tended, intermixed with tropical flowers and Japanese gardens. A full breakfast is delivered to your room each morning. The hotel's pool and Jacuzzi combine intricate and colorful tile work with a view of the jungle-covered hillsides and the Pacific Ocean.

Makanda's **Sunspot Bar & Grill** ★★ is one of the better restaurants in Manuel Antonio, with just a few tables set under open-sided cloth tents, serving creative Continental dishes and rich desserts. Be sure to make reservations in the high season.

Manuel Antonio (A.P. 29, Quepos). © **777-0442**. Fax 777-1032. www.makanda.com. 11 units. $230 studio; $300–$350 villa. Rates include full breakfast. Rates lower in the off season. V. No children under 16. **Amenities:** Restaurant; bar; midsize outdoor pool; Jacuzzi; watersports equipment and bike rental; concierge; tour desk; limited room service (noon–10pm); in-room massage and spa services; laundry service. *In room:* Kitchenette, stocked minibar, coffeemaker, safe.

EXPENSIVE

Hotel Casitas Eclipse ★ Located close to the top of the hill between Quepos and Manuel Antonio, these beautiful casitas are some of the most boldly styled structures in the area. Although the villas have a distinctly Mediterranean flavor, the owner swears they're inspired by Mesoamerican and Pueblo Indian villages. All are painted a blinding white and are topped with red-tile roofs. Simply furnished, the rooms are quite comfortable and attractive inside.

You can either rent the entire casita or split it up. The larger downstairs suites have tile floors, built-in banquettes, high ceilings, large patios, and full kitchens. If you don't need all that space, you can opt for the upstairs room, which has a separate entrance, a private bathroom, and a balcony of its own. Three attractive tiled pools are spread out among the lush grounds. Only the restaurant and a couple of villas have ocean views here, and even these are rather blocked by trees. I personally prefer the units farther from the road, where you're more likely to hear and see squirrel monkeys passing than trucks and buses.

Manuel Antonio (A.P. 11-6350, Quepos). © **777-0408**. Fax 777-1738. www.casitaseclipse.com. 30 units. Dec 16–Apr 15 $112–$155 double, $275 2-bedroom casita; Apr 16–Dec 15 $86–$103 double, $172 2-bedroom casita. Rates include continental breakfast. AE, DC, MC, V. **Amenities:** Restaurant; bar; 3 outdoor pools; small spa and exercise room; concierge; tour desk; laundry service. *In room:* A/C, TV, fridge, safe.

MODERATE

In addition to the hotels mentioned below, the **Best Western Hotel Kamuk** (© **777-0811;** www.kamuk.co.cr) is a dependable option right in downtown Quepos; it's popular with sport fishermen.

El Mono Azul Hotel *Value* Located on the road to Manuel Antonio, just outside of Quepos, the "Blue Monkey" offers clean and comfortable rooms at a good price. The more expensive rooms feature air-conditioning and/or a small television with cable. One room even has a Jacuzzi tub. The whole place has a lively, hostel-like feel. The owner is active in a children's arts program aimed at helping preserve the local rainforest and the endangered squirrel monkey. In fact, 10% of your bill goes to this program. The simple restaurant and pizzeria here is quite popular. These folks can also arrange longer-term rentals of fully equipped apartments and villas.

Manuel Antonio (A.P. 297-6350, Quepos). © **777-1548** or ©/fax 777-1954. www.monoazul.com. 20 units. $50–$65 double. Rates $10 lower in the off season, $10 higher during peak weeks. V. **Amenities:** Restaurant; bar; lounge; 2 small pools; small gym; tour desk; game room; laundry service. *In room:* A/C and TV in some units, no phone.

Hotel and Cabinas Playa Espadilla These are actually two separate sister projects located across the street from each other. The newer hotel has rooms with air-conditioning and cable television, and most have full kitchenettes. There's a tennis court here, as well as a bordering private reserve with a small trail system. The older (and less expensive) *cabinas* are more basic, although most have been well maintained, and a few even have air-conditioning. Ask about bed distribution before you take or reserve a room because a fair number of rooms have one double and a bunk bed. There's a small swimming pool and well-tended green areas at each site. This place started out as a popular budget option down near the national park entrance. Despite the expansion and improvements, I'm not sure that the facilities and amenities merit the prices they're now charging. You'll find both of these places down the side road that runs inland, perpendicular to Playa Espadilla, the first beach outside the national park.

Manuel Antonio (A.P. 195, Quepos). ℂ/fax 777-0903. www.espadilla.com. 32 units. $68–$72 cabina; $108–$122 double. The rates for the hotel rooms include a full breakfast. Rates lower in the off season. AE, MC, V. **Amenities:** Restaurant; bar; 2 small outdoor pools; tennis court; tour desk; laundry service. *In room:* A/C and TV in some units, fridge, safe, no phone.

Hotel Costa Verde ★ *Value*   This longstanding and constantly evolving hotel has consistently offered up good values, ocean views, and reasonable proximity to the beaches and national park. Located more than halfway down the hill to Manuel Antonio, about a 10-minute walk from the beach, Costa Verde has continued to add new rooms and new buildings over the years. Today there are rooms in a wide range of sizes and prices. Some of the buildings are located quite a hike from the hotel's reception and restaurants, so be sure you know exactly what type of room you'll be staying in and where it's located. Management has recently added rooms with air-conditioning and cable TV. The nicest rooms here have ocean views, kitchenettes, private balconies, and loads of space; some of these don't have air-conditioning, but that's no problem because they feature huge screened walls to encourage cross ventilation. There is also a huge penthouse suite with a commanding view of the spectacular surroundings. Three small pools are set into the hillside, with views out to the ocean, and the hotel has a couple of miles of private trails through the rainforest.

Manuel Antonio (mailing address: SJO 1313, P.O. Box 025216, Miami, FL 33102). ℂ **866/854-7958** in the U.S. and Canada, or 777-0584. Fax 777-0560. www.costaverde.com. 43 units. $79–$155 double. Rates lower in the off season, higher during peak weeks. AE, MC, V. **Amenities:** 2 restaurants, 3 bars; 3 small outdoor pools; tour desk; laundry service. *In room:* A/C and TV in some units, no phone.

Hotel Plinio *Value*   For many years, the Plinio was a favorite of budget travelers visiting Manuel Antonio, and although its room rates have crept up over the years, it's still a good value. The hotel is built into a steep hillside, so it's a bit of a climb from the parking lot up to the guest rooms and restaurant (roughly the equivalent of three flights of stairs). when you're up top, though, you'll think you're in a treehouse. Floors and walls are polished hardwood, and there are even rooms with tree-trunk pillars.

The hotel's suites are the best value. These are built on either two or three levels. Both have sleeping lofts; the three-story rooms also have rooftop decks. My favorite room is known as the "jungle house" and is set back in the forest. Behind the hotel there's a private reserve with 15km (9⅓ miles) of trails and, at the top of the hill, a 15m (49-ft.) tall observation tower with an incredible view. In addition to the popular **Plinio Restaurant** (p. 278), there's a poolside grill where lunches are served. Plinio is located just outside of Quepos on the road toward the national park, so it is a fair distance from the park entrance and beaches.

Manuel Antonio (A.P. 71-6350, Quepos). ℂ 777-0055. Fax 777-0558. www.hotelplinio.com. 12 units. Dec–Apr $60–$70 double; $85–$110 suite or house. Rates include breakfast buffet in high season. Rates lower May–Nov. AE, MC, V (7% surcharge). **Amenities:** Restaurant; bar; small outdoor pool in lush garden setting; laundry service. *In room:* No phone.

Hotel Verde Mar   This hotel is one of the best choices for proximity to the national park and the beach. From your room, it's just a 50m (164-ft.) walk to the beach (Playa Espadilla) via a raised wooden walkway. All of the rooms here have plenty of space, nice wrought-iron queen-size beds, red-tile floors, a desk and chair, a fan, and a small porch. All but two of the rooms come with a basic kitchenette. Some of the larger rooms even have two queen-size beds. The hotel has no restaurant, but there are plenty within walking distance. There's a small pool here, for when the surf is too rough. You'll find Verde Mar on the beach side of the road just before the Mar y Sombra.

Manuel Antonio (A.P. 348-6350), Quepos. 🅒 **777-1805** or 777-2122. Fax 777-1311. www.verdemar.com. 21 units. $70–$90 double; $105 suite. Rates lower in the off season. AE, MC, V. **Amenities:** Small pool; laundry service. *In room:* A/C, kitchenette in some units, no phone.

Karahé The Karahé has long been one of the few beachfront hotels in Manuel Antonio. If you stay in one of the more expensive beachfront units, you'll have a newer room with cool tile floors, two double beds, air-conditioning, and a small patio. The least-expensive rooms are located just off the reception and offer neither views nor easy access to the ocean. Be aware that if you opt for one of the villas (the cheapest and oldest rooms in the hotel), you'll have a steep uphill climb from the beach; on the other hand, a couple of these have great views. The gardens here are quite lush and are planted with flowering ginger that often attracts hummingbirds.

The hotel can arrange a wide variety of tours and charters, including sportfishing ($850 for a full day). Karahé is located on both sides of the road about 450m (1,476 ft.) before you reach Playa Espadilla.

Manuel Antonio (A.P. 100-6350, Quepos). 🅒 **777-0170.** Fax 777-1075. www.karahe.com. 24 units, 9 villas. $70–$110 double. Rates include continental breakfast. Rates lower in the off season. AE, MC, V. **Amenities:** Restaurant; bar; small outdoor pool and Jacuzzi; exercise room; tour desk; laundry service. *In room:* A/C, no phone.

La Colina 🅐 *Value* This casual little place started out as a quaint little B&B offering just four simple budget rooms. The hotel has grown considerably, and there are now a variety of rooms in a variety of price ranges. Although the original rooms here are fairly small, they're decorated with style. They have cool tile floors, louvered French doors, and a good writing desk. Outside each room there's a small patio area with a few chairs. The newer suites are built on the highest spot on this property and have front and back balconies with views of both the ocean and the mountains, in addition to more space and natural light. All rooms are nonsmoking. There's a two-tiered swimming pool with a swim-up bar, and the restaurant here is pretty good. La Colina also rents out two fully equipped apartments and can accommodate longer-term stays. The hotel is on your right as you head out of Quepos toward Manuel Antonio, right at a sharp switchback on a steep hill (hence the name, which means "The Hill").

Manuel Antonio (A.P. 191, Quepos). 🅒 **777-0231.** Fax 777-1553. www.lacolina.com. 13 units. Dec–Apr $45–$85 double; May–Nov $39–$70 double. Rates include full breakfast. AE, MC, V. **Amenities:** Restaurant; bar; small pool; small day spa; tour desk; limited room service (8am–9pm); babysitting; laundry service. *In room:* A/C, TV, safe, no phone.

Villas Nicolás 🅐 *Value* These large villas offer bang for your buck. Built as terraced units up a steep hill in deep forest, they really give you the feeling that you're in the jungle. Most are quite spacious and well appointed, with wood floors, throw rugs, and comfortable bathrooms; some rooms even have separate living rooms and full kitchenettes, which make longer stays comfortable. My favorite features, though, are the balconies, which come with sitting chairs and a hammock. Some of these balconies are massive and have incredible views. In fact, the rooms highest up the hill have views that I'd be willing to pay a lot more for, and a few of them even have air-conditioning. During the high season, the hotel usually opens an informal restaurant/bar near the pool that serves breakfast and sometimes lunch and dinner, depending on demand.

Manuel Antonio (A.P. 236, Quepos). ℂ 777-0481. Fax 777-0451. www.villasnicolas.com. 20 units. $75–$135 double. Weekly, monthly, and low-season (May–Nov) rates available. AE, MC, V. **Amenities:** Small outdoor pool; laundry service. *In room:* A/C in some units, fridge.

INEXPENSIVE

In addition to the places listed below, **Didi's Charming House B&B** (ℂ 777-0069; www.didiscr.com) pretty much lives up to its name.

Cabinas Pedro Miguel   Located a kilometer outside Quepos on the road to Manuel Antonio (across from Hotel Plinio), these *cabinas* are very basic, with cement floors and cinder-block walls, but at least they're away from the fray and surrounded by forest. The second-floor rooms are newer and cleaner and have carpeting, as well as a glimpse of the water from the common veranda. One of them is huge, with a kitchen and a back wall made entirely of screen. From it, guests can look out over a lush stand of trees. During the high season (late Nov to late Apr), there's a breakfast buffet, which will run you about $5. In the evening you can dine at the restaurant, which serves Costa Rican standards.

Manuel Antonio (A.P. 17, Quepos). ℂ/fax 777-0035. pmiguel@racsa.co.cr. 16 units. $30–$40 double; $60 quad. MC, V. **Amenities:** Restaurant; postage stamp–size pool. *In room:* No phone.

Cabinas Vela-Bar   You'll find this little hotel up the narrow road that leads off to the left just before the end of the road to Manuel Antonio National Park. It has a wide variety of room choices: If you're on a tight budget, you can stay in a tiny room, or if you have a little more money to spend, you can opt for a spacious one-bedroom house that has tile floors and arched windows. There are double beds and tiled bathrooms in all rooms. Quite a few rooms come with air-conditioning and small refrigerators, and a couple have full kitchenettes. The open-air restaurant/bar is deservedly popular; check the chalkboard for the day's special. If you can bear the soft beds, this is one of the better budget options in Manuel Antonio, and it's only 100m (328 ft.) from the beach.

Manuel Antonio (A.P. 13, Quepos). ℂ 777-0413. Fax 777-1071. www.velabar.com. 11 units. $45–$85 double. Rates lower in the off season. AE, MC, V. **Amenities:** Restaurant; bar; laundry service. *In room:* A/C, kitchenette, and fridge in some units; no phone.

Hotel Malinche   A good choice for budget travelers, the Hotel Malinche is located on the first street to your left as you come into Quepos. Look for the hotel's arched brick entrance. Inside you'll find bright rooms with louvered windows. The rooms are small but have hardwood or tile floors and clean bathrooms. The more expensive rooms are newer and larger, and have air-conditioning, TVs, and carpets.

Quepos. ℂ 777-0093. Fax 777-1833. 24 units. $20–$50 double. V. *In room:* No phone.

Hotel Quepos   This little budget hotel is both comfortable and clean, offering hardwood floors, ceiling fans, a large and sunny TV lounge, and a protected parking lot. The management is very friendly, and there's an interesting souvenir shop and a charter-fishing office on the first floor. This hotel is hard to miss: It's directly across from the soccer field on the way out of town toward Manuel Antonio, and it's painted hot pink with green trim.

Quepos. ℂ/fax 777-0274. 20 units, 11 with private bathroom. $15 double with shared bathroom; $22 double with private bathroom. No credit cards. *In room:* No phone.

WHERE TO DINE

There are scores of dining options around Manuel Antonio and Quepos, and almost every hotel has some sort of restaurant. In addition to the places listed below, the downtown Quepos **El Banco Bar** is deservedly popular, with excellent American-style bar food and fresh seafood. For the cheapest meals around, try a simple soda in Quepos, or head to one of the open-air joints on the beach road before the National Park entrance. The standard Tico menu prevails, with prices in the $3-to-$8 range. Of these, **Marlin Restaurant,** right in front of Playa Espadilla, and **Mar Luna,** on the main road just beyond Hotel La Colina, are your best bets. For simple pasta, pizzas, and Italian gelato, head to **Escalofrío,** right downtown.

If you have a room with a kitchenette, you can shop at one of several supermarkets in Quepos, or brave the cluttered stalls of its central market, right next to the bus station. Two other options for light meals, deli items, and well-prepared sandwiches are **L'Angelo Italian Deli** and **Green Valley Gourmet,** both located in downtown Quepos.

Barba Roja SEAFOOD/CONTINENTAL   Perched high on a hill, with stunning views over jungle and ocean, the Barba Roja has long been one of the more popular restaurants in Manuel Antonio, although more for its lively ambience and stellar location than for culinary excellence. The rustic interior is done with local hardwoods and bamboo, which gives the open-air dining room a warm glow, and there's an outdoor patio where you can sit for hours taking in the view or the stars. There's even a gallery attached to the restaurant that displays original art by local artists. On the blackboard are daily specials such as grilled fish steak served with a salad and a baked potato. Portions here are massive. The restaurant is open for breakfast and serves delicious whole-wheat French toast. For lunch, there are a number of different sandwiches, all served on whole-wheat bread.

Manuel Antonio. © 777-0331. Reservations needed for groups of 6 or more. Main courses $5–$20; sandwiches $3–$6. AE, MC, V. Tues–Sun 7am–11pm; Mon 4–11pm. Closed for breakfast throughout the low season.

El Gran Escape SEAFOOD   This Quepos landmark is consistently one of the top restaurants in the region. The fish here is fresh and expertly prepared, and the prices are reasonable. If that's not enough of a recommendation, the atmosphere is lively, the locals seem to keep coming back, and the service is darn good for a beach town in Costa Rica. Sturdy wooden tables and chairs fill up the large indoor dining room, and sportfishing photos and an exotic collection of masks fill up the walls. If you venture away from the fish, there are hearty steaks, giant burgers, and a wide assortment of delicious appetizers, including fresh tuna sashimi. El Gran Escape's Fish Head Bar is usually crowded and spirited, and if there's a game going on, it will be on the television here.

On the main road into Quepos, on your left just after the bridge. © 777-0395. Reservations recommended in the high season. Main courses $5–$20. V. Daily 6am–11pm.

Karola's SEAFOOD/INTERNATIONAL   The steep driveway leading down to this open-air restaurant is within a few feet of the Barba Roja parking lot but is easily overlooked (watch closely when you're up at the top of the hill). The restaurant is across a footbridge from its parking lot and is set against a jungle-covered hillside. Far below, you can see the ocean if you're here during the day. Grilled seafood is the specialty, but there's also a wide range of international treats including sashimi, fish burritos, and Caribbean chicken. I highly recommend starting things off with the Honduran tuna ceviche. Desserts are decadent, and you can order a variety of margaritas by the pitcher.

Manuel Antonio. © 777-1557. Reservations recommended. Main courses $10–$22. V. Daily 11am–11pm.

Plinio Restaurant ⚝ INTERNATIONAL   This is a long-standing, popular restaurant in Manuel Antonio, located at an equally popular hotel. The open-air restaurant is about three stories above the parking lot, so be prepared to climb some steps. It's worth it, though. The broad menu features an enticing mix of international dishes. The chef uses organically grown herbs and veggies. Thai, Indian, and Indonesian dishes are found alongside German and Italian fare, and there are always vegetarian options and a nightly special. Lunch is served poolside throughout the high season.

In the Hotel Plinio, 1km (½ mile) out of Quepos toward Manuel Antonio. © 777-0055. Reservations recommended in the high season. Main courses $5–$18. AE, MC, V (7% surcharge). Daily 5–10pm.

Restaurant Vela-Bar INTERNATIONAL   The Vela-Bar is a small and casual place that serves some of the more creative cuisine in Manuel Antonio. This is also the best of the restaurants closest to the park entrance. Seafood and vegetarian meals are the specialties. The most interesting dishes are almost always the specials posted on the blackboard. A typical day's choice might include fresh fish in sherry or wine sauce with curried vegetables.

100m (328 ft.) down the side road near the park entrance. © 777-0413. Reservations recommended in the high season. Main courses $5–$17. AE, MC, V. Daily 7–10pm.

Sunspot Bar & Grill ⚝⚝ (Finds) INTERNATIONAL   Dining by candlelight under a purple canvas tent at one of the few poolside tables here is one of the most romantic dining experiences to be had in Manuel Antonio. The food's some of the best in town as well. The menu changes regularly but features prime meats and poultry and fresh fish, excellently prepared. The rack of lamb might get a light jalapeno-mint or tamarind glaze, and the chicken breast might be stuffed with feta cheese, Kalamata olives, and roasted red peppers and topped with a blackberry sauce. There are nightly specials and a good selection of salads, appetizers, and desserts.

At Makanda-by-the-Sea (p. 272). © 777-0442. Reservations recommended. Main courses $10–$25. AE, MC, V. Daily 11am–10pm.

Tropical Sushi ⚝ SUSHI/JAPANESE   As the name implies, the ambience here is decidedly tropical, with lively pastel colors and Caribbean architectural highlights, but don't let the surroundings fool you: This is still an excellent sushi joint. In addition to fresh tuna, dorado, mackerel, and grouper brought in daily by local fishermen, you can get maki, sushi, and sashimi made with Chilean salmon, smoked eel, and deep-fried soft-shell crabs. The sushi bar itself is tiny, and the main dining room is similarly small. The nicest seating here is in the open-air patio. Start things off with some *edamame,* an appetizer of steamed soybeans in their husks, and be sure to try the Crocodile Roll, with its mix of crab, eel, and avocado.

Next to El Gran Escape, on a side street, Quepos. © 777-0395. Reservations recommended. Maki rolls $3–$7; main courses $5–$18. V. Wed–Mon 5–10pm.

MANUEL ANTONIO AFTER DARK

Discos are becoming almost as common in Manuel Antonio as capuchin monkeys. Night owls and dancing fools have their choice. Down near the beach, folks get going at the restaurant **Mar y Sombra** ⚝. This is my favorite spot—you can walk off the dance floor and right out onto the beach, and there's usually no cover. For real late-night action, the local favorite appears to be the **Arco Iris,** which is located just before the bridge heading into town. Admission is usually around $2.50.

The bars at the **Barba Roja** restaurant (p. 277) and the **Hotel Sí Como No** (p. 272) are good places to hang out and meet people in the evenings. You can also check out the **Vela-Bar,** which seems to be popular with gay men. Back in Quepos, **El Banco Bar, Mar y Blues, Sargento Garcia's,** and the **Fish Head Bar** at El Gran Escape are the most popular gringo hangouts.

If you enjoy the gaming tables, the **Hotel Kamuk** in Quepos has a small casino and will even foot your cab bill if you try your luck and lay down your money.

If you want to see a flick, check what's playing at **Hotel Sí Como No**'s little theater, although you have to eat at the restaurant or spend a minimum at the bar to earn admission.

EN ROUTE TO DOMINICAL: PLAYA MATAPALO

Playa Matapalo is a long expanse of flat beach that's about midway between Quepos and Dominical. It's an easy but bumpy 26km (16 miles) south of Quepos on the Costanera Sur. It's nowhere near as developed as either of those two beaches, but that's part of its charm. The beach here seems to stretch on forever, and it's usually deserted. The surf and strong riptides frequently make Matapalo too rough for swimming, although surfing and boogie-boarding can be good. Foremost among this beach's charms are peace and quiet.

WHERE TO STAY

Matapalo is basically a little village; the beach is about 1km (½ mile) away. There are a few very small and intimate lodges right on the beach. Of these, the **Jungle House** (©/fax **834-6633;** www.junglehouse.com) is the nicest.

El Silencio *Finds*   A bit before you reach Matapalo, you'll pass one of the more interesting tourism developments in Costa Rica. El Silencio is a project run by the 60 or so families of an agricultural cooperative. There are 10 simple rooms in thatch-roofed cabins here. Each comes with two single beds on the ground floor and another two in a sleeping loft. All have private bathrooms, and some even have water. This is a grass-roots tourism venture, and not many of the folks here (at times, not even the guides) speak much English. A stay here, however, allows you to mix hikes in the forest and horseback rides with a look into the rural life of Costa Rica. Tours range in price from $10 to $25, and meals will run you around $20 per person per day. El Silencio is located about 6km (3¾ miles) inland from the Coastal Highway, about 23km (14 miles) south of Quepos. Volunteer stays are available.

Cooperativa El Silencio (A.P. 6939-1000, San José). ©/fax **779-8250** or © 248-2538. www.turismorural.cr. com. 10 units. $40 double; student rates available. No credit cards. **Amenities:** Restaurant; bar; laundry service. *In room:* No phone.

4 Dominical ⊙

29km (18 miles) SW of San Isidro; 42km (26 miles) S of Quepos; 160km (99 miles) S of San José

This area might not be the best-kept secret in Costa Rica any longer, but Dominical and the coastline just south of it remain excellent places to find isolated beaches, spectacular views, remote jungle waterfalls, and abundant budget lodgings. The beach at Dominical itself has both right and left beach breaks, which means there are usually plenty of surfers in town. In fact, the beach in Dominical really has appeal only to surfers; it's generally too rough and rocky for regular folks. However, you will find excellent swimming, sunbathing, and strolling beaches just a little farther south at **Dominicalito, Playa Hermosa,** and **Ballena Marine National Park** ⚲.

Leaving Manuel Antonio, the road south to Dominical runs by mile after mile of oil-palm plantations. However, just before Dominical, the mountains again meet the sea. From Dominical south, the coastline is dotted with tide pools, tiny coves, and cliff-side vistas. Dominical is the largest village in the area and has several small lodges both in town and along the beach to the south. The village enjoys an enviable location on the banks of Río Barú, right where it widens considerably before emptying into the ocean. There's good bird-watching along the banks of the river and throughout the surrounding forests.

ESSENTIALS
GETTING THERE & DEPARTING **By Plane** The nearest airport with regular service is in Quepos (see "Essentials," in "Manuel Antonio National Park," earlier in this chapter). From there you can hire a taxi, rent a car, or take the bus.

By Car From San José, head south (toward Cartago) on the Interamerican Highway. Continue on this road all the way to San Isidro de El General, where you turn right and head down toward the coast. The entire drive takes about 4 hours.

You can also drive here from Manuel Antonio/Quepos. Just take the road out of Quepos toward the hospital and airport. Follow the signs for Dominical. It's a straight, albeit bumpy, shot. However, the road is slated to be paved, and if that happens, it should no longer take more than an hour to cover the mere 40km (25 miles).

By Bus To reach Dominical, you must first go to San Isidro de El General or Quepos. Buses leave San José for San Isidro roughly every hour between 5:30am and 6:30pm. See "Getting There & Departing" in "San Isidro de El General: A Base for Exploring Chirripó National Park," below. The trip takes 3 hours; the fare is $3. Leave no later than 9am if you want to be sure to catch the 1:30pm bus to Dominical.

From San Isidro de El General, buses (© **257-4121** or 771-4744) leave for Dominical at 7 and 9am and 1:30 and 4pm. The bus station for Dominical is 1 block south of the main bus station and 2 blocks west of the church. Trip duration is 1½ hours; the fare is $1.50.

From **Quepos,** buses leave daily at 5 and 9:30am and 1:30 and 7pm. Trip duration is 2 hours; the fare is $3.50.

When you're ready to leave, buses depart Dominical for San Isidro at 6:40 and 7:10am, and 2:45 and 3:30pm. If you want to get to San José the same day, you should catch the morning bus. Buses leave San Isidro for San José roughly every hour between 5am and 6pm. Buses to Quepos leave Dominical at approximately 5:45 and 8am, and 1 and 2:30pm.

ORIENTATION Dominical is a small village on the banks of Río Barú. The village is to the right after you cross the bridge and stretches out along the main road parallel to the beach. As you first come into town, there's a soccer field and a general store, where there are a couple of public telephones. Just beyond the turnoff into town, on the Costanera highway heading south, is a little strip mall, **Plaza Pacífica,** with a couple of restaurants and the village's main grocery store.

FAST FACTS   Taxis tend to congregate in front of the soccer field. The gas station is located about 2km (1¼ miles) north of town on the road to Quepos. You can purchase stamps and send mail from the **San Clemente Bar & Grill.**

EXPLORING THE BEACHES & BALLENA MARINE NATIONAL PARK

Because the beach in the village of Dominical itself is unprotected and at the mouth of a river, it's often too rough for swimming; however, you can go for a swim in the calm waters at the mouth of the Río Barú, or head down the beach a few kilometers to the little sheltered cove at **Roca Verde.**

If you have a car, you should continue driving south, exploring beaches as you go. You will first come to **Dominicalito,** a small beach and cove that shelters the local fishing fleet and can be a decent place to swim, but continue on a bit. You'll soon hit **Playa Hermosa,** a long stretch of desolate beach with fine sand. As in Dominical, this is unprotected and can be rough, but it's a nicer place to sunbathe and swim than Dominical.

At the village of Uvita, 16km (10 miles) south of Dominical, you'll reach the northern end of the **Ballena Marine National Park** ⭐ (© 743-8236), which protects a coral reef that stretches from Uvita south to Playa Piñuela and includes the little Isla Ballena, just offshore. To get to **Playa Uvita** (which is inside the park), turn in at the village of Bahía and continue until you hit the ocean. The beach here is actually well protected and good for swimming. At low tide, an exposed sandbar allows you to walk about and explore another tiny island. This park is named for the whales that are sometimes sighted close to shore in the winter months. If you ever fly over this area, you'll also notice that this little island and the spit of land that's formed at low tide compose the perfect outline of a whale's tail. A parks office at the entrance here regulates the park's use and even runs a small turtle-hatching shelter and program. Although this is a national park, it charges only 400 colones (around $1) per person as an entrance fee. Camping is allowed here for around $2 per person per day, with access to a public bathroom and shower.

Dominical is a major surf destination. The long and varied beach break here is justifiably popular. In general, this is a powerful wave best suited for experienced surfers. Nevertheless, beginners should check in with the folks at the **Green Iguana Surf Camp** (© 825-1381; www.greeniguanasurfcamp.com), who offer lessons and comprehensive "surf camps."

OTHER ACTIVITIES IN THE AREA

Although the beaches stretching south from Dominical should be beautiful enough to keep most people content, there are lots of other things to do. Several local farms offer horseback tours through forests and orchards, and at some of these farms you can even spend the night. **Hacienda Barú** ⭐ (© 787-0003; fax 787-0004; www.haciendabaru.com) offers several different hikes and tours, including a walk through mangroves and along the riverbank (for some good bird-watching), a rainforest hike through 80 hectares (198 acres) of virgin jungle, an all-day trek from beach to mangrove to jungle that includes a visit to some Indian petroglyphs, an overnight camping trip, and a combination horseback-and-hiking tour. It even has tree-climbing tours and a small canopy platform 30m (98 ft.) above the ground. Tour prices range from $20 (for the mangrove hike) to $60 (for the jungle overnight). If you're traveling with a group, you'll be charged a lower per-person rate, depending on the number of people in your group. Hacienda Barú also has six comfortable cabins with two bedrooms each, full kitchens, and even a living room ($60 double, $70 triple). Hacienda Barú is located about 1.5km (1 mile) north of Dominical on the road to Manuel Antonio.

The jungles just outside of Dominical are home to two spectacular waterfalls. The most popular and impressive is the **Santo Cristo** or **Nauyaca Waterfalls** ⭐, a two-tiered beauty with an excellent swimming hole. Most of the hotels in town can arrange for the horseback ride up here, or you can call **Don Lulo** at ✆ **771-3187.** A half-day tour, with both breakfast and lunch, should cost around $35 per person. This site has become so popular that Don Lulo has set up a little welcome center at the entrance (just off the road into Dominical from San Isidro), and even allows camping here. Round-trip car transportation can be arranged for a nominal charge. It is also possible to reach these falls by horseback from an entrance near the small village of Tinamaste. (You will see signs on the road.) Similar tours (at similar prices) are offered to the **Diamante Waterfalls,** which are a three-tiered set of falls with a 360m (1,180-ft.) drop, but not quite as spacious and inviting a pool as the one at Santo Cristo.

Other adventure activities offered in Dominical include kayak tours of the mangroves, river floats in inner tubes, ultra light flights over the beaches and waves, and sport fishing. To arrange any of these activities, check in with **Dominical Adventures** (✆ **787-0191,** at the San Clemente Bar & Grill), **Southern Expeditions** (✆ 787-0100; www.costarica-southern-expeditions. com), or the folks at the **Hotel Roca Verde** (✆ 787-0036).

WHERE TO STAY
MODERATE

Hotel Diuwak ⭐   This little complex offers the most modern and comfortable accommodations right near the surf break, although it is located about 50m (164 ft.) inland from the beach. The rooms are clean, bright, and relatively spacious. About half the rooms come with air-conditioning, and there are a few bigger suites and bungalows for larger groups and families. Most have some sort of private or semiprivate veranda facing lush gardens. At the center of the complex, you'll find a refreshing pool, and in the adjacent shopping center there's a coffee shop, an Internet cafe, and a minimarket. This place is the best option for surfers seeking a little extra comfort just steps away from the waves.

Dominical. ✆ 787-0087. Fax 787-0089. www.diuwak.com. 18 units. $50–$65 double. Rates lower in the off season. MC, V. **Amenities:** Restaurant; bar; midsize pool; tour desk; laundry service.

Hotel Roca Verde ⭐   This popular hotel offers the nicest beachfront accommodations in Dominical. The setting is superb—on a protected little cove with rocks and tide pools. The rooms are located in a two-story building beside the swimming pool. Each room comes with one queen-size and one single bed, and a small patio or balcony. There's a large open-air restaurant with a popular bar that keeps folks dancing most weekend nights. The rooms are a bit close to the bar, so it can sometimes be hard to get an early night's sleep, especially during the high season on weekends. These folks also rent out some stunning luxury villas located in the hills behind the hotel.

1km (½ mile) south of Dominical, just off the coastal highway. ✆ 787-0036. Fax 787-0013. www.rocaverde.net. 12 units. $75 double. Rates lower in the off season. MC, V. **Amenities:** Restaurant; bar; small pool; tour desk; laundry service. *In room:* A/C, no phone.

Villas Río Mar   This is the closest thing to a resort in this neck of the woods. The bamboo-accented rooms are in 20 separate thatch-roofed duplex bungalows. Although the rooms themselves seem a bit overwhelmed by the queen-size beds, each has a small couch, coffee table, wet bar, and minifridge, plus a spacious and comfortable porch with several chairs. At night, you can drop the tulle drapes that enclose each patio for some privacy and mosquito protection. The grounds have beautiful flowering plants, and the bird-watching is excellent. A wide range of tours is offered, including inner-tube floats on the nearby Río Barú.

Up a dirt road a few hundred meters up the Río Barú, just on the right as you enter Dominical; Dominical, Pérez Zeledó. © 787-0052. Fax 787-0054. www.villasriomar.com. 40 units. Jan–Apr $70 double; May–Dec $55 double. Children under 12 stay free in parent's room. AE, MC, V. **Amenities:** Restaurant; bar; large out-door pool w/swim-up bar; tennis court; exercise room; Jacuzzi; bike rental; tour desk; laundry service. *In room:* Fridge, hair dryer, no phone.

INEXPENSIVE

As a popular surfer destination, budget lodgings abound in Dominical. I've tried to list the best below, but if you're really counting pennies, it's always a good idea to walk around and check out what's currently available. There are plenty of camping options as well. I recommend **Piramys** (© **787-0196;** piramys@ hotmail.com), which is right on the beach and offers reasonably clean bath and shower facilities.

In addition to the places listed here, if you continue south another 16km (10 miles), you'll find a campground at Playa Ballena and a couple of basic *cabinas* in Bahía and Uvita. The most popular of these is **El Coco Tico Ecolodge** (© **743-8032;** $22 double), owned and operated by Jorge Díaz, a local legend and enjoyable raconteur who also arranges trips to a nearby waterfall. Coco Tico allows camping as well for around $4 per person. You'll see a sign for Coco Tico on your left as you reach Uvita, traveling south from Dominical. Turn here; the hotel is 500m (1,640 ft.) up the dirt road. Closer to the beach, in Bahía, **Cabinas Hegalva** (© **743-8016**) offers clean, basic rooms at $15 for a double, and also allows camping.

Cabinas San Clemente *Value*   In addition to running the town's most popular restaurant and serving as the social hub for the surfers, beach bums, and expatriates passing through, this place offers a variety of accommodations to fit most budgets. Located about 1km (½ mile) from the in-town restaurant, San Clemente offers rooms in three separate buildings, right on the beach. Some of the newer second-floor rooms have wood floors and wraparound verandas and are a real steal in this price range. The grounds are shady, and there are plenty of hammocks.

The cheapest rooms are bunk-bed hostel-style affairs in a separate building dubbed the **Dominical Backpacker's Hostel.** Rooms here come with access to a communal kitchen. There are also a few budget rooms above the downtown restaurant. These are very basic budget affairs, with wood walls and floors, shared bathrooms, and floor or ceiling fans.

Dominical (A.P. 703-8000, Pérez Zeledón). © 787-0026 or 787-0055. Fax 787-0158. 19 units, 16 with private bathroom. $10 per person with shared bathroom; $25–$65 double with private bathroom. AE, MC, V. **Amenities:** Restaurant; bar; surf- and boogie-board rental; bike rental; tour desk; laundry service. *In room:* No phone.

Pacific Edge ★ *Finds*   This place is away from the beach, but the views from each individual bungalow are so breathtaking that you might not mind. Spread along a lushly planted ridge on the hillside over Dominical, these comfortable cabins have wood floors, solar-heated water, and solar reading lights. Their best feature is surely the private porch with a comfortable hammock in which to laze about and enjoy the view. The restaurant serves breakfast and dinner daily, with an emphasis on well-prepared international cuisine. A wide range of tours and activities can be arranged here, and there's a refreshing swimming pool if you're too tired or lazy to head down to the beach. Pacific Edge is 4km (2½ miles) south of Dominical and then another 1.2km (¾ mile) up a steep and rocky road; four-wheel-drive vehicles are highly recommended—I'd say required.

Dominical (A.P. 531-8000, Pérez Zeledón). ©/fax **787-8010**. pacificedge@pocketmail.com. 4 units. $48–$73 double. AE, MC, V (10% surcharge). **Amenities:** Restaurant; midsize outdoor pool. *In room:* Kitchenette, no phone.

Tortilla Flats   This long-standing surfer hotel is a good budget option on the beach, especially if all of the best rooms at San Clemente are booked. There are several styles of rooms located in a cluster of buildings, including older rooms with fans, older rooms with air-conditioning, and newer rooms with air-conditioning, skylights, carved wooden headboards, and louvered windows. I recommend the second-floor rooms with ocean views but no air-conditioning. Because the rooms differ so much in size and comfort levels, you should definitely take a look at a few of them before choosing.

Dominical. ©/fax **787-0033**. 18 units. $30–$50 double or triple. Rates lower in the off season. AE, MC, V (7% surcharge). **Amenities:** Restaurant; bar; laundry service. *In room:* No phone.

DINING & NIGHTTIME FUN

The social center of Dominical is definitely the **San Clemente Bar & Grill** (© **787-0055**), located right at the entrance to town beside the soccer field. This gringo/surfer hangout and sports bar specializes in massive breakfasts, nightly dinner specials (usually seafood), and a regular menu of hefty sandwiches and tasty Mexican-American food (expect main courses to run between $5 and $15). One interesting (and sobering) thing here is the ceiling full of broken surfboards. If you break a board out on the waves, bring it in, and they'll hang it and even buy you a bucket of beer.

Right in town, in front of the soccer field, there's **Su Raza,** which serves basic Tico meals and good seafood at great prices, and even has a nice view of the river mouth. A little farther down the main road is the **Soda Nanyoa.** Dishes at these places range in price from $2 to $7. If you head a little bit south of town, you can check out the restaurant at the **Hotel Roca Verde** (p. 282), which is usually pretty good for freshly grilled fish, steaks, and burgers.

Don't come to Dominical expecting a raging nightlife. In addition to the aforementioned **San Clemente, Thrusters** is a popular surfer bar with pool tables and dartboards, and the bar at **Roca Verde** is one of the livelier places in town, with occasional live music.

SOUTH OF DOMINICAL

The beaches south of Dominical are some of the nicest and most unexplored in Costa Rica. Basic *cabinas* and hotels are starting to pop up all along this route. This is a great area to roam in a rental car—it's a **beautiful drive**, and the broad southern highway (Costanera Sur) was recently paved. One good itinerary is to make a loop from San Isidro to Dominical, down the Costanera Sur, hitting several deserted beaches and then returning along the Interamerican Highway.

Among the beaches you'll find are **Playa Ballena, Playa Piñuela, Playa Ventanas,** and **Playa Tortuga.** There's a bit of development in the area around

Playa Tortuga and Ojochal, and some in the works around playas Piñuela and Ventanas.

A REMOTE NATURE LODGE

Hotel Villas Gaia ✪   Located off the Costanera Sur just before the town of Ojochal, this small hotel has the nicest accommodations down in this neck of the woods. All the rooms are separate, spacious wood bungalows. Each has one single and one double bed, a private bathroom, a ceiling fan, and a small veranda with a jungle view. I prefer the bungalows farthest from the restaurant, up on the high hill by the swimming pool. The pool can accommodate scuba instruction—Villa Gaia hopes to lure divers with its proximity to Isla del Caño. There's a large, open-air dining room down by the parking lot, which is too close to the highway for my taste but serves tasty, well-prepared international fare. A wide range of tours is available, including trips to Isla del Caño, Corcovado National Park, and Wilson Botanical Gardens.

Playa Tortuga (A.P. 11516-1000, San José). ℂ/fax **244-0316.** www.villasgaia.com. 12 units. $59 double. AE, MC, V. **Amenities:** Restaurant; bar; small outdoor pool w/wonderful ocean view; tour desk; laundry service. *In room:* No phone.

120km (74 miles) SE of San José; 123km (76 miles) NW of Palmar Norte; 29km (18 miles) NE of Dominical

San Isidro de El General is the largest town in this region and is located just off the Interamerican Highway in the foothills of the Talamanca Mountains. Although there isn't much to do right in town, this is the jumping-off point for trips to Chirripó National Park. This is also the principal transfer point if you're coming from or going to Dominical, and most buses traveling the Interamerican Highway stop here.

ESSENTIALS

GETTING THERE & DEPARTING By Car The long and winding stretch of the Interamerican Highway between San José and San Isidro is one of the most difficult sections of road in the country. Not only are there the usual car-eating potholes and periodic landslides, but you must also contend with driving over the 3,300m (10,824-ft.) **Cerro de la Muerte (Mountain of Death).** This aptly named mountain pass is legendary for its dense afternoon fogs, blinding torrential downpours, steep drop-offs, severe switchbacks, and unexpectedly breathtaking views. (Well, you wanted adventure travel, so here you go!) Drive with extreme care, and bring a sweater or sweatshirt—it's cold up at the top. It'll take you about 3 hours to get to San Isidro.

By Bus Plenty of daily buses will take you to San Isidro. **Musoc** (ℂ 222-2422 in San José, or 771-3829 in San Isidro) buses leave from their modern terminal at Calle Central and Avenida 22 roughly hourly between 5:30am and 6:30pm. **Tuasur** (ℂ 222-9763 or 771-0419) runs express buses between San José and San Isidro that leave roughly every hour between 5am and 5pm from Calle 16 between avenidas 1 and 3. Whichever company you choose, the trip takes around 3 hours, and the fare is roughly $3. There are buses from **Quepos** to San Isidro daily at 5 and 9:30am and 1:30 and 4pm. Trip duration is 3½ hours; the fare is $3.50. Buses to or from **Golfito** and **Puerto Jiménez** will also drop you off in San Isidro.

Buses depart San Isidro for **San José** roughly every hour between 5am and 6pm.

> ⎛ *Tips* **Little Devils**
>
> If you're visiting this area in February, head out to nearby **Rey Curré** village for the **Fiesta of the Diablitos,** where costumed Boruca Indians perform dances representative of the Spanish conquest of Central America. There are fireworks and an Indian handicraft market. The date varies, so it's best to call the **Costa Rica Tourist Board** (© **800/327-7033**) for more information.

ORIENTATION   Downtown San Isidro is just off the Interamerican Highway. A large church fronts the central park. The main bus station is 2 blocks west of the north end of the central park.

EXPLORING CHIRRIPO NATIONAL PARK ★★

At 3,759m (12,330 ft.) in elevation, Mount Chirripó is the tallest mountain in Costa Rica. If you're headed up this way, come prepared for chilly weather. Actually, dress in layers and come prepared for all sorts of weather: Because of the great elevations, temperatures frequently dip below freezing, especially at night. However, during the day, temperatures can soar—remember, you're still only 9 degrees from the equator. The elevation and radical temperatures have produced an environment here that's very different from the Costa Rican norm. Above 3,000m (9,840 ft.), only stunted trees and shrubs survive in *páramos.* If you're driving the Interamerican Highway between San Isidro and San José, you'll pass through a *páramo* on the Cerro de la Muerte.

Hiking up to the top of Mount Chirripó is one of Costa Rica's great adventures. On a clear day (usually in the morning), an unforgettable **view** ★★★ is your reward: You can see both the Pacific Ocean and the Caribbean Sea from the summit. You can do this trip fairly easily on your own if you've brought gear and are an experienced backpacker. Although it's possible to hike from the park entrance to the summit and back down in 2 days (in fact, some daredevils even do it in 1 day), it's best to allow 3 to 4 days for the trip, to give yourself time to enjoy your hike fully and spend some time on top because that's where the glacier lakes and *páramos* are. For much of the way, you'll be hiking through cloud forests that are home to abundant tropical fauna, including the spectacular **quetzal,** Costa Rica's most beautiful bird. However, quetzal sightings on summit climbs are rare. If you really want to see one of these birds, head to one of the specialized lodges listed below. These cloud forests are cold and damp, so come prepared for rain and fog.

There are several routes to the top of Mount Chirripó. The most popular, by far, leaves from **San Gerardo de Rivas.** However, it's also possible to start your hike from the nearby towns of **Herradura** and **Canaan.** All these places are within a mile or so of each other, reached by the same major road out of San Isidro. San Gerardo is the most popular because it's the easiest route to the top and has the greatest collections of small hotels and lodges, as well as the National Parks office. Information on all of these routes is available at the parks office.

When you're at the summit lodge, there are a number of hiking options. Just in front of the lodge are Los Crestones (The Crests), an impressive rock formation, with trails leading up and around them. The most popular, however, is to the actual summit (the lodge itself is a bit below), which is about a 2-hour hike that passes through the Valle de los Conejos (Rabbit Valley) and the Valle de los Lagos (Valley of Lakes). Other hikes and trails lead off from the summit lodge, and it's easy to spend a couple of days hiking around here. A few trails will take you to the summits of several neighboring peaks. These hikes should be undertaken only after carefully studying an accurate map and talking to park rangers and other hikers.

ENTRY POINT, FEES & REGULATIONS   Although it's not that difficult to get to Chirripó National Park from nearby San Isidro, it's still rather remote. And to see it fully, you have to be prepared to hike. To get to the trail head, you have three choices: car, taxi, or bus. If you choose to drive, take the road out of San Isidro, heading north toward San Gerardo de Rivas, which is some 20km (12 miles) down the road. Otherwise, you can catch a bus in San Isidro that will take you directly to the trail head in San Gerardo de Rivas. Buses leave daily at 5am from the western side of the central park in San Isidro. It costs 85¢ one-way and takes 1½ hours. Another bus departs at 2pm from a bus station 200m (656 ft.) south of the park. Buses return to San Isidro daily at 7am and 4pm. A taxi from town should cost around $15 to $20. Because the hike to the summit of Mount Chirripó can take between 6 and 12 hours, depending on your physical condition, I recommend taking the earlier bus so that you can start hiking when the day is still young, or, better still, arriving the day before and spending the night in San Gerardo de Rivas (there are inexpensive *cabinas* there) before setting out early the following morning.

Before climbing Mount Chirripó, you must check in with the National Parks office in San Gerardo de Rivas. The office is open from 6am to 4:30pm daily. I highly recommend checking in the day before you plan to climb, if possible. If you plan to stay at the lodge near the summit, you must make reservations in advance because accommodations there are limited (see "Staying at the Summit Lodge," below). Note that camping is not allowed in the park. It's possible to have your gear carried up to the summit by horseback during the dry season (Dec–Apr). Guides work outside the park entrance in San Gerardo de Rivas. They charge between $20 and $25 per pack, depending on size and weight. In the rainy season, the same guides work, but they take packs up by themselves, not by horseback. The guides like to take up the packs well before dawn, so arrangements are best made the day before.

STAYING AT THE SUMMIT LODGE   Reservations for lodging on the summit of Mount Chirripó must be made with the **National Parks office** in San Isidro de El General (Ⓒ/fax **771-3155,** 771-5116, or 771-4836). This is an increasingly popular destination, and you must reserve well in advance during the dry season. The lodge holds only 60 people and fills up quite frequently. There are bunk beds, bathrooms, and a common kitchen area, complete with pots, pans, plates, and silverware. There is good drinking water at the lodge and blankets, lanterns, and cook stoves for rent, although you have to pack in your own food and water for the hike up. *Be forewarned:* It gets cold up here at night, and the lodge seems to have been designed to be as cold, dark, and cavernous as possible. No consideration was made to take advantage of the ample passive solar potential. The showers are freezing. It costs $10 per person per night to stay here; the entrance fee to the national park is $15 for your first 2 days, and then $10 for each additional day.

WARNING   It can be dangerous for more inexperienced or out-of-shape hikers to climb Chirripó, especially by themselves. It's not very technical climbing, but it is a long, arduous hike. If you're not sure you're up for it, you can just take day hikes out of San Isidro and/or San Gerardo de Rivas, or ask at your hotel about guides.

OTHER ADVENTURES IN & AROUND SAN ISIDRO

If you want to undertake any other adventures while in San Isidro, contact **Selva Mar** (② 771-4582; fax 771-8841; www.exploringcostarica.com). Selva Mar has branched off to form **Costa Rica Trekking Adventures** (www.chirripo.com), offering organized treks through Chirripó National Park. A 4-day/3-night trip costs between $325 and $500 per person, depending on group size and specific routes.

Just 7km (4⅓ miles) from San Isidro is **Las Quebradas Biological Center** (②/fax 771-4131), a community-run private reserve with 2.7km (1¾ miles) of trails through primary rainforest. There's a rustic lodge for visitors and researchers ($25 per person; $15 students, including three meals), and camping is also permitted. There's an information center here and a small souvenir store. You can hike the trails here and visit the small information center for $6. From San Isidro, you can take a local bus to Quebradas, but you'll have to walk the last mile to the entrance. You can also take a taxi for around $8. If you're driving, take the road to Morazán and Quebradas.

WHERE TO STAY & DINE

There are no notable restaurants in San Isidro. The town has its fair share of local joints, but most visitors are content at their hotel restaurant. If you do venture beyond your hotel, your best options are the **Mexico Lindo** (② 771-8222) and the **Pizzería El Tenedor** (② 771-0881), both located just off the Central Park.

Hotel del Sur   This midsize hotel fancies itself a destination resort. Although it has far better facilities and a wider range of services than anything within a couple of hours of here, it's seen better days and is definitely not worth going out of your way to visit. Rooms are generally large. The nicer (and more expensive) rooms have air-conditioning, loads of space, and plenty of light, and tile floors; the cheaper rooms feel cramped and dingy. The whole place has the feel of a cut-rate country club. There's a large pool, as well as a basketball court and one tennis court with its own tiny pro shop. The newest addition here is a small casino that is quite popular with locals.

6km (about 3¾ miles) south of San Isidro, right on the Interamerican Hwy. (A.P. 4-8000), San Isidro de El General. ② 771-3033. Fax 771-0527. www.hoteldelsur.co.cr. 57 units. $40–$60 double. AE, MC, V. **Amenities:** 2 restaurants; bar; large outdoor pool; tennis court; game room; tour desk; laundry service. *In room:* A/C in some units, TV.

Hotel Iguazú   This is a good, clean, safe choice in San Isidro. The rooms are basic and come in different sizes, with a different arrangement of beds, but all have small televisions. The rooms are definitely in better shape than those at the more popular budget choice, the Hotel Chirripó. The hotel is a half block away from the Musoc bus station. Some might find this convenient; others might find it too noisy. The hotel is actually on the second and third floors of the Gallo Mas Gallo department store.

San Isidro de El General (above the Gallo Mas Gallo store). ② 771-2571. Fax 771-4451. 22 units, 17 with private bathroom. $10 double with shared bathroom; $20 double with private bathroom. V. *In room:* TV.

Tips Rest Your Weary Muscles Here

If you're tired and sore from so much hiking, be sure to check out the small natural hot springs located a short hike off the road between San Gerardo de Rivas and Herradura. The entrance to the springs is 1km (½ mile) beyond San Gerardo de Rivas. From here you'll have to hike about 10 minutes and pay a $3 entrance fee before getting in to soak.

Hotel Los Crestones   This two-story hotel doesn't have much in the way of character or style, but it offers the cleanest and most comfortable rooms in San Isidro. All rooms are relatively large and come with air-conditioning, but it costs an extra $10 to turn it on. I prefer the units on the second floor, which share a broad tiled veranda. Hotel Los Crestones is located 4 blocks south of San Isidro's Central Park.

San Isidro de El General (southwest side of the stadium). (C) 771-1200. Fax 771-6012. www.hotelloscrestones.com. 12 units. $40–$55 double. Rates include breakfast. MC, V. **Amenities:** Restaurant; tour desk; laundry service. *In room:* A/C (for a fee), TV, no phone.

WHERE TO STAY CLOSER TO THE TRAIL HEAD

If you're climbing Mount Chirripó, you'll want to spend the night as close to the trail head as possible. As mentioned above, several basic *cabinas* right in San Gerardo de Rivas charge between $5 and $10 per person. The best of these are **El Descanso** ((C) **369-0067**) and **Roca Dura** ((C) **771-1866**). If you're looking for a little more comfort, check out the lodge listed below.

Talari Mountain Lodge ⭐   This small mountain getaway is nothing fancy, but it is one of the nicer options right around San Isidro, and it also makes a good base for exploring or climbing Mount Chirripó. The rooms are in two separate concrete-block buildings. Most come with one double and one single bed, although one room can handle a family of four in one double and two single beds. Each of the rooms comes with a small fridge and a small patio. I prefer the four rooms that face the Talamanca Mountains. There are plenty of fruit trees around and good bird-watching right on the grounds. (They've identified more than 200 bird species here.) The hotel borders the Rió General and maintains some forest trails. Talari is located 8km (5 miles) outside of San Isidro, and a staff member picks you up in town for free with advance notice. Remember, if you're here just to climb the mountain, this lodge is about 11km (6¾ miles) from San Gerardo de Rivas, so you'll probably also have to arrange transportation to and from the park entrance.

Rivas, San Isidro (A.P. 517-8000, Pérez Zeledón). (C)/fax 771-0341. www.talari.co.cr. 9 units. $52 double; $72 triple. Rates include full breakfast. AE, MC, V. Closed Sept 16–Oct 31. **Amenities:** Restaurant; bar; small pool and separate children's pool; tour desk; laundry service. *In room:* Fridge, no phone.

EN ROUTE TO SAN JOSE: THREE PLACES TO SEE QUETZALS IN THE WILD

Between San Isidro de El General and San José, the Interamerican Highway climbs to its highest point in Costa Rica and crosses over the Cerro de la Muerte. This area has recently acquired a newfound importance as one of the best places in Costa Rica to see quetzals. March, April, and May make up nesting season for these birds; this is usually the best time to see them, but it's often possible to spot them year-round. On one 2-hour hike here, without a guide, my small group spotted eight of these amazing birds.

All of the lodges listed below, along with some new ones, are located along a 20km (12-mile) stretch of the Interamerican Highway, between the cities of Cartago and San Isidro. You'll probably start seeing their billboards and quetzal-painted placards long before you see any birds.

In addition to the lodges listed below, if you're looking for a rustic (although not cheap) escape on a private reserve with a great trail system, check in with the folks at the **Genesis II Cloudforest Preserve** ((C)/fax **381-0739**; www.genesis-two.com). This place recently opened a small canopy tour of three platforms connected by two zip-lines. You can hike the trails for $10 per person or get a guided hike for an additional $5 per person. There's a very modest canopy tour here ($35), with just three platforms connected by two cables. If you want to stay here ($95 per person, including three meals, tour, and guide), there are only five simple rooms with shared bathrooms, so reservations are highly recommended. Camping is also allowed for $5 per person per day. You'll see signs for this place along the Interamerican Highway. The road down into Genesis is very rugged, and a four-wheel-drive vehicle is necessary.

Albergue Mirador de Quetzales This family-run lodge is also known as Finca Eddie Serrano. The rooms in the main lodge are quite basic, with wood floors, bunk beds, and shared bathrooms. Eight newer A-frames provide a bit more comfort and a private bathroom. Meals are served family style in the main lodge. But quetzals, not comfort, are the main draw here, and if you come between December and May, you should have no trouble spotting plenty of them. There are good hiking trails through the cloud forest, and the Serrano family members are genial hosts and good guides. On a clear day, you can see the peaks of five volcanoes from the hotel's lookout—but it's not that clear too often. The lodge is located about 1km (½ mile) down a dirt road from the main highway.

Carretera Interamericana Sur Km 70 (A.P. 985-7050, Cartago). ℭ/fax **381-8456.** 12 units, 8 with private bathroom. $29–$37 per person. Rate includes breakfast, dinner, a 2-hr. tour, and taxes. No credit cards. **Amenities:** Restaurant; bar. *In room:* No phone.

Savegre Mountain Hotel ✸ This working apple-and-pear farm, which also has more than 240 hectares (593 acres) of primary forest, has acquired a reputation for superb bird-watching—it's one of the best places in the country to see quetzals. The rustic farm has long been popular as a weekend vacation and picnicking spot for Ticos, but now people from all over the world are searching it out. The rooms are basic, but if you're serious about birding, this shouldn't matter. In addition to the quetzals, some 150 other species have been spotted. Hearty Tico meals are served, and if you want to try your hand at trout fishing, you might luck into a fish dinner. You'll find this lodge 9km (5½ miles) down a dirt road off the Interamerican Highway. This road is steep and often muddy, and four-wheel-drive is recommended, although not necessary.

Carretera Interamericana Sur Km 80, San Gerardo de Dota (A.P. 482, Cartago). ℭ **740-1028.** Fax 740-1027. www.savegre.co.cr. 30 cabins. $78 per person. Rates include all meals and taxes. AE, MC, V. **Amenities:** Restaurant; bar; tour desk; laundry service. *In room:* No phone.

Trogon Lodge ✸ *Finds* This is by far the most attractive and comfortable of the lodges in the area. The rooms are still rather basic, but the grounds, setting, amenities, and sense of style are much nicer than those found at the lodges listed above. The rooms are all of good size, with wood floors, wood walls, a shared veranda, and one double and one twin bed. Room nos. 15 and 16 are my favorites; they are the farthest from the main lodge and have a great view of the river. The family-style meals often feature fresh trout from their well-stocked trout ponds; as at Savegre Lodge, more than half the fun is catching it yourself. There's a pool table, satellite TV, and an inviting bar in the main lodge, as well as a top-notch industrial espresso machine. There are some well-maintained trails right at the lodge, and a host of tour and activities is available.

Carretera Interamericana Sur Km 80, San Gerardo de Dota (A.P. 10980-1000, San José). ℭ **293-8181.** Fax 239-7657. www.grupomawamba.com. 16 units. $62 double. A full meal package runs $33 per person. AE, MC, V. **Amenities:** Restaurant; bar; tour desk; laundry service. *In room:* No phone.

The Southern Zone

The southern zone is an area of rugged beauty, with vast expanses of virgin lowland rainforest and few cities or settlements. Lushly forested mountains tumble into the sea, streams still run clear and clean, scarlet macaws squawk raucously in the treetops, and dolphins frolic in the Golfo Dulce. The Osa Peninsula is the most popular attraction in this region and one of the premier ecotourism destinations in Costa Rica. It's home to **Corcovado National Park** ★★★, the largest single expanse of lowland tropical rainforest in Central America, and its sister, **Piedras Blancas National Park** ★. Scattered around the edges of these national parks and along the shores of the Golfo Dulce are some of the country's finest nature lodges. These lodges, in general, offer comfortable to nearly luxurious accommodations, attentive service, knowledgeable guides, and a wide range of activities and tours, all close to the area's many natural wonders.

But this beauty doesn't come easy. You must have plenty of time (or plenty of money—or, preferably, both) and a desire for adventure. Because it's so far from San José (it's an 8-hr. drive from San José to Golfito or Puerto Jiménez) and there are so few roads, most of the really fascinating spots can be reached only by small plane or boat, although hiking and four-wheeling will get you into some memorable surroundings as well. In many ways, this is Costa Rica's final frontier, and the cities of Golfito and Puerto Jiménez are nearly as wild as the jungles that surround them. Tourism is still underdeveloped here; there are no large resorts in this neck of the woods. Moreover, the heat and humidity are more than many people can stand. So it's best to put some forethought into planning a vacation down here, and it's usually wise to book your rooms and transportation in advance.

1 Drake Bay ★★

145km (90 miles) S of San José; 32km (20 miles) SW of Palmar

Located on the northern end of the Osa Peninsula, Drake Bay is what adventure travel is all about. Little more than a small collection of lodges catering to naturalists, anglers, scuba divers, and assorted vacationers, Drake Bay is a good place to get away from it all. Accommodations vary from cement-walled *cabinas* to very comfortable lodges that border on the luxurious. There are few conventional phones and no power lines in Drake Bay, so most lodges make do with radio and cellular phones and gas-powered electrical generators.

Until 1997, there was no road into Drake Bay and no airstrip in town. Currently, both exist, but how reliable they are is another story—the road is often closed by heavy rains and mudslides, and the airstrip is serviced by a limited number of scheduled and charter flights. Because of the bay's remoteness, development has been very slow here. Unfortunately, it's starting to increase and it could someday change the face of this pristine destination. The town itself is

---

Tips   **Helping Out**

If you want to help local efforts in protecting the fragile rainforests and wild areas of the Osa Peninsula, contact the **Corcovado Foundation** at ℂ **281-0656** or www.corcovadofoundation.org.

---

starting to grow a bit, and massive logging is underway all along the road into Drake Bay and around—and even in—the national park.

The bay is named after Sir Francis Drake, who is believed to have anchored here in 1579. Emptying into the bay is the tiny **Río Agujitas,** which acts as a protected harbor for small boats and is a great place to do a bit of canoeing or swimming. It's here that many of the local lodges dock their boats. Stretching south from Drake Bay are miles of deserted beaches. Adventurous explorers will find tide pools, spring-fed rivers, waterfalls, forest trails, and some of the best bird-watching in all of Costa Rica. If a paradise such as this appeals to you, Drake Bay makes a good base for exploring the peninsula.

South of Drake Bay lay the wilds of the **Osa Peninsula,** including **Corcovado National Park.** This is one of Costa Rica's most beautiful regions, yet it's also one of its least accessible. Corcovado National Park covers about half of the peninsula and contains the largest single expanse of virgin lowland rainforest in Central America. For this reason, Corcovado is well known among naturalists and researchers studying rainforest ecology. If you come here, you'll learn first-hand why they call them rainforests: Some parts of the peninsula receive more than 250 inches of rain per year. In addition to producing lush forests, this mas-sive amount of rain produces more than a few disgruntled visitors.

Puerto Jiménez (see section 2, later in this chapter) is the best base to choose if you want to spend a lot of time hiking in and camping inside Corcovado National Park. Drake Bay is primarily a collection of mostly high-end hotels, very isolated and mostly accessible only by boat. Travelers using these hotels can have great day hikes and guided tours into Corcovado park, but Puerto Jiménez is the place if you want to have more time in the park or explore independently. (It has a range of budget hotels, the parks office, and "taxi/bus" service to Carate and Los Patos, from which visitors can hike into the various stations.) From the Drake Bay side, you're much more dependent on a boat ride/organized tour from one of the lodges to explore the park; these lodges offer many other guided outings in addition to visits to the park.

ESSENTIALS

Because Drake Bay is so remote, it's highly recommended that you have a room reservation and transportation arrangements (usually arranged with your hotel) before you arrive. Most of the lodges listed here are scattered along several kilome-ters of coastline, and it is not easy to go from one to another looking for a room.

A flashlight and rain gear are always useful to have on hand in Costa Rica; they're absolutely essential in Drake Bay.

GETTING THERE   By Plane   More people are flying directly into the little airstrip at Drake Bay, although a sizeable number of tourists still fly to Palmar Sur. Most lodges include transportation in their packages, so check with them about where you will be flying into. **Sansa** (ℂ 221-9414; www.flysansa.com) flies directly to Drake Bay daily at 9:30am and 2:05pm from San José's Juan Santa-maría International Airport. The return flights leave Drake Bay at 10:30am and

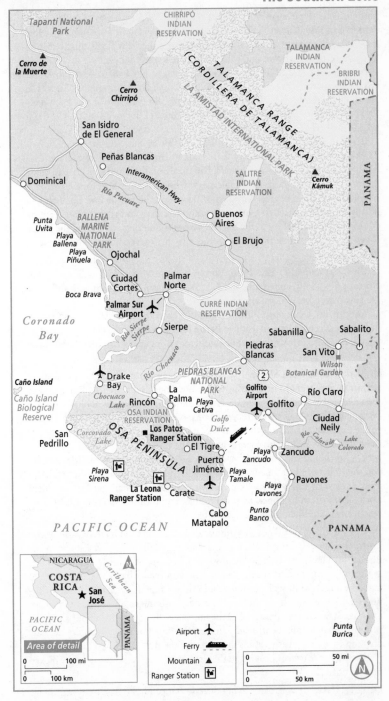

The Southern Zone

Tapantí National Park

CHIRRIPÓ INDIAN RESERVATION

TALAMANCA INDIAN RESERVATION

BRIBRI INDIAN RESERVATION

▲ Cerro de la Muerte

▲ Cerro Chirripó

TALAMANCA RANGE (CORDILLERA DE TALAMANCA)

LA AMISTAD INTERNATIONAL PARK

San Isidro de El General

PANAMA

Peñas Blancas

Interamerican Hwy.

Dominical

Río Pacuare

SALITRE INDIAN RESERVATION

▲ Cerro Kámuk

Punta Uvita

BALLENA MARINE NATIONAL PARK

Buenos Aires

Playa Ballena

Playa Piñuela

Ojochal

El Brujo

Ciudad Cortes

Palmar Norte

Boca Brava

Palmar Sur Airport ✈

CURRÉ INDIAN RESERVATION

Coronado Bay

Río Sierpe Sierpe

Sierpe

Sabanilla

Sabalito

Piedras Blancas

San Vito

Río Chocuaco

Wilson Botanical Garden

Caño Island

✈ Drake Bay

PIEDRAS BLANCAS NATIONAL PARK

[2]

Golfito Airport ✈

Río Claro

Caño Island Biological Reserve

Chocuaco Lake

Rincón

La Palma

Playa Cativa

Golfito

Ciudad Neily

OSA INDIAN RESERVATION

Golfo Dulce

San Pedrillo

Corcovado Lake

OSA PENINSULA

■ Los Patos Ranger Station

El Tigre

Río Colorado

Lake Colorado

Zancudo

Playa Sirena

Puerto Jiménez ✈

Playa Zancudo

Playa Tamale

Pavones

La Leona Ranger Station

Carate

Playa Pavones

PACIFIC OCEAN

Cabo Matapalo

Punta Banco

PANAMA

NICARAGUA

Caribbean Sea

COSTA RICA

★ San José

PACIFIC OCEAN

PANAMA

Area of detail

0 —— 100 mi

0 —— 100 km

Airport ✈
Ferry 🚢
Mountain ▲
Ranger Station 🏕

0 ——— 50 mi

0 ——— 50 km

N

Punta Burica

293

3:05pm. The flight takes 50 minutes; the fare is $73 each way. Another flight departs San José daily at 9:30am for Palmar Sur; the fare is $66 each way. Note that Sansa frequently alters its schedule and routing; this flight might stop in Quepos on the way down and thus could take slightly longer.

Nature Air (© 220-3054; www.natureair.com) has a direct flight to Drake Bay that departs daily at 8:30am from Tobías Bolaños International Airport in Pavas. Flight duration is 50 minutes; the fare is $85 each way. It also has a daily flight to Palmar Sur that departs at 9am and stops at Quepos en route. The flight takes a little over an hour, and the fare is $73 each way.

If your travels take you to Drake Bay via Palmar Sur, you must then take a 15-minute bus or taxi ride over dirt roads to the small town of **Sierpe.** This bumpy ride takes you through several banana plantations and quickly past some important archaeological sites. In Sierpe, you board a small boat for a 40km (25-mile) ride to Drake Bay; see "By Taxi & Boat from Sierpe," below. The first half of this trip snakes through a maze of mangrove canals and rivers before heading out to sea for the final leg to the bay. *Be warned:* Entering and exiting the Sierpe River mouth is often treacherous, and I've had several very white-knuckle moments here.

By Bus   Tracopa (© 222-2666) express buses leave San José daily for Palmar Norte at 5, 7, 8:30, and 10am, and 1, 2:30, and 6pm from Avenida 5 and Calle 14. Bus trips take 6 hours; the fare is $4.75.

You can also catch any Golfito-bound bus from this same station and get off in Palmar Norte. Once in Palmar Norte, ask when the next bus goes out to Sierpe. If it doesn't leave for a while (buses aren't frequent), consider taking a taxi (see below).

By Taxi & Boat from Sierpe   When you arrive at either the Palmar Norte bus station or the Palmar Sur airstrip, you'll most likely first need to take a taxi to the village of Sierpe. The fare should be around $15. If you're booked into one of the main lodges, chances are, your transportation is already included. Even if you're not booked into one of the lodges, a host of taxi and minibus drivers offer the trip. When you get to Sierpe, head to the dock and try to find space on a boat. This should run you another $15 to $20. If you don't arrive early enough, you might have to hire an entire boat, which usually runs around $70 to $90 for a boat that can carry up to six passengers. Make sure that you feel confident about the boat and skipper, and, if possible, try to find a spot on a boat from one of the established lodges in Drake Bay.

By Car   Driving is still not a recommended way to get to Drake Bay. But if you insist, you should drive down the Interamerican Highway, past Palmar to the turnoff for Puerto Jiménez (at the town of Chacarita; it's clearly marked). Then at Rincón, turn onto the rough road leading into Drake Bay. I've received mixed reports on the viability of this road, and I'm not sure if it remains passable during the rainy season. It certainly reaches only into the small heart of the village of Drake Bay, whereas almost all of the hotels I've listed are farther out along the peninsula, where only boats reach. In fact, the only hotels that you can actually drive up to are very basic cabins in town. For the rest, you'd have to find someplace secure to leave your car and either haul your bags quite a way or get picked up in a boat.

DEPARTING   If you're not flying directly out of Drake Bay, have your lodge arrange a boat trip back to Sierpe for you. Be sure that the lodge also arranges for a taxi to meet you in Sierpe for the trip to Palmar Sur or Palmar Norte. (If you're on a budget, you can ask around to see whether a late-morning public bus is still running from Sierpe to Palmar Norte.) In the two Palmars, you can make onward plane and bus connections. At the Palmar Norte bus terminal, almost any bus heading north will take you to San José, and almost any bus heading south will take you to Golfito.

WHAT TO SEE & DO

Beaches, forests, wildlife, and solitude are the main attractions of Drake Bay. Although Corcovado National Park (see "Puerto Jiménez: Gateway to Corcovado National Park," later in this chapter) is the area's star attraction, there's plenty to soak up in Drake Bay. The Osa Peninsula is home to an unbelievable variety of plants and animals: more than 140 species of mammals, 267 species of birds, and 117 species of amphibians and reptiles. You aren't likely to see a high percentage of these animals, but you can expect to see quite a few, including several species of monkeys, coatimundis, scarlet macaws, parrots, and hummingbirds. Other park inhabitants include jaguars, tapirs, sloths, and crocodiles. If you're lucky, you might even see one of the region's namesake *osas,* the giant anteaters.

Around Drake Bay and within the national park, there are many miles of trails through rainforests and swamps, down beaches, and around rock headlands. All of the lodges listed below offer guided excursions into the park. It's also possible to begin a hike around the peninsula from Drake Bay.

One of the most popular excursions from Drake Bay is a trip out to **Caño Island** and the **Caño Island Biological Reserve** 🐾🐾 for a bit of exploring and snorkeling or scuba diving. The island is located about 19km (12 miles) offshore from Drake Bay and was once home to a pre-Columbian culture about which little is known. A trip to the island will include a visit to an ancient cemetery, and you'll also be able to see some of the stone spheres that are commonly believed to have been carved by the people who once lived in this area (see "Those Mysterious Stone Spheres," above). Few animals or birds live on the island, but the coral reefs just offshore teem with life and are the main reason most people come here. This is one of Costa Rica's prime scuba spots. Visibility is often quite good, and there's even easily accessible snorkeling from the beach. All of the lodges listed below offer trips to Caño Island.

All of the lodges in the area also offer a host of half- and full-day tours and activities, including hikes in Corcovado National Park, horseback rides, and sportfishing. In some cases, tours are included in your room rate or package; in others, they must be bought a la carte. Other options include mountain biking and sea kayaking. Most of these tours run between $60 and $100, depending on the activity, with scuba diving ($100–$120 for a two-tank dive) and sportfishing ($450–$1,200, depending on the size of the boat and other amenities) costing a bit more.

One of the most interesting tour options in Drake Bay is a 2-hour **night tour** (www.thenighttour.com; $35 per person) offered by Tracie Stice, who is affectionately known as the "Bug Lady." Equipped with flashlights and night-vision glasses, participants get a bug's-eye view of the forest at night. Also, the folks from the **Original Canopy Tour** (© 257-5149; www.canopytour.com) have set up an operation in Drake Bay in the forest behind the Cabinas Jinetes de Osa. The 2½-hour tour costs $45 per person. Any hotel in the area can book either of the above tours for you.

Those Mysterious Stone Spheres

Although Costa Rica lacks the great cities, giant temples, and bas-relief carvings of the Maya, Aztec, and Olmec civilizations of northern Mesoamerica, its pre-Columbian residents did leave a unique legacy that continues to cause archaeologists and anthropologists to scratch their heads and wonder. Over a period of several centuries, hundreds of painstakingly carved and carefully positioned granite spheres were left by the peoples who lived throughout the Diquis Delta, which flanks the Terraba River in southern Costa Rica. The orbs, which range from grapefruit size to more than 2m (6½ ft.) in diameter, can weigh up to 15 tons, and many reach near-spherical perfection.

Archaeologists believe that the spheres were created during two defined cultural periods. The first, called the Aguas Buenas period, dates from around A.D. 100 to 500. Few spheres survive from this time. The second phase, during which spheres were created in apparently greater numbers, is called the Chiriquí period and lasted from approximately A.D. 800 to 1500. The "balls" believed to have been carved during this time frame are widely dispersed along the entire length of the lower section of the Terraba River. To date, only one known quarry for the spheres has been discovered, in the mountains above the Diquis Delta, which points to a difficult and lengthy transportation process.

Some archaeologists believe that the spheres were hand-carved in a very time-consuming process, using stone tools, perhaps aided by some sort of firing process. However, another theory holds that granite blocks were placed at the bases of powerful waterfalls, and the hydraulic beating of the water eventually turned and carved the rock into these near-perfect spheres. And more than a few proponents have credited extraterrestrial intervention for the creation of the stone balls.

Most of the stone balls have been found at the archaeological remains of defined settlements and are associated with either central plazas or known burial sites. Their size and placement have been interpreted to have both social and celestial importance, although their exact significance remains a mystery. Unfortunately, many of the stone balls have been plundered and are currently used as lawn ornaments in the fancier neighborhoods of San José. Some have even been shipped out of the country. The **Museo Nacional de Costa Rica** (p. 119) has a nice collection, including one massive sphere in its center courtyard. It's a never-fail photo op. You can also see the stone balls near the small **airport in Palmar Sur** and on **Caño Island** (which is located 19km/12 miles off the Pacific coast near Drake Bay).

WHERE TO STAY & DINE

Given the remote location and logistics of reaching Drake Bay, as well as the individual isolation of each hotel, nearly all of the hotels listed below deal almost exclusively in package trips that include transportation, meals, tours, and taxes.

I've listed the most common packages, although all of the lodges will work with you to accommodate longer or shorter stays. I've listed nightly room rates only where they're available and practical, generally at the more moderately priced hotels.

VERY EXPENSIVE

Aguila de Osa Inn ⍟   This luxurious hillside lodge has long been a popular choice for serious sportfishers. Situated high on a hill overlooking Drake Bay and the Pacific Ocean, the Aguila de Osa Inn offers large, attractively decorated rooms (with hardwood or tile floors, ceiling fans, large bathrooms, and excellent views), located a vigorous hike up a steep hillside. This could pose a problem for those with mobility or health issues because the restaurant, reception, and docks are located far below, around river level. There's a bar built atop some rocks on the bank of the Río Agujitas, and the dining room has a good view of the bay. Meals are simply prepared but tasty and filling, and the kitchen leaves a fresh thermos of coffee outside each room every morning.

Because most folks are out for the day fishing or taking one of the organized tours, lunches are often picnic affairs on the boat, in Corcovado National Park, or on Caño Island. Dinners feature fresh fish, meat, and chicken, often prepared with a tropical or Caribbean flair.

Drake Bay (mailing address: Interlink 898, P.O. Box 025635, Miami, FL 33102). ℂ **296-2190**. Fax 232-7722. www.aguiladeosainn.com. 13 units. $528 per person for 3 days/2 nights; $683 for 4 days/3 nights. Rates are based on double occupancy and include round-trip transportation from San José, all meals, and taxes. AE, MC, V. **Amenities:** Restaurant; bar; modern fleet of sportfishing and dive vessels; laundry service. *In room:* No phone.

Casa Corcovado Jungle Lodge ⍟   This very isolated jungle lodge is the closest accommodation to Corcovado National Park from this end of the Osa Peninsula. The rooms are all private bungalows built on the grounds of an old cacao plantation on the jungle's edge. The bungalows are all spacious, with one or two double beds (each with mosquito netting) and a large tiled bathroom. Electricity and hot water are supplied by a combination solar and hydroelectric energy system. Family-style meals are served in the main lodge, although most guests take lunch with them to the beach or on one of the various tours available. Late afternoons are usually enjoyed from a high point overlooking the sea and sunset, with your beverage of choice in hand. Access is strictly by small boat here, and sometimes the beach landing can be a bit rough, so it's recommended that guests be in decent physical shape. When the sea's not too rough, the beach is great for swimming; when it is rough, it's a great place to grab a hammock in the shade and read a book. A wide range of tours and activities is available.

Osa Peninsula (mailing address: Interlink 253, P.O. Box 526770, Miami, FL 33152). ℂ **888/896-6097** in the U.S., or 256-3181. Fax 256-7409. www.casacorcovado.com. 14 units. $765 per person for 3 days/2 nights with 1 tour; $925 for 4 days/3 nights with 2 tours. Rates are based on double occupancy and include round-trip transportation from San José, all meals, park fees, and taxes. Rates slightly higher peak weeks, lower in the off season. AE, MC, V. **Amenities:** Restaurant; 2 bars; small, spring-fed pool surrounded by lush jungle; laundry service. *In room:* Stocked minibar, safe, no phone.

La Paloma Lodge ⍟⍟ *(Finds)*   Set on a steep hill overlooking the Pacific, with Caño Island in the distance, the individual bungalows at La Paloma offer expansive ocean views that, combined with the attentive and amiable service, make this my top choice in Drake Bay. The main lodge building is a large, open-air structure with a long veranda that has a sitting area and swing chairs, where you can mingle with other guests. All of the cabins are built on stilts, feature private verandas, and are set among lush foliage facing the Pacific. The large Sunset Ranchos are the choice rooms here: Four screen walls keep you in touch with nature and let the ocean breezes blow through, and the views are to die for. The A-frame cabins are a little smaller but provide amazing ocean views from their main sleeping lofts as well. The standard rooms, which were recently remodeled, are much smaller and less private than the cabins, but they're still quite attractive and have good views from their verandas (which, like the cabins, have hammocks). The beach is about a 10-minute hike down a winding jungle path, and the lodge also offers scuba certification courses. There are single and double kayaks free for guests to use.

Hearty and delicious meals are served family style, and the kitchen will accommodate vegetarians or those with special dietary needs with advance warning. There's scrumptious freshly baked bread served with almost every meal here.

Drake Bay (mailing address: SJO Dept. 229, Box 025216, Miami, FL 33102-5216). (C) **239-2801** or (C)/fax 239-0954. www.lapalomalodge.com. 11 units. $910–$1,100 per person for 4 days/3 nights with 2 tours; $1,025–$1,270 per person for 5 days/4 nights with 2 tours. Rates are based on double occupancy and include round-trip transportation from San José, all meals, park fees, indicated tours, and taxes. Rates slightly lower in the off season. AE, MC, V (5% surcharge). **Amenities:** Restaurant; bar; small tile pool w/spectacular view; laundry service. *In room:* No phone.

MODERATE

Cabinas Jinetes de Osa   This former budget hotel in the village of Drake Bay has been spruced up, expanded, and turned into a good option for serious divers and adventure tourists. Although it's now far from a budget lodging, it does offer a reasonable alternative to the more upscale options in the area. The wooden construction, attention to detail, and location directly above the beach give Jinetes an edge over other lodgings right in the village of Drake Bay. The nicest rooms here are quite comfortable and even have a view of the bay. The hotel is pretty close to the docks on the Río Agujitas, which is a plus for those traveling independently or with heavy bags. A wide range of tours and activities is available, as are dive packages, weekly packages, and PADI certification courses. The latest word is that they plan to add a swimming pool.

Drake Bay (mailing address: P.O. Box 833, Conifer, CO 80433). (C) **800/317-0333** or 303/838-0969 in the U.S. and Canada, or 236-5637 in Costa Rica. Fax 303/838-1914. www.drakebayhotel.com. 9 units, 7 with private bathroom. $120–$150 double. Rates include 3 meals daily. DISC, MC, V. **Amenities:** Restaurant; bar. *In room:* No phone.

Drake Bay Wilderness Resort   This is one of the best-located lodges at Drake Bay. It backs onto the Río Agujitas and fronts the Pacific. The rooms here are decidedly less fancy than those at the more expensive resort lodges listed above, but they are clean and comfortable, with ceiling fans, small verandas, good mattresses on the beds, and private bathrooms. The newest additions here are five budget cabins that share bath and shower facilities. A few of the rooms have actually been nicely upgraded in recent years, and they have added a deluxe honeymoon suite on a little hill toward the rear of the property. The family-style meals are filling, with an emphasis on fresh seafood and fresh fruits. My favorite treats here are the freshly baked chocolate-chip cookies frequently served for dessert.

Because it's on a rocky spit, there isn't a good swimming beach on-site (it's about a 15-min. walk away), but there's a saltwater pool in front of the bay, and, depending on the tide, you can bathe in a beautiful small tide pool formed by the rocks. The resort offers a wide range of tour options. The lodge runs a small butterfly farm and iguana-breeding project on some land inland from Drake Bay, and you can even spend the night there, if you want.

Drake Bay (A.P. 13710-1000, San José). (C) **770-8012** or 256-7394. Fax 221-4948. www.drakebay.com. 25 units. $65 per person per day with shared bath; $95–$130 per person per day standard and deluxe. Rates include all meals and taxes. $680–$810 per person for 4 days/3 nights with 2 tours, including round-trip transportation from San José, all meals, and taxes. Rates lower in the off season. AE, MC, V. **Amenities:** Restaurant; bar; small saltwater pool; free use of canoes and kayaks; free same-day laundry service. *In room:* Hair dryer, no phone.

2 Puerto Jiménez ✸: Gateway to Corcovado National Park

35km (22 miles) W of Golfito by water (90km/56 miles by road); 85km (53 miles) S of Palmar Norte

Despite its small size and languid pace, Puerto Jiménez is a bustling little burg, where rough jungle gold panners mix with wealthy ecotourists, budget backpackers, and a surprising number of celebrities seeking a small dose of anonymity and escape. Located on the southeastern tip of the Osa Peninsula, the town itself is just a couple of gravel streets with the ubiquitous soccer field, a block of general stores, some inexpensive *sodas,* a butcher shop, and several bars. Scarlet macaws fly overhead, and mealy parrots provide wake-up calls.

On first glance, it's hard to imagine anything ever happening here, but looks are often deceiving. Signs in English on walls around town advertise a variety of tours, with most of the excursions going to nearby Corcovado National Park. The national park has its headquarters here, and this town makes an excellent base for exploring this vast wilderness. If the in-town accommodations are too budget-oriented, you'll find several far more luxurious places farther south on the Osa Peninsula. However, not only the highbrow are making their way to this remote spot—you will also find a burgeoning surfer community. **Cabo Matapalo** (the southern tip of the Osa Peninsula) is home to several very dependable right point breaks.

If you're worried that the nightlife is going to be too sleepy for you, don't forget about all those gold miners lurking about. As the home base and resupply station for miners (most of them panning illegally) seeking to strike it rich in the jungles in and around the park, Puerto Jiménez can actually get pretty rowdy at night, especially when panners cash in a find.

ESSENTIALS

GETTING THERE & DEPARTING   By Plane   Sansa (✆ **221-9414;** www.flysansa.com) has flights to Puerto Jiménez daily at 6 and 9:30am, and 2:05pm from San José's Juan Santamaría International Airport. The flight takes 55 minutes; the cost is $71 each way. Sansa flights depart Puerto Jiménez for San José daily at 7 and 10:30am, and 3pm.

Nature Air (✆ **220-3054;** www.natureair.com) has flights to Puerto Jiménez departing from Tobías Bolaños International Airport in Pavas at 6, 8:30, and 11am, and 2:30pm daily. The flight takes between 55 minutes and 1½ hours, depending on whether it stops en route; the fare is $84 each way. Nature Air flights to San José depart daily at 7 and 9:50am, and 12:15 and 3:30pm.

Note that due to the remoteness of this area and the unpredictable flux of traffic, both Sansa and Nature Air frequently improvise on scheduling. Sometimes this means an unscheduled stop in Quepos or Golfito either on the way down from or back to San José, which can add some time to your flight. Less frequently it might mean a change in departure time, so it's always best to confirm. Also, lodges down here sometimes run charters, so it pays to ask them as well.

By Car   Take the Interamerican Highway east out of San José (through San Pedro and Cartago) and continue south on this road. In about 3 hours, you'll pass through San Isidro de El General. In another 3 hours or so, take the turnoff for La Palma and Puerto Jiménez. This road is paved at first, but at Rincón it turns to gravel. The last 35km (22 miles) are slow and rough, and, if it's the rainy season (mid-Apr to Nov), it'll be too muddy for anything but a four-wheel-drive vehicle.

By Bus   Express buses (© **257-4121**) leave San José daily at 6am and noon from Calle 12 between avenidas 7 and 9. The trip takes 8 hours; the fare is $6. Buses depart Puerto Jiménez for San José daily at 5 and 11am.

By Boat   There is daily passenger launch service from Golfito to Puerto Jiménez at 11:30am. The boat leaves from the municipal dock. Trip duration is 1½ hours; the fare is $3. The return trip departs Puerto Jiménez for Golfito from the public dock at 6am. It's also possible to charter a water taxi in Golfito for the trip across to Puerto Jiménez. You'll have to pay between $40 and $60 for an entire launch, some of which can carry up to 12 people.

ORIENTATION   Puerto Jiménez is a dirt-lane town on the southern coast of the Osa Peninsula. The public dock is over a bridge past the north end of the soccer field; the bus stop is 2 blocks east of the center of town. There are a couple of Internet cafes in town; the best of these is **Cafe Net El Sol** (© **735-5718;** www. soldeosa.com), which is run by the folks who publish the local paper *El Sol de Osa.*

EXPLORING CORCOVADO NATIONAL PARK ✸✸✸

Although a few gringos have, over the years, come to Puerto Jiménez to try their luck at gold panning, the primary reason for coming here now is to visit Corcovado National Park. Within a couple of hours of the town (by 4WD vehicle), there are several entrances to the park; however, there are no roads in the park, so once you reach any of the entrances, you'll have to start hiking.

Exploring Corcovado National Park is not something to be undertaken lightly, but neither is it the expedition that some people make it out to be. The weather is the biggest obstacle to overnight backpacking trips through the park. The heat and humidity are often unbearable, and frequent rainstorms cause the trails to be quite muddy. If you choose the alternative—hiking on the beach— you'll have to plan your hiking around the tides. Often there is no beach at all at high tide, and some rivers are impassable at high tide.

Because of its size and remoteness, Corcovado National Park is best explored over several days; however, it is possible to enter and hike a bit of it for day trips. The best way to do this is to book a tour with your lodge on the Osa Peninsula, from a tour company in Puerto Jiménez, or through a lodge in Drake Bay (see "Where to Stay & Dine," above).

GETTING THERE & ENTRY POINTS   There are four primary entrances to the park, which are really just ranger stations reached by rough dirt roads. When you've reached them, you'll have to strap on a backpack and hike. Perhaps the easiest one to reach from Puerto Jiménez is **La Leona ranger station,** accessible by car, bus, or taxi.

⌜*Tips*   **Trail Distances in Corcovado National Park**

It's 16km (10 miles) from La Leona to Sirena. From Sirena to San Pedrillo, it's 25km (16 miles) along the beach. From San Pedrillo, it's 9km (5½ miles) to Marenco Biological Reserve. It's 19km (12 miles) between La Sirena and Los Patos.

If you choose to drive, take the dirt road from Puerto Jiménez to Carate (Carate is at the end of the road). From Carate, it's a 3km (1¾-mile) hike to La Leona. To travel there by "public transportation," pick up one of the collective buses (actually, a 4WD pickup truck with a tarpaulin cover and slat seats in the back) that leave Puerto Jiménez for Carate daily at 6am and 1pm, returning at 8am and 4pm. Remember, these "buses" are very informal and change their schedules regularly to meet demand or avoid bad weather, so always ask in town. One-way fare is around $7. A small fleet of these pickups leaves from the main road in town, more or less in front of the Soda Carolina, and will stop to pick up anyone who flags them down along the way. Your other option is to hire a taxi (© 735-5222), which will charge approximately $60 to $70 each way to Carate.

En route to Carate, you will pass several campgrounds and small lodges as you approach the park. If you are unable to get a spot at one of the campsites in the park, you can stay at one of these and hike the park during the day.

You can also travel to **El Tigre,** about 14km (8¾ miles) by dirt road from Puerto Jiménez, where there's another ranger station. But note that trails from El Tigre go only a short distance into the park.

The third entrance is in **Los Patos,** which is reached from the town of La Palma, northwest of Puerto Jiménez. From here, there's a 19km (12-mile) trail through the center of the park to **Sirena,** a ranger station and research facility (see "Beach Treks & Rainforest Hikes," below). Sirena has a landing strip that is used by charter flights.

Tips Important Corcovado Tips

If you plan to hike the beach trails from La Leona or San Pedrillo, be sure to pick up a tide table at the park headquarters' office in Puerto Jiménez. The tide changes rapidly; when it's high, the trails and river crossings can be impassable.

  If you plan to spend a night or more in the park, you'll want to stock up on food, water, and other essentials while you're in Puerto Jiménez. There's a minimarket in Carate, but the selection is limited. Although most of the stations have simple sodas, you need to reserve in advance if you plan to take your meals at any of these.

The northern entrance to the park is **San Pedrillo,** which you can reach by hiking from Sirena or by taking a boat from Drake Bay or Sierpe (see "Beach Treks & Rainforest Hikes," below). It's 14km (8¾ miles) from Drake Bay.

FEES & REGULATIONS   Park admission is $8 per person per day. Only the Sirena station is equipped with dormitory-style lodgings and a simple soda, but the others have basic campsites and toilet facilities. All must be reserved in advance by contacting the Parks Service in Puerto Jiménez (© 735-5036; fax 735-5276). Its offices are adjacent to the airstrip. Only a limited number of people are allowed to camp at each ranger station, so make your reservations well in advance.

BEACH TREKS & RAINFOREST HIKES   There are quite a few good hiking trails in the park. Two of the better-known ones are the beach routes, starting at either the La Leona or San Pedrillo ranger stations. None of the hikes is easy, but the forest route from the Los Patos ranger station to Sirena, although long, is less taxing than either of the beach treks, which can be completed only when the tide is low. The route between the Los Patos/Sirena hike is 19km (12 miles) through beautiful rainforest.

  Sirena is a fascinating destination. As a research facility and ranger station, it's frequented primarily by scientists studying the rainforest. One of the longest hikes, from San Pedrillo to Sirena, can be done only during the dry season. Between any two stations, the hiking is arduous and takes all day, so it's best to rest for a day or so between hikes, if possible.

  Remember, this is quite a wild area. Never hike alone, and take all the standard precautions for hiking in the rainforest. In addition, be especially careful about swimming in any isolated rivers or river mouths because most rivers in Corcovado are home to crocodiles.

WHERE TO STAY & DINE IN THE PARK: CAMPSITES, CABINS & CANTINAS   Reservations are essential at the various ranger stations if you plan to eat or sleep inside the park (see "Fees & Regulations," above). **Sirena** has a modern research facility with dormitory-style accommodations for 28 persons, as well as a campground, soda, and landing strip for charter flights. There is also camping at the **La Leona, Los Patos,** and **San Pedrillo** ranger stations. Every ranger station has potable water, but it's advisable to pack in your own; whatever you do, don't drink stream water. Campsites in the park are $4 per person per night. A dorm bed at the Sirena station will run you $8—you must bring your own sheets, and a mosquito net is highly recommended—and meals here are another $30 per day. Everything must be reserved in advance.

ACTIVITIES OUTSIDE THE PARK

Closer to Puerto Jiménez, **kayaking trips** around the estuary and up into the mangroves and out into the gulf are popular. Contact **Escondido Trex** ★ (© **735-5210;** www.escondidotrex.com), which has an office in the Soda Carolina (see "Where to Dine in Puerto Jiménez," below). There are daily paddles through the mangroves, as well as sunset trips, where you can sometimes see dolphins. These folks also do guided rainforest hikes and can have you rappelling down the face of a jungle waterfall. More adventurous multiday kayak and camping trips are also available, in price and comfort ranges from budget to luxury (staying at various lodges around the Golfo Dulce and Matapalo). They'll even take you gold panning (although there are no guarantees that your panning will pay for the trip).

Osa Aventura (©/fax **735-5670;** www.osaaventura.com) and **Osa Natural** (© **735-5440;** www.osanatural.com) also offer a host of guided tours around the Osa Peninsula and into Corcovado National Park.

If you're interested in doing some **billfishing** or **deep-sea fishing,** you'll probably want to stay at or fish with **Crocodile Bay Lodge** (© **800/733-1115** in the U.S. and Canada, or 735-5631; www.crocodilebay.com). This upscale fishing lodge is close to the Puerto Jiménez airstrip. If you want a more budget-oriented fishing outing, check around the public dock for notices put up by people with charter boats, or call **Marco "Taboga" Loaiciga** (© **735-5265**). Rates can run between $250 and $1,200 for a full day, or between $100 and $600 for a half day, depending on the boat, tackle, number of anglers, and fishing grounds.

If you're not into hiking in the heat, you can charter a plane in Puerto Jiménez to take you to Carate, Sirena, Drake Bay, or even Tiskita Jungle Lodge (see "Where to Stay & Dine" in "Playa Pavones: A Surfer's Mecca," later in this chapter), which is across the gulf, south of Playa Pavones. A five-passenger plane should cost around $150 to $200 one-way, depending on your destination. Contact **Alfa Romeo Aero Taxi** (© **775-1515** or ©/fax 735-5178) for details.

WHERE TO STAY IN PUERTO JIMENEZ
MODERATE

Parrot Bay Village   This collection of individual cabins is located on a spit of land jutting out into the gulf, just east of town and the airstrip. The smaller cabins are octagonal and have just one double bed, while the larger ones each feature a sleeping loft with a double and single bed above and a double bed below. There's a small restaurant and bar here and a large central deck built under and around a large fig tree that's frequented by scarlet macaws. The grounds also include a small patch of beach and a semigroomed trail through the mangroves. This place was formally known as Doña Leta's Bungalows. There's a small-resort feel to the whole operation.

A.P. 91, Puerto Jiménez. © **735-5180** or ©/fax 735-5568. www.parrotbayvillage.com. 8 units. $85–$105 double. Rates lower in the off season. V. **Amenities:** Restaurant; bar; limited watersports equipment rental and free kayak use; laundry service. *In room:* A/C, no phone.

INEXPENSIVE

Agua Luna   Agua Luna is located right at the foot of the town's public dock and backs up to a mangrove forest. The six older rooms directly face the gulf across a fenced-in gravel parking area. The most surprising feature in each of these rooms is the bathroom, which includes both a shower and a tub facing a picture window that looks into the mangroves. (The most disappointing feature is that these windows let you watch the gray water discharge directly into the mangroves.) There are two double beds in each room, and on the tiled veranda out front you'll find hammocks for lounging. The newer rooms are located a half-block away and are smaller and less attractive than those in the original building. The higher prices are for the larger rooms, which have tubs and mini-refrigerators.

In front of the public dock, Puerto Jiménez. ℂ **735-5034**. Fax 735-5393. 14 units. $40–$60 double. V. **Amenities:** Restaurant; laundry service. *In room:* A/C, TV, and fridge in some units; no phone.

Cabinas Oro Verde   The rooms at this budget hotel are on the second floor of a basic restaurant of the same name. The rooms are kept clean and have fans and fresh sheets. The five rooms in the front of the hotel share a narrow veranda over a sleepy street in Puerto Jiménez. The owners can help arrange a variety of tour and adventure options.

On a cross street in the center of town, 50m (164 ft.) east of the main road, Puerto Jiménez. ℂ **735-5241**. 10 units. $14 double; $21 triple. No credit cards. **Amenities:** Restaurant; laundry service. *In room:* No phone.

Cabinas Puerto Jiménez   Located right on the waterfront at the north end of the soccer field, this inexpensive accommodation even offers one room with a view of the bay. The exterior of the building, with its varnished wood, is more appealing than the guest rooms. Although large, the basic rooms have cement floors and either a floor or table fan. However, they're kept clean and are the best choice in town for travelers on a real shoestring budget.

50m (164 ft.) north of Bar y Restaurant El Rancho, Puerto Jiménez. ℂ **735-5090** or 735-5215. 10 units. $16 double; $24 triple. No credit cards. *In room:* No phone.

WHERE TO DINE IN PUERTO JIMENEZ

In addition to the places listed below, locals and visitors alike love the margaritas and California-style Mexican food at **Juanitas Mexican Bar & Grille** (ℂ **735-5056**), in the center of town.

Bar Restaurant Agua Luna COSTA RICAN/SEAFOOD   The first restaurant you come to after arriving in Puerto Jiménez by boat is also one of the best. The restaurant is a large, mostly open building built between the dirt road and the mangroves. I recommend a table overlooking the mangroves. Seafood is plentiful and fresh, and prices for fish dinners are low even for Costa Rica. They also serve a host of well-prepared Chinese dishes. The bar and its dance floor are popular, and the music is usually loud, so don't expect a quiet, romantic dinner for two.

25m (82 ft.) north of the public pier. ℂ **735-5033**. Main courses $4–$18. V. Daily 10am–10pm.

Soda Carolina COSTA RICAN   Set in the center of the town's main street, and otherwise known as the "Bar, Restaurante y Cabinas Carolina," this is the town's budget travelers' hangout and also serves as an unofficial information center. The walls are painted with colorful jungle and wildlife scenes. As for the fare, seafood is the way to go. There's good fried fish as well as a variety of ceviches. The black-bean soup is usually tasty, and the casados are filling and cost less than $3.

If you need a place to stay, there are five basic rooms with cement floors and private bathrooms behind the kitchen. The rooms cost around $10 per person and front a very unattractive yard.

On the main street. ℂ **735-5185**. Main courses $3–$8. V. Daily 7am–10pm.

WHERE TO STAY & DINE AROUND THE OSA PENINSULA

As with most of the lodges in Drake Bay, the accommodations listed in this section include three meals a day in their rates and do a large share of their business in package trips. Per-night rates are listed, but the price categories have been adjusted to take into account the fact that all meals are included. Ask about package rates if you plan to take several tours and stay a while: They could save you money.

In addition to the lodges listed below, there are several other options, ranging from small bed-and-breakfasts to fully equipped home rentals. Surfers, in particular, might want to inquire into one of the several rental houses located close to the beach at Matapalo. Your best bet for any of the above is to contact Isabel at **Osa Tropical** (© 735-5062; www.osatropical.com). In addition to being the local Sansa agent, Isabel arranges bookings via radio with a host of small remote lodges around the area.

Finally, there's a very isolated option up in the hills above Carate. **Luna Lodge** ★ (© 888/409-8448 in the U.S., or 380-5036; www.lunalodge.com) has five rustically luxurious cabins with great views over the jungle.

VERY EXPENSIVE

In addition to the places listed below, **El Remanso** ★ (© 735-5569; www.el remanso.com) is a beautiful option in Matapalo, run by a couple with a strong commitment to conservation and environmental protection.

Bosque del Cabo Rainforest Lodge ★★ *Finds* This secluded jungle lodge is my favorite place in this neck of the woods. The cabins are all spacious and attractively furnished, have wooden decks or verandas to catch the ocean views, and are set amid beautiful gardens. Bosque del Cabo is located 150m (492 ft.) above the water at the southern tip of the Osa Peninsula, where the Golfo Dulce meets the Pacific Ocean. The deluxe cabins come with king-size beds and slightly larger deck space. The Congo cabin is my choice for its spectacular view of the sunrise from your bed. All of the cabins have indoor bathrooms, although the tiled showers are set outdoors amid flowering heliconia and ginger.

There's a trail down to a secluded beach that has some tide pools and ocean-carved caves. Another trail leads to a jungle waterfall, and several others wind through the rainforests of the lodge's private reserve. The wildlife viewing here is excellent. If you're too lazy to hike down to the beach, there's a small pool by the main lodge. Surfing is a popular activity here, as are hiking and horseback riding. Attractions include a canopy platform 36m (118 ft.) up a Manu tree, reached along a 90m (295-ft.) zip line, as well as a bird- and wildlife-watching rancho set beside a little lake on the edge of their tropical gardens and surrounded by forest. Trips to the national park or fishing excursions can be arranged, as can guided hikes, sea kayaking, and a host of other activities and tours. These folks also rent out two separate, fully equipped houses that are quite nice and popular, along with a couple of new cabins set inland by their gardens.

Osa Peninsula (mailing address: Interlink 528, P.O. Box 02-5635, Miami, FL 33102). ©/fax **735-5206** or 381-4847. www.bosquedelcabo.com. 10 units. $280–$310 double. Rates include 3 meals daily and taxes. $25 round-trip transportation from Puerto Jiménez. MC, V. **Amenities:** Restaurant; bar; small pool; surfboard and bike rental; in-room or rainforest massage; laundry service. *In room:* No phone.

Lapa Ríos ★★ This is Costa Rica's most famous ecolodge. However, keep in mind that there are no TVs, no telephones, no air-conditioning, no discos, no shopping, no paved roads, and no crowds. Moreover, the beach is a good 15-minute hike away, and it's not the best for swimming. In fact, other than a beautiful little pool, miles of hiking trails, an array of adventure tours and activities, and a quiet tropical bar, there is nothing around to distract your attention from the stupendous views of the rainforest all around and the ocean far below.

The hotel consists of seven duplex buildings perched along a steep ridge. Each spacious room is totally private and oriented toward the view. Walls have open screening, and the ceiling is a high-peaked thatched roof. Mosquito nets drape languidly over the two queen-size beds. A large deck and small tropical garden, complete with outdoor shower, more than double the living space of each room. *Note:* It's a bit of a hike back and forth from the main lodge to the rooms located farthest down the ridge.

The centerpiece of the lodge's large open-air dining room is a 15m (49-ft.) spiral staircase that leads to an observation deck tucked beneath the peak of the building's thatched roof. Lapa Ríos is surrounded by its own 400-hectare (988-acre) private rainforest reserve, which is home to scarlet macaws, toucans, parrots, hummingbirds, monkeys, and myriad other wildlife. Tour and activity options include guided walks, horseback riding, boat tours, sportfishing, sea kayaking, and yoga classes, as well as day trips to Corcovado National Park, Casa Orquideas, and Wilson Botanical Gardens.

Osa Peninsula (mailing address: SJO-706, Box 025216, Miami, FL 33102). ☎ **735-5130.** Fax 735-5179. www.laparios.com. 14 units. $428 double. Rates include 3 meals daily and taxes. Discounts for children under 11; rates lower in the off season, higher during peak periods. AE, MC, V. **Amenities:** Restaurant; bar; small pool; tour desk; in-room massage; laundry service; nonsmoking rooms. *In room:* Safe, no phone.

EXPENSIVE

Corcovado Lodge Tent Camp ★   If you're looking for a balanced blend of comfort and adventure, check out Corcovado Lodge Tent Camp, which is built on a low bluff right above the beach. Forested mountains rise up behind the tent camp, and just a few minutes' walk away is the entrance to the national park. Accommodations are in large tents pitched on wooden decks. Each tent has two twin beds, a table, a couple of plastic garden chairs on the front deck, and an ocean view. Toilets and showers are a short walk away, but there are enough that there's usually no waiting.

Meals are served family style in a large open-air dining room furnished with picnic tables. A separate screen-walled building is furnished with hammocks, a small bar, a Ping-Pong table, and a few board games. Services at the lodge include guided walks and excursions, including hikes through the national park and horseback rides on the beach. The latest addition to the lodge is a canopy platform located 36m (118 ft.) up an ancient Guapinol tree. If you're truly adventurous, you can spend the night in a tent atop the platform. (Just don't wake up on the wrong side of the tent.) Package rates that include transportation and tours are also available and are the way most people come here.

Just reaching this lodge is an adventure in itself. Most guests take a five-seat chartered plane to the gravel landing strip at Carate and then walk for around 30 minutes along the beach to the lodge. Don't worry: Your bags are hauled in on a mule-drawn cart. If you have a four-wheel-drive vehicle, you can get as far as Carate, arrange for safe parking, and then walk the remaining 1.6km (1 mile). When you're there, you have a real sense of being very away from it all.

Osa Peninsula (mailing address: SJO 235, P.O. Box 025216, Miami, FL 33102-5216). ☎ **257-0766.** Fax 257-1665. www.costaricaexpeditions.com. 20 tents, all with shared bathrooms. $134 double. Rates include 3 meals daily and all taxes. 3-day/2-night package $1,138 double, including air transportation (pickup and delivery from any San José hotel), 3 meals daily, 1 treetop/canopy tour, park entrance fee, and all taxes. Add $65 per person per day for extra days. Rates lower in the off season, slightly higher during peak periods. AE, MC, V. **Amenities:** Restaurant; bar; laundry service. *In room:* No phone.

3 Golfito: Gateway to the Golfo Dulce

87km (54 miles) S of Palmar Norte; 337km (209 miles) S of San José

Golfito is an odd and unlikely destination for foreign travelers. In its prime, this was a major banana port, but United Fruit pulled out in 1985 following a few years of rising taxes, falling prices, and labor disputes. Now Ticos come here in droves on weekends and throughout December to take advantage of cheap prices on name-brand goods and clothing sold at the duty-free zone, and sometimes all these shoppers make finding a room difficult.

Golfito is also a major sportfishing center and a popular gateway to a slew of nature lodges spread along the quiet waters, isolated bays, and lush rainforests of the Golfo Dulce, or "Sweet Gulf." In 1998, much of the rainforest bordering the Golfo Dulce was officially declared the **Piedras Blancas National Park** ✮, which includes 12,000 hectares (29,640 acres) of primary forests, as well as newly protected secondary forests and pasturelands.

Golfito is set on the north side of the Golfo Dulce, at the foot of lush green mountains. The setting alone is enough to make this one of the most attractive cities in the country, but Golfito also has a certain charm all its own. Sure, the areas around the municipal park and public dock are kind of seedy and the "downtown" section is quite run-down, but if you go a little bit farther along the bay, you come to the old United Fruit Company housing. Here you'll find well-maintained wooden houses painted bright colors and surrounded by neatly manicured gardens. Toucans are commonly sighted. It's all very lush and green and clean—an altogether different picture from that painted by most port towns in this country. These old homes are experiencing a sort of renaissance, as they become small hotels catering to shoppers visiting the adjacent duty-free shopping center.

Sportfishing cognoscenti know that Golfito's real draw is the marlin and sailfish just beyond its bay. Arguably one of the best fishing spots in Costa Rica, it provides pleasant, uncrowded surroundings in which die-hard sportfishers can indulge their greatest fantasies of landing the great one to end all great ones. Landlubbers, take heed: Golfito has great opportunities for bird-watching and is also close to some lovely botanical gardens that you can easily spend a day or more touring.

ESSENTIALS

GETTING THERE & DEPARTING By Plane Sansa (© **221-9414;** www.flysansa.com) has three daily flights to Golfito departing at 6 and 10:30am, and 2:15pm from San José's Juan Santamaría International Airport. Trip duration is 1 hour; fare is $71 each way. Sansa flights return to San José daily at 7:10 and 11:40am, and 3:25pm.

Nature Air (© **220-3054;** www.natureair.com) flies to Golfito daily at 6am from the Tobías Bolaños International Airport in Pavas. The flight returns to San José at 7:20am. The flight takes 1 hour; the fare is $84 each way.

By Car The Interamerican Highway goes almost all the way to Golfito from San José, but even the main highway is a long and arduous trip. In the 6 hours it takes to drive the 337km (209 miles) from San José, you'll pass over the Cerro de la Muerte, which is famous for its dense fog and torrential downpours. Also, you'll have to contend with potholes of gargantuan proportions for almost the entire length of this road. Just remember, if the road is suddenly smooth and in great shape, you can bet that around the next bend there will be a bottomless pothole that you can't swerve around. Take it easy. When you get to Río Claro, you'll notice a couple of gas stations and quite a bit of activity. Turn right here and follow the signs to Golfito. If you end up at the Panama border, you've missed the turnoff by about 32km (20 miles).

By Bus   Express buses leave San José daily at 7am and 3pm from the Tracopa station at Avenida 5 and Calle 14 (© **222-2666**). The trip takes 8 hours; the fare is $6.50. Buses depart Golfito for San José daily at 5am and 1pm from the bus station near the municipal dock.

By Boat   A passenger launch leaves **Puerto Jiménez,** on the Osa Peninsula, for Golfito daily at 6am. The trip takes 1½ hours; the fare is $3. You can also hire a boat to take you across the Golfo Dulce to Golfito. However, there are often not very many available in Puerto Jiménez; they tend to be based in Golfito. You're likely to have to pay between $40 and $60 for a boat that can carry up to 12 passengers. The passenger launch departs Golfito for Puerto Jiménez daily at 11:30am.

GETTING AROUND   If you can't get to your next destination by boat, bus, commuter airline, or car, **Alfa Romeo Aero Taxi** (© 775-1515) runs charters to most of the nearby destinations, including Carate, Drake Bay, Sirena, and Puerto Jiménez. A regular taxi ride anywhere in town should cost around 75¢.

FAST FACTS   To avoid the bureaucracy and frequently long lines at the banks, you can **exchange money** at the gas station, or "La Bomba," in the middle of town. There's a **laundromat** on the upper street of the small downtown that charges around $3 for a normal-size load.

EXPLORING THE AREA

There aren't any really good swimming beaches right in Golfito. The closest spot is **Playa Cacao,** a short boat ride away, although this is not one of my favorite beaches in Costa Rica. You should be able to get a ride here for around $5 per person from one of the boat taxis down at the public docks, however, you might have to negotiate hard because these boatmen like to gouge tourists whenever possible. If you really want some beach time, I recommend staying at one of the hotels in the Golfo Dulce (see "Where to Stay," below) or heading over to **Playa Zancudo** (see section 4, later in this chapter).

The waters off Golfito also offer some of the best **sportfishing** in Costa Rica. If you'd like to try hooking into a possible world-record marlin or sailfish, contact **Banana Bay Marina** (© 775-0838; www.bananabaymarina.com) or **King and Bartlett** (© 775-1624; www.kingandbartlettsportfishing.com). Both of these operators have a full-service marina, a few waterside rooms for guests, and a fleet of sportfishing boats and captains. A full-day fishing trip costs between $600 and $1,500. You can also try either **Golfito Sportfishing** (© 776-0007; www.costaricafishing.com) or **Roy's Zancudo Lodge** (© 776-0008; www.roys zancudolodge.com). Both of these operations are based in nearby Playa Zancudo. They can arrange pickup in Golfito, although I prefer the lodgings and scenery out in Zancudo.

There's no steady charter fleet here, but itinerant sailors often set up shop here for a season or so. If you're looking to charter a sailboat, you should check with Banana Bay Marina, King and Bartlett, or **Las Gaviotas Hotel** (p. 310).

About 30 minutes by boat out of Golfito, you'll find **Casa Orquídeas** ★★, a private botanical garden lovingly built and maintained by Ron and Trudy MacAllister. Most hotels in the area offer trips here, including transportation and a 2-hour tour of the gardens. During the tour, you'll sample a load of fresh fruits picked right off the trees. If your hotel can't, you can book a trip out of

Golfito with the folks at **Land Sea Tours** (© 775-1614). The entrance and guided tour is only $5 per person, but it will cost you between $50 and $60 for the round-trip boat ride.

If you have a serious interest in botanical gardens or bird-watching, consider an excursion to **Wilson Botanical Gardens** ✦✦✦ at the Las Cruces Biological Station (© **240-6696** in San José, or 773-4004 at the gardens; www.ots.ac.cr), located just outside the town of San Vito, about 65km (40 miles) to the northeast. The gardens are owned and maintained by the Organization for Tropical Studies and include more than 7,000 species of tropical plants from around the world. Among the plants grown here are many endangered species, which make the gardens of interest to botanical researchers. Despite the scientific aspects of the gardens, there are so many beautiful and unusual flowers amid the manicured grounds that even a neophyte can't help but be astounded. All this luscious flora has attracted at least 330 species of birds. A full-day guided walk, including lunch, will cost you $34; a half-day guided walk costs $10. If you'd like to stay the night here, there are 12 well-appointed rooms. Rates, which include one guided walk, three meals, and taxes, run around $65 per person; you definitely need to make reservations beforehand if you want to spend the night, and it's usually a good idea to make a reservation for a simple day visit and hike. You'll find the gardens about 6km (3¾ miles) before San Vito. To get here from Golfito, drive back out to the Interamerican Highway and continue south toward Panama. In Ciudad Neily, turn north. A taxi from Golfito should cost around $40 each way.

WHERE TO STAY

In addition to the listings below, the **Wilson Botanical Gardens** offer simple yet beautiful rooms in a spectacular setting. See "Exploring the Area," above.

IN GOLFITO

Complejo Turístico Samoa del Sur   It's hard to miss the two giant spires that house this popular hotel, restaurant, and bar. The rooms are spacious and clean. Varnished wood headboards complement two firm and comfortable double beds. With red-tile floors, modern bathrooms, and carved-wood doors, the rooms all share a long, covered veranda that's set perpendicular to the gulf, so the views aren't great. If you want to watch the water, you're better off grabbing a table at the restaurant. The most recent addition here is a small full-service marina. Future plans include a swimming pool, tennis and volleyball courts, and more rooms.

100m (328 ft.) north of the public dock, Golfito. © **775-0233.** Fax 775-0573. www.samoadelsur.com. 14 units. $40–$50 double. AE, MC, V. **Amenities:** Restaurant; bar; kayak rental; laundry service. *In room:* A/C, TV.

El Gran Ceibo *(Value)*   This little motel-like option at the entrance to Golfito is a good choice. It's named after the giant ceibo tree you'll see standing over it near the entrance. The rooms are clean, bright, comfortable, and relatively spacious. All feature a small veranda with some sitting chairs. About half of them come with air-conditioning and cable TV; although you pay more for these, they're still quite affordable. The others have just fans and cold-water showers. From the grounds and some of the rooms, there are nice views over the gulf.

On the left, just as you enter Golfito. © **775-0403.** Fax 775-2303. www.hotelelgranceibo.com. 27 units. $20–$45 double. AE, MC, V. **Amenities:** Restaurant; bar; outdoor pool; laundry service. *In room:* A/C and TV in some units, no phone.

Golfo Azul   Azul offers clean rooms and a quiet location in an attractive section of the old banana company compound near the Depósito Libre (free port).

Most of the guests here are Ticos in town to shop at the duty-free shops. The smallest rooms are cramped, but there are larger rooms, some with high ceilings, making them feel even more spacious. Some rooms come with cable TV. Bathrooms are tiled and have hot water. The hotel's restaurant serves breakfast only.

Barrio Alameda, 300m (984 ft.) south of the Depósito Libre, Golfito. (C) **775-0871.** Fax 775-1849. 20 units. $20–$40 double. V. **Amenities:** Restaurant. *In room:* A/C, TV in some units, no phone.

Las Gaviotas Hotel   Situated just at the start of Golfito proper—a short taxi or bus ride from the "downtown"—Las Gaviotas has long been a popular choice. The waterfront location is this hotel's greatest asset. There is a long pier that attracts the sailboat and sportfishing crowd. For landlubbers, there's a small pool built out near the gulf. Guest rooms, which are set amid attractive gardens, all face the ocean, and although they're quite large, they're a bit spartan and definitely show their age. There are small, tiled patios in front of all the rooms, and the cabanas have little kitchens. A large, open-air restaurant looks over the pool to the gulf; it's a great view, but the food leaves much to be desired. Just around the corner is a large, open-air bar.

A.P. 12-8201, Golfito. (C) **775-0062.** Fax 775-0544. lasgaviotas@hotmail.com. 18 units, 3 cabanas. $40–$55 double; $85 cabana. AE, DC, MC, V. **Amenities:** Restaurant; bar; small outdoor pool; tour desk; laundry service. *In room:* A/C, TV.

FARTHER AFIELD ON THE GOLFO DULCE

The lodges listed here are all located on the shores of the Golfo Dulce. There are no roads into this area, so you must get to the lodges by boat. I recommended that you have firm reservations when visiting this area, so your transportation should be arranged. If worse comes to worst, you can hire a boat taxi at the *muellecito* (little dock), which is located on the water just beyond the gas station, or "La Bomba," in Golfito, for between $25 and $35, depending on which lodge you are staying at.

This area is experiencing a bit of a boom. In addition to the lodges listed below, the new **Playa Nicuesa Lodge** ((C) 735-5237; www.nicuesalodge.com) is a promising option. **Dolphin Quest** ((C) 382-8630) is the closest thing to a budget place in this area. It has a variety of lodging options and even allows camping. The folks there are particularly hard to contact, and an advance reservation is necessary; if you have any problems, you can try contacting them through **Osa Tropical** ((C) 735-5062).

Very Expensive

Caña Blanca Beach & Rainforest Lodge ★★ *Finds*   This small, isolated nature lodge is perfect for a romantic getaway or some serious relaxation. The three individual cabins are nestled on the edge of a 360-hectare (889-acre) private reserve. All are spacious, wooden affairs built on stilts, with private bathrooms and outdoor garden showers. From your balcony, you can watch the waters of the Golfo Dulce lap onto Caña Blanca's palm-lined black-sand beach. There are kayaks for paddling around the gulf, as well as a few kilometers of trails and a resident naturalist guide. Your hosts, Earl and Carol Crews, prepare gourmet meals featuring fresh fruits, herbs, and vegetables, and quite often fresh fish. There are no TVs and there's only an erratic cellphone connection out here, so be prepared to get away from it all. However, the bird-watching is fabulous, and you're guaranteed to see some monkeys, pizotes, and much more of the rich local fauna.

Golfo Dulce (A.P. 48-8203, Puerto Jiménez). (C) **813-3803.** Fax 735-5043. canablan@racsa.co.cr. 3 units. $250–$300 double. Rates include all meals, drinks, daily tours and activities, taxes, and transfers to and from either Golfito or Puerto Jiménez. 3-day minimum stay. MC, V (with surcharge). **Amenities:** Restaurant; bar; limited watersports equipment; laundry service. *In room:* No phone.

Rainbow Adventures ⭐⭐   The open architecture, varnished hardwoods, four-poster beds and scattered antiques, stained glass, and Oriental rugs make this one of the more unique jungle lodges in Costa Rica. The grounds immediately surrounding the lodge are neatly manicured gardens planted with exotic fruit trees, flowering shrubs, and palms from around the world. The second-floor rooms in the main lodge are the smallest and least expensive. But for just a little more, you can have the penthouse, a large third-floor room with four open walls and treetop views of the gulf. The individual cabins, which are set off 90m (295 ft.) or so from the main building, have open living rooms and a large bedroom that can be divided into two small rooms.

Days are spent lounging in hammocks, swimming, sunning, exploring the jungle, reading, bird-watching, wild animal–watching, and maybe fishing a bit. A private (albeit rocky) beach provides protected swimming, and, when it's calm, there's some good snorkeling nearby. (Equipment is available at no charge.) Boat charters and guided tours to neighboring attractions are available. The hotel has an air-conditioned library and reading room, with one of the most extensive collections of natural-history books I've ever seen. There are several well-maintained trails through primary rainforest, with jungle waterfalls and wonderful swimming holes. Creative and tasty meals are served either family or buffet style.

The owner has eight more rooms in the sister lodge, Buena Vista, located several hundred meters up Playa Cativa, but the level of comfort, service, and general ambience are not quite as appealing there.

Playa Cativa (mailing address: 5849 Cornell Rd., Portland, OR 97210). ℂ **800/565-0722** in the U.S., or ℂ/fax 735-5062 in Costa Rica. www.rainbowcostarica.com. 6 units. $355–$395 double. Extra person $95. Rates include 3 meals daily, round-trip transportation between the lodge and Golfito, all nonalcoholic drinks, snacks, and taxes. MC, V. **Amenities:** Restaurant; small outdoor spring-fed pool; limited watersports equipment; laundry service. *In room:* No phone.

Expensive

Golfo Dulce Lodge ⭐   This small Swiss-run lodge is just down the beach from Casa Orquideas, about a 30-minute boat ride from Golfito. The five separate cabins and main lodge buildings are all set back away from the beach about 500m (1,640 ft.) into the forest. The cabins are spacious and airy, and feature either a twin and a double bed or three single beds. In addition, there are large modern bathrooms, solar hot-water showers, a small sitting area, and a porch with a hammock. The rooms are all comfortable and well appointed, and even feature private verandas, but they are not nearly as nice as the cabins. Meals are served in a two-story open rancho with an observation deck, located beside the small swimming pool. The lodge offers jungle hikes, river trips, and other guided tours.

Golfo Dulce (A.P. 137-8201, Golfito). ℂ **232-0400** or 821-5398. Fax 775-0573. www.golfodulcelodge.com. 8 units. $190–$210 double; $225–$255 triple. Rates include 3 meals daily and taxes. Add $20 per person for transportation to and from Golfito. Rates lower in the off season. No credit cards. **Amenities:** Restaurant; bar; small outdoor pool; laundry service. *In room:* No phone.

WHERE TO DINE

In addition to the restaurants listed below, a local favorite for fresh seafood and simple Tico fare is the funky waterfront **Mar y Luna** (ℂ **775-0192**).

Bar & Restaurant La Cubana COSTA RICAN   This small, open-air restaurant with a basic menu commands a good view of the gulf from its location on the bluff of a small hill. It serves hearty meals at rock-bottom prices. A fresh whole fish in garlic sauce costs around $3.50. The bar is a quiet spot to have a drink in the evening.

150m (492 ft.) east of the gas station, on the upper road through downtown Golfito. No phone. Main courses $3–$8. No credit cards. Tues–Sun 6am–10pm.

Samoa del Sur CONTINENTAL   It's hard to miss the Samoa del Sur: It's that huge twin-towered rancho just north of the public dock. The restaurant features an extensive menu of Continental and French dishes (the owners are French), including such specialties as onion soup, salad Niçoise, filet of fish meunière, and, in a nod to their southern neighbor, paella. There are also pizzas and spaghetti. The view of the gulf makes this a great spot for a sunset drink. In addition to the food, the giant rancho houses a pool table, several high-quality dartboards, and a big-screen TV. The bar sometimes stays open all night.

100m (328 ft.) north of the public dock. ✆ 775-0233. Main courses $4–$20. AE, MC, V. Daily 7am–midnight.

GOLFITO AFTER DARK

Golfito is a rough-and-tumble port town, and it pays to be a bit careful here after dark. Right in town, about 1½ blocks inland and uphill from the *muellecito,* **Latitude 8** is the most popular spot. Most folks stick pretty close to their hotel bar and restaurant. Of these, the bar/restaurants at **Las Gaviotas** (p. 310) and **Samoa del Sur** (see above) are by far the liveliest.

4 Playa Zancudo ⭐

19km (12 miles) S of Golfito by boat; 35km (22 miles) S of Golfito by road

Playa Zancudo remains one of Costa Rica's most isolated beach getaways. It's a popular backpacker hangout, which means there are plenty of cheap rooms, some cheap places to eat, and lots of young gringos and Europeans around. These factors alone are enough to keep Zancudo jumping through the winter months. The beach itself is long and flat, and because it's protected from the full force of Pacific waves, it's one of the calmest beaches on this coast and relatively good for swimming, especially toward the northern end. There's a splendid view across the Golfo Dulce, and the sunsets are hard to beat. Because there's a mangrove swamp directly behind the beach, mosquitoes and biting sand flies can be a problem, so be sure to bring insect repellent.

ESSENTIALS

GETTING THERE   By Plane   The nearest airport is in Golfito. See "Golfito: Gateway to the Golfo Dulce," earlier in this chapter, for details. To get from the airport to Playa Zancudo, you can take a boat (see "By Boat," below) or a taxi (see "By Car," below).

By Boat   Water taxis can be hired in Golfito to make the trip out to Playa Zancudo; however, trips depend on the tides and weather conditions. When the tide is high, the boats take a route through the mangroves. This is by far the calmest and most scenic way to get to Zancudo. When the tide is low, they must stay out in the gulf, which can get choppy at times. Currently, it costs around $12 per person for a water taxi, with a minimum charge of $25. If you can round up any sort of group, be sure to negotiate. The ride takes about 30 minutes.

Also, there's a passenger launch from the *muellecito* (little dock) in Golfito, which normally leaves daily at around noon. Because the schedule sometimes changes, be sure to ask in town about current departure times. The trip lasts 40 minutes; fare is $5. The *muellecito* is located next to the town's principal gas station, or "La Bomba."

If you plan ahead, you can call **Zancudo Boat Tours** (✆ 776-0012) and arrange for pickup in Golfito or Puerto Jiménez. The trip costs $13 per person each way from Golfito and $15 per person from Puerto Jiménez, with a two-person minimum from Golfito and a three-person minimum from Puerto Jiménez. Zancudo Boat tours also include land transportation to your hotel in Playa Zancudo—a very nice little perk because there are no taxis in town.

By Car   If you've got a four-wheel-drive vehicle, you should be able to make it out to Zancudo even in the rainy season, but be sure to ask in Golfito before leaving the paved road. The turnoff for playas Zancudo and Pavones is at El Rodeo, about 4km (2½ miles) outside of Golfito, on the road in from the Interamerican Highway. About 20 minutes past the turnoff, you'll have to wait and take a small diesel-operated crank ferry. (Fare is $2 per vehicle.) After the ferry, you should make a left at every major intersection, although the road is fairly well marked. A four-wheel-drive taxi costs around $40 from Golfito. It takes about 1 hour when the road is in good condition, and about 2 hours when it's not. To get here from San José, see "By Car" under "Essentials" in "Golfito: Gateway to the Golfo Dulce," earlier in this chapter.

By Bus   It's possible to get to Zancudo by bus, but I recommend the above waterborne routes. If you insist, you can catch the 2pm Pavones bus in front of the gas station "La Bomba" in downtown Golfito and get off in the village of Conte (at around 3:30pm). A Zancudo-bound bus should be there waiting. The whole trip takes about 3 hours; the fare is $3.

DEPARTING   The public launch to Golfito leaves daily at 7am from the Arena Alta dock near the school, in the center of Zancudo. You can also arrange a water taxi back to Golfito, but it's best to work with your hotel owner and make a reservation at least 1 day in advance. **Zancudo Boat Tours** (© 776-0012) will take you for $13 per person, with a two-person minimum. If you're heading to **Pavones** or the **Osa Peninsula** next, **Zancudo Boat Tours** will also take you to these two places. It costs around $15 per person, with a minimum charge of $45. The bus to Golfito leaves Zancudo each morning at 5:30am. You can catch the bus anywhere along the main road.

ORIENTATION   Zancudo is a long, narrow peninsula (sometimes only 90m/295 ft. or so wide) at the mouth of the Río Colorado. On one side is the beach; on the other is a mangrove swamp. There is only one road that runs the length of the beach, and along this road, spread out over several kilometers of long, flat beach, you'll find the hotels I mention here. It's about a 20-minute walk from the public dock near the school to the popular Cabinas Sol y Mar.

WHAT TO SEE & DO (OR HOW NOT TO DO ANYTHING)

The main activity at Zancudo is relaxing, and people take it seriously. There are hammocks at almost every lodge, and if you bring a few good books, you can spend quite a number of hours swinging slowly in the tropical breezes. The beach along Zancudo is great for swimming. It's generally a little calmer on the northern end and gets rougher (good for bodysurfing) as you head south. There are a couple of bars and even a disco, but visitors are most likely to spend their time just hanging out at their hotel or in restaurants meeting like-minded folks, reading a good book, or playing board games. If you want to take a horseback ride on the beach, ask at your hotel; it should be able to arrange it for you.

Susan and Andrew Robertson, who run Cabinas Los Cocos (p. 314), also operate **Zancudo Boat Tours** (© 776-0012), which offers snorkeling trips, trips to the Casa Orquídeas Botanical Garden, a trip up the Río Coto to watch birds and wildlife, and others. Tour prices are $40 per person per tour, with discounts available for larger groups.

For fishing, contact **Golfito Sportfishing** (℗ 776-0007; www.costaricafishing. com), which, despite the name, is located in Zancudo, or **Roy's Zancudo Lodge** (see below). A full day of fishing with lunch and beer should cost between $600 and $1,200 per boat.

WHERE TO STAY
EXPENSIVE

Roy's Zancudo Lodge ✪✪   Primarily a fishing lodge, this comfortable hotel is located at the north end of Zancudo. All of the rooms look out onto a bright green lawn of soft grass and the small swimming pool and Jacuzzi; the beach is just a few steps beyond. The rooms are in several long row buildings on stilts. All have hardwood floors; small, clean bathrooms; and small verandas. There are four suites that have separate sitting rooms and stocked minifridges. The lodge offers many different types of fishing excursions and packages, and boasts more than 50 world-record catches.

Playa Zancudo (A.P. 41, Golfito). ℗ 877/529-6980 in the U.S., or 776-0008. Fax 776-0011. www.roys zancudolodge.com. 20 units. $110 per person nonfishing; $550 per person double occupancy for full-day fishing. Rates include all meals, drinks (alcoholic and soft), and taxes. Multiday packages available. V. **Amenities:** Restaurant; bar; pool; Jacuzzi; laundry service. *In room:* A/C, TV, stocked minibar, coffeemaker, hair dryer.

INEXPENSIVE

Cabinas Los Cocos ✪ *Finds*   If you've ever pondered throwing it all away and setting up shop in a simple house by the beach, these kitchen-equipped cabins might be a good place for a trial run. Set under the trees and only a few meters from the beach, the four cabins are quiet and semi-isolated from one another. Two of them served as banana-plantation housing in a former life, until they were salvaged and moved here. These wood houses have big verandas and bedrooms, and large eat-in kitchens. Bathrooms are down a few steps in back and have hot water. The two newer cabins also offer plenty of space, small kitchenettes, and a private veranda, as well as comfortable sleeping lofts. If you plan to stay in Zancudo for a while, this is a perennially good choice. The owners, Susan and Andrew Robertson, also run Zancudo Boat Tours, so if you want to do some exploring or need a ride into Golfito or Puerto Jiménez, they're the folks to see.

Playa Zancudo (A.P. 88, Golfito). ℗/fax **776-0012.** www.loscocos.com. 4 units. $58–$64 double. Rates lower in the off season, and weekly discounts available. No credit cards. *In room:* Kitchenette, no phone.

Cabinas Sol y Mar ✪ *Value*   This friendly owner-run establishment is one of the most popular lodgings in Zancudo. All of the accommodations were recently rebuilt from the ground up. There are two individual bungalows and two rooms in a duplex building with a shared veranda. I prefer the individual rooms for their privacy. The bathrooms in these have unusual showers that feature a tiled platform set amid smooth river rocks. There's also a small budget cabin that is quite a good deal, as well as a fully equipped house for longer stays. All of the options are just steps away from the sand. The hotel's open-air restaurant is one of the most popular places to eat in Zancudo. Seafood dishes are the specialty here; there's usually a few selections of freshly caught fish, and prices are very reasonable.

Playa Zancudo (A.P. 87-8201, Golfito). ℗ **776-0014.** www.zancudo.com. 5 units. $21–$48 double. Rates lower in the off season. V (6.5% surcharge). **Amenities:** Restaurant; bar. *In room:* No phone.

WHERE TO DINE

I've gotten great reports recently about the wood-oven pizza and nightly specials at the **Zancudo Beach Club** (℗ 776-0087). You might also try the tasty Italian meals at **Restaurante Macondo** (℗ 776-0157) or **Alberto's Puerta Negra.** And if you want basic Tico fare and some local company, head to **Soda Sussy** (© 776-0107) or **Soda Katherine** (© 776-0124). The most popular restaurant and bar in Zancudo has traditionally been at **Cabinas Sol y Mar** ★ (© 776-0014). This small open-air spot is a classic hangout for resident gringos as well as travelers.

5 Playa Pavones: A Surfer's Mecca
40km (25 miles) S of Golfito

Touted as the world's longest rideable left break, Pavones is a legendary destination for surfing. It takes around 1.8m (6 ft.) of swell to get this wave cranking, but when the surf's up, you're in for a long, long ride—so long, in fact, that it's much easier to walk back up the beach to where the wave is breaking than to paddle back. The swells are most consistent during the rainy season, but you're likely to find surfers here year-round. Locals tend to be pretty possessive around here (both the wave and local properties have engendered bitter disputes), so don't be surprised if you receive a cool welcome in Pavones.

Other than surfing, nothing much goes on here; however, the surrounding forests are quite nice, and the beaches feature some rocky areas that give Pavones a bit more visual appeal than Zancudo. If you're feeling energetic, you can go for a horseback ride or hike into the rainforests that back up this beach town, or stroll south on the beaches that stretch toward Punta Banco and beyond, all the way to the Panamanian border. Various lodges are starting to sprout up, but so far most accommodations are very basic—Pavones is a tiny village with few amenities.

ESSENTIALS
GETTING THERE & DEPARTING   By Plane   The nearest airport with regularly scheduled flights is in Golfito (see earlier in this chapter). See "By Car," and "By Bus," below, for how to get to Pavones from the Golfito airport. There is a private strip at Tiskita Jungle Lodge (p. 316). Depending on space, you might be able to arrange transportation to Pavones on one of its charter flights even if you are not staying there.

By Car   If you have a four-wheel-drive vehicle, you should be able to get to Pavones even in the rainy season, but be sure to ask in Golfito before leaving the paved road. The turnoff for playas Zancudo and Pavones is at El Rodeo, about 4km (2½ miles) outside of Golfito, on the road in from the Interamerican Highway. Pretty quickly after the turnoff, you'll have to wait and take a small diesel-operated crank ferry. (The fare is $2 per vehicle.) A four-wheel-drive taxi from Golfito to Pavones will cost between $50 and $60. It takes around 2 hours.

By Bus   There are two daily buses (© 775-0365) to Pavones from Golfito at 10am and 3pm. Trip duration is 3 hours; the fare is $2.25. Buses to Golfito depart Pavones daily at 5:30am and 12:30pm. This is a very remote destination, and the bus schedule is subject to change, so it always pays to check in advance.

WHERE TO STAY & DINE
Right in Pavones, there are several very basic lodges catering to itinerant surfers and renting rooms for between $10 and $20 per night for a double room. There are also a couple of sodas where you can get Tico meals. The most popular spot for both cheap meals and cheap rooms is **Esquina del Mar,** which is located right on the beach's edge, in front of the fattest part of the surf break. However, for budget lodgings, I prefer **Cabinas Cazaolas** (no phone), located about 100 yards uphill from the soccer field. For meals, I recommend **Café de la Suerte,** a

lively little joint located across from Esquina del Mar that serves breakfasts and lunches and specializes in vegetarian items, fresh baked goods, and fresh-fruit smoothies.

EXPENSIVE

Tiskita Jungle Lodge ★★ *Finds* This small ecolodge is nearly on the Panamanian border, with the beach on one side and rainforest-clad hills behind. Originally an experimental fruit farm growing exotic tropical fruits from around the world, Tiskita has become a great place to get away from it all. The lodge itself is set on a hill a few hundred meters from the beach and commands a superb view of the ocean. There's a dark-sand swimming beach, tide pools, jungle waterfalls, a farm and forest to explore, and great bird-watching—285 species have been sighted. Of the 160 hectares (395 acres) here, 100 hectares (247 acres) are in primary rainforest; the rest are in secondary forest, reforestation projects, orchards, and pastures.

Accommodations are in deluxe rustic cabins with screen walls and verandas. Constructed of local hardwoods, the cabins have a very tropical feel. If you're a bird-watcher, you can just sit on the veranda and add to your life list. My favorite cabin is no. 6, which has a great view and ample deck space. Some of the cabins have two or three rooms, making them great for families but less private for couples. Most of the bathrooms are actually outdoors, although they are private and protected, allowing you to take in the sights and sounds as you shower and shave.

Meals are served family style in the open-air main lodge. Although they're not fancy, they're certainly tasty and filling, and you'll be eating plenty of ingredients straight from the gardens.

The lodge is well over 8 hours from San José by car, so most guests take advantage of the package tours, which include air transportation to Tiskita's private landing strip. If you've already driven all the way to Pavones, Tiskita is only 6km (3¾ miles) farther down the road.

Pavones (A.P. 13411-1000, San José). © **296-8125.** Fax 296-8133. www.tiskita-lodge.co.cr. 16 units. $240 double. Rates include 3 meals and 1 guided walk daily, and all taxes. Packages with transportation to and from Golfito or Puerto Jiménez are available. AE, MC, V. **Amenities:** Restaurant; bar; small outdoor pool; limited watersports equipment; laundry service. *In room:* No phone.

MODERATE

Casa Siempre Domingo This small hillside inn offers up the nicest accommodations right in Pavones. The rooms all feature high ceilings, tile floors, and two double beds (one room has two doubles and a twin). The high beds are custom-made constructions, and they're uncommonly high off the ground. The owner says the design helps capture every bit of breeze from the picture windows. Meals are served on picnic tables in the large interior common space, and there is also a separate sitting room with satellite TV. The nicest feature is the huge deck, with its ocean view. Casa Siempre Domingo is located several hundred meters south and then several hundred more uphill from downtown Pavones.

Pavones (A.P. 91, Golfito). © **820-4709.** www.casa-domingo.com. 4 units. $50 double. Rate includes breakfast. No credit cards. *In room:* No phone.

The Caribbean Coast

Costa Rica's Caribbean coast feels a world apart from the rest of the country. The pace is slower, the food is spicier, the tropical heat is more palpable, and the rhythmic lilt of patois and reggae music fills the air.

Although Christopher Columbus landed here in 1502 and christened Costa Rica (Rich Coast), this region has until recently remained terra incognita. The Guápiles Highway between San José and Limón was not completed until 1987. Before that, the only routes down to this region were the famous jungle train (which is no longer in operation) and the narrow, winding road from Turrialba to Siquirres. More than half of this coastline is still inaccessible except by boat or small plane. This inaccessibility has helped preserve large tracts of virgin lowland rainforest, which are now set aside as **Tortuguero National Park** ★★ and **Barra del Colorado National Wildlife Refuge** ★. These two parks, on the northern reaches of this coast, are among Costa Rica's most popular destinations for adventurers and ecotravelers. Of particular interest are the sea turtles that nest along this stretch of coast. **Cahuita National Park** ★ is another popular national park in this area, located just off its namesake beach village. It was set up to preserve 200 hectares (494 acres) of coral reef, but its palm tree–lined beaches and gentle trails are stunning.

So remote was the Caribbean coast from Costa Rica's population centers in the Central Valley that it developed a culture all its own. The original inhabitants of the area included people of the Bribri, Cabécar, and Kékõldi tribes, and these groups maintain their cultures on indigenous reserves in the Talamanca Mountains. In fact, until the 1870s, there were few non-Indians in this area. However, when Minor Keith built the railroad to San José and began planting bananas, he brought in black laborers from Jamaica and other Caribbean islands to lay the track and work the plantations. These workers and their descendants established fishing and farming communities up and down the coast. Today dreadlocked Rastafarians, reggae music, Creole cooking, and the English-based patois of this Afro-Caribbean culture give this region a quasi-Jamaican flavor. Many visitors find this striking contrast with the Spanish-derived Costa Rican culture fascinating.

Over the past few years, the Caribbean coast has garnered a reputation as being a dangerous, drug-infested zone, rife with crime and danger. Part of this reputation is deserved because there have been several high-profile crimes; marijuana, cocaine, and crack are readily available in Limón and at the beach towns here. However, part of this reputation is exaggerated. The same crime and drug problems exist in San José and most of the more popular beach destinations on the Pacific coast. Use common sense and take normal precautions, and you should have no problems on the Caribbean coast.

1 Barra del Colorado ★

115km (71 miles) NE of San José

Named for its location at the mouth of the Río Colorado up near the Costa Rica–Nicaragua border, Barra del Colorado is an isolated little town, accessible only by boat or small plane. There are no roads in or to Barra del Colorado. The town itself is a small, ramshackle collection of raised stilt houses, and it supports a diverse population of Afro-Caribbean and Miskito Indian residents, Nicaraguan emigrants, and transient commercial fishermen.

Visitors come here for the fishing. Tarpon and snook fishing are world class, or you can head farther offshore for some deep-sea action. Barra del Colorado is part of the same ecosystem as Tortuguero National Park (see below); as in Tortuguero, there's an abundance of wildlife and rainforest fauna in the rivers and canals, which are accessible only by small boat. It's hot and humid here most of the year, and it rains a lot, so although some of the lodges have at times risked offering a "tarpon guarantee," they're generally hesitant to promise anything in terms of the weather.

ESSENTIALS

GETTING THERE & DEPARTING **By Plane** Sansa (© 221-9414; www.flysansa.com) has a daily flight that departs at 6am for Barra del Colorado from San José's Juan Santamaría International Airport. The return flight to San José leaves Barra del Colorado daily at 6:55am. Flight duration is 40 minutes; the fare is $58 each way.

Nature Air (© 220-3054; www.natureair.com) has a daily flight that departs the Tobías Bolaños International Airport in Pavas at 6:15am. Flight duration is between 35 and 55 minutes, depending on whether the flight stops first at Tortuguero. Fare is $66 each way. The return flight leaves Barra del Colorado at approximately 7am.

Most folks come here on multiday fishing packages, and most of the lodges in this area either operate charter flights as part of their package trips or will book you a flight.

By Boat It is also possible to travel to Barra del Colorado by boat from **Puerto Viejo de Sarapiquí** (see chapter 6). Expect to pay $200 to $250 each way for a boat that holds up to 10 people. Check at the public dock in Puerto Viejo de Sarapiquí. **Río Colorado Lodge** (© 800/243-9777 in the U.S. and Canada, or 232-4063) runs its own launch, the *Tucan,* between Barra del Colorado and Puerto Viejo de Sarapiquí (and sometimes between Barra and Limón), including land transportation between Puerto Viejo de Sarapiquí and San José. If you're staying at the Río Colorado Lodge, be sure to ask about this option (for at least one leg of your trip) when booking; the hotel doesn't discriminate—you can arrange transportation even if you aren't staying there. For $196 per person, you can arrange a pickup in San José, a minibus to the boat, a trip down the river to Barra, overnight accommodations at Río Colorado Lodge, and a return trip the next day, all meals and taxes included.

ORIENTATION The Río Colorado neatly divides the town of Barra del Colorado in two. The airstrip is in the southern half of town, as are most of the lodgings. The lodges that are farther up the canals will meet you in a small boat at the airstrip.

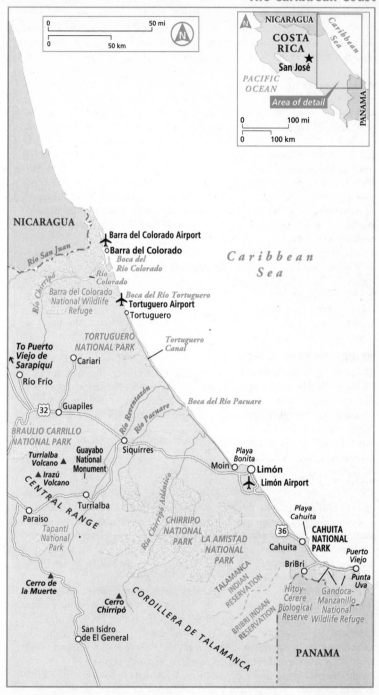

0   50 mi

0   50 km

N

NICARAGUA

COSTA RICA

San José ★

PACIFIC OCEAN

Caribbean Sea

Area of detail

PANAMA

0   100 mi

0   100 km

NICARAGUA

Río San Juan

Río Chirripó

Barra del Colorado Airport

Barra del Colorado

Boca del Río Colorado

Río Colorado

Barra del Colorado National Wildlife Refuge

Boca del Río Tortuguero

Tortuguero Airport

Tortuguero

TORTUGUERO NATIONAL PARK

Tortuguero Canal

To Puerto Viejo de Sarapiquí

Cariari

Río Frío

Río Reventazón

Río Pacuare

Boca del Río Pacuare

32

Guapiles

BRAULIO CARRILLO NATIONAL PARK

Turrialba Volcano ▲

Guayabo National Monument

Siquirres

▲ Irazú Volcano

CENTRAL RANGE

Turrialba

Paraiso

Tapantí National Park

Río Chirripó Atlántico

CHIRRIPO NATIONAL PARK

LA AMISTAD NATIONAL PARK

Caribbean Sea

Playa Bonita

Moín

Limón

Limón Airport

Playa Cahuita

36

CAHUITA NATIONAL PARK

Puerto Viejo

Cahuita

BriBri

Punta Uva

Cerro de la Muerte ▲

Cerro Chirripó ▲

San Isidro de El General

CORDILLERA DE TALAMANCA

TALAMANCA INDIAN RESERVATION

BRIBRI INDIAN RESERVATION

Hitoy-Cerere Biological Reserve

Gandoca-Manzanillo National Wildlife Refuge

PANAMA

FISHING, FISHING & MORE FISHING

Almost all of the lodges here specialize in fishing and fishing packages. If you don't fish, you might wonder just what in the world you are doing here. Even though there are excellent opportunities for bird-watching and touring the jungle waterways, most lodges are still merely paying lip service to ecotourists and would rather see you with a rod and reel.

Fishing takes place year-round. You can do it in the rivers and canals, in the very active river mouth, or offshore. Most anglers come in search of the tarpon, or silver king. **Tarpon** can be caught year-round, both in the river mouth and, to a lesser extent, in the canals; however, they are much harder to land in July and August—the 2 rainiest months—probably because the river runs so high and is so full of runoff and debris. **Snook,** an aggressive river fish, peak in April, May, October, and November; fat snook, or **calba,** run heavy November through January. Depending on how far out to sea you venture, you might hook up with **barracuda, jack, mackerel** (Spanish and king), **wahoo, tuna, dorado, marlin,** or **sailfish.** In the rivers and canals, fishermen regularly bring in **mojarra, machaca,** and *guapote* (rainbow bass).

Following recent developments in fishing, anglers have been using traditional rod-and-reel setups, as well as fly rods, to land just about all the fish mentioned above. To fish here, you'll need both salt- ($10) and freshwater ($40) fishing licenses. The lodges here either include these in your packages or can readily provide the licenses for you.

Nonfishers should see whether their lodge has a good naturalist guide or canoes or kayaks for rent or use.

WHERE TO STAY & DINE

Almost all of the hotels here specialize in package tours, including all your meals, fishing and tackle, taxes, and usually your transportation and liquor, too, so rates are high. There are no dependable budget hotels here, and Barra remains a remote and difficult destination for independent and budget travelers. In addition to the places listed below, **Casa Mar Lodge** (© 800/543-0282 in the U.S. and Canada; www.casamarlodge.com) is a long-standing fishing lodge that is popular with hard-core anglers.

VERY EXPENSIVE

Río Colorado Lodge ⚐ This rustic old lodge, one of the country's best-known fishing lodges, was founded and built more than a quarter of a century ago by local legend Archie Fields. The rooms are comfortable but rustic, with some showing the wear and tear of the years. Several have televisions, and two are wheelchair accessible. There's even a "honeymoon suite," which is basically a standard room with a small mirror hung by ropes over the bed. As at Silver King Lodge, the whole complex is tied together by covered walkways.

The nicest feature here is the large covered deck out by the river, where breakfast is served. Dinner is served family style in the second-floor dining room. There's also a large bar (where lunch is served) with satellite TV, pool table, and dartboard, as well as a conference room and a well-stocked tackle shop. The most disappointing aspect for me here is the sad little zoo, which houses a wide range of local birds and mammals in small chicken-wire cages.

This lodge runs the *Tucan* riverboat (see "Essentials," above) for those interested in cruising to either Puerto Viejo de Sarapiquí or Limón, as well as several other smaller launches for a variety of tours and outings.

Barra del Colorado (A.P. 5094-1000, San José). ✆ **800/243-9777** in the U.S. and Canada, or 232-4063. Fax 231-5987. www.riocoloradolodge.com. 18 units. $2,245 per person double occupancy for 7 days/6 nights with 4 full days of fishing, including 2 nights' lodging in San José, all meals and drinks at the lodge, boat, guide, fuel, licenses, and taxes. Nonfishing guests $120 per person per day. AE, MC, V. **Amenities:** Restaurant; bar; Jacuzzi; laundry service. *In room:* A/C, no phone.

Silver King Lodge ★★ *Finds*   This is by far the most upscale lodge in Barra del Colorado. They take their fishing seriously here—there's a large selection of modern boats and equipment, as well as a full tackle shop—but Silver King also emphasizes comfort. The rooms are immense, with two double beds, a desk and chair, luggage racks, fishing racks, air-conditioning, an overhead fan, and a roomy closet. The floors and walls are all varnished hardwood, and the ceilings are finished in bamboo. The entire complex is built on raised stilts and connected by covered walkways (useful during the frequent downpours).

The meals here are truly exceptional, some of the best buffet-style lodge cooking I've ever had. Each all-you-can-eat meal is anchored with at least two main dishes and a wide variety of appetizers, salads, side dishes, and dessert. You should be eating plenty of fish during your stay—coconut-battered snook nuggets with a pineapple-wasabi dip were just one of the highlights of my culinary indulgences here.

Barra del Colorado (mailing address: Interlink 399, P.O. Box 02-5635, Miami, FL 33102). ✆ **800/847-3474** in the U.S., or ✆/fax 381-1403 in Costa Rica. ✆ 381-1403 direct at lodge. www.silverkinglodge.net. 10 units. $2,075 per person double occupancy for 4 full days of fishing, air transportation to and from Barra del Colorado from San José, all meals at the lodge, liquor, taxes, and 1 night's lodging in San José; $550 per person per day, including all fishing, meals, liquor, and taxes; $130 per person for nonfishers. AE, MC, V. Closed June 15–Aug 31 and Nov 15–Dec 31. **Amenities:** Restaurant; bar and lounge w/satellite TV; small outdoor pool and enclosed Jacuzzi; free daily laundry service. *In room:* A/C, coffeemaker, no phone.

2 Tortuguero National Park ★★

250km (155 miles) NE of San José; 79km (49 miles) N of Limón

"Tortuguero" comes from the Spanish name for the giant sea turtles *(tortugas)* that nest on the beaches of this region every year from early March to mid-October. The chance to see this nesting attracts many people to this remote region, but just as many come to explore the intricate network of jungle canals that serve as the region's main transportation arteries. This stretch of coast is connected to Limón, the Caribbean coast's only port city, by a series of rivers and canals that parallel the sea, often running only about 90m (295 ft.) from the beach. This aquatic highway is lined for most of its length with a dense rainforest that is home to howler and spider monkeys, three-toed sloths, toucans, and great green macaws. A trip up the canals is a bit like cruising the Amazon, but on a much smaller scale.

Very important: Consider the climate in this region. More than 200 inches of rain fall annually, so you can expect a downpour at any time of the year. Most of the lodges in the area will provide you with sturdy rain gear (including ponchos and rubber boots), but it can't hurt to carry your own.

Independent travel is not the norm in this area, although it's possible. Most folks rely on their lodge for boat transportation through the canals and into town. At most of the lodges around Tortuguero, almost everything (bus rides to and from, boat trips through the canals, and even family-style meals) is done in groups. Depending on a variety of factors, this group feeling can be intimate and rewarding, or overwhelming and impersonal.

ESSENTIALS

GETTING THERE & DEPARTING   By Plane   Nature Air (© **220-3054;** www.natureair.com) has one flight that departs daily at 6:15am for Tortuguero from Tobías Bolaños International Airport in Pavas. The flight takes 35 minutes; the fare is $66 each way. The return flight leaves Tortuguero daily at 7:05am for San José.

Sansa (© **221-9414;** www.flysansa.com) has one flight daily that departs at 6am for Tortuguero from San José's Juan Santamaría International Airport. Flight duration is 40 minutes; the fare is $48 each way. The return flight leaves Tortuguero daily at 6:55am for San José.

It always pays to check with both Sansa and Travelair. Additional flights are often added during the high season, and departure times can vary according to weather or the whim of the airline.

In addition, many lodges in this area operate charter flights as part of their package trips.

By Car   It is not possible to drive to Tortuguero. If you have a car, your best bet is to either leave it in San José and take an organized tour; or drive it to Limón or Moín, find a secure hotel or public parking lot, and then follow the directions for arriving by boat below. You can also leave your car at the lot at Caño Blanco Marina, but you should try to arrange your boat transportation and lodging in advance. There is actually a road sign declaring TORTUGUERO at the turnoff for Caño Blanco Marina.

By Boat   Flying to Tortuguero is convenient if you don't have much time, but a boat trip through the canals and rivers of this region is often the highlight of any visit to Tortuguero. However, be forewarned: Although this trip can be stunning and exciting, it can also be uncomfortable. You'll first have to ride by bus or minivan from San José to Moín, Caño Blanco, or one of the other embarkation points; then it's 2 to 3 hours on a boat, usually with hard wooden benches or plastic seats. All of the more expensive lodges listed offer their own bus and boat transportation packages, which include the boat ride through the canals. However, if you're coming here on the cheap and plan to stay at one of the less expensive lodges or at a budget *cabina* in Tortuguero, you will have to arrange your own transportation. In this case, you have a few options.

The most traditional option is to get yourself first to Limón (see "Limón: Gateway to Tortuguero National Park & Southern Coastal Beaches," later in this chapter) and then to the public docks in **Moín,** just north of Limón, and try to find a boat on your own. You can reach Limón easily by public bus from San José (see "Getting There & Departing" in "Limón: Gateway to Tortuguero National Park & Southern Coastal Beaches," later in this chapter). If you're coming by car, make sure you drive all the way to Limón or Moín, unless you have arrangements out of Cariari or Caño Blanco Marina.

If you arrive in Limón by bus, you might be able to catch one of the periodic local buses to Moín right there at the main bus terminal; it costs 50¢. Otherwise, you can take a taxi for around $5 (for up to four people). At the docks, you should be able to negotiate a fare of between $50 and $70, depending on how many people you can round up to go with you. These boats tend to depart between 8 and 10am every morning. Usually, the fare you pay covers the return trip as well, and you can arrange with the captain to take you back when you're ready to leave. The trip from Moín to Tortuguero takes between 3 and 4 hours. **Laura's Tropical Tours** (© **758-2410**) also offers boat tours to Tortuguero from Moín.

As I mentioned above, it is possible to get to Tortuguero by bus and boat from Cariari. This is the cheapest and most adventurous means of reaching Tortuguero from San José, but it's also more work—and if you miss a connection or the boats aren't running, you could get stuck in a backwater banana village. To take this route, begin by catching the 9am direct bus to Cariari from the **Gran Terminal del Caribe,** on Calle Central, 1 block north of Avenida 11 (© **222-0610**). The fare is $2. This bus will actually drop you off in a new terminal in Cariari, from which you'll have to walk 5 blocks north to catch the noon bus to "La Pavona." The bus fare is around $1.75. A boat will be waiting to meet the bus at the dock at the edge of the river at around 1:30pm. The fare to Tortuguero should be between $7 and $10 each way. Return boats leave Tortuguero for Cariari every morning at 6am and 11:30am, making return bus connections. **Warning:** Be careful if you decide to take this route. I've received reports of unscrupulous operators providing misinformation to tourists. Be especially careful if the folks selling you boat transportation aggressively steer you to a specific hotel option, claim that your first choice is full, or insist that you must buy a package with them that includes the transportation, lodging, and guide services. If you have doubts or want to check on the current state of this route, contact Daryl Loth in Tortuguero (© **833-0827;** safari@racsa.co.cr).

Finally, it's also possible, albeit expensive, to travel to Tortuguero by boat from **Puerto Viejo de Sarapiquí** (see chapter 6). Expect to pay $250 to $350 each way for a boat that holds up to 10 people. Check at the public dock in Puerto Viejo de Sarapiquí if you're interested. The ride usually takes about 3 to 4 hours, and the boats tend to leave in the morning.

ORIENTATION   Tortuguero is one of the most remote locations in Costa Rica. There are no roads into this area and no cars in the village, so all transportation is by boat or foot. Most of the lodges are spread out over several kilometers to the north of the village of Tortuguero on either side of the main canal; the small airstrip is at the north end of the beachside spit of land. At the far northern end of the main canal, you'll see the **Cerro de Tortuguero (Turtle Hill),** which, at some 119m (390 ft.), towers over the area. The hike to the top of this hill is a popular half-day tour and offers some good views of the Tortuguero canals and village, as well as the Caribbean Sea.

Tortuguero Village is a tiny collection of houses connected by footpaths. The village is spread out on a thin spit of land, bordered on one side by the Caribbean Sea and on the other by the main canal. At most points, it's less than 300m (984 ft.) wide. In the center of the village you'll find a small children's playground and a soccer field, as well as a kiosk that has information on the cultural and natural history of this area.

If you stay at a hotel on the ocean side of the canal, you'll be able to walk into and explore the village at your leisure; if you're across the canal, you'll be dependent on the lodge's boat transportation. However, some of the lodges across the canal have their own network of jungle trails that might appeal to naturalists.

FAST FACTS   There are no banks, ATMs, or currency-exchange houses in Tortuguero, be sure to bring sufficient cash in colones to cover any expenses and incidental charges. The local hotels and shops generally charge a hefty commission to exchange dollars. There is an **information center** (© **833-0827**) in town in front of the Catholic church. This is a good place for independent travelers looking to arrange local tours and onward travel. It was also planning to have an Internet cafe operational by the time you read this.

EXPLORING THE NATIONAL PARK

According to existing records, sea turtles have frequented Tortuguero National Park since at least 1592, largely due to its extreme isolation. Over the years, turtles were captured and their eggs were harvested by local settlers; by the 1950s, this practice became so widespread that the turtles faced extinction. Regulations ·controlling this mini-industry were passed in 1963, and in 1970, Tortuguero National Park was established.

Today four different species of sea turtles nest here: the green turtle, the hawksbill, the loggerhead, and the giant leatherback. The prime nesting period is from **July to mid-October** (with Aug–Sept being the peak months). The park's beaches are excellent places to watch sea turtles nest, especially at night. Appealingly long and deserted, however, the beaches are not appropriate for swimming. The surf is usually very rough, and the river mouths have a nasty habit of attracting sharks that feed on the turtle hatchlings and many fish that live here.

Green turtles are perhaps the most common turtle found in Tortuguero, so you're more likely to see one of them than any other species if you visit during the prime nesting season. **Loggerheads** are very rare, so don't be disappointed if you don't see one. The **giant leatherback** is perhaps the most spectacular sea turtle to watch laying eggs. The largest of all turtle species, the leatherback can grow to 2m (6½ ft.) long and weigh well over 1,000 pounds. It nests from early March to mid-April, predominantly in the southern part of the park.

You can also explore the park's rainforest, either by foot or by boat, and look for some of the incredible varieties of wildlife that live here: jaguars, anteaters, howler monkeys, collared and white-lipped peccaries, some 350 species of birds, and countless butterflies, among others. Boat tours are far and away the most popular way to visit this park, although one frequently very muddy trail here starts at the park entrance and runs for about 2km (1¼ miles) through the coastal rainforest and along the beach.

ENTRY POINT, FEES & REGULATIONS   The Tortuguero National Park entrance and ranger station are at the south end of Tortuguero Village. Admission to the park is $7. A 3-day pass can be purchased for $10. However, there are some caveats: Most people visit Tortuguero as part of a package tour. Be sure to confirm whether the park entrance is included in the price. Moreover, only certain canals and trails leaving from the park station are actually within the park. Many hotels and private guides take their tours to a series of canals that border the park, and are very similar in terms of flora and fauna but don't require a park entrance. When the turtles are nesting, you will have to arrange a night

---

Turtle Tips

- Visitors to the beach at night must be accompanied by a licensed guide. Tours generally last between 2 and 4 hours.
- Sometimes you must walk quite a bit to encounter a nesting turtle. Wear sneakers or walking shoes rather than sandals. The beach is very dark at night, and it's easy to trip or step on driftwood or other detritus.
- Wear dark clothes. White T-shirts are not permitted.
- Flashlights, flash cameras, and lighted video cameras are prohibited on turtle tours.
- Smoking is prohibited on the beach at night.

tour in advance with either your hotel or one of the private guides working in town. These guided tours generally run between $10 and $15. Flashlights and flash cameras are not permitted on the beach at night because the lights discourage the turtles from nesting.

ORGANIZED TOURS   Most visitors come to Tortuguero on an organized tour. All of the lodges listed below, with the exception of the most inexpensive accommodations in Tortuguero Village, offer complete package tours that include various hikes and river tours; this is generally the best way to visit the area.

In addition, several San José–based tour companies offer budget 2-day/1-night excursions to Tortuguero, including transportation, all meals, and limited tours around the region. Prices for these trips range between $95 and $200 per person, and—depending on price—guests are lodged either in one of the basic hotels in Tortuguero Village or one of the nicer lodges listed below. Reputable companies offering these excursions include **Ecole Travel** (© 223-2240; www. ecoletravel.com) and **Caño Blanco Marina** (© 256-9444). There are even 1-day trips that spend almost all their time coming and going but that do allow for a quick tour of the canals and lunch in Tortuguero. These trips are good for travelers who like to be able to say, "Been there, done that," and they generally run between $85 and $110 per person. However, if you really want to experience Tortuguero, I recommend staying for at least 2 nights.

Alternately, you could go with **Fran and Modesto Watson** (© 226-0986; www.tortuguerocanals.com), who are pioneering guides in this region and operate their own boat. The couple offers a range of overnight and multiday packages to Tortuguero.

BOAT CANAL TOURS   Aside from watching the turtles nest, the unique thing to do in Tortuguero is tour the canals by boat, keeping your eye out for tropical birds and native wildlife. Most of the lodges can arrange a canal tour for you, but you can also arrange a tour through one of the operators in Tortuguero Village. I recommend **Ernesto Castillo,** who can be reached through Cabinas Sabina or by just standing anywhere in the village and shouting his name—Tortuguero's that small. I also recommend **Daryl Loth** (© 833-0827; safari@ racsa.co.cr), who runs the Casa Marbella Bed and Breakfast in the center of the village. If neither of these guides is available, ask for a recommendation at the **Jungle Shop** (© 391-3483) or at the **Caribbean Conservation Corporation's Museum** (© 711-0680). Most guides charge between $10 and $15 per person for a tour of the canals. If you travel through the park, you'll also have to pay the park entrance fee ($6 per person).

EXPLORING THE VILLAGE

The most popular attraction in town is the small **Caribbean Conservation Corporation's Visitors' Center and Museum** ☆ (© 711-0680; www.cccturtle. org). The museum has information and exhibits on a whole range of native flora and fauna, but its primary focus is on the life and natural history of the sea turtles. Most visits to the museum include a short, informative video on the turtles. There's a small gift shop here, and all the proceeds go toward conservation and turtle protection. The museum is open Monday through Saturday from 10am to noon and 2 to 5:30pm, and Sunday from 2 to 5pm. There's a $1 admission charge, but more generous donations are encouraged.

In the village, you can also rent dugout canoes, known in Costa Rica as *cayucos* or *pangas*. Be careful before renting and taking off in one of these; they tend to be heavy, slow, and hard to maneuver, and you might be getting more than you bargained for. **Miss Junie** (✆ **709-8102**) rents more modern, lighter fiberglass canoes for around $10 for a half-day.

There are a couple of souvenir shops on the main footpath near the center of the village. About 182m (597 ft.) of this path was recently paved with concrete. The **Jungle Shop** donates 10% of its profits to local schools. The **Paraíso Tropical Gift Shop** has the largest selection of gifts and souvenirs, by far.

WHERE TO STAY & DINE

Although the room rates below appear quite high, keep in mind that they usually include round-trip transportation from San José (which amounts to approximately $100–$140 per person), plus all meals, taxes, and usually some tours. When broken down into nightly room rates, most of the lodges are really charging only between $50 and $100 for a double room.

Most visitors take all their meals, as part of a package, at their hotel. There are a couple of simple *sodas* and local restaurants in town. The best of these is **La Caribeña,** which is located on the corner of the soccer field.

EXPENSIVE

Tortuga Lodge ★★   This is Costa Rica Expeditions' oldest hotel, but thanks to steady renovations, maintenance, and additions, it has not only aged well, but has improved over time. The nicest feature here is the long multilevel deck located off the main dining room, where you can sit and dine, sip a cool tropical drink, or just take in the view as the water laps against the docks at your feet. There's also a lovely little pool built by the water's edge and designed to create the illusion that it blends into Tortuguero's main canal. All the rooms are considered standards, with either one double and one twin bed or one king-size bed, ceiling fans, and a comfortable private bathroom. I'd opt for the second-floor rooms, which feature varnished wood walls and floors and come with a small, covered veranda. Of these, room no. 13 is definitely a better amongst equals.

Despite the high rates (considerably higher than at other area lodgings), the rooms are not substantially larger or more luxurious than those at the Mawamba, Laguna, or Pachira lodges (see below); what you're paying for is all the years of experience that Costa Rica Expeditions brings to Tortuguero. Service here is generally quite good, as are the family-style meals. There are several acres of forest behind the lodge, and a few kilometers of trails wind their way through the trees. This is a great place to look for howler monkeys and colorful poison-arrow frogs.

Tortuguero (mailing address: SJO 235, P.O. Box 025216, Miami, FL 33102-5216). ✆ **257-0766** in San José, or 710-8016 at the lodge. Fax 257-1665. www.costaricaexpeditions.com. 24 units. $578 double for 2 days/1 night; $758 double for 3 days/2 nights. Rates include round-trip transportation (bus and boat one-way, charter flight the other) from San José, tours, taxes, and 3 meals daily. Rates lower in the off season, slightly higher during peak periods. AE, MC, V. **Amenities:** Restaurant; bar; small pool; laundry service. *In room:* No phone.

MODERATE

Laguna Lodge ★   This comfortable lodge is another good choice, located 2km (1¼ miles) north of Tortuguero Village, on the ocean side of the main canal (which allows you to walk along the beach and into town, at your leisure). The rooms are all spacious and attractive. Most have wood walls, waxed hardwood floors, and tiled bathrooms with screened upper walls to let in air and light. Each room also has a little shared veranda overlooking flowering gardens.

The large dining room, where basic buffet-style meals are served, is located on a free-form deck that extends out over the Tortuguero Canal. Another covered deck, also over the water, is strung with hammocks for lazing away the afternoons. Several covered palapa huts strung with hammocks have also been built among the flowering ginger and hibiscus. There's a large and inviting pool, with a poolside bar and grill. All the standard Tortuguero tours are available.

Tortuguero (A.P. 173-2015, San José). © **225-3740.** Fax 283-8031. www.lagunalodgetortuguero.com. 52 units. $398 double for 2 days/1 night; $498 double for 3 days/2 nights. Rates include round-trip transportation from San José, tours, taxes, and 3 meals daily. AE, DC, MC, V. **Amenities:** Restaurant; 2 bars; large free-form pool; laundry service. *In room:* No phone.

Mawamba Lodge ★ Located about 500m (1,640 ft.) north of Tortuguero Village on the ocean side of the canal, Mawamba is quite similar to Laguna Lodge. (In fact, they are owned by brothers.) Rooms have varnished wood floors, twin beds, hot-water showers, ceiling fans, and verandas with rocking chairs. A recent remodeling has spruced things up, and rooms are now painted in bright Caribbean colors. The gardens are lush and overgrown with flowering ginger, heliconia, and hibiscus. There are plenty of hammocks around for anyone who wants to kick back, and a beach volleyball court for those who don't.

The family-style meals here are above average for Tortuguero. Rates include a 4-hour boat ride through the canals and a guided forest hike. These folks have also recently added an extensive menu of kayaking tours and excursions, including one package in which you actually kayak part of the way into Tortuguero. There's a small gift shop on the premises, a small butterfly garden, and nightly lectures and slide shows that focus on the natural history of this area.

Tortuguero (A.P. 10980-1000, San José). © **293-8181** or 711-0670. Fax 239-7657. www.grupomawamba. com. 54 units. $418 double for 2 days/1 night; $524 double for 3 days/2 nights. Rates include round-trip transportation from San José, 3 meals daily, taxes, and some tours. Rates lower in the off season. AE, MC, V. **Amenities:** 2 restaurants; bar; free-form pool; laundry service. *In room:* No phone.

Pachira Lodge ★ The rooms in this lodge are in a series of four-plex buildings perched on stilts and connected by covered walkways in a dense section of secondary forest set in a little bit from the main canal. Each room is spacious and clean, with varnished wood floors, painted wood walls, two double beds, ceiling fans, and plenty of cross ventilation. The covered walkways come in handy when it rains. Standard buffet meals are served in a large, screened-in dining room. There's a large, refreshing pool in the shape of a turtle, with children's wading pools built into the flippers. Bilingual guides and all the major tour options are available.

Tortuguero (A.P. 1818-1002, San José). © **256-7080.** Fax 223-1119. www.pachiralodge.com. 34 units. $376 double for 2 days/1 night; $502 double for 3 days/2 nights. Rates include round-trip transportation from San José, 3 meals daily, taxes, and tours. AE, MC, V. **Amenities:** Restaurant; bar; pool; laundry service. *In room:* No phone.

INEXPENSIVE

There are several basic *cabinas* in the village of Tortuguero, offering budget lodgings for between $7 and $15 per person. **Cabinas Miss Junie** (© **709-8102**) and **Cabinas Sabinas** (no phone) are the traditional favorites, although the best of the batch are the newer **Cabinas Aracari** (© **709-8006**) and **Cabinas Tortuguero** (© **839-1200**). If you choose one of these, you'll likely be taking your meals at one of the several small sodas in town and will have to make your own arrangements for touring the canals or renting a canoe.

Casa Marbella *Value* This in-town house is a great choice for budget travelers looking for a bit more comfort and care than that offered at most of the more inexpensive in-town options. The four rooms here all have high ceilings, tile floors, firm mattresses, and white walls with varnished wood trim. Owner Daryl Loth is a long-time resident and well-respected naturalist guide. Breakfast is served on a little patio facing the main Tortuguero canal in back of the house. A wide range of tours and onward travels can be arranged. They're planning to add a library, lounge, and small Internet cafe.

Tortuguero, Limón. ℂ/fax **709-8011** or ℂ 833-0827. http://casamarbella.tripod.com. 4 units. $48 double. Rates include breakfast. Rates lower in the off season. No credit cards. *In room:* No phone.

El Manati Lodge   For budget travelers looking for some of the trappings of an ecolodge experience, this is a good alternative. El Manati is located across the canal from Laguna Lodge, about 2km (1¼ miles) north of Tortuguero Village. Most of the rooms are fairly basic, with cement floors and floor fans, but they're kept clean and painted. There's even hot water. Some of the cabins have several rooms, with a variety of sleeping arrangements, including bunk beds; these are a good deal for families. The owners live here and have slowly built the lodge themselves over the years; they're also very active in a local project to protect the manatees that inhabit these waters. Canal tours and turtle-watching walks can be arranged, and you can rent canoes for $5 per hour. The honor bar is housed in a separate screened-in building and features a dartboard and Ping-Pong table.

Tortuguero, Limón. ℂ/fax **383-0330**. 10 units. $50 double. Rates include breakfast. No credit cards. **Amenities:** Restaurant; bar. *In room:* No phone.

3 Limón: Gateway to Tortuguero National Park & Southern Coastal Beaches

160km (99 miles) E of San José; 55km (34 miles) N of Puerto Viejo

It was just offshore from present-day Limón, in the lee of Isla Uvita, that Christopher Columbus is believed to have anchored in 1502, on his fourth and last voyage to the New World. He felt that this was potentially a very rich land and named it Costa Rica (Rich Coast), but it never quite lived up to his expectations.

The spot where he anchored, however, has proved over the centuries to be the best port on Costa Rica's Caribbean coast, so his judgment wasn't all bad. From here the first bananas were shipped to North America in the late 19th century. Today Limón is primarily a rough-and-tumble port city that ships millions of pounds of bananas northward every year and accepts a fair share of the country's ocean-borne imports and a modest number of cruise-ship callings.

Limón is not generally considered a tourist destination, and I don't recommend it except during Carnaval or as a brief logistical stop on your way to someplace else. Most travelers use it primarily as a gateway to Tortuguero to the north or the beaches of Cahuita and Puerto Viejo to the south.

If you do spend some time in Limón, you can take a seat in Parque Vargas along the seawall and watch the city's citizens go about their business. There are even some sloths living in the trees here—maybe you'll spot them. Take a walk around town if you're interested in architecture. When banana shipments built this port, many local merchants erected elaborately decorated buildings, several of which have survived the city's many earthquakes. There's a certain charm in the town's fallen grace, drooping balconies, rotting woodwork, and chipped paint. Just be careful, particularly after dark and outside of the city center—Limón has earned a reputation for frequent muggings and robberies.

If you want to get in some beach time while you're in Limón, hop in a taxi or a local bus and head north a few kilometers to **Playa Bonita,** a small public

---

Tips **A Fall Festival**

The biggest event of the year in Limón, and one of the liveliest festivals in Costa Rica, is the annual **Carnaval**, which is held around Columbus Day (Oct 12). For a week, languid Limón shifts into high gear for a nonstop bacchanal orchestrated to the beat of reggae, soca, and calypso music. During the revelries, residents don costumes and take to the streets in a dazzling parade of color. In recent years, the central government has tried to rein in Carnaval, citing health and safety concerns. The effort has somewhat dampened the party, but the city still gets pretty boisterous. If you want to experience Carnaval, make your reservations early because hotels fill up fast. (This advice goes for the entire coast.)

---

beach. Although the water isn't very clean and is usually too rough for swimming, the setting is much more attractive than downtown. This beach is popular with surfers.

ESSENTIALS

GETTING THERE & DEPARTING By Plane The small Limón airstrip was severely damaged by flooding in late 2002. It received a major facelift and expansion in 2003 and 2004, although at press time there were no regularly scheduled commuter flights here. You can always check with **Sansa** (© 221-9414; www.flysansa.com) or **Nature Air** (© 220-3054; www.natureair.com) to see if that's changed.

By Car The Guápiles Highway heads north out of San José on Calle 3 before turning east and passing close to Barva Volcano and through the rainforests of Braulio Carrillo National Park, en route to Limón. The drive takes about 2½ hours and is spectacularly beautiful, especially when it's not raining or misty. Alternately, you can take the old highway, which is also scenic but much slower. This highway heads east out of San José on Avenida Central and passes through San Pedro before reaching Cartago. From Cartago on, the road is narrow and winding and passes through Paraiso and Turrialba before descending out of the mountains to Siquirres, where the old highway meets the new. This route will take you around 4 hours, more or less, to get to Limón.

By Bus Buses (© 222-0610) leave San José roughly every half-hour daily between 5am and 7pm from the Caribbean bus terminal (Gran Terminal del Caribe) on Calle Central, 1 block north of Avenida 11. Trip duration is 2½ to 3 hours. The buses are either direct or local *(corriente),* and they don't alternate in any particularly predictable fashion. The local buses are generally older and less comfortable, and stop en route to pick up passengers from the roadside. I highly recommend taking a direct bus, if possible. The fare is $3.50 for the local and $5 for the direct.

Buses leave Limón (© 758-2575) for San José roughly every half-hour between 5am and 7:30pm, and similarly alternate between local and direct. The bus stop is 1 block east and half a block south of the municipal market. Buses (© 758-0618) to **Cahuita** and **Puerto Viejo** leave roughly every hour from 5am to 6pm daily. The Cahuita/Puerto Viejo bus stop is on Avenida 4, near the Radio Casino building, 1 block north of the municipal market. Buses to **Punta Uva** and **Manzanillo,** both of which are south of Puerto Viejo, leave Limón daily at 6am and 2:30 and 6pm, from the same block.

ORIENTATION Nearly all addresses in Limón are measured from the central market, which is aptly located smack-dab in the center of town, or from Parque Vargas, which is at the east end of town fronting the sea. The stop for buses out to Moín and Playa Bonita is located in front of the prominent Radio Casino building, just to the north of the Cahuita/Puerto Viejo bus stop.

FAST FACTS There is a host of private and national banks in the small downtown area. You can reach the **local police** at ℂ 758-1148 and the **Red Cross** at ℂ 758-0125. The **Tony Facio Hospital** (ℂ 758-0580) is just outside of the downtown area on the road to Playa Bonita.

WHERE TO STAY & DINE

Two of the hotels listed here are actually a few kilometers out of town toward Playa Bonita, and I recommend them over the options you'll find in Limón proper.

Hotel Acón This older in-town choice is a decent bet in Limón proper, if you can't get a room at the Park Hotel (see below). The rooms are clean, each with two twin beds with bright yellow bedspreads. The architecture and decor could best be described as Art Deco decay. The restaurant on the first floor just off the lobby is a cool, dark haven on steamy afternoons. The second-floor disco here is open every night and is particularly lively on weekends, so if your room is anywhere near it, don't count on a quiet night.

Av. 3 and Calle 3 (A.P. 528-7300), Limón. ℂ **758-1010.** Fax 758-2924. 39 units. $32 double; $48 triple. AE, MC, V. **Amenities:** Restaurant; bar/disco. *In room:* A/C, TV.

Hotel Cocori Located on the water just before you reach Playa Bonita, this hotel commands a fine view of the cove, a small beach, and crashing surf. A pair of two-story, peach-colored buildings houses the rooms, most of which are small and basic. Those on the second floor have better sea breezes and views. A long veranda runs along both floors. The grounds are in need of landscaping, and the rooms are a bit desultory, but all come with air-conditioning and a small television with cable. The restaurant serves basic Tico fare but has a great setting overlooking the sea.

Playa Bonita, Limón. ℂ **795-1670.** Fax 795-2930. 22 units. $40–$45 double. Rates include breakfast. AE, MC, V. **Amenities:** Restaurant. *In room:* A/C, TV, no phone.

Hotel Maribu Caribe Located on top of a hill overlooking the Caribbean and built to resemble an Indian village, the Maribu Caribe is a pleasant (if not overly luxurious) choice if you're looking to spend some time close to Limón. The hotel is popular with Tico families from San José because it's easy to get to for weekend trips. The guest rooms are in circular bungalows with white-tile floors and varnished wood ceilings. The furnishings are comfortable but a bit old.

The hotel's restaurant has the best view in or around Limón. It's built out over the edge of a steep hill, with tide pools and the ocean below. In addition to the formal dining room, there are tables outside on a curving veranda that make the most of the view. The Maribu Caribe can help you with tour arrangements and has a gift shop.

Playa Bonita, Limón (mailing address: A.P. 623-7300, San José). ℂ **795-2543** or 253-1838. Fax 234-0193. 56 units. $78 double; $88 triple. Rates lower in the off season. AE, DC, MC, V. **Amenities:** Restaurant; bar; attractive outdoor pool; laundry service. *In room:* A/C.

Park Hotel You can't miss this pastel peach building facing the ocean, across the street from the fire station. It's certainly seen better years, but in Limón there aren't too many choices, so I often end up staying here. This place is periodically painted and spruced up, but the climate and sea breezes really take their toll. Still, part of what makes this hotel memorable is the aging tropical ambience. Try to see the room you'll be getting before putting down any money. Ask for a room on the ocean side of the hotel because these are brighter, quieter, and cooler than those that face the fire station, although they're also slightly more expensive. The suites are generally kept in much better condition and have private oceanview balconies and larger bathrooms with tubs. The large, sunny dining room off the lobby serves standard Tico fare at very reasonable prices.

Av. 3, between calles 1 and 3 (A.P. 35-7300), Limón. (C) **758-3476** or 798-0555. Fax 758-4364. 35 units. $40 double; $50 triple; $60 suite. AE, MC, V. **Amenities:** Restaurant. *In room:* A/C, TV.

EN ROUTE SOUTH

Staying at one of the places below is a great way to combine some quiet beach time on the Caribbean coast with a more active ecolodge or bird-watching experience into one compact itinerary.

Aviarios del Caribe ✪   If you prefer bird-watching to beaching, this B&B, located on the edge of a small river delta, is the place to stay on this section of the Caribbean coast. The lodge's owners have spotted more than 325 species within the immediate area. You can work on your life list from the lawns, the second-floor open-air dining room and lounge, or a canoe paddling around the nearby canals. This small hotel is surrounded by a private wildlife sanctuary, comprised mainly of the estuary, mangroves, and an uninhabited island, but it also includes several well-groomed forest trails adjacent to the main building.

The guest rooms are all large and comfortable and have fans, tile floors, potted plants, fresh flowers, and modern bathroom fixtures. Some rooms even have king-size beds.

In the lounge area, you'll find an interesting collection of mounted insects, as well as terrariums that house live poison-arrow frogs. You'll also certainly make friends with Buttercup, the resident three-toed sloth. In fact, you're guaranteed to see sloths because they run a sloth rehabilitation and breeding program here. Only breakfast is offered, so you'll have to take your other meals in Cahuita or at one of the nearby roadside sodas.

30km (19 miles) south of Limón, or 9km (5½ miles) north of Cahuita, just off the main road (A.P. 569-7300, Limón). (C)/fax **750-0775.** www.ogphoto.com/aviarios. 6 units. $75–$85 double. No credit cards. *In room:* No phone.

Selva Bananito Lodge ✪✪ *(Finds)*   This remote nature lodge is a welcome addition to the Caribbean coast, allowing you to combine some rainforest adventuring with some serious beach time in Cahuita or Puerto Viejo. The individual raised-stilt cabins are all spacious and comfortable, with an abundance of varnished woodwork. Inside you'll find two double beds, a desk and chair, and some fresh flowers, as well as a large private bathroom. Outside there's a wraparound veranda with a hammock and some chairs. It all adds up to what I call rustic luxury. Half the cabins have views of the Bananito River and a small valley; the other half have views of the Matama Mountains, part of the Talamanca mountain range.

There are no electric lights at Selva Bananito, but each evening as you dine by candlelight, your cabin's oil lamps are lit for you. Hot water is provided by solar panels. Tasty family-style meals are served in the large, open *rancho,* which is also a great spot for morning bird-watching. There's a wide range of tours and activities, including rainforest hikes and horseback rides in the jungle, tree climbing, self-guided trail hikes, and even the opportunity to rappel down the face of a jungle waterfall. The owners are very involved in conservation efforts in this area, and approximately two-thirds of the 2,100 acres here are primary forest managed as a private reserve. You'll need a four-wheel-drive vehicle to reach the lodge, or you should arrange pickup in Bananito beforehand. You can also arrange to be picked up in San José.

Bananito (A.P. 2333-2050, San Pedro). ⓒ 253-8118. Fax 280-0820. www.selvabananito.com. 11 units. $200–$220 double. Rates include 3 meals daily and all taxes. Rates lower in the off season. No credit cards. **Amenities:** Restaurant; activity desk. *In room:* No phone.

4 Cahuita ⓐ

200km (124 miles) E of San José; 42km (26 miles) S of Limón; 13km (8 miles) N of Puerto Viejo

Cahuita is a sleepy Caribbean beach village and the first "major" tourist destination you'll reach heading south out of Limón. The boom going on in Puerto Viejo and the beaches south of Puerto Viejo have in many ways passed Cahuita by. Any way you slice it, Cahuita is one of the most laid-back villages in Costa Rica. The few dirt and gravel streets here are host to a languid parade of pedestrian traffic, parted occasionally by a bicycle, car, or bus. After a short time, you'll find yourself slipping into the heat-induced torpor that affects anyone who ends up here.

The village traces its roots to Afro-Caribbean fishermen and laborers who settled in this region in the mid-1800s, and today the population is still primarily English-speaking blacks whose culture and language set them apart from other Costa Ricans.

People come to Cahuita for its miles of pristine beaches, which stretch both north and south from town. The southern beaches, the forest behind them, and the coral reef offshore (one of just a handful in Costa Rica) are all part of **Cahuita National Park.** Silt and pesticides washing down from nearby banana plantations have taken a heavy toll on the coral reefs, so don't expect the snorkeling to be world-class. But on a calm day, it can be pretty good, and the beaches are idyllic every day. It can rain almost any time of year here, but the most dependably dry season is in September and October.

ESSENTIALS

GETTING THERE & DEPARTING　By Car　Follow the directions above for getting to Limón. As you enter Limón, about 500m (1,640 ft.) from the busiest section of downtown, watch for a paved road to the right, just before the railroad tracks. Take this road south to Cahuita, passing the airstrip and the beach on your left as you leave Limón. Alternatively, there's a turnoff with signs for Sixaola and La Bomba several miles before Limón. This winding shortcut skirts the city and puts you on the coastal road several miles south of town.

By Bus　Express buses (ⓒ 257-8129) leave San José daily at 6 and 10am, and 1:30 and 3:30pm from the new Caribbean bus terminal (Gran Terminal del Caribe) on Calle Central, 1 block north of Avenida 11. The trip's duration is 4 hours; fare is $5.30. During peak periods, extra buses are often added. However, it's wise to check because this bus line **(Mepe)** is one of the most fickle.

Alternatively, you can catch a bus to **Limón** (see section 3, above) and then transfer to a Cahuita- or Puerto Viejo–bound bus (ⓒ 758-0618) in Limón. These latter buses leave roughly every hour between 5am and 6pm from Radio Casino, which is 1 block north of the municipal market. Buses from Limón to Manzanillo also stop in Cahuita and leave daily at 6am and 2:30pm. The trip takes 1 hour; the fare is $1.50.

Grayline (© 220-2126; www.graylinecostarica.com) has a daily bus that leaves San José for Cahuita at 7am; the fare is $25. **Interbus** (© 283-5573; www.costaricapass.com) has a daily bus that leaves San José for Cahuita at 10am; the fare is $25. Both companies will pick you up at most San José–area hotels.

Buses departing **Puerto Viejo** and Sixaola (on the Panama border) stop in Cahuita at approximately 7:30, 9:30, and 11:30am, and 4:30pm en route to San José. However, this schedule is far from precise, so it's always best to check with your hotel. Moreover, these buses are often full, particularly on weekends and throughout the high season. To avoid standing in the aisle all the way to San José, it is sometimes better to take a bus first to Limón and then catch one of the frequent Limón–San José buses. Buses to Limón leave regularly throughout the day.

Another tactic I've used is to take a morning bus to Puerto Viejo, spend the day down there, and board a direct bus to San José at its point of origin, thereby snagging a seat.

ORIENTATION   There are only about eight dirt streets in Cahuita. The highway runs parallel to the coast, with three main roads running perpendicular. The northernmost of these bypasses town and brings you to the northern end of Playa Negra. It's marked with signs for the Magellan Inn and other hotels up on this end. The second road in brings you to the southern end of Playa Negra, a half-mile closer to town. Look for signs for Atlantida Lodge. The third road is the principal entrance into town. The village's main street in town, which runs parallel to the highway, dead-ends at the entrance to the national park (a footbridge over a small stream).

Buses usually drop their passengers in front of Coco's Bar, which is still sometimes called Salon Vaz, its legendary prior incarnation. If you come in on the bus and are staying at a lodge on Playa Negra, head out of town on the street that runs between Coco's Bar and the small park. This road curves to the left and continues a mile or so out to Playa Negra.

FAST FACTS   You can wash your clothes at the self-service **laundromat** in front of Cabinas Vaz (about 1½ blocks south of the former Salón Vaz). One load in the washer or dryer costs $1.50. The **police station** (© 755-0217) is located where the road from Playa Negra turns into town. The **post office,** next door to the police station, is open Monday through Friday from 8am to 5pm. If you can't find a **cab** in town, try calling **René** (© 755-0243), **Wayne** (© 755-0078), or **Dino** (© 755-0012).

EXPLORING CAHUITA NATIONAL PARK ⚐

On arrival, you'll immediately feel the call of the long scimitar of beach that stretches south from the edge of town. This beach can be glimpsed through the trees from Cahuita's sun-baked main street and extends a promise of relief from the heat. Although the lush coastal forest and picture-perfect palm lines are a tremendous draw, the park was actually created to preserve the 240-hectare (787-acre) **coral reef** that surrounds it. The reef contains 35 species of coral and provides a haven for hundreds of brightly colored tropical fish. You can walk on the beach itself or follow the trail that runs through the forest just behind the beach to check out the reef.

The best place to swim is just before or beyond the **Río Perezoso (Lazy River),** several hundred meters inside Cahuita National Park. The trail behind the beach is great for bird-watching, and if you're lucky, you might see some monkeys or a sloth. The loud grunting sounds you hear off in the distance are the calls of howler monkeys, which can be heard from more than a kilometer away. Nearer at hand, you're likely to hear crabs scuttling amid the dry leaves on the forest floor—there are half a dozen or so species of land crabs living in this region. My favorites are the bright orange-and-purple ones.

The trail behind the beach stretches a little more than 6.4km (4 miles) to the southern end of the park at **Puerto Vargas,** where you'll find a beautiful white-sand beach, the park headquarters, and a primitive campground with showers and outhouses. It's a nice, flat walk, but a rewarding one because there's good wildlife viewing and access to the beach. The reef is off the point just north of Puerto Vargas, and you can snorkel here. If you don't dawdle, the hike to Puerto Vargas should take no more than 2 hours each way. Bring plenty of mosquito repellent because this area can be buggy.

Although there's snorkeling at Puerto Vargas, the nicest coral heads are located several hundred meters offshore, and it's best to have a boat take you out. A 3-hour **snorkel trip** should cost between $15 and $25 per person with equipment. These can be arranged with any of the local tour companies listed below. *Note:* These trips are best taken when the seas are calm—for safety's sake, visibility, and comfort.

ENTRY POINTS, FEES & REGULATIONS   The **in-town park entrance** is just over a footbridge at the end of the village's main street. It has bathroom facilities, changing rooms, and storage lockers. This is the best place to enter if you're just interested in spending the day on the beach and maybe taking a little hike in the bordering forest.

The main park entrance is at the southern end of the park in **Puerto Vargas.** This is where you should come if you plan to camp at the park or if you don't feel up to hiking a couple of hours to reach the good snorkeling spots. The road to Puerto Vargas is approximately 5km (3 miles) south of Cahuita on the left.

Officially, **admission** is $6 per person per day, but this is collected only at the Puerto Vargas entrance. You can enter the park from the town of Cahuita for free or with a voluntary contribution. The park is open from dawn to dusk for day visitors.

There is an extra $2 per person charge for **camping.** The 50 campsites at Puerto Vargas stretch along for several kilometers and are either right on or just a few steps from the beach. My favorite campsites are those farthest from the entrance. There are basic shower and bathroom facilities at a small ranger station, but these can be a bit far from some of the campsites.

GETTING THERE   **By Car**   The turnoff for the Puerto Vargas entrance is clearly marked, 7km (4⅓ miles) south of Cahuita.

By Bus   Your best bet is to get off of a Puerto Viejo– or Sixaola-bound bus at the turnoff for the Puerto Vargas entrance (well marked, but tell the bus driver in advance). The actual guard station/entrance is only about 500m (1,640 ft.) down this road. However, the campsites are several kilometers farther, so it's a long hike with a heavy pack.

BEACHES & ACTIVITIES OUTSIDE THE PARK

Outside the park, the best place for swimming is **Playa Negra.** The stretch right in front of the Atlantida Lodge is my favorite spot.

If you want to take advantage of any organized adventure trips or tours while in Cahuita, there are plenty of options. I recommend **Cahuita Tours and Adventure Center** (© **755-0232**), on the village's main street heading out toward Playa Negra. Cahuita Tours offers glass-bottom-boat and snorkeling trips

($20 per person), jungle tours ($25), white-water rafting trips ($95), and Jeep tours to the Bribri Reservation ($60).

Turística Cahuita Information Center (①/fax **755-0071**), also on the main road heading toward Playa Negra, and **Roberto Tours** (① **755-0117**), 50m (164 ft.) south of the bus stop, offer similar tours at similar prices. Most of the companies offer multiday trips to Tortuguero, as well as to Bocas del Toro, Panama.

Brigitte (① **755-0053;** www.brigittecahuita.com) rents horses for $10 per hour (you must have experience) and offers guided horseback tours for $35 to $40. She also rents mountain bikes for $8 per day or $25 per week.

Bird-watchers who have cars should head north 9km (5½ miles) to the **Aviarios del Caribe** ※ (①/fax **750-0775**), where more than 325 species of birds have been sighted in the immediate area. The 3½-hour canoe tour through the surrounding estuary costs $30 per person and leaves at 6am and 3pm. The 6am tour includes breakfast. There's also a 1¼-hour canoe tour combination that includes a visit to the company's sloth rehabilitation center and self-guided hike on its trails, for $20 per person. This option is available between 8am and 2:30pm. It's best to make reservations in advance.

SHOPPING
For a wide selection of beachwear, local crafts, cheesy souvenirs, and batik clothing, try **Boutique Coco Miko** or **Boutique Bambata,** which are both on the main road near the entrance to the park. The latter is also a good place to have your hair wrapped in colorful threads and strung with beads. Out toward Playa Negra, similar wares are offered at the gift shop at **Cahuita Tours.** Handmade jewelry and crafts are sold by local and itinerant artisans in makeshift stands near the park entrance.

Ask around town, and you might be able to pick up a copy of Paula Palmer's *What Happen: A Folk-History of Costa Rica's Talamanca Coast* (Publications in English, 1993). The book is a history of the region, based on interviews with many of the area's oldest residents. Much of it is in the traditional Creole language, from which the title is taken. It makes fun and interesting reading, and you just might bump into someone mentioned in the book.

If you are interested in the local music scene, you should definitely buy the recently issued *Babylon,* by Walter Gavitt Ferguson. The 85-year-old calypso singer and songwriter is a local legend and has finally recorded a CD of his original songs. Ask around town, and you should be able to find a copy. If you're lucky, you might even bump into Gavitt as well.

WHERE TO STAY
MODERATE
Atlántida Lodge   This quiet, comfortable hotel is your best bet if you want to be just steps away from the beach, with a nice pool and a few basic amenities. The guest rooms have a rustic feel to them, yet they are clean and comfortable, with pale-yellow stucco walls, red-tile floors, a ceiling fan, and plenty of bamboo trim. Each has a small patio with a bamboo screen divider for privacy, which opens onto the hotel's lush gardens. A host of different tours can be arranged here, from snorkeling to horseback riding, to white-water rafting.

Beside the soccer field on the road to Playa Negra, .8km (½ mile) north of town, Cahuita, Limón. ① **755-0115.** Fax 755-0213. www.atlantida.co.cr. 30 units. $55 double; $65 triple or quad. Rates lower in the off season. AE, MC, V. **Amenities:** Restaurant; bar; midsize tile pool; small gym; Jacuzzi; tour desk, laundry service. *In room:* No phone.

Chalet Hibiscus If you're planning a long stay in Cahuita, I advise checking into this place. The largest house has two bedrooms and sleeps up to six people. There's hardwood paneling all around, a full kitchen, hot water, red-tile floors, a *pila* (wash basin) for doing your laundry, and even a garage. A spiral staircase leads to the second floor, where you'll find the bedrooms, as well as hammocks on a balcony that looks over a green lawn to the ocean. The other houses are similarly simple yet elegant, and the setting is serene and beautiful. The small cabins are much more basic and have wicker furniture and walls of stone and wood. Be sure to ring the bell outside the gate—there are guard dogs on the grounds. You're a kilometer north of Playa Negra here, on a section of exposed coral coastline, so you'll have to walk, ride a bike, or drive a bit to enjoy the beach.

A.P. 943, Limón. ℂ 755-0021. Fax 755-0015. hibiscus@racsa.co.cr. 7 units. Dec–Apr $45–$60 double; $100–$120 house; lower rates May–Nov. AE, MC, V. **Amenities:** Bar; tiny pool. *In room:* No phone.

El Encanto Bed and Breakfast 🏆 *Value* The individual bungalows at this little bed-and-breakfast are set in from the road, on spacious and well-kept grounds. The bungalows themselves are also spacious and have attractive touches such as wooden bed frames, arched windows, Mexican-tile floors, Guatemalan bedspreads, and framed Panamanian *molas* hanging on the walls. There is a separate two-story, three-bedroom, two-bathroom house with a full kitchen at the rear of the grounds, as well as a new deluxe room. Hearty breakfasts are served in the small open dining room surrounded by lush gardens. Recent additions here include a meditation hall, a covered garden gazebo, and an open-air massage room.

Cahuita (A.P. 7302-7), Limón (just outside of town on the road to Playa Negra). ℂ/fax **755-0113.** www. elencantobedandbreakfast.com. 7 units. $55 double. Rates include full breakfast. Rates slightly lower in the off season. MC, V. *In room:* No phone.

Magellan Inn 🏆 This small inn is the most sophisticated hotel in the area. The rooms are all carpeted and have French doors, vertical blinds, tiled bathrooms with hardwood counters, and two joined single beds. Although there's a ceiling fan over each bed, the rooms could use a bit more ventilation. Two of the units just got wall-mounted air-conditioners. Each room has its own tiled veranda with a Persian rug and bamboo sitting chairs. The combination bar/lounge and dining room features even more Persian-style rugs and wicker furniture. Most memorable of all are the hotel's sunken pool and lush gardens, both of which are built into a crevice in the ancient coral reef that underlies this entire region—which leads to good bird-watching.

At the far end of Playa Negra (about 2km/1¼ miles north of Cahuita), Cahuita (A.P. 1132), Limón. ℂ/fax **755-0035.** http://magellaninn.toposrealestate.org. 6 units. $69 double; $89 double with A/C. Rates include continental breakfast. AE, MC, V. **Amenities:** Restaurant; bar/lounge; small pool; tour desk; laundry service. *In room:* No phone.

INEXPENSIVE

Alby Lodge *Value* With the feel of a small village, Alby Lodge is a fascinating little place hand-built by its German owners. Although the four small cabins are close to the center of the village, they're surrounded by a large lawn and feel secluded. The cabins are quintessentially tropical, with thatched roofs, mosquito nets, hardwood floors and beams, big shuttered windows, tile bathrooms, and a hammock slung on the front porch. There's no restaurant here, but there is a communal kitchen area if you want to cook your own meals. The turnoff for the lodge is on your right just before you reach the national park entrance; the hotel is located about 136m (446 ft.) down a narrow, winding lane from here.

Cahuita (A.P. 840), Limón. ©/fax **755-0031**. alby_lodge@racsa.co.cr. 4 units. $40 double; $45 triple; $50 quad. Children under 12 stay free in parent's room. No credit cards. *In room:* Safe, no phone.

Cabinas Arrecife   Located near the water, next to Restaurant Edith (p. 338), this row of basic rooms is an excellent budget choice in Cahuita. Each room comes with a double and a single bed, a table fan, and tile floors. There's not a lot of room to move around, but things are pretty clean and new for this price range. There's a shared veranda with some chairs for sitting, where you can catch a glimpse of the sea through a dense stand of coconut palms. If you want to be closer to the sea, grab one of the hammocks strung on those palms, or sit in the small, open restaurant, which serves breakfast every day and dinners according to demand.

Cahuita (about 100m/328 ft. east of the post office), Limón. ©/fax **755-0081**. 12 units. $20 double; $25 triple. AE, MC, V. **Amenities:** Restaurant. *In room:* No phone.

Jenny's Cabinas   This place has been popular for years, and the rooms, although decidedly basic, have arguably the best views and location in town, just a few meters away from and overlooking the Caribbean Sea. All of the rooms have shuttered windows, and there are sling chairs and hammocks on their porches. The most expensive rooms are on the second floor, and I think it's worth a few extra dollars for the added elevation and private balcony. There are hammocks strung up between palms, and a few tables and chairs around the grounds in front of the hotel, where you'll likely spend hours trading tales with fellow travelers.

Cahuita, Limón. ©/fax **755-0256**. cabinasjenny@racsa.co.cr. 9 units. $20–$30 double. Rates slightly lower in the off season. AE, MC, V. *In room:* No phone.

WHERE TO DINE

Coconut meat and milk figure in a lot of the regional cuisine. Most nights, local women cook up pots of various local specialties and sell them from the front porches of the two discos or from street-side stands around town; a full meal will cost you around $2 to $4.

In addition to the places listed below, **Sobre Las Olas** (© **755-0109**) serves a mix of local and Italian cuisine. The restaurant has a stunning location on a low bluff over the ocean, with waves breaking on coral just below. Another local favorite is **Relax** (© **755-0322**), which serves a mix of local, Italian, and Mexican fare in a lovely open-air dining room above **Ricky's Bar.**

Casa Creole ★★ FRENCH/CREOLE   The rest of Cahuita might feel like a misplaced piece of Bob Marley's Jamaica, but this restaurant takes its inspiration from islands a little farther south in the Caribbean—and far more French. Tables in the open first-floor dining room are set with linen tablecloths and candles in glass lanterns. There's a sense of informal elegance about the whole affair. Start with a dish of the pâté *maison* or a shrimp, coconut, and pineapple cocktail. The spiced shrimp *martiniquaise* and the jumbo coconut shrimp soup are both excellent, as is the fresh fish, seasoned and baked inside a banana leaf. The emphasis here is on seafood, but the ample menu includes meat, chicken, and pasta dishes. Top it off with some fresh raspberry coulis, homemade profiteroles, or exquisite homemade fresh-fruit sherbet.

At the Magellan Inn, Playa Negra Rd., 2.5km (1½ miles) north of Cahuita. © **755-0035**. Reservations recommended during the high season. Main courses $7–$20. AE, MC, V. Mon–Sat 6–9pm.

Cha Cha Cha ★★ SEAFOOD/INTERNATIONAL   Fresh seafood and grilled meats, simply and expertly prepared. What more could you ask from a casual, open-air restaurant in a funky beach town? In addition to the fresh catch of the day and filet mignon, the menu here is an eclectic mix, including everything from jerk chicken and Thai shrimp salad to pasta primavera and fajitas. The grilled squid salad with a citrus dressing is one of the house specialties and a great light bite. The restaurant occupies the ground floor of an old wooden building. Everything is painted pure white, with some blue trim and accents. There are only a half-dozen or so tables, so the place fills up fast.

On the main road in town, 3 blocks north of Coco's Bar. ⓒ **394-4153.** Reservations recommended during the high season. Main courses $6–$20. MC, V. Tues–Sun 2–10pm.

Restaurant Edith ⭐ *Finds* CREOLE/SEAFOOD   This place has become a tradition, and deservedly so. Quite some years ago, Miss Edith decided to start serving home-cooked meals to all the hungry visitors hanging around. If you want a taste of the local cuisine in a homey, sit-down environment, this is the place. While Miss Edith's daughters take the orders, Mom cooks up a storm out back. The menu, when you can get hold of it, is long, with lots of local seafood dishes and Creole combinations such as yuca in coconut milk with meat or vegetables. The sauces here have spice and zest and are a welcome change from the typically bland fare served up throughout the rest of Costa Rica. After you've ordered, it's usually no more than 45 minutes until your meal arrives. It's often crowded here, so don't be bashful about sitting down with total strangers at any of the big tables. Miss Edith's place is at the opposite end of town from the park entrance; just turn right at the police station/post office.

By the police station, Cahuita. ⓒ **755-0248.** Main courses $3.50–$12. No credit cards. Mon–Sat 7–10am, noon–3pm, and 6–10pm; Sun 4–9pm. Sometimes closed without warning.

CAHUITA AFTER DARK
Coco's Bar ⭐, a classic Caribbean watering hole, has traditionally been the place to spend your nights (or days, for that matter) if you like cold beer and very loud reggae and soca music. **Ricky's Bar,** located just across the street, is giving Coco's a run for its money. Check them both out; on any given night, you might be more drawn to one or the other. There are usually local women hanging out on the front porches of each establishment, selling fresh *pati* pies or bowls of rundown stew (see "That Rundown Feeling" on p. 347). Toward the park entrance, the **National Park Restaurant** has a popular bar and disco on most nights during the high season and on weekends during the low season.

5 Puerto Viejo ⭐⭐
200km (124 miles) E of San José; 55km (34 miles) S of Limón

Although Puerto Viejo is farther down the road from Cahuita, it's become increasingly more popular and has a livelier atmosphere, due in part to the many surfers who come here from around the country (and around the world) to ride the village's famous Salsa Brava wave. For nonsurfers, there are also some good swimming beaches, plenty of active vacation options, nearby rainforest trails, and some great local and international restaurants. This area gets plenty of rain, just like the rest of the coast (Sept–Oct are your best bets for sun, although it's not guaranteed even in those months).

As you head still farther south, you will come to the most beautiful beaches on this coast, with white sand and turquoise seas. When it's calm (Aug–Oct), the waters down here are some of the clearest anywhere in the country, with good snorkeling among the nearby coral reefs. The recent paving of the road, all the way to Manzanillo, has made these beaches much more accessible, and there's been a slew of small moderately priced and budget hotels built along this stretch of coast.

This is the end of the line along Costa Rica's Caribbean coast. After the tiny town of Manzanillo, some 15km (9⅓ miles) south of Puerto Viejo, a national wildlife reserve stretches a few final kilometers to the Panamanian border.

You might notice as you make your way into town from the highway that there are cacao trees planted along the road. Most of these trees suffer from a blight that has greatly reduced the cacao-bean harvest in the area. However, there is still a modest harvest, and you can get delicious locally made cocoa candies here.

ESSENTIALS

GETTING THERE & DEPARTING   By Car   To reach Puerto Viejo, continue south from Cahuita for another 16km (10 miles). Watch for a prominent fork in the highway. The right-hand fork continues on to Bribri and Sixaola. The left-hand fork (it actually appears to be a straight shot) takes you into Puerto Viejo on 5km (3 miles) of paved road.

By Bus   MEPE express buses (© 257-8129) to Puerto Viejo leave San José daily at 6 and 10am, and 1:30 and 3:30pm from the new Caribbean bus terminal (Gran Terminal del Caribe) on Calle Central, 1 block north of Avenida 11. The trip's duration is 4½ to 5 hours; fare is $5.75. During peak periods, extra buses are sometimes added. Always ask if the bus is going into Puerto Viejo (you do not want to end up getting dropped off at the turnoff for Sixaola) and if it's continuing on to **Manzanillo** (especially helpful if you're staying in a hotel south of town). Regardless, don't be surprised if it doesn't do exactly what you were told.

Grayline (© 220-2126; www.graylinecostarica.com) has a daily bus that leaves San José for Puerto Viejo at 7am; the fare is $25. **Interbus** (© 283-5573; www. costaricapass.com) has a daily bus that leaves San José for Puerto Viejo at 10am; the fare is $25. Both companies will pick you up at most San José–area hotels.

Alternatively, you can catch a bus to **Limón** (see section 3, earlier in this chapter, for details) and then transfer to a Puerto Viejo–bound bus in Limón. These latter buses (© 758-0618) leave roughly every hour between 5am and 6pm from Radio Casino, which is 1 block north of the municipal market. Buses from Limón to Manzanillo also stop in Puerto Viejo and leave daily at 6am and 2:30pm. The trip takes 1½ hours; the fare is $2.

If you arrive by bus, be leery of hucksters offering you hotel rooms. In most cases, they just work on a small commission from whatever hotel or *cabina* is hiring, and, in some cases, they'll steer you away from one of my recommended hotels or falsely claim that it is full.

Express buses leave Puerto Viejo for San José daily at 7, 9, and 11am, and 4pm. Buses for Limón leave daily at 6 and 9am, and 1, 4, and 5pm. Buses to **Punta Uva** and **Manzanillo** leave Puerto Viejo daily around 7:30am and 4 and 7:30pm. These buses return from Manzanillo at 5 and 8:30am and 5pm.

ORIENTATION   The road in from the highway runs parallel to Playa Negra, or Black Sand Beach, for a couple hundred meters before entering the village of Puerto Viejo, which has all of about 10 dirt streets. The sea will be on your left and forested hills on your right as you come into town. It's another 15km (9⅓ miles) south to Manzanillo. This road is paved almost all the way to Manzanillo (at press time, there were a few small sections of gravel between Punta Uva and Manzanillo).

FAST FACTS   Public phones are located at Hotel Maritza, El Pizote lodge, and the Manuel Leon general store (next to Johnny's Place), as well as in front of the **ATEC office** (see below), across the street from the Soda Tamara. Those looking to change money should head to the new **Banco de Costa Rica** branch, located on the main road in town. There's also a **Banco Nacional** branch in **Bribri,** about 10km (6 miles) away. You'll find the **post office** in the tiny strip mall behind Café Viejo. There is a **Guardia Rural police** (© 750-0230) post on the beach, near Johnny's Place.

In addition to the ATEC office, there are a few little Internet cafes around town. The town's main **taxi** driver is named **Bull** (© 750-0112), and he drives a beat-up old Isuzu Trooper. You might find him hanging around the *parquecito* (little park), or you can ask a local to point you to his house. If Bull's not around or he's busy, you could try **Delroy** (© 750-0132).

WHAT TO SEE & DO

SUNNING & SURFING   **Surfing** has historically been the main draw here, but increasing numbers of folks are coming here for the miles of beautiful and uncrowded **beaches** ★★, acres of lush rainforests, and laid-back atmosphere. If you aren't a surfer, the same activities that prevail in any quiet beach town are the norm here—sunbathe, go for a walk on the beach, read a book, or take a nap. If you have more energy, there's a host of tours and hiking options, or you can rent a bicycle or a horse. (Watch for signs.) For swimming and sunbathing, locals like to hang out on the small patches of sand in front of Stanford's Disco and Johnny's Place. There are small, protected tide pools in front of each of these bars for cooling off.

If you want a more open patch of sand and sea, head north out to **Playa Negra** (this is not the same one I talked about in Cahuita), along the road into town, or, better yet, to the beaches south of town around Punta Uva and all the way down to Manzanillo, where the coral reefs keep the surf much more manageable (see "Manzanillo & the Manzanillo-Gandoca Wildlife Refuge," below).

Just offshore from the tiny village park is a shallow reef where powerful storm-generated waves sometimes reach 6m (20 ft.). **Salsa Brava,** as it's known, is the prime surf break on the Caribbean coast. Even when the waves are small, this spot is recommended only for very experienced surfers because of the danger of the reef. There are also popular beach breaks south of town on Playa Cocles.

Atlántico Tours (© 750-0004) rents boogie boards, snorkel gear, and bicycles (all for $10 per day). **Reef Runners Dive Shop** (© 750-0480) rents dive equipment and mask and fins (around $10); see below for details on its dive trips. Right in the heart of town, there's a makeshift stand (with no name or face) that faces the water and rents full-size surfboards.

CULTURAL & ADVENTURE TOURS   The **Asociación Talamanqueña de Ecoturismo y Conservación (ATEC)** ★, across the street from the Soda Tamara (© 750-0398 or ©/fax 750-0191; www.greencoast.com), is concerned with preserving both the environment and the cultural heritage of this area and promoting ecologically sound development. (If you're looking to stay in Puerto Viejo for an extended period of time and would like to contribute to the community, you can ask here about volunteering.) In addition to functioning as the local information center and traveler's hub, ATEC runs a little shop that sells T-shirts, maps, posters, and books.

ATEC also offers quite a few tours, including **half-day walks** that focus on nature and either the local Afro-Caribbean culture or the indigenous Bribri culture. These walks pass through farms and forests, and along the way you'll learn about local history, customs, medicinal plants, and Indian mythology, and have an opportunity to see sloths, monkeys, iguanas, keel-billed toucans, and other

---

Tips South Caribbean Music Festival

Each year, the folks at Playa Chiquita Lodge (p. 347) organize a month-long festival of concerts and workshops featuring local and national musical groups and solo artists. The dates vary, but the festival tends to fall somewhere during the months of March and April, and always ends the week before Easter. Concerts are usually held on Friday and weekends at Playa Chiquita Lodge and other venues around the area.

---

wildlife. There is a range of different walks through the nearby Bribri Indians' Kéköldi Reserve; there are also more strenuous hikes through the primary rainforest. **Bird walks** and **night walks** will help you spot more of the area wildlife; there are even overnight treks. The local guides who lead these tours have a wealth of information and make a hike through the forest a truly educational experience. Half-day walks (and night walks) are $15, and a full day costs between $25 and $40. ATEC can arrange snorkeling trips to the nearby coral reefs, as well as snorkeling and fishing trips in dugout canoes. A half day of snorkeling or fishing costs around $20 to $40 per person.

ATEC can also help you arrange overnight and multiday **camping trips** into the Talamanca Mountains and through neighboring indigenous reserves, as well as trips to Tortuguero and even a 7- to 10-day transcontinental trek to the Pacific coast. Some tours require minimum groups of 5 or 10 people and several days' advance notice. The ATEC office is open daily from 8am to 9pm.

Atlántico Tours (© 750-0004), **Puerto Viejo Tours & Rentals** (© 750-0411), and **Terraventuras** (© 750-0426; www.terraventuras.com) all offer a whole host of half- and full-day adventure tours into the jungle or sea for between $30 and $90 per person. Scuba divers can check in with the **Reef Runners Dive Shop** (© 750-0480); these folks charge $60 for a two-tank dive, including all your equipment and a guide. They frequent about 10 different dive sites between Punta Uva and Manzanillo, and when the seas are calm and visibility is good, this is some good diving.

NOT YOUR EVERYDAY GARDENS One of the nicest ways to spend a day in Puerto Viejo is to visit the **Tropical Botanical Gardens** ★★ (© **750-0046;** jardbot@racsa.co.cr), located a couple hundred meters inland from the Black Sand Beach on a side road just north of El Pizote lodge. Hosts Peter and Lindy Kring have poured time and love into the creation of this meandering collection of native and imported tropical flora. There are medicinal, commercial, and just plain wild flowering plants, fruits, herbs, trees, and bushes. Visitors get to gorge on whatever is ripe at the moment. There is also a rigorous rainforest loop trail leaving from the grounds. The gardens are generally open Friday through Monday from 10am to 4pm, but visits can sometimes be arranged for other days with advance notice. Entrance to the garden or loop trail is $3 per person, or $8 with the guided tour.

Farther down the road, near Punta Uva, you'll find the **Punta Uva Butterfly Garden** ★ (© **750-0086**). This small yet well-run facility is the only butterfly-breeding and production facility along the coast, and is open daily from 8am to 4pm. Admission is $5 for adults; children enter free.

A LITTLE MIND & BODY REVITALIZATION Check in with **Samasati** ★ (© **800/563-9643** in the U.S., or 224-1870 in Costa Rica; www.samasati.com), a lovely jungle yoga retreat with spectacular hillside views of the Caribbean Sea and surrounding forests. Rates here run between $62 and $148 per person per day, depending on occupancy and room type, and include three vegetarian meals per day. A wide range of tour, massage, and yoga packages are available. If you're staying elsewhere in Puerto Viejo or Cahuita, you can come up for yoga classes ($12), meditations ($5), or private massages ($60) with advance notice. Samasati is located a couple of kilometers before Puerto Viejo (near the turnoff for Bribri) and roughly 1.6km (1 mile) up into the jungle.

MANZANILLO & THE MANZANILLO-GANDOCA WILDLIFE REFUGE ★★

If you continue south on the coast road from Puerto Viejo, you'll come to a couple of even smaller villages. **Punta Uva** ★★ is 8km (5 miles) away, and **Manzanillo** ★★ is about 15km (9⅓ miles) away. For a good day trip, you can catch the 7:30am bus from Puerto Viejo down to Manzanillo and then catch the 5pm bus back. (It's always wise to check with ATEC about current local bus schedules.) You could also hire a cab for around $6 to Punta Uva or $9 to Manzanillo. Alternatively, it's about 1½ hours each way by bicycle, with only two relatively small hills to contend with; except for a couple of short washed-out patches, the road is paved all the way to Manzanillo. It's even possible to walk along the beach all the way from Puerto Viejo to Manzanillo, with just a couple of short and well-worn detours inland around rocky points.

Manzanillo is a tiny village with only a few basic *cabinas* and funky *sodas,* although this is starting to change. The most popular place to eat and hang out is **Restaurant Maxi** ★ (© 759-9073), an open-air joint located on the second floor of an old wooden building facing the sea. This place gets packed on weekends, especially for lunch.

The **Manzanillo-Gandoca Wildlife Refuge** ★★ encompasses the small village and extends all the way to the Panamanian border. Manatees, crocodiles, and more than 350 species of birds live within the boundaries of the reserve. The reserve also includes the coral reef offshore—when the seas are calm, this is the best **snorkeling** and **diving** spot on this entire coast. Four species of **sea turtles** nest on one 8.9km (5½-mile) stretch of beach within the reserve between March and July. Three species of dolphin also inhabit and frolic in the waters just off Manzanillo. Many local tour guides and operators offer boat trips out to spot them. If you're looking for a more in-depth experience, including research internships, contact the **Talamanca Dolphin Foundation** (© 759-9115; www.dolphinlink.org).

If you want to explore the refuge, you can easily find the single, well-maintained trail by walking along the beach just south of town until you have to wade across a small river. On the other side, you'll pick up the trail head. Otherwise, you can ask around the village for local guides or check out **Aquamor** (© 759-9012; aquamor1@racsa.co.cr), a kayak and dive operation located on the one main road in town. These folks rent kayaks for $6 per hour and offer a variety of guided excursions for between $15 and $55 per person. Depending on tides and sea conditions, this is a great way to explore the mangroves and estuaries, visit several nearby beaches, and even snorkel or dive the nearby coral reef. A one-tank beach dive, with equipment and guide, costs $30 per person. They have a whole variety of tour and diving options, including PADI dive-certification courses, hikes into the Talamanca Mountains, dolphin-watching excursions, and trips to Bocas del Toro, Panama.

Serious fishermen looking to hook a tarpon should check in with **Manzanillo Tarpon Expeditions** (℗ 759-0715; www.tarponville.com).

SHOPPING

Puerto Viejo attracts a lot of local and international bohemians, who seem to survive solely on the sale of handmade jewelry, painted ceramic trinkets (mainly pipes and cigarette-lighter holders), and imported Indonesian textiles. You'll find them at makeshift stands set up by the town's *parquecito* (little park), a few wooden benches in front of the sea between Soda Tamara and Stanford's.

In addition to the makeshift outdoor stands is a host of well-stocked gift and crafts shops in town. **Boutique Tabu,** located near the Mepe bus stop, sells hand-painted T-shirts, batik beachwear, and coconut-shell jewelry. **Luluberlu,** located inland across from Cabinas Guaraná, features locally produced craft-work, including shell mobiles and mirrors with mosaic-inlaid frames, as well as imports from Thailand and India. **The Jewelry Factory** and **Color Caribe,** both on the main road into town, sell a wide range of jewelry, crafts, and gift items, as well as Costa Rican hammocks.

WHERE TO STAY
IN PUERTO VIEJO

True budget hounds will find a host of basic *cabinas* in downtown Puerto Viejo in addition to the hotels listed below. Of these, **Cabinas Guaraná** (℗ 750-0024), **Hotel Pura Vida** (℗ 750-0002; fax 750-0296), and **Cabinas Maritza** (℗ 750-0003; fax 750-0313) are all good bets; however, the new **Rocking J's** (℗ 750-0657; www.rockingjs.com), a sprawling compound offering simple rooms, camping spaces, and a "hammock hotel," is quickly becoming the preferred spot for backpackers, surfers, and students.

For more isolated options, try **Cabinas Black Sands** (℗ 750-0124; fax 750-0188), on the northern end of Black Beach, or **Escape Caribeño** (℗ 750-0103; www.escapecaribeno.com), just south of Salsa Brava.

Moderate

El Pizote   El Pizote is the largest and most modern hotel in Puerto Viejo proper, but that's not necessarily saying much: None of the rooms here has a television or telephone, some are actually quite old and are showing their age, and some even have shared bathrooms. The hotel is located 100m (328 ft.) or so inland from a long, quiet stretch of black sand beach, about 400m (1,312 ft.) before you reach downtown proper.

The four deluxe bungalows are modern concrete-block affairs, with a small kitchenette, two separate bedrooms, one small bathroom, air-conditioning, and a private porch. Although they are older and funkier, the standard bungalows have much more character. These raised wooden buildings have dark, stained wood walls; steeply pitched roofs; ceiling fans; private porches; and larger step-down bathrooms. The most basic rooms are in a U-shape wooden building. These rooms are cool, and come with two double beds, a ceiling fan, a shared wraparound veranda, and shared bathroom facilities. Everything is set amid lush gardens, assorted tropical fruit trees, and a few towering rainforest trees. For activity, there are hiking trails in the adjacent forest, and there's good bird-watching here, too.

Just off the main road, about 275m (902 ft.) before you enter downtown, Puerto Viejo, Limón. ℗ 750-0088. Fax 750-0226. 8 units, none with bathroom; 10 bungalows. $48 double; $60 double bungalow; $86 double deluxe bungalow. AE, MC, V. **Amenities:** Restaurant; bar; pool and adjacent kid's pool; laundry service. *In room:* No phone.

Inexpensive

Cabinas Casa Verde ⭐ *Value*   This little hotel is located on a side street on the south side of town and is my favorite hotel right in Puerto Viejo, regardless of price. A quiet sense of tropical tranquillity pervades this place. The rooms with shared bathrooms are housed in a raised building with a wide, covered breezeway between the rooms. The front and back porches of this building are hung with hammocks and surrounded by lush gardens, where you'll find the showers and toilets. The rest of the rooms are spread around the small complex. Most are larger, with high ceilings, tile floors, private bathrooms, and a private veranda. There's also a small separate bungalow with a kitchenette. Everything is very well maintained, and even the shared bathrooms are kept immaculate. There's also a small but well-stocked gift shop, a coffee shop, and a poison-dart frog garden. Even though it's an in-town choice, there's great bird-watching all around the grounds here.

A.P. 1115, Puerto Limón. ⓒ 750-0015. Fax 750-0047. www.cabinascasaverde.com. 17 units, 9 with private bathroom. $22–$26 double with shared bathroom; $37 double with private bathroom. Rates slightly higher during peak weeks, lower in the off season. AE, MC, V. *In room:* Fridge in some units, no phone.

Cabinas Jacarandá *Value*   This basic backpackers' special has a few nice touches that set it apart from the others. Guatemalan bedspreads add a dash of color and tropical flavor, as do the tables made from sliced tree trunks. Most rooms and walkways feature intricate and colorful tilework, Japanese paper lanterns cover the lights, mosquito nets hang over the beds, and covered walkways connect the various buildings in this budding compound. If you're traveling in a group, you'll enjoy the space and atmosphere of the big room. If the hotel is full, the owners also rent a few nearby bungalows.

1½ blocks inland from Marco's Pizzería, Puerto Viejo, Limón. ⓒ/fax 750-0069. 10 units, 7 with private bathroom. $15 double with shared bathroom; $20 double with private bathroom. MC, V. *In room:* No phone.

BETWEEN PUERTO VIEJO & MANZANILLO

All the hotels listed below are located along the road south of Puerto Viejo heading toward Manzanillo. This is one of the most beautiful and isolated stretches of beach in Costa Rica. The single coastal road here has been paved all the way to Manzanillo, greatly improving access to this area. I recommend that you have a vehicle if you plan to stay at one of these hotels because public transportation is sporadic. If you arrive by bus, however, a rented bicycle might be all you need to get around once you are settled.

In addition to the hotels listed below, budget travelers should check out **La Isla** (ⓒ/fax **750-0109**), a simple hotel catering to surfers, located at the start of Playa Cocles.

Moderate

Almonds & Corals Tent Camp   This isn't camping in any traditional sense, so don't expect to rough it. You'll find large raised platforms, big enough so that within the stretched-tarp roof and screened walls there's another large standing-room tent, providing double protection against rain and mosquitoes. This second tent takes up about half of the platform's screened-in floor space and still leaves room for a hammock, a table, chairs, and a bathroom area with a cold-water shower and toilet. Inside the tent you'll find either two single beds or one double bed, a small table, two oil lamps, and a small closet. The tents are in dense secondary forest, with nothing but screen and cloth for walls, so you'll feel very close to nature. There are wooden walkways connecting the tents to the main lodge and dining area. Perhaps the best part of the whole setup is the fact that Manzanillo Beach is just about 180m (590 ft.) away through the jungle. Snorkel equipment, sea kayaks, and a variety of tours are also available, and there's a zip-line canopy tour through the forest here that ends right at the beach.

Manzanillo, Limón (A.P. 681-2300, San José). ✆ 272-2024, or 759-9057 at the lodge. Fax 272-2220. www.almondsandcorals.com. 24 tents. $130 double. Rates include breakfast, dinner, and taxes. Rates slightly lower in the off season. AE, MC, V. **Amenities:** Restaurant; bar; Jacuzzi; watersports equipment rental; laundry service. *In room:* No phone.

Azania Bungalows ★ *Finds*
This new collection of private bungalows is yet another excellent option for those seeking a quiet, romantic tropical getaway. The spacious bungalows are set apart from each other amid the hotel's high flowering gardens, giving each a sense of seclusion. All come with one queen-size bed and one double bed downstairs, and another double bed in the small loft. The thatch roofs are high-pitched and, combined with large, screened windows, allow for good cross ventilation. The lounge area features a television with DirecTV, a small lending library, and a collection of board games. When I last visited, there were plans to add a swimming pool.

Playa Cocles, Puerto Viejo, Limón. ✆ 750-0540. Fax 750-0371. www.azania-costarica.com. 8 bungalows. $65 double. Rates include full breakfast. Rates lower in the off season. AE, DC, MC, V. **Amenities:** Restaurant; lounge; bike and boogie-board rental; laundry service. *In room:* Fridge, no phone.

Cariblue Bungalows ★
This Italian-owned bed-and-breakfast is a wonderful choice in this neck of the woods. The rooms are spread around the well-tended and lush grounds. My favorites are the raised-stilt wood bungalows, with spacious bedrooms featuring either one king-size bed and one single bed, or two queen-size beds. The beds are covered with mosquito nets, and there's a small veranda with a hammock. The nicest features here are the bathrooms, with their intricate mosaic tile designs. The standard rooms are in a couple of concrete-block buildings with high-pitched thatch roofs. They are also spacious and comfortable, but not quite as private or charming as the bungalows. There's also a two-bedroom house with a full kitchen, for families or for longer stays. The most recent and welcome addition here is a free-form swimming pool with swim-up bar. There are also plans to add an open-air yoga and exercise room. Cariblue is located about 90m (295 ft.) or so inland from the southern end of Playa Cocles.

Playa Cocles, Puerto Viejo (A.P. 51-7304), Limón. ✆ 750-0035 or ✆/fax 750-0057. www.cariblue.com. 14 units, 1 house. $75–$90 double; $185 house. Rates include breakfast buffet. AE, MC, V. **Amenities:** Restaurant; bar/lounge; pool; bike and boogie-board rental; laundry service. *In room:* Coffeemaker, hair dryer, iron, safe, no phone.

Casa Camarona
Casa Camarona has the enviable distinction of being another of the handful of hotels in this area right on the beach. There's no road to cross and no path through the jungle—just a small section of shady gardens separates you from a quiet section of Playa Cocles and the Caribbean Sea. The rooms are in two separate two-story buildings. Definitely get a room on the second floor. Up there you'll find spacious rooms painted in pleasant pastels, with plenty of cross ventilation and a wide shared veranda. I don't know who designed the first-floor rooms, but several of them have such low ceilings that I felt as tall as Yao Ming—and believe me, I'm not. The hotel keeps some chaise longues on the beach under the shade of palm trees, and there's even a beach bar open during the day, so you barely have to leave that chaise to quench your thirst.

Playa Cocles, Puerto Viejo, Limón (mailing address: A.P. 2270-1002, Paseo de los Estudiantes, San José). ✆ 283-6711 or 750-0151. Fax 222-6184. www.casacamarona.co.cr. 16 units. $55–$76 double. Rates include continental breakfast. AE, MC, V. **Amenities:** Restaurant; bar. *In room:* A/C in some units, no phone.

Shawandha Lodge ★★ *Finds*   If you're looking for an isolated and romantic getaway, in a style best described as rustic luxury, this small collection of individual bungalows is a great choice. Set in a lush patch of forest about 180m (590 ft.) or so inland from Playa Chiquita, Shawandha has the feel of a small village. Artistic flourishes abound. The thatch-roofed, raised bungalows feature painted exterior murals, high-pitched ceilings, varnished wood floors, and either one king-size bed or a mix of queen-size and single beds. The bathrooms are practically works of art, each with original, intricate mosaics of hand-cut tile highlighting a large, open shower. Every bungalow has its own spacious balcony, with both a hammock and a couch, where you can lie and look out on the lush, flowering gardens. The beach is easily accessed by a private path, and a host of activities and tours can be arranged.

There's a large open-air restaurant and lounge where meals and drinks are served. The menu is an eclectic mix, featuring fresh fish and meats in a variety of French, Caribbean, and Polynesian sauces.

Puerto Viejo, Limón. © **750-0018.** Fax 750-0037. www.shawandhalodge.com. 14 units. Dec 15–Apr 30 $90 double; May 1–Dec 14 $75 double. Rates include full breakfast. AE, MC, V. **Amenities:** Restaurant; laundry service. *In room:* No phone.

Villas del Caribe ★   If you want to be right on the water's edge and have spacious, comfortable accommodations, there isn't a better choice in this area. Villas del Caribe offers two-story villas with full kitchens and a choice of one or two bedrooms. The living rooms have built-in sofa beds, and just outside there is a large terrace complete with a barbecue grill. The kitchens are attractively designed with blue-and-white–tile counters and are fully equipped. Bathrooms feature wooden-slat shower doors, potted plants on a platform by the window, louvered and screened walls that let in light and air, and more blue-tile counters. Upstairs you'll find either a large single bedroom with a king-size bed or two smaller bedrooms (one with bunk beds). Either way, there's a balcony with a hammock and an ocean view.

The water, which is usually fairly calm, is only steps away through the coconut palms. Sand beaches can be found a couple hundred meters in either direction, and right in front of the hotel are some coral reefs and tide pools that make for good snorkeling. The hotel offers beach towels and beach chairs.

Puerto Viejo, Limón (A.P. 8080-1000, San José). © **750-0202** or 233-2200. Fax 750-0203. www.villasdel caribe.com. 12 units. $69–$89 double. Rates include continental breakfast. AE, DC, MC, V. **Amenities:** Restaurant; limited watersports equipment rental; tour desk; babysitting; laundry service. *In room:* Kitchen, no phone.

Inexpensive

Cabinas Selvyn   The atmosphere here is friendly and funky. Rooms are located in a few two-story buildings behind the small open-air restaurant. All the rooms come with mosquito nets and fans, but beyond that, the accommodations are spartan. If you land a second-floor room facing the sea, you might get a bit of a breeze. The hotel is located about 100m (328 ft.) down a dirt lane from one of the most isolated and beautiful beaches in Costa Rica. The hotel's owner, Selvyn Brown, is a great cook and wonderful raconteur.

Punta Uva, Limón. No phone. 10 units, all with shared bathroom; 2 apts. $10–$15 double; $200–$250 per month for apt. No credit cards. **Amenities:** Restaurant. *In room:* No phone.

La Costa del Papito *Value*   This small collection of individual and duplex cabins offers some of the same feel and character as Shawandha and Cariblue, with fewer amenities and less luxury—but at lower rates. La Costa del Papito is located just across from Cocles beach, about 1.6km (1 mile) south of Puerto Viejo. The wooden bungalows, which are a little dark inside, come with one or two double beds, artfully tiled bathrooms, and an inviting private porch with a table and chairs and either a hammock or a swing chair. Only breakfast, snacks, and drinks are served here, so you'll have to head into Puerto Viejo or farther down the road for the rest of your meals.

Playa Cocles, Puerto Viejo, Limón. ©/fax 750-0080. www.greencoast.com/papito.htm. 10 units. $39–$56 double. Rates lower in the off season. AE, MC, V. *In room:* No phone.

Playa Chiquita Lodge *Value* *Kids*   Set amid the shade of large old trees a few kilometers south of Puerto Viejo toward Punta Uva (watch for the sign), the lodge consists of several wooden buildings set on stilts and connected by a garden walkway. There are wide verandas with built-in seating and rocking chairs. The whole place received a bit of an overhaul in 2003. The spacious rooms were again repainted in bright colors, and the bathrooms were remodeled, with gas water heaters replacing the electric showerhead elements. There is a short trail that leads down to a semiprivate little swimming beach with tide pools and beautiful turquoise water. This stretch of beach is the site of a daily 4pm volleyball game.

Throughout the day, there are free bananas and coffee. The owners have three children, ranging from a toddler to a teenager, and travelers with kids often feel like part of the family. The owners also rent out fully equipped houses for those interested in longer stays or more privacy and independence.

Puerto Viejo, Limón. © 750-0062 or ©/fax 750-0408. www.playachiquitalodge.com. 10 units. $46 double. Rates lower in the off season. Rates include breakfast. AE, MC, V. **Amenities:** Restaurant. *In room:* No phone.

WHERE TO DINE
IN PUERTO VIEJO

To really sample the local cuisine, you need to look up a few local women. Ask around for **Miss Dolly, Miss Daisy, Miss Sam, Miss Isma,** and **Miss Irma,** who all serve up sit-down meals in their modest little *sodas.* In addition to locally seasoned fish and chicken served with rice and beans, these joints are usually a great place to find some *pan bon* (a local sweet, dark bread), ginger cakes, *paty* (meat-filled turnovers), and *rondon* (see below). Just ask around for these women, and someone will direct you to them.

Puerto Viejo has become a very popular destination for Italian immigrants, and it seems there's a pretty decent Italian restaurant everywhere you turn. In addition to the restaurants listed below, you can get good Italian cuisine at **Café Viejo,** right in town. If you're looking for a light bite for breakfast, lunch, or a snack, check out **Pan Pay,** a French-run bakery and sandwich shop located next to Johnny's Place (see "Puerto Viejo After Dark," below).

My favorite restaurant in the area, **The Garden** (© 750-0069), located next to Cabinas Jacaranda, has been closed more often than not in recent years. When you get to Puerto Viejo, it's worth your while to see if it's open again.

Reservations are not needed at any of the restaurants in town.

Tips **That Rundown Feeling**

Don't be discouraged by signs advertising "rundown" soup or stew. It's not what you think. Rundown (or *rondon*) soup is a spicy coconut-milk stew made with anything the cook can run down. Be sure to try this authentic taste of the Caribbean.

Amimodo ✦ NORTHERN ITALIAN   You can't find better Italian food in Puerto Viejo proper. The dining room occupies the open-air bottom floor of a traditional local raised stilt house. It's airy, and there's lots of whitewashed wood and gingerbread trim. On good days, you can feel the sea breeze coming in off the ocean about 100m (328 ft.) away. The sturdy wood tables have hand-painted trim patterns that match the painted chairs. Be sure to begin your meal with the *jamón de tiburón,* thin slices of home-smoked shark served with freshly baked bread and a light avocado dressing. I also recommend the homemade ravioli stuffed with lobster in a lobster and cognac–based red sauce, and the gnocchi, which melt in your mouth. If you've got room for dessert, opt for the chocolate salami. There's a small bar that sometimes fills with locals and a big-screen TV that broadcasts the most important soccer games and Italian television programs.

On the left-hand side of the main road heading south of Puerto Viejo, just after Cabinas Salsa Brava. ℰ 750-0257. Main courses $5–$19. AE, MC, V. Mon–Fri 6–11pm; Sat–Sun noon–4pm and 6–11pm.

El Loco Natural ✦✦ INTERNATIONAL   A funky, hippy vibe pervades this second-floor open-air restaurant. Seating is at heavy wooden tables, and if the few smaller, more private tables are all taken, you can take any empty seat at one of the larger communal tables. The short menu features several vegetarian items, as well as fresh fish and some chicken and meat dishes, prepared in curry, Thai, and Mexican sauces. There's often live music here, running the gamut from reggae to jazz, to Latin American folk.

On the main road. ℰ 750-0263. Main courses $4–$10. AE, MC, V. Thurs–Sun 5–10pm.

The Place INTERNATIONAL   If you want a quick, casual meal, check out this humble little restaurant located on a side street just off the bus stop. The Place features a small menu with daily specials and excellent sandwiches. The menu is eclectic—it might feature anything from vegetarian nori rolls to curried chicken, to the local *rondon* stew.

On a side street ½ block inland from the bus stop. ℰ 750-0195. Main courses $3–$8. AE, MC, V. Fri–Wed 8am–10pm.

Soda Tamara COSTA RICAN   This little Tico-style restaurant has long been popular with budget-conscious travelers and has an attractive setting for such an economical place. There's an open-air dining area, which is larger and more comfortable than the somewhat cramped indoor dining room. The painted picket fence in front gives the restaurant a homey feel. The menu features standard fish, chicken, and meat entrees, served with a hefty helping of Caribbean-style rice and beans. You can also get *patacones* (fried chips made out of plantains) and a wide selection of fresh-fruit juices. At the counter inside, you'll find homemade cocoa candies and unsweetened cocoa biscuits made by several women in town. They're definitely worth a try. Soda Tamara also has a second-floor open-air bar that's open nightly from 6pm until the last straggler calls it quits.

On the main road. ℰ 750-0148. Main courses $3.50–$15. AE, MC, V. Daily 7am–10pm.

BETWEEN PUERTO VIEJO & MANZANILLO

As the beaches stretching south of Puerto Viejo keep getting more popular, there has been a corresponding increase in the number of places to grab a meal. In addition to the restaurants listed above and below, **Cabinas Selvyn,** at Punta Uva, and **Bar & Restaurant Elena's,** at Playa Chiquita (ℰ 750-0265), are two very popular and dependable spots for local cuisine. **El Duende Feliz** is yet another excellent little Italian joint, out toward Playa Cocles.

If you make it as far south as Manzanillo, **Restaurant Maxi** ★ (© **759-9073**) is your best bet. This open-air spot is always packed, especially for lunch. A fresh-fish plate will cost you between $5 and $7; lobster, in season, will cost around $12. Whatever you order comes with rice and beans, patacones, and a small side of cabbage salad. For fancier fare, check out the restaurant at **Shawandha Lodge** (p. 346).

La Pecora Nera ★★ *Finds* ITALIAN   This open-air joint on the jungle's edge has handily replaced Amimodo as the finest Italian restaurant in the region, if not the country. Owner Ilario Giannoni is a whirlwind of enthusiasm and activity, switching hats all night long from maitre d' to chef to waiter to busboy and back in an entertaining blur. Sure, he's got some help, including his grandmother making gnocchi, but it seems like he's doing it single-handedly. The menu has a broad selection of pizzas and pastas, but your best bet is to just ask Ilario what's fresh and special for that day, and to trust his instincts and inventions. I've had fabulous fresh pasta dishes and top-notch appetizers every time I've visited.

50m (164 ft.) inland from a well-marked turnoff on the main road south just beyond the soccer field in Cocles. © **750-0490.** Reservations recommended. Main courses $8–$25. AE, MC, V. Tues–Sun noon–10pm.

PUERTO VIEJO AFTER DARK

There are two main disco/bars in town. **Johnny's Place** ★★ is near the Rural Guard station, about 100m (328 ft.) or so north of the ATEC office. You'll find **Stanford's** overlooking the water out near Salsa Brava just as the main road heads south of town. Both have small dance floors with ground-shaking reggae, dub, and rap rhythms blaring. The action usually spills out from the dance floor at both joints on most nights. I like the atmosphere better at Johnny's, where they have tables and candles set out on the sand, near the water's edge.

Another place I like is **El Bambú** ★, just beyond Stanford's on the road toward Punta Uva. It's smaller and more intimate than either of the other bars, yet it still packs them in and gets them dancing on the Monday or Friday reggae nights.

Visitors and locals alike take advantage of the pool table, board games, and DirecTV (usually showing sporting events) at **El Dorado,** in front of the ATEC office, as an alternative to the loud music and dance scenes of the other joints mentioned above. There's also an open-air bar on the second floor of **Soda Tamara** (p. 348), which has become a casual and quiet place to gather after dark. **Neptunos Bar** has begun hosting open jam sessions on Wednesday night.

Appendix A:
Costa Rica in Depth

Costa Rica is, and has historically been, a sea of tranquillity in a region that has been troubled by turmoil for centuries. For more than 100 years, it has enjoyed a stable democracy and a relatively high standard of living for Latin America. The literacy rate is high, as are medical standards and facilities. Perhaps most significant, at least for proud Costa Ricans, is that this country does not have an army. When former Costa Rican president Oscar Arias Sánchez was awarded the Nobel Peace Prize for negotiating a peace settlement in Central America in 1987, Costa Rica was able to claim credit for exporting a bit of its own political stability to the rest of the region.

1 The Natural Environment

Costa Rica occupies a central spot in the isthmus that joins North and South America. For millennia, this land bridge served as a migratory thoroughfare and mating ground for species native to the once-separate continents. It was also the meeting place of Mesoamerican and Andean pre-Columbian indigenous cultures.

The country comprises only .01% of the earth's landmass, yet it is home to 5% of the planet's biodiversity. More than 10,000 identified species of plants, 850 species of birds, 800 species of butterflies, and 500 species of mammals, reptiles, and amphibians are found here.

The key to this biological richness lies in the many distinct life zones and ecosystems found in Costa Rica. It might all seem like one big mass of green to the untrained eye, but the differences are profound.

In any one spot in Costa Rica, temperatures remain relatively constant year-round. However, they vary dramatically according to altitude, from tropically hot and steamy along the coasts to below freezing at the highest elevations.

Costa Rica's **lowland rainforests** are true tropical jungles. Some are deluged with more than 200 inches of rainfall per year, and their climate is hot and humid. Trees grow tall and fast, fighting for sunlight in the upper reaches. In fact, life and foliage on the forest floor are surprisingly sparse. The action is typically 30m (98 ft.) above, in the canopy, where long vines stream down, lianas climb up, and bromeliads grow on the branches and trunks of towering hardwood trees. You can find these lowland rainforests along the southern Pacific coast and Osa Peninsula, as well as along the Caribbean coast. **Corcovado, Cahuita,** and **Manuel Antonio** national parks, as well as the **Manzanillo-Gandoca Wildlife Refuge,** are fine examples of lowland rainforests.

At higher altitudes, you'll find Costa Rica's famed **cloud forests.** Here the steady flow of moist air meets the mountains and creates a nearly constant mist. Epiphytes—resourceful plants that live cooperatively on the branches and trunks of other trees—grow abundantly in the cloud forests, where they must extract moisture and nutrients from the air. Because cloud forests are found in generally steep, mountainous terrain, the canopy here is lower and less uniform than in lowland rainforests, providing better chances for viewing elusive fauna.

Costa Rica's most spectacular cloud forest is the **Monteverde Biological Cloud Forest Reserve** in Guanacaste province (see chapter 6).

At the highest reaches, the cloud forests give way to **elfin forests** and *páramos.* More commonly associated with the South American Andes, a páramo is characterized by a variety of tundralike shrubs and grasses, with a scattering of twisted, windblown trees. Reptiles, rodents, and raptors are the most common residents here. **Mount Chirripó, Chirripó National Park,** and the **Cerro de la Muerte (Mountain of Death)** are the principal areas of páramo in Costa Rica.

In a few protected areas of Guanacaste, you will still find examples of the otherwise vanishing **tropical dry forest.** During the long and pronounced dry season (late Nov to late Apr), no rain relieves the unabated heat. In an effort to conserve much-needed water, the trees drop their leaves but bloom in a riot of color: purple jacaranda, scarlet poró, and brilliant orange flame-of-the-forest are just a few examples. Then during the rainy season, this deciduous forest is transformed into a lush and verdant landscape. Because the foliage is not so dense, the dry forests are excellent places to view a variety of wildlife species, especially howler monkeys and pizotes (coati). Dry forests are found in **Santa Rosa** and **Guanacaste** national parks.

Along the coasts, primarily where river mouths meet the ocean, you will find extensive **mangrove forests** and **swamps.** Around these seemingly monotonous tangles of roots exists one of the most diverse and rich ecosystems in the country. All sorts of fish and crustaceans live in the brackish tidal waters. Caimans and crocodiles cruise the maze of rivers and unmarked canals, and hundreds of herons, ibises, egrets, and other marsh birds nest and feed along the silty banks. Mangrove swamps are often havens for water birds: cormorants, frigate birds, pelicans, and herons. The larger birds tend to nest up high in the canopy, while the smaller ones nestle in the underbrush. The **Gulf of Nicoya** is particularly popular among frigate birds and brown pelicans, as well as all manner of terns and seagulls.

Over the last decade or so, Costa Rica has taken great strides toward protecting its rich biodiversity. Thirty years ago, it was difficult to find a protected area anywhere, but now more than 11% of the country is protected within the national park system. Another 10% to 15% of the land enjoys moderately effective preservation as part of private and public reserves, Indian reserves, and wildlife refuges and corridors. Still, Costa Rica's precious tropical hardwoods continue to be harvested at an alarming rate, often illegally, while other primary forests are clear-cut for short-term agricultural gain. Many experts predict that Costa Rica's unprotected forests will be gone by the early part of this century.

This is also a land of high volcanic and seismic activity. There are three major **volcanic mountain ranges** in Costa Rica, and many of the volcanoes are still active, allowing visitors to experience the awe-inspiring sight of steaming fumaroles and intense lava flows during their stay. Two volcanoes near the capital—Poás and Irazú—are currently active, although relatively quiet. The best places to see volcanic activity are farther north in **Rincón de la Vieja National Park** and at **Arenal Volcano** (see chapters 5 and 6).

SEARCHING FOR WILDLIFE

Animals in the forests are predominantly nocturnal. When they are active in the daytime, they are usually elusive and on the watch for predators. Birds are easier to spot in clearings or secondary forests than they are in primary forests.

Unless you have lots of experience in the tropics, your best hope for enjoying a walk through the jungle lies in employing a trained and knowledgeable guide. (By the way, if it's been raining a lot and the trails are muddy, a good pair of rubber boots comes in handy. These are usually provided by the lodges or at the sites, where necessary.)

Here are a few helpful hints:

- **Listen.** Pay attention to rustling in the leaves; whether it's monkeys up above or pizotes on the ground, you're most likely to hear an animal before seeing one.
- **Keep quiet.** Noise will scare off animals and prevent you from hearing their movements and calls.
- **Don't try too hard.** Soften your focus and allow your peripheral vision to take over. This way you can catch glimpses of motion and then focus in on the prey.
- **Bring your own binoculars.** It's also a good idea to practice a little first, to get the hang of them. It would be a shame to be fiddling around and staring into space while everyone else in your group oohs and aahs over a quetzal.
- **Dress appropriately.** You'll have a hard time focusing your binoculars if you're busy swatting mosquitoes. Light, long pants and long-sleeved shirts are your best bet. Comfortable hiking boots are a real boon, except where heavy rubber boots are necessary. Avoid loud colors; the better you blend in with your surroundings, the better your chances are of spotting wildlife.
- **Be patient.** The jungle isn't on a schedule. However, your best shot at seeing forest fauna is in the very early-morning and late-afternoon hours.
- **Read up.** Familiarize yourself with what you're most likely to see. Most lodges and hotels have a copy of *A Guide to the Birds of Costa Rica* (Cornell University Press, 1990) and other wildlife field guides, although it's always best to have your own.

2 Costa Rica Today

Costa Rica has a population of roughly four million, more than half of whom live in the Central Valley and are classified as urban. Nearly 96% of the population is of Spanish or otherwise European descent, and it is not at all unusual to see fair-skinned and blond Costa Ricans. This is largely because the indigenous population in place when the first Spaniards arrived was small and thereafter was quickly reduced to even more of a minority by wars and disease. There are still some remnant indigenous populations, primarily on reservations around the country; the principal tribes include the Bribri, Cabécar, Boruca, and Guaymí. In addition, on the Caribbean coast and in the big cities, there is a substantial population of English-speaking black Creoles who came over from the Antilles to work on the railroad and in the banana plantations. Racial tension isn't palpable, but it exists, perhaps more out of standard ignorance and fear rather than an organized or articulated prejudice.

In general, Costa Ricans (who call themselves Ticos, a practice that stems from their tendency to add a diminutive, either "tico" or "ito," to the ends of words to connote familiarity or affection) are a friendly and outgoing people. In conversation and interaction with visitors, Ticos are very open and helpful. Time has relative meaning to Ticos. Although most tour companies and other establishments operate efficiently, don't expect punctuality, in general.

In a region plagued by internal strife and civil wars, Costa Ricans are proud of their peaceful history, political stability, and relatively high level of development.

However, this can also translate into arrogance and prejudice toward immigrants from neighboring countries, particularly Nicaraguans, who make up a large percentage of the workforce on the banana and coffee plantations.

Roman Catholicism is the official religion of Costa Rica, although freedom to practice any religion is guaranteed by the country's constitution. More than 90% of the population identifies itself as Roman Catholic, yet there are small but visible evangelical Christian, Protestant, and Jewish communities. By and large, Ticos are relatively religious. Although many city dwellers lead quite secular lives, those in small villages and towns attend Mass regularly.

Modern Costa Rica is a nation of contrasts. On one hand, it's the most technologically advanced and politically stable nation in Central America, and it has the largest middle class. Even the smallest towns have electricity, the water is mostly safe to drink, and the phone system is relatively good. On the other hand, Costa Rica finds itself in the midst of a huge economic transition. In real terms, the gap between rich and poor is widening. The government and banking institutions are regularly embroiled in scandal. To come to terms with decades of trade deficits and pay back its debt, there has been a move toward economic austerity and privatization, overburdening and underfunding the country's vast network of social services, particularly its health-care system and its educational institutions. This has led to public protests and demonstrations, increased unemployment, lower wages, higher taxes, and more expensive goods and services. And there are no immediate signs of this condition changing. Several "Free Zones" and some high-tech investments and production facilities have dramatically changed the face of Costa Rica's economy. Intel, which opened two side-by-side assembly plants in Costa Rica in 1997, currently accounts for more than 20% of the country's exports, compared with traditional exports such as coffee (3.5%) and bananas (10%). Although Intel and other international companies are used to trumpet a growing gross domestic product, very little of the profits actually make their way into the Costa Rican economy. In early 2004, Costa Rican and U.S. negotiators signed a Free Trade Agreement, although it was very unclear whether it would be ratified by the legislature in either, much less both, countries.

Tourism has quickly grown to become the nation's true principal source of income, surpassing both cattle ranching and exports of coffee and bananas. In 1999, for the first time, a million tourists visited Costa Rica. Increasingly, Ticos whose fathers and grandfathers were farmers find themselves hotel owners, tour guides, and waiters. Although most have adapted gracefully and regard the industry as a source of new jobs and opportunities for economic advancement, restaurant and hotel staff can seem gruff and uninterested at times, especially in rural areas. And, unfortunately, an increase in the number of visitors has led to an increase in crime, prostitution, and drug trafficking. Common sense and street savvy are required in San José and Limón, and in some of the more popular tourist destinations.

3 History 101

EARLY HISTORY Little is known of Costa Rica's history before its colonization by Spanish settlers. The pre-Columbian Indians who made their home in this region of Central America never developed the large cities or

Dateline

- 13,000 B.C. Earliest record of human inhabitants in Costa Rica.
- 1000 B.C. Olmec people from Mexico arrive in Costa Rica searching for rare blue jade.

continues

advanced culture that flowered farther north in what would become Guatemala, Belize, and Mexico. However, from scattered excavations around the country, primarily in the northwest, ancient artifacts have been unearthed, indicating a strong sense of aesthetics. Beautiful gold and jade jewelry, intricately carved grinding stones, and artistically painted terracotta objects point to a small but highly skilled population.

SPAIN SETTLES COSTA RICA   In 1502, on his fourth and last voyage to the New World, Christopher Columbus anchored just offshore from present-day Limón. Whether he actually gave the country its name is open to discussion, but it wasn't long before the inappropriate moniker took hold.

The earliest Spanish settlers found that, unlike the Indians farther north, the native population of Costa Rica was unwilling to submit to slavery. Despite their small numbers, scattered villages, and tribal differences, they fought back against the Spanish until they were overcome by superior firepower and European diseases. When the fighting was finished, the European settlers in Costa Rica found that there were very few Indians left to force into servitude. The settlers were thus forced to till their own lands, a situation unheard of in other parts of Central America. Few pioneers headed this way because they could settle in Guatemala, where there was a large native workforce. Costa Rica was nearly forgotten, as the Spanish crown looked elsewhere for riches to plunder and souls to convert.

It didn't take long for Costa Rica's few Spanish settlers to head for the hills, where they found rich volcanic soil and a climate that was less oppressive than in the lowlands. Cartago, the colony's first capital, was founded in 1563, but it was not until the 1700s that additional cities were established in this agriculturally rich region. In

- 1000 B.C.–A.D. 1400 City of Guayabo is inhabited by as many as 10,000 people.
- 1502 Columbus lands in Costa Rica in September, at what is now Limón.
- 1519–61 The Spanish explore and colonize Costa Rica.
- 1563 City of Cartago is founded in the Central Valley.
- 1737 San José is founded.
- Late 1700s Coffee is introduced as a cash crop.
- 1821 On September 15, Costa Rica, with the rest of Central America, gains independence from Spain.
- 1823 San José is named the capital. The decision is disputed and isn't officially settled until 1835.
- 1848 Costa Rica is proclaimed an independent republic.
- 1856 Battle of Santa Rosa: Costa Ricans defeat the United States, which backed proslavery advocate William Walker.
- 1870s First banana plantations are established.
- 1889 First election is won by an opposition party, establishing democratic process in Costa Rica.
- 1890 Inauguration of the railroad connecting San José with the Caribbean coast.
- 1899 The United Fruit Company is founded by railroad builder Minor Keith.
- 1941 Costa Rica's social security and health system is instituted by President Rafael Angel Calderón.
- 1948 After aborted revolution and short civil war, Costa Rican army is abolished.
- 1949 Women and blacks are given the right to vote.
- 1956 Costa Rica's population tops one million.
- 1963 Cabo Blanco Reserve becomes Costa Rica's first national park.
- 1987 President Oscar Arias Sánchez is awarded the Nobel Peace Prize for orchestrating the Central American Peace Plan.
- 1994 President Rafael Angel Calderón hands over the reigns of government to José María Figueres, in a peaceful replay of their fathers' less amenable and democratic transfer of power in 1948.

the late 18th century, the first coffee plants were introduced, and because these plants thrived in the highlands, Costa Rica began to develop its first cash crop. Unfortunately, it was a long and difficult journey transporting the coffee to the Caribbean coast and then onward to Europe, where the demand for coffee was growing.

■ 1999 More than a million tourists visit Costa Rica for the first time in a single year.

■ 2002 For the first time in history, the presidential elections are forced into a second-round runoff. Abel Pachecho of the Social Christian Unity Party (PUSC) emerges as the winner.

FROM INDEPENDENCE TO THE PRESENT   In 1821, Spain granted independence to its colonies in Central America. Costa Rica joined with its neighbors to form the Central American Federation, but in 1838, it withdrew to form a new nation and pursue its own interests. By the mid-1800s, coffee was the country's main export. Free land was given to anyone willing to plant coffee on it, and plantation owners soon grew wealthy and powerful, creating Costa Rica's first elite class. Coffee plantation owners were powerful enough to elect their own representatives to the presidency.

This was a stormy period in Costa Rican history. In 1856, the country was invaded by William Walker, a soldier of fortune from Tennessee who, with the backing of U.S. President James Buchanan, was attempting to fulfill his grandiose dreams of presiding over a slave state in Central America (before his invasion of Costa Rica, he had invaded Nicaragua and Baja California). The people of Costa Rica, led by their own president, Juan Rafael Mora, marched against Walker and chased him back to Nicaragua. Walker eventually surrendered to a U.S. warship in 1857, but in 1860, he attacked Honduras, claiming to be the president of that country. The Hondurans, who had had enough of Walker's shenanigans, promptly executed him.

Until 1890, coffee growers had to transport their coffee either by oxcart to the Pacific port of Puntarenas or by boat down the Río Sarapiquí to the Caribbean. In the 1870s, a progressive president proposed a railway from San José to the Caribbean coast to facilitate the transport of coffee to European markets. It took nearly 20 years for this plan to reach fruition, and more than 4,000 workers lost their lives constructing the railway, which passed through dense jungles and rugged mountains on its journey from the Central Valley to the coast. Partway through the project, as funds were dwindling, the second chief engineer, Minor Keith, proposed an idea that not only enhanced his fortunes, but also changed the course of Central American history. Banana plantations would be developed along the railway right-of-way (land on either side of the tracks). The export of this crop would help to finance the railway, and, in exchange, Keith would get a 99-year lease on 1,976,000 hectares (800,000 acres) of land with a 20-year tax deferment. The Costa Rican government gave its consent, and in 1878, the first bananas were shipped from the country. In 1899, Keith and a partner formed the United Fruit Company, a business that eventually became the largest landholder in Central America and caused political disputes and wars throughout the region.

In 1889, Costa Rica held what is considered the first free election in Central American history. The opposition candidate won the election, and the control of the government passed from the hands of one political party to those of another without bloodshed or hostilities. Thus, Costa Rica established itself as the region's only true democracy. In 1948, this democratic process was challenged by Rafael Angel Calderón, who had served as the country's president from 1940 to 1944. After losing by a narrow margin, Calderón, who had the backing of the communist labor unions and the Catholic Church, refused to concede the country's leadership to the rightfully elected president, Otillio Ulate, and a civil war ensued. Calderón was eventually defeated by José "Pepe" Figueres. In the wake of this crisis, a new constitution was drafted; among other changes, it abolished Costa Rica's army so that such a revolution could never happen again.

In 1994, history seemed to repeat itself—peacefully this time—when José María Figueres took the reins of government from the son of his father's adversary, Rafael Angel Calderón. In 2001, Otton Solis and his new Citizen's Action Party (PAC) forced the presidential elections into a second round, breaking the two-party system that had become seemingly entrenched for good, although Solis himself finished third and didn't make it to the runoff. Abel Pacheco of the Social Christian Unity Party (PUSC) ultimately defeated National Liberation Party (PLN) candidate Rolando Araya. The National Assembly is rather fractured, with no one party having a clear majority. The upstart Citizen's Action Party won quite a few deputy slots.

More than a century of nearly uninterrupted democracy has helped make Costa Rica the most stable country in Central America. This stability, adherence to the democratic process, and staunch position of neutrality in a region that has been torn by 200 years of nearly constant strife are a source of great pride to Costa Ricans, who like to think of their country as the "Switzerland of Central America."

4 *Gallo Pinto,* Ceviche & *Frescos:* Costa Rican Food & Drink

Costa Rican food is not especially memorable. Perhaps that's why there's so much international food available throughout the country. However, if you really want to save money, you'll find that Costa Rican, or *típico,* food is always the cheapest nourishment available. It's primarily served in *sodas,* Costa Rica's equivalent of diners.

MEALS & DINING CUSTOMS

Rice and beans are the basis of Costa Rican meals—all three of them. At breakfast, they're called *gallo pinto* and come with everything from eggs to steak to seafood. At lunch or dinner, rice and beans are an integral part of a *casado* (which translates as "married" and is the name for the local version of a blue-plate special). A *casado* usually consists of cabbage-and-tomato salad, fried plantains (a starchy, bananalike fruit), and a chicken, fish, or meat dish of some sort.

Dining hours in Costa Rica are flexible but generally follow North American customs. Some downtown restaurants in San José are open 24 hours; however, expensive restaurants tend to be open for lunch between 11am and 3pm and for dinner between 6 and 11pm.

APPETIZERS Known as *bocas* in Costa Rica, appetizers are served with drinks in most bars. Often the *bocas* are free, but even if they aren't, they're very inexpensive. Popular *bocas* include *gallos* (tortillas piled with meat, chicken, cheese, or beans), ceviche (a marinated seafood salad), tamales (stuffed cornmeal patties wrapped and steamed inside banana leaves), *patacones* (fried green plantain chips), and fried yuca.

SANDWICHES & SNACKS Ticos love to snack, and there's a large variety of tasty little sandwiches and snacks available on the street, at snack bars, and in sodas. *Arreglados* are little meat-filled sandwiches, as are *tortas,* which are served on little rolls with a bit of salad tucked into them. Tacos, *tamales,* and empanadas (turnovers) also are quite common. *Gallos* (see above) are popular snacks as well.

MEAT   Costa Rica is beef country—one of the tropical nations that has converted much of its rainforest land to pastures for raising beef cattle. Consequently, beef is cheap and plentiful, although it might be a bit tougher than it is back home. In general, steaks are cut and served thinner here than in the United States or Europe. One very typical local dish is called *olla de carne,* a bowl of beef broth with large chunks of meat, local tubers, and corn. Spit-roasted chicken is also very popular here and is surprisingly tender.

SEAFOOD   Costa Rica has two coasts, and, as you'd expect, there's plenty of seafood available everywhere in the country. Corvina (sea bass) is the most commonly served fish and is prepared innumerable ways, including as ceviche. (***Be careful:*** In many cheaper restaurants, particularly in San José, shark meat is often sold as *corvina.*) You should also come across *pargo* (red snapper), dorado (mahimahi), and tuna on some menus, especially along the coasts. Although Costa Rica is a major exporter of shrimp and lobster, both are relatively expensive and in short supply here.

VEGETABLES   On the whole, you'll find vegetables surprisingly lacking in the meals you're served in Costa Rica—usually nothing more than a little pile of shredded cabbage topped with a slice or two of tomato. For a much more satisfying and filling salad, order *palmito* (hearts of palm salad). The heart (actually the stalk or trunk of these small palms) is first boiled and then chopped into circular pieces and served with other fresh vegetables, with a salad dressing on top. If you want something more than this, you'll have to order a side dish such as *picadillo,* a stew or purée of vegetables with a bit of meat in it. Most people have a hard time thinking of *plátanos* (plantains) as vegetables, but these giant relatives of bananas require cooking before they can be eaten. Green plantains have a very starchy flavor and consistency, but they become as sweet as candy as they ripen. Fried *plátanos* are one of my favorite dishes. *Yuca* (manioc root or cassava in English) is another starchy staple root vegetable in Costa Rica.

One more vegetable worth mentioning is the *pejibaye,* a form of palm fruit that looks like a miniature orange coconut. Boiled *pejibayes* are frequently sold from carts on the streets of San José. When cut in half, a *pejibaye* reveals a large seed surrounded by soft, fibrous flesh. You can eat it plain, but it's usually topped with a dollop of mayonnaise.

FRUITS   Costa Rica has a wealth of delicious tropical fruits. The most common are mangoes (the season begins in May), papayas, pineapples, melons, and bananas. Other fruits include the *marañón,* which is the fruit of the cashew tree and has orange or yellow glossy skin; the *granadilla* or *maracuyá* (passion fruit); the *mamón chino,* which Asian travelers will immediately recognize as the rambutan; and the *carambola* (star fruit).

DESSERTS   *Queque seco,* which literally translates as "dry cake," is the same as pound cake. *Tres leches* cake, on the other hand, is so moist that you almost need to eat it with a spoon. Flan is a typical custard dessert. It often comes as either *flan de caramelo* (caramel) or *flan de coco* (coconut). Many other sweets are available, many of which are made with condensed milk and raw sugar. *Cajetas* are popular handmade candies, made from sugar and various mixes of evaporated, condensed, and powdered milk. They are sold in differing-size bits and chunks at most *pulperías* and street-side food stands.

BEVERAGES

Frescos, refrescos, and *jugos naturales* are my favorite drinks in Costa Rica. They are usually made with fresh fruit and milk or water. Among the more common fruits used are mangoes, papayas, blackberries *(mora),* and pineapples *(piña).* You'll also come across *maracuyá* and carambola. Some of the more unusual frescos are *horchata* (made with rice flour and a lot of cinnamon) and *chan* (made with the seed of a plant found mostly in Guanacaste—definitely an acquired taste). The former is wonderful; the latter requires an open mind (it's reputed to be good for the digestive system). Order *un fresco con leche sin hielo* (a *fresco* with milk but without ice) if you are trying to avoid untreated water.

If you're a coffee drinker, you might be disappointed here. Most of the best coffee has traditionally been targeted for export, and Ticos tend to prefer theirs weak and sugary. The better hotels and restaurants are starting to cater to gringo and European tastes and are serving up better blends. If you want black coffee, ask for *café negro;* if you want it with milk, order *café con leche.*

If you want to try something different for your morning beverage, ask for *agua dulce,* a warm drink made from melted sugar cane and served either with milk or lemon, or straight.

WATER   Although water in most of Costa Rica is safe to drink, bottled water is readily available and is a good option if you're at all worried about an upset stomach. *Agua mineral,* or simply soda, is sparkling water in Costa Rica. If you like your water without bubbles, be sure to request *agua mineral sin gas,* or *agua en botella.*

BEER, WINE & LIQUOR   The German presence in Costa Rica over the years has produced several fine beers, which are fairly inexpensive. Most Costa Rican beers are light pilsners. The most popular brands are Bavaria, Imperial, and Pilsen. I personally can't tell much of a difference between any of them. Licensed local versions of Heineken and Rock Ice are also available.

Imported wines are available at reasonable prices in the better restaurants throughout the country. You can usually save money by ordering a Chilean wine rather than a Californian or European one.

Costa Rica distills a wide variety of liquors, and you'll save money by ordering these rather than imported brands. The national liquor is *guaro,* a rather crude cane liquor that's often combined with a soft drink or tonic or mineral water. If you're looking to buy or try some *guaro,* stick to the Cacique brand. Both the Café Britt and Salicsa brands produce a couple of types of coffee-based liqueurs. Café Rica is similar to Kahlúa and quite good. You can also find delicious cream-style coffee liqueurs.

Appendix B:
Glossary of Spanish
Terms & Phrases

Costa Rican Spanish is neither the easiest nor the most difficult dialect to understand. Ticos speak at a relatively relaxed speed and tend to enunciate clearly, without dropping too many final consonants. The *y* and *ll* sounds are very subtly pronounced, almost inaudible. Perhaps the most defining idiosyncrasy of Costa Rican Spanish is the way Ticos have of overemphasizing, almost chewing, their *r*'s.

1 Basic Words & Phrases

English	Spanish	Pronunciation
Hello	**Buenos días**	*bweh*-nohss *dee*-ahss
How are you?	**¿Cómo está usted?**	*koh*-moh ehss-*tah* oo-*stehd*
Very well	**Muy bien**	mwee byehn
Thank you	**Gracias**	*grah*-syahss
Good-bye	**Adiós**	ad-*dyohss*
Please	**Por favor**	pohr fah-*vohr*
Yes	**Sí**	see
No	**No**	noh
Excuse me (to get by someone)	**Perdóneme**	pehr-*doh*-neh-meh
Excuse me (to begin a question)	**Disculpe**	dees-*kool*-peh
Give me	**Deme**	*deh*-meh
Where is . . . ?	**¿Dónde está . . . ?**	*dohn*-deh ehss-*tah*
the station	**la estación**	la ehss-*tah*-syohn
the bus stop	**la parada**	la pah-*rah*-dah
a hotel	**un hotel**	oon oh-*tehl*
a restaurant	**un restaurante**	oon res-tow-*rahn*-teh
the toilet	**el servicio**	el ser-*vee*-syoh
To the right	**A la derecha**	ah lah deh-*reh*-chah
To the left	**A la izquierda**	ah lah ees-*kyehr*-dah
Straight ahead	**Adelante**	ah-deh-*lahn*-teh
I would like . . .	**Quiero . . .**	*kyeh*-roh
to eat	**comer**	ko-*mehr*
a room	**una habitación**	oo-nah ah-bee-tah-*syohn*
How much is it?	**¿Cuánto?**	*kwahn*-toh
The check	**La cuenta**	la *kwen*-tah
When?	**¿Cuándo?**	*kwan*-doh
What?	**¿Qué?**	keh
What time is it?	**¿Qué hora es?**	keh *oh*-rah ehss

Yesterday	**Ayer**	ah-*yehr*
Today	**Hoy**	oy
Tomorrow	**Mañana**	mah-*nyah*-nah
Breakfast	**Desayuno**	deh-sah-*yoo*-noh
Lunch	**Comida**	coh-*mee*-dah
Dinner	**Cena**	*seh*-nah
Do you speak English?	**¿Habla usted inglés?**	ah-blah oo-*stehd* een-*glehss*
Is there anyone here who speaks English?	**¿Hay alguien aquí que hable inglés?**	eye *ahl*-gyehn ah-*kee* keh *ah*-bleh een-*glehss*
I speak a little Spanish.	**Hablo un poco de español.**	ah-bloh oon *poh*-koh deh ehss-pah-*nyohl*
I don't understand Spanish very well.	**No (lo) entiendo muy bien el español.**	noh (loh) ehn-*tyehn*-do mwee byehn el ehss-pah-*nyohl*

NUMBERS

1	**uno** (*oo*-noh)		16	**dieciséis** (dyeh-see-*sayss*)
2	**dos** (dohss)		17	**diecisiete** (dyeh-see-*syeh*-teh)
3	**tres** (trehss)		18	**dieciocho** (dyeh-see-*oh*-choh)
4	**cuatro** (*kwah*-troh)		19	**diecinueve** (dyeh-see-*nweh*-beh)
5	**cinco** (*seen*-koh)		20	**veinte** (*bayn*-teh)
6	**seis** (sayss)		30	**treinta** (*trayn*-tah)
7	**siete** (*syeh*-teh)		40	**cuarenta** (kwah-*rehn*-tah)
8	**ocho** (*oh*-choh)		50	**cincuenta** (seen-*kwehn*-tah)
9	**nueve** (*nweh*-beh)		60	**sesenta** (seh-*sehn*-tah)
10	**diez** (dyehss)		70	**setenta** (seh-*tehn*-tah)
11	**once** (*ohn*-seh)		80	**ochenta** (oh-*chehn*-tah)
12	**doce** (*doh*-seh)		90	**noventa** (noh-*behn*-tah)
13	**trece** (*treh*-seh)		100	**cien** (syehn)
14	**catorce** (kah-*tohr*-seh)		1,000	**mil** (meel)
15	**quince** (*keen*-seh)			

DAYS OF THE WEEK

Monday	**lunes**	(*loo*-nehss)
Tuesday	**martes**	(*mahr*-tehss)
Wednesday	**miércoles**	(*myehr*-koh-lehs)
Thursday	**jueves**	(*wheh*-behss)
Friday	**viernes**	(*byehr*-nehss)
Saturday	**sábado**	(*sah*-bah-doh)
Sunday	**domingo**	(doh-*meen*-goh)

2 Some Typical Tico Words & Phrases

Birra   Slang for beer.

Boca   Literally means "mouth," but also a term to describe a small appetizer served alongside a drink at many bars.

Brete   Work, or job.

Choza   Slang for house or home.

Chunche   Knicknack; thing, as in "whatchamacallit."

Con mucho gusto   With pleasure.

De hoy en ocho   In 1 week's time.

Diay   An untranslatable but common linguistic punctuation, often used to begin a sentence.

Goma   Hangover.

La sele   Short for *la selección,* the Costa Rican national soccer team.

Macha or **machita**   A blond woman.

Mae   Translates like "man"; used by many Costa Ricans, particularly teenagers, as frequent verbal punctuation.

Maje   A lot like *mae,* above, but with a slightly derogatory connotation.

Mejenga   An informal, or pickup, soccer game.

Ponga la maría, por favor   This is how you ask taxi drivers to turn on the meter.

Pulpería   The Costa Rican version of the "corner store" or small market.

Pura vida   Literally, "pure life"; translates as "everything's great."

Qué torta   What a mess; what a screw-up.

Si Dios quiere   God willing. You'll hear Ticos say this all the time.

Soda   A casual diner-style restaurant serving cheap Tico meals.

Tuanis   Means the same as *pura vida,* above, but is used by a younger crowd.

Una teja   100 colones.

Un rojo   1,000 colones.

Un tucán   5,000 colones.

3 Menu Terms

FISH

Almejas Clams	**Langosta** Lobster
Atún Tuna	**Langostinos** Prawns
Bacalao Cod	**Lenguado** Sole
Calamares Squid	**Mejillones** Mussels
Camarones Shrimp	**Ostras** Oysters
Cangrejo Crab	**Pargo** Snapper
Ceviche Marinated seafood salad	**Pulpo** Octopus
Corvina Sea bass	**Tiburón** Shark
Dorado Dolphin, or mahimahi	**Trucha** Trout

MEATS

Albóndigas Meatballs	**Costillas** Ribs
Bistec Beefsteak	**Jamón** Ham
Cerdo Pork	**Lengua** Tongue
Chicharrones Fried pork rinds	**Mondongo** Tripe
Chuleta Cutlet	**Pato** Duck
Conejo Rabbit	**Pavo** Turkey
Cordero Lamb	**Pollo** Chicken

VEGETABLES

Aceitunas Olives	**Palmito** Heart of palm
Alcachofa Artichoke	**Papa** Potato
Berenjena Eggplant	**Pepino** Cucumber
Cebolla Onion	**Remolacha** Beet
Elote Corn on the cob	**Repollo** Cabbage
Ensalada Salad	**Tomate** Tomato
Espárragos Asparagus	**Vainica** String beans
Espinacas Spinach	**Yuca** Cassava, or manioc
Hongos Mushrooms	**Zanahoria** Carrot

FRUITS

Aguacate Avocado
Banano Banana
Carambola Star fruit
Cereza Cherry
Ciruela Plum
Fresa Strawberry
Limón Lemon or lime
Manzana Apple
Melocotón Peach

Mora Raspberry
Naranja Orange
Pera Pear
Piña Pineapple
Plátano Plantain
Sandía Watermelon
Toronja Grapefruit
Uvas Grapes

BASICS

Aceite Oil
Ajo Garlic
Arreglado Small meat sandwich
Azúcar Sugar
Bocas Appetizers
Casado Plate of the day
Frito Fried
Gallo Corn tortilla topped with meat or chicken
Gallo pinto Rice and beans
Hielo Ice
Mantequilla Butter

Miel Honey
Mostaza Mustard
Natilla Sour cream
Olla de carne Meat and vegetable soup
Pan Bread
Patacones Fried plantain chips
Picadillo Chopped vegetable side dish
Pimienta Pepper
Queso Cheese
Sal Salt
Tamal Filled cornmeal pastry
Tortilla Flat corn pancake

Index

See also Accommodations index, below.

GENERAL INDEX

Accommodations, 13–17, 41, 54–56. *See also* Accommodations Index
Adventure trips, best, 8
Aerial Tram, 209
Airfares, 40–41, 45
Airlines, 43–44, 48–49
Air travel, 43–46
Alajuela, 120–121
Allegro Papagayo Resort, 12–13
Alma Ata Archaeological Park, 209
American Express, 28–29, 93
Arenal, Lake, 8, 226–230
Arenal Botanical Gardens & Butterfly Sanctuary, 227
Arenal National Park, 10, 79, 213, 216
Arenal Volcano, 3, 213, 216–218
Aserri, 113
ATMs (automated teller machines), 27–28
Aviarios del Caribe, 12, 67, 331, 335
Azufrale hot springs, 151

Bahía Culebra, 154
Bajo del Tigre Trail, 236
Baldi Termae, 217
Ballena Marine National Park, 281
Ballooning, 73
Barra del Colorado, 318–321
Barra del Colorado National Wildlife Refuge, 208, 317
Barra Honda National Park, 78, 189–190
Basílica de Nuestra Señora de los Angeles (Cartago), 140
Beaches. *See also Entries starting with "Playa"*
best, 6–8
Cahuita, 332, 333–334

Corcovado National Park, 302
Dominical, 281
La Cruz area, 153
within Manuel Antonio National Park, 267
outside Manuel Antonio National Park, 268
Puerto Viejo, 340
south of Dominical, 284
Bees, 34–35
The Big Bazaar (Tamarindo), 19, 181
Bijagual, 255
Biking, 174, 190, 269. *See also* Mountain biking tours, 66–67
Bird-watching, 67–68
Aviarios del Caribe, 12, 67, 331, 335
best places for, 11–12
Cabo Blanco Absolute Nature Reserve, 198
Cahuita, 335
Caño Negro National Wildlife Refuge, 11, 79–80, 219
Carara Biological Reserve, 11, 255–256
Cerro de la Muerte, 11–12, 67, 69, 289
La Selva Biological Station, 11, 67
Monteverde area, 235–236
Osa Peninsula, 295
Parque del Este, 11, 123
Playa Nosara, 185
Puerto Viejo, 340–341
quetzals, 69, 232, 235, 286, 289, 290
Río Tempisque Basin, 11, 149
San José, 123
Wilson Botanical Gardens (near San Vito), 12, 309
Zoo Ave (Alajuela), 122
Blue Lake, 149
Boat trips and cruises, 71, 136, 137
Barra del Colorado, 318
La Fortuna, 215

Playa Flamingo, 167
Playa Zancudo, 312–313
Puerto Jiménez, 300
Puerto Viejo de Sarapiquí, 208
Puntarenas, 248, 250
Quepos/Manuel Antonio, 268–269
Tortuguero canal tours, 325
Tortuguero National Park, 322
Bosque Eterno de Los Niños, 236
Botanical gardens. *See* Gardens
Braulio Carrillo National Park, 3, 79
Bullfighting (San José), 123
Bungee jumping, 68, 136
Business hours, 60
Bus travel, 46, 49
Butterflies, 121, 122, 227, 237, 269, 341
Butterfly Farm (Alajuela), 121
Butterfly Garden (Monteverde), 237

Cabo Blanco Absolute Nature Reserve, 198
Cabo Matapalo, 299
Cabuya, 198
Café Britt Farm (near Heredia), 121
Cahuita, 332–338
Cahuita National Park, 11, 80, 317, 332, 333–334
Camping, 68
Ballena Marine National Park, 281
Corcovado National Park, 302
Dominical, 283
Genesis II Cloudforest Preserve, 290
Las Quebradas Biological Center, 288
Playa Brasilito, 169
Playa Junquillal, 183
Playa Sámara, 190

Camping *(cont.)*
Playa Tamarindo, 178
Rincón de la Vieja National
Park, 148
Santa Rosa National Park,
153
Talamanca Mountains, 341
Canaan, 286
Cañas, 147
Canoeing, 76–77, 218,
325–326
Caño Island, 295
Caño Negro National
Wildlife Refuge, 11, 79–80,
219
Canopy tours, 8, 70–71
Drake Bay, 295
Genesis II Cloudforest
Preserve, 289–290
La Fortuna area, 218
Malpais area, 203
Monteverde, 236–237
near San José, 137–139
Playa de Jacó, 253–254
Playa Hermosa area, 156
Playa Montezuma, 198
Playa Sámara, 190
Quepos/Manuel Antonio,
269–270
Tamarindo, 175
Cantarrana trail, 209
Canyoning, 218
Capuchin monkeys, 81
Carara Biological Reserve,
11, 255–256
Caribbean coast, 2, 21, 24,
317–349
Caribbean Conservation
Corporation's Visitors'
Center and Museum
(Tortuguero Village), 325
Carnaval, Limón, 329
Car rentals, 41, 51–52
Carrera de San Juan, 31
Cartago, 140
Car travel, 46–47, 49–53
Casa Orquídeas (near
Golfito), 308–309
Casinos (San José), 134
Caves (caverns),
78, 189–190, 219
Cellphones, 43
Center for Agronomy
Research and
Development (CATIE;
Turrialba), 141
Central Pacific Coast, 22
Centro Nacional de Arte y
Cultura (San José), 118
Centro Neotrópico
Sarapiquís, 209–210
Cerro Chato, 217

Cerro de la Muerte, 11–12,
67, 69, 289
Cerro de Tortuguero, 323
Chester Field Biological
Gardens, 209
Chirripó, Mount,
18, 286–287
Chirripó National Park,
80, 286–288
Climate, 30
Cloud forests, 232, 350–351.
*See also specific cloud
forests*
Cocos Island, 249
Coffee, 57, 84, 125
Copa del Café (San José), 31
Coral reefs, 78, 80, 281, 295,
317, 332, 333, 340–342
Corcovado National Park, 6,
10, 80, 292, 295, 300–303
Corobicí River, 156, 175
Coter, Lake, 227
Credit cards, 28–29
Cruise ships, 47
Cuisine, 109, 356–357
Currency and currency
exchange, 26–27
Curú Wildlife Refuge
(near Tambor), 193
Customs regulations, 25–26

Damas Island, 268
Dengue fever, 33–34
Día de la Pólvora, 32
Día del Boyero (San Antonio
de Escazú), 31
Día de los Muertos, 32
Día de San Ramón, 32
Diamante Waterfalls, 282
Diarrhea, 34
Disabilities, travelers
with, 36
Dominical, 279–285
Dominicalito, 281
Drake Bay, 291–299
Driving rules, 52
Drug laws, 60

Ecolodges and wilder-
ness resorts. *See also
Accommodations Index*
best, 15–16
Ecologically oriented volunteer and study programs,
82–83
Eco Termales (La Fortuna),
2, 217
El Chorro (near Montezuma),
197

El Cuartel de la Boca del
Monte (San José), 19, 132
El Mirador Ehecatl, 18, 152
El Rincón de los Monos, 197
El Tigre, 301
El Tope and Carnival (San
José), 32
Embassies, 60
Emergencies, 60
Entry requirements, 24–25
Etiquette in the
wilderness, 82

Families with children,
12–13, 37–38
Ferries, 53
Festejos Populares
(San José), 32
Festival Internacional de las
Artes (San José), 130
Festivals and special events,
31–32
Fincas Naturales/The Nature
Farm Reserve (Quepos),
269
Fishing, 8, 72
Barra del Colorado, 320
Golfito, 308
La Fortuna area, 218
Lake Arenal, 226, 227
Playa de Jacó, 254
Playa del Coco/Playa
Ocotal, 161
Playa Flamingo, 166–167
Playa Junquillal, 182
Playa Nosara, 185
Playa Sámara, 190
Playa Zancudo, 314
Puerto Jiménez, 303
Puerto Viejo, 343
Puntarenas, 248
Quepos, 269
Tamarindo, 175
Four-wheeling, 8, 174,
218, 269
Frog Pond of Monteverde,
237–238

Gardens
Arenal Botanical Gardens
& Butterfly Sanctuary,
227
Casa Orquídeas (near
Golfito), 308–309
Chester Field Biological
Gardens, 209
Lankester Gardens
(near Cartago), 122, 140
La Paz Waterfall Gardens,
122

Orchid Garden
(Monteverde), 238
Pura Vida Botanical
Gardens (Bijagual), 256
Solera Botanical Gardens
(near Cóbano), 198
Tropical Botanical Gardens
(Puerto Viejo), 341
Wilson Botanical Gardens
(near San Vito), 309
Gay and lesbian travelers,
36–37, 134
Genesis II Cloudforest
Preserve, 289–290
Golf, 72–73, 123, 167, 174
Golfito, 307–312
Golfo Dulce, 9, 310–311
Grecia, 143
Grecia Regional Museum,
143
Guanacaste, 1, 8, 22,
144–146
Guápiles Highway, 206, 208,
209, 317
Guaro, 128–129
Guayabo National
Monument, 78, 136

H andicrafts, 57, 127–128,
143, 149, 227–228,
238–239, 343
Hang gliding, 73
Health concerns, 32–35, 82
Heredia, 142–143
Herradura, 286
High season, 29–30
Hikes and nature walks
best, 9–11
Chirripó National Park,
286–287
Corcovado National Park,
302
Dominical area, 281
Genesis II Cloudforest
Preserve, 289–290
La Fortuna area, 216–218
Lake Arenal, 227
Las Quebradas Biological
Center, 288
Los Angeles Cloud Forest
Reserve, 136, 225
Manuel Antonio National
Park, 268
Monteverde area, 235–236
Mount Chirripó, 9,
286–287
Playa de Jacó, 256
Puerto Viejo (Caribbean
coast), 340–341

Puerto Viejo de Sarapiquí,
209
Rincón de la Vieja National
Park, 148–149
History, 353–356
Hitchhiking, 53
Holidays, 30–31
Holy Week, 31
Horseback riding, 73–74
Cahuita, 335
Dominical, 281
La Fortuna area (Arenal
National Park), 216–217
Lake Arenal, 227
Manuel Antonio, 270
Monteverde, 237
Playa de Jacó, 254
Playa Flamingo, 167
Playa Montezuma,
197, 198
Playa Nosara, 185
Santa Ana, 137
Tamarindo, 174
Hot springs, 79, 217, 219,
221, 223, 224, 288
Howler monkeys, 81, 149,
193, 198, 321, 324, 326,
333, 351

I NBio Park (Heredia),
121, 142–143
Independence Day, 32
India Point, 185
Insurance, 33, 35–36
auto, 47, 51–52
Internet access, 41–43
Irazú Volcano, 18, 138–139
Irazú Volcano National
Park, 78
Isla del Coco, 9, 249

J acó. See Playa de Jacó
Jewels of the Rainforest
insect museum (Puerto
Viejo de Sarapiquí), 209
Jogging (San José), 124
Johnny's Place (Puerto
Viejo), 19, 349
Juan Santamaría Day
(Alajuela), 31
Juan Santamaría Historical
Museum (Alajuela),
120–121
Juan Santamaría Interna-
tional Airport (San José),
43, 85
Jungla y Senderos Los Lagos
(near La Fortuna), 219
Junquillal, 181–183

K ayaking, 76–77, 137
Golfo Dulce (Puerto
Jiménez area), 9, 303
Manuel Antonio National
Park, 268
Playa de Jacó, 254
Playa Flamingo, 167
Playa Nosara, 185
Puerto Viejo, 342
Puerto Viejo de Sarapiquí,
208–209
Tamarindo, 175, 176
Kazam Canyon, 151
Kiteboarding, 77, 153, 227

L a Cangrejo Waterfall,
149
La Casa de la Cultura
(Puntarenas), 248
La Casa del Soñador
(near Cachí), 141
La Casona (Santa Rosa
National Park), 153
La Cruz, 152–154
La Fortuna, 213–219
La Fortuna Falls, 216
La Negrita (Cartago), 140
Language, 60. See also
Spanish-language
programs and courses
Lankester Gardens
(Cartago), 9, 122, 140
La Paz Waterfall Gardens,
122, 209
La Sabana Park (San José),
122–124
Las Corridas a la Tica
(San José), 123
La Selva Biological Station,
10, 11, 67
Las Fuentes Termales,
217, 218
Las Pailas loop, 148
Las Pailas ranger station, 148
Las Posadas, 32
Las Quebradas Biological
Center (near San Isidro),
288
Leather goods (San José),
128
Leptospirosis, 34
Liberia, 146–152
Limón, 32, 317, 321, 322,
328–332
Liquor laws, 61
Los Angeles Cloud Forest
Reserve, 136, 225
Los Patos, 301

M ahogany Park, 137
Mail, 61
Malaria, 33
Malpais (Mal País), 7, 202–205
Manuel Antonio National Park and environs, 6, 13, 80, 262–279
  accommodations, 271–276
  activities near, 269–270
  beaches, 7
  exploring, 267–268
  nightlife, 278–279
  orientation, 266
  restaurants, 277–278
  shopping, 270–271
  transportation, 266–267
  traveling to, 264–266
Manzanillo, 7–8, 342
Manzanillo-Gandoca Wildlife Refuge, 342
Maps, road, 52, 61
Markets (San José), 126
Marriages, 38–39
Mar y Sombra (Manuel Antonio), 19
Mercado Central (San José), 126
Miradores, 113
Money matters, 26–29
Monkeys, 81, 193, 198, 208, 235, 236, 262, 264, 267, 268, 295, 306, 321, 324, 326, 333, 340, 351
Monteverde, 230–244
Monteverde Biological Cloud Forest Reserve, 6, 10, 13, 80
  exploring, 234–235
Monteverde Conservation League, 236
Monteverde Music Festival, 238
Monteverde Serpentarium, 237
Motorcycles, 74
Mountain biking, 8
  Lake Arenal, 227
  near San José, 137
Museo de Arte Costarricense (San José), 118
Museo de Cultura Popular (Heredia), 143
Museo de Jade Marco Fidel Tristán (San José), 118–119
Museo de Los Niños (San José), 119
Museo de Oro Banco Central (San José), 119
Museo Nacional de Costa Rica (San José), 119–120
Music stores (San José), 129

N ational Autonomous University (Heredia), 142
National Orchid Show (San José), 31
National parks, 77–78
National Symphony Orchestra (San José), 130
Natural environment, 350–352
Nature parks and reserves (bioreserves), 77–78
  Bosque Eterno de Los Niños, 236
  Cabo Blanco Absolute Nature Reserve, 198
  Caño Island Biological Reserve, 295
  Carara Biological Reserve, 11, 255–256
  Centro Neotrópico Sarapiquís, 209–210
  Genesis II Cloudforest Preserve, 289–290
  INBio Park (Heredia), 121, 142–143
  Los Angeles Cloud Forest Reserve, 136
  Monteverde Biological Cloud Forest Reserve, 6, 10, 13, 80
  Reserva Sendero Tranquilo, 236
  Santa Elena Cloud Forest Reserve, 236
Nauyaca Waterfalls, 282
Newspapers and magazines, 61, 94
Nicoya Peninsula, 22
Northern Zone, 22, 206–244
Nosara, 183–184. *See also* Playa Nosara
Nosara Wellness Center, 185
Nuevo Arenal, 226–230

O jo de Agua (near San José), 124
Orchid Garden (Monteverde), 238
Orosi Valley, 140–141
Osa Peninsula, 6, 292, 295, 303–306

P acific coast, 21
Palo Verde National Park, 78–79, 149
Papagayo Peninsula, 155
Paragliding, 73
Páramos, 9, 245, 286, 351
Parque del Este (San José), 11, 123, 124

Parque La Sabana (San José), 122–124
Parque Marino del Pacífico (Puntarenas), 248
Parque Zoológico Simón Bolívar (San José), 120
Paseo de los Turistas (Puntarenas), 246, 248
Piedras Blancas National Park, 307
Playa Avellanas, 181
Playa Ballena, 284
Playa Barrigona, 7, 189
Playa Blanca, 153, 253
Playa Bonita, 328–329
Playa Brasilito, 165, 166, 169–170
Playa Buena Vista, 7, 189
Playa Cacao, 308
Playa Carillo, 7, 189
Playa Conchal, 164–168
Playa de Jacó, 13, 251–262
Playa del Coco, 160–164
Playa Doña Aña, 248
Playa Escondida, 254
Playa Espadilla, 267, 268
Playa Espadilla Sur, 267
Playa Esterillos, 253
Playa Flamingo, 165, 166, 168–170
Playa Grande, 172, 175–176, 179, 197
Playa Guiones, 184
Playa Hermosa de Jacó, 253, 254, 261–262
Playa Hermosa (Dominical), 281
Playa Hermosa (Guanacaste province), 12, 154–156
Playa Herradura, 253
Playa Junquillal, 153, 181–183
Playa La Penca, 165, 166
Playa Manta, 253
Playa Manuel Antonio, 267
Playa Matapalo, 279
Playa Montezuma, 7, 195–202
Playa Nacascolo, 155
Playa Nancite, 153
Playa Naranjo, 153, 193
Playa Negra (Cahuita), 334
Playa Negra (Guanacaste), 181
Playa Negra (Puerto Viejo), 340
Playa Nosara, 183–188
Playa Ocotal, 160–163
Playa Panamá, 154
Playa Pan de Azúcar, 165, 166
Playa Pavones, 315–316
Playa Pelada, 184–185
Playa Piñuela, 284
Playa Potrero, 165, 166, 169

Playa Sámara, 7, 188–192
Playa Tamarindo, 7, 13, 170–181. *See also* Tamarindo
Playa Tambor, 193–195
Playa Tivives, 248
Playa Tortuga, 284
Playa Uvita, 281
Playa Ventanas, 284
Playa Zancudo, 308, 312–315
Poás Volcano, 139
Poás Volcano National Park, 78
Police, 61
Pre-Columbian ruins, 136
Puerto Escondido, 267
Puerto Jiménez, 292, 299–306
Puerto Vargas, 334
Puerto Viejo (Caribbean coast), 338–349
Puerto Viejo de Sarapiquí, 206–213
Punta Catedral, 268
Puntarenas, 245–251
Punta Surrucho, 268
Punta Uva, 7–8, 342
Punta Uva Butterfly Garden, 341
Pura Vida Botanical Gardens, 256

Q uepos, 264–279. *See also* Manuel Antonio National Park
Quetzals, 69, 232, 235, 286, 289, 290

R adio stations, 61–62
Rafting (river floats), 8, 149, 175, 268. *See also* White-water rafting
Rain Forest Aerial Tram Caribbean, 137–138
Rain Forest Aerial Tram Pacific (near Jacó), 2, 253
Rainforests, 350. *See also* Canopy tours; Cloud forests; Nature parks and reserves
Rainmaker Nature Refuge (near Quepos), 269
Rainy season, 30
Reserva Sendero Tranquilo, 236
Restaurants, 17–18, 56–57
Restrooms, 62
Reventazón River, 141
Rey Curré, 286

Rincón de la Vieja National Park, 3, 9–10, 79, 146, 148
accommodations near, 150–151
Río Agujitas, 292
Río Fortuna waterfall, 216
Río Perezoso, 333
Río Sarapiquí region, 3
Río Tempisque Basin, 11, 149
Riptides, 34
River floats. *See* Rafting
Roca Verde, 281
Rock climbing, 74

S abanero Museum (Liberia), 147
Safety, 37, 62
in the wilderness, 82
Sailboarding, 227
Sailboat charters, 166–167, 174, 308
Salsa Brava, 340
Sámara, 188–192
San Clemente Bar & Grill (Dominical), 19, 284
San Gerardo de Rivas, 286
San Isidro de El General, 285–290
San José, 1, 21–22, 84–143
accommodations, 96–109
arriving in, 85, 88
bars, 131–132
car rentals, 92
emergencies, 93
express mail services, 93
for families with children, 12
finding addresses in, 89
gay and lesbian scene, 134
hospitals, 94
Internet access, 94
layout of, 89–90
maps, 94
neighborhoods, 90–91
nightlife, 129–134
organized tours, 117
outdoor activities and spectator sports, 122–124
photographic needs, 94
post office, 95
restaurants, 109–117
restrooms, 95
safety, 95
shopping, 124–129
side trips from, 134–143
sights and attractions, 117–122
suggested itineraries, 117–118

telephones, 95–96
temperatures and rainfall in, 30
transportation, 91–92
visitor information, 88–89
water, 96
weather, 96
San Pedrillo, 302
San Pedro (San José), 19, 132–134
Santa Elena, 234
Santa Elena Cloud Forest Reserve, 236
Santa María ranger station, 148
Santa Rosa National Park, 7, 79, 152–153
Santa Teresa, 202–205
Santo Cristo Waterfalls, 282
Sarapiquí River, 208
Sarchí, 143
Scarlet macaws, 255
Scuba diving, 71–72
Cabo Blanco, 203
Caño Island, 295
Isla del Coco (Cocos Island), 9, 249
Manzanillo-Gandoca Wildlife Refuge, 342
Playa de Jacó, 254
Playa del Coco/Playa Ocotal, 161
Playa Flamingo, 166
Playa Hermosa, 156
Playa Junquillal, 182
Playa Montezuma, 198
Puerto Viejo, 340, 341
Quepos/Manuel Antonio, 269
Tamarindo, 174–175
Sea kayaking. *See* Kayaking
Seasons, 29–30
Sea turtles, 76, 175–176, 185, 321, 324–325, 342
Seniors, 37
Serpentarium (San José), 120
Shopping, tips on, 57–58
Sierpe, 294
Sirena, 301, 302
Sky Trek (Monteverde), 236, 237
Sky Walk (Monteverde), 236
Snakes, 35
Snorkeling, 71–72, 176, 295, 334, 342
Soccer (fútbol), San José, 124
Solera Botanical Gardens (near Cóbano), 198
South Caribbean Music Festival (Puerto Viejo), 341

Southern Zone, 22, 24, 291–316
Spanish-language programs and courses, 53–54, 167, 174, 187, 190, 203, 238, 270
Spanish terms and phrases, glossary of, 359–362
Spas and yoga retreats, 74–75, 123, 162, 185, 254, 270, 341
Spider monkeys, 81, 321
Spirogyra Butterfly Garden (San José), 120
Squirrel monkeys, 81, 262, 264, 268
Stone spheres, 296
Students, 38–40
Study programs, 82
Sun exposure, 34
Surfing, 8, 9, 75–76, 161, 176, 182, 185, 203, 253, 254, 281, 340
Swimming, 124, 227

Tabacón Hot Springs Resort & Spa (near La Fortuna), 3, 6
Tamarindo, 170–181
Tapantí National Park, 141
Taxes, 62
Taxis, 63
Telephones, 63
Television stations, 61
Tennis, 123, 175
Terciopelo Cave, 78, 190
Termales del Bosque, 218, 224
Tilarán, 226–230
Time zone, 63
Tipping, 63
Tirimbina Biological Reserve, 209–210
Tobías Bolaños International Airport (near San José), 48–49, 88
Tortuga Island, 198, 248
Tortuguero National Park, 80, 137, 208, 321–328
Tortuguero Village, 6, 323–327
Tour operators, 65–66
Tours, 19, 47–48. See also Canopy tours
Traveler's checks, 29
Tropical Botanical Gardens (Puerto Viejo), 341
Tropical diseases, 33–34
Turrialba, 141–142
Turrialtico (near Turrialba), 141–142

Turtles, 76, 175–176, 185, 321, 324–325, 342
Turu BaRi Tropical Park, 2, 70, 139, 254

U jarrás, 141
University of Costa Rica (San José), 123
Upper Reventazón River, 8

V enado Caverns, 219
Visitor information, 24
Volcanoes, 138–139
Volunteer and study programs, ecologically oriented, 82–83

W ater, drinking, 63, 358
Waterfalls, 149, 197, 209, 216, 218, 255, 282
Watersports, 156, 176. See also specific sports
Websites, 20, 42
Weddings, 38–39
White-water rafting, 76–77, 137, 208, 218
Wildlife, 351–352
Wilson Botanical Gardens (near San Vito), 12, 309
Windsurfing, 8–9, 77, 153, 227
World of Insects (Santa Elena), 2, 238
World of Snakes (Grecia), 143

Z arcero, 143
Zoo Ave (Alajuela), 122

ACCOMMODATIONS

Agua Luna (Puerto Jiménez), 303–304
Aguila de Osa Inn (Drake Bay), 297
Albergue Mirador de Quetzales (near San Isidro), 290
Alby Lodge (Cahuita), 336–337
Allegro Papagayo Resort, 157
Almonds & Corals Tent Camp (Manzanillo), 344–345
Almost Paradise (Playa Nosara), 186
Amalia's Inn (La Cruz), 152

Amor de Mar (Montezuma), 199
Apartotel Flamboyant (Playa de Jacó), 256
Apartotel Girasol (Playa de Jacó), 256
Arco Iris Lodge (Monteverde), 17, 241–242
Arenal Lodge, 221–222
Arenal Observatory Lodge, 15, 222
Arenal Pacífico (Playa de Jacó), 256–257
Atlántida Lodge (Cahuita), 335
Auberge du Pélican (Playa Esterillos Este), 261
Aurola Holiday Inn (San José), 97
Azania Bungalows (Puerto Viejo), 345
The Backyard (Playa Hermosa), 261–262
Barceló Playa Tambor Beach Resort, 194
Best Western Coco Verde (Playa del Coco), 162
Best Western El Sitio Hotel & Casino (Liberia), 149
Best Western Hotel Kamuk (Quepos), 273
Best Western Jacó Beach Hotel, 257
Best Western Tamarindo Vista Villas, 178
Bosque del Cabo Rainforest Lodge, 16, 305
Britannia Hotel (San José), 98
Buena Vista Lodge (Rincón de la Vieja National Park), 150
Cabañas Arenal Paraíso (La Palma de la Fortuna), 223
Cabinas Aracari (Tortuguero), 327
Cabinas Arco Iris (Tamarindo), 178
Cabinas Arrecife (Cahuita), 337
Cabinas Black Sands (Puerto Viejo), 343
Cabinas Bosque Mar, 204
Cabinas Casa Verde (Puerto Viejo), 17, 344
Cabinas Cazaolas (Playa Pavones), 315
Cabinas Conchal, 169
Cabinas Cristina (Playa Potrero), 169
Cabinas Dolly (Tamarindo), 178

Cabinas Guaraná (Puerto Viejo), 343
Cabinas Hegalva (Dominical), 283
Cabinas Jacarandá (Puerto Viejo), 344
Cabinas Jinetes de Osa (Drake Bay), 298
Cabinas Las Olas (Playa Avellanas), 181
Cabinas Las Olas (Playa Hermosa), 262
Cabinas Los Cocos (Playa Zancudo), 17, 314
Cabinas Los Guayabos (near La Fortuna), 223
Cabinas Marielos (Tamarindo), 178–179
Cabinas Maritza (Puerto Viejo), 343
Cabinas Mar y Cielo (Montezuma), 200
Cabinas Mary (Tilarán), 229
Cabinas Miss Junie (Tortuguero), 327
Cabinas Oro Verde (Puerto Jiménez), 304
Cabinas Pedro Miguel (Manuel Antonio), 276
Cabinas Puerto Jiménez, 304
Cabinas Sabinas (Tortuguero), 327
Cabinas San Clemente (Dominical), 283
Cabinas Selvyn (Punta Uva), 346
Cabinas Sol y Mar (Playa Zancudo), 314
Cabinas Tortuguero, 327
Cabinas Vela-Bar (Manuel Antonio), 276
Cabinas Zully Mar (Tamarindo), 179
Café de París (Playa Nosara), 186
Camping Brasilito, 169
Camping Coco's (Playa Sámara), 191
Camping Los Malinches (Playa Junquillal), 183
Camping Río Lagarto (Playa Sámara), 191
Caña Blanca Beach & Rainforest Lodge (Golfo Dulce), 310
Caño Negro Natural Lodge, 225
Cariblue Bungalows (Puerto Viejo), 15, 345
Casa Camarona (Puerto Viejo), 345
Casa Corcovado Jungle Lodge (Osa Peninsula), 297

Casa de las Tías (San José), 105
Casa del Mar (Playa Sámara), 191
Casa Marbella (Tortuguero), 327–328
Casa Mar Lodge (Barra del Colorado), 320
Casa Ridgeway (San José), 100
Casa Siempre Domingo (Playa Pavones), 316
Casa Valeria (Playa Sámara), 191
Ceiba Tree Lodge (Tilarán), 228
Centro Neotrópico Sarapiquís, 211
Chalet Hibiscus (Limón), 336
Chalet Nicholas (Tilarán), 228
Claro de Luna (Monteverde), 241
Club del Mar Condominiums & Resort (Playa de Jacó), 256
Comfort Hotel Real Santa Ana (San José), 104–105
Complejo Turístico Samoa del Sur (Golfito), 309
Corcovado Lodge Tent Camp (Playa Carate), 16, 306
Costa Nera (Playa Hermosa), 261
Costa Rica Backpackers (San José), 100
Courtyard San José, 104
Didi's Charming House B&B (Manuel Antonio), 276
Dolphin Quest (Golfo Dulce), 310
Dominical Backpacker's Hostel, 283
Drake Bay Wilderness Resort, 298–299
Ecoplaya Beach Resort (La Cruz), 153–154
El Bosque (Monteverde), 242
El Coco Tico Ecolodge (Dominical), 283
El Descanso (San Isidro), 289
El Diriá (Tamarindo), 176–177
El Encanto Bed and Breakfast (Cahuita), 336
El Gran Ceibo (Golfito), 309
El Hicaco (Playa de Jacó), 257
El Manati Lodge (Tortuguero), 328
El Mono Azul Hotel (Manuel Antonio), 273

El Ocotal Beach Resort (Playa del Coco), 162
El Pargo Feliz (Montezuma), 200
El Pizote (Puerto Viejo), 343
El Remanso (Matapalo), 305
El Rincón de los Monos (Playa Montezuma), 200
El Sano Banano Beach Resort (Playa Montezuma), 15, 199
El Silencio (near Playa Matapalo), 279
El Sol (Monteverde), 239
El Velero Hotel (Playa Hermosa), 158
Escape Caribeño (Puerto Viejo), 343
Esquina del Mar (Playa Pavones), 315
Fiesta Premier Resort & Spa (Guanacaste), 1, 157–158
Finca Rosa Blanca Country Inn (Santa Bárbara de Heredia), 16, 105–106
Flamingo Beach Resort (Playa Flamingo), 168
Flamingo Marina Resort Hotel and Club (Playa Flamingo), 169
Flor Blanca Resort (Playa Santa Teresa), 14, 203
Four Seasons Resort Costa Rica (Papagayo Peninsula), 1, 13, 156–157
Frank's Place (Malpais), 204
Gavilán Sarapiquí River Lodge (near Puerto Viejo de Sarapiquí), 212
The Gilded Iguana (Playa Nosara), 186
Golfo Azul (Golfito), 309–310
Golfo Dulce Lodge, 311
Gran Hotel Costa Rica (San José), 98
Hacienda Dorada (Playa Sámara), 190
Hacienda Lodge Guachipelin (near Liberia), 150–151
Hampton Inn & Suites (San José), 107–108
Harbor Reef Lodge (Playa Nosara), 186
Hibiscus Hotel (Playa Junquillal), 183
Hotel Acón (Limón), 330
Hotel Alta (San José), 104
Hotel Amón Plaza (San José), 97–98
Hotel and Cabinas Playa Espadilla (Manuel Antonio), 273–274

Hotel and Villas Cala Luna (Tamarindo), 176

Hotel Aranjuez (San José), 100

Hotel Ayi Con (Puntarenas), 250

Hotel Belmar (Monteverde), 239

Hotel Belvedere (Playa Sámara), 191

Hotel Bougainvillea (San José), 108

Hotel Boyeros (Liberia), 150

Hotel Brasilito (Playa Brasilito), 169–170

Hotel Cacts (San José), 102–103

Hotel Camino Verde (Monteverde), 241

Hotel Capitán Suizo (Tamarindo), 177

Hotel Casitas Eclipse (Manuel Antonio), 273

Hotel Cocal (Playa de Jacó), 257

Hotel Cocori (Limón), 330

Hotel Costa Verde (Manuel Antonio), 274

Hotel Del Rey (San José), 98

Hotel del Sur (San Isidro), 288

Hotel Diuwak (Dominical), 282

Hotel Doña Ines (San José), 100

Hotel Don Carlos (San José), 99

Hotel Dos Largatos (Tambor), 194

Hotel El Bucanero (Playa Grande), 179

Hotel El Castillo Divertido (Playa Junquillal), 183

Hotel El Establo (Monteverde), 239–240

Hotel El Jardín del Edén (Tamarindo), 177

Hotel El Jardín (Playa Montezuma), 198–199

Hotel El Sapo Dorado (Monteverde), 15, 240

Hotel Finisterra (Playa Hermosa), 158–159

Hotel Fonda Vela (Monteverde), 240

Hotel 1492 Jade y Oro, 103

Hotel Giada (Playa Sámara), 191–192

Hotel Grano de Oro (San José), 14–15, 101

Hotel Guanacaste (Liberia), 150

Hotel Heliconia (Monteverde), 240–241

Hotel Iguazú (San Isidro), 288

Hotel La Aurora (Montezuma), 200

Hotel La Fortuna, 219

Hotel La Garza (Plantanar), 223

Hotel La Mariposa (Quepos), 18, 271

Hotel La Punta (Puntarenas), 250

Hotel Las Brisas del Pacífico (Playa Sámara), 190–191

Hotel Las Brisas (Puntarenas), 250

Hotel Las Colinas (La Fortuna), 219–220

Hotel Le Bergerac (San José), 15, 103

Hotel Los Crestones (San Isidro), 289

Hotel Los Mangos (Montezuma), 200

Hotel Lucy (Montezuma), 200–201

Hotel Malinche (Quepos), 276

Hotel Mar de Luz (Playa de Jacó), 258

Hotel Maribu Caribe (Limón), 330

Hotel Mirador Pico Blanco (San José), 105

Hotel Naralit (Tilarán), 229

Hotel Occidental El Tucano (Aguas Calientes de San Carlos), 223–224

Hotel Parador (Manuel Antonio), 271–272

Hotel Pasatiempo (Tamarindo), 178

Hotel Playa Hermosa, 159

Hotel Playa Junquillal, 183

Hotel Playa Negra, 181

Hotel Plinio (Manuel Antonio), 274

Hotel Poco a Poco (Monteverde), 239

Hotel Presidente (San José), 99

Hotel Punta Islita (Playa Islita), 14, 192

Hotel Pura Vida (Puerto Viejo), 343

Hotel Quepos, 276

Hotel Roca Verde (Dominical), 282

Hotel Rosa del Paseo (San José), 102

Hotel San Bosco (La Fortuna), 220

Hotel Santo Tomás (San José), 99

Hotel Sí Como No (Manuel Antonio), 14, 272

Hotel Sugar Beach (Playa Pan de Azúcar), 168–169

Hotel Tilawa (Tilarán), 228

Hotel Tioga (Puntarenas), 250

Hotel Torremolinos (San José), 102

Hotel Verde Mar (Manuel Antonio), 274–275

Hotel Villa Casa Blanca (Playa Ocotal), 162

Hotel Villas Gaia (Playa Tortuga), 285

Hotel Villa Taype (Playa Nosara), 186

Hotel Zabamar (Playa de Jacó), 258

Iguanazul Hotel (Playa Junquillal), 18, 182–183

Jenny's Cabinas (Cahuita), 337

Joluva Guesthouse (San José), 100–101

Jungle House (Playa Matapalo), 279

Kap's Place (San José), 100

Karahé (Manuel Antonio), 275

La Carolina Lodge (near Liberia), 150

La Colina Lodge (Monteverde), 242

La Colina (Manuel Antonio), 275

La Costa del Papito (Puerto Viejo), 346–347

Lagarta Lodge (Playa Nosara), 187

Laguna Lodge (near Tortuguero Village), 326–327

La Isla (near Puerto Viejo), 344

La Laguna del Lagarto Lodge (Boca Tapada), 213

La Mansion Inn Arenal (Tilarán), 228

La Paloma Lodge (Drake Bay), 16, 297–298

Lapa Ríos (Osa Peninsula), 305

La Quinta de Sarapiquí Country Inn (Chilamate), 212

La Selva Biological Station, 15, 211

Las Gaviotas Hotel (Golfito), 310

Las Tortugas Hotel (Playa Grande), 179

Los Inocentes Lodge (La Cruz), 154

Luigi's Hotel (La Fortuna), 220

Luna Lodge (near Carate), 305

Madrigal (Playa de Jacó), 257

Magellan Inn (near Cahuita), 336

Maiyra's (Playa Potrero), 169

Makanda-by-the-Sea (Manuel Antonio), 272–273

Mal País Surf Camp & Resort, 204–205

Mariner Inn (Playa Flamingo), 169

Marriott Costa Rica Hotel (San Antonio de Belén), 13, 106

Marriott Los Sueños Ocean & Golf Resort (Playa Herradura), 14, 258

Mawamba Lodge (Tortuguero), 327

Meliá Cariari (San José), 106

Montaña de Fuego Inn (La Palma de la Fortuna), 222–223

Monteverde Biological Cloud Forest Reserve, 241

Monteverde Lodge, 241

Mystica (near Tilarán), 228–229

Nature Lodge Finca Los Caballos (Cóbano de Puntarenas), 199

Nosara Beach Hotel (Playa Nosara), 187

Orquídeas Inn (San José), 108–109

Pachira Lodge (Tortuguero), 327

Pacific Edge (Dominical), 283–284

Palma Real (San José), 101

Paradisus Playa Conchal, 14, 167–168

Park Hotel (Limón), 330–331

Parrot Bay Village (Puerto Jiménez), 303

Peace Lodge (San José), 1, 107

Pensión de la Cuesta (San José), 101

Pensión Flor de Monteverde, 241

Pensión Monteverde Inn (Monteverde), 241

Pensión Santa Elena (Monteverde), 241

Piramys (Dominical), 283

The Place (Santa Teresa), 203

Playa Chiquita Lodge (Puerto Viejo), 347

Playa Nicuesa Lodge, 310

Pochote Grande (Playa de Jacó), 257

Posada Andrea Cristina (near Puerto Viejo de Sarapiquí), 212

Posada del Tope (Liberia), 150

Radisson Europa Hotel (San José), 97

Rainbow Adventures (Playa Cativa), 311

Rara Avis (near Las Horquetas), 210

Raya Vida Villa (San José), 99–100

Real InterContinental San José, 104

Rincón de la Vieja Mountain Lodge, 151

Río Colorado Lodge (Barra del Colorado), 320–321

Roca Dura (San Isidro), 289

Rocking J's (Puerto Viejo), 343

Rock River Lodge (Tilarán), 229

Roy's Zancudo Lodge (Playa Zancudo), 314

Savegre Mountain Hotel (San Gerardo de Dota), 290

Selva Bananito Lodge, 16, 331–332

Selva Verde Lodge (Chilamate), 210

Shawandha Lodge (Playa Chiquita), 17, 346

Silver King Lodge (Barra del Colorado), 321

Sueño Azul Resort (Las Horquetas), 211–212

Sueño del Mar (Playa Tamarindo), 16–17, 177

Tabacón Hot Springs Resort & Spa, 2, 6, 18, 75, 217, 221

Talari Mountain Lodge (San Isidro), 289

Tambor Tropical, 195

Tango Mar Resort (Playa Tambor), 195

Taylor's Inn (San José), 100

Termales del Bosque (Ciudad Quesada), 224

Terraza del Pacífico (Playa Hermosa de Jacó), 262

Tilajari Resort Hotel (Muelle), 224–225

Tiskita Jungle Lodge (Playa Pavones), 316

Tito's Camping (Tamarindo), 178

Tortilla Flats (Dominical), 284

Tortuga Lodge (Tortuguero), 16, 326

Toruma Youth Hostel (San José), 103

Tranquilo Backpackers (San José), 100

Trogon Lodge (San Gerardo de Dota), 290

Trópico Latino Lodge (Santa Teresa), 204

Tryp Corobicí (San José), 102

Villa Alegre (Tamarindo), 178

Villablanca Hotel (San Ramón), 225–226

Villa Caletas (near Jacó), 14, 18, 259

Villa Decary (near Nuevo Arenal), 229

Villa del Sol B&B (Playa del Coco), 163

Villa del Sueño Hotel (Playa Hermosa), 15, 159

Villa Flores B&B (Playa del Coco), 162

Villa Lapas (Tárcoles), 259

Villas del Caribe (Puerto Viejo), 346

Villas Nicolás (Manuel Antonio), 275–276

Villas Playa Sámara, 190

Villas Río Mar (Dominical), 283

Villas Sol Hotel & Villas Beach Resort (Playa Hermosa), 158

Vista del Valle Plantation Inn (near Grecia), 16, 108

Volcano Lodge (La Fortuna), 223

Wilson Botanical Gardens (near San Vito), 309

Xandari Resort & Spa (San José), 107

Great Trips Like Great Days Begin with a Plan

FranklinCovey and Frommer's Bring You *Frommer's Favorite Places*® Planner

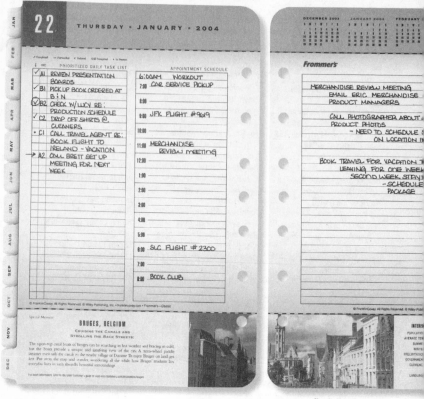

Classic Size Planning Pages $39.95

The planning experts at FranklinCovey have teamed up with the travel experts at Frommer's. The result is a full-year travel-themed planner filled with rich images and travel tips covering fifty-two of Frommer's Favorite Places.

- Each week will make you an expert about an intriguing corner of the world
- New facts and tips every day
- Beautiful, full-color photos of some of the most beautiful places on earth
- Proven planning tools from FranklinCovey for keeping track of tasks, appointments, notes, address/phone numbers, and more

Save 15%

when you purchase Frommer's Favorite Places travel-themed planner and a binder.

Order today before your next big trip.

www.franklincovey.com/frommers
Enter promo code 12252 at checkout for discount. Offer expires June 1, 2005.

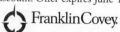
FranklinCovey.

Frommer's is a trademark of Arthur Frommer.

FROMMER'S® COMPLETE TRAVEL GUIDES

Alaska
Alaska Cruises & Ports of Call
American Southwest
Amsterdam
Argentina & Chile
Arizona
Atlanta
Australia
Austria
Bahamas
Barcelona, Madrid & Seville
Beijing
Belgium, Holland & Luxembourg
Bermuda
Boston
Brazil
British Columbia & the Canadian
  Rockies
Brussels & Bruges
Budapest & the Best of Hungary
Calgary
California
Canada
Cancún, Cozumel & the Yucatán
Cape Cod, Nantucket & Martha's
  Vineyard
Caribbean
Caribbean Cruises & Ports of Call
Caribbean Ports of Call
Carolinas & Georgia
Chicago
China
Colorado
Costa Rica
Cuba
Denmark
Denver, Boulder & Colorado
  Springs
England
Europe
Europe by Rail
European Cruises & Ports of Call

Florence, Tuscany & Umbria
Florida
France
Germany
Great Britain
Greece
Greek Islands
Halifax
Hawaii
Hong Kong
Honolulu, Waikiki & Oahu
India
Ireland
Israel
Italy
Jamaica
Japan
Kauai
Las Vegas
London
Los Angeles
Maryland & Delaware
Maui
Mexico
Montana & Wyoming
Montréal & Québec City
Munich & the Bavarian Alps
Nashville & Memphis
Newfoundland & Labrador
New England
New Mexico
New Orleans
New York City
New York State
New Zealand
Northern Italy
Norway
Nova Scotia, New Brunswick &
  Prince Edward Island
Oregon
Ottawa
Paris

Peru
Philadelphia & the Amish
  Country
Portugal
Prague & the Best of the Czech
  Republic
Provence & the Riviera
Puerto Rico
Rome
San Antonio & Austin
San Diego
San Francisco
Santa Fe, Taos & Albuquerque
Scandinavia
Scotland
Seattle
Shanghai
Sicily
Singapore & Malaysia
South Africa
South America
South Florida
South Pacific
Southeast Asia
Spain
Sweden
Switzerland
Texas
Thailand
Tokyo
Toronto
USA
Utah
Vancouver & Victoria
Vermont, New Hampshire &
  Maine
Vienna & the Danube Valley
Virgin Islands
Virginia
Walt Disney World® & Orlando
Washington, D.C.
Washington State

FROMMER'S® DOLLAR-A-DAY GUIDES

Australia from $50 a Day
California from $70 a Day
England from $75 a Day
Europe from $70 a Day
Florida from $70 a Day
Hawaii from $80 a Day

Ireland from $80 a Day
Italy from $70 a Day
London from $90 a Day
New York from $90 a Day
Paris from $90 a Day
San Francisco from $70 a Day

Washington, D.C. from $80 a
  Day
Portable London from $90 a Day
Portable New York City from $90
  a Day
Portable Paris from $90 a Day

FROMMER'S® PORTABLE GUIDES

Acapulco, Ixtapa & Zihuatanejo
Amsterdam
Aruba
Australia's Great Barrier Reef
Bahamas
Berlin
Big Island of Hawaii
Boston
California Wine Country
Cancún
Cayman Islands
Charleston
Chicago
Disneyland®
Dominican Republic
Dublin

Florence
Frankfurt
Hong Kong
Las Vegas
Las Vegas for Non-Gamblers
London
Los Angeles
Los Cabos & Baja
Maine Coast
Maui
Miami
Nantucket & Martha's Vineyard
New Orleans
New York City
Paris

Phoenix & Scottsdale
Portland
Puerto Rico
Puerto Vallarta, Manzanillo &
  Guadalajara
Rio de Janeiro
San Diego
San Francisco
Savannah
Vancouver
Vancouver Island
Venice
Virgin Islands
Washington, D.C.
Whistler

FROMMER'S® NATIONAL PARK GUIDES

Algonquin Provincial Park
Banff & Jasper
Family Vacations in the National
  Parks

Grand Canyon
National Parks of the American
  West
Rocky Mountain

Yellowstone & Grand Teton
Yosemite & Sequoia/Kings
  Canyon
Zion & Bryce Canyon

FROMMER'S® MEMORABLE WALKS

Chicago
London

New York
Paris

San Francisco

FROMMER'S® WITH KIDS GUIDES

Chicago
Las Vegas
New York City

Ottawa
San Francisco
Toronto

Vancouver
Walt Disney World® & Orlando
Washington, D.C.

SUZY GERSHMAN'S BORN TO SHOP GUIDES

Born to Shop: France
Born to Shop: Hong Kong,
  Shanghai & Beijing

Born to Shop: Italy
Born to Shop: London

Born to Shop: New York
Born to Shop: Paris

FROMMER'S® IRREVERENT GUIDES

Amsterdam
Boston
Chicago
Las Vegas
London

Los Angeles
Manhattan
New Orleans
Paris
Rome

San Francisco
Seattle & Portland
Vancouver
Walt Disney World®
Washington, D.C.

FROMMER'S® BEST-LOVED DRIVING TOURS

Austria
Britain
California
France

Germany
Ireland
Italy
New England

Northern Italy
Scotland
Spain
Tuscany & Umbria

THE UNOFFICIAL GUIDES®

Beyond Disney
Central Italy
Chicago
Cruises
Disneyland®
England
Florida
Florida with Kids
Inside Disney

Hawaii
Las Vegas
London
Maui
Mexico's Best Beach Resorts
Mini Las Vegas
Mini-Mickey
New Orleans
New York City

Paris
San Francisco
Skiing & Snowboarding in the
  West
Walt Disney World®
Walt Disney World® for
  Grown-ups
Walt Disney World® with Kids
Washington, D.C.

SPECIAL-INTEREST TITLES

Athens Past & Present
Cities Ranked & Rated
Frommer's Best Day Trips from London
Frommer's Caribbean Hideaways
Frommer's China: The 50 Most Memorable Trips
Frommer's Exploring America by RV
Frommer's Gay & Lesbian Europe
Frommer's Best RV and Tent Campgrounds
  in the U.S.A.

Frommer's Road Atlas Europe
Frommer's Road Atlas France
Frommer's Road Atlas Ireland
Frommer's Wonderful Weekends from
  New York City
The New York Times' Guide to Unforgettable
  Weekends
Retirement Places Rated
Rome Past & Present

Travel Tip: He who finds the best hotel deal has more to spend on facials involving knobbly vegetables.

Hello, the Roaming Gnome here. I've been nabbed from the garden and taken round the world. The people who took me are so terribly clever. They find the best offerings on Travelocity. For very little cha-ching. And that means I get to be pampered and exfoliated till I'm pink as a bunny's doodah.

*** travelocity®

1-888-TRAVELOCITY / **travelocity.com** / **America Online Keyword: Travel**

Travel Tip: Make sure there's customer service for any change of plans — involving friendly natives, for example.

One can plan and plan, but if you don't book with the right people you can't seize le moment and canoodle with the poodle named Pansy. I, for one, am all for fraternizing with the locals. Better yet, if I need to extend my stay and my gnome nappers are willing, it can all be arranged through the 800 number at, oh look, how convenient, the lovely company coat of arms.

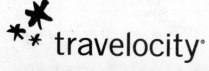